Channeling Violence

Channeling Violence

THE ECONOMIC MARKET FOR
VIOLENT TELEVISION PROGRAMMING

· *JAMES T. HAMILTON* ·

PRINCETON UNIVERSITY PRESS

PRINCETON, NEW JERSEY

Copyright © 1998 by Princeton University Press
Published by Princeton University Press, 41 William Street,
Princeton, New Jersey 08540
In the United Kingdom: Princeton University Press,
3 Market Place, Woodstock, Oxfordshire OX20 1SY

Second printing, and first paperback printing, 2000
Paperback ISBN 0-691-07024-5

The Library of Congress has cataloged the cloth edition of this book as follows

Hamilton, James, 1961–
Channeling violence : the economic market for violent
television programming / James T. Hamilton.
Includes bibliographical references and index.
ISBN 0-691-04848-7 (cloth : alk. paper)
1. Violence in television—United States. 2. Television
broadcasting—Economic aspects—United States. I. Title.
PN1992.8.V55H36   1998   303.6'0973—dc21   97-41417

This book has been composed in Times Roman

The paper used in this publication meets the minimum requirements of
ANSI/NISO Z39.48-1992 (R1997) (Permanence of Paper)

www.pup.princeton.edu

Printed in the United States of America

3 5 7 9 10 8 6 4 2

TO MY PARENTS •

MARTHA AND MILTON HAMILTON

· C O N T E N T S ·

PEOPLE interested in television violence can often trace their concern about the issue to an incident from a particular movie, a graphic scene portrayed on television, or the reaction of a child or friend to watching a violent program. My interest in television violence came through a more prosaic source—a series of academic articles about pollution control. For several years I had been studying the Toxics Release Inventory, a U.S. Environmental Protection Agency program that requires over 20,000 industrial plants each year to make public their pollution releases for over 300 chemicals. I wrote articles on the origin of the program, the reaction of stock prices to the release of polluter information, and the reductions in facility emissions that took place once the data became public. Reading an article about television violence one day, I was struck by a proposal to have the Federal Communications Commission develop "violence reportcards" that would link companies to the violent programs they sponsored on television. This possible use of information as a policy tool to influence firm behavior sparked the insight that serves as the basis for this book—that television violence is fundamentally a problem of pollution.

My goal in writing this book is to use economics to explain how the pursuit of individual self-interest by consumers, producers, and distributors of violent programming leads to undesirable social outcomes, such as the current rates of children's exposure to violent programming. I try to explore how policies designed to deal with environmental pollution also offer opportunities to reduce the harms associated with television violence. In researching this book I have benefited from discussing its results with academics and interest group participants at the Duke Conference on Media Violence and Public Policy; with the chairman of the Federal Communications Commission, Reed Hundt, and his staff at an agency seminar; and with industry participants at meetings organized by the TV Ratings Executive Committee (the group that coordinated the design of the current program rating system for television shows). In these discussions, in presentations at academic panels, and in conversations with journalists, I have received much encouragement from individuals who have come to view television violence as an economic problem. Still, four questions seem to arise when I present my analysis: What about *Schindler's List*? What about the *Road-runner* cartoons? What about Japan? What about the First Amendment?

The research presented here will address each of the concerns implicit in these four questions. Hollywood producers and network executives rightfully point to *Schindler's List* as a movie where violence is used to dramatize the horror and brutality of the Holocaust. Yet in chapter 4 I find that for 5,000 movies with indicators for violence shown on broadcast and cable television in 1995–96, only 2.8% were four-star films. Though high-quality violent films exist, they are not the norm in critics' eyes among the violent films shown on television. The question about *Roadrunner* often arises from a sense that cartoons cannot be harmful or that many children have consumed cartoons and grown up to be nonviolent adults. The review of the literature on media effects in chapters 1 and 3 underscores that for some children "fantasy" or cartoon violence does stimulate aggression. These effects may be more pronounced for younger children less likely to distinguish cartoon characters from "real" villains.

The third question is often phrased "Japan is said to have violent programming, but it has a low crime rate—how would you explain this?" This often boils down to a question about whether television violence is a major cause of violence in American society. My response is that violence in America has many causes, including television violence. I believe that the better question is whether policies designed to deal with television violence would on net yield benefits to society, a question I begin to explore in chapter 1 through a discussion of how to estimate the risks from the violent content in a particular television program. The last question about the First Amendment is a reminder that attempts to deal with problems arising from television violence must recognize that media products enjoy constitutional protections that constrain government policies, a point that I support and incorporate in my policy analysis.

I have benefited greatly from discussing questions about television violence with many colleagues at Duke, including Sara Beale, John Brehm, Charles Clotfelter, Phil Cook, Jerome Culp, Mark Fischle, Joel Fleishman, Helen Ladd, Fritz Mayer, Ellen Mickiewicz, Madeline Morris, David Paletz, Stan Paskoff, Dee Reid, Chris Schroeder, William Van Alstyne, and Redford Williams. I have also learned a great deal from conversations with Joanne Cantor, Brandon Centerwall, Joel Federman, Julius Genachowski, Raymond Handlan, Dale Kunkel, Joel Marcus, Kathryn Montgomery, Eli Noam, Victoria Rideout, Herbert Schlosser, and Ellen Wartella. Larry Bartels, Colin Shaw, and Matthew Spitzer read the entire draft manuscript and provided expert advice, which I have tried to follow. Madhuri Bhat, Lisa Cioci, Francisco Escalante, Justin Hoagland, Dan Lipinski, Aaron Miller, Andre Robinson, Matthew Schruers, Richard Senzel, and Theodore Tatos provided extremely able research assistance. Tad Bashore, Robert Carscadden, Nancy Torre Dauphinais, and Robert Malme each worked for over a year as a research assistant on the project. Their dedication made the project much more productive and enjoyable. I also benefited greatly from the suggestions of Peter Dougherty, Beth Gianfagna, and Brian MacDonald of Princeton University Press. Grants from the New York Times Company Foundation and others to the DeWitt Wallace Center for Communications and Journalism at the Terry Sanford Institute of Public Policy at Duke University made this research possible.

I also owe much to people who have had a long-term influence on my work. In undergraduate and graduate courses, Richard Caves encouraged my interest in industrial organization. Ken Shepsle instilled an appreciation for rational choice models of politics. Joseph Kalt introduced me to economic models of media markets and planted the questions about information exchange that in-

• P R E F A C E •

spired my interest in analyzing the media. The steadfast encouragement and support of my wife, Nancy, made it possible for me to finish the manuscript. Finally, this book is in some ways a product of the vacations deferred and experiences forgone by my parents, Martha and Milton Hamilton. Their gift of an education left me free to explore any career without the burden of student loans and choose any path opened by the opportunities they made possible. This book is lovingly dedicated to them.

Channeling Violence

Why Is Television Violence a Public Policy Issue?

ECONOMICS determines the supply and demand of violent images in American television programming. The portrayal of violence is used as a competitive tool in both entertainment and news shows to attract particular viewing audiences. The likelihood that a television program will contain any violent acts and the type of violence portrayed depend on a number of economic factors: the size and demographic composition of the potential viewing audience; the distribution of tastes for violent programming; the values placed by advertisers on viewing audiences and the willingness of viewers to pay for programming; the costs of different types of shows; the market for different types of U.S. programs abroad; and the interactions among the theatrical, video, cable, network broadcast, and syndication television markets. In a world where consumers face a variety of entertainment options, violence is an element of product differentiation that allows a programmer to distinguish a show from other viewing options.

Although television violence is a product of market forces, it is also an example of a market failure. Television violence generates negative externalities, which economists define as costs that are borne by individuals other than those involved in the production activity.[1] Environmental pollution is a familiar example of an externality, since a firm that generates hazardous wastes may not incorporate the full costs to society of its production decisions if it is not led to consider the damage to the environment from its wastes. Similarly, broadcasters attempting to deliver audiences to advertisers or attract viewers to a cable system may not fully incorporate the costs to society of their violent programming if these costs include such factors as increased levels of aggression and crime. The parallel to pollution is important, since in the United States the remedies proposed to deal with violent programming such as zoning provisions (e.g., restricting violent broadcasts to certain times) and information provision (e.g., reporting on the violent content of programming and its advertiser support) are similar to policies already adopted to deal with environmental pollution. The parallel depends, however, on the question to be addressed here of whether violence on television adds to violence in society.

Economics explains television violence as the product of rational, self-interested decisions made by viewers and television programmers. The top consumers of television violence are males aged 18–34, followed by females 18–34. Advertisers are willing to pay a premium for these viewers, which means that some programmers will face incentives to offer violent shows. Violent content becomes a way to build audiences for a television movie, attract viewers for a local news broadcast, or lead consumers to subscribe to cable. A majority of viewers may prefer less violent programming, especially older audience members (who are less valued by advertisers). Viewers offended by the levels of violent programming may be an attractive audience for others assembling a popular audience, politicians seeking election. The difference between the marginal viewers sought by particular programmers and the marginal voters sought by some politicians gives rise to a conflict between Hollywood and Washington over the use of violence in television and movies.

The theory of externalities underscores how the damage to society that arises from television violence remains outside the calculations of most programmers, producers, and viewers. Children are not the target audience for the products advertised on violent shows aimed at adults, and broadcasters are not rewarded by advertisers targeting adult consumers for attracting additional child viewers to an adult-oriented program. Yet the times when substantial numbers of adults aged 18–34 are in the audience are those when numerous children are also viewing, so that the decision to broadcast violent content results in the exposure of substantial numbers of viewers aged 2–11 or 12–17 to programs that social science research indicates may be hazardous for them.

Progress in dealing with the negative impacts of television violence is slowed by the same incentives for individuals and firms that impede efforts to deal with environmental pollution. Consider a parent concerned about media violence who believes that violence on television does have an impact on violence in society. Even if she knew which companies supported violent shows through their advertising, she would be unlikely to boycott their products. Although she might view the benefits to society of a drop in television violence as large, the probability that her actions would lead an advertiser to withdraw sponsorship is so small that the expected benefits from boycotting would be swamped by the additional costs to her of searching for other items to buy instead of the advertised product. This logic of collective action (described in chapter 5) explains why the threat of consumer boycotts on issues such as television violence or environmental pollution may be low, even if a large number of consumers is concerned about these issues. Broadcasters conscious of government and interest group scrutiny generated by television violence may wish to reduce their use of violent imagery. Even if broadcasters jointly would be better off reducing levels of television violence, however, each individual broadcaster has a dominant strategy of continuing to broadcast television violence. The logic of the prisoners' dilemma (described in chapter 8) means that individual networks and stations may continue to face a profit-maximizing strategy of using violence to attract viewers.

The recognition that television violence is fundamentally a problem of externalities and economics suggests that solutions should focus on the individual incentives faced by viewers, producers, programmers, and advertisers. Just as the optimal amount of pollution from society's perspective is not zero, the optimal amount of violence on television is not zero. Analysis of television violence should focus on the marginal benefits and costs involved in attempts to influence how violence is portrayed in the media. Remedies often adopted to deal with negative externalities, such as zoning provisions that restrict the location of polluting facilities and tax plans that discourage pollution, may not be readily applied to television violence because of the First Amendment. Information provision about the existence and extent of externalities, a common feature of pollution policies, may offer a way to reduce the damage of television violence.

Information provision about violent content has a number of desirable features as a policy tool. It lowers the costs to parents of determining what programs they want to shield their children from. It raises the scrutiny of board members, entertainment executives, and advertisers, so that the link between company decisions and the prevalence of television violence is more explicit. The discussion generated by the information may also foster the development of norms about violent content, so that parents see protecting their children from violent content as part of a social obligation or board members view decisions about media content as having a moral element. The advantage of relying on information is that its success depends not on government force but on the strength of belief about the true impacts of television violence. The disadvantage of relying on information provision is that its success depends in part on the degree that people are willing to pay a price, in terms of time spent monitoring children's viewing or profits forgone by avoiding violent programming, for the satisfaction of furthering social goals. Questions also remain about the type of program content information that will be produced in the market and the extent to which government as a speaker can encourage the provision of information about program content.

The TV Parental Guidelines initially implemented by the television industry in 1997 used information provision by placing adult programs other than sports or news into four different viewing categories (TV-G; TV-PG; TV-14; or TV-MA) and children's programs into two categories (TV-Y and TV-Y7). Although these ratings offered parents some guidance, the system was heavily criticized for not offering viewers information on the degree of violence, sexual content, or adult language in a program. In response to this criticism, changes in the rating system were to be implemented in the fall of 1997 to provide additional content indicators for violence, sexual situations, language, and suggestive dialogue. The evidence developed in this book offers an explanation for why the industry initially chose to provide only limited rating information. Chapter 3 shows that the parental discretion warnings placed on prime-time network movies reduced the numbers of children 2–11 watching a program by 14%, but did not affect the size of teen or adult audiences. This is consistent with the notion that if the costs to parents of learning which programs are violent are substantially reduced, more parents will shield their children from the potentially harmful impacts of these programs. Although adult audiences remained the same for movies with warnings, the labeling discouraged some companies from advertising because they feared associating their product image with controversy. This advertiser backlash can reduce the returns to violent programming and, ultimately, change the type and quantity of violence offered on television. When faced with the decision in 1996 of how to design a program rating system, the industry chose a program rating system less likely to change advertiser incentives. The formation and implementation of policies designed to deal with television violence, like the production and consumption of the product itself, are ultimately a matter of such economic trade-offs.

This book offers the first combined theoretical and empirical examination of television violence from an economic perspective. Large literatures exist on the impact of television violence on society, the prevalence of violence in broadcast and cable programming, and the legal issues involved with attempts to influence the content and consumption of television programming.[2] Research efforts in these areas have formed the basis of current debates over what role, if any, the government should play in protecting children from television violence. Economics adds to this debate the view that television programming in general and violent programming in particular emerge as information products consciously shaped by programmers to maximize profits. Economics treats shows as endogenous, as commodities designed to sell and survive in a marketplace. This viewpoint leads one to explore the individual incentives operating in media markets. What incentives do parents have to monitor their children's television viewing? Why do advertisers sponsor violent programming? What calculations go through news directors' minds as they decide to lead the news with a violent crime story? Why does HBO show violent movies on Thursday evenings at 9 PM?

Economics helps answer these questions, by focusing on the incentives of individuals in the television marketplace. Separate chapters in the book examine the decisions of the people whose actions determine programming outcomes: adult viewers; children; broadcast and cable executives; program producers; advertisers; news directors; and policy makers. The book concludes with an examination of the political constraints on policy makers, a discussion of the range of policies to deal with television violence, and a focus on information provision efforts such as the TV Parental Guidelines. Before examining the different participants in the market for violent programming, I analyze in this chapter how television violence is akin to pollution and develop a simple economic programming model to explain the prevalence of violence in both entertainment and news programming.

DOES VIOLENCE ON TELEVISION CAUSE VIOLENCE IN SOCIETY?

If television violence generates negative externalities such as increased aggression and crime in society, then it should conceptually be susceptible to the same type of analysis as an externality such as pollution. Consider the parallels between answering the questions, What impact does a site contaminated by hazardous waste have on society? and What impact do violent action adventure programs have on society? At a hazardous waste site targeted for federal cleanup money under the Superfund program of the U.S. Environmental Protec-

For an individual, the basic lifetime excess cancer risk (LECR) for ingestion of contaminated groundwater at a hazardous waste site can be calculated as:

Human intake factor × (Concentration) × Toxicity = Individual lifetime excess cancer risk

where the Human intake factor (HIF) is defined as:

(Ingestion rate × Exposure frequency × Exposure duration)/(Body weight × Averaging time)

with the variables defined in units of

Ingestion rate	Liters/day	Body weight	Kilograms (kg)
Exposure frequency	Days/year	Averaging time	Days
Exposure duration	Years	Concentration	Miligrams/liter
		Toxicity	$(Mg/Kg\text{-}Day)^{-1}$

The total expected cancer cases arising from ingestion of contaminated groundwater will equal the sum across demographic groups of (Individual lifetime excess cancer risk) × (Number of individuals in a demographic group potentially exposed at the site).

Figure 1.1a. Estimating the Risks from Ingestion of Contaminated Groundwater

tion Agency (EPA), the government targets $1.1 million to analyze potential threats to human health and alternative remedies to deal with contamination. Figures 1.1a and 1.1b detail the steps entailed in calculating the lifetime excess cancer risk to an individual arising from contamination of groundwater at a hazardous waste site. The "human intake factor" for an individual depends in part on the ingestion rate (e.g., how much contaminated water the child or adult ingests per day), exposure frequency (i.e., how many days per year the person comes into contact with contaminated groundwater), and exposure duration (i.e., how long a person lives on or near the site). Analysts sample the soil and groundwater at the site to determine the concentration of the chemical contaminant. The EPA then uses a toxicity factor that reflects the likelihood that an individual will develop cancer based on ingestion of a given dose of the chemical. The product of these factors yields the lifetime excess cancer risk to an individual arising from exposure to a given chemical at a contaminated site. The total lifetime excess cancer risk from ingestion of contaminated groundwater is treated as the sum of the risk calculated to arise from each chemical contaminant.

The individual probability calculations of cancer risks at hazardous waste sites help form the basis of EPA remediation decisions, even though the figures

From society's perspective, the increase in the expected number of crimes an individual will commit that arises from consumption of action adventure programs can be calculated as:

Human intake factor × (Concentration of violence) × Toxicity of program violence = Individual lifetime excess number of crimes

where the Human intake factor (HIF) is defined as:

(Ingestion rate × Exposure frequency × Exposure duration)

with the variables defined in units of

Ingestion rate	Number of action adventure programs per week
Exposure frequency	Weeks/year of viewing
Exposure duration	Years of viewing
Concentration of violence	Number of particular types of violent acts per program
Toxicity	Number of crimes committed/violent act viewed

The total number of crimes arising from consumption of action adventure programs will equal the sum across demographic groups of (Individual lifetime excess number of crimes) × (Number of individuals in demographic group exposed to action adventure programs).

Figure 1.1b. Estimating the Expected Number of Crimes from Consumption of Action Adventure Programs

are controversial. Numerous questions surround the calculations of individual risks.[3] Should risks be calculated for individuals with a relatively high exposure duration or a mean exposure duration? How accurate are the toxicity factors, given that they are often developed by taking laboratory experiment data on animals and extrapolating to human health effects? Should mean concentrations be used, or the highest concentration found in a chemical sample at the site? The estimated lifetime excess cancer risks arising from site contamination often equal 1 in 1,000, while the baseline probability an individual will contract cancer over the course of a lifetime is 1 in 3. Can risk assessment accurately capture such relatively small additional risks from contamination? How much of the variation in risks to individuals is due to variations in people (e.g., in ingestion rates) versus uncertainty (e.g., our ignorance of the true values of the ingestion rates of people)? Aside from cancer risks, hazardous waste sites also generate noncancer risks, such as damages to reproductive health, and natural resource damages, such as destruction of habitats. These would also need to be quantified in a complete assessment of risks. Finally, individual risk estimates would need to be combined with information on how many people live around a site to get a calculation of the total number of expected cancer cases arising from contamination at a site. Since demographic groups will vary in terms of their intake factors (e.g., children consume less water than adults), one can calculate individual risks for different demographic groups, multiply these risk numbers by the number of individuals in the demographic groups living around the site, and add these numbers to yield a total number of expected cancers arising at a site over a given time period.

Each of the calculations and controversies associated with risk assessments at hazardous waste sites has a parallel in the debate over the impact of television violence. In estimating the expected number of crimes arising from exposure to violent action adventure programs on television, each program is akin to a potentially dangerous chemical. As figure 1.1b denotes, estimating the human intake factor for a show involves calculating who watches what programs over a given period of time. The corollary to the calculation of contaminant concentration is estimating the amount and types of violent acts in a given program. The toxicity factor for a program would be an estimate of the increased number of crimes that arise from the consumption of a given media image. Additional adverse outcomes could also be considered, such as increases in noncriminal aggression and changes in opinions, which may lead to increased levels of fear or discontent. Complete information on all of these factors would allow one to quantify the risks to society, if any, arising from a particular violent television program. The additional crimes estimated to arise from viewing each program would be summed across the set of violent action adventure programs consumed by an individual to yield an estimate of the increased number of expected crimes by the individual that arise from consuming these programs. Since the impact of programs varies by demographic factors such as age (e.g., lab research indicates that children are more likely to be affected by media violence than adults), one would want to calculate the risks by demographic group, multiply by the number of individuals in the demographic group that watch violent action adventure programs, and then add these figures to get the total expected number of crimes that will arise because of consumption of action adventure programming over a given time period. I investigate each of these factors in turn to see how far current research is from providing estimates of the dangers of particular violent programs.

Human Intake Factors

The degree that information exists to answer the questions in figure 1.1 depends, not surprisingly, on the degree that the information would help private decision makers maximize profits. Substantial information exists in the private sector on who watches what television shows, for these figures are compiled by the Nielsen corporation and sold to networks, advertisers, and local stations. If one were concerned primarily about exposure of children to violent television shows, figures 1.2a and 1.2b indicate that data exist on when children are likely

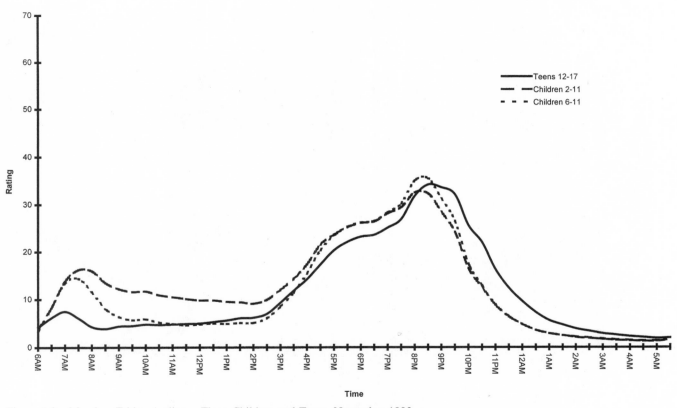

Figure 1.2a. Monday–Friday Audience Flow, Children and Teens, November 1993

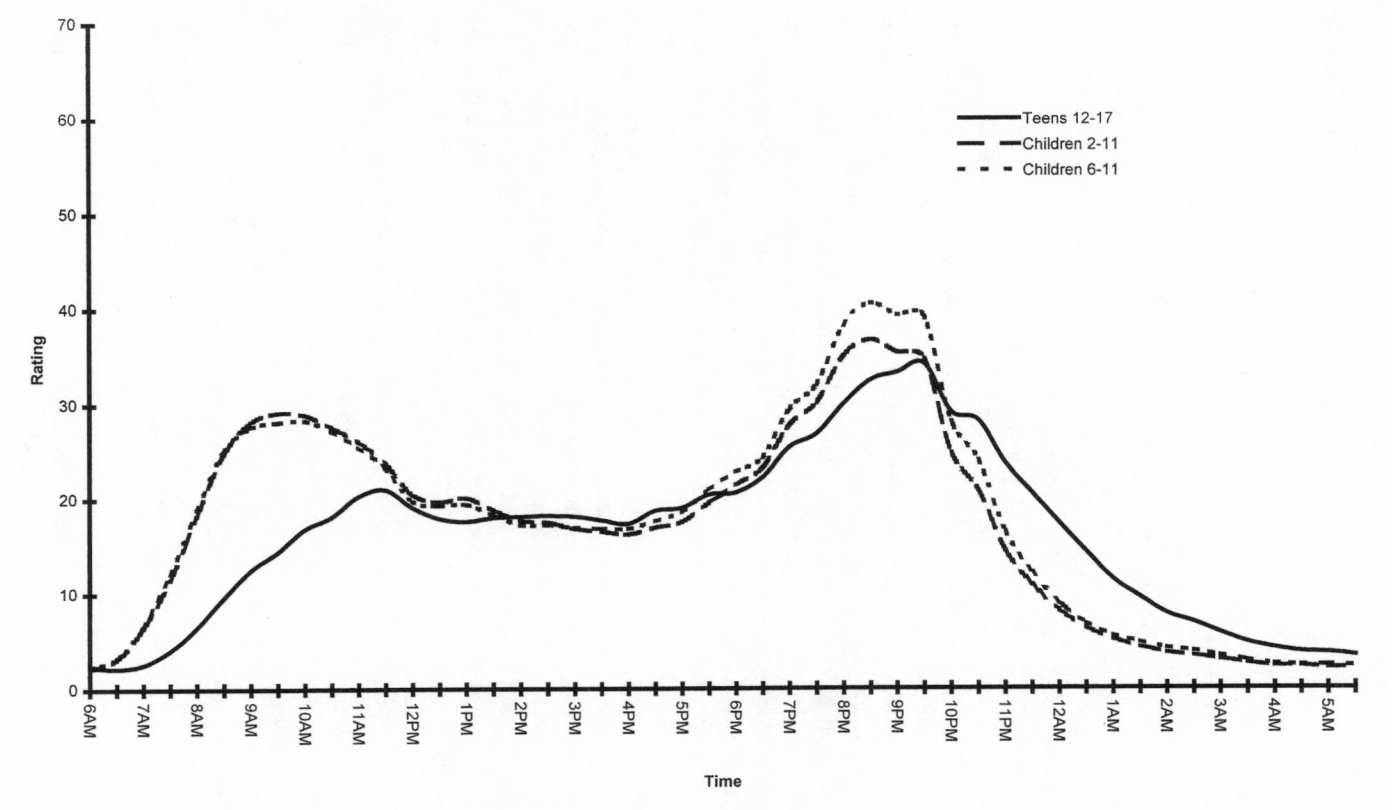

Figure 1.2b. Saturday Audience Flow, Children and Teens, November 1993

to be in the viewing audience. For Monday through Friday, children 2–11 or 6–11 and teens 12–17 gradually start coming into the audience at 3 PM and peak at 8 PM, when nearly one in three children is watching television. The interpretation of what rating constitutes a "substantial" number of children is often dependent on the interests of the interpreter.[4] In claiming that broadcasters are meeting their obligations to air educational shows for children by scheduling such programs at 7 AM on Saturdays, broadcasters have noted that fully 10% of children 6–11 are in the viewing audience at this time. Note that 10% of all children aged 6–11 are still in the viewing audience at 11 PM, although broadcasters have argued that this audience is so small that on balance indecent programming should be allowed in this time period. As expected, at least 20% of all children are in the viewing audience at most hours during Saturday, which generates incentives for programmers to schedule children's shows during the Saturday morning hours.

If one defines particular types of programming as violent, it is easy to calculate the average ratings for children 2–11 and teens for these programs. Table 1.1 is based on a snapshot of the television market from the fall of 1993.[5] For children 2–11, the average ratings for network animated children's programs was 4.8, which (since there were approximately 37.7 million children aged 2–11 in television households) translates into 1.8 million children on average watching one of these cartoons. While local news and talk shows may contain programming unsuitable for children, the information in table 1.1 reveals that situation comedies showing at the dinner hour average ratings among children 2–11 that are at least three times greater (mean 6.1) than those for local news or talk shows. During prime time, broadcast network programs in nonviolent genres average a 5.6 rating among children 2–11 versus 2.9 for violent programs. Although children are not the audience targeted by advertisers for programming such as feature films on broadcast television, they still may watch these shows in numbers that are substantial. Movies that *TV Guide* described as particularly violent earned a 3.4 rating among children 2–11 (which translates into 1.3 million children). More children on average watch these violent films than view the average network children's nonanimated program (the genre that includes many children's educational programs).

With ratings data and an accepted definition of programs of concern, one could calculate the expected number of hours of viewing a given show for children and adults based on average ratings. Ratings information also allows one to take into account the variation in television consumption across children, information that exists since advertisers value viewing of children differently depending on their demographic characteristics. For example, though the mean rating among children 2–11 for network "noneducational" children's programs was 5.4, the mean was 6.5 for children in households with income $20,000–$30,000, 6.4 in black households, and 4.5 in households headed by a person with 4 years of college. Just as environmental calculations of risk often focus on more sensitive populations, the data on differences in consumption of television allow one to calculate the amount of hours of particular types of program-

TABLE 1.1
Ratings for Children and Teens by Type of Show, Fall 1993

	Children 2–11		Teens 12–17	
	Mean	No. of Shows	Mean	No. of Shows
Network Children's Programs	4.8	40	2.3	40
Children's Animated	5.5	32	2.4	32
Children's Nonanimated	2.0	8	1.7	8
Syndicated Children's Programs	2.1	44	1.0	44
Children's Animated	2.4	35	1.1	35
Children's Nonanimated	1.1	9	0.6	9
Dinner Hour Programming	3.4	652	3.5	679
Children's Animated	6.1	57	3.9	58
Children's Nonanimated	4.3	61	3.8	31
Foreign Language	1.6	37	1.6	37
Local News	1.3	125	1.8	156
National News	1.2	20	1.5	27
News, Syndicated	1.3	15	1.8	17
Official Police	1.9	13	2.8	13
Quiz/Game	2.0	11	2.2	11
Quiz/Game—Children's	2.1	15	1.4	5
Science Fiction	2.4	10	3.6	11
Situation Comedy	6.1	148	6.7	145
Talk	1.4	52	2.5	75
Other	3.3	88	3.8	93
Network Prime-time Programs	5.0	128	5.8	128
Violent Genre	2.9	27	3.3	27
Nonviolent Genre	5.6	101	6.4	101
Syndicated Series	1.3	30	1.7	30
Violent Genre	1.3	15	1.7	15
Nonviolent Genre	1.2	15	1.7	15
Feature Films (1993)	3.4	414	4.7	414
TV Guide Violence	3.4	8	5.4	8
Murder Theme	2.6	143	3.6	143
No Murder Theme	3.9	271	5.3	271
Warning	3.0	5	3.7	5
No Warning	3.4	409	4.7	409
Late Hour	1.7	272	2.8	343
Local News	1.1	48	1.8	77
Reality-Based Adventure	1.2	12	1.9	17
Other	1.9	197	3.3	220

ming viewed by children who are heavy watchers (such as those from low-income families).[6]

Calculating the number of hours of a particular type of television programming consumed by a child or adult is akin to estimating an individual's consumption of groundwater at a waste site. For the set of action adventure programs on broadcast and cable, one can extrapolate from Nielsen data to estimate the number of hours of this type of violent programming consumed over the course of a given time period on average by individuals within a given demographic group. The next step in determining the impact of violence on television is determining the amount of different types of violent acts in a given show over time, which is like calculating the level of chemical contaminants in the groundwater at a hazardous waste site. Information on violent acts per episode of shows comes from interest groups and academics concerned with media violence, since there is not a private market demand for an exact specification of violence in shows that children are exposed to.

Concentration

Researchers concerned with quantifying the level of violence in television programming face at least three questions: how should violent programming be defined; what constitutes the unit of observation; and how many programs or broadcast days should be included in the sample of shows monitored?[7] The longest ongoing monitoring program in America is the Cultural Indicators Project at the University of Pennsylvania headed by George Gerbner. This project defines violence in television programming as

the overt expression of physical force (with or without a weapon, against self or other) compelling action against one's will on pain of being hurt or killed, or actually hurting or killing.[8]

This definition has proved controversial in part because it includes violence that occurs during cartoons, accidents, and acts of nature. The Cultural Indicators project counts a violent action as a scene of violence confined to the same participants (hence the introduction of different participants would involve a count of another violent action). The project has sampled 1 week of network broadcasts yearly and reported for each year since 1967 on measures such as the percentage of programs containing violence, the number of violent episodes per program and per hour, the percentage of characters involved in violence or killing, and an index that combines information on all these measures. These measures are all recorded with high intercoder reliability—for example, different coders tend to observe similar amounts of violence when they view the same programs.[9] The pattern of violence has generally been very stable over the years, with the percentage of prime-time shows containing some violence remaining around 70 percent and the number of violent acts on network prime time averaging between 5 and 6 per hour.[10] For the 1992–93 prime-time season, however, the number of violent acts in prime time recorded by the Cultural

Indicators project dropped to 2.9 per hour, the lowest figure in 20 years. Gerbner interpreted this result as indicating that "the threat of legislation was taken seriously and seems to have had some effect."[11]

Lichter and Amundson (1992) provided a different overview by examining programming on ten television channels (including network, independent, and cable) for a single day and counting the number of violent scenes, where violence is defined as:

any deliberate act involving physical force or the use of a weapon in an attempt to achieve a goal, further a cause, stop the action of another, act out an angry impulse, defend oneself from attack, secure a material reward or intimidate others.[12]

This definition ruled out accidents but did include comedic violence. The researchers counted 1,980 violent scenes across these ten channels for 1 day's programming, with 93% in fictional programming and 7% in news, talk shows, and tabloid television shows. Types of violence included serious assaults (389 scenes), gunplay (362), isolated punches (273), pushing/dragging (272), and menacing threats with a weapon (226). In terms of violence per hour, cartoons and toy commercials made mornings 6–9 AM (158.3 violent acts per hour across these ten channels) and late afternoon 2–5 PM (191.3 violent acts per hour) more violent than early evening 5–8 PM (40.7 violent acts per hour) or prime time 8–11 PM (102.0 violent acts per hour). Nearly half of the violent scenes showed no physical outcome for the victim of the violence, such as injuries or fatalities. Another quarter of the scenes showed no outcomes to the violence at all, as when violence in commercials for upcoming shows or theatrical movies showed violent scenes where the object of the violence was not shown. Commercials for television shows produced the second highest amount of violence by program category.

Licther's Center for Media and Public Affairs used the same definition of violence to study violent scenes in the 1992 and 1993 television seasons, where a scene was defined as:

A group of interconnected actions and dialogue that take place in the same location, in the same time frame, between a similar group of characters. A scene may consist of one act or multiple acts of violence. If there are multiple violent acts as in a beating or a brawl, then the individual blows should be grouped together and coded as one scene that depicts an assault. If there is any break in the action or change in locale or time frame or the characters involved, then the material following the change is considered a new scene.[13]

The researchers looked at the first episode during the 1993 season of each prime-time network fictional series. For these seventy-three network shows, they found that twenty-three contained no violent scenes and ten contained only one minor act of violence. The ten most violent series, however, accounted for 58% of the 361 violent scenes counted. These shows were generally ones categorized as police detective or action adventure series. About a quarter of the violence was classified as "serious violence" involving armed or unarmed assaults, gunplay, sexual assaults, or suicides. The commercials during these shows contained 354 violent scenes, almost as much as the shows themselves. Almost half of the commercial violence involved promotions for movies (theatrical and movies on television).

While academic research efforts have tried to develop measures of television violence, interest groups have also produced their own indicators of television violence and used them to label particular programs as violent. During the mid-1970s the National Citizens Committee on Broadcasting (NCCB) produced lists of violent programs and their advertisers. The program was discontinued, however, after a short-term drop in monitored levels of violence on broadcast network television.[14] The American Family Association (AFA), led by the Reverend Donald Wildmon, has labeled particular shows as violent and targeted particular sponsors for consumer boycotts based on advertising on these shows. The AFA also monitors shows for sexual content, use of profanity, and adult themes, but the group varies in the degree that it provides counts of the incidents it deems objectionable in specific shows.[15]

From 1981 through 1992, the National Coalition on Television Violence (NCTV) published the most comprehensive list of violence counts for individual programs and movies. Calculations of violent acts per hour used the following methodology:

NCTV's violence scores are actual counts of physically violent acts, hostile acts committed with the intention of hurting another person. NCTV uses a weighting system so the minor acts of violence, such as an angry push or shove, count very little (1/3 of an act of violence), and violence with serious consequences such as an attempted murder, murder, rape, or suicide count as somewhat more than a standard act of violence (1 2/3 acts of violence).[16]

Table 1.2 indicates that there are clear trends in the number of violent acts across different programming genres. The mean numbers of violent acts per episode were higher for programs in such genres as action adventure (27.6 violent acts per hour), crime (20.2), westerns (22.6), science fiction (22.8), and mystery (25.5). Each of these genres had nearly three times the rate of violence as the mean for network prime-time programming (8.4 violent acts per hour).

The NCTV data indicate that the rate of violence in most violent prime-time programming genres is greater than that for PG-13 movies. The NCTV data reveal that in terms of violent acts per hour there are really only three levels indicated by the Motion Picture Association of America (MPAA) ratings: G, PG/PG-13, and R. There is no statistically significant difference in the number of violent acts per hour in the PG movies in the sample (20.1 violent acts per hour) and the number per hour in the PG-13 movies in the sample (19.8 violent acts per hour).[17] PG and PG-13 movies are more distinguishable on the 0–5 scale for sexual content used by the NCTV to evaluate movies. These figures point out the difficulty for a parent in using MPAA ratings as a guide to violent content.

The increased congressional scrutiny of television violence in the early 1990s

TABLE 1.2
Number of Violent Acts per Hour by Show Genre and Movie Rating

	Mean	Standard deviation	Min.	Max.	No. of Shows or Movies
Network Prime-Time Programming					
All Shows	8.4	12.3	0	63	770
Narrowly Defined Genres					
Action Adventure	27.6	16.5	2	63	29
Crime	20.2	12.1	0	55	127
Western	22.6	19.9	2	55	11
Family Drama	0.7	1.1	0	4	16
Family	1.0	1.6	0	6	90
Legal	3.1	2.5	0	7	10
Medical	1.7	1.4	0	5	20
Miscellaneous	8.3	13.5	0	61	79
News	2.8	2.8	0	12	43
Occupational Comedy	1.4	2.8	0	22	156
Spin-offs	4.4	7.7	0	31	57
Romance	3.1	4.2	0	14	13
Real People	7.6	10.1	0	35	34
Science Fiction	22.8	11.4	10	50.5	20
Soap Opera	3.7	3.2	0	15	42
Mystery	25.5	4.5	18	34	16
Broadly Defined Genres					
Action Adventure	23.5	14.0	0	63	175
Drama	3.2	4.4	0	31.5	122
Fantasy–Science Fiction	19.4	11.5	2	50.5	28
News	5.6	9.0	0	50	83
Situation Comedy	1.9	4.3	0	31	326
Mystery	11.5	5.2	0	19.5	20
Variety	3.8	3.0	0	10	11
Movies					
All Movies	25.7	31.5	0	273	1210
MPAA Ratings					
G					
Violent Acts per Hour	12.9	13.4	0	62	34
PG					
Violent Acts per Hour	20.1	24.4	0	137	242
Sexual Content (scale 0–5)	0.5	1.1	0	4	45
PG-13					
Violent Acts per Hour	19.8	26.3	0	160	165
Sexual Content (scale 0–5)	1.1	1.4	0	4	65

TABLE 1.2 (Continued)

	Mean	Standard deviation	Min.	Max.	No. of Shows or Movies
R					
Violent Acts per Hour	33.1	37.0	0	273	483
Sexual Content (scale 0–5)	2.34	1.97	0	5	161

Source: Violent acts per hour were calculated by National Coalition on Television Violence for 770 shows from 1980 to 1991 and 1,210 movies from 1982 to 1992. Narrowly defined genre definitions came from Wakshlag and Adams 1985. Broadly defined genre definitions came from Tiedge and Ksobiech 1987.

generated new attempts to convey which types of programming contain violence. The UCLA Center for Communication Policy conducted a study funded by the network broadcasters to monitor television content for 3 years. Rather than develop quantitative measures of violent content, the report on the first year of programming (1994–95) adopted a qualitative approach to the assessment of the use of violence.[18] The researchers sampled each prime-time series program and all movies on the broadcast networks and examined the violence presented in terms of context, motivation, relevance of the violence to plot or character development, consequences of violence, and the nature of the violence (e.g., real, fantasy, comedic?). The researchers then presented qualitative descriptions of violence on the particular shows they felt raised issues of concern based on their monitoring factors. Of the 121 prime-time series reviewed, 10 had frequent problems with the use of violence and 8 raised occasional issues.[19] Among 161 miniseries and made-for-television movies examined, the researchers felt 23 were problematic in terms of violence. This compares to 50 out of the 118 theatrical movies broadcast on the networks during this period that the UCLA researchers found raised issues of concern with respect to violence. These findings are consistent with earlier work that indicates action adventure, police, reality, and theatrical movies are sources of potentially objectionable or damaging violence on television.

The most ambitious quantitative depiction of television violence emerged from a 3-year monitoring program funded by the National Cable Television Association, a program that drew upon research teams from four universities to produce the National Television Violence Study (NTVS). The NTVS researchers designed a coding framework specifically related to the social science literature on the impact of violent programming. The explicit definition of violence used in the content analysis is:

Violence is defined as any overt depiction of a credible threat of physical force or the actual use of such force intended to physically harm an animate being or group of beings. Violence also includes certain depictions of physically harmful consequences against an animate being or group that occur as a result of unseen violent means. Thus, there are three primary types of violent depictions: credible threats, behavioral acts and harmful consequences.[20]

This definition rules out most harmful speech as violence, includes superhero and cartoon violence, and includes as violent scenes to be coded instances where the violent act is not seen but the outcomes (such as injuries) are.[21] The broad unit of analysis used is the violent incident, defined as an interaction between a perpetrator, an act, and a target. The researchers coded the context of the violent incident based on factors found in the social literature to be related to the harms from media violence. The researchers identified three types of undesirable outcomes arising from exposure to media violence: learning aggression, fear, and desensitization. They then identified a set of contextual factors that the social science literature indicates leads to outcomes such as increased learning of aggression: attractive perpetrators, justified violence, presence of weapons, graphic violence, realistic violence, violence that is rewarded, and the mixture of humor and violence. They noted that violence shown with punishment and with pain and harm cues was less likely to stimulate the learning of aggression, so that these factors were also tracked in their content analysis.

The NTVS methodology for analyzing content can provide the inputs into a risk assessment of particular types of programming, for it describes programming in terms of content known to be harmful to children or adults. The researchers point out that it is difficult to come up with a summary measure of the risk of a program based on contextual factors for several reasons:

Because the experimental studies to date have only tested these context factors in isolation from one another, we have no solid information about which factors may be most critical or how such factors might interact with one another. For example, it might be that pain and harm cues are most influential when shown within a realistic portrayal of violence than in the context of a fantasy program. Until more detailed analyses are conducted, we must assume that each factor is somehow important to the overall risk associated with a given portrayal. In that case, a violent program that contains several contextually-based risk factors presumably is more problematic than a portrayal featuring only one.[22]

The results from the first year of the NTVS research demonstrate how content analysis can be used to describe variations in the nature of violence used in television programming. The researchers found that violence was frequently used in contexts that laboratory evidence suggests increases the likelihood that aggression will be stimulated. Perpetrators were not punished in 73% of the violent scenes examined. Nearly half of the violent actions did not show the harm associated with the victim of violence, and 58% did not show any pain. The presentation of violence varied across genres, so that the researchers were able to indicate potential dangers associated with given types of programming. Movies were notable, for example, in that they were "more likely to present violence in realistic settings (85%), and include blood and gore in violent scenes (28%) than other program types."[23] A methodology such as that developed by the NTVS allows one to describe the "concentration" of violence in a given set of programming by analyzing the context and frequency of violent acts in these shows.

Toxicity

Once the viewership of a particular show is established and the nature and number of violent acts it contains are determined, the final step in conducting a risk assessment of television violence is determining what (if any) effects the program has on individuals. There are numerous reviews of the literature on the impacts of violent television programming. An early overview by Andison (1977) determined that among 67 studies done between 1956 and 1976, 77% found a positive association between the consumption of violent television programming and aggression, 4% found the reverse effect, and 19% discovered no impact on aggression. Paik and Comstock (1994) conducted a metaanalysis of 217 studies of the impact of television violence and determined that in these studies there was a highly statistically significant positive association of "medium magnitude" between exposure and aggressive behavior.[24] About three-quarters of the tests examined came from experimental studies, where one set of viewers was shown violent programming, another set was shown neutral programming or no programming, and their subsequent behaviors were compared. One-quarter were from correlational studies that surveyed individuals' amount of TV viewing, expressed preferences for particular programs, or frequency of viewing actual TV programs, and related these exposure measures to differences in aggressive or criminal behavior. In terms of the age distribution of participants, 85% of the total sample of participants were aged 6–21, a testament in part to the use of school subjects for testing. The range of antisocial behaviors cataloged by the studies included criminal acts and physical violence (studied in the survey responses), verbal aggression, reported aggressive intent through survey questions, and willingness to administer electric shocks to others in the laboratory setting. Of the antisocial effects measured, 45% were based on self-reports of violent intentions or performance in tests for willingness to shock a third party, 25% dealt with interpersonal aggression observed during play or other social interactions, and 10% involved illegal behavior (as measured through survey responses or crime statistics). Paik and Comstock found that these measures revealed that television violence affected both children and adults, although the size of the effect is greatest for preschool age children and smallest for adults. The measured magnitude of the effect is greatest when the indicator is aggression directed against an object and smallest when the measure is criminal violence directed against another person.

Although lab experiments and field surveys both indicate that higher consumption of violent programming is associated with more aggressive behavior, correlation does not prove causation. To investigate whether consumption of violent programming causes increased aggression, one needs to examine the design of experiments, see if factors other than TV consumption explain the association, and consider the theoretical explanations offered for the positive association. Spitzer notes that there are at least four psychological theories that hypothesize a positive relationship between increased aggression and the viewing of violent television programming by children: disinhibition, whereby children who view violent acts on TV become more comfortable with such behavior and less likely to be affected by social sanctions against this behavior; social learning, which posits that children imitate adult role models, including adult role models on TV who may engage in violent actions; conditioning, which means that children who are exposed to television scenes where violence is used to solve problems may automatically adopt violent solutions when they face similar situations in the real world; and the theory that violence on TV acts as a commercial for aggressive behavior, so that children grow up with a taste for violent activity, which is often portrayed as pleasurable.[25] Although a catharsis theory posits that youths may satisfy aggressive impulses through the viewing of violent material and thus violent programming could lead to a net reduction of such behavior, the finding of a consistently positive association in the lab between exposure and aggression contradicts the catharsis theory.

In terms of proving that consumption of violent TV causes aggressive behavior, lab experiments offer strong evidence for causation since the experimenter can attempt to control for differences among participants so that the factor being varied relates almost exclusively to the amount of violent television consumed. In such studies (see Bandura, Ross, and Ross 1963), children who view violent programming in the experiment are more likely to behave aggressively (e.g., act out aggression against toys) than those exposed to no programming or nonviolent programming. What these studies establish is that consumption of violent programming can cause short-term increases in aggressive behavior by children. These results have also been confirmed when behavior was observed outside the lab, for Steuer, Applefield, and Smith (1971) found that nursery school children exposed to violent programming were more aggressive in playground interactions than those exposed to nonviolent programming.

Atkin's study (1983) shows how investigators have used lab experiments to vary the presentation of violence in TV programming to see how context can influence viewer reactions. Atkin showed elementary school students randomly assigned to three separate groups a 6-minute newscast with commercials. Each group saw the same program, except one group saw a segment that contained a fight sequence presented as part of the newscast, one group saw the same fight in a commercial as part of a movie promotion, and the third (control) group saw a newscast without the fight scene. Atkin surveyed the students afterward and developed measures of aggression based on responses to hypothetical situations and responses to statements about aggression. Children who viewed the violence segments were more likely to exhibit aggression in the hypothetical situations than the students in the control group, and the aggressive responses were higher for those who viewed the fight as part of a news segment than as part of an entertainment promotion. The news version also generated more attention among the students and was perceived as more realistic than the entertainment version of the fight.

Numerous lab studies also reveal that teenagers and college students exposed to violent programming are more likely to exhibit aggressive behavior, measured by survey responses after the exposure or a willingness to administer electric shocks to others in the lab setting (note that although the subjects believe they control the setting of shocks, they are not actually administering shocks to others in the lab). Violent programming can thus be said to cause aggression among young adults, in a short-term manner as measured in experiments. As Comstock and Paik note, however, "The experimental setting for teenagers and young adults departs from the everyday in the perceptions of the subjects, in the brevity of the television exposure, in the absence of the possibility of retaliation for aggression, in the exclusion of competing and countervailing communications, and in the criterion of immediacy as the measure of effects."[26]

Survey evidence relating the amount of violent programming watched or expressed preferences for such programming to measures of aggression and criminal acts helps test whether the results of the lab experiments extend to the real world. The survey results that are discussed here do indicate a statistically significant, positive association between consumption of violent programming and aggressive or criminal behavior. Again, however, the problem arises of attributing causation to correlation. If one finds that children who consume more violent programming are more aggressive, one might conclude that exposure to violent programming causes children to be more violent, that aggressive behavior causes children to consume more violent programming (e.g., their aggression leads children to be in situations where they watch more TV or more violent TV), that a third variable not captured in models influences both aggression and consumption of violent programming (e.g., children with certain personality traits are more likely to be aggressive, and these same traits also lead them to be more likely to consume violent programming), or that some combination of these explanations accounts for the relationship.

Belson (1978) examined the viewing patterns and behavior of a sample of 1,565 teenage London males. The youths were asked about the frequency of viewing a sample of violent television programs aired during their childhood and teenage years, information that was also combined with information on how violent the particular programs were perceived to be by a panel of television viewers. Data on violent behavior were also collected from the youths, which ranged from questions about swearing or aggressive behavior to queries about criminal acts. Belson concluded that:

The evidence gathered through this investigation is very strongly supportive of the hypothesis that high exposure to television violence increases the degree to which boys engage in serious violence. Thus for serious violence by boys: (i) heavier viewers of television violence commit a great deal more serious violence than do lighter viewers of television violence who have been closely equated to the heavier viewers in terms of a wide array of empirically derived matching variables; (ii) the reverse form of this hypothesis is not supported by the evidence.[27]

Milavsky et al. (1982) tracked approximately 2,400 elementary school children and 800 male teenagers for over 3 years to examine the relationship between consumption of violent television programming and antisocial behavior. Among the elementary school children, an index of exposure to violent programming was derived from data on children's reported viewing frequencies for particular programs and information on violence rankings of these programs, and an index of aggressive behavior was derived from peers' reports on how often the child engaged in behavior such as pushing or hitting others. Data on the teenagers were derived from questions about their viewing habits and aggressive or criminal behavior. Students in the panel were interviewed multiple times during the study to investigate the lagged effects of exposure to violent programming. Although the authors found that measures of current exposure to television violence and current aggression were positively correlated, they determined that there was evidence that once one controlled for past levels of aggressive behavior there was not a statistically significant impact of past consumption of violent programming on current aggressive behavior. They concluded that their study "did not find evidence that television violence was causally implicated in the development of aggressive behavior patterns among children and adolescents over the time periods studied."[28] The report has attracted much criticism and reanalysis of the data, with the result that Comstock and Paik (1991) conclude that "these data are consistent with and add to the support given by the data from other surveys for the proposition that greater exposure to violent television entertainment heightens subsequent aggressive and antisocial behavior."[29]

In a study tracking a group of individuals from childhood to adulthood, Eron and Huesmann report:

The more violent the programs children watched at age 8, the more aggressive they were at age 19, as indicated both by self-ratings and peer ratings; the more serious were the crimes for which they were convicted by age 30; the more aggressive was their behavior while under the influence of alcohol; and . . . the harsher was the punishment of their own children. These relations held up even when the subjects' initial aggressiveness, social class and IQ were controlled.[30]

These authors found there was no relation between the amount of violence viewed as an adult and aggression as an adult. They interpret these findings as indicating that the impact of consumption of violent programming is large during childhood, when a youth who watches heavy amounts of violent programming is "more likely to develop and maintain cognitive scripts emphasizing aggressive solutions to social problems."[31] In another study of elementary school children, Eron and Huesmann (1986) found that, when they controlled for initial levels of aggression, later aggression was higher among girls who had consumed more violent programming and boys who had consumed more violent programming and identified with the violent characters. They also found some evidence that current viewing of violent programming can be predicted in part by past aggressive behavior.

The introduction of television into communities and nations at different rates also provides evidence on the impact of consumption of programming. Joy, Kimball, and Zabrack (1986) found that physical and verbal aggression on the playground increased among children tested in the first and second grades and again in the third and fourth grades when television was introduced into a Canadian community but that this pattern did not hold in two control communities where television had already been introduced. Hennigan et al. (1982) found that among U.S. cities in the 1950s, which received television station licenses at different times, the introduction of television was associated with an increase in larceny in cities but not with an increase in violent crime. Centerwall (1992) used information on the introduction of television in Canada, South Africa, and the United States to argue that the long-term exposure of children to television is a significant factor in explaining the homicide rate in the United States.

In sum, a substantial number of laboratory studies show that consumption of violent programming by children and young adults can cause short-term increases in aggressive behavior or attitudes. The data from field surveys relating to consumption of violent programming and aggressive or criminal behavior are also consistent with the theory that such programming leads to long-term effects. Deducing causation from the correlations in the field studies alone is always problematic, since one must try to determine whether a third omitted variable could be driving both aggression and viewing of violent programming or whether aggression can lead to the viewing of violent programming. Comstock and Paik (1991) conclude:

The question of whether a portion (and if so how great) of the positive association between the viewing of violent entertainment and aggressive and antisocial behavior is attributable to young persons higher in such behavior seeking out that type of diversion remains open. . . . In sum, some of the association may be attributable to the influence of behavior on viewing, but it is unlikely that any such influence is as large as that of viewing on behavior, and unlikely that such influence entirely explains the association.[32]

Comstock (1986) found in his review of field surveys that exposure to violent programming explained 4% to 10% of the variance in aggression among the subjects.

Most researchers assess this information and conclude that violent television programming does cause increases in aggression among children and teenagers. A report prepared in 1982 for the National Institute of Mental Health declared that:

The consensus among most of the research community is that violence on television does lead to aggressive behavior by children and teenagers who watch the programs. This conclusion is based on laboratory experiments and on field studies. Not all children become aggressive, of course, but the correlations between violence and aggression are positive. In magnitude, television violence is as strongly correlated with aggressive behavior as any other behavioral variable that has been measured. The research question has moved from asking whether or not there is an effect to seeking explanations for the effect.[33]

When sixty-eight researchers who had done research on television and youths were surveyed about the preceding statement, more than 80% strongly or moderately agreed with it.[34]

While these studies allow one to conclude that certain genres are more likely to contain violent acts that are harmful to viewers and that children are more likely to be harmed than adults by violent programming, the studies are not specific enough to allow one to state a "toxicity factor" for a given program that would translate exposure into an expected increase in criminal activity or aggressive behavior. The ideal "toxicity factor" for a show would allow one to estimate the change in the expected number of crimes committed per violent act viewed by an individual in a given demographic group, a figure that studies indicate could be higher for children since they are more likely to be influenced by violent programming. One could then take the toxicity factor for a given demographic group and multiply it by the concentration of violence and the human intake factor for violent programming, which would yield an estimate of the increase in the expected number of crimes arising from a person's consumption of action adventure programming. These individual crime estimates would be multiplied by the number of individuals exposed to violent programming in each demographic group, to yield the expected number of crimes arising from exposure of children and adults to action adventure programming over a given time period. The increase in expected numbers of crimes or aggressive actions corresponds to the expected number of cancer cases estimated in the hazardous waste risk assessment.

A second possible source of negative externalities from violent programming is its impact on viewers' construction of reality and values.[35] This theory suggests that exposure to more television or violent programming may make children and adults more likely to adopt a vision of reality as a "mean world," which may translate into fearfulness about personal safety (e.g., being afraid to walk alone at night) and pessimism. A positive association between television viewing and "mean world" perceptions has frequently been found in surveys (Gerbner et al. 1978, 1979), although the size and statistical significance of these relationships often decline once one controls for socioeconomic variables such as the age, income, and gender of the viewers.[36] As evidence that television cultivates a "mean world" syndrome among viewers, Gerbner, Morgan, and Signorelli (1994) point out that

heavy viewers are more likely than comparable groups of light viewers to overestimate one's chances of involvement in violence; to believe that one's neighborhood is unsafe; to state that fear of crime is a very serious personal problem; and to assume that crime is rising, regardless of the facts of the case. Heavier viewers in every subgroup (defined by education, race, age, income, gender, newspaper reading, neighborhood, etc.) express a greater sense of apprehension than do light viewers in the same groups. Other results show that heavy viewers are also more likely to have bought new locks, watchdogs, and guns "for protection."[37]

More recent research has demonstrated that "mean world" perceptions are related more to the viewing of crime shows and the news than simply television viewing in general.[38] A difficulty with the attribution of causation from exposure to attitude formation remains the fact that individuals who vary in attitudes may also vary in the quantity and types of programming they select, so that some differences in attitudes may predate or exist independent of exposure to different shows.

A new area of research indicates that violence may affect the health of the viewer through physiological responses to viewing. Pilot studies by Williams and his colleagues (1996a, 1996b) indicate that adult subjects who viewed violent movies in a lab setting had higher blood pressure measurements after watching violent movie sequences, if the victim of the violence was of the same gender as the viewer. Stress hormone levels also increased after viewing violent movie sequences. Both effects were greater for female subjects viewing violent sequences than for male subjects. While sample sizes in both studies were small ($N = 40$ subjects), the results suggest that for some individuals viewing violent films may lead to physiological effects that contribute to heart disease.

Another potential loss to society from television violence arises from the "existence values" that some individuals place on living in a culture free from violent images on television. Just as some people derive satisfaction from pristine environmental areas even if they will never visit them, some individuals derive pleasure from living in a society free from media violence, independent of the negative impacts television violence may have on behavior. This ideological satisfaction in part helps explain why some individuals may be active in interest groups on this issue. A full analysis of the costs of media violence levels would include a value (derived from survey evidence) of the benefits to these individuals.[39] Incorporating the value that individuals place on preventing the consumption of television programming by others, however, may generate controversy among those who place a value on individuals' freedom to choose whatever media products they wish to consume. If one is guided by existence values in this area, then in a cost-benefit framework one may well end up recommending that majority preferences about media content should take precedence over an individual's freedom to consume.[40]

Figure 1.3 summarizes the risk assessment parallels between estimating the number of expected cancer cases likely to arise at a hazardous waste site and the number of crimes generated by action adventure programming. In both cases, data can be readily collected on the number of people likely to be exposed to the externality. Census data track housing figures that indicate likely exposure to contaminated groundwater, while Nielsen data provide profiles of the likely viewers of programs. The levels of contaminants, whether they are

Pollution: Hazardous Waste Site	Television Violence: Action Adventure Programming
1. How many people are exposed to the contaminant?	1. How many people view a particular television program?
2. What chemical concentrations are individuals exposed to?	2. What levels and types of violence are viewers exposed to in a given program?
3. What evidence from animal tests or human epidemiological studies indicates the magnitude of a chemical's toxicity?	3. What evidence from lab experiments or epidemiological studies indicates the dangers of particular types of television violence?
4. Aside from elevated risks of cancer, how does the contaminant elevate risks of noncancerous diseases? Natural resources damages?	4. Aside from elevated risks of crime commission, how do violent programs effect levels of fear? Desensitization? Aggression?
5. How large are the existence and bequest values involved?	5. How much do individuals value living in a society free of media violence, independent of its impact on crime and attitudes?
6. What is the value of a statistical cancer averted?	6. What is the value of a statistical crime averted?

Figure 1.3 Risk Assessment Parallels

contaminants in groundwater or violent acts in programs, can be assayed through sampling. EPA regulatory guidance provides a framework for estimating exposures to carcinogens. The NTVS study provides a framework for measuring the presence of violent contexts that are thought to increase the generation of aggression, fear, or desensitization.

Both the generation of cancers and crimes involve long lag times, so that it is difficult to trace particular adverse outcomes to particular exposures. For chemicals this has meant that toxicity factors are generally derived from laboratory experiments with animals, so that dose-response relationships observed in lab animals become the basis for estimating the reaction of humans to chemical exposures. In media violence research, lab experiments also serve as the basis for studying the contextual factors associated with the generation of aggression. The limits of the lab, primarily that one is measuring short-term effects and that the lab outcomes measured (e.g., aggressive play) may not be the subject of the policy debate (e.g., violent crime), mean that to date toxicity factors that relate consumption of images to increases in the expected number of crimes have not been developed for specific television programs.

Ideally, the outputs from risk assessments can be incorporated in cost-benefit analysis of proposals to deal with externalities. At a hazardous waste site, this would involve accepting a value for the avoidance of a statistical case of cancer and multiplying this by the number of cancers averted by a given remediation proposal, such as treatment of the contaminated groundwater at the site. For example, Viscusi (1992) indicates that value of life estimates derived from data on consumer reactions to product risks and worker reaction to jobsite risks cluster in a range from $3 to $7 million (1990$).[41] If one assumed a value of averting a statistical cancer case of $10 million, then the costs of groundwater treatment at a hazardous waste site could then be balanced against the dollar value of the averted cancer cases (e.g., $10 million per cancer case averted times the number of cancer cases averted).

Consider how the risk assessment figures would factor into a cost-benefit analysis of television violence policies, such as the placement of parental discretion warnings on a given movie. Evidence from chapter 3 establishes that a short-run effect of this may be to reduce the audience of children 2–11 for a movie with a warning label by approximately 220,000, while the teen and adult audience remains constant. Chapter 5 indicates that some advertisers may pull sponsorships from the movie, which can lead the network to run an internal promotion rather than a commercial. Assume that the value to society of the net change in advertising is approximately $200,000.[42] The cost of the labeling of a movie is thus $200,000, which yields a benefit of 220,000 fewer children being exposed to the violence in the film. If one values a life at $10 million, then placing a label on the film would pass a rough cost-benefit test if it reduced the expected number of murders potentially committed at some time by these children by .02 murders. Incorporating the reduction in the expected number of other crimes would lower even further the number of expected murders averted required for the labeling to appear desirable.[43]

There may be additional long-run implications for a general policy of labeling movies with parental discretion warnings. If these labels caused advertising returns to drop, then broadcasters might shift production to other genres of programming. The financial impact on producers, actors, and writers of a policy would not show up as a loss in the cost-benefit analysis since the assumption is generally made that "workers" in an industry can costlessly move on to other employment. There could, however, be a reduction in the utility of adult viewers who would have preferred to see violent programming but now end up consuming nonviolent programming. The impact of media violence policies on the viewing utility of adult consumers, who face a much lower probability of being adversely affected by its consumption, should thus factor into analysis of policies aimed at reducing the exposure of children to violent programming. Note that the source of the label policy may also affect cost-benefit calculations. If the warning labels were required by the government rather than voluntarily adopted, then one would need to factor in the disutility of First Amendment activists who value the freedom of broadcasters to program without having to label their products.

The questions involved in cost-benefit analyses of externalities, whether they arise from hazardous waste sites or violent television programs, underscore why they are costly to undertake. In cleaning up a hazardous waste site, the EPA does not conduct a full analysis of costs and benefits. The difficulty of isolating health effects through epidemiology leads the EPA to rely on health impact models derived from lab experience with animals to derive lifetime excess cancer risks for humans at waste sites. For noncancer effects, the agency simply calculates (again generally from lab animal evidence) the lowest dose of the chemical associated with no adverse health effects and determines whether individuals are exposed to higher doses at a site. Cleanup decisions are made on the basis of risk assessments and exposure standards from other regulatory programs, which establish concentration levels that the agency must use as cleanup standards. New legislation considered by Congress in 1995 would have required federal agencies to conduct a risk assessment and cost-benefit analysis of regulations costing more than $25 million annually or environmental cleanups costing more than $5 million.[44] This would have entailed estimating cancer cases and noncancer effects at sites and trying to put a dollar value on these effects. Had this legislation passed and media violence proposals also passed, such as the measure that would have banned broadcasters from airing violent television when children were likely to be in the audience, a full cost-benefit analysis of regulations dealing with television violence would have been required by law.[45]

This chapter reveals what questions can and cannot be answered in such a cost-benefit analysis. Excellent data exist, from Nielsen and other survey sources, on when children and adults are in the television audience and what programs they are watching. One knows historically what program genres generally contain violence, such as action adventure, crime, and mystery series; movies that are rated as violent by critics or program guides; and children's action adventure and cartoon programming. More detailed data on specific violent acts and their context can be derived from monitoring projects, although these data often simply confirm the distinctions among genres discussed earlier. One can thus estimate the number of hours of viewing by children 2–11 of prime-time broadcast movies that contain violence. The American Psychological Association estimates, for example, that a child consuming 2 to 4 hours of television per day will have seen by the end of his or her elementary school years 8,000 murders and 100,000 violent acts on television.[46]

Given current research, one cannot link specific acts of violence on a particular television program with the generation of specific crimes or quantify the expected increase in crime from the program.[47] The strongest evidence on the impact of television violence comes from the laboratory experiments involving children. Yet what is measured in the lab is aggression rather than criminal acts. In terms of specific shows, one can say whether the program contains violent elements that have been linked to increases in aggressive behavior or attitudes. Thus one can identify which programs contain violent elements that are likely to generate negative externalities, though the extent of the impact of a particular program cannot be isolated. One could attempt to quantify the impacts of media violence as a whole on society, rather than proceeding from a summation of effects from individual programs.[48] This global approach is made difficult by the fact that estimates would generally be based on the impact of television as a whole rather than the specific effects of consumption of violent television.

This book is written from the perspective that violence on television does have a negative impact on society. I believe that the laboratory evidence firmly establishes that violence on television causes children to be more aggressive and that evidence on the introduction of television is consistent with the theory that children learn scripts of behavior from television that lead them to be violent in later life. Survey evidence is consistent with this theory since more violent youths and adults also report higher consumption of violent television as children. Throughout the book I thus analyze violent television programs in part in terms of the audiences they attract among children. Although children are not the audience targeted by advertisers on adult series and movies, their viewership influences the extent of negative externalities generated by the program. Readers may differ in their interpretation of whether particular types of programming are harmful. In each empirical analysis I explicitly state what constitutes a violent program. In analysis of adult series I generally will identify particular genres as violent, such as action adventure, crime, and mystery programs. In examining movies, I use ratings by the Motion Picture Association of America, reviews by critics of violent content, and warning labels or content indicators from broadcasters and cable networks used to identify violent films. Among children's shows, I distinguish between "educational" programs less likely to be violent and the noneducational shows, which often include violent cartoons. In examining local news broadcasts, I develop measures of story content and styles that help differentiate "high-crime" broadcasts.

A MODEL OF THE MARKET FOR VIOLENT PROGRAMMING

If violent programming is harmful to society, what explains its commercial success? Since the first congressional hearing on the topic in 1954, policy makers have debated why violent programming is a persistent part of programming schedules despite periodic public outcries about the impacts of such programs. Journalists, legal scholars, network executives, and industry participants have generated (sometimes competing) explanations for how the market for violent programming operates. This section lays out the "stylized facts" about television violence frequently made in policy debates. Although many of these "facts" may be true, they have not until now been collected into explicit economic models or extensively tested. I will first describe these commonly held beliefs (without examining whether they are internally consistent) and then incorporate part of them into a more formal economic model.

Violence sells. The acknowledgment that violent programming emerges from market interactions often begins with the observation that "violence sells": programmers schedule violent shows because they attract both viewers and advertisers in profitable quantities. As the journalist Bill Moyers put it, "It is the bottom line that is driving the violence in television, videos and other forms of the media. The message of violence in the media is if you want juice, money, power, ratings, respect, use violence because violence sells."[49] In legislative debate, Senator Paul Simon observed that, "The networks obviously continue to believe that in order to earn ratings, they must put on their share of guns and blood. There is still the feeling that if violence sells, they will air it."[50] The assertion that programmers use violence to attract viewers almost appears prosaic, yet some deny this choice is a conscious business strategy. Broadcasters are much more likely to discuss the function of violence as a plot device than a profit mechanism. The link between sales and violent content is even denied in public forums, perhaps because describing violent content as a business strategy rather than artistic expression might undercut the efforts of broadcasters to resist changes in schedules. In response to questioning at a congressional hearing on television violence, a CBS executive declared, "We disagree with the statement . . . that violence attracts both audience and advertiser dollars and for that reason broadcasters are unwilling to air programming which might be less violent."[51]

Violent programs are proof that television programmers are not responsive to viewer preferences. In contrast to the idea that violent programs are aired because they attract viewers, some analysts emphasize that factors other than viewer preferences lead to the provision of violent programming. Describing the market for violent content, George Gerbner has observed, "television violence is an overkill of 'happy violence'—swift, cool, effective, without graphic consequences and in other ways divorced from real life and crime statistics. 'Happy violence' is the byproduct of a manufacturing and marketing process that defies popular taste and imposes uniformity on creative people and viewers. There is no evidence that, other factors being equal, violence per se is giving most viewers 'what they want.'"[52] The notion here is that elements of market structure (described in additional detail later) restrict the types of programs that are offered and that viewers are dissatisfied with these options. As one scholar put it, "Faced with the choice between violent material and violent material, then, viewers not surprisingly reach for what is available. Greater diversity in program selection combined with more precise measures of viewer preference could lead program executives to reformulate their assumptions about what people want to see."[53]

Violent shows generate higher or lower ratings than other programs. People who stress that violence sells often indicate that this means violent programs will have higher ratings than other programs. Those who stress viewer dissatisfaction with violent programming often go on to assert that violent shows attract lower ratings. Summarizing the factors that influence television programmers, Senator Simon noted, "One is the plain fact that violence sells. Programmers, producers and advertisers have discovered the axiom that violence is nearly a sure-fire ratings booster. It moves the numbers."[54] The same incentives are also said to operate in news coverage. As journalist David Nyhan put it, "Violence boosts TV news ratings; the gorier the pictures, the higher the ratings and thus the ad rates."[55] George Gerbner stresses, however, that "the most highly rated programs are seldom violent." He compared the average Nielsen ratings and shares for 104 violent programs and 103 nonviolent programs aired from 1988 to 1993 and found that the average rating and average share for the violent shows were 11.1 and 18.9 versus a mean rating of 13.8 and mean share of 22.5 for the nonviolent shows. He concluded that this "test of the relationship between violence and ratings refutes the standard rationalization for violent programming. . . . violence per se consistently receives lower ratings."[56] The debate over violent programming thus proceeds with contradictory claims about the degree that violence attracts ratings.

Competitive pressure yields violent programming. Although industry participants sometimes acknowledge the social problems entailed with violent programming, they go on to point out that any attempt by one network or cable channel to reduce violence on its own would place it at a competitive disadvantage against other networks or channels that continued to schedule violent programming. Though cooperation among competitors could theoretically lead to a joint agreement to reduce violence levels, the prospect that this would be a violation of antitrust laws led Congress to pass the Television Violence Act of 1990, which gave television executives a 3-year exemption from antitrust provisions so they could jointly develop voluntary guidelines to reduce television violence. In debates over such legislation, competitive pressures were frequently invoked as a rationale for the bill. Representative Dan Glickman noted, "An obstacle to a voluntary reduction in violence by networks is that, in this intensely competitive business, it is commonly held that violence sells. Each network is reluctant to take unilateral steps to reduce violent programming for fear of slipping in the ratings."[57] Senator Simon observed, "It is difficult for one member of the television industry to impose internal standards on violence when the others can gain a commercial advantage by going in the opposite direction."[58] Although broadcasters often publicly disavow that violent programming is driven by competitive pressures, privately they often point to such pressures as an obstacle to reducing television violence. As one executive said during a private meeting in the 1970s at the Federal Communications Commission (FCC), "The networks are only part, and in some cases only a small part, of the problem of violence and tasteless material. There are times when CBS rejects a program only to find it turning up on other stations, to our competitive disadvantage. It seems pointless for the FCC to direct its attention to the networks alone while nonnetwork independent stations play very violent, syndicated programs such as *The Untouchables* in the late afternoon and early evening."[59]

Television violence is a market-driven commodity. Emphasis on television as part of a marketplace of ideas leads some analysts to conclude that respect for market outcomes should lead to tolerance of television violence. As one legal scholar put it, "the viewers have manifested in the market their enjoyment of violent television and their willingness to pay for it. The television industry is part of the marketplace and is likely to respond to market pressures. . . . Because the purpose of our communication system is to allow, where possible, the free market to determine matters, television violence should be left to the control of the market."[60] This emphasis on television violence as an outcome of private market decisions is consistent with the deregulatory approach toward television instituted in the 1980s by FCC Chairman Mark Fowler, who declared that television was simply a "toaster with pictures," and held that the same market mechanisms which worked well in appliance markets would also work in the broader marketplace of ideas.[61] If one believes that television violence yields violence in society, however, then the externalities generated by violent programs can be viewed as an instance of market failure.

The stylized facts about the economics of television can be helpful if they focus attention on the incentives faced by the different participants in the television industry. The problem with these hypotheses is that they are not often brought together to see how different factors interact, they tend to focus on violent programming without placing this genre in a larger programming market, and they are not formally specified so that their implications can be more easily tested. In the remainder of the chapter I remedy these defects by explicitly modeling the economics behind violent programming and proposed policies to deal with this problem. I start by constructing a simple model of the market for violent programming.[62]

Television viewers vary in preferences for different types of programming. Assume that there are three distinct groups of television viewers: those who watch low-violence programming, those who prefer shows with moderate levels of violence, and those who view programs with heavy amounts of violence. In a market where broadcasters value viewers on the basis of their value to advertisers, the revenues from capturing viewers in a particular market will vary depending on the demographics of those watching the programs. A programmer selecting what show to air will consider both the number of viewers for that genre (e.g., number of high-violence viewers overall), the value that advertisers place on the genre's viewers, and the number of channels that will be contending for the attention of the viewing group (e.g., the number of stations airing programs aimed at audiences who watch low-violence shows). Profits for a station will also depend on the cost of the program, which may vary by genre. Technology limits the number of channels vying for viewer attention, either because of spectrum signal or cable channel capacity. A programmer will choose to offer low-, medium-, or high-violence programming depending on the profits offered in each of these genres. In equilibrium, channels will be distributed so that the profits of a firm are equal across these three types of programming.

This description can be formalized in the following manner. Consider the market for programming at a particular time of day. Let X_l be the number of viewers (in thousands) who prefer nonviolent programming, X_m the number that watch shows with moderate levels of violence, and X_h be the number of viewers who watch high-violence shows. Viewers in each group are assumed to watch their preferred type of programming only (e.g., high-violence viewers select programs to view only among high-violence shows). The values in terms of dollars per thousand viewers placed by advertisers on viewers of particular programs are denoted by P_l, P_m, and P_h (e.g., advertisers will pay P_h for one thousand viewers of a program with high violent content). The costs of programming vary with genre. The cost to a programmer is C_l, for a low-violence program, C_m for a moderate-violence program, and C_h for a high-violence show. The additional cost to a programmer of providing the programming to an additional customer is zero, so a channel's cost is assumed to equal what it pays for programming. The combination of technology (e.g., spectrum scarcity, cable capacity) and property rights (e.g., FCC licenses, local cable regulation) yields a total of N independent competitors in this market. Each channel is viewed as an independent firm trying to maximize its profits. The number of channels that choose to offer low-violence, moderate-violence, and high-violence programming will be defined as N_l, N_m, and N_h. Channels offering a particular type of programming are assumed to face identical costs and to split the number of viewers for that genre equally. The profits for a channel offering moderate levels of violent programming, for example, are thus defined as $P_m*(X_m/N_m) - C_m$.

In equilibrium, the profits of channels across the three genres will be equal. If they were not, then a channel would have an incentive to switch programming into the genre with the higher profits. Thus we know in equilibrium that

$$P_l*(X_l/N_l) - C_l = P_m*(X_m/N_m) - C_m = P_h*(X_h/N_h) - C_h$$ and

$$N_l + N_m + N_h = N.$$

With these conditions, we can conduct comparative statics analyses (see appendix 1.1) to see how changes in exogenous variables in the market (P_l, P_m, P_h, X_l, X_m, X_h, C_l, C_m, C_h, N) affect the number of channels offering particular types of programming (N_l, N_m, N_h). This simplified model yields the following programming predictions.[63]

Violent shows will be more prevalent if advertisers value their viewers more highly. In the terms of the model, the number of violent shows (N_h) will increase as the value of violent-genre consumers (P_h) rises. An increase in advertising rates makes the violent-programming market more profitable, which draws programmers to this genre until profits are equalized across the three types of programming (low, medium, and high violence). If viewer satisfaction is related to the number of channels offering particular types of programming, this implies that consumers of violent programming should be more satisfied with television offerings since they will have more viewing options as the number of channels offering violent programming increases. Chapter 2 explores why consumers of violent programming may be more highly valued by advertisers than consumers of other types of shows. Note that if the value of consumers of low- or moderate-violence programming were to increase, the number of shows in these genres would increase and the offerings of violent programming would decline.

If programmers pay less for violent shows, then they will be more likely to program violent offerings. In equilibrium, the profits of firms in each of the three markets of low, medium, and high violence will be equal. Consider what happens, however, if violent programming becomes less costly. Profits in this genre increase. More firms will leave the low and moderate programming options and start to offer violent programming, until profits are once again equalized. Relative to a world where all programs cost the same, if violent programming is cheaper, then it will be more likely to be offered by channels. Thus as C_h decreases, N_h increases and N_m and N_l decrease. Similarly, if low-violence programming were to decrease in cost, then the number of channels offering this genre would increase and N_h would decline. Costs here refer to the fee that channels pay for the program, which may be the cost of producing the program if it is produced internally or the price paid to outside production companies if the show is produced by another company. Later in chapter 6 I will explore how the decision to invest in a program may vary with the number of different outlets (e.g., export markets, video sales) for a production.

As the number of channels increases the number of violent programs will increase. Technology often sets constraints on the number of channels contending for viewers in a given area. The FCC's allocation of the broadcast spectrum limits the number of over-the-air signals broadcast in a market. The physical capacity of cable technology limits the number of cable networks offered in a given franchise area. Over time these constraints have relaxed, so that viewers can choose from an increasing number of channels. Reception of television programming through satellite dishes has also expanded the number of channels. The model demonstrates that as channels are added, the number of violent programs will increase. New entrants distribute themselves across programming genres so that equilibrium profits remain equal across the low-, medium-, and high-violence market niches. As the number of programs offered increases, the number of competitors in each of these market niches will increase. Markets across the United States currently differ in the number of channels offered within a viewing area. The model predicts that the number of violent programs offered should be higher in areas with a higher number of stations or channels overall.

The number of violent shows grows as the number of viewers attracted to violent programs increases. Broadcasters sell audiences to advertisers. As the number (X_h) of viewers attracted to violent programming increases, profits from offering this type of programming will attract more channels into this market so that N_h increases. The demographic audience for televisions changes by the hour each day. As the number of viewers of violent programming increases, holding other factors constant, programmers will find it more profitable to offer violent shows to attract these viewers. Thus one would predict that violent offerings will vary in part as the television audience changes during the day. Cities also vary in their demographic makeup, so that cities with higher numbers of consumers of violent programming should have more programs aimed at these viewers.

In equilibrium, there is no reason to expect violent programs to have higher or lower ratings or lower or higher costs. Much of the attention focused on violent programming has considered this genre as a special type of programming in terms of ratings or costs. Consider, however, the relationships among costs, ratings, and advertiser values that hold in equilibrium. Since profits are the same across the programming niches, one knows that $P_m*(X_m/N_m) - C_m = P_h*(X_h/N_h) - C_h$, or

$$P_m*(X_m/N_m) - P_h*(X_h/N_h) = C_m - C_h.$$

Rearranging the terms in this manner underscores that in equilibrium it is the values that advertisers place on viewers, the number of viewers in a given market niche, the number of competitors, and the costs of programming that help determine the relationships one would predict among costs and ratings. If the difference on the left-hand side of the equation is positive, then one will predict that violent programming is cheaper for programmers to purchase than shows with moderate levels of violence (i.e., $C_m > C_h$). If the left-hand side were negative, then one would predict that violent programming is more costly than shows with moderate levels of violence.

One can also derive different predictions about the ratings of violent programs. Many predictions of the relationship between violent content and viewership focus on the overall ratings for a show—that is, the percentage of total television households watching a particular program. Broadcasters focus, however, on the viewing of particular demographic groups (e.g., women 18–34 , men 18–49). The model predicts that the relationship between the number of people watching a show with moderate levels of violence (X_m/N_m) and the number of viewers watching a violent program (X_h/N_h) will depend on both the values that advertisers place on these viewing groups (P_m for each thousand viewers of the moderate programming and P_h for each thousand viewers of the violent programming). Assume, for example, that $P_h = P_m$—that is, that advertisers valued these two groups equally. This would mean $X_m/N_m - X_h/N_h = (C_m - C_h)/P_h$. One would then expect in equilibrium that the number of viewers for a program with moderate levels of violence would be higher than a show with high violence if the costs of moderate programming were higher than the costs of violent programming (i.e., $C_m > C_h$). If violent programming were more expensive, then one would predict more viewers for a program with high violent content.

The average rating for violent programs goes down as the number of violent programs increases. By assumption the number of viewers attracted to programming with high violent content (as opposed to moderate or low violent content) is fixed at X_h. Consider what happens as the number of overall channels expands or the values that advertisers place on consumers of violent programming increases. The model predicts in both cases the number of competitors offering violent programs (N_h) will increase. This means that the number of viewers of a high violence program, X_h/N_h, will decline. This is another reminder that if programming in a particular niche becomes more attractive to broadcasters—as, for example, because of an increase in advertising rates—this does not mean that the rating for a show in that niche will increase.

If broadcasters were led to internalize the costs to society of violent programming, fewer violent programs would be offered. If violence on television contributes to violence and aggression in society, these effects are not generally reflected in the decisions of broadcasters since they are not led to consider the full costs to society of their shows. If broadcasters did consider these costs, their decision-making calculus would change.[64] Assume that channels offering high-violence programming were led to consider the negative externalities generated by their shows. One could express the value of these externalities by a cost to society E per thousand viewers multiplied by the number of thousands of viewers of the program. E would reflect the dollar value of increases in aggression, crime, fear, and desensitization that occur in society for each thousand viewers of a program. Then in equilibrium the market equations become

$$P_l*(X_l/N_l) - C_l = P_m*(X_m/N_m) - C_m = P_h*(X_h/N_h) - C_h - E*(X_h/N_h)$$
$$\text{and } N_l + N_m + N_h = N.$$

As the costs of the externalities generated by a program (E) increase, programs with high violent content become less profitable. This causes programmers to shift out of this program niche and into the provision of shows with low or moderate levels of violence. Hence as the externalities generated by high-violence programs increase, fewer high-violence shows would be offered if channels were led to consider the total costs to society of these programs. Appendix

1.2 further analyzes the welfare implications of the failure of broadcasters to internalize the negative and positive externalities generated by their shows.

This simplified model of programming decisions clarifies many of the "stylized facts" that are currently used to describe the market for violent programming. The notions that violence sells, that violent content is a market-driven commodity, and that competition creates pressures for violent programming are captured in the model. The model emphasizes that there is a set group of viewers who prefer violent programming and that channels compete for these viewers depending on the relative profits of serving other market niches. As the number of violent viewers increases during the viewing day, the number of channels offering this fare should increase. Similarly, if a city has a larger population that prefers this programming, then, if one controls for other factors, the number of high-violence programs should be higher in that market. If advertisers value viewers of violent programming more, perhaps because of demographic reasons explored in chapter 2, then viewers of violent programming should be more satisfied with television's offerings since the number of channels offering violent programming will be higher.

Some segments of viewers will prefer low and moderate levels of violence in their programming. These consumers may even constitute a majority of viewers. Some have reasoned from this that the presence of violent programming means that channels are not responsive to viewer preferences. The model indicates that programming with high violent content is responsive to viewing preferences, those of the set of consumers who prefer such programming as opposed to less violent fare. The model also demonstrates that in equilibrium there is no definitive relationship between violent content and ratings or costs. Equilibrium profits will be equal across programming niches and will depend on advertiser values, the number of viewers who watch particular types of shows, programming costs, and the number of channels that divide up viewership.

Although the model yields many hypotheses that will be tested later in the book, some questions important to the debate over television violence are not addressed directly in this simplified model. Children do not appear directly in this model, yet they are often the focus of concerns about the harms of television violence.[65] In programming decisions during most parts of the day and week, advertisers are not concerned about the viewership of children because they are trying to reach an adult market. The audiences that programmers sell to advertisers denoted by X_l, X_m, and X_h refer to adult viewers. The externality costs E associated with viewership by adults can be interpreted in at least two ways. One could define E as the increased levels of aggression, fear, and desensitization caused among adults by the consumption of violent programming. Or one could assume that viewership by children in part moves with viewership by adults, so that a given number of adults viewing a program translates into viewing by children. The costs to society of viewership by children, which may lead to increased aggression and crime in the long run and other adverse consequences in the short run, would thus be captured in part by E. Since the model assumes that the number of adult viewers (and hence children viewers) of high-violence programs is constant, this would mean that the exposure of children to violent programming would remain constant. If children's viewing is seen as a function of the number of channels offering violent programming, then reductions in the number of high-violence channels would reduce the externalities generated by such programming by lowering the number of children exposed.

Many other questions remain outside this programming model. How does the existence of additional markets for programs, such as export or syndication markets, affect investment in programs? What are the implications for social welfare of violent programming on broadcast television or cable television? How do parents make their decisions to monitor their children's consumption of television? How might consumer boycotts, sweeps months, or government scrutiny factor into programming decisions? These are explored in more detail in the following chapters.

CONCLUSIONS

Violence on television is a commercial product. Yet the market for television violence is characterized by the same market failure created by pollution. Laboratory evidence and field experience confirm that the portrayal of violent acts on television can lead to aggression and violence in society. Broadcasters and advertisers do not incorporate these costs into their programming decisions, however. The resulting levels of violence on television have generated a demand for government policies, a demand based in part on policy impacts and in part on political impacts. The following chapters will explore how the individual decisions of viewers and programmers and voters and politicians have led to the current debate about television violence.

THE MARKET FOR VIOLENT PROGRAMMING

COMPARATIVE STATICS ANALYSIS allows one to examine how changes in an exogenous variable (i.e., a variable whose value is determined outside the model) can affect the values of the variables that are endogenous (i.e., determined by the operation of the model). As described in the chapter, variables whose values are set outside the model are the values of different types of programming viewers in thousands (X_l, X_m, X_h) in the different programming niches, the number of advertisers place on viewers of different types of programming, the number of viewers in thousands per thousand viewers (P_l, P_m, P_h) that (C_l, C_m, C_h) of producing the different show types, and the total number of channels (N). Given these values, the model yields the number of channels in each programming niche (N_l, N_m, N_h). In equilibrium we know that profits are equal across the programming niches and that the N channels are distributed across these niches so that

$$\frac{P_l X_l}{N_l} - C_l = \frac{P_m X_m}{N_m} - C_m = \frac{P_h X_h}{N_h} - C_h \text{ and}$$

$$N_l + N_m + N_h = N.$$

We can rewrite these conditions as three separate simultaneous equations

$$\frac{P_l X_l}{N_l} - C_l - \frac{P_m X_m}{N_m} + C_m = 0$$

$$\frac{P_m X_m}{N_m} - C_m - \frac{P_h X_h}{N_h} + C_h = 0 \text{ and}$$

$$N_l + N_m - N_h - N = 0.$$

Each of these equations is assumed to have continuous partial derivatives with respect to the exogenous and endogenous variables. The relevant Jacobian determinant is

$$
\begin{vmatrix}
\dfrac{-P_l X_l}{N_l^2} & \dfrac{P_m X_m}{N_m^2} & 0 \\[2ex]
0 & \dfrac{-P_m X_m}{N_m^2} & \dfrac{P_h X_h}{N_h^2} \\[2ex]
1 & 1 & 1
\end{vmatrix}
= \dfrac{P_l X_l}{N_l^2}\dfrac{P_m X_m}{N_m^2} + \dfrac{P_m X_m}{N_m^2}\dfrac{P_h X_h}{N_h^2} + \dfrac{P_l X_l}{N_l^2}\dfrac{P_h X_h}{N_h^2} \neq 0.
$$

This means that we can consider N_l, N_m, and N_h to be implicit functions of $(P_l, P_m, P_h, C_l, C_m, C_h, N)$ at the equilibrium solution. We can use this fact and Cramer's rule to solve for how the equilibrium values $\overline{N_l}, \overline{N_m}, \overline{N_h}$ vary with changes in a given exogenous variable. Consider what happens to the number of channels in each programming niche when the value that advertisers place on consumers of high-violence programming increases. We know that

$$
\begin{bmatrix}
-\dfrac{P_l X_l}{N_l^2} & \dfrac{P_m X_m}{N_m^2} & 0 \\[2ex]
0 & -\dfrac{P_m X_m}{N_m^2} & \dfrac{P_h X_h}{N_h^2} \\[2ex]
1 & 1 & 1
\end{bmatrix}
\begin{bmatrix}
\dfrac{\delta \overline{N_l}}{\delta P_h} \\[2ex]
\dfrac{\delta \overline{N_m}}{\delta P_h} \\[2ex]
\dfrac{\delta \overline{N_h}}{\delta P_h}
\end{bmatrix}
=
\begin{bmatrix}
0 \\[2ex]
\dfrac{X_h}{N_h} \\[2ex]
0
\end{bmatrix}
$$

solving for

$$
\frac{\delta \overline{N_h}}{\delta P_h} = \frac{
\begin{vmatrix}
-\dfrac{P_l X_l}{N_l^2} & \dfrac{P_m X_m}{N_m^2} & 0 \\[2ex]
0 & -\dfrac{P_m X_m}{N_m^2} & \dfrac{X_h}{N_h} \\[2ex]
1 & 1 & 0
\end{vmatrix}
}{|J|}
= \frac{\dfrac{P_m X_m}{N_m^2}\dfrac{X_h}{N_h} - \left(-\dfrac{P_l X_l}{N_l^2}\right)\dfrac{X_h}{N_h}}{\dfrac{P_l X_l}{N_l^2}\dfrac{P_m X_m}{N_m^2} + \dfrac{P_m X_m}{N_m^2}\dfrac{P_h X_h}{N_h^2} + \dfrac{P_l X_l}{N_l^2}\dfrac{P_h X_h}{N_h^2}} > 0.
$$

Since both the numerator and denominator are positive, we know that $\dfrac{\delta \overline{N_h}}{\delta P_h}$ is positive. Cramer's rule also yields

$$
\frac{\delta \overline{N_l}}{\delta P_h} = \frac{
\begin{vmatrix}
0 & \dfrac{P_m X_m}{N_m^2} & 0 \\[2ex]
\dfrac{X_h}{N_h} & -\dfrac{P_m X_m}{N_m^2} & \dfrac{P_h X_h}{N_h^2} \\[2ex]
0 & 1 & 1
\end{vmatrix}
}{|J|}
= \frac{-\dfrac{P_m X_m}{N_m^2}\dfrac{X_h}{N_h}}{\dfrac{P_l X_l}{N_l^2}\dfrac{P_m X_m}{N_m^2} + \dfrac{P_m X_m}{N_m^2}\dfrac{P_h X_h}{N_h^2} + \dfrac{P_l X_l}{N_l^2}\dfrac{P_h X_h}{N_h^2}} < 0
$$

and

$$\frac{\delta \bar{N}_m}{\delta P_h} = \frac{\begin{vmatrix} \dfrac{-P_l X_l}{N_l^2} & 0 & 0 \\[2mm] 0 & \dfrac{X_h}{N_h} & \dfrac{P_h X_h}{N_h^2} \\[2mm] 1 & 0 & 1 \end{vmatrix}}{|J|} = \frac{\dfrac{P_l X_l}{N_l^2}\dfrac{P_m X_m}{N_m^2} + \dfrac{P_m X_m}{N_m^2}\dfrac{P_h X_h}{N_h^2} + \dfrac{P_l X_l}{N_l^2}\dfrac{P_h X_h}{N_h^2}}{\dfrac{-P_l X_l}{N_l^2}\dfrac{X_h}{N_h}} < 0.$$

These results demonstrate that if P_h increases, the number of channels offering high-violence programming (N_h) will increase while the number of channels offering moderate-violence (N_m) or low-violence programming (N_l) will decline.

The application of Cramer's rule also allows one to calculate how channel distribution varies with changes in other exogenous variables. The same reasoning can be used to determine the following results:

changes in costs (C_l, C_m, C_h):

$$\frac{\delta \bar{N}_l}{\delta C_l} < 0, \quad \frac{\delta \bar{N}_m}{\delta C_l} > 0, \quad \frac{\delta \bar{N}_h}{\delta C_l} > 0; \quad \frac{\delta \bar{N}_l}{\delta C_m} > 0, \quad \frac{\delta \bar{N}_m}{\delta C_m} < 0, \quad \frac{\delta \bar{N}_h}{\delta C_m} > 0;$$

$$\frac{\delta \bar{N}_l}{\delta C_h} > 0, \quad \frac{\delta \bar{N}_m}{\delta C_h} > 0, \quad \frac{\delta \bar{N}_h}{\delta C_h} < 0$$

changes in advertising values (P_l, P_m):

$$\frac{\delta \bar{N}_l}{\delta P_l} > 0, \quad \frac{\delta \bar{N}_m}{\delta P_l} < 0, \quad \frac{\delta \bar{N}_h}{\delta P_l} < 0; \quad \frac{\delta \bar{N}_l}{\delta P_m} < 0, \quad \frac{\delta \bar{N}_m}{\delta P_m} > 0, \quad \frac{\delta \bar{N}_h}{\delta P_m} < 0$$

changes in viewing audience sizes (X_l, X_m, X_h):

$$\frac{\delta \bar{N}_l}{\delta X_l} > 0, \quad \frac{\delta \bar{N}_m}{\delta X_l} < 0, \quad \frac{\delta \bar{N}_h}{\delta X_l} < 0; \quad \frac{\delta \bar{N}_l}{\delta X_m} < 0, \quad \frac{\delta \bar{N}_m}{\delta X_m} > 0, \quad \frac{\delta \bar{N}_h}{\delta X_m} < 0;$$

$$\frac{\delta \bar{N}_l}{\delta X_h} < 0, \quad \frac{\delta \bar{N}_m}{\delta X_h} < 0, \quad \frac{\delta \bar{N}_h}{\delta X_h} > 0$$

changes in total channels (N):

$$\frac{\delta \overline{N}_l}{\delta N} > 0, \ \frac{\delta \overline{N}_m}{\delta N} > 0, \ \frac{\delta \overline{N}_h}{\delta N} > 0.$$

In the expanded model which includes the externality costs E, the profit for high violence is modified if stations are led to "internalize" their externality costs so that in equilibrium:

$$\frac{P_l X_l}{N_l} - C_l = \frac{P_m X_m}{N_m} - C_m = \frac{P_h X_h}{N_h} - C_h - \frac{E X_h}{N_h} \quad \text{and}$$

$$N_l + N_m + N_h = N.$$

Again we can rewrite the conditions as three separate simultaneous equations:

$$\frac{P_l X_l}{N_l} - C_l - \frac{P_m X_m}{N_m} + C_m = 0$$

$$\frac{P_m X_m}{N_m} - C_m - \frac{P_h X_h}{N_h} + C_h + \frac{E X_h}{N_h} = 0 \quad \text{and}$$

$$N_l + N_m + N_h - N = 0.$$

The Jacobian determinant of this matrix is:

$$
\begin{vmatrix}
-\dfrac{P_l X_l}{N_l^2} & \dfrac{P_m X_m}{N_m^2} & 0 \\[2ex]
0 & -\dfrac{P_m X_m}{N_m^2} & \dfrac{P_h X_h - E X_h}{N_h^2} \\[2ex]
1 & 1 & 1
\end{vmatrix}
$$

$$= \frac{P_l X_l}{N_l^2} \frac{P_m X_m}{N_m^2} + \frac{P_m X_m}{N_m^2} \frac{P_h X_h - E X_h}{N_h^2} + \frac{P_l X_l}{N_l^2} \frac{P_h X_h - E X_h}{N_h^2} \neq 0.$$

This is positive if $P_h > E$, which is assumed to hold. We know that:

$$
\begin{bmatrix}
-\dfrac{P_l X_l}{N_l^2} & \dfrac{P_m X_m}{N_m^2} & 0 \\[2ex]
0 & -\dfrac{P_m X_m}{N_m^2} & \dfrac{P_h X_h - E X_h}{N_h^2} \\[2ex]
1 & 1 & 1
\end{bmatrix}
\begin{bmatrix}
\dfrac{\delta \overline{N}_l}{\delta E} \\[2ex]
\dfrac{\delta \overline{N}_m}{\delta E} \\[2ex]
\dfrac{\delta \overline{N}_h}{\delta E}
\end{bmatrix}
=
\begin{bmatrix}
0 \\[2ex]
-\dfrac{X_h}{N_h} \\[2ex]
0
\end{bmatrix}.
$$

Using Cramer's rule we find that:

$$\frac{\delta \bar{N}_m}{\delta E} = \frac{\begin{vmatrix} \dfrac{-P_l X_l}{N_l^2} & 0 & 0 \\[2mm] 0 & \dfrac{-X_h}{N_h} & \dfrac{P_h X_h}{N_h^2} - EX_h \\[2mm] 1 & 0 & 1 \end{vmatrix}}{|J|} = \frac{\dfrac{X_h}{N_h}\,\dfrac{P_l X_l}{N_l^2}}{\dfrac{P_l X_l}{N_l^2}\dfrac{P_m X_m}{N_m^2} + \dfrac{P_m X_m}{N_m^2}\dfrac{P_h X_h - EX_h}{N_h^2} + \dfrac{P_l X_l}{N_l^2}\dfrac{P_h X_h - EX_h}{N_h^2}} > 0.$$

Similarly, one can use Cramer's rule to show that

$$\frac{\delta \bar{N}_l}{\delta E} > 0 \text{ and } \frac{\delta \bar{N}_H}{\delta E} < 0.$$

SOCIAL WELFARE: ENTERTAINMENT AND EXTERNALITIES

FROM society's perspective, how can one analyze the contribution of a particular television program to overall social welfare? Economists approach this question by using people's valuations, their willingness to pay for a good, as a measurement of the worth of a product. Calculating the net social benefit from a program thus involves determining the values that viewers and potential viewers place on the show, the value to advertisers of an audience's viewing of commercials and the costs of producing these commercials, and the costs to society of the production and distribution of the program. Several types of economic models exist that analyze the social welfare aspects of the programming market. Yet these models do not generally incorporate the externalities generated by programs, such as the positive externalities associated with educational programming for children or the negative externalities in the form of increased aggression, crime, fear, or desensitization associated with consumption by some viewers of violent programming. This appendix considers how the welfare analysis developed by Owen and Wildman (1992) would change with the incorporation of externalities into the model.

Consider first a competitive pay television industry where the costs of adding an additional viewer to a channel's audience is assumed to be zero.[1] Figure A1.1a (from Owen and Wildman 1992) outlines one of the drawbacks of a competitive pay television system.[2] A channel considering how to price its program will equate the marginal revenue from adding another viewer with the marginal cost of attracting this viewer (which is assumed to be zero). The channel will charge a price p^* and earn revenues of $p^* \times v^*$. These revenues are assumed to at least cover the cost of the program, else the channel would not offer the show. There is a welfare loss to society from this pricing policy, which economists refer to as a "deadweight loss" to society. A set of viewers (those beyond v^*) places a positive value on the program and would consume it if the price were zero. From society's perspective, the additional cost of adding these consumers to the audience is zero. There thus exist viewers whose benefits exceed the cost to society of allowing them to view the program who nevertheless do not see the show because their willingness to pay is less than p^*.

Some shows have benefits beyond those reflected in the private demands expressed by viewers for entertainment. Educational shows for children and public affairs programming for adults both share this characteristic. Parents will consider the value to their children of consuming educational shows, but they will not consider the extra value to society of their children's consumption of educational programming (such as the increased probability the child will de-

a. Competitive Pay Television   b. Positive Externalities

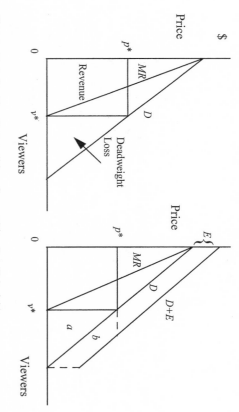

Figure A1.1. Positive Externalities, Competitive Pay Television

velop into an educated, productive citizen). Similarly, adults will express a willingness to pay for public affairs programming based on the entertainment value they derive from politics as sport or the ideological satisfaction of doing the right thing by being better informed. Viewers, however, will not factor in the benefits to society of their becoming informed voters and thus will not reflect these benefits in their willingness to pay for public affairs programming.

Figure A1.1b shows the additional losses to society created by a programmer's failure to internalize the positive benefits to society involved with public affairs programming. If the positive externalities are a constant E per viewer, then the total value to society of a program is reflected in the curve that sums the private value individuals place on programming and the positive externalities. Note that here the deadweight loss to society has increased because of the existence of these positive externalities. The channel will still charge $p*$ and attract $v*$ viewers, but the deadweight loss will now be equal to the areas $a + b$.[3] The failure of the viewers beyond $v*$ to consume the programming (even though their consumption would have a marginal cost of zero) results in even larger benefits forgone from society's perspective because these potential viewers do not generate the positive externalities associated with consumption. If pay cable programmers were able to realize the benefits to society E per person from the viewing of educational shows for children or public affairs programming, more of these programs would be produced. Shows where private revenues were slightly outweighed by program costs would be profitable if programmers captured the broader benefits to society.

Chapter 1 emphasizes the difficulty in determining the magnitude of the negative externalities associated with violent television programs. The harm to society generated by a particular show varies with factors such as the frequency of violent acts, context of violence, and the audience exposed to the show. Even among "violent genres," the externalities generated will vary among theatrical films, action adventure series, and reality crime programs. In figure A1.2, the externalities generated by a violent program are assumed to be a constant E per person and are reflected by the curve labeled MCe. E represents the costs in dollar terms to society of the exposure of a viewer to violent programming.[4] Figure A1.2a analyzes the case where E is relatively high. For ease of analysis, assume that production costs of a program are zero in figure A1.2. The marginal costs to a channel of adding viewers is still assumed to be zero. The marginal costs to society of adding a viewing is E, which represents the increase in expected crime or fear resulting from viewer exposure. Absent negative externalities, a deadweight loss to society arises because too few people consumed the program (see figure A1.1a). If the negative externalities generated by a show are extremely high, however, it is clear that the opposite problem may occur. In figure A1.2a, the externality cost is above the private willingness to pay for every viewer. From society's perspective, each additional viewer adds to social losses. Since the channel does not factor in externalities, it will charge p^* and attract v^* viewers. The trapezoid a represents the amount by which costs to society of these viewers' consumption exceeds the benefits they derive. If a channel were forced to incorporate the externalities, in this example social costs would always outweigh revenues and the program would not be offered.

Figure A1.2b reflects the case where externality values are moderate, relative to the value placed on shows by viewers. The channel would still charge a price p^* to maximize its profits, which would attract v^* viewers. The loss to society is captured by triangle b. For each of the viewers from v' through v^*, the value each viewer places on the program is less than the expected cost to society of his or her exposure to violent programming. Here again, negative externalities give rise to "too much" consumption of a program from society's perspective. From society's perspective, the optimal number of viewers of violent programming would be v'. Up until v', the benefits an individual derives from the program outweigh the expected cost to society of his or her viewing. At v', these costs and benefits exactly balance.

The externalities associated with some violent programs could be quite low, especially for program genres that do not contain a high frequency of violent acts or in which violence is portrayed in a manner less likely to give rise to aggressive behavior. Figure A1.2c reflects this assumption about the value of E. The channel continues to price at p^* and attract v^* viewers. The deadweight loss in the absence of externalities would be $a + b$. Once the externality costs are incorporated, however, the deadweight loss drops to b. From society's perspective, the optimal number of consumers drops from v''' to v'' once the externality costs are factored in. In the case of low externalities from violent programming, too few viewers consume the program rather than too many (which was the case when externalities were high or moderate).

Advertiser-supported television is also subject to a set of market biases.

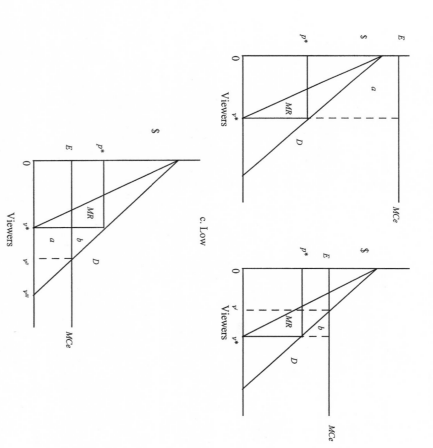

a. High

b. Moderate

c. Low

Figure A1.2. Negative Externalities, Competitive Pay Television

Owen and Wildman (1992) stress that the biases against programs that cater to minority tastes and against expensive programs evident in the pay television industry are even more pronounced in the advertiser-supported market. Although intensity of demand is reflected in part through the prices paid in the pay television market, advertisers care about the number of viewers in a show's audience rather than the value these consumers place on the show. Figure A1.3a (reproduced from Owen and Wildman) represents a case of two television programs that are valued differently by consumers, as represented by demand curves $D1$ and $D2$. In the case of pure advertiser-supported television, a channel charges a zero monetary price to the viewer and attracts v^* viewers at this price. This audience is sold to advertisers, who anticipate the commercial viewing of a segment of the v^* viewers. If the two programs are equally costly, the channel will be indifferent between the two programs. If program 1 were slightly

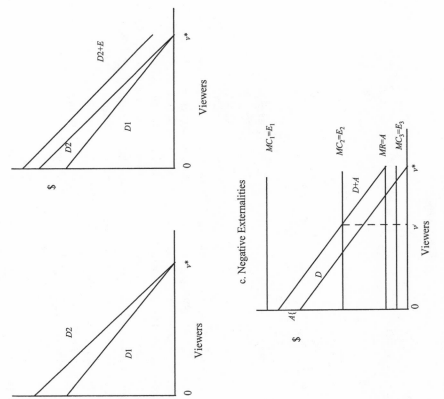

a. No Externalities

b. Positive Externalities

c. Negative Externalities

Figure A1.3. Advertiser-Supported Television

cheaper, the channel would show this program even though from society's perspective the greater viewer benefits from program 1 compared with those from program 1 (defined by the area between the two demand curves) would outweigh the additional costs of program 2. If program 2 generated positive externalities per viewer measured by E, then the difference between the showing of program 1 versus program 2 from society's perspective is represented in figure A1.3b by the area between the curves $D1$ and $D2 + E$. Positive externalities thus exaggerate some of the problems associated with advertiser-supported television.

Assume that an advertiser places a value A on each viewer and pays the television channel A per viewer. From society's perspective, the value of viewing is reflected in figure A1.3c by the line D (reflecting the entertainment value derived by consumers) plus A (reflecting the value to an advertiser of the individual's viewing). The negative externalities generated by the program again may vary in magnitude. If the expected value of these negative externalities is E_1, figure A1.3c demonstrates that social welfare decreases as an additional viewer is added to the program. At price zero there will be v^* viewers. For each of these viewers, however, the externality cost exceeds the sum of the value placed by the viewer on the program and placed by the advertiser on the viewer. If externality costs are lower, as in E_2, then the social losses are lower than with E_1. For each of the viewers beyond v' through to v^*, the additional costs to society arising from exposure to violent programming outweigh the viewer and advertiser benefits. Again, from society's perspective there are too many viewers of a violent program with externality costs of E_2 per viewer. If externality costs per viewer were E_3, the marginal costs per viewer would be below the additional value to society from a viewer's consumption (as reflected in the curve $D + A$). The optimal number of viewers would be v', which is the number derived by the channel's policy of charging zero for the program.

Adult Audiences: Who Watches Violent Programming?

TASTES FOR violent programming vary. Chapter 1 assumed that there was a distinct group of viewers who watched programs with high violent content and that these viewers were valued differently by advertisers. This chapter demonstrates that viewing of violent programming varies greatly with age and gender. Young adults are much more likely to consume larger amounts of violent programming, and men are more likely to watch particularly violent programming than women. Ranked by adult demographic groups, the highest consumers of violent entertainment are men 18–34, followed by women 18–34 and men 35–49. Advertisers trying to reach younger viewers, especially the highly valued female 18–34 demographic, may find violent programming as a way to target these consumers. The willingness of sponsors to pay more for young adult viewers translates into greater incentives to program violent content. A majority of American viewers may report that there is too much violence in entertainment programming, that violence on television bothers them, and that television violence is harmful to society. Yet there exists a segment of viewers valued by advertisers, the high consumers of violent entertainment, who are much less likely to view television violence as a problem or be bothered by it.

This chapter uses survey data on general television viewing and Nielsen rating information for particular shows to describe the demographic audiences among adults for violent programming. These data reveal that a taste for some type of violent programming is evident among most adult demographic groups. Older viewers watch mystery films, women have higher ratings for family crime dramas, and males of all adult age groups are more likely to watch movies noted for high levels of violence. The evidence presented in this chapter shows that adult viewers are not likely to be surprised by the level of violence in the programming they watch, for the addition of viewer discretion warnings to prime-time broadcast films has no impact on the ratings among adults. In terms of the cost per thousand (cpt) viewers reached by commercial, violent prime-time shows are cheaper than nonviolent programs for advertisers buying audiences of males or females aged 18–49. For violent programs, broadcasters gain additional ad revenues by attracting viewers 18–49 but not by adding more viewers aged 50+. This underscores how violent programs are used by advertisers and programmers primarily to target younger adult viewers. For prime-time broadcast shows, the number of children 2–11 watching has no impact on ad prices. This indicates that their viewing is a true externality to programmers, who gain no additional revenue from children's viewing of adult programs since children are not the audiences sought by advertisers of adult products.

Advertisers and programmers know who watches specific programs through analysis of the data collected by Nielsen Media Research.[1] Ratings data are now available to corporate clients down to the minute level, so that networks can track the ratings for individual stories on a program such as a newsmagazine.[2] Before examining ratings data, I first explore survey data collected by the Times Mirror Center in February 1993.[3] The Times Mirror survey asked a nationwide sample of 1,516 adults about their television viewing habits, their personal reactions to violence on television, their beliefs about the effects of television violence on society, and a number of questions relating to their demographic characteristics. Using the individual responses provided by the center, I am able to explore who watches different types of television programs and how opinions about television content vary.

Analyzing viewing of violence requires a definition of violent programming. The Times Mirror Center created an indicator of whether viewers were heavy, medium, or light consumers of violent entertainment based on responses to nine survey questions about whether a person regularly watched "fictional crime drama shows about detectives and police"; regularly watched "shows that present footage of real life crimes and emergencies such as *Cops, Rescue 911*, and *Top Cops*"; regularly or sometimes watched *American Gladiators*; reported being very interested in real-life crime programs; or saw *The Silence of the Lambs, Alien 3, Bloodsport, Hard to Kill*, or *Cape Fear*. A yes answer to a question was scored as a 1 and the results of these nine viewing questions were summed. If the person had a 0 on this scale, they were classified as a light viewer of violent entertainment. If the viewer scored a 1 or a 2 they were termed moderate viewers, while those with 3 or higher were classified as heavy viewers of violent entertainment programming. Using these definitions, 45% of the respondents were heavy viewers of violent programming, while 35% were medium and 20% were light consumers.

The age and gender of who holds preferences for violent programming are important in the broadcast television market, since products advertised on a program often have specific target audiences based on these characteristics. Advertisers buy television audiences based on the match between the demographics of the consumers of their products and the demographics of the viewers of the programs, the total numbers of viewers among their target demographic groups who watch a show, the frequency with which they can reach viewers with a particular message that is effective, the ability of the advertising that is viewed to sway the purchasing decisions of the viewers, and the costs of reaching their targeted demographics through a particular program as opposed to other advertising avenues. The end result of all these factors is that programmers often focus on the value of younger demographic groups (e.g., viewers aged 18–49) to advertisers, especially women aged 18–34.

Many considerations are cited as reasons for why younger viewers may be more highly valued by television advertisers on the whole. Per capita spending actually peaks among those aged 45–54, but these are not the viewers who are said to command the attention of television advertisers.[4] Young viewers are often sought after because they may be more easily influenced by ad exposure since they have not yet established consistent purchasing patterns for particular brands. According to advertising analysts:

Younger consumers are more inexperienced consumers. It's often easier to persuade them to buy something than it is to persuade a more experienced older consumer. When the ratio of novice consumers to experienced consumers goes down, the result is a lower net response to a mass-marketing ad campaign. People who market to older consumers know that as a person's age rises, so too does the cost of marketing needed to make the first sale. It takes more money, time, and effort to persuade older consumers to switch brands or try something new.[5]

Another factor that increases the price advertisers are willing to pay for younger viewers is the fact that they are in the viewing audience for fewer hours, so that scarcity drives up the price on shows that command their attention. Women 18–24 watch 29 hours of television a week, compared to 44 hours a week for women aged 55 and older. According to one advertiser, the result is that, "There is more competition among advertisers for younger viewers, so that runs up the air-time charges for shows that are popular with them. . . . Because older people watch more television, we can have them any time."[6]

In addition, women may be more highly valued than men by some companies if they are the consumers making the purchasing decision for a given product. Survey data on the relative volume of consumption of products indicate that women often account for a high percentage of the purchases of products used routinely by many households.[7] Some products break down clearly along gender lines, so that women account for 67% of the consumption of hairspray and males account for 75% of the use of shaving cream. Within a given category of products such as alcoholic beverages, there are differences in consumption based on types of product. Men account for 74% of the consumption of regular domestic beer, whereas women account for 53% of the consumption of domestic dinner wines. Since women may be the principal shoppers in a large set of households, they also make the purchase decisions that affect products used by many families. Purchases by women account for 58.7% of grocery food shopping, 56.4% of consumption of headache and pain relievers, and 54.5% of consumption of toothpaste. The fact that women make the purchase decisions for a substantial fraction of products increases their value to advertisers. If younger consumers are potentially more susceptible to advertising since they are less experienced in using particular products, then young women (e.g., 18–34) may be highly valued by companies seeking to market their products through television. Since advertisers thus value viewers differently, understanding the attraction of violent shows for advertisers and programmers should start with a demographic analysis of who consumes these programs.

In this chapter I divide the adult viewing audience into six mutually exclusive demographic groups: males 18–34, 35–49, and 50+, and females 18–34, 35–49, and 50+. I selected these categories because of the way that advertisers segment the viewing audience. The Nielsen company is able to breakdown viewer information by many different demographic classifications, including age, gender, race, income, education, cable status, and region of the country. The broad classifications by which Nielsen reports show ratings data include women 18+, 18–34, 18–49, and 25–54 and men 18+, 18–34, and 18–49. I have divided the Times Mirror survey data into mutually exclusive categories so that one can examine how viewing varies among demographic groups that may be valued differently by advertisers. For January 1994, there were in the U.S. television household audience approximately 37.7 million children 2–11, 20.9 million teens 12–17, 32.7 million females 18–34, 32.1 million males 18–34, 28.7 million females 35–49, 27.7 million males 35–49, 35.1 million females 50+, and 28.4 million males 50+.[8]

Whereas the model in chapter 1 simply assumed that there was a distinctive set of viewers who watch violent programming, table 2.1 confirms this assertion. Overall, 45% of the sample respondents were classified as heavy viewers of violent programming. For males 18–34, 73% were heavy consumers of violent programs. Females 18–34 were the next highest group in violent viewing (60% were heavy viewers), followed by males 35–49 (52%). At the other end of the spectrum, viewers over 50 were much more likely to fall into the light-violence consumers (i.e., viewers who did not answer yes to any of the nine viewing questions dealing with violent programming in the survey). While 20% of the survey respondents were light viewers of violent programming, 31% of males aged 50 or older were light viewers and 44% of females 50 and older were in this category. This is not because older viewers are less likely to be watching television. In fact, older viewers watch more television per week than younger viewers. Women 18–24 averaged 29 hours of viewing per week and men 18–24 averaged 24 hours per week (for November 1992), whereas women 55+ watched television 44 hours per week versus 39 hours per week for men 55+.[9] Even though younger adults watch less television, they are more likely to consume larger amounts of violent programming because of the types of shows and movies that they choose to watch. Younger viewers are also more likely to report that they are interested in such programming. When asked in the Times Mirror survey whether they are interested in "real life crime programs that show crime and violence in actual situations," 70% of males 18–34 and 60% of females 18–34 reported they were very or somewhat interested in such programs. Older viewers found such programming much less attractive (40% of males 50+ and 36% of females 50+ said they found these real-life crime shows interesting).

Table 2.1 underscores that viewership of violent programming, while highest among young males, is also popular among young females. On a 10-point scale based on responses to ten questions about viewing violent shows, men 18–34 averaged 4.7 yes answers to questions about whether they watched particular

TABLE 2.1
Viewing of Violent Entertainment

		Males 18–34	Females 18–34	Males 35–49	Females 35–49	Males 50+	Females 50+
	Total			% of Column Respondents			
Violent Entertainment Viewing							
Heavy	44.7	72.8	59.9	52.0	36.8	22.9	18.2
Medium	35.4	22.9	32.5	35.9	40.7	46.3	38.2
Light	19.9	4.3	7.6	12.1	22.5	30.7	43.6
Very/Somewhat Interested in Real-life Crime Programs	50.3	69.8	59.9	50.8	41.6	39.5	35.7
Violent Viewership Index Mean (0–10 scale)	3.1	4.7	4.0	3.4	2.7	2.1	1.5

types of violent programs or movies.[10] Women 18–34 had the next highest rating, 4.0. This was higher than the 3.4 registered for men 35–49. These differences between the mean index for men 18–34 versus women 18–34 and women 18–34 versus men 35–49 are both statistically significant at the .01 level. The figures reinforce the notion that viewing violent television programs and movies is thus popular among men and women aged 18–34.

For advertisers trying to reach younger adult viewers with frequent exposures to a particular commercial, the Times Mirror information suggests that sponsoring different types of violent programming (e.g., fictional crime, real-life police, action adventure feature films) may be one avenue to reach these viewers.[11] Males 18–34 constituted 33% of the heavy viewers of violent programming versus 4% of the light-viewing category (see table 2.2). Nearly 75% of the heavy viewers of violent programming are concentrated in three of the demographic groups, males 18–34, females 18–34 (21% of heavy viewers), and males 35–49 (19%). These three groups accounted for only 21% of the light

TABLE 2.2
Demographics of Violent Entertainment Viewing

		% of Column Respondents		
	Total	Light	Medium	Heavy
Males 18–34	20.0	4.4	13.0	32.5
Females 18–34	15.8	6.0	14.5	21.1
Males 35–49	16.5	10.1	16.8	19.2
Females 35–49	15.4	17.5	17.7	12.6
Males 50+	13.6	21.1	17.9	7.0
Females 50+	18.6	40.9	20.2	7.6

viewers. Thus 79% of the light-viewing category came from the other three adult demographic groups: females 50+ (41% of the light viewers), males 50+ (21%), and females 35–49 (18%). In terms of income distribution, heavy viewers of violent programming mirror the distribution for the sample as a whole. Total respondents in the Times Mirror survey had the following income distribution: 23% reported less than $20,000 annual income; 18%, $20,000–$29,000; 27%, $30,000–$49,000; and 21%, $50,000 and over. The percentages for heavy viewers of violent programming are nearly identical: 25%, 20%, 27%, 19%.

Age is the single strongest influence on the viewing of violent television programming. Many different factors may affect whether an adult is a heavy viewer of violent television programming: age, gender, race, education, income, region of the country, residence (city, town, suburb, rural) and amount of daily television viewing (see table A2.1 for a model predicting who will be a heavy consumer of violent shows). Table 2.3 reports how the probability a person will be a heavy consumer of violent television programming changes with demographic characteristics (all of which were statistically significant at the .01 level).[12] The predicted probability for a person with the "mean" demographic characteristics of the sample is .44. The model indicates that younger viewers, males, minorities, those with less education, and people who watch more television overall are more likely to be heavy consumers of violent programming. Relative to viewers aged 50+, viewers who are 18–34 have a .49 higher probability of heavy violence consumption (i.e., the predicted probability is .19 for 50+ viewers and .68 for viewers 18–34). Viewers 35–49 have a .27 higher probability than the oldest viewers. Women have a .15 lower probability of

TABLE 2.3

Impact of Demographic Factors on Probability of Heavy Violence Viewing

Variables	Change in Probability of Heavy Violence Viewing
Female vs. Male	−.15
White vs. Nonwhite	−.23
Aged 18–34 vs. 50+	.49
Aged 35–49 vs. 50+	.27
Some College vs. College Graduate	.11
HS vs. College Graduate	.16
Less Than HS vs. College Graduate	.17
4+ Hours of Daily Television Viewing vs. Less Than 2 Hours	.28
2–3.5 Hours of Daily Television Viewing vs. Less Than 2 Hours	.14

Note: Change in probability = probability of heavy violence viewing for a person with first characteristic − probability for person with the second characteristic. Evaluated at the means for all characteristics, the predicted probability of heavy violence viewing is .44. See table A2.1.

viewing then men. After one controls for education, income is not statistically significant in predicting who will watch higher quantities of violent programming. Those who watched more television overall are, other things being equal, also more likely to consume violent programming.

Programmers and advertisers aiming for particular demographic groups can thus predict how audiences will vary by program type. The survey data reveal that some genres draw viewers from many different demographic groups. Table 2.4 indicates the percentage of people who report that they regularly watch fictional crime dramas is similar across males 18–34 (19%), females 18–34 (22%), males 50+ (24%), and females 50+ (24%). There is a continuum of violent content even within this genre ranging from *Murder, She Wrote* (a mystery with little violence) to *Walker, Texas Ranger* (noted for graphic violence), so that these groups may not be watching the same crime dramas.[13] A given show may draw evenly from many different viewing groups. The percentage of people regularly viewing shows such as *A Current Affair* and *Hard Copy* is remarkably similar across different ages and genders (e.g., 18% of males 18–34 regularly watch these programs versus 19% of women 50+). Other programs draw more heavily from particular groups. News magazines such as *60 Minutes* or *20/20* are more popular among older viewers (59% of males and 64% of females 50+ are regular viewers, compared with 37% for males and females 18–34). The national news and local news programs also are more popular among viewers 50+. *Married with Children* is three times as popular among

TABLE 2.4

Percentage of Demographic Group Watching Show

| | | % of Column Respondents | | | | | |
	Total	Males 18–34	Females 18–34	Males 35–49	Females 35–49	Males 50+	Females 50+
Fictional Crime Dramas	21.4	18.6	21.9	20.2	20.8	23.9	23.6
Shows Such As *Cops, Rescue 911*	33.2	40.2	42.6	30.2	32.0	25.9	26.8
Local News	76.5	72.1	68.4	75.8	76.2	82.0	85.0
National News	58.8	47.5	43.0	62.1	55.8	69.8	73.9
News Magazine Shows Such As *60 Minutes, 20/20*	49.5	37.2	36.7	51.2	50.6	58.5	64.3
Talk Shows	18.9	13.5	37.9	15.3	17.7	12.3	18.5
Shows Such As *A Current Affair, Hard Copy*	20.6	18.3	23.2	23.0	21.2	20.5	19.3
Roseanne	19.7	22.9	34.6	15.3	19.9	9.8	14.6
Married with Children	15.9	27.6	20.3	18.1	11.3	9.3	6.1

younger viewers than older viewers (e.g., 28% of males 18–34 are regular viewers versus 9% for males 50+). Talk shows are regularly watched by 19% of viewers, but among women 18–34 this figure jumps to 38%. Shows such as *Cops* and *Rescue 911* are much more popular among men 18–34 (40% are regular viewers) and women 50+ (27%).

The Times Mirror data bear out the assumption made in chapter 1 that there is a continuum of consumption of violent programming and that groups of particular types of programs are distinctive demographically. If one categorizes viewers based on the *frequency* of viewing different types of violence programming, the survey data indicate that males 18–34, females 18–34, and males 35–49 are heavy consumers of violent shows. Though these viewers watch less television than older demographic groups, their preferences for violent programming make them more frequent viewers of shows such as reality police programs, fictional crime, and violent movies. By contrast, males 50+ and females 50+ are much more likely to populate the ranks of light viewers of television violence.

Within the category of violent programming, one can also ask the question of how the audience for violent shows varies by the degree (e.g., frequency, context) of violence in a program. Table 2.5 reveals that the viewership of violent movies varies greatly by the *quantity* of violence in the film. The Times Mirror survey asked respondents whether they had seen a particular set of violent movies at home or in theater. With the exception of *Dances with Wolves*, *Home Alone II*, and *Robin Hood: Prince of Thieves* (each rated PG-13 by the MPAA), all of these movies were rated R. Content summaries for each of these films in movie reviews or television viewing guides all carry an indicator for violence, indicating that these movies are seen as "violent" in the viewing market. There are gradations of violence within these violent movies, however. The National Coalition on Television Violence (NCTV) calculated violent acts per hour for

TABLE 2.5
Composition of Violent Movie Audiences

% of Movie's Adult Audience

	Dances with Wolves	Home Alone II	Robin Hood: Prince of Thieves	The Silence of the Lambs	Lethal Weapon III	Terminator 2	Cape Fear	Alien 3	Hard to Kill	Blood-sport
Males 18–34	21.5	24.8	25.7	26.7	30.5	30.8	31.3	35.6	35.8	49.6
Females 18–34	15.9	14.7	19.3	20.4	20.9	20.7	23.1	19.7	19.7	18.1
Males 35–49	18.7	18.7	19.9	18.8	18.2	20.3	18.2	22.2	21.9	18.5
Females 35–49	16.8	16.4	15.9	14.4	15.6	13.2	12.1	12.0	11.5	7.5
Males 50+	12.7	11.8	9.8	9.6	7.8	9.8	8.7	5.6	5.5	5.1
Females 50+	14.4	13.7	9.5	10.2	7.0	5.2	6.6	4.9	5.5	1.2

Note: Movies are listed by the increasing percentage of the adult audience accounted for by males 18–34.

three of the films: *Dances with Wolves* (26 acts per hour), *Robin Hood* (63 acts per hour), and *Hard to Kill* (96 acts per hour).[14] The NCTV also reported violent acts per hour for the original offerings of the sequels listed here: *Terminator* had 84 violent acts per hour; *Home Alone* had 17; *Lethal Weapon* had 63; and *Aliens* had 45. Audience data for these movies thus allow one to examine how viewership varies with the degree of violence.

Table 2.5 lists for each movie the percentage of the film's audience accounted for by a particular age group. The results indicate that for movies with relatively high levels of violence, such as *Hard to Kill* or *Bloodsport*, males 18–34 made up a high percentage of the adult survey population that reported seeing the film.[15] Half of the adult audience for *Bloodsport* came from males 18–34, as did 36% of the audience for *Hard to Kill*. For the less violent of these films with violence, males 18–34 still accounted for the highest percentage of the audience but they were not as dominant a factor in a film's overall attendance (e.g., they accounted for 22% of the widely popular *Dances with Wolves* and 25% of the *Home Alone II* audience). For the high violence movies, there is substantial patronage by females 18–34 and males 35–49, who account for similar percentages of these films' audiences. There is a substantial drop in viewing for the high-violence films when one compares the viewing of males 35–49 and females 35–49. The overall consumption of violent films is concentrated among a core of younger viewers. If one counts each yes response in the sample of movie questions as a viewing, 24% of the viewers in the survey had seen seven or more of the ten violent films in the survey and accounted for 41% of the total viewing of these violent films. The core of violent movie viewers that had seen at least seven of the ten violent films in the survey was 65% male and younger than the sample as a whole (62% were aged 18–34).

Table 2.6 analyzes how the attraction to different gradations of violent content varies by examining the percentage of a particular demographic group that reported seeing a film. Males 18–34 were more likely to see each of the violent films than members of any other demographic group, consistent with their higher reported tendency to view movies in theaters overall.[16] For the blockbuster film *Terminator 2*, 80% of males 18–34 reported seeing this film. For violent movies with lower frequencies of violence such as *Dances with Wolves* or *Home Alone II*, males 35–49 and females 35–49 see these films in similar percentages. Extremely violent films such as *Hard to Kill* and *Bloodsport* are characterized by at least two audience patterns. Viewership drops off dramatically with age. The ratio between the percentage of males 18–34 and the percentage of males 50+ who saw *Bloodsport* is 7:1 and for *Hard to Kill* is 5:1 (versus 1.2:1 for the *Dances with Wolves* and 1.4:1 for *Home Alone II*). There is also a dramatic difference in the viewership of males versus females in the 35–49 age category for the films with high violent content. Males 35–49 were much more likely to see than women in the same age category *Hard to Kill* (37% vs. 21%) and *Bloodsport* (19% vs. 8%).

In sum, the Times Mirror data show that viewers of violent programs are characterized primarily by their age (18–34) and then by their gender (male).

Table 2.6
Percentage of Demographic Group Watching Movie

		% of Column Respondents					
	Total	Males 18–34	Females 18–34	Males 35–49	Females 35–49	Males 50+	Females 50+
Dances with Wolves	69.7	74.8	70	79	76.2	64.9	53.9
Home Alone II	31.7	39.2	29.5	35.9	33.8	27.3	23.2
Robin Hood: Prince of Thieves	54.9	70.4	67.1	66.1	56.7	39.5	27.9
The Silence of the Lambs	57.5	76.7	74.3	65.3	53.7	40.5	31.4
Lethal Weapon III	40.8	62.1	54	45.2	41.6	23.4	15.4
Terminator 2	52	80.1	68.4	64.1	44.6	37.6	14.6
Cape Fear	38	59.5	55.7	41.9	29.9	24.4	13.6
Alien 3	18.9	33.6	23.6	25.4	14.7	7.8	5
Hard to Kill	27.6	49.5	34.6	36.7	20.8	11.2	8.2
Bloodsport	16.9	41.9	19.4	19	8.2	6.3	1.1

Men 18–34 are the highest consumers of violent content, both in terms of the frequency of consumption of violent shows and their viewing among violent programs of those with the highest violence. Women 18–34 report the next highest consumption of violent programming, followed by men 35–49.

PRIME-TIME NIELSEN RATINGS

Nielsen ratings for prime-time movies carried on the broadcast networks offer many advantages in studying how the adult television audience is segmented. Advertisers and programmers make their decisions based on Nielsen ratings, so patterns analyzed here reflect the type of information used in the television marketplace. There are wide variations in viewing across genres and detailed indications of content for these movies, so that one can isolate more precisely for these shows what types of programming attract specific viewers. The networks have historically placed viewer advisories on a fraction of these films because of violent or adult content, so these movies also offer an opportunity to test the impact of providing viewers with information about program content. The ratings for prime-time movies reveal there is a taste for some type of violent programming across all age and gender categories. Men are more likely to watch films described by critics as particularly violent, while women have higher ratings for family crime stories. Viewer advisories did not change the ratings among adult demographic groups for these films, demonstrating that adults seeking to find or avoid violent programming are generally not surprised by the content in these films.

The sample of movies analyzed here consists of all movies (2,295) with complete listings in *TV Guide* and ratings information from Nielsen shown on the four major broadcast networks (ABC, CBS, NBC, and Fox [as of October 8, 1990]) from September 14, 1987 to September 26, 1993. During this time period, 44 movies were listed in *TV Guide* with the notation that the network "is advising viewer discretion." Of the 24 of these films with ads in *TV Guide*, 23 contained printed warnings from the networks that included general parental discretion warnings (17 ads), warnings about "mature themes"(4), warnings about language (1), and warnings about "violent content" (1). Though the print warnings provided in *TV Guide* or supplied by the networks did not often provide detailed information on why discretion was advised, the movies selected for warning did tend to be more violent than the other films in the set.[17] The tests, described later, examine how variations in content affect viewership and what the net impact of viewer discretion warnings are on adult audience sizes.

Ratings are often a function of scheduling, since audiences overall and among different demographic groups vary by time, day, and month.[18] The regressions described here predicting the ratings for prime-time broadcast movies control for these factors as well as for the year the movie was broadcast. One would expect declining ratings for films over the period 1987–93 since ratings for network shows in general have fallen over this period with increasing competition from cable. The rating of the lead-in show (i.e., the program preceding the movie) is also an important factor in a program's audience size. The regressions here use network dummy variables and the scheduling control variables as proxies for lead-in ratings. Since tastes for different genres of movies may vary across demographic groups, the program category assigned by *TV Guide* to a movie (e.g., comedy, drama) is also included in the rating regressions.

Movies that receive warnings are often films previously released in theaters, which means that they are produced with larger budgets than made for television movies and may contain more violent scenes. One thus needs to control for movie quality and content in a regression before examining the impact of viewer warnings to avoid potential problems of omitted variable bias (which could lead to conclusions about warning labels' impact on ratings that are driven by factors other than the addition of the viewer discretion designation). The ratings regressions thus control for whether the network promoted the film through an ad in *TV Guide* and whether the movie was described in a "Close-up" description in the magazine (writeups that highlight shows likely to attract viewer interest such as those with star actors or shows that reviewers wish to point out as worth watching). These two measures help capture a degree of expected audience interest and film quality. *TV Guide* information was also used to classify each movie based on whether it dealt with murder (e.g., did the description mention murder or attempted murder). Since true stories and family crime stories are thought to evoke viewer interest, the descriptions were also used to code for these variables. The networks themselves use these categories in analyzing movie programming. Assessing the performance of films during the 1993–94 television season, Ted Harbert, then president of ABC Entertainment and the network's head programmer, said, "this season, ABC's best performance was with family crime. The domestic crisis movies that were nonviolent averaged a point lower than the true crime movies and two points lower than the family crime movies."[19] *TV Guide* at times mentions whether a movie is particularly violent in its film descriptions, apart from the viewer warnings provided by networks. The ratings regressions include an indicator for this factor to determine whether movies with extremely violent content attract particular audiences. The ratings regressions allow one to examine whether, controlling for movie scheduling and content (including violent content), movies that receive a discretion warning have ratings that differ from other films.

Table 2.7 offers summary statistics for the set of 2,295 movies on network broadcast television shown in prime time for the 1987–92 television seasons. A plurality (46%) of the films were listed in *TV Guide* as dramas. Films in violent genres accounted for a significant proportion of these films: crime drama, 13%; western, 3%; science fiction, 2%; adventure, 6%; mystery, 4%; and thriller, 3%. In terms of themes associated with violent content, stories including murder were involved in 30% of the films and family crime stories accounted for 4% of the programs. *TV Guide* specifically described 4% of the films as particularly violent, using language much more descriptive than that in network advisories. The descriptions of these violent films included phrases such as "bloodbath," "gruesome nonstop action," and an "unrelenting exercise in gore, sex, and drugs." *TV Guide* contained network viewer discretion warnings on 2% of the films (note that of the 44 films with network viewer discretion warnings, 8 had specific mentions of violence in the description provided by *TV Guide*).

Overall, the average household rating for these prime-time network films was 11.7. This translates into approximately 11 million households viewing one of these films on average. The average share figure of 19.6 means that nearly 1 in 5 households watching television when these films were showing were watching one of these movies. Note that, as is true of television watching in general, ratings for these movies increase with viewer age. If one controls for age, women had higher average ratings for these films then men. The mean rating for children 2–11 was 4.2, which indicates that on average 1.6 million children in this age group were watching one of these broadcast network films when it aired in prime time. The impacts of viewer warnings on children's ratings are discussed in chapter 3.

Table 2.8 provides information on overall ratings and shares among the population of television households.[20] As indicated in previous research, scheduling plays a large role in audience size. Ratings vary with starting time, day of the week, and month. Relative to movie ratings in 1987, ratings in later years decline as competition from cable has increased. The overall ratings also provide evidence that violence does attract viewers to prime-time films.[21] Movies with murder or family crime themes do have higher ratings. Films that *TV Guide* specifically describes as violent also have higher ratings, indicating that on net some viewers are attracted to these types of films. The viewer discretion warn-

TABLE 2.7

Content and Audience Indicators: Prime-Time Broadcast
Network Movies, 1987–93 ($N = 2{,}295$)

Genre (% Movies)	
Drama	46.1
Comedy Drama	5.3
Crime Drama	12.5
Comedy	13.0
Western	2.6
Science Fiction	1.9
Adventure	6.4
Mystery	3.7
Thriller	2.5
Fantasy	3.0
Other	2.9
Type (% Movies)	
Theatrical	28.6
Closeup Summary	12.9
TV Guide Ad	51.9
Murder	30.2
True Story	18.0
Family Crime	4.0
TV Guide Violence	3.8
Warning	1.9
Audience (Mean Ratings)[a]	
Children, 2–11	4.24 (2.84)
Teens, 12–17	5.52 (3.42)
Women, 18+	9.03 (3.66)
Women, 18–34	7.11 (3.44)
Women, 18–49	7.78 (3.34)
Women, 25–54	8.50 (3.50)
Women, 55+	11.23 (5.61)
Men, 18+	7.01 (3.01)
Men, 18–34	5.44 (2.88)
Men, 18–49	6.06 (3.27)
Men, 25–54	6.69 (3.01)
Men, 55+	9.30 (4.35)
Household Ratings	11.67 (3.91)

[a] The 2,295 movies in the main regression sample were shown in prime time on broadcast network television from September 14, 1987, to September 26, 1993. Standard deviations of ratings are in parentheses.

ings had no impact on a film's overall household rating or share. Although debates about discretion warnings are occasionally framed as helping to prevent adults from being surprised and offended about viewing violent content, household ratings from movies with warnings are not significantly different in statistical terms from other films.

TABLE 2.8
Determinants of Movie Ratings on Network Television, 1987–93

	Household Ratings	Household Share (%)
Drama	−.23 (.86)	−.36 (.86)
Crime Drama	−.03 (.10)	.07 (.15)
Comedy	−.56 (1.92)*	−.98 (2.14)**
Western	1.08 (2.52)**	1.63 (2.45)**
Science-Fiction	−.64 (1.35)	−1.06 (1.42)
Adventure	−.42 (1.26)	−.54 (1.04)
Mystery	.13 (.33)	.43 (.69)
Thriller	−.83 (1.95)*	−1.27 (1.91)*
Fantasy	−.23 (.55)	−.28 (.44)
Other Genre	−.93 (2.25)**	−1.40 (2.18)**
Theatrical	−.07 (.46)	.00052 (.002)
Closeup Summary	.27 (1.52)	.30 (1.06)
TV Guide Ad	1.83 (11.64)***	2.22 (9.06)***
Murder	.47 (3.22)***	.64 (2.85)***
True Story	.40 (2.46)**	.60 (2.37)**
Family Crime	1.00 (3.32)***	1.62 (3.45)***
TV Guide Violence	.52 (1.74)*	.61 (1.31)
Warning	−.30 (.72)	−.47 (.71)
Adjusted R^2	.54	.44

Note: Absolute values of T statistics are in parentheses. *** = statistically significant at the .01 level; ** = significant at the .05 level; * = significant at the .10 level. Genre dummies are relative to comedy drama. Each regression also contains controls for the network, starting hour, day, month, and year the movie was aired. Sample contains 2,295 movies shown on broadcast network television between September 14, 1987, and September 26, 1993.

Since the model in chapter 1 predicts that violent programming will be popular with particular viewing segments, tables 2.9 and 2.10 explore how ratings for these films vary based on age and gender. Table 2.9 breaks down viewing among women by age groups. Relative to the comedy drama genre, the regressions indicate that crime dramas, adventure films, and mysteries are less popular with younger women (though women 55+ do have higher ratings for mystery films). Theatrical movies have lower ratings for women than made-for-television movies, which could be because men are viewed as the marginal consumers for movies in theaters while women are the target of television movie themes because of their value to advertisers. Women overall have higher ratings for movies with murder themes, a trend more apparent among women 25–54 and 55+. Women 18–34, 18–49, and 25–54 are attracted to true stories, and women of all age groupings have higher ratings for family crime stories. Movies that are described as violent by *TV Guide* had ratings for women that are not significantly different from other films. Viewer discretion warnings had no impact on ratings among any of the female demographic groups.

TABLE 2.9
Determinants of Movie Ratings on Network Television, 1987–93, for Female Demographic Groups

	18+	18–34	18–49	25–54	55+
Drama	−.01 (.04)	−.80 (3.10)***	−.48 (2.02)**	−.27 (1.12)	.85 (2.18)**
Crime Drama	−.25 (.84)	−1.57 (5.26)***	−.96 (3.49)***	−.61 (2.17)**	.70 (1.55)
Comedy	−.87 (3.09)***	−.28 (.99)	−.54 (1.42)	−.07 (.19)	1.35 (2.16)**
Western	.03 (.07)	−1.29 (3.12)***	−.05 (.11)	−.24 (.54)	−4.70 (6.73)***
Science Fiction	−1.64 (3.57)***	−.08 (.16)	−.75 (2.51)**	−.64 (2.10)**	−2.12 (4.33)***
Adventure	−1.21 (3.77)***	−1.16 (3.58)***	−.75 (2.51)**	−.64 (2.10)**	−2.12 (4.33)***
Mystery	.36 (.93)	−2.28 (5.90)***	−1.26 (3.52)***	−.66 (1.81)*	3.82 (6.55)***
Thriller	−.90 (2.20)**	−.14 (.35)	−.09 (.24)	−.26 (.66)	−2.53 (4.05)***
Fantasy	−.77 (1.95)*	.27 (.68)	.19 (.51)	.08 (.21)	−2.54 (4.23)***
Other Genre	−.94 (2.38)**	−.61 (1.53)	−.56 (1.51)	−.57 (1.52)	−1.54 (2.57)**
Theatrical	−.94 (6.18)***	.48 (3.11)***	−.05 (.38)	−.36 (2.49)**	−2.60 (11.21)***
Closeup Summary	.32 (1.84)*	.17 (.97)	.27 (1.71)*	.32 (1.96)*	.35 (1.32)
TV Guide Ad	1.42 (9.40)***	1.47 (9.64)***	1.56 (11.09)***	1.70 (11.85)***	1.07 (4.67)***
Murder	.30 (2.12)**	−.14 (1.03)	.07 (.51)	.25 (1.89)*	.57 (2.68)***
True Story	.26 (1.64)	.81 (5.12)***	.61 (4.21)***	.54 (3.66)***	−.36 (1.52)
Family Crime	1.35 (4.65)***	1.55 (5.32)***	1.41 (5.23)***	1.32 (4.79)***	1.38 (3.14)***
TV Guide Violence	.11 (.37)	.22 (.78)	.24 (.90)	.25 (.93)	−.16 (.36)
Warning	−.46 (1.13)	−.11 (.28)	−.29 (.78)	−.50 (1.30)	−.56 (.91)
Adjusted R^2	.51	.44	.49	.52	.52

Note: See footnote on table 2.8.

TABLE 2.10
Determinants of Movie Ratings on Network Television, 1987–93, for Male Demographic Groups

	18+	18–34	18–49	25–54	55+
Drama	−.10 (.43)	−.64 (3.13)***	−.44 (1.73)*	−.37 (1.80)*	.70 (2.37)**
Crime Drama	.93 (3.60)***	−.24 (1.00)	.36 (1.23)	.64 (2.66)***	2.65 (7.71)***
Comedy	−.04 (.15)	.35 (1.53)	.51 (1.84)*	.21 (.91)	−.78 (2.39)**
Western	2.96 (8.28)***	.91 (2.75)***	1.87 (4.63)***	2.38 (7.18)***	5.80 (12.17)***
Science Fiction	1.06 (2.64)***	2.47 (6.68)***	2.57 (5.68)***	2.43 (6.57)***	−2.63 (4.93)***
Adventure	.93 (3.32)***	.85 (3.28)***	1.26 (3.99)***	1.40 (5.39)***	.14 (.37)
Mystery	.44 (1.31)	−1.26 (4.07)***	−.59 (1.56)	−.26 (.86)	3.64 (8.17)***
Thriller	−.21 (.58)	.42 (1.28)	.34 (.83)	.28 (.85)	−1.70 (3.58)***
Fantasy	.23 (.66)	.98 (3.07)***	1.10 (2.81)***	1.11 (3.48)***	−1.32 (2.88)***
Other Genre	−.19 (.55)	−.05 (.17)	.12 (.30)	.08 (.26)	−.71 (1.54)
Theatrical	.72 (5.44)***	1.60 (13.05)***	1.41 (9.40)***	1.25 (10.17)***	−.85 (4.79)***
Closeup Summary	.07 (.47)	.05 (.34)	.05 (.32)	.15 (1.08)	.23 (1.14)
TV Guide Ad	1.02 (7.78)***	1.13 (9.35)***	1.11 (7.48)***	1.23 (10.10)***	1.07 (6.09)***
Murder	.73 (5.99)***	.16 (1.46)	.22 (1.62)	.44 (3.88)***	1.21 (7.48)***
True Story	.19 (1.42)	.49 (3.86)***	.35 (2.27)**	.42 (3.33)***	−.15 (.84)
Family Crime	−.33 (1.32)	.13 (.58)	−.11 (.38)	−.22 (.95)	−.50 (1.48)
TV Guide Violence	.92 (3.68)***	.78 (3.35)***	.99 (3.49)***	1.15 (4.94)***	.66 (1.96)**
Warning	−.28 (.79)	.08 (.26)	−.06 (.15)	−.15 (.47)	−.60 (1.27)
Adjusted R^2	.46	.49	.41	.53	.54

Note: See footnote on table 2.8.

Table 2.10 provides evidence that males turn out for particularly violent films. Among movie genres, younger men are more likely to view science fiction and adventure movies. Men overall have higher ratings for crime drama, especially men 25–54 and 55+ (who, like their female counterparts, view mysteries more too). Men aged 18–34, 18–49, and 25–54 are also more likely to view movies made for theater release. Movies with murder themes gain higher ratings from men overall, especially among men 55+. Note that the preference for family crime stories evident among female demographic groups is absent among men. Consistent with the Times Mirror survey results that men are less likely to be offended by violence and more likely to watch violent shows than women, men in all age categories had higher ratings for movies described as violent by *TV Guide*. Viewer discretion warnings had no statistically significant effect on ratings among men.

These results reveal that preferences for some type of violent programming exist across many different demographic groups. Older viewers prefer movies in the mystery genre, women favor family crime stories (which often portray women as victims of domestic violence), and men register higher ratings for movies described by critics as particularly violent. Among the prime-time network broadcast movies shown during the 1987–92 television seasons examined here, movies with references to murder, that focused on family crime, and were noted as violent by reviewers all enjoyed higher household ratings.

VALUING ADULT VIEWERS

The Times Mirror survey and the Nielsen data indicate that violent content is more popular with younger and male viewers. The prevalence of violent programming depends not only on the number of viewers interested in violent genres but also on the value that advertisers place on these consumers. This section explores how advertisers, and hence broadcast programmers, value different adult demographic groups. Companies advertising on broadcast network television view advertising transactions in terms of the cost per thousand viewers reached in a particular demographic group. While a given show may attract a large number of viewers, from an advertiser's perspective, the question will be how the combination of viewers and ad price translates into a cost per thousand of reaching particular demographic groups with a commercial. From a broadcaster's perspective, the profitability of a show will depend in part on the ad prices the network can charge and the production fees (explored more in chapter 6) paid for the right to air the programming. This section analyzes the differences between violent and nonviolent shows in terms of cost per thousand viewers and advertising prices for November 1993.

The costs per thousand viewers for reaching different demographic groups were available for a total of 297 shows on broadcast network television shown in November 1993. These programs were from many different parts of the day, including morning programs such as news shows, afternoon shows such as soap operas, prime time ($N = 140$ shows), late night programming such as talk shows, and weekend sports programming. One way to analyze these programs is to compare cost per thousand (cpt) for the prime-time violent shows ($N = 27$) with those for all other network broadcast programs ($N = 270$).[22] Overall the cpt for reaching total households was nearly identical for violent and non-violent shows. The cpt for total households was $8.4 for the 270 nonviolent shows and $8.0 for the 27 violent shows. For women 18–49 the cpt was lower for violent shows, $21.3, than for nonviolent shows, $26.8 ($T = 2.9$). For men 18–49 the cpt was also lower for violent programs (25.2) than for nonviolent (31.5) ($T = 2.8$). For teens (nonviolent cpt $97.0, violent cpt $109.1) and children 2–11 (nonviolent cpt $68.4, violent cpt $72.9) the difference in cost per thousand for violent versus nonviolent programs was not statistically significant.

These cpt results show that for a company considering advertising on broadcast television the cost of reaching a thousand television households is the same for nonviolent programs and violent programs. From an advertiser's perspective, however, all television households are not equally desirable. A firm may place a premium on reaching particular demographic groups that are more likely to be swayed by an ad to purchase a given product. Once television viewers are disaggregated into rough demographic groups, it becomes clearer that violent prime-time shows have a lower cpt for both women 18–49 and men 18–49. On the other hand, the difference between the cpt for nonviolent versus violent programs is not statistically significant for teens or children. This suggests that violent programs may be a less expensive way for advertisers to reach both men and women in the 18–49 demographic range and that these programs would not be good buys for advertisers targeting teens or children. The latter result underscores that exposure of children to violent programming is truly an externality since advertisers are not likely to be aiming at these viewers in sponsoring violent adult shows.

Broadcasters focus on a different indicator in the advertising market, the price per 30 seconds of advertising they can charge on a program. For the 140 prime-time shows in the November 1993 sample, the price per 30-second ad (hereafter referred to as the "ad price") ranged from a high of $298,300 for *Seinfeld* to a low of $28,500 for *Front Page*. The mean ad price for the 113 nonviolent network prime-time broadcasts was $110,000, while the mean ad price for the 27 violent prime-time shows as $68,000. The lower ad prices are consistent with the finding that violent shows draw lower ratings (see chapter 6). The violent genres also include some shows such as *Murder, She Wrote* that draw heavily on viewers over 50+, who are less valued by advertisers.

Though violent shows draw lower overall audiences, the particular composition of those audiences in terms of age, gender, and income may affect the price that broadcasters are ultimately able to charge for these shows. Viewers 18–49 are said to be more valued by advertisers because their brand loyalties are not as firmly established and because of the products they buy during this part of the life cycle. Women 18–34 are said to be especially valued, since they may often make purchasing decisions within a household.

Table 2.11 bears out these hypotheses of how the composition of an audience affects ad prices. The program audience for each prime-time show was divided into children 2–11, teens 12–17, males 18–34, females 18–34, adults 35–49, adults 50+. For the 140 shows in prime-time broadcast by the networks, the mean ad price for 30 seconds was $102,000. The number of teens and children in the audience did not have a statistically significant impact on prime-time broadcast ad prices, indicating that in general these are not the target audiences of these particular television shows. This would be consistent with children being targeted through other programs (e.g., weekend programming) and teens being targeted through particular niche shows rather than general prime-time broadcasts.

For prime-time shows in general, increases in male viewers aged 18–34 and viewers over 49 did not have a statistically significant impact on ad prices, which suggests that these are not the general target audiences for advertisers on prime-time. An increase in the number of women 18–34 did increase ad rates. The addition of 100,000 viewers in this demographic group raises 30-second ad prices by $1,450. Increases in viewers 35–59 also increase ad prices. The addition of 100,000 audience members from this viewing group raises prime-time network broadcast ad prices by $1,740. When one controls for the number of viewers in these different demographic groups, specification (2) in table 2.11 shows that ads on violent programs sold for $18,000 less than ads on non-violent shows. Several factors may account for this ad differential. If viewers of violent programs had lower incomes or education, then they might be less sought after by advertisers. There may also be a premium for certain advertisers in reaching a large number of viewers at once, so that programs that draw smaller absolute ratings sell at a discount.

Table 2.11 provides additional support for the hypothesis that violent programs are aimed primarily at viewers 18–49. If the 140 prime-time network shows are split into violent and nonviolent samples—specifications (3) and (4)—it becomes clear the ad prices for shows in different genres are driven by different demographic groups. For the violent set of shows, an increase in viewers 18–49 had a statistically significant impact on ad prices, while changes in viewers aged 50+ did not impact ad rates. This would occur if the companies using violent programming were focusing on reaching 18–49 viewers and did not value additional viewers aged 50+ since these were not the targets of the ads. Increasing the audience for a violent show by 100,000 viewers age 18–49 resulted in an increase in ad rates of $560. For nonviolent programs, viewing by both those aged 18–49 and 50+ has an impact on ad prices. If 100,000 more viewers aged 18–49 tune into a program, the ad price increases by $1,300, while an increase in 100,000 viewers age 50+ increases ad rates by $250. Note that the return to capturing the younger demographic group is nearly five times that of garnering additional older viewers. This provides support for the notion that broadcasters will focus on the viewing preferences of those aged 18–49, which may leave older viewers reporting greater dissatisfaction with broadcast television. Increases in viewing by teens had no impact on the ad rates of prime-time programs in either regression, consistent with the

TABLE 2.11
Determinants of Prime-Time Broadcast Network Advertising Rates, Fall 1993

	(1) Prime-Time Rate, 30-Second Ad, Full Sample (N = 140 Programs)	(2)	(3) Prime-time Rate, 30-Second Ad, Violent Programs (N = 27)	(4) Prime-time Rate, 30-Second Ad, Nonviolent Programs (N = 113)
Intercept	-7.82 (7.15)	-0.67 (7.45)	1.52 (14.97)	-3.78 (8.10)
Children, 2–11 Viewing	-1.80e-3 (3.34e-3)	-1.30e-3 (3.27e-3)		
Teens, 12–17 Viewing	4.63e-3 (8.93e-3)	1.47e-3 (8.79e-3)	0.03 (0.02)	-5.77e-3 (4.62e-3)
Males, 18–34 Viewing	2.98e-4 (6.48e-3)	2.76e-3 (6.39e-3)		
Females, 18–34 Viewing	1.45e-2*** (5.01e-3)	1.29e-2*** (4.93e-3)		
Women and Men, 18–49 Viewing			5.56e-3* (2.87e-3)	1.30e-2*** (1.11e-3)
Women and Men, 35–49 Viewing	1.74e-2*** (3.94e-3)	1.67e-2*** (3.85e-3)		
Women and Men, 50+ Viewing	9.83e-4 (1.26e-3)	1.25e-3 (1.23e-3)	2.29e-3 (1.45e-3)	2.47e-3** (1.10e-3)
Violent Program		-18.14*** (6.62)		
Adjusted R^2	0.71	0.72	0.44	0.72

Note: Dependent variable in each OLS regression is the November 1993 ad rate (in $000) for a 30-second ad during the program. All viewing figures are in terms of the number of thousands of viewers in the demographic group watching the program. Standard errors are in parentheses. *** = statistically significant at the .01 level, ** = significant at the .05 level, * = significant at the .10 level.

notion that these prime-time broadcast programs are not primarily targeted at these viewers.

Overall these advertising results indicate that network broadcasters will take into account the preferences of both those aged 18–49 and those 50+ in broadcasting nonviolent shows. Increases in viewing by both these groups are rewarded with higher ad rates for nonviolent genres. In selling audiences for violent programs to advertisers, however, the networks face incentives to focus on the preferences of the younger adult demographic group. Additional viewers aged 18–49 for violent programs bring higher ad prices, while increases in viewing by those 50+ do not affect ad prices for violent shows.

OPINIONS ABOUT VIOLENT PROGRAMMING

General dissatisfaction with violence in news and entertainment programming is a frequent topic of surveys and news reports. The majority of Americans report that television news gives "too much attention to stories about violent crimes" (58% in the Times Mirror survey) and that there is also "too much violence" in nonnews (e.g., entertainment) programming (72% in the Times Mirror survey). Programmers and advertisers do not necessarily focus on what the "majority" of Americans believe, since few decision makers have a constituency or consumer base where obtaining a majority of the American populace is the relevant goal. With advertisers and broadcasters aiming at the marginal viewer or consumer within set demographic groups, the differences of opinion about violent programming among different demographic groups become potentially more important than the overall mean response in the general population.

The simplified model in chapter 1 predicted that if advertisers value consumers of violent programming more, then a higher number of channels will program to reach them. This implies that these consumers may be happier with viewing options, if satisfaction is in part a function of the number of viewing options available. This chapter has established that violent programming is consumed particularly by younger viewers, a group more highly valued by advertisers. One would thus predict that these viewers would be happier with the offerings of programs than consumers in demographic groups less valued by advertisers (i.e., the 50+ viewing audience). The Times survey bears this out. When asked to "compare TV entertainment shows these days with TV entertainment 5 years ago," 43% of males 18–34 and 37% of females 18–34 said current television entertainment programming was better. This compares with 18% for males 50+ and 10% for females 50+. The differences are also as stark when one compares the opinions of heavy consumers of violent programming (43% of whom felt the current entertainment programming was better) and light consumers (80% of whom responded that current entertainment programming was worse). These results are not simply a generational dissatisfaction with all of television. When asked whether local news in their area was better now than in the past 5 years, 60% of males 18–34 said it was better and 65% of females 50+ reported the same opinion. National news was similarly seen as improving by a majority in each of the six age and gender categories.

Table 2.12 describes the distribution of opinions about violent programming. When the Times Mirror survey asked adults about satisfaction with levels of violence in news and entertainment programming, whether violence on television personally bothers them, and the degree that they felt television violence

• *C H A P T E R 2* •

TABLE 2.12
Views of Violent Programming

	Total	Males 18–34	Females 18–34	Males 35–49	Females 35–49	Males 50+	Females 50+
			% of Column Respondents				
How do you feel about the amount of violence portrayed on TV programs today, not including news programs?							
Too Much Violence	71.9	53.8	65.4	65.7	80.1	77.1	91.1
Reasonable Amount	24.9	43.5	31.2	29.4	17.7	17.6	7.5
Very Little Violence	1.5	2.0	2.1	1.2	0.9	2.0	1.1
Do you think TV news is too full of violence?							
Yes	52.2	41.9	56.1	40.7	59.7	52.7	62.9
No	44.5	56.5	42.2	55.6	37.7	43.4	30.7
Would you say violence on TV shows bothers you?							
Bothers a Great Deal	24.9	10.3	26.2	15.7	35.9	21.5	41.1
Does not Bother	39.4	65.4	32.1	50.8	19.0	46.3	19.6
Would you say that violence on TV shows is harmful or harmless to society?							
Very Harmful	47.4	29.6	46.8	36.7	55.0	51.7	67.1
Harmless	15.1	24.3	14.3	21.4	8.7	14.6	5.7
Do you feel that violence on TV and in movies is a cause of the breakdown in law and order?							
Major Cause	38.9	22.9	32.9	23.0	47.6	47.8	61.4
Minor Cause	39.8	43.9	48.9	49.2	37.2	36.1	23.6
Hardly a Cause	17.7	31.9	16.9	25.8	9.5	11.2	8.2

was harmful to society, three patterns were clear across all of these questions. Younger viewers were less pessimistic about violent programming than older viewers. Within a given age group, women were more dissatisfied with violent content than men. Males 18–34 reported the most favorable reaction to violent programming, while women 50+ looked upon violent content with the most disfavor.

Dissatisfaction was much higher with violence in entertainment programming than with violence in news. While 52% of the sample agreed that television news is too full of violence, 72% expressed this sentiment about nonnews programming. Gender and age gaps in opinions are particularly evident in these views toward entertainment shows.[23] For example, 54% of males 18–34 agreed that nonnews programming has too much violence, compared with 91% of females 50+. Within a given age group, women were twice as likely as men to report that violence on television bothers them "a great deal." In the 18–34 age group, 10% of males 18–34 versus 26% of females agreed with that statement, versus 22% of males 50+ and 41% of females 50+. Among males 18–34 65% said that violence on television "does not bother" them, compared with only 20% for females 50+. These age and gender differences also exist in views about the impact of violence on society. For example, 30% of males 18–34 agree with the statement that television violence is very harmful to society versus 67% of females 50+. Only 23% of males 18–34 see television violence as a major cause of the breakdown in law and order in society, compared with 61% of females 50+. Ranked by their opinions about the impact of television violence, males 18–34 report the most favorable views about the impact of television violence, followed by males 35–49 and then females 18–34. This is a reversal from the earlier viewing patterns, where females 18–34 ranked second in terms of heavy consumption of violent programming.[24]

The differences in reactions to violent programming affect advertiser incentives. Consider two companies deciding whether to advertise on a violent program (a topic covered more thoroughly in chapter 5). If advertising on a violent program attracts public scrutiny, then a firm's brand image could be damaged among consumers who felt that violence on television affects violence in society. Companies primarily trying to reach 18–34 consumers would face less fallout from supporting a violent program, for these consumers are much less likely to find violent programming personally bothersome or believe it has a negative impact on society. A firm whose target customers contained older consumers, however, might be less willing to risk advertising on a violent program because of the greater risk of brand name damage among older consumers (who in general voice greater objections to violent content). Politicians may be similarly more responsive to the views of constituents older than 18–34 since they are more likely to vote, although the particular political benefits from voicing concern for television violence will depend on the distribution of opinions (discussed in chapter 8) among those viewed as marginal voters by particular candidates or parties.

It could be the case that people consume violent programming and believe it is harmful to society, but continue to do so because the logic of collective action leads them to decide that they should not forgo viewing because their actions would have little impact on scheduling decisions. But Table 2.13 demonstrates that this possible gap between viewing and opinions does not exist. Heavy consumers of violent programming are much less likely to report that television violence bothers them a great deal (13%, versus 45% of light viewers) or agree that violence on television shows is very harmful to society (agreed to by 37% of heavy viewers versus 67% of light viewers of television

TABLE 2.13
Opinions of the Impact of Violent Programming by Amount of
Violent Programming Consumed

	% of Column Respondents		
	Light	*Medium*	*Heavy*
Would you say violence on TV shows bothers you?			
Bothers a Great Deal	45.2	28.1	13.3
Does Not Bother	19.9	34.6	51.9
Would you say that violence on TV shows is harmful or harmless to society?			
Very Harmful	67.4	49.5	36.9
Harmless	7.3	8.6	23.8
Do you feel that violence on TV and in movies is a cause of the breakdown in law and order?			
Major Cause	59.1	42.5	27.1
Minor Cause	27.2	41.7	43.8
Hardly a Cause	7.3	12.5	26.6

violence).[25] When asked whether television violence is a major cause of the "breakdown of law and order" in society, 27% of heavy viewers agreed with this versus 59% of light viewers.

Advertisers on violent programming risk few adverse reactions from the viewers of such shows, for they are much less likely to see violence on television as harmful to society. Since this segment of the viewing population is highly valued by advertisers (85% of heavy violence consumers are age 18–49), advertising on violent programming may remain cost-effective for companies trying to reach younger viewers, even if such sponsorship generates negative reactions among older viewers and consumers.

CONCLUSIONS

While the model in chapter 1 assumed that the consumers of violent programming were a distinct group of viewers, analysis of the Times Mirror survey and Nielsen ratings confirms this. Males 18–34 are the highest consumers of violent programming, followed by females 18–34 and males 35–49. These groups are less likely to be offended by television violence or believe that it is harmful to society. They are also more likely to be highly valued by advertisers, and hence programmers. Advertisers primarily targeting these demographic groups may find it profitable to sponsor violent programs because the consumers of their products are less likely to see such programming as controversial. Much of the controversy surrounding violent programs centers around an unintended viewing audience, children. The next chapter explores children's viewing of both adult programs and shows targeted specifically at their age group.

TABLE A2.1
Determinants of Heavy Viewing of Violent Entertainment

Variable	Coefficient (Standard Error)
Intercept	-1.30***
	(0.34)
Female	-0.62***
	(0.12)
White	-0.94***
	(0.19)
Aged 18–34	2.19***
	(0.16)
Aged 35–49	1.31***
	(0.16)
Less Than HS Education	0.71***
	(0.24)
HS Education	0.67***
	(0.17)
Some College/Post-HS Education	0.47***
	(0.16)
East	0.09
	(0.20)
Midwest	0.02
	(0.18)
South	-0.13
	(0.18)
Annual Income Less Than $20K	-0.10
	(0.21)
Annual Income $20K–$29K	0.05
	(0.20)
Annual Income $30K–$49K	-0.04
	(0.18)
Don't Know/Refused to Give Income	-0.16
	(0.24)
City	0.09
	(0.18)
Town	-0.04
	(0.18)
Suburb	0.01
	(0.20)
Medium Amount of TV watching (2–3.5 Hours per Day)	0.59***
	(0.15)
Heavy Amount of TV Watching (4 + Hours per Day)	1.16***
	(0.16)
Log Likelihood	-826.9

Note: Dependent variable in logit analysis equals 1 if viewer was a heavy viewer of violent television and movies.

*** = significant at the .01 level; ** = significant at the .05 level; * = significant at the .10 level.

Children as Viewers

ALTHOUGH CHILDREN 2–11 on average watch 23 hours of television per week, many of these hours are spent viewing programs where children are an unintended audience.[1] Nearly 6 hours per week of a child's viewing occurs during prime time, a time when advertising rates on network programs are unaffected by the number of children watching since the advertised products are generally targeted at adults. Yet the ratings for children watching prime-time broadcast network shows are often higher than those for programs particularly aimed at children. The mean rating for children 2–11 for the forty-three prime-time sitcoms broadcast on network television in November 1993 was a 7.1, while the mean rating for children 2–11 for the thirty-four weekend children's programs on the broadcast networks was a 4.8.[2] Children's viewing is often associated with Saturday morning, since on average 23% of children 2–11 are watching television on Saturday from 7 AM to 1 PM. In the first hour (8–9 PM) of prime time, however, 33% of all children 2–11 are viewing television. Analyzing children's consumption of television programming should thus involve both an examination of their viewership of adult programming and their viewership of shows targeted specifically at children.

This chapter first examines children's viewership of violent programming aimed at adults. The absolute number of children watching such violent programming is often large. For the movies described by *TV Guide* as particularly violent that aired during prime time on the broadcast networks in 1993, the average movie-viewing audience contained 1.3 million children aged 2–11. These large numbers do not mean that children have higher ratings overall for violent adult shows. Violent programs actually earn lower ratings than those for other types of prime-time shows among children 2–11. The analysis of another source of violent content, syndicated programming, reveals that part of the exposure of children to violent content arises from the consumption of programs scheduled for early evening and weekend daytime hours. Although these time periods provide access to young adults, they also generate significant numbers of children in the audience for violent programs.

This chapter offers the first analysis using ratings data to examine how information provision about program content may be used to reduce the exposure of children to television violence. In theory, if parents are provided with information about objectionable content, this will lower their costs of shielding their children and thus decrease the number of children remaining in the audience for violent programs. Analysis of the impact of viewer discretion warnings on prime time movies on broadcast television from 1987 to 1993 reveals that placing a viewer discretion warning on a movie resulted in a decrease in children's ratings of approximately 14%. If one controls for the other factors that drive program ratings, those films with warnings had 220,000 fewer children in the audience. This suggests that, on net, viewer discretion warnings in prime time do assist parents in monitoring their children's viewing. The implications of these results for the TV Parental Guidelines rating system implemented in 1997 by the television industry are discussed more fully in chapter 8.

One of the strongest explanations for why television violence represents a market failure is that producers of programs aimed at adults often do not consider the costs to children of viewing these programs. Yet programs produced directly for children also generate negative externalities, even though producers realize that their prime audiences are children. Many of the programs aimed at children are cartoons (e.g., of the television shows in syndication for children in November 1993, 80% were animated). The analysis of National Coalition on Television Violence (NCTV) data in this chapter indicates that as a genre children's programs are extremely violent. For the sample of 363 children's programs examined by NCTV from 1982 through 1991, the average number of violent acts per hour on the four broadcast networks was 22.4. This compares with a mean of 8.6 for adult programs shown over the same time period. This level of violence would place children's programs (primarily cartoons) among the most violent television genres, such as action adventure (27.6 violent acts per hour) and crime shows (20.2). The chapter further demonstrates that there is some market segmentation in children's programming that is similar to the product differentiation in adult programming discussed in chapter 4. Broadcast network children's shows had slightly lower levels of violent acts per hour than those shown in syndication (26.4) or on cable (25.4), and just as within adult programming there was a wide range of violence levels across children's programming on cable channels.

Whereas violent cartoons generate negative externalities, another genre of children's shows, often called "educational" programming, produces positive externalities. This chapter underscores why educational programming for children involves a market failure, based largely in the failure of parents or broadcasters to internalize fully the benefits to society of what children learn from educational programs. The analysis here demonstrates that educational programs for children on average earn lower ratings than noneducational shows in both the broadcast network market and the syndicated children's market. For the 1993 fall season the mean rating among children 2–11 for broadcast network educational shows was 3.3, versus 5.4 for the other children's programs on the networks. Lower ratings translate into lower ad rates. The mean price per 30-second commercial for network children's educational shows was $20,900, compared with $29,700 for noneducational shows aimed at children. Even controlling for the ratings that the programs generate, the results in this chapter indicate that educational shows generate lower advertising rates.

Currently, broadcasters receive their licenses essentially for free in return for a promise to broadcast in the "public interest, convenience, and necessity." The Children's Television Act of 1990 clarified in part what this "public interest" obligation entails by requiring the FCC to "consider the extent to which the licensee . . . has served the educational and informational needs of children through the licensee's overall programming, including programming specifically designed to serve such needs."[3] This transformed children's programming in part into a "price" that local broadcasters had to pay in order to get their licenses renewed. Yet in the absence of significant scrutiny of their programming efforts, stations tried to lower the price they paid by placing educational programming in early hours (when fewer revenues were lost by using such programming) and by claiming that noneducational programs were actually educational. These efforts reached such extremes as stations claiming that *GI Joe* was educational programming since it dealt with "issues of social consciousness and responsibility" and that *Geraldo* and *Beverly Hills, 90210* were educational since they dealt with issues of sexuality.[4]

This chapter explores the incentives for stations to shirk their public interest requirements by looking at the scheduling of children's programming. Though network affiliates generally follow the programming times suggested by the network in airing prime-time programming, they sometimes decide to shift when children's programs provided by the networks are aired so that they can program more profitable shows. Using information on such program "deviations" from November 1993, I find that for noneducational programs for children on Saturdays 10.3% of these showings were shifted to another time by network affiliates. Twice the percentage, 20.2%, of the scheduled educational programs were shifted. The pattern is even starker when one examines the shifting of Saturday shows to an air time prior to 8 AM. Only 3.5% of the noneducational shows were shifted to air before 8 AM, whereas 9.7% of the total Saturday network educational programs aired by affiliates were shifted to air before 8 AM.

The patterns of deviations demonstrate that stations do calculate the lost potential profits associated with educational programming and that there are consistent patterns of behavior with how stations treat their public interest programming obligations in educational programming targeted for children and in public affairs shows aimed at adults. The opportunity cost in terms of forgone revenues associated with airing an educational show should be higher in larger markets, since local advertising rates are higher in areas where programs reach larger audiences. This should mean that deviations on educational programs are more likely in larger markets. The results indicate that in the top twenty-five television markets 27.6% of the airings of network educational programs are shifted, versus 16.9% in the nation's smaller television markets (i.e., those with market size rankings of 101 or higher). There is no statistically significant difference in the treatment of noneducational children's programs across these two market categories, which is what one would expect if it is the educational nature of the children's programming that draws lower ratings and ad rates and hence raises incentives for scheduling deviations.

Evening news programming may also generate positive externalities, in the form of viewers who become more informed voters as a result of the coverage of public affairs issues. Some stations deviate on the time scheduled by the network for the airing of national evening news, so that they can offer more profitable programs. The analysis here indicates that how stations treat public affairs programming for *adults* is related to how they treat educational shows for *children*. Controlling for factors such as market size and number of competing stations, those affiliates that shifted their evening news programs were also more likely to deviate on their children's programs. For ABC affiliates, those which deviated when they programmed *Nightline* (a late night news program) were also more likely to deviate on children's programs, especially if the program was educational. Stations that chose to use crime to generate local news audiences were also more likely to shift children's programs to air before 8 AM. The greater the amount of local news "teasers" (the promotions for upcoming stories) that dealt with crime, the greater the likelihood the station would deviate on scheduling children's programs. There were also clear differences in network behavior toward educational shows. The local affiliates owned by ABC and CBS were less likely to deviate, while those owned by NBC and Fox were more likely. These results on deviations demonstrate how stations face incentives to shirk their public interest requirements in the scheduling of educational programs and that those stations which deviate in children's programming are also those with lower standards in public affairs programming.

In sum, this chapter underscores that children's television viewing involves two types of market failures. The consumption of violent adult programming and violent cartoons generates negative externalities, since programmers do not incorporate the impact on society of the viewing of these shows by substantial numbers of children. While children are overexposed to violent content from society's perspective, they are underexposed to the positive impacts of educational programming. The chapter explores how information provision as a policy tool may be used both to reduce exposures to television violence and increase the provision of educational programming.

Consumption of Violent Programming Aimed at Adults

Children's ratings for violent programs targeted at adults are low relative to their ratings for nonviolent shows aimed at adults, but these relatively low ratings still translate into large numbers of viewers 2–11 for violent programs. The evidence from table 1.1 demonstrates that many other genres of programming garner higher ratings among children. For the fall of 1993, children 2–11 had average ratings of 2.9 for prime-time network programs in violent genres, 1.3 for local news programs and 1.9 for official police shows on during the dinner hour, 1.3 for violent series in syndication, and 1.1 for the late local evening news. Each of these types of programs has been criticized for exposing children to violent content. Children, however, have much higher ratings for nonviolent genres of programs. The ratings for viewers 2–11 were 5.6 for nonviolent prime-time network programs and 6.1 for situation comedies on during the dinner hour. For teens 12–17, ratings are similarly higher for network prime-time nonviolent shows (6.4) than for violent programs (3.3). During the dinner hour, local news programs averaged a 1.8 among teens while situation comedies garnered a mean rating of 6.7.

Even low ratings for genres of violent programming targeted at adults can translate into large absolute numbers of children viewing a program. Since there were approximately 37.7 million children 2–11 in television homes in 1993, the 3.4 rating for prime-time network films described in *TV Guide* as particularly violent meant that on average 1.3 million children viewed each of these violent shows. Chapter 1 underscores the difficulties of calculating the impact of particular genres of programming; since reactions to content will vary across children, impacts may not appear until long after viewing, and it is difficult to link viewing with behavior. Yet these ratings data indicate that for the types of programming described by content analysis as likely to contain violence, a large number of children 2–11 may be exposed to potentially harmful content.

These figures demonstrate that if one compares the audiences of children and teens for violent programming across many different time periods, the ratings for these demographic groups are low relative to their consumption of nonviolent shows. Another way to examine the popularity of violent programming is to see whether, within a particular time period, violent shows attract larger audiences. To examine this, I analyzed the ratings of all prime-time violent shows on network broadcast television for November 1993, a sample of 140. For each of these shows I modeled a particular demographic's rating for the program as a function of day of the week, starting time, and network. In addition, I added a dummy variable to control for whether the program was in a violent genre. Of the 140 shows in the sample, 27 were in violent genres.[5]

Table 3.1 reports the coefficient on the violent program genre by age and gender demographic groups. Of the 54 groups examined, the coefficient for violent programs was negative and statistically significant for 23, negative and insignificant for 25, and positive and insignificant for 6. None of the 54 groups had statistically significant higher ratings for prime-time broadcast network programs in violent genres. Ratings for both children and teens dropped by at least 2 ratings points for violent programs, a large drop considering that the average ratings for these 140 programs were 5.0 for children 2–11 and 5.8 for teens 12–17. In contrast, among the 22 different demographic groups examined for men 18+ (average rating, 6.2) only three subsets had a negative, statistically significant coefficient for programs in violent genres. For men with 4 or more years of college, ratings for violent programs dropped by 1.1 ratings points. Adult men with children 6 or younger had lower ratings (1.2 ratings points) for violent programs as did those with children 12 or younger (1.0). For the 22 different demographic groups for women 18+ (average rating, 7.9), 10 had negative and statistically significant violent genre coefficients. Violent programs had ratings nearly 2 points lower for women with 4 or more years of college, in households with higher incomes and education, in higher-income households with children,

TABLE 3.1

Change in Rating for Violent Broadcast Network Programs, Fall 1993

Demographic Group	Children, 2–11	Teens, 12–17	Men, 18+	Women, 18+
Total	−2.5***	−2.7***	−0.2	−0.7
Any Cable	−2.5***	−2.9***	−0.2	−0.7
No Cable	−2.5***	−2.4***	9e−2	−0.9
Pay Cable	−2.8***	−3.1***	−0.3	−0.9
Own VCR	−2.5***	−2.8***	−0.2	−0.8
Counties in Large Metropolitan Areas			−0.6	−1.1
Counties in Medium Metropolitan Areas			3e−2	−0.7
All Other Counties			0.4	−0.3
4+ Years of College			−1.1*	−1.8**
No College			0.5	1e−2
Income $20K–30K			0.2	−0.3
Income $30K–40K			−0.3	−0.9
Income $40K–60K			−0.6	−1.1
Income $60K+			−0.8	−1.5*
Presence of Children under 6			−1.2**	−2.3***
Presence of Children 12–17			−0.3	−1.3**
Presence of Children under 12			−1.0*	−2.2***
Presence of Children under 18			−0.7	−1.9***
Black			−0.5	−1.9*
Income $40K+ and Head of Household			0.2	−1.9**
Income $40K+, Presence of Non-adults			−1.0	−2.0***
Income $40K+/Professional, Owner, Manager			−1.1	−1.9**

Note: Table reports the regression coefficient for violent program genre in a ratings equation controlling for day of week, show time, and network for 140 shows broadcast in network prime-time for the fall of 1993.

*** = Statistically significant at the .01 level; ** = significant at the .05 level; * = significant at the .10 level.

and in higher-income households with professional workers. Women with children also had lower ratings for violent programs by about 2 ratings points.

Overall, these detailed demographics indicate that children and teens are less likely to be in the audience for programs that are violent. Since the data do not indicate what combination of factors leads to this pattern, one cannot separate out the influence of the viewing preferences of children and intervention by adults. The pattern is encouraging, however, since many of the negative externalities associated with violent programming are predicated on the exposure of children and teens to these shows. The data indicate that, overall, the different demographic groups of men examined were not attracted to or deterred from viewing violent programming, while for many female demographic groups women were less likely to turn out for violent shows. The presence of children in a household caused ratings to drop for violent shows (who are more likely to be offended by violent programming and believe it is harmful) than men. This suggests that parents with children may avoid watching violent programming themselves as part of a way to shield their children from violent content.

As another measure of the popularity of these 140 prime-time programs, I ranked these shows by the absolute number of children 2–11 and the percentage of a program's audience made up of children, and repeated this analysis for teens 12–17. There were no violent programs in the top twenty prime-time shows viewed by children or teens in terms of absolute number of viewers or percentage composition of the program's audience.[6]

SCHEDULING AND THE CONSUMPTION OF VIOLENT SYNDICATED PROGRAMMING

Part of the exposure of children to violent programming arises from the scheduling of syndicated series in time periods when large numbers of children are likely to be in the audience. Data from the November 1993 sweeps period allow me to examine the audiences of children and teens (and adults) for violent syndicated programs. While a few programs in syndication such as *Cobra* and *Renegade* were listed in Nielsen data as action adventure programs, other programs such as *Highlander* or *Acapulco H.E.A.T.* were listed as general drama, a genre that includes both violent and nonviolent programming. This section will define different types of violent programming used in syndication as including violent series (e.g., action adventure programs or those that focus on crime), violent movies (e.g., theatrical films with indicators of violence in reviews), and violent reality programming (e.g., shows that use real footage or recreations of police and emergency squad work). The rationale for including action adventure and general dramas dealing with crime as violent arises in part from the UCLA Center for Communication Policy (1995) and NTVS (1996a, 1996b) reports. Assessing the 1994–95 episodes of some of the syndicated shows on TV in the 1993 season, the UCLA study described these syndicated shows as containing multiple acts of violence:

Highlander: . . . While the intensity of the violence is not of concern, there are as many as 14 different scenes of violence in an episode, making it apparent that violence is the thread that holds the show together. There are many fight scenes, typically involving weapons such as swords, knives, and fists. In one particularly disturbing scene, a character is kicked in the face.

Renegade: A show about a loner who rides a motorcycle, *Renegade* compresses more scenes of violence into its one hour than any other original program monitored. Most of the acts of violence are more mean-spirited than are the violent acts in the other shows in syndication. Most of the time the violence is not very graphic. The program is about little other than violence. The quantity of scenes is excessive even though most individual scenes are not. One episode features more than 20 acts of violence.

Kung Fu: The Legend Continues: . . . contains many scenes of violence, a good number of which are prolonged. In the opening credits, the viewer sees pistols, shotguns and a man being kicked in the face. At the end of that scene the man is kicked through a plate glass window. Although the program's theme is based on the world of martial arts, a surprising number of the many acts of violence involve guns and explosives.[7]

In their study of violence in reality programming, the National Television Violence Study researchers discovered that reality police shows (i.e., *America's Most Wanted, Cops, Highway Patrol, Real Stories of the Highway Patrol,* and *Top Cops*) contained a high level of violence. Of the reality police shows examined, 100% contained violence. The researchers also found that these shows were more likely to portray extreme violence and more likely to show violence as rewarded.[8] The UCLA Center for Communication Policy study (1995) also cited violence in reality programming as particularly problematic. In their summary of *Real Stories of the Highway Patrol,* the researchers declare:

As a show that uses re-creations, it raises the recurring issue of how graphically to illustrate the crime. Frequently the re-creation is excessive and seems more likely to sensationalize the crime than to offer any real understanding to the viewer or any assistance to law enforcement. Several of the re-creations are horribly excessive, graphic, and prolonged. In one episode the scene of violence lasted over eight minutes. It starts with the criminals shooting at a bus and ends with four police officers being killed in a shoot-out. The point of the scene is to demonstrate the horror and senselessness of the crime. However noble the purpose, the scene is overly long and excessively graphic, going far beyond whatever is necessary to demonstrate that point.[9]

Qualitative and quantitative assessments of syndicated violent series programming and reality shows thus suggest the potential dangers of exposures by children to these programs. Table 3.2 analyzes the audiences for particular types of syndicated programming by examining for each program the fraction of the show's total audience composed of different demographic groups. Series in violent genres on prime-time broadcasts networks are often broadcast later in prime time, when children make up a declining share of the audience. During the November 1993 sweeps children 2–11 made up only 4% of the audience of

• *CHAPTER 3* •

TABLE 3.2
Percentage of a Program's Viewing Audience by Demographic Groups

	Children 2–11	Teens 12–17	Women 18–49	Men 18–49	Women 50+	Men 50+
Violent Series						
Acapulco H.E.A.T.	13	8	24	27	15	13
Cobra	11	6	25	26	17	14
Highlander	9	7	30	30	12	11
Kung Fu	11	7	25	28	16	12
Renegade	11	6	25	26	17	15
Violent Reality						
Cops	11	8	27	27	15	13
Emergency Call	7	7	26	25	19	16
Real Stories of the Highway Patrol	7	7	28	29	14	16
Violent Syndicated Movies						
Nightmare on Elm Street 5	12	17	31	30	5	5
Amityville: The Evil Escapes	15	9	31	22	15	9
Crucifer of Blood	8	3	23	27	18	21
Talk/Entertainment/ "News"						
A Current Affair	6	5	26	21	25	17
Entertainment Tonight	6	4	28	20	25	16
Geraldo	5	3	32	19	29	11
Hard Copy	4	5	26	17	31	18
Oprah Winfrey Show	4	5	33	12	33	11

Note: Audience percentages are based on national average audiences for each program during the November 1993 sweeps period.

NYPD Blue (shown on ABC on Tuesdays at 10:00 PM) and 8% for Walker, Texas Ranger (CBS, Saturdays, 10:00 PM). Syndicated shows containing violence are often scheduled in early evening or weekend daytime hours, so children are more likely to be in the total potential viewing audience. Table 3.2 reveals that children 2–11 represent between 9% and 13% for violent crime shows such as Renegade and Kung Fu: The Legend Continues, which is nearly twice the rate as that for violent prime-time network series. Note that children 2–11 are not the target audiences for advertisers on these programs, which are generally aimed at men and women 18–34 and 18–49 (see chapter 5). The presence of children in the viewing audience at times when younger adult viewing groups can be reached more easily generates child viewers who are not sought after by advertisers. Although males 18–34 consume more violent television, the survey data in chapter 2 suggest that younger women also consume this type of programming. Additional evidence in chapter 5 establishes that advertisers seek female customers through violent series programming. The results in table 3.2 show that women 18–49 make up nearly the same percentage of the audience for violent syndicated series as men 18–49 (e.g., women 18–49 are 25% of the audience for an average episode of *Renegade*, while men 18–49 makeup 26% of the audience).

Children constitute a slightly lower percentage of the audiences of reality programs. Children 2–11 are 11% of the audience for syndicated episodes of *Cops*, 7% for *Emergency Call*, and 7% for *Real Stories of the Highway Patrol*. Men and women 18–49 still constitute similar percentages of the audiences for these programs. Note that syndicated movies have higher percentages of children 2–11 and teens than the other types of violent programming. Critical reviews describe *Nightmare on Elm Street 5: The Dream Child* as "a grisly terror fantasy of supernatural terror masterminded by the seemingly unconquerable Freddy Krueger" and *Amityville: The Evil Escapes* as involving "two exorcists [who] fight to finally lay the curse of the infamous house when a young girl is possessed by sinister forces."[10] These movies, however, may be scheduled on weekend afternoons, so that they are easily accessible to children. Teens 12–17 made up 17% and children 2–11 made up 12% of the audience for the syndicated showing of *Nightmare on Elm Street 5*. Women 18–49 made up a similar percentage (31%) of this film's audience as men 18–49 (30%).

Talk and entertainment news programs have also come under attack for the exposure of children and teens to content potentially objectionable to parents. Much of the attention has focused on the discussion of sexuality and adult themes on these daytime or early evening programs. For example, Senator Joseph Lieberman and former Education Secretary William Bennett joined together in a campaign in 1995 to urge talk shows to reduce their reliance on sexual content.[11] Some of these programs may also contain violence as part of their entertainment strategy. Lasorsa et al. (1996) found that for the tabloid news programs they examined (defined as *American Journal*, *A Current Affair*, *Extra*, *Hard Copy*, and *Inside Edition*) 86% contained a visual representation of violence. They also found that although entertainment news programs were much less likely to contain violence (only 21% in their sample of 1994–95 programs), the violence selected by entertainment programs for inclusion was much more likely to go unpunished and more likely to focus on extreme violent acts.[12] The UCLA study also found that the tabloid news program *Hard Copy* raised issues of concern. In their sample of 2 weeks of programming, they found that:

On 11/10/94 there was film footage of a man, surrounded by a group of people, shooting at the White House. This was an important news story and was covered by all the mainstream news media. What *Hard Copy* did differently than anyone else was air the same shooting scene 13 times in a 30-minute program. It was used as a preview at the front of the show and as a teaser before each commercial. . . . On the next day's episode, the scene was shown five more times. This excessive use qualifies as gratuitous by any definition.[13]

Table 3.2 indicates that children 2–11 make up a much smaller percentage of the audiences for talk and entertainment shows such as *Hard Copy* and *Geraldo* than for the other types of syndicated programs. The targeting of the talk shows and entertainment news programs toward women rather than men is evident in the higher audience percentage accounted for by women 18–49 than men 18–49 for these types of programs.

Table 3.2 allows one to judge the externalities generated by programs by the percentage of a program's audience composed of children 2–11 and teens 12–17. Viewed from this perspective, violent syndicated films and violent series generate a higher rate of externalities than reality programs or talk/entertainment programs since children compose a higher fraction of their audiences. Table 3.3 examines the externalities from another perspective, the absolute size of the audiences exposed to different types of programming. These results indi-

TABLE 3.3
Total Number of Viewers for a Program Episode by Demographic Group (000s), November 1993

	Children 2–11	Teens 12–17	Women 18–49	Men 18–49	Women 50+	Men 50+
Violent Series						
Acapulco H.E.A.T.	640	397	1,294	1,137	629	629
Cobra	490	271	1,109	1,137	729	629
Highlander	490	459	1,602	1,615	623	591
Kung Fu	829	522	1,849	2,094	1,151	907
Renegade	720	438	1,726	1,735	1,177	1,001
Violent Reality						
Cops	828	626	2,095	2,094	1,194	995
Emergency Call	301	271	1,048	1,017	791	660
Real Stories of the Highway Patrol	301	292	1,233	1,316	703	626
Violent Syndicated Movies						
Nightmare on Elm Street 5	490	668	1,233	1,197	219	216
Amityville: The Evil Escapes	678	417	924	1,017	711	395
Crucifer of Blood	339	146	986	1,137	756	893
Talk/Entertainment "News"						
A Current Affair	565	397	2,280	1,855	2,171	1,500
Entertainment Tonight	678	459	3,082	2,274	2,821	1,787
Geraldo	230	125	1,417	838	1,292	486
Hard Copy	339	250	2,034	1,376	1,424	1,010
Oprah Winfrey Show	565	626	4,252	1,556	4,166	1,446

Note: Figures represent the average national audience for a program episode during the November 1993 sweeps period.

cate that within each type of programming genre there are shows that generate significant audiences of both children and teens. *Kung Fu* averages 829,000 children 2–11 and 522,000 teens 12–17 per episode for its martial arts style of violence. *Cops* averages 828,000 children and 626,000 teens for the showing of its syndicated episodes. In terms of the audiences that advertisers are likely to focus on for a program such as *Cops*, each episode drew over 2 million women 18–49 and an equal number of men 18–49. Although syndicated movies rarely attract critical debate in congressional hearings or journalistic accounts, table 3.3 indicates that *Amityville: The Evil Escapes* attracted 678,000 children 2–11 during its airing on local television stations during November 1993, a figure comparable with children's exposures to a syndicated crime series program.

Many of the exposures of children to syndicated violence arise from the frequent scheduling of these programs during times when children are likely to be in the audience, such as weekend daytimes and the early evening hours before prime time on weekdays and weekends. Table 3.4 analyzes the viewing by children and adults of the twenty-eight action or crime shows in syndication during the November 1993 sweeps months. The largest audiences were for programs produced originally for syndication, such as *Kung Fu: The Legend Continues*, *Renegade*, *Highlander*, and *The Untouchables*. Yet the violent crime shows in syndication also included programs released earlier on broadcast network television, such as *Hunter* and *The A Team*.[14] If the viewing of children 2–11 of these twenty-eight action or crime programs are added, the average weekly audience for these violent programs translates into 3.5 million exposures of children 2–11. This contrasts to 11.8 million viewings by women 18–49 and 11.2 million viewings by men 18–49, groups that are prime targets for advertisers on these programs. Note that women and men in this age group account for nearly the same amount of viewers, consistent with the survey evidence from chapter 2 that women 18–34 and men 18–34 are the second highest consumers of violent programming after men 18–34.

Although syndicated programming is often used by independent stations as prime-time programming, prime-time viewing accounts for just slightly more than a third of the weekly viewing by adults, teens, or children for violent action or crime shows in syndication. Late night scheduling (11 PM–2 AM) totals roughly 15% of the exposure of adults. Scheduling in this time period also lowers the chances that children will be in the audience, as confirmed by the fact that viewing after prime time accounts for just 4.4% of weekly exposures of children to these programs. Scheduling in weekend daytime and early evening, however, results in greater likelihood of exposure of children and teens. These are times that network affiliates may often need programming to fill gaps, and these are also times when adults 18–49 may be more likely to be in the audience than during weekdays. If one compares the viewing of children 2–11 and men 18–49, it is clear that these weekend time periods play a greater role in the exposure of children than they do in the exposure of one of the prime audiences targeted by advertisers, men 18–49. Weekend daytime viewing accounted for 21.5% of weekly viewing by children versus 17.2% for men 18–

TABLE 3.4
Percentage Distribution of Viewing Exposures by Time Period for Syndicated Action Crime Series

Time Period	% of Exposures to Syndicated Action/Crime Series					
	Children 2–11	Teens 12–17	Women 18–49	Men 18–49	Women 18+	Men 18+
Daytime (M–F, 6AM–4PM)	6.7	4.9	7.7	6.6	9.7	8.2
Early Fringe (M–F, 4–7:30 PM)	2.0	2.4	1.9	1.7	3.0	2.7
Prime Access (Mon–Sat, 7:30–8 PM)	1.4	1.3	1.9	4.0	2.5	4.0
Prime (Mon–Sat, 8–11 PM, Sun 7–11 PM)	37.9	35.0	34.1	38.7	32.1	37.3
Postprime (Sun–Sat, 11 PM–2 AM)	4.4	9.3	15.3	13.7	15.4	13.3
Weekend Daytime (Sat, Sun 6 AM–5 PM)	21.5	25.2	18.8	17.2	18.2	16.1
Weekend Preprime, (Sat, 5–7:30 PM, Sun, 5–7 PM)	27.3	23.0	21.9	21.8	21.3	22.1
Total Weekly Exposures (000s)	3,523.0	3,023.4	11,836.7	11,240.9	20,115.9	17,527.0

Note: Percentages indicate the fraction of total weekly viewing by a demographic group of syndicated action crime series that occurs within a given time period. Total exposures reflect the average weekly audience figures for these syndicated programs summed across markets.

49, while weekend early evening viewing accounted for 27.3% of exposures of children versus 21.8% for men 18–49.

If one expands the definition of violent programming to include science fiction shows (such as *Star Trek: The Next Generation* and *Star Trek: Deep Space Nine*) and reality programs (such as *Cops* and *Rescue 911*), there were forty-four violent series in syndication during November 1993.[15] This boosts the estimate of weekly exposures by children 2–11 to violent syndication to 11.7 million (see table 3.5). The scheduling of reality programs and science fiction in time slots prior to prime time makes these time periods of more concern if one defines violent programming to include science fiction and reality programs. Early fringe, the weekday period from 4 to 7:30 PM, and prime access (Mon-

TABLE 3.5

Percentage Distribution of Viewing Exposures by Time Period for Violent Syndicated Programming

Time Period	% of Exposures to Syndicated Action Crime, Science Fiction, and Reality Series					
	Children 2–11	Teens 12–17	Women 18–49	Men 18–49	Women 18+	Men 18+
Daytime (M–F, 6 AM–4 PM)	2.6	2.1	2.9	2.2	4.0	3.0
Early Fringe (M–F, 4–7:30 PM)	15.6	13.1	11.0	10.5	11.3	11.1
Prime Access (Mon–Sat, 7:30–8 PM)	7.8	6.2	5.3	5.7	5.4	5.8
Prime (Mon–Sat, 8–11 PM, Sun 7–11 PM)	27.2	30.4	29.5	31.9	27.4	30.7
Postprime (Sun–Sat, 11 PM–2 AM)	4.4	8.3	14.4	14.0	14.8	13.9
Weekend Daytime (Sat, Sun 6 AM–5 PM)	10.3	13.1	10.3	8.9	11.1	9.4
Weekend Pre-prime, (Sat, 5–7:30 PM, Sun, 5–7 PM)	32.1	26.7	26.6	26.7	26.1	26.3
Total Weekly Exposures (000s)	11,702.1	9,095.5	37,049.5	39,202.6	54,886.7	53,752.0

Note: Percentages indicate the fraction of total weekly viewing by a demographic group of these syndicated programs that occurs within a given time period. Total exposures reflect the average weekly audience figures for these syndicated programs summed across markets.

day–Saturday 7:30–8 PM) account for 15.6% and 7.8% of the exposures by children 2–11. Early fringe accounts for a much higher proportion of children's exposures than those for adults 18–49, an indication that scheduling in this time period reaches a relatively larger number of children. Weekend before prime time accounts for 32.1% of exposures of children versus 26.6% for women 18–49 and 26.7% for men 18–49, another sign that this time period generates a significant number of exposures by children.

Overall, tables 3.4 and 3.5 demonstrate that prime-time viewing of syndicated violence accounts for at most a third of the viewing of violent syndicated programming. It is the scheduling of these programs before prime time and in weekend daytime hours that generates significant exposures to children. These are popular times for scheduling syndicated programming both because they are times when networks may not be providing affiliates with programming and because men and women 18–49 may be in the television audience. The exposures of children thus arise as a true externality, since they are not the likely target of advertisers during these programs but are exposed as a by-product of attempts to reach adults 18–49.

MEASURING THE IMPACT OF VIEWER ADVISORIES

The ratings data presented demonstrate that while violent adult programming is not among the most frequently chosen viewing options for children 2–11, substantial numbers of children are exposed to violent shows targeted at adults. A frequent refrain in discussions of violent programming is that parents who are worried can simply intervene and shield their children by switching channels or simply turning off the television. A brief review of the incentives that parents face in dealing with television, however, indicates that they will fail to engage in the optimal amount of monitoring from society's perspective. After describing the incentives that parents face in intervening in children's viewing, this section offers the first empirical evidence from ratings data on the impact of a particular type of intervention aimed at helping parents—the provision of viewer discretion warnings on programs. The results indicate that viewer discretion warnings placed on prime-time broadcast movies do result in lower audiences among children 2–11, consistent with parents and children acting upon content information provided by programmers.

Consider the television monitoring decisions faced by parents of a young child. They will consider the benefits from shielding a child from violent programming in deciding how much effort to exert in monitoring what their child watches. The benefits they consider will include reduced chances that the child will be stimulated to aggression in the short run or long run, a lowered probability the child will be frightened, a diminished chance the child will become desensitized to violence, and other effects on the child's development. The marginal benefits from another hour's monitoring is assumed to decline since not all hours of viewing are equally damaging. The parent may screen out the most damaging viewing first, but eventually the parent would be monitoring programs that might present fewer risks to the child. There is an additional set of benefits to society that the parents will not consider in their calculations. If the child is shielded from television violence, society also benefits from the reduction in the costs of aggression and expected punishment costs. The marginal benefits to the parents are reflected in the curve MBp in figure 3.1, while the social marginal benefits curve MBs reflects the benefits to the parents plus the added benefits to society. The gap between the two curves represents the additional benefits to society that parents do not consider in their decision making (a

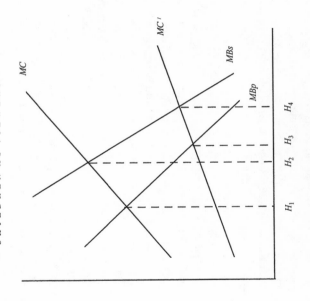

Hours of Monitored Viewing

Figure 3.1. Parental-Monitoring

gap that declines since the social benefits of shielding also decline as less dangerous shows are screened).

A parent faces significant costs in monitoring a child's consumption of violent programming. There are information costs, such as the costs of determining what programming is on which channels at what times. There are decision-making costs, such as determining what programs are likely to contain violence or other material the parent might find objectionable. There are "enforcement costs," which involve checking in on the viewing of the child. There are also other transaction costs, which arise out of the negotiations or disagreements with children over viewing decisions. These costs may be substantial for parents. Consider the question of which programs are violent. A study of the implementation of the 1993 network and cable violence advisory program found that television grids in newspapers did not carry the violence advisories provided by the networks and that many of the warnings in the listing were changed to parental guidance notices rather than specific warnings about violent content.[16] The monitoring report produced by the center hired by broadcast networks to assess television violence found that the networks often failed to place warnings on shows that merited them. Of the 161 made for television movies examined by the UCLA Center for Communications Policy during the 1994–95 season, the authors felt that 23 raised issues of concern in terms of violence. Yet only 6 of these shows carried viewer discretion warnings. Of the 50 (out of a total 118) theatrical films shown on broadcast network television that raised issues of concern about the use of violence during the 1994–95 season, the networks placed advisories on only 28.[17] The TV Parental Guidelines system initially implemented in 1997 provides parents with some information about the mix of language, violence, and sexual content in a show, but the categories used do not explicitly reveal the level of violence or sexual content in a program.[18]

Even if parents are fully informed about the violent content of programs, they still must monitor children's viewing to make sure that programs are not viewed. Cable operators provide parents with the opportunity to block particular channels, and parents concerned especially about violence or sexual content may choose not to subscribe to premium channels (which program films with relatively high levels of both—see chapter 4). Alternative technologies also exist for monitoring viewing.[19] For many parents, however, monitoring consists of checking on viewing. Some parents, especially those who work when children are viewing, face extremely high opportunity costs to monitoring. Figure 3.1 captures the total of these information, decision, transaction, and monitoring costs in the curve MC. The additional cost to a parent of monitoring another hour of programming is assumed to increase with the number of hours monitored since the opportunity costs of the parents rise as they divert more attention to this effort.

Parents trading off the personal marginal benefits MBp with the marginal costs MC will choose to monitor H_1 hours of viewing. If they incorporated the full benefits to society of their efforts in their calculations, however, the parents would engage in H_2 hours of monitoring. The added benefits to society generated by protecting children from violent programming thus lead to an argument for changing the incentives that parents currently face. If programs were rated based on program content and a V-chip allowed parents to set the level of violent content they wished their children to be exposed to, then for parents the information, decision-making, transaction, and monitoring costs would all drop dramatically. Parents could set the violence level they find acceptable and then check occasionally to see if the ratings were appropriate and the system was working (e.g., to see if the chip mechanism had been disabled). Curve MC′ reflects these lower information and monitoring costs. Note that it is lower and rises more slowly than the MC curve since the fixed costs of becoming informed and the opportunity costs of additional hours of monitoring are reduced by the V-chip (e.g., the parent only needs to check on viewing intermittently). The number of hours that are effectively monitored thus increases to H_3. Parents faced with lower costs take steps that result in an increasing number of hours of viewing that are monitored. Although parents will still fail to engage in the optimal level of monitoring (H_4), a content-based ratings system and V-chip would lead to an increase in total number of hours that are effectively monitored by parents.[20]

Although no prior study has examined the impact of viewer discretion warnings on program ratings, results in television research indicate that such warnings could help parents influence the shows viewed by young children. Survey evidence indicates that viewers do report dissatisfaction with the level of violence on television and believe parents should influence viewing selections of children. The 1993 Times Mirror survey found that 59% of those interviewed said they were bothered by violence on television, with a split of 74% of women and 42% of men sharing this sentiment.[21] Of parents with children 8–13 in the sample, 61% were worried more about violence on fictional television shows, 14% were more concerned about violence on news and real-life programming, 11% were equally worried about these sources, and 12% reported that they did not worry about the amount of violence seen by their children on television. In a Roper query (1993) about who should have the most say about what children see on television, 82% stated it should be parents by deciding what they will allow their children to view.

Parents do report that they act on their objections to television programming. In a Times Mirror question about news viewing, 53% of parents responded that they had switched channels or turned off the set because of program content they did not want their children to see. Of these parents, 72% said the last time they did this it was in part because of the violence in the news (57% said it was because of sex, 17% language, and 11% drugs). A majority of parents surveyed in 1980 reported that they often or occasionally restricted the amount of viewing for their children, decided what programs they could watch, changed channels when programming was objectionable, and forbade the watching of certain programs.[22] The proportion of parents with "definite rules" about children's viewing, however, varied by education level with 46% of those with high school educations versus 58% of those with college educations reporting the use of television viewing rules. Parents also have the opportunity to monitor directly what children watch since some viewing occurs with the entire family watching. In multiset families in 1980, about one-third of the time the entire family viewed television together while about one-quarter of the time children watched by themselves. Reviewing the involvement of parents with children's viewing, Comstock and Paik (1991) found that level of parental education strongly influences the level of parental involvement with child viewing. They concluded that "despite signs of increased concern, parental involvement in the television viewing of their children, on the whole, is at the most moderate and at the least nonexistent."[23]

Parents also generally report that they find information about program content useful. In a survey about the MPAA rating system for theatrical movies, 76% of parents surveyed said they found the system very or fairly useful.[24] In a small sample of parents, Slater and Thompson (1984) found that 90% approved of the uses of parental discretion warnings on broadcast television, 70% had seen these warnings frequently, three-quarters stated that they used them in deciding what is suitable for children's viewing, and a majority favored more detailed ratings. They conclude that parents who are involved in regulating or monitoring their children's viewing are those most influenced by the viewer discretion warnings. Greenberg, Abelman, and Cohen (1990) found that when they gave parents and children television guides with information about program content and viewing recommendations, the parents did not use the data and the children were attracted to programs labeled as "warranting parental supervision or discretion."[25]

If shows are designated with a warning, television listings would be a good source of information for viewers to receive this data. In determining what to watch, 40% of cable viewers report using a television listing or guide (19% refer to *TV Guide* explicitly), 37% say they simply flip channels, and 19% report they use both methods.[26] A study of the implementation of the 1993 network and cable advisory program, however, found that television grids in newspapers did not carry the violence advisories and that many of the warnings in listings were changed to parental guidance notices rather than specific warnings about violent content.[27] The degree that warnings reach viewers may thus affect the likelihood that parents can act upon them. The amount of information contained in warnings may also vary, as indicated by the more detailed information on violent movies provided by rating systems in countries other than the United States.[28]

Following pressure from both Congress and the Federal Communications Commission to reduce levels of media violence, broadcast networks and major cable programmers voluntarily adopted a new policy of providing viewers with information about violent program content in the summer of 1993. The new policy had a number of facets: parental advisories would be provided for violent shows; each network would determine the programs to carry the warning; shows with advisories would carry an audiovisual warning when broadcast; and the warning would also be carried on all promotional materials for the particular program. Studies following the implementation of this policy began to examine the impact of discretion warnings on viewer behavior. In an experimental setting where children were given descriptions of programs to select for viewing, Cantor and Harrison (1996) found that on net children's selections of "reality-action" programs were not influenced by a parental advisory (e.g., "Parental discretion advised"). Boys 10–14, however, were more likely to select programs with a parental discretion advisory. If the warning is phrased as "viewer discretion advised," children overall and especially girls 5–9 were less likely to select the program. The influence of MPAA ratings similarly varied by age and gender. The authors found that "although younger children and girls showed a tendency to shy away from the movie when it had the restrictive rating 'R,' older boys were attracted to the more restrictive ratings and avoided the 'G' rating."[29] In a separate experiment, Cantor and Krcmar (1996) found that when a parent and child were offered the chance to select programs to watch, the joint decision was nearly always to avoid programs with parental discretion warnings. The authors conclude that the increased interest by boys in movies and programs with parental discretion warnings and PG-13 or R ratings suggests a need to study further how ratings are used and interpreted by children.

Bushman and Stack (1996) found experimental evidence that warning labels can increase interest among college students in violent films. Students reported an increased interest in viewing movies labeled with warnings, especially when the U.S. surgeon general was mentioned in the warning. If the viewer advisory is phrased as informational (e.g., "Viewer discretion is advised"), students were not more attracted to violent films with the informational label. These results, combined with those of Cantor and colleagues, indicate the importance of investigating how ratings are worded and understood by different demographic groups.

Even prior to the 1993 industry announcement, broadcast networks attached viewer discretion warnings to a fraction of films shown during prime time. Because of the wider product differentiation among movies and the difficulty for some films of assessing movie content, viewer warnings may be especially valuable on films since consumers may not have as much information to predict content as they would with a familiar television series. This section examines the impact of warning labels on movie audiences for films shown on the four major broadcast networks (ABC, CBS, NBC, and Fox [as of October 8, 1990]) from September 14, 1987 to September 26, 1993.

The sample consists of all movies (2,295) with complete listings in *TV Guide* and ratings information from Nielsen. The mean rating for children 2–11 for these movies was a 4.2, which indicates that on average 1.6 million children in this age group were watching one of these broadcast network films when it aired in prime time. Using the same methodology described in chapter 2, I develop in table 3.6 models of movie ratings for children 2–11 and teens 12–17. The dependent variable in each regression is the rating among the demographic group, so that the coefficients in the regressions indicate the change in ratings points associated with the given movie characteristic. Viewing by children 2–11 obviously reflects a combination of preferences of parents, children, and older siblings. In terms of genre, young children are less likely to watch crime drama and mysteries and more likely to watch science fiction, fantasy, and adventure (relative to the omitted genre variable of comedy drama). As expected among viewers with early bedtimes, ratings decline substantially as the starting time of the movie comes later in prime time. Movies with murder themes receive fewer young viewers, perhaps reflecting some parental intervention. Movies that *TV Guide* specifically cites as violent do not have ratings that differ statistically from other movies. The impact of the network viewer advisory, however, is negative and statistically significant.

Movies carrying the warning label lost .6 ratings points among children. Since the average rating for broadcast network television movies in prime time for this age group was 4.2, this means that viewership declines by about 14% for films that carry the warnings. Another way to view the impact is that since a rating point represented approximately 377,000 children in 1993, movies that carried the viewer discretion warnings had 222,000 fewer children in the audience than those without this label. This evidence casts doubt on assertions that warnings have no impact on children's viewing or that labels effectively serve as magnets to attract younger consumers. The negative net impact of the warnings on children's ratings is consistent with a model of parental mediation of viewing, as are the lower ratings for crime dramas or movies with murder

TABLE 3.6
Determinants of Movie Ratings on Network Television, Children and Teens, 1987–93

	Children 2–11 Ratings	Teens 12–17 Ratings
Drama	−.72 (3.36)***	−1.36 (5.11)***
Crime Drama	−.88 (3.54)***	−1.74 (5.65)***
Comedy	.83 (3.48)***	.87 (2.97)***
Western	−.32 (.92)	−.94 (2.20)**
Science Fiction	1.33 (3.43)***	1.08 (2.26)**
Adventure	.59 (2.17)**	−.03 (.08)
Mystery	−1.44 (4.46)***	−2.35 (5.87)***
Thriller	.13 (.37)	.46 (1.07)
Fantasy	3.24 (9.73)***	1.15 (2.79)***
Other Genre	.64 (1.92)*	−.57 (1.39)
Theatrical	.80 (6.21)***	1.15 (7.24)***
Closeup Summary	−.20 (1.41)	−.07 (.39)
TV Guide Ad	.76 (5.99)***	1.21 (7.69)***
Murder	−.36 (3.05)***	−.45 (3.12)***
True Story	.26 (1.98)*	.38 (2.32)**
Family Crime	.32 (1.31)	.45 (1.49)
TV Guide Violence	.31 (1.30)	.43 (1.43)
Warning	−.59 (1.74)*	−.01 (.02)
Adjusted R²	.43	.40

Note: Absolute values of T statistics are in parentheses. *** = Statistically significant at the .01 level; ** = significant at the .05 level; * = significant at the .10 level. Genre dummies are relative to comedy drama. Each regression also contains controls for the network, starting hour, day, month, and year the movie was aired. Sample contains 2,295 movies shown on broadcast network television between September 14, 1987 and September 26, 1993.

themes. The fact that the coefficient on *TV Guide's* mention of violence is not statistically significant while the warning label is indicates that parents do not simply screen out all violent movies. It is the violent movies that carry explicit viewer discretion warnings that have lower ratings among children.

Comparisons between the ratings regressions for children 2–11 and teens 12–17 indicate that the adolescents share interests in comedies, science fiction, and fantasy. The bedtime effect of movie starting times disappears for teens. The viewer discretion warning has no statistically significant impact on the viewing by teens for the movies in this sample. There is thus no evidence that teens on balance use the viewer discretion warnings to search out violent movies.

As another test of the impact of viewer discretion warnings on the ratings of children 2–11, the regression for children's ratings from table 3.6 was rerun with the ratings of men 18–49, women 18–49, and teens 12–17 added as independent variables. The ratings for other demographic groups were included as further indicators of a movie's popularity, so that positive or negative coefficients on the warning variable can be interpreted as reflecting the impact of labeling rather than the impact of characteristics of movies that get labeled that may make them more or less popular with particular demographic groups. The results indicate that ratings among children 2–11 increase with ratings among both women 18–49 (a 1-point increase in ratings for women 18–49 increases ratings for children by .1) and teens 12–17 (a point increase in teen ratings leads to a .53 increase in ratings for children). These effects could arise because of joint viewing in a family or because of preferences that lead to viewing of similar movies. The impact on children's ratings is strongest for the teen variable, which is consistent with the finding that most coviewing occurs among people of similar age groups.[30] Even controlling for how popular a movie is with adult males, females, and teens, the warning label causes ratings for children 2–11 to drop by .56 (T statistic = 2.4). When the teen specification in table 3.6 was rerun with controls for ratings for men 18–49 and women 18–49, the warning label was still not statistically significant for this demographic group.

Controlling for other factors such as genre and scheduling, one thus finds that for children 2–11 ratings are lower for movies dealing with murder and that movies dealing with family crime or extreme violence did not have statistically different ratings among children. The results demonstrate that the placement of warnings on films does have an additional, independent impact on ratings for children. The fact that ratings drop by about 14% for children 2–11 with the placement of a warning does not mean that information provision "solves" the television violence problem. Knowing the "optimal" number of children exposed to television violence through network prime-time broadcast movies would involve the calculation, as outlined in chapter 1, of factors such as the costs to parents of monitoring their children's viewing and the benefits to society of reducing the consumption of violent programming by children. The numbers do indicate that the warnings did reduce the audiences for films by approximately 220,000 children 2–11, a large figure in absolute terms considering the small change (e.g., provision of a warning label on the movie).

A common concern in the political debate over television violence is how active parents are in protecting their children from violent television and who those parents who are active are. When ratings systems and the V-chip were debated, many analysts asserted that only high-income, high-education parents would intervene in the viewing habits of their children. The results from table 3.6 do not allow one to explore which families react to the provision of viewer discretion warnings on movies. The Times Mirror survey discussed in chapter 2, in gathering data relevant to this question, asked about parental action to shield children from viewing in a particular context: "Have you ever switched the channel or turned off the TV because there was something on the news that you didn't want your child to see?" Table A3.1 reports the results of analyzing the responses of parents to this question, while table 3.7 translates these results into changes in the probability a parent said he or she had taken action to shield a child from viewing. Note that at least three decisions are implicitly involved

TABLE 3.7
Which Parents Switch Channels to Shield Children during News Viewing?

Variable	Change in Probability
White vs. Nonwhite	.15
Female vs. Male	.18
HS vs. College Graduate	.18
Some College vs. College Graduate	.18
Income $20K–29K vs. Income $50+	−.15
Income $30K–49K vs. Income $50+	−.17
Bothered by Violence on TV Shows vs. Not	.18
2–3.5 Hours per Day of TV Viewing vs. Less Than 2 Hours	.13

Note: See table A3.1. The probability of a parent switching channels during news viewing (based on mean sample values) was .53.

in determining the answer to this question. Does the parent watch the news with a child? Did the parent find something objectionable? Did the parent act on this by switching the channel or turning the television off? About half the parents answered yes to the question (the mean estimated probability that a parent said yes in the sample was .53). Overall, women were much more likely than men to report that they had intervened in viewing (the probability is .18 higher for women). Middle-income parents (those with incomes $20,000–29,000 or $30,000–$49,000) were less likely than higher-income parents to intervene. Controlling for these factors, one finds (contrary to frequent assertions) that parents with less education were more likely to intervene in viewing by their children. Relative to parents with a college degree, parents with a high school education or some college had a .18 higher probability of intervening during the news. Parents who said they were personally bothered by violence on television news were more likely to switch channels during the news.[31]

CHILDREN'S PROGRAMS AND VIOLENCE

The previous sections demonstrate that violent programming targeted at adults attracts substantial numbers of children viewers, although these exposures may be reduced if information about program content is provided to parents. Ironically, much of programming aimed directly at children contains high levels of violence, although this violence is often portrayed through animated characters. In debates about violent programming for children, defenders of network programming often frame the issue of television's impact by asking whether *Road-runner* cartoons cause violence in society.[32] For example, in discussing why cartoons were unlikely to carry violence advisories that the broadcast networks agreed to air in 1993 MPAA President Jack Valenti said:

I think you graze the outer edge of incredulity when you say cartoons are too violent and causing all sorts of horrendous things in the marketplace. Millions and millions of American children grew up on cartoons and millions and millions of American children today have their values intact, their integrity preserved and they are good citizens and the idea that Willie the Whale or Road Runner or Superman is having anything to do with the causing of violence, I think takes the whole arena of research and expands it into an era [sic] where it becomes distended and distorted.[33]

Yet children have often been the subject of laboratory experiments involving violent programming, including violent programming produced specifically for children. The lab research indicates that while realistic portrayals of violence lead to more aggressive behavior than fantasy (e.g., cartoon) violence, cartoons can still cause an increase in short-term aggression among child viewers.

The National Television Violence Study researchers cite three studies that relate to the relative power of realistic portrayals versus fantasy programming on the behavior of children.[34] Hapkiewicz and Stone (1974) found that children 6–10 who viewed the violence among the human actors in the *Three Stooges* behaved more aggressively after viewing than children who watched the cartoon violence in *Mighty Mouse*. For children 9–11 who watched a violent scene either as a news story or a theatrical film, Feshbach (1972) determined that those who saw the footage as more realistic behaved more aggressively after viewing. Atkin (1983) exposed sets of children aged 10–13 to the same violent scene, with one group seeing the scene as part of a news cast and another as part of a movie promotion. Those who viewed the violence as part of a news show behaved more aggressively after viewing the scene. In sum, these studies suggest that "realistic violence" in television programming generates more aggression in older children than fantasy or fictional violent programming.

The conclusion that realism generates greater aggression does not mean, however, that cartoons do not generate aggression in children. A substantial body of research indicates that children's programming, including cartoons, can generate short-term increases in aggression (the type of aggression that can be measured among children in lab experiments). Bandura, Ross, and Ross (1963) found that preschoolers who viewed a violent cartoon were as aggressive after viewing as those who watched a human perform similar acts of violence. The NTVS researchers note that many studies (Friedrich and Stein 1972; Steur, Applefield, and Smith 1971; Boyatzis, Matillo, and Nesbitt 1995) demonstrate that young children "readily imitate violent cartoon characters such as *Batman* . . . and superheros with magical powers like the *Power Rangers*."[35] When Liss, Reinhardt, and Fredriksen (1983) exposed a set of children to a violent cartoon featuring a superhero and another set to a violent cartoon without a superhero, those children who viewed the superhero violence were more likely to act aggressively. This demonstrates that children are influenced in their reaction to violence in part based on the nature of the perpetrator. Adults too are found to be more likely to be aggressive after viewing violence if they identify with the hero (Leyens and Picus 1973, Turner and Berkowitz 1972).

Summarizing the literature on the particular impacts of violence on children, the NTVS researchers note that:

Younger viewers are more likely to perceive fantasy and animated violence as realistic, thus increasing the risk of imitation and fear when this age group is exposed to such content. They also are less able to link scenes together that are temporally separated. Thus, punishments may not serve as effective inhibitors of imitation and aggression unless such restraints are depicted in the same scene or immediately adjacent to the violence.[36]

In assessing the impact of children's programming, a survey of children's television experts by the group Children Now yielded the conclusion that these programs should be rated so that parents can understand the potentially harmful content of children's programs, including cartoons.[37] As Dale Kunkel, one of the NTVS researchers, put it:

One of the contextual elements that is important in shaping the effect of violence on the audience is the viewer's perceived reality of that action. To the young child, everything on television is "real." Therefore you cannot draw the conclusion that cartoon violence is acceptable or excusable merely because it is presented in a fantasy setting or context. Cartoon violence or violence in fantasy settings can still pose significant risks of antisocial effects for child viewers, and therefore should be rated accordingly.[38]

The NTVS study analyzed children's programming as a separate genre, so that its content for the 1994–95 season can be analyzed along the same lines as adult programming. For the composite week of television examined, these researchers found that 66% of the children's shows contained at least one violent act (compared with 57% for the overall sample).[39] In contrast to adult programming, where nearly half of violent movies were preceded with advisories, the NTVS found that 0% of the violent children's programming carried advisories about content.[40] In assessing the context surrounding the use of violence, they found that children's programs were less likely to show the pain of violence or long-term consequences, which means that the violence may be more likely to be imitated by child viewers. Overall, children's programs that were violent relied less on the use of guns and were slightly less likely to use "blood and gore." The fact that many children's' programs involved cartoon violence meant that these shows were less likely to use violence in realistic settings. The researchers note however that although in children's programming "most depictions of violence avoid realistic settings . . . the importance of this factor is minimized by the knowledge that young child-viewers lack full ability to discriminate fantasy from reality in television programming."[41] In the second year of their study (focusing on the 1995–96 season), the NTVS researchers found (1997a) that children's programming often involves a combination of contexts likely to increase aggression (e.g., attractive perpetrators, violence that appears justified and goes unpunished, and violence with minimal consequences shown for the victim). They conclude that "Portrayals that have a high risk of teaching aggression to children under 7 are concentrated in the very programs and channels targeted to young viewers."[42]

In sum, the media effects literature demonstrates that children's programs stimulate aggressive behavior, the NTVS research confirms that children's programming in the 1994–95 and 1995–96 seasons contained violence used in contexts likely to generate aggression, and the Children Now survey indicates that children's experts believe that programs such as cartoons should carry some type of content rating or indicator. The information from the National Coalition on Television Violence that will be analyzed here allows one to explore how violence in children's programming has varied across time and across channels, with the results indicating that many of the patterns evident in the market for violent programming for adults are also evident in the market for violent children's programming.

The NCTV used the same definition of violence to count violent acts per hour in both children's and prime-time programming.[43] The organization's newsletter published information on violence in children's programming for the broadcast networks throughout the 1980s and included data on syndicated and cable programs in their assessments for 1985 and 1989–91.[44] Table 3.8 analyzes this information by channel. Broadcast network children's programs overall

TABLE 3.8
Violent Acts per Hour in Children's Programming

	No. of Violent Acts per Hour	No. of Shows
Broadcast Networks		
ABC	22.0	113
CBS	22.0	128
Fox	35.7	10
NBC	22.1	112
Network Average	22.4	363
Syndication	26.4	48
Cable Channels		
Disney	26.3	7
Family Channel	15.1	20
HBO	4.0	4
TBS	57.0	2
TNT	54.5	4
USA	18.8	9
WGN	46.1	8
Cable Average	25.4	54
NCTV Rating Category		
Low Violence	3.3	89
Some Violence	13.9	78
High Violence	24.9	52
Very High Violence	45.7	103

Note: The number of violent acts per hour was calculated by the National Coalition on Television Violence. Figures for broadcast networks are from 1982–87 and 1989–91, and for syndication and cable channels from 1985 and 1989–91.

evaluated by NCTV from 1982 through 1991 had a mean number of violent acts per hour of 22.4. This would place children's programs as comparable to the adult genres of action adventure (27.6) and crime (20.2) in terms of violent acts per hour. Among the broadcast networks, Fox had the highest number of violent acts per hour—35.7 versus 22 for the other three networks. Note that chapter 4 will demonstrate that Fox was also the outlier among these networks in terms of the use of violent acts in prime time. Among ABC, CBS, and NBC, the use of violence in children's programming was nearly identical, with none of these networks staking out a claim to being more nonviolent or violent in their programming targeted at children.

As in programming aimed at adults (described more in chapter 4), children's programs in syndication (26.4 violent acts per hour) were more violent than those on the four broadcast networks. Cartoons on cable were also slightly more violent than those on the broadcast networks, with a mean of 25.4 acts per hour.[45] Although the sample sizes for individual cable channels are small, the differences across cable channels in children's programming are consistent with the brand identities established in the use of violence in programming aimed at adults. The Family Channel had 15.1 violent acts per hour, lower than the broadcast network and cable network averages. The Disney figure of 26.3 is heavily influenced by the rate of 122 violent acts per hour for *Superman*, without which the Disney channel would have rated an average of 10.4 violent acts per hour. TNT, TBS, and WGN each broadcast cartoons with twice the rate of violence as the broadcast networks, consistent with their brand image in adult programming as using more violent programming. Note that some of the cartoons on TNT, TBS, and WGN were more likely to be older cartoons such as *Tom and Jerry* and *Bugs Bunny and Friends*, so that part of these differences may arise from the use of older programming on these channels.

Another parallel in the use of violence between adult and children's programming is the decline of violence on network broadcast television. Chapter 4 establishes that in prime time the mid-1980s marked the high-water point for the use of violent series programming on the broadcast networks, with violent shows declining from 51% of series programming hours in 1984 to 23% in 1993. This is consistent with cable, both basic and premium, airing violent programs and the networks responding by making less use of this type of programming. The NCTV data suggest a similar pattern in children's programming. For 1982 the NCTV estimated that children's programming on ABC, CBS, and NBC averaged 30.7 violent acts per hour. This figure declined throughout the 1980s, so that by 1990 the three networks averaged 16.0 acts per hour, a large and statistically significant difference ($T = 3.7$) from 1982.

In the debate over rating children's programs, industry officials have often stated there is an inherent difficulty in rating violence in children's programs since the violence often occurs in cartoons.[46] Yet the NCTV was able to develop and apply a rating code for children's programs based generally on the number of violent acts. The organization classified shows as having low violence (13.9), high violence (24.9), and very high violence (45.7). Note that the mean historical number of violent acts per hour on network broadcast children's shows would place these programs in the high-violence category. More than a third of the shows merited the very high category. These results demonstrate that there is a distribution in the use of violence in programming for children just as there is one in programming for adults. The high prevalence of violence in children's shows means most have the rates of violent acts similar to violent programs in adult genres. The children's programs with low violence, such as *CBS Storybreak*, are often those referred to as educational programs. These shows too generate externalities, but as the section below details they are positive rather than negative.

THE MARKET FOR CHILDREN'S EDUCATIONAL PROGRAMS

Theories

Many explanations are offered for what parents, interest group members, industry participants, and government officials have termed a lack of educational programs for children on television. Some observers believe that educational programs are more costly to produce because they involve more intelligent writing and production, which means that they may be less likely to be offered if stations can attract children with cheaper fare. The FCC noted in its 1996 order on children's programming that educational shows for children are best tailored to narrow audiences, since what is educational for children aged 2–5 may differ from what is educational for children 6–11.[47] Stations may find it more profitable to broadcast to the larger adult audiences since these programs may be aimed at larger demographic segments that may be more highly valued by advertisers than children 2–5 or 6–11 are. The FCC also notes that over-the-air broadcasting prevents parents who do value educational programming highly from expressing this preference in ways that reward local broadcasters, who simply sell audiences to advertisers and who are not able to capture the intensity of programming preferences in their sales to advertisers.

These complaints are not unique to children's educational programming. They rather embody inherent problems involved in broadcast and pay television. As Owen and Wildman observed in their analysis of television economics:

Relative to the viewer benefits provided, both advertiser-supported television and pay television have three biases: against programs that cater to minority-interest tastes, against expensive programs, and in favor of programs that produce large audiences. These biases are less pronounced for pay television, because the intensity of viewers' preferences is reflected in the prices they pay.[48]

Intervention in the market for children's programming based on these rationales could also justify intervention in the many different types of programming that exhibit these characteristics, such as cultural programming for adult viewers that is highly valued by a small number of viewers and is expensive to produce. Children's programming also has another characteristic that sets it apart from

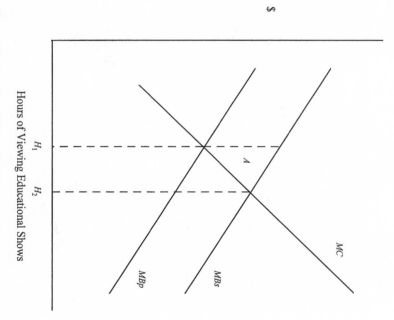

Figure 3.2. Benefits of Educational Programming

many other types of shows, for the consumption of educational programs by children generates positive externalities for society. The failure of broadcasters or cable operators to gain rewards for generating these positive benefits for society means that the market for children's educational programming is characterized by an additional market failure.

Consider the case of a parent who wants her child to gain exposure to educational television. Figure 3.2 captures the incentives for this parent to search out educational shows for her child to consume. Each additional hour of viewing educational shows per week brings the child happiness in terms of entertainment and brings the parent satisfaction that the child is learning. These values are reflected in the marginal benefits curve labeled MBp. The private benefits to a child's viewing are assumed to decline with diminishing returns to consuming (e.g., the child may gain less from the tenth hour of educational programming consumed each week than from the first hour). Getting a child to watch educational programming entails costs for a parent, including searching out what is educational and making sure that the child is watching these programs. Watching educational programming also entails opportunity costs for a child, who could be pursuing other interests. These costs are reflected in the curve MC, which rises with each hour of viewing on the assumption that it is increasingly costly for a parent to monitor what is watched and that a child's opportunity cost may also increase. With this set of private incentives the parent will guide a child to watch H_1 hours of educational shows.

From society's perspective, H_1 is not the optimal amount of educational programming hours for the child to watch. As the child watches educational programs, there are benefits to society that arise from this viewing that are not captured by the interest expressed by the parent or the child. A parent will value the learning generated by these programs, but his or her value will not reflect the full benefits to society of the child's learning (represented by the curve Mbs). The knowledge gained by a child will increase the probability that she or he will grow up to be a productive citizen and benefit others. The failure of parents' (and a child's) interest in a child's learning to reflect fully the gains to education for society in part explains the existence of support for public education in general and helps explain why the market for educational programs may yield less than optimal results. Figure 3.2 does not predict that a child will watch zero hours of educational programming; it simply illustrates that the child will watch less than the optimal amount (H_2) from society's perspective. Although the private costs to viewing outweigh the private benefits between H_1 and H_2, society misses out on the potential gains marked by triangle A since for these hours the marginal private benefits are less than the marginal private costs of monitoring and viewing.

The failure of parents and children to take into account the full benefits to society from educational programs leads to less educational programming in the marketplace. The gap between H_1 and H_2 means that fewer children turn up in the broadcast and cable audiences for educational programs, which means fewer children to sell to advertisers or less demand for educational programs on pay cable channels. This argument that educational programs generate positive externalities rests on the assumption that these shows do teach children skills valuable to society. This assumption has been tested as a hypothesis for particular educational programs, however, and the evidence indicates that viewing educational programs does yield quantifiable, statistically significant improvements in learning. Huston and Wright (1995) found that children 2–4 from low- or moderate-income families performed better on vocabulary, math, and school readiness tests if they viewed *Sesame Street* and other educational programs, a result obtained even after controlling for children's initial language skills and characteristics of family environment. Children exposed to *Barney and Friends* demonstrated greater knowledge of colors, shapes, vocabulary, and counting skills than those who were not viewers.[49]

These results are also obtained for older children who watch educational programming. Fay et al. (1995) evaluated the impact of *CRO*, a show created by the Children's Television Workshop. *CRO* is an animated series about an 11-year-old Cro-Magnon boy that "aims to introduce six- to 11-year-old children to some basic concepts in science and technology, to simulate their interests to learn more, and to show them that science and technology is an integral part of everyday life."[50] The researchers tested the impact of eight episodes of *CRO* on

101 inner city children aged 5–10 in Pittsburgh, a market where the show was not aired. The study found that the show had high appeal among these children, increased interest and understanding of science concepts presented in the episodes, and had stronger comprehension effects for both girls and low science achievers.[51]

While the existence of positive externalities provides one argument for the scrutiny of the market for educational programming, the licensing of local broadcast stations affords another reason to consider the amount of educational programs aired. Currently, local broadcast stations essentially receive their licenses for free in exchange for the promise to broadcast in the "public interest, convenience, and necessity." Congress and the FCC have varied over the years in their willingness to specify exactly what these terms mean for broadcast content, in part out of respect for the First Amendment freedoms of broadcasters. In 1990 Congress passed the Children's Television Act (CTA), which directed the FCC to "consider the extent to which the licensee . . . has served the educational and informational needs of children through the licensee's overall programming, including programming specifically designed to serve such needs." The debate in Congress recognized that children's educational programs have broader benefits for society and that such programs may not be aired frequently by broadcasters since they may be less profitable than other shows. By passing the 1990 act Congress transformed children's programming into a "price" that local broadcast stations would have to pay to retain their licenses. The following analysis of a snapshot of the children's television market from the fall of 1993 demonstrates the incentives broadcasters have to show educational programs and their responses to these incentives.

Data and Analysis

Children in search of television programming in the fall of 1993 faced the same channel outlets as adult viewers: broadcast networks, syndicated broadcast programming, basic cable, and premium channels. Many of the programs that attracted critical acclaim for serving the educational needs of children were on PBS, including *Sesame Street* and *Barney and Friends*. In addition, the cable channels such as Nickelodeon and Disney offered a slate of children's programs that earned favorable reviews and favorable audiences.[52] Much of the debate over the quantity and quality of children's educational shows centered on the programming of the commercial broadcast networks and local independent stations, since broadcast stations were required under the Children's Television Act to air programs that "served the educational and informational needs of children." This section focuses on the incentives that face broadcast stations in their decisions of whether and when to schedule educational programs for children.

In the debate over the implementation of the CTA, commentators in the federal rule-making process offered many suggestions for how to define "educational programs" for children: shows with specifically enumerated educational goals, programs that had educational advisors on scripts and production; and offerings that could demonstrate through testing (e.g., focus groups, surveys) that they had a positive impact on the education of children.[53] Disputes arose over whether a program had to have "education" as its prime mission, or whether a show centered around entertainment could also be considered educational. Industry programmers stressed that entertainment programs could often draw larger child audiences, which might then be exposed to educational messages interwoven into engaging stories. This argument was often summarized by the statement that for a television program "you have to reach before you teach."[54] A related definitional issue was whether interstitials, short program segments run during entertainment programs, could count as fulfilling the educational programming requirements of the CTA. *Schoolhouse Rock*, an interstitial series on ABC that included such memorable segments as "Conjunction Junction" and "I'm Just a Bill," attempted to teach children grammar, math, and civics lessons in between entertainment shows. The Fox Network argued that its interstitial segments during entertainment programs were "a most compelling means of conveying information," which ultimately might yield more exposures than if such programming had been offered as a solo educational show.[55]

Given this debate over what shows were "educational" for children, I have chosen to define a children's show as educational if there were frequent claims in the entertainment press or FCC rule-making docket that a program was "educational" or "FCC friendly" (e.g., would help a station comply with the CTA). For the set of 51 programs designated as children's programs in Nielsen infor-

TABLE 3.9
Ad Rates and Audiences for Broadcast Network Children's Programs, Fall 1993

	Educational Programs	N	Noneducational Programs	N	Difference of Means Test (T Statistic)
Mean Price for 30-Second Commercial	$20,900	15	$29,700	36	3.1***
Mean Cost per Thousand Children 2–11 Delivered	$24.20	15	$16.80	35	–1.4
Mean Program Audience (000 Viewers)					
Children 2–5	530.0	14	862.0	35	3.9***
Children 6–11	732.1	14	1,133.4	35	2.6**
Teen Females	200.0	15	209.0	34	0.2
Teen Males	201.3	15	336.8	34	3.2***
Mean Program Ratings					
Children 2–5	3.3	12	5.4	28	3.2***
Children 6–11	3.4	12	5.2	28	2.2**
Teen Females	1.6	12	2.0	28	1.2
Teen Males	1.7	12	2.5	28	2.2**

Note: *** = statistically significant at the .01 level; ** = significant at the .05 level.

mation on advertising prices and audiences, table 3.9 indicates that 15 children's programs were referred to as educational in descriptions of the fall 1993 programming lineups on ABC, CBS, Fox, and NBC.[56] These shows included *Citykids* (ABC), *Beakman's World* (CBS), *Bobby's World* (Fox), and *Saved by the Bell* (NBC). The other programs listed as children's programs by Nielsen are labeled "noneducational" in this analysis. These shows included *Teenage Mutant Ninja Turtles*, *Bugs Bunny/Tweety Show*, *Tales from the Cryptkeeper*, and *Power Rangers*.

Table 3.9 confirms several claims made during the debate over the incentives that broadcasters face in the children's television market. The mean price of 30-second commercials on educational programs ($20,900) was nearly a third lower than that on noneducational shows ($29,700). From an advertiser's perspective, the mean cost of reaching a thousand viewing children aged 2–11 was higher on educational programs ($24.20) than on noneducational shows ($16.80), although this difference is not statistically significant. Educational shows on average attract much smaller audiences than noneducational programs. The average audience for an educational program was 530,000 children 2–5 and 732,100 children 6–11. The mean audiences for noneducational children's shows were 862,000 children 2–5 and 1,133,400 children 6–11. Audiences for educational shows were over one-third lower for children 2–5, children 6–11, and teenage males 12–17. For teenage females, there was no statistical difference between audiences for educational versus noneducational programs. The ratings data for children's educational programs (3.3 for children 2–5 and 3.4 for children 6–11) reveal that these shows earn much lower children's audiences than such prime-time adult programming as situation comedies (7.1 rating among children 2–11) or feature films (4.2 rating). Noneducational children's shows had a mean rating of 5.4 for children 2–5 and 5.2 for children 6–11, which are nearly identical to the mean rating of 5.5 for children 2–11 for prime-time network shows shown from 7 to 9 PM. Children were thus less likely to watch educational shows targeted directly at their age group than they were to watch adult prime-time programs aimed at adult viewers.[57]

Across many different demographic groups, children 2–11 turn out in lower numbers for broadcast network educational programs. Table 3.10 shows that the mean rating for noneducational shows for children 2–11 was 3.3 versus 5.4 for noneducational shows. The gap is particularly large in households where the head of household did not go to college and in black households. Note that in households without cable educational shows earned higher ratings (4.1) than those households with cable (2.9), consistent with the assertions that cable does supply programs that may be educational and that households without cable rely on broadcast stations for educational shows.

Table 3.11 reveals that the gap in viewership also holds for children's syndicated programming. If one defines educational programs "broadly" as those syndicated programs referred to in press and rule-making accounts as educational or "FCC friendly," then fourteen of the forty-four children's syndicated programs listed in Nielsen data for Fall 1993 were educational.[58] This broad

TABLE 3.10

Ratings for Broadcast Network Children's Programs by Program Type and Demographic Groups, Fall 1993

Ratings for Children 2–11 for	Ratings for Noneducational Programs	Ratings for Educational Programs	Difference of Means Test (T Statistic)
Households with Cable	4.7	2.9	2.8***
Households without Cable	6.7	4.1	3.5***
Head of Household, 4 Years of College	4.5	3.0	2.1**
Head of Household, No College	5.6	3.5	2.9***
Household with Income $20K–$30K	6.5	3.8	2.9***
Household with Income $60K +	4.2	3.0	2.0***
Black Households	6.4	3.2	2.8***
Total Households	5.4	3.3	3.1***

Note: *** = statistically significant at the .01 level; ** = significant at the .05 level.

definition included animated shows such as *Biker Mice from Mars* and *Exosquad*. One could also restrict the syndicated shows that were defined as educational shows to the narrower subset of programs that were claimed to be educational and were in the genres of children's news or children's live programs (as opposed to animated). This yields a smaller subset of eight educational syndicated programs tracked in the fall 1993 Nielsen data. Table 3.11 shows that the ratings for educational shows in syndication are lower than those for educational shows on the broadcast networks. These ratings for syndicated educational programs are even lower once one excludes programs more geared toward entertainment such as *Biker Mice from Mars*. For the narrowly defined set of educational syndicated programs, the ratings for children 2–11 were 1.1, compared to 2.3 for noneducational shows. If one uses the narrow definition of educational programs, ratings were lower for these shows among all the demographic groups in table 3.11. Note again that for syndicated programs, ratings for educational shows were higher in households without cable than those with cable, in households where the household head had not gone to college, and in households were incomes were lower (e.g., $20,000–$30,000). This indicates that these broadcast programs may be consumed more in households where children could obtain a higher marginal benefit from consumption of such programming.[59]

The differences in audience size help explain the lower returns to children's educational programs for network broadcasters. Consider the advertising rates for the forty-one weekend children's program slots tracked by Nielsen in November 1993. The mean advertising price for a 30-second ad was $28,300. The target age ranges for these broadcast programs are large, ranging from the teen-oriented offerings on NBC such as *Saved by the Bell* to *Garfield and Friends*, which is aimed at a younger audience.[60] Analysis of the ad rates for these

TABLE 3.11
Ratings for Children's Programs by Program Type and Demographic Groups,
Syndicated Programs

Ratings for Children 2–11 for	Ratings for Noneducational Programs	Ratings for Educational Programs	Difference of Means Test (T Statistic)
Educational Programs Broadly Defined			
Households with Cable	2.0	1.3	1.6
Households without Cable	3.2	1.9	2.3**
Head of Household, 4 Years of College	1.9	1.1	2.1**
Head of Household, No College	2.7	1.7	2.0**
$30K			
Household with Income $60K+	3.1	1.8	2.0**
Black Households	2.0	1.2	2.1**
Household with Income $20K–	2.9	1.9	1.6
Total Households	2.4	1.5	2.0**
Educational Programs Narrowly Defined			
Households with Cable	1.9	0.8	4.2***
Households without Cable	3.0	1.6	2.1**
Head of Household, 4 Years of College	1.8	0.7	4.2***
Head of Household, No College	2.6	1.1	4.2***
$30K			
Household with Income $60K+	3.0	1.3	3.6***
Black Households	1.9	0.7	4.2***
Household with Income $20K–	2.9	1.1	4.5***
Total Households	2.3	1.1	4.0***

Note: *** = Statistically significant at the .01 level; ** = significant at the .05 level.

programs will thus mix returns to different types of audiences for programs in different market niches. Overall, the regression analysis in table 3.12 indicates that advertising rates on weekend broadcast network children's shows increase with the viewership of children 2–5, children 6–11, and teen females 12–17. Additional viewers among males 12–17 do not bring higher advertising prices, perhaps because advertisers in search of these consumers may find them through other avenues such as sports programming. The coefficients indicate that advertising prices per 30 seconds increases by $7.7 for an additional thousand viewers age 2–5, $6.6 for an additional thousand viewers age 6–11, and $20.0 for an additional thousand teen female viewers.

The coefficient on the dummy variable for educational programs indicates that, if one controls for the audiences generated by a program, an educational show will have an advertising price that is $3,910 lower than a noneducational

TABLE 3.12

Determinants of 30-Second Ad Prices on Weekend Broadcast Network Children's Programs ($N = 41$)

	Parameter Estimate (Standard Error)
Intercept	12.61***
	(3.26)
Children 2–5 Viewing	7.71e-3**
	(3.73e-3)
Children 6–11 Viewing	6.62e-3**
	(3.14e-3)
Teen Females Viewing	0.02**
	(8.96e-3)
Teen Males Viewing	−6.10e-4
	(0.01)
Educational Program	−3.91*
	(2.05)
Adjusted R^2	0.68

Note: Data are from November 1993. Viewing audience numbers and ad prices are in thousands. The mean ad price was 28.3 (e.g., $28,300 per 30 seconds). *** = Statistically significant at the .01 level, ** = significant at the .05 level, * = significant at the .10 level.

program. There are several possible explanations for this lower advertising rate. The demographic mix of children watching educational programs (e.g., income, education status of the households) may mean that advertisers have a lower willingness to pay for these viewers, either because they can be reached easily through other programs or because they are less likely to be influenced to purchase products advertised. The type of products that find advertising on educational programs consistent with their brand image may differ from those that sponsor noneducational programs. Producers of violent toys, for example, may find it easier to reach children who would desire these products through noneducational programming. These manufacturers might also believe that there would be a possibility of consumer backlash in response to advertising for violent products on educational programs. The net result for broadcasters is that, even after one controls for audience size, educational children's programs earn lower advertising prices.

In light of these market conditions, the Children's Television Act can be viewed in at least two different ways in economic terms. The requirement that a station broadcast educational programming for children can be seen as an attempt to remedy the market failure caused by firms' failures to take into account the larger benefits to society (e.g., positive externalities) of children's educational programs. Or the legislation can be seen as an addendum to the spectrum-leasing contract that the government has with a broadcaster, in which case educational shows are part of the "price" that licensees pay for their (currently free) use of the spectrum. From the perspective of a local broadcast station, the Children's Television Act requires the station to broadcast programs that may be less profitable than the alternative programming the station would choose to broadcast in the absence of this legislation.[61] Economic theories of regulation would predict that stations will attempt to evade this requirement or comply in a low-cost manner, predictions borne out in the analysis in the remainder of the chapter.

One way for stations to avoid the lost profits associated with airing educational shows is to air entertainment programs but claim they are educational. The Center for Media Education, for example, found that stations claimed that programs such as *Leave It to Beaver* and *Yo! Yogi* were educational.[62] In a separate analysis of station license renewal applications filed in 1994, Dale Kunkel found that stations were still claiming entertainment programs such as *America's Funniest Home Videos* and *Mighty Morphin Power Rangers* as educational.[63]

The rationales offered for calling entertainment shows educational themselves are often entertaining. A Fox affiliate (WLFL) claimed in regulatory filings that episodes of *Geraldo* with titles such as "Underaged and Oversexed," "Overweight Kids and Their Mothers," and "When Love Doesn't Make the Grade" were educational-instructional for children 16 and under. In describing why the last-named episode fulfilled these goals, the station asserted: "This edition of Geraldo addresses teacher-student affairs. Information on how parents can recognize the warning signs of this situation and the psychological affects [*sic*] it can have on young, impressionable teenaged girls, and how to prevent it from happening."[64] The same station went on to claim that episodes of *Beverly Hills, 90210* were also educational-instructional programming for children. The rationale for this assertion for the episode "Beverly Hills, 90210: Spring Dance/Beach Blanket Brandon" stated: "In this episode of 90210, the gang at West Beverly High goes to the prom after which Brenda and Dylan confront the responsibilities and potential repercussions of having sex. Although Brenda finds out she is not pregnant, the scare makes her think more clearly about the issue of sex and causes her to want to slow things down with Dylan. And Steve deals with the news that he's adopted."[65]

These statements were contained in filings that the FCC requires a station to maintain in its public inspection file. Stations rationally concluded during early years of the implementation of the CTA that the high costs of monitoring their compliance meant that it would be easy to mislabel entertainment as education. The logic of collective action predicts that few parents would visit stations to examine public inspection files and few interest groups would attempt to sift through information on license renewal applications at the FCC headquarters in Washington. The lack of graduated sanctions also made it unlikely that the FCC would fail to renew a license if a station did not fully comply with the spirit of the CTA.

Another way for stations to lower the cost of showing educational programming is to shift such programs to hours when potential audiences are lower, so that the potential revenues lost by programming that complies with the CTA are lower. One area to test whether stations strategically shift educational programs is in the deviation of network affiliates from regularly scheduled network air times for children's programs. Local network affiliates may choose to air a network program at a time other than that suggested by the network's schedule, a practice referred to as a program deviation. Nielsen tracks these deviations, so that advertisers can see when programs aired in local markets.[66] If stations are trying to shift educational programs to times that minimize lost revenues, then one may expect educational programs to be shifted more than noneducational programs. If one analyzes which programs experienced deviations that shifted air times to a showing before 8 AM, then one would also expect this pattern to be more pronounced for educational shows.

Table 3.13 bears out both these predictions. For the 27 Saturday children's programs aired on the four major networks in November 1993, the scheduling times for each local station affiliated with a network were examined. A program was defined as having a scheduling deviation in a particular market if the local affiliate aired the program at a time other than that scheduled by the network during the month of November.[67] The unit of observation is thus the "showing," with a station's monthly showing of a program defined as deviating if the station scheduled the program at a time other than that suggested by the network. The combination of 27 shows and network affiliates in 210 markets yields a total sample of 1,655 showings to examine for deviations for children's educational programs and 5,381 showings to examine for deviations for noneducational children's programs. Table 3.13 indicates that stations deviated for 20.2% of educational program showings versus 10.3% of noneducational programs, a difference of proportions statistically significant at the .01 level. For educational program showings, 9.7% were shifted to starting times prior to 8 AM, consistent with the attempt to lower the reduction in revenues associated with these programs. Only 3.5% of noneducational shows were shifted to airtimes before 8 AM.[68]

Since ad rates on the alternative programs stations run in place of educational shows may be higher in larger markets, then one may expect that the forgone revenues from airing educational shows in larger markets will be greater.[69] License values will be larger and scrutiny of programming may be greater in larger markets, so that stations would be less likely to deviate if they felt that the probability of FCC license renewal were affected by shifting educational programs to less desirable hours. Stations in smaller markets might be more likely to be owned locally, which could translate into greater incentives to serve the "public interest" in providing educational programs. Table 3.13 reveals that on net it appears that the gains to shifting educational programs win out more often in the largest markets. For educational programs in the largest twenty-five television markets in the United States, 27.6% of showings for educational programs experienced deviations in November 1993. This figure was 16.9% for educational programs in the smallest television markets (i.e., those that rank 101+ based on number of television households). There is no statistically significant difference in the deviations on noneducational programs in the top

TABLE 3.13

Deviations for Broadcast Network Saturday Children's Programs

	% of Showings Deviating	% Showings Deviating and Aired before 8 AM	N
Top 25 Markets			
Educational Programs	20.2	9.7	1,655
Noneducational Programs	10.3	3.5	5,381
26–100 Markets			
Educational Programs	27.6	10.3	243
Noneducational Programs	12.3	4.5	799
101+ Markets			
Educational Programs	21.1	11.5	706
Noneducational Programs	11.1	4.2	2,381
Top 25 Markets, Network Owned			
Educational Programs	16.9	7.8	706
Noneducational Programs	8.7	2.3	2,201
Top 25 Markets, Not Owned by Network			
Educational Programs	23.3	5.0	60
Noneducational Programs	10.9	3.6	220
Educational Programs	20.1	9.9	1,595
Noneducational Programs	10.3	3.5	5,161

twenty-five markets versus markets 101+, which suggest that the scheduling differences observed relate to the amount of revenues the stations in larger markets can gain in shifting children's educational programs.

Each of the broadcast networks owns a handful of local stations in the largest television markets. If the networks were concerned about the possible brand image damage of shifting educational shows, then one would expect network-owned stations to be less likely to change the air times of children's educational programs. Table 3.13, however, indicates that within the top twenty-five television markets there is no statistically significant difference in the deviations for educational programs on stations owned by the networks (23.3% deviations) versus those on local affiliates not owned by the networks (20.1%). For the more stringent test of deviations before 8 AM, there is no difference between deviations prior to 8 AM for educational (5.0%) versus noneducational programs (3.6%) on the network-owned stations. There is evidence for strategic scheduling changes in the early hours for the affiliates not owned by the networks, since deviations where the program was shifted to air before 8 AM accounted for 9.9% of showings for educational programs on these stations versus 3.5% for noneducational shows.[70]

Table A3.2 reports show deviations calculated for each Saturday network children's program. The programs with the highest incidence of being shifted to airtimes prior to 8 AM are those most frequently cited as educational for children: *CRO* (20.2% showings involved deviations where the program was shifted to air before 8 AM), *Beakman's World* (18.1% deviations prior to 8 AM), and *CBS Storybreak* (16.0% deviations prior to 8 AM). Note that if one simply examined the regularly scheduled program times for educational shows, then one might believe that some of these programs were aired at times aimed at large children's audiences. *Beakman's World* was scheduled by CBS to run at noon and *CBS Storybreak* to run at 12:30 PM on Saturdays. Yet *Beakman's World* had the highest deviation rate (31.6%) for any of the network children's shows, in part because a noon time slot on Saturdays may guarantee interruption during the fall by college football programming in many parts of the country. Although *Disney's Little Mermaid* was cited in some press accounts as being educational, this animated program could be viewed as more of an entertainment vehicle than educational show. The program's high entertainment value may have posed a lower likelihood of reduced profits for airing it at its normally scheduled time. Deviation patterns bear this out, since the program was shifted to airtimes prior to 8 AM at half the rate (8.2%) of that for the other two CBS educational programs.

Although educational children's shows earn lower ratings than noneducational programs, part of these lower audiences are attributable to the early time slots stations chose for educational programs. The impact of schedule deviations on ratings for *Beakman's World* demonstrates how scheduling can affect an educational program's audience. Table 3.14 contains regressions modeling the rating for children 2–11 for *Beakman's World* across the top 100 local television markets in November 1993. Although this educational program was scheduled to air on Saturdays at noon on the East Coast, some network affiliates switched the program to air at 7:30 AM or earlier. Based on the first specification in Table 3.14, airing the program at 7:30 AM or earlier decreased ratings by 1.75 ratings points, for a program that averaged a 3.44 rating in the 88 markets with Nielsen ratings reported. In some markets the number of children watching the program was so low that the numbers were not sufficient to meet Nielsen's reporting requirements to estimate a rating. If one makes the assumption that these markets had a zero rating, then specification (3) in table 3.14 indicates that the early deviations drop ratings by 2.20 ratings points. Shifting *Beakman's World* to early time slots caused the program to have audiences that were between one-half and two-thirds lower than they would be if the program aired at its noon time slot. Though stations may bemoan the failure of educational programs to attract audiences, Table 3.14 demonstrates that part of this failure lies in the scheduling of these programs in early morning slots.

If stations shift the scheduled showings of educational and noneducational

TABLE 3.14
Impact of Schedule Deviations on Children's Ratings for *Beakman's World* in the Top 100 Markets among Children 2–11

	(1) Reported	(2) Calculated	(3) Imputed
Intercept	1.92*	1.94*	1.83*
	(1.14)	(1.15)	(1.11)
Number of Broadcast Stations	0.07	0.07	0.09
	(0.11)	(0.11)	(0.11)
Total Television Households	−3e−5	−7.09e−5	−9.75e−5
	(3.34e−4)	(3.37e−4)	(3.37e−4)
Eastern	0.78	0.68	0.76
	(0.87)	(0.87)	(0.81)
Central	2.13**	2.11**	2.00**
	(0.88)	(0.88)	(0.84)
Mountain	0.94	0.92	0.96
	(1.25)	(1.25)	(1.23)
Station Deviates and Schedules at 7:30 AM or Earlier	−1.75**	−1.77**	−2.20***
	(0.78)	(0.78)	(0.66)
Adjusted R^2	.14	.15	.18
Number of Markets	88	90	94
Mean Rating for Children 2–11	3.44	3.37	3.23

Note: Specification (1) includes ratings as reported in Nielsen 1994. Specification (2) includes calculated ratings for two markets where the number of children watching was reported but a rating was not reported. Specification (3) assigns a 0 rating for those four markets where viewership was not high enough to meet Nielsen reporting requirements. Standard errors in parentheses. *** = statistically significant at the .01 level; ** = significant at the .05 level; * = significant at the .10 level.

programs for children based on the prospect of higher returns on alternative programs, then these decisions can be modeled based on the market and station characteristics that reflect these financial incentives. Table 3.15 offers empirical models of a network affiliate station's decision of whether to deviate on the scheduling of a children's program. If the values of all variables are set to their means in specification (1), the predicted probability that a station will deviate on a children's show is .11. The time zone a station is in will affect the incentives to shift programs on Saturday mornings, since stations in time zones other than the East Coast may face financial incentives to air sports programming live as it originates from the East Coast.[71] Relative to a program aired in the Pacific time zone (the omitted time zone dummy), a children's program aired in the eastern time zone has a .08 lower probability of being shifted in the schedule and a program in the central time zone has a .15 lower probability of being shifted.[72] The more local broadcast stations there are in the market (controlling for the size of the market), the more likely a station is to deviate on children's programs. A shift in the number of broadcast stations in a local market from four to ten increases the probability a station will deviate on a children's pro-

gramming live as it originates from the East Coast. The more local broadcast stations there are in the market (controlling for the size of the market), the more likely a station is to deviate on children's programs. A shift in the number of broadcast stations in a local market from four to ten increases the probability a station will deviate on a children's program.

gram by .02. This is consistent with statements that "competitive pressures" affect the willingness of broadcasters to schedule children's programs in desirable time slots.[73] If a children's program is educational, the probability that the station will shift it from its normally scheduled time increases by .09. This is consistent with the percentage figures in table 3.13 that indicate that educational programs are shifted at twice the rate of noneducational programs.

The estimated probability in specification (2) that a station will deviate and air a program before 8 AM is .04. Stronger competition in the number of local broadcast stations (e.g., a shift from four to ten local broadcast stations) increases this probability by .01. A program's chance of being shifted to air before 8 AM increases markedly if the program is educational. If one controls for the other sets of factors that influence scheduling, the probability a network children's show will be switched to air before 8 AM increases by .05 if the program is educational.

The shifting of children's programs away from the time periods scheduled by the networks reflects a willingness by a local station to gain additional revenues by running alternative programming in place of these network shows aimed at children. Some of these children's shows will have positive externalities in the form of increasing the educational development of children. Network affiliates offer another type of programming that generates positive externalities, network news coverage of public affairs issues.[74] Affiliates of ABC, CBS, and NBC face a decision of whether to air the nightly network evening news programs at the times scheduled by the networks or to switch these programs to another time period to show alternative programming. In the New York market, for example, the network-owned affiliate WCBS attracted considerable attention for shifting *The CBS Evening News* by one-half hour so that it could air a game show (*Win, Lose, or Draw*) that it expected would be more profitable in the time slot.[75] If stations vary in their concern for the positive externalities generated by their programs (e.g., the education of both children and adults), then those stations that slight audiences for public affairs programming may also be those that shift the air times of educational programs for children.

Specification (3) in table 3.15 confirms that whether a station is willing to reduce the potential audience for children's shows can be predicted in part by its willingness to shift public affairs programming aimed at adults. The estimated mean probability that an ABC, CBS, or NBC station would deviate on a children's program was .13. If a station deviated on its scheduling of the network evening news, the probability that it rescheduled children's programming increased by .02. The coefficient on educational programs indicated that for affiliates of the three main networks that educational programs had a .09 higher probability of being rescheduled. Overall, stations owned by the network affiliates were less likely to deviate on children's show. Network ownership lowers the probability of deviating by .06.

Table A3.3 reveals that the deviation behavior of stations will vary across networks. Estimates for the probability of deviations were .13 for ABC, .11 for CBS, .01 for Fox, and .20 for NBC. For each set of network affiliates educa-

TABLE 3.15
Predicting Deviations for Saturday Children's Programming

	(1) Deviations	(2) Deviations before 8 AM	(3) Deviations
Intercept	−1.47***	−3.18***	−1.52***
	(0.13)	(0.21)	(0.17)
Number of Broadcast Stations in Market	0.03**	0.06**	0.05***
	(0.02)	(0.02)	(0.02)
Total Television Households	−8.0e−5	−1.2e−4	7.5e−5
	(7.9e−5)	(1.3e−4)	(8.8e−5)
Eastern	−0.91***	−0.13	−0.77***
	(0.10)	(0.16)	(0.14)
Central	−1.77***	−1.37***	−1.47***
	(0.12)	(0.19)	(0.16)
Mountain	−0.03	−0.26	−0.72***
	(0.13)	(0.22)	(0.16)
Network-Owned Station	0.03	−0.31	−0.61**
	(0.13)	(0.40)	(0.15)
Educational Program	0.81***	1.10***	0.72***
	(0.24)	(0.11)	(0.31)
Station Deviates on Network Evening News			0.21*
	(0.08)		(0.09)
Log Likelihood	−2,453.4	−1,292.8	−1,958.9
Number of Showings	7,036	7,036	5,017

Note: Dependent variable in logit = 1 for (1) and (3) if the station did not air the children's program at its regularly scheduled network time and in (2) = 1 if the station deviated and aired the program before 8 A.M. *** = Statistically significant at the .01 level; ** = significant at the .05 level; * = significant at the .10 level.

tional programs were more likely to be rescheduled, with an estimated increase in the probability of deviation of .08 for ABC, .08 for CBS, .01 for Fox, and .02 for NBC (although for this network the impact was not statistically significant). Part of the difference in incentives to deviate on educational programs across networks may relate to the amount of educational content of a network's programs and the likely reduction in potential revenues that arise from running an educational program. The educational programs run by ABC and CBS such as *CRO, Beakman's World,* and *CBS Storybreak* have been lauded for their educational content and potential impact.[76] NBC adopted the strategy to aim its children's programming at the upper end of the definition of childhood, the early teenage years. The programs that the network labels as educational, such as *Saved by the Bell* and *California Dreams,* are sitcoms that may sometimes focus on "societal problems like drugs, violence, alcohol and racism and personal concerns like dating, sportsmanship and final exams."[77] The fact that these shows are closer to entertainment than education may explain why NBC affiliates treat educational and noneducational programs alike in deviations.[78] The networks with shows that have the highest perceived educational content, ABC and CBS, were less likely to deviate on their scheduling of children's programs at the affiliates that they owned. Relative to the other stations in their affiliate pools, a children's program on an affiliate owned by ABC was .09 less likely to be shifted and on one owned by CBS was .04 less likely to experience a scheduling deviation. For children's programs aired on Fox affiliates, a program's probability of deviation increased by .15 if the station were owned by the parent company. For NBC programs, the deviation probability increased by .25 if the program was aired on a network-owned station. The lower apparent commitment of offering children's educational shows by the Fox and NBC networks thus extends to the scheduling of children's programs on the network-owned stations.

Table 3.16 offers additional ways to test the relation between how a station handles positive externalities in one area, children's programming, and positive externalities in another area, public affairs coverage. *Nightline*, the ABC late night news program hosted by Ted Koppel, has elements of entertainment and public affairs reporting in its style and substance. During Mondays in November, *NFL Monday Night Football* will often extend past prime time, which will further push the schedules of local stations back in terms of late local news and other programming. Some stations may decide to switch the airing of *Nightline* on Mondays to an even later time than that suggested by the network so that they can run more profitable programming in their local markets. Specifications (1) and (2) in table 3.16 model the decisions of ABC affiliates to deviate on the Saturday children's programming offered by the network. The mean estimated probabilities of deviation are .13 for rescheduling a program and .04 for shifting a program to air before 8 AM. If the children's program is educational, the probability that the station will deviate increases by .08. If the station deviates on *Nightline*, then the probability that the station deviates on a children's program also increases by .08. If the children's program is educational *and* the station deviates in airing *Nightline* on Mondays, then the probability that the station will deviate on the children's educational program jumps by .29.[79] Stations willing to sacrifice part of the audience for public affairs programming are thus much more likely to shift a children's program when it is educational. These effects also hold for rescheduling children's programs to air before 8 AM. If the program is educational, the probability increases by .12, and if the station deviates on *Nightline* on Mondays, the early morning deviation probability grows by .03. If the program is educational and the station is one that deviates on *Nightline*, then the probability the station will reschedule the program to air before 8 AM increases by .31.

Offering children's educational programs and providing public affairs coverage are two ways that stations may demonstrate that they are complying with their license requirement to "serve the public interest, convenience, and necessity." Stations may vary in the brand names that they develop for providing such "public interest" programming, with some stations offering children's pro-

TABLE 3.16
Relationship between Public Affairs Coverage and Deviations for
Saturday Children's Programming

	(1) Deviations	(2) Deviations before 8 AM	(3) Deviations before 8 AM (55 Station Local News Subset)
Intercept	-0.50* (0.27)	-2.37*** (0.39)	-0.61 (1.41)
Number of Broadcast Stations in Market	0.05 (0.03)	0.08 (0.05)	5.37e-3 (0.09)
Total Television Households	6.9e-5 (1.6e-4)	7.3e-5 (2.07e-4)	-3.4e-4 (3.74e-4)
Eastern	-1.93*** (0.21)	-1.48*** (0.28)	-1.62 (1.17)
Central	-2.58*** (0.23)	-2.69*** (0.28)	-1.64 (1.25)
Mountain	-1.97*** (0.30)	-0.92*** (0.36)	-2.58* (1.58)
Network-Owned Station	-0.92* (0.49)	-0.55 (0.64)	-1.26 (0.90)
Educational Program	0.36 (0.26)	1.47*** (0.31)	0.93*** (0.32)
Station Deviates on *Nightline*	0.52*** (0.19)	0.63** (0.29)	
Nightline Deviates on Monday	0.85** (0.43)	0.81* (0.49)	
% of Local News Teasers Dealing with Crime			0.05** (0.02)
Log Likelihood	-570.8	-313.8	-142.9
Number of Showings	1,543	1,543	460

Note: Dependent variable in logit = 1 if the station did not air the children's program at its regularly scheduled network time. Standard errors are in parentheses. *** = statistically significant at the .01 level; ** = significant at the .05 level; * = significant at the .10 level.

grams with higher educational content and public affairs programs with higher "news" content. In chapter 7 I explore how the content of evening local news programs can be modeled using the same framework established in chapter 1 that explains the distribution of entertainment programming. For the analysis in chapter 7 I coded the content of local news broadcasts in fifty-seven stations in nineteen television markets for November 1993.[80] One of the variables used to indicate the style of newscast chosen by a station is the percentage of story "teasers" in a newscast that deal with crime. This variable is negatively correlated with coverage of stories dealing with local government, education, or business and positively correlated with coverage of accidents or disasters and positively correlated with the number of stories per broadcast. The percentage of teasers dealing with crime thus may serve as an indicator of the degree that a station focuses on entertainment content rather than "hard news" in its newscasts.

Specification (3) in table 3.16 examines the deviation on children's programs for the fifty-five stations in the local news subset that overlapped with the November 1993 children's television data. The estimated mean probability of deviation for the programs in this sample is .09. As in previous models, educational programs were more likely to be switched to a time different than that scheduled by the network (e.g., the probability of deviation increases by .09 if a program was educational). Stations that emphasized crime in their story teasers were also more likely to deviate on children's programs. An increase in the percentage of teasers dealing with crime from 2% to 17% leads to a .05 increase in the probability that a station will switch a children's program from the network's scheduled time.[81] This demonstrates that a station's treatment of positive externalities in children's programming and public affairs content are related, which suggests these two elements are part of the brand identities that stations choose in developing reputations within local television markets.

ENCOURAGING (POSITIVE) EXTERNALITIES

While much of this book focuses on how to limit the negative impacts generated by violence on television, educational programming for children represents a type of market failure where too little programming will be provided and consumed. Because parents will not internalize the full benefits to society of their children's viewing of educational shows, fewer children than optimal will be in the viewing audience, which results in smaller audiences to market to advertisers or cable channels. While the existence of these positive externalities is clear, their magnitude has not been well established, which makes it difficult to determine the optimal amount of educational programming that should be offered in a local television market. This has given rise to at least three classes of suggested policies for encouraging educational programming.[82]

Since local broadcast stations currently receive their licenses for free, the requirements to air educational and informational programming for children can be seen as a "price" the Congress requires that stations pay for their license. In this sense, the 1996 rule issued by the FCC can be viewed as clarifying the terms of these license renewal contracts. Under this rule, the FCC states that stations that air 3 hours of "core" educational programming for children per week will be certain of staff-level approval that they have complied with the

CTA, whereas those stations that do not meet this requirement will have a stricter scrutiny of their assertion that they have complied with the CTA. To reduce the likelihood that broadcasters will attempt to schedule programs in early AM hours or claim entertainment equals education, the commission defines core programming as shows that serve "the educational and information needs of children as a significant purpose," air between 7 AM and 10 PM, and are identified as educational when aired.[83] To discourage broadcasters from claiming shows such as *Beverly Hills, 90210* are educational, the commission has also proposed an Internet accessible database that will list the reports filed by stations in which they state what programs they air are educational for children. The prospect that parents and interest groups will scrutinize these assertions, which previously lay dormant in the public inspection files kept at local broadcast stations, should discourage stations from evading the CTA by claiming that prime-time entertainment programs aimed at adults are educational programming for children.

A second class of solutions would rely on the creation of norms that encourage individuals to produce and consume educational programming. Cass Sunstein provides a useful definition of norms as "social attitudes of approval and disapproval, specifying what ought to be done and what ought not to be done."[84] This could be seen as trying to affect through public discussion and examination the ideological returns associated with educational programming. At the ownership level, this would mean that the individuals that were identified with ownership of a specific network (e.g., Ted Turner, Rupert Murdoch) would be willing to trade off a measure of profits for the ideological satisfaction of helping to educate children through television. Station owners local to a market would earn greater respect within the community for airing educational programs. The problem with norm creation at the ownership level is that for the networks ownership has shifted away from individuals to publicly traded stock corporations, which dissipates the responsibility and moral returns to any one individual within a network's management from championing the cause of educational programming. Those individual owners who are associated with a network, such as Turner and Murdoch, have controlled channels that developed brand identities for violent programming within the marketplace.[85] While local ownership of stations might provide a link between a station and a community, increasingly stations are owned by groups rather than a local individual within the community.[86] Norm creation among owners alone will not provide sufficient incentives for additional educational programming.

While the ownership of broadcast stations by publicly traded stock corporations reduces the prospects that owners will identify with the broadcast product, the problems associated with the separation of ownership and control offer another possible role for norms to influence the market. Broadcast companies operate based on the principal-agent relationship, where owners of the firms delegate to managers the decisions to maximize profits, who in turn delegate more detailed choices about how to maximize profits to those lower down the company hierarchy. If network managers and station programmers came to believe in the importance of educational programs, then they might be willing to trade off profits for public approval since the profits come from the owners rather than the managers. Advertising buyers within companies could similarly choose to purchase ads on educational programs, a more costly strategy since it may take more purchases to reach a given amount of children through educational shows. Norms could thus influence the decisions of broadcast and advertising managers, although the constant scrutiny of decisions within these industries means that actions would be less likely to go unnoticed by those concerned with profit maximization.[87]

An alternative approach to norm creation would be to focus on parents as those most concerned with the educational needs of children. If parents came to believe that directing their children toward educational programs was the "right thing to do" in terms of its broader benefits to society, then they might be more willing to invest the time to search out educational programs for their children. If parents came to view advertising on educational programs as part of a prosocial activity, then returns to the brand image of corporate sponsors would be increased and private market incentives would lead to additional sponsorship of children's educational programs.

While norm creation could influence the amount of children's programming ultimately offered and viewed, there are significant obstacles to this strategy. Norms, like ideas in general, are public goods. They will thus tend to be underprovided.[88] Norm creation about broadcasting is difficult for the government, in part because the notion of the First Amendment appears to mitigate against government attempts to influence broadcast content. To date the current owners of broadcast properties have not viewed educational programming as an area that they choose to become identified with. Managers in charge of show selection and advertising purchases operate in an environment where results, measured in terms of ratings achieved and costs of audiences delivered, are continuously monitored, which would make the pursuit of goals other than profit maximization more difficult. Parents may respond more to appeals about the importance of educational programming, but these appeals may be more likely to succeed if they stress the personal benefits to a parent's child rather than the broader benefits to society.

Both the contract and norm approach recognize that the marketplace emphasis on audiences and advertisers does not lead broadcasters to factor in the positive externalities generated by educational shows. Both advertisers and programmers will often state clearly that it is not their job to educate children through television. A third class of solutions would focus on greater support for the set of broadcasters who do view providing educational programs for children as part of their job. Public broadcasters have a well-established track record for creating shows that successfully educate and entertain children. One way to provide additional support for these broadcasters, in an era of declining government appropriations, would be an auction of the broadcast spectrum. The auction could place spectrum rights in their most highly valued use in the private marketplace. If a subset of the spectrum fees were set aside to generate an endowment for public broadcasting, this would give those broadcasters who do desire to meld education and entertainment additional funds to develop programs. Although parents and children will watch educational programs in less than optimal amounts, educational shows with larger budgets may be better able to attract viewers. This incentive-compatible approach would provide more government support for broadcasters attempting to generate the positive externalities associated with educational programs.

CONCLUSIONS

The exposure of children to violent television programming often arises as an unintended by-product of attempts by advertisers to reach adult viewers. Ratings for children and teens demonstrate that within a time period such as prime time, audiences for nonviolent network shows are larger among these groups than those for violent programs. Though violent programs aimed at adults earn relatively low ratings among children, these figures still can translate into more than a million children 2–11 in the audience for a violent network movie in prime time. Children and teens constitute a substantial number of viewers of syndicated violent programming, which is often aired during times such as weekend daytime and pre-prime-time slots when children are likely to be in the audience.

The results in this chapter indicate that when programmers target children directly as viewers, they often use programming that is as violent as the violent programming aimed at adults, if one views cartoon violence as problematic. Substantial research exists that indicates that cartoon violence may pose dangers for children since they are unable when young to distinguish fantasy from reality, are more likely to imitate the attractive perpetrators who may use violence in cartoons, and may be more likely to be influenced by violence which lacks indications of harm (a frequent problem with children's programming). Disputes over defining and rating violence in cartoons may be particularly contentious since companies advertising on children's programs may be especially reluctant to have their brand image associated with "violent" programs.

While the failure of firms to internalize the negative impacts of violent programming will lead to an overprovision of these shows, this chapter has also explored how companies' failure to capture the broader benefits of children's educational programs will lead to an underprovision of these types of shows. Although the Children's Television Act requires that local broadcasters provide educational and informational programming for children as part of their license requirement to serve the public interest, the analysis in this chapter indicates that stations treat this requirement as an economic regulation to be complied with at the lowest possible cost. Network affiliates are much more likely to shift the airing of children's educational programs than children's noneducational shows, especially to program times before 8 AM. Shifting of an educational program such as *Beakman's World* to air at 7:30 AM or earlier reduces its audience among children 2–11 in some local markets by at least 50%. The shifting of programs that generate benefits to children is also related to the station's treatment of public affairs reporting, an area that involves positive externalities for adult viewers. Stations that shift the evening news broadcast or alter the airing of a show such as *Nightline* are also more likely to deviate on children's programs. Broadcast stations face multiple economic incentives to ignore both the negative externalities generated by children's exposure to violent programming and the positive externalities generated by children's consumption of educational programs. The next chapter explores in greater depth how economic incentives can help explain the content and scheduling decisions of broadcast and cable programmers.

TABLE A3.1
Which Parents Switch Channels to Shield Children from News Viewing?

Variable	Coefficient (Standard Error)
Intercept	−2.27**
	(1.11)
Female	0.72***
	(0.27)
White	0.61*
	(0.36)
Aged 18–34	0.42
	(0.55)
Aged 35–49	0.21
	(0.53)
Less Than HS Education	0.22
	(0.57)
HS Education	0.74**
	(0.36)
Some College/Post-HS Education	0.74**
	(0.35)
Annual Income Less Than $20K	−0.65
	(0.48)
Annual Income $20K–$29K	−0.61*
	(0.42)
Annual Income $30K–$49K	−0.71**
	(0.36)
Don't Know/Refused to Give Income	−0.06
	(0.49)
East	0.35
	(0.47)
Midwest	0.47
	(0.41)
South	0.39
	(0.41)

TABLE A3.1 (*Continued*)

Variable	Coefficient (Standard Error)
City	0.38
	(0.39)
Town	0.40
	(0.37)
Suburb	0.23
	(0.41)
Bothered by Violence on TV Shows	0.73***
	(0.28)
Watches 2–3.5 Hours of TV per Day	0.51*
	(0.31)
Watches 4+ Hours of TV per Day	0.11
	(0.33)
Republican	−0.04
	(0.77)
Democrat	−0.01
	(0.76)
Independent	−0.13
	(0.75)
Voted in 1992 Presidential Election	−0.01
	(0.35)
Log Likelihood	−189.0

Note: Dependent variable in logit analysis equals 1 if viewer was the parent of a child between the ages of 8 and 13 who answered "yes" to the question "Have you ever switched the channel or turned off the TV because there was something on the news that you didn't want your child to see?". *** = statistically significant at the .01 level; ** = significant at the .05 level; * = significant at the .10 level.

TABLE A3.2
Deviations by Program, Saturday Children's Programs

	Program Air Time (EST)	% of Showings Deviating	% Showings Deviating and Aired before 8 AM	N
ABC Educational				
CRO	8 AM	22.8	20.2	193
ABC Noneducational				
Addams Family	9:30 AM	8.8	4.1	194
Bugs Bunny/Tweety Show	10:30 AM	21.1	4.6	194
	11:00 AM	20.1	4.1	194
C.O.W.-Boys of Moo Mesa	11:30 AM	22.3	4.7	193
Sonic the Hedgehog	9 AM	11.9	10.4	193
Tales from the Cryptkeeper	10 AM	10.4	3.1	193
CBS Educational				
Beakman's World	12 PM	31.6	18.1	193
CBS Storybreak	12:30 PM	25.3	16.0	194
Disney's Little Mermaid	8:30 AM	11.3	8.2	194
CBS Noneducational				
Cadillacs & Dinosaurs	10 AM	14.0	8.8	193
Garfield & Friends	9 AM	8.2	3.6	194
Marsupilami	8 AM	8.2	5.6	195
New Dennis the Menace	11 AM	15.0	10.9	193
Teenage Mutant Ninja Turtles	11:30 AM	6.2	1.6	193
Fox Educational				
Bobby's World	9 AM	9.7	0.0	145
Dog City	8 AM	9.7	6.9	145
Fox Noneducational				
Droopy	8:30 AM	9.7	6.9	145
Eek the Cat	9:30 AM	8.3	0.0	145
Mighty Morphin Power Rangers	11:30 AM	11.0	0.7	145
Taz-Mania	10:30 AM	9.7	0.0	145
Tiny Toons	10 AM	9.7	0.0	145
X-Men	11 AM	9.7	0.0	145
NBC Educational				
California Dreams	10:30 AM	18.4	4.6	196
Name Your Adventure	10 AM	26.8	7.1	198
Saved by the Bell	11 AM	21.3	3.6	197
NBC Noneducational				
Running the Halls	11:30 AM	20.0	5.1	195

• *C H A P T E R 3* •

TABLE A3.3
Predicting Deviations for Saturday Children's Programming by Network

	(1) ABC	(2) CBS	(3) Fox	(4) NBC
Intercept	−0.25	−3.65***	−0.13	0.66*
	(0.25)	(0.34)	(0.63)	(0.35)
Number of Broadcast Stations in Market	0.03	0.05	−0.25***	4.03e−3
	(0.03)	(0.04)	(0.10)	(0.04)
Total Television Households	1.4e−4	1.5e−4	−1.31e−3**	2.28e−4
	(1.6e−4)	(2.3e−4)	(5.51e−4)	(1.98e−4)
Eastern	−2.04***	0.78***	−1.00***	−1.01***
	(0.20)	(0.26)	(0.33)	(0.26)
Central	−2.49***	−0.39	−4.99***	−1.54***
	(0.22)	(0.30)	(1.04)	(0.26)
Mountain	−1.67***	−2.13***	3.55***	−0.16
	(0.28)	(0.30)	(1.04)	(0.28)
Network-Owned Station	−1.14**	−2.94**	3.29***	1.18*
	(0.50)	(0.75)	(1.08)	(0.65)
Educational Program	0.62***	1.29***	0.66**	0.13
	(0.20)	(1.23)	(0.30)	(0.21)
Log Likelihood	−589.8	−585.4	−250.3	−379.5
Number of Showings	1,547	2,708	1,994	786

Note: Dependent variable in logit = 1 if the station did not air the children's program at its regularly scheduled network time. *** = statistically significant at the .01 level; ** = significant at the .05 level; * = significant at the .10 level.

Programming Violence

MOVIES ARE the most violent programming genre on television. While 57% of the programs in the 1994–95 National Television Violence Study (NTVS) contained violence, 90% of the movies in the composite week of television analyzed had at least one violent act. Nearly 60% of the violent films examined had nine or more violent interactions, the highest rate for any programming genre.[1] Part of the high incidence of violence in movies on television arises because premium cable channels rely primarily on unedited theatrical films for their programming. Although broadcast networks later edit these films when they are shown, theatrical films still account for the most violent programming on their schedules.[2] Films attract large audiences for both broadcast and cable channels, audiences that often include a substantial number of children. In 1995, for example, the average prime-time movie broadcast on the four major networks attracted an audience of 1.4 million children 2–11 and 900,000 teens 12–17. This chapter examines the scheduling of movies to explore how channels use violence to establish brand identities, the strategic use of violent content in different months and parts of the day, and the degree that channels take into account the possible exposure of children in their scheduling of violent films.

Drawing on content information from a sample of over 11,000 films shown during prime time and 16,000 movies shown during the 24-hour viewing cycle on thirty-two channels from February 1995 to March 1996, I first explore in this chapter how channels differ in their use of violent and sexual content. The analysis demonstrates that, as predicted in the model of programming competition presented in chapter 1, channels do use movies to help establish specific brand identities. Channels such as Disney, aimed primarily at children, and Lifetime, aimed primarily at female viewers, have much lower rates of violence in the movies they show. For Cinemax, HBO, and Showtime, however, each of these premium cable channels chooses to program so that at least 65% of the films carry content indicators of violence. Network executives defend the prevalence of violence in theatrical films on television in part as a by-product of creative expression in critically acclaimed films, such as *Schindler's List*. Little of the violence in films shown on television during this time period, however, can be equated with the narrative drive of *Schindler's List*. Of the 5,030 films with program indicators for violent content that were rated by critics on a scale of one to four stars, only 2.8% were four-star films. A low level of critical acclaim for violent films was true for films on broadcast networks (among films with violence indicators, 3.1% were four-star movies), basic cable (4.8% were four-star), and premium cable (1.8% were four-star).[3]

The scheduling of violent movies demonstrates how programmers use violence to build audiences. During the sweeps months when ratings are measured, some channels respond by rapidly increasing the level of violent films shown. WGN, an independent broadcast station carried nationally on basic cable, increased its use of violent movies from 70.1% in nonsweeps months to 88.7% during the periods when ratings were measured. NBC, in contrast, decreased its use of violence as a programming strategy during sweeps, so that the percentage of violent movies dropped from 46.1% to 25.0%. When ABC carried *NFL Monday Night Football* during the fall and early winter months, several networks responded to the likely attraction of young male viewers to these games. TNT actually increased its use of violent movies on *Monday Night Football* evenings, while TBS and Cinemax were less likely to show violent movies on the Mondays when ABC was broadcasting football than on those when it was not. HBO instituted a counterprogramming strategy termed "Testosterone Thursday" to compete with NBC's *Seinfeld*. Since the premium channel's programmers believed that a segment of young adult males would choose action films over a show "about nothing," they consistently scheduled one-star violent films on Thursday evenings at 9 PM.[4] TNT explicitly advertised its regular showing of violent films on Saturday night by branding this programming block as "Saturday Nitro."

The scheduling of violent movies depends primarily on the attempts of broadcasters and cable programmers to reach adult audiences. During the week-days, the violence content of films increases rapidly after the dinner hour as more young adult viewers (e.g., 18–34, 18–49) enter the viewing audience. On basic cable, the percentage of films that are violent increases from 33.8% percent at 7 PM to 48.2% percent at 8 PM. On premium channels the pattern is repeated, with an increase from 52.6% percent violent at 7 PM to 62.9% percent violent at 8 PM. This level of violence generally persists over the next 3 hours. Although television in the 1970s briefly enjoyed a "family hour" from 8 to 9 PM, these figures demonstrate that cable programmers focus on adult audiences rather than factoring in potential exposures of children in early evening programming. During the summer months, school-age children may watch television in greater numbers during the day than during the school year. Yet in terms of violence, there is no statistically significant difference between summer programming and nonsummer programming in the percentage of violent films shown between noon and 2 PM or 2 PM and 4 PM on premium or basic channels. Similarly, movie programming on television contains higher levels of violence and nudity on Saturday afternoons than weekday afternoons, despite the larger number of children in the audience at these times.[5] Overall, the analysis here reveals that channels use violent content strategically to build audiences. The use of violent movie content varies in predictable ways across particular months (sweeps period), days (Is *Monday Night Football* on?), and time periods (Thursdays at 9 PM, the *Seinfeld* time slot).

PRIME-TIME BRAND NAMES

The model in chapter 1 predicts that channels will choose different levels of violence in their programming content to attract particular viewing audiences. While the simple model refers to programming chosen at a given time period, one can also think of the model as applying to the establishment of a consistent "brand name" for a particular type of programming. In a world of increasing numbers of viewing options, programmers stress the importance of creating an image in viewers' minds of what type of programming one can expect on a given channel. This section looks primarily at how channels use movie programming during prime time to establish "brand identities" for particular types of programming.

The analysis draws on a unique sample of 11,603 movies shown on thirty-two channels from February 26, 1995, through March 10, 1996. During this time period an Internet service, *What's On Tonite!*, posted daily programming schedules for these channels. These listings were downloaded and translated into a database of movie schedules. For each movie the service provided the Motion Picture Association of America (MPAA) rating, genre, release year, content indicators for violence, adult language, adult situations, and nudity, and a critics' ranking ranging from one to four stars for movie quality.[6] The general lack of content indicators on movies not rated by the MPAA may reflect a lack of information about a movie's content or the absence of this content in the program.[7] To address the potential problem with relying solely on content indicators, I created another content classification called "violent films." For those movies rated by the MPAA, a film was defined as violent if it carried a violent indicator in the programming guide. For those unrated movies, the film was defined as violent if it was in one of the violent genres.[8] Violent genres in turn were defined by the percentage of MPAA-rated films in each genre that carried violence warnings. The violent genres included action adventure (94.1% violent indicators for rated films), crime mystery (71.4%), horror (96.2%), science fiction–fantasy (79.7%), suspense (87.2%), war (92.7%), and western (89.8%). For the MPAA-rated films, the percentages of films that carried violence indicators for the other genres were biography 51.4%, children 8.0%, comedy 42.3%, documentary 21.6%, drama 54.5%, miniseries 9.1%, musical 18.4%, and romance 19.8%.

Violence and adult content are mainstays of movie programming on television. In terms of the prevalence of violence in evening movies, figure 4.1 indicates that 56.7% of the 11,603 movies shown from 6 PM to midnight during this time period were violent. Nearly half of the movies carried indicators for adult language (57%), adult situations (49.6%), and violence (46.5%). Nudity indicators were present on a quarter of these films.[9] Nearly 15% of these evening movies had indicators for all four types of content. G-rated films accounted for 3.4% of the films; PG-13, 13.4%; PG, 20.4%; and R, 31.7%. In terms of critics' ratings of the quality of films, the most frequent critics' rating was two stars

• *C H A P T E R 4* •

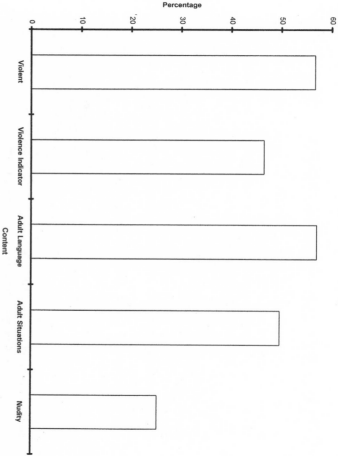

Figure 4.1. Content Characteristics of 1995–96 Evening Movies, Percentage of Movie Content

(43.2%), with only 4.1% getting four stars. If one focuses only on MPAA-rated films (7,989 movies), the levels of content indicators are even higher. For rated films, 63% carry violence indicators and 33.8% carry indicators for nudity.[10]

These high levels of content warnings arise in part because the sample includes numerous channels on basic cable and premium cable, which carry movies with higher levels of violence. Table A4.1 breaks down the sample by channel. The four major broadcast networks account for only 3.8% of the total number of films scheduled during prime time over this period. Basic cable channels such as AMC (10.2%) and Disney (6.3%) account for a large fraction of the films, although the largest contributors are the premium movie channels: HBO (8.6%); Encore (9.5%), Showtime (9.9%), the Movie Channel (10.1%), and Cinemax (11.7%). In terms of release year, over half of the films scheduled during these evening hours were released in the 1990s, with the highest fraction coming from 1993 and 1994 (consistent with the time lag during which movies progress from screen to video to premium or broadcast channels). A significant fraction of these films are distributed across seven violent genres: action adventure (10.7%), suspense (9.4%), science fiction–fantasy (7.8%), western (4.8%), horror (4.4%), crime mystery (2.0%), and war (1.5%).

Table 4.1 breaks down the early evening and prime-time movies by the three channel types of broadcast networks (i.e., ABC, CBS, Fox, NBC), basic cable channels, and premium cable channels.[11] The variation in content across these

TABLE 4.1
Content Characteristics of 11,587 Evening Movies, 1995–96, by Channel Type (%)

	Broadcast (N = 441)	Basic Cable (N = 5,362)	Premium Cable (N = 5,784)
Violent	41.3	47.8	66.3
Violence Indicator	23.1	29.1	64.5
Adult Language	29.0	32.2	82.2
Adult Situations	23.6	30.0	69.8
Nudity	10.9	13.5	36.9
Total Warnings			
0	62.8	53.3	6.7
1	10.0	10.9	11.0
2	10.2	17.7	28.2
3	11.6	14.0	29.0
4	5.4	4.2	25.1
Star Ratings			
Not Rated	48.3	6.6	7.8
1	3.6	9.3	18.8
2	29.5	40.0	47.4
3	17.5	37.4	24.2
4	1.1	6.8	1.8
MPAA Ratings			
Not Rated	61.0	49.5	11.7
G	1.8	5.6	1.5
PG	10.7	19.5	22.0
PG-13	10.7	6.2	20.3
R	15.9	19.2	44.5
NC-17	—	0.0	0.1

three channel types is consistent with variations in advertiser constraints and legal treatment of content across the three outlets. The broadcast networks reach the largest audiences, are solely dependent on advertiser revenue, and face federal regulation in terms of explicit indecency rules and implicit expectations about programming content necessary to gain license renewal. Basic cable in total attracts higher ratings than the premium channels, depends on a mix of cable fees and advertiser support, and is treated by the court as midway between broadcast and premium channels in terms of accessibility to children and prevalence in U.S. households. Premium channels as a segment attract the smallest audiences, depend solely on subscription decisions implicitly made each month by cable subscribers, are not dependent on advertisers, and are free to broadcast indecent programming under the theory that viewers invite these channels into their home by taking the affirmative step of subscribing.[12]

The broadcast television networks are close to basic cable channels in their selection of violent content in movies. Table 4.1 shows that 41.3% of prime-time broadcast movies were violent, versus 47.8% of basic cable and 66.3% of premium channels. Basic cable channels are also much closer to broadcast networks in terms of sexual content. For broadcast network movies, 29% had content indicators for adult language and 23.6% for adult situations, which were very close to the basic cable figures of 32.2% for language and 30% for adult situations. Premium cable movies had nearly three times the rate of nudity as films on the other two types of outlets, consistent with the different legal constraints, advertiser constraints, and audience expectations facing programmers across these media. Nearly 37% of the movies on premium cable had indicators for nudity, versus 13.5% for basic cable and 10.9% for broadcast television.

Premium channels are much more likely to rely on movies with a higher number of content warnings and on lower-quality films. Fully 25% of the evening films on premium channels carry all four warnings for violence, adult language, adult situations, and nudity, while only 4.2% of the movies on basic cable and 5.4% of the evening films on the four major broadcast networks merit this number of warnings. In terms of critics' ratings, basic cable carries a higher percentage of films viewed favorably by critics than premium channels. Nearly 19% of the films on premium channels are one-star movies while only 1.8% are four stars. By contrast, basic cable relies on one-star movies 9.3% of the time and carries four-star films 6.8% of the time. Note that critics' assessment of four-star movies are weighted heavily toward less recent films. Of four-star movies, 95.8% were made before 1990. Only four movies in the sample that were released after 1989 carried a four-star critics' rating: *Aladdin*, *Dances with Wolves*, *Howard's End*, and *Raise the Red Lantern*. The majority of premium films are recently produced (e.g., two-thirds were made after 1990). R-rated films account for 44.5% of the films on premium channels, versus 15.9% and 19.2% for broadcast networks and basic cable. This again demonstrates how premium channels have established themselves as providing movies with the higher levels of violence and sexual content associated with R-rated films.

One explanation for the differences among channel type might be that premium channels simply rely more on recent MPAA-rated movies, rather than the made for television movies associated with broadcast networks or the older theatrical films associated with basic cable. Only 11.7% of the films on premium channels did not have an MPAA rating, which indicates they may have been original programming made for cable or older films. Of the films on broadcast and basic cable, 61% and 49.5% were not rated by the MPAA. Age of films does explain part of these figures. While two-thirds of the films on premium were released after 1990, half of the films on basic cable were released before 1980. Consistent with the large role played by made for television movies on broadcast networks, half of the films shown on prime-time broadcast television during the sample period were made in 1994–96. Yet, if one examines only the films rated by the MPAA, table A4.2 demonstrates that premium channels still rely on movies with higher levels of violence and sexual content.[13]

Differences in content are clear across the three types of television channels. Within each type of programming outlet, there are also evident attempts to establish brand names for different types of content. Table 4.2 focuses on this

TABLE 4.2
Brand Positions of Television Channels, by Content of 11,587 Evening Movies, 1995–96 (%)

Channel	Violent	Violence Indicator	Adult Language	Adult Situations	Nudity
Broadcast					
ABC	42.5	32.1	35.1	28.4	13.4
CBS	35.7	15.1	17.5	13.5	6.3
Fox	56.1	33.3	50.9	43.9	14.0
NBC	38.8	17.2	23.3	18.1	10.3
Basic Cable					
A&E	63.0	50.0	33.3	46.3	29.6
AMC	40.3	6.3	6.6	7.7	1.5
Bravo	39.1	34.3	51.9	49.7	30.8
Comedy Central	37.3	37.3	83.4	75.1	29.6
Disney Channel	30.3	20.0	20.2	14.1	2.2
E!	55.0	45.0	33.3	38.3	23.3
Family Channel	57.2	15.5	8.0	11.2	0.0
Lifetime	25.7	9.8	19.3	21.3	8.7
Science Fiction	89.6	49.1	30.7	27.6	17.2
TBS	71.8	57.8	54.7	44.9	18.7
TNT	61.6	41.4	39.7	35.1	13.6
USA	63.0	49.7	55.9	55.1	31.1
WGN	75.9	67.1	52.4	54.7	18.8
Premium Cable					
Cinemax	74.7	74.1	92.4	78.0	51.4
Encore	43.5	38.6	57.0	54.9	19.2
HBO	72.8	72.4	92.6	70.9	35.6
Showtime	68.2	65.4	81.1	66.0	34.2
Movie Channel	70.7	70.0	86.6	77.3	40.6

"product differentiation" within each type of television channel. Consider first the four broadcast networks. The movies selected by Fox during prime time clearly set it apart from the other networks in terms of sex and violence, consistent with the network's general reputation among critics, viewers, advertisers, and government officials for using higher levels of potentially objectionable content.[14] Of the evening films on Fox, 56% were violent, compared with 42.5% for ABC, 38.8% for NBC, and 35.7% for CBS. Fox again was the outlier in terms of adult language, with 50.9% of its films carrying this warning versus 17.5% for CBS. Note that the relative rankings of Fox, ABC, NBC, and CBS are the same for indicators of violence, language, adult situations, and nudity. The gap between Fox and CBS in the use of violence and sex in movies is consistent with the age gap evident in the viewing audiences for these networks. For the May 1996 sweeps Fox finished second in the 18–34 demographic group, the adult viewers most likely to view violent programming. CBS finished fourth among the 18–34 demographic group and was said to be "moving back appealing to a slightly older audience," an audience less likely to consume violent programming.[15]

Within broadcast networks there is a definite brand image established for Fox as an outlier for violence and sexual content.[16] The networks are closer together in their use of violent content than in their use of adult language or situations. The span from low to high was smaller for violent content (Fox 56.1% vs. CBS 35.7%, roughly 20%) than for adult language (Fox 50.9% vs. CBS 17.5%, 33%) and adult situations (Fox 43.9% vs. CBS 13.5%, 30%). The span for nudity, which is used sparingly in films on broadcast movies, is much smaller (Fox 14.0% vs. CBS 6.3%, 8%). The results in table 4.2 for basic cable channels reveal that they span a larger range than the four broadcast networks and are more likely to be at the tails of the distribution of channels in terms of content indicators. In terms of violent films, the percentage of violent movies ranges from a high of 89.6% on the Science Fiction Channel to a low of 25.7% for Lifetime, the network aimed primarily at women 18–49, which yields a span of 64%. There are numerous basic channels with higher percentages of violent films than the broadcast channels, such as WGN (75.9%) and TBS (71.8%) (which are both also superstations—local broadcast stations that are carried nationally as part of basic cable packages). There are also several basic cable stations positioned below the broadcast networks in percentage of violent films, such as Comedy Central (37.3% violent) and the Disney Channel (30.3%). The Family Channel has a relatively high level of violent films (57.2%), traceable in part to the channel's heavy reliance on the western (19.8% of its evening films) and crime mystery genres (14.4% of its films).

If one examines the use of films most likely to contain heavy amounts of violence, those with violent indicators, the channels with likely brand names for nonviolence become clearer. AMC, which relies on earlier Hollywood movies, has violent indicators on only 6.3% of its programs (note that 91% of its films were made before 1968 and 51% before 1954). Lifetime, which markets itself as "the channel for women," programs movies with violent indicators for only 9.8% of its early evening and prime time films.[17] While the Family Channel ranked high in violent films because of its use of westerns, it used the type of recently released MPAA-rated movie that gets a violent indicator only sparingly. Only 15.5% of the Family Channel movies carried violence indicators. Films on the Disney Channel had violent indicators 20.0% of the time, compared with 67.1% by WGN, the top use among basic cable channels.

The span in adult language indicators runs on basic cable from a low of 6.6% for AMC (home to movies less likely to be released after 1968, when MPAA ratings started) to a high of 83.4% for Comedy Central, a figure consistent with the channel's use of comedy that often involves adult topics.[18] The Family Channel also had an extremely low percentage of movies with language indicators, 8.0%, which fits with concern among parents with the extent of adult language on television.

There is a correlation between use of movies with violent indicators and those with indicators for adult situations. Since these types of content often appear within the same movie, it is not surprising that table 4.2 indicates that basic cable channels with moderate to high levels of violence indicators also have moderate to high levels of adult situations. When the two types of content are compared, however, it becomes clear that among basic cable channels with moderate to high levels of both types of content that programmers will choose to use either violence or sexual content more heavily in their evening films. In terms of the percentage of films with violent indicators versus the percentage with adult situations, WGN (67.1% vs. 54.7%), TBS (57.8% vs. 44.9%), and the Science Fiction Channel (49.1% vs. 27.6%) program films with moderate or high levels of both content but use more violence than sex; in contrast, Bravo (34.3% vs. 49.7%) and Comedy Central (37.3% vs. 75.1%) are much more likely to attract audiences by using films with adult situations. Consistent with family brand images, the Disney Channel and the Family Channel are unlikely to program films in prime time that involve adult situations (14.1% and 11.2%, respectively). Lifetime uses a relatively low percentage of films with indicators for adult situations (21.3%), although, given its extremely low use of violence, this means that its programming mix has more adult situations than violence.

Use of films with indicators for nudity also appears to be part of establishing brand positions in prime time on basic cable. The Family Channel (0%) and Disney Channel (2.2%) are free of this type of content in evening movie programming. The outliers at the other end of the spectrum may represent different uses of nudity in film programming strategies. The highest percentage of films using nudity among basic cable channels is on the USA Network, whose 31.1% of films with nudity indicators is comparable with the level of nudity on premium channels such as HBO and Showtime. This network has a brand reputation in part for showing films with little critical acclaim and higher than average nudity, including movies with such titles as *Campus Hustle, Hardbodies,* and *Illicit Behavior.* For the films on USA with nudity warnings, the average critics' rating was 1.9 stars. In contrast, Bravo has a reputation for programming "art films," where nudity may be associated more with a narrative story. Movies with nudity indicators on Bravo included *La Dolce Vita, Romeo and Juliet,* and *The Last Metro.* For the programs on Bravo with nudity, the average star rating was 2.5. On the Arts and Entertainment Network, 29.6% of the films have nudity indicators, with an average star rating of 3.0. Excluding the Disney and Family Channels, the channels with the two lowest percentages of nudity either rely on older films (AMC, 1.5%) or target female viewers (Lifetime, 8.7%). The average star ratings for films with nudity indicators was 2.0 on TNT, 2.1 on TBS, 2.5 on Lifetime, and 2.8 on AMC. There thus appears to be a range of quality in the films that carry nudity indicators, with a channel such as USA programming films that contain nudity with low critical appeal and Bravo programming films that contain nudity used in stories that earn higher critical reviews.

Part of these differences in content arises from the differences in channels' use of recent MPAA-rated (which tend to have higher warning levels) versus older MPAA-rated films, of theatrical films released before the MPAA started rating films in 1968, or original programming.[19] If one totals the number of warning indicators per film for violence, adult language, adult situations, and nudity, the trend in average warnings per film is increasing over time. For the MPAA-rated films in the sample produced during the 1970s, the average number of warning indicators per films was 2.0. This grew to 2.4 for films produced in the 1980s to 2.7 for those MPAA-rated films produced in the 1990s. Even within this decade the trend has continued, with the mean number of warnings growing from 2.5 for films produced in 1990 to 3.0 for those produced in 1995.[20]

Premium cable channels generally show recently released unedited theatrical films, which in part creates a brand name for programming films with higher levels of controversial content than are available on broadcast television. Table 4.2 shows that, in general, the individual premium channels rank higher than broadcast or basic cable in terms of content indicators. Even within premium channels, however, there are identifiable differences in programming strategy.[21] If these five channels are ranked in terms of indicators, Encore has much lower rates of controversial content than the other channels, consistent with its attempt to develop a brand identity for high-quality, low-violence programming. Consider the contrast between Cinemax and Encore on violence indicators (74.1% vs. 38.6%), adult language (92.4% vs. 57%), adult situations (78.0% vs. 54.9%), and nudity (51.4% vs. 19.2%). Encore has clearly positioned itself as less likely to use controversial content than the other premium channels. As the channel's director of marketing put it: "We don't have gratuitous sex or violence. We think the country is ready for a lot less violence. Our movies are more wholesome and family oriented."[22] The other four channels are clustered together in terms of their use of violence, adult language, and adult situations, although Cinemax tends to rank number 1 and Showtime number 4 in the use of these types of programming. The widest difference among premium channels is in the use of nudity. Cinemax is clearly more likely to use films involving nudity (51.4%) than HBO, Showtime, or the Movie Channel.[23]

Brand positioning is also evident in decisions about what combinations of potentially controversial types of programming to use and what quality of films to schedule. Table 4.3 offers evidence on these programming decisions by describing the distribution of a channel's movies by indicator warning count (the sum of indicators for violence, adult language, adult situations, and nudity) and star ratings by films critics. ABC (7.5%) and Fox (5.3%) had the highest percentage of movies with four warnings among the broadcast channels, consistent with the earlier evidence on the use of controversial content by these networks. These percentages would place them toward the middle of the spectrum in basic cable. Three channels appeared to avoid using movies with four warnings: AMC (0%), Family Channel (0%), and Disney (.4%). WGN (12.4%) and the Science Fiction Channel (11.0%) had nearly double the rate of use of movies with four warnings when compared to broadcast channels. Movies with warnings for each category of violence, adult language, adult situations, and nudity, however, play their most prominent role in premium cable programming.

TABLE 4.3
Distribution of Content Indicators for 11,587 Evening Movies, 1995–96, by Channel (%)

Channel	Warning Indicators					Star Ratings					Mean Stars, Violent Indicator Movies
	0	1	2	3	4	NR	1	2	3	4	
Broadcast											
ABC	53.0	13.4	11.9	14.2	7.5	38.8	4.5	34.3	20.1	2.2	2.3
CBS	76.2	8.7	5.6	5.6	4.0	60.3	2.4	20.6	15.9	0.8	2.5
Fox	42.1	8.8	19.3	24.6	5.3	36.8	8.8	33.3	21.1	0.0	2.2
NBC	69.8	8.6	8.6	8.6	4.3	50.9	1.7	31.9	14.7	0.9	2.4
Basic Cable											
A&E	40.7	5.6	18.5	24.1	11.1	13.0	3.7	29.6	44.4	9.3	2.7
AMC	89.0	2.4	6.2	2.4	0.0	0.1	1.9	36.8	49.9	11.3	2.7
Bravo	26.9	16.3	26.1	24.4	6.2	1.0	7.2	25.7	58.0	8.1	2.5
Comedy Central	3.0	14.2	43.2	33.7	5.9	1.2	17.8	45.6	35.5	0.0	2.3
Disney Channel	64.8	18.3	12.8	3.7	0.4	8.2	4.1	43.5	36.8	7.5	2.5
E!	45.0	15.0	10.0	15.0	15.0	3.3	33.3	48.3	15.0	0.0	1.6
Family Channel	81.8	4.3	11.2	2.7	0.0	13.4	3.7	51.9	28.3	2.7	2.4
Lifetime	74.3	6.5	8.5	7.0	3.7	18.7	4.6	60.0	16.5	0.2	2.5
Science Fiction	47.2	12.3	20.2	9.2	11.0	4.9	22.7	44.2	22.1	6.1	2.1
TBS	25.1	11.7	30.9	26.3	6.0	6.4	15.0	39.5	33.5	5.6	2.2
TNT	44.3	11.0	20.8	18.2	5.7	10.5	17.6	33.1	30.0	8.8	2.1
USA	18.1	15.9	29.5	28.4	8.1	14.9	20.3	44.3	18.4	2.2	2.0
WGN	21.8	15.9	22.4	27.6	12.4	3.5	15.3	47.1	27.1	7.1	2.2
Premium Cable											
Cinemax	0.9	6.5	24.8	29.2	38.6	8.5	24.7	50.9	15.4	0.5	1.9
Encore	22.3	18.2	31.6	23.3	4.6	1.3	10.2	36.3	46.9	5.3	2.5
HBO	1.6	10.3	28.3	33.8	25.9	11.6	15.7	56.2	16.2	0.3	2.0
Showtime	7.4	11.6	29.7	27.5	23.8	15.3	18.4	46.6	18.7	1.0	1.9
Movie Channel	2.2	9.5	27.6	31.6	29.1	2.6	23.1	46.8	25.2	2.2	2.0

Again, Cinemax offers the most controversial programming mix—38.6% of its movies have indicators for all four content areas. Encore has carved out a niche more resembling broadcast programming, for it has only 4.6% of its films with 4 warnings (a percentage lower than that for Fox and ABC). The percentages are clustered for the Movie Channel (29.1%), HBO (25.9%), and Showtime (23.8%).

Channels may also choose to compete in movie quality. A number of movie types, such as made for television movies and other original programming genres, are not often evaluated in the critics' star ratings provided in viewer guides. Of the 1,022 films in the prime-time sample without a critic's rating, 72% also lacked MPAA ratings, which indicates that these were probably films made originally for broadcast or cable networks.[24] A channel might thus broadcast a "four-star" original program that would end up in a viewing guide as unevaluated (no stars). The star ratings still allow one to examine how the distribution of "critically acclaimed" films varies across channels. Table 4.3 indicates that basic cable channels have the highest percentage of films with four stars. The four-star movies are populated heavily by older films. Of the 476 offerings that rated four stars, half were released before 1960 and 70% were released before 1971. The most recently released four-star movies in the sample were *Aladdin* and *Howard's End*, released in 1992. With their emphasis on older films, it is thus not surprising that basic cable channels rated higher use of four-star films. AMC (11.3%), A&E (9.3%), Bravo (8.1%), and Disney (7.5%) ranked high in use of these four star films. Two stations noted in the previous analysis for showing violent films also showed more four-star movies, TNT (8.8%) and WGN (7.1%). Among premium channels, Encore is the outlier with 5.3% four-star films. HBO's .3% is nearly the lowest percentage of these films, except for Comedy Central (0%) and Fox (0%).

While broadcast networks rarely show four-star movies, they also rarely program one-star movies. Fox had the highest percentage of one-star films (8.8%). In the basic cable universe, USA (20.3%) and the Science Fiction Channel (22.7%) had the highest percentages of one-star films, consistent with the expectation that both these channels may sometimes feature "low-budget," low-quality programming.[25] Within the premium channel world there are stark differences in the quality locations chosen by Encore and Cinemax. Nearly a quarter (24.7%) of the films shown by Cinemax are one-star films, versus 10.2% for Encore.[26] Half of the films shown by Cinemax are two-star, as contrasted with the 46.9% for three-star films on Encore.

Table 4.3 indicates that brand positions for quality are evident even among the set of movies that carry content indicators for violence. Among films marked with an indicator for violence, Fox has the lowest mean star rating (2.2) and CBS the highest (2.5). Within the basic cable networks, channels with reputations for using "higher-quality" films also program violent films of higher quality. The mean critics' ratings for films with violent indicators on AMC (2.7) and Bravo (2.5) are much higher than those on USA (2.0), TNT (2.1), and WGN (2.2). Differentiations evident among premium cable channels in film quality also hold true among the subset of films with violent indicators. When Encore does program a film with a violent indicator, the mean critics' rating is 2.5, in contrast with 1.9 for Cinemax and Showtime. While few violent films garner four-star ratings, there are evident differences in the interaction of violent content and critical ratings in the programming selections of the channels in the sample.

Another way to summarize the brand positions chosen by the channels in their use of films is to examine evening movie programming by the MPAA ratings for films, as reported in table A4.4. Note that many channels rely on films not rated by the MPAA, since in the case of broadcast networks they may be showing made-for-television films or in the case of AMC or the Family Channel they may be showing older theatrical films not rated by the MPAA (94% of AMC's offerings were made before 1970, as were 40% for the Family

Channel). For broadcast networks, Fox leads in terms of the percentage of R-rated films it shows (40.4%), followed by ABC at 17.9%. Neither Fox (aimed at young adults) nor CBS (aimed at older viewers) broadcast a G-rated movie during this time period. If one restricts the analysis to only MPAA-rated films, Fox has the highest use of R-rated films (67.6%) and NBC relies the least on these films (21.6%). In terms of rated films, NBC relies much more heavily on PG-13 films (40.5%) than Fox (17.6%) or the other broadcast networks.

For basic cable, the patterns established earlier by use of sex and violence are confirmed by the distribution of film ratings by channel. Disney has the highest percentage of films that are G-rated at 24% and the lowest use (next to the Family Channel's 0%) of R-rated films. R-rated films comprise 42.6% of the offerings on Comedy Central, 39.5% on USA, and 46.5% on WGN. Use of R-rated films peaks on premium channels. For Cinemax, 57.1% of its prime-time programming involves R-rated films, versus 20.7% for Encore. In contrast, 44.8% of Encore's films are rated PG, consistent with its emphasis on family friendly programs.[27]

The provision of content indicators, MPAA ratings, and star rankings in the viewer guide allows one to analyze how content varies across MPAA and critic ratings.[28] Table 4.4 indicates that there is a clear jump in content potentially objectionable to parents between G and PG. None of the G movies had indicators for language or nudity, and only 4.3% had indicators for violence and 1.5% for adult situations. For PG and PG-13, there are again clear differences between language (81.6% for PG-13 vs. 68.8% PG), adult situations (71.9% vs. 57.9%), and nudity (24.0% vs. 8.2%). There is very little difference in terms of

TABLE 4.4
Content by MPAA Ratings and Star Ratings

	% of Movies Rating Category					Mean Number by Category		
	V	VI	AL	AS	N	Warnings	Stars	N
MPAA Rating								
Not Rated	42.9	10.0	9.5	10.2	5.6	0.4	2.5	3,612
G	4.3	4.3	0.0	1.5	0.0	0.1	2.6	393
PG	52.5	52.5	68.8	57.9	8.2	1.9	2.4	2,364
PG-13	56.3	56.3	81.6	71.9	24.0	2.3	2.1	1,553
R	78.7	78.7	91.8	78.6	58.1	3.1	2.0	3,673
Star Rating								
Not Rated	56.1	35.2	37.7	32.9	22.9	1.3	—	1,022
1	69.5	66.7	81.3	69.6	45.9	2.7	—	1,600
2	59.8	50.2	61.6	51.2	25.3	1.9	—	5,016
3	48.2	37.4	49.3	45.6	18.1	1.5	—	3,489
4	44.8	29.4	25.6	30.3	8.0	0.9	—	476

Note: Categories include violent movies (V) and movies with indicators for violence (VI), adult language (AL), adult situations (AS), and nudity (N). Mean star ratings are for movies receiving a star rating on the 1–4 scale.

the percentage of violence indicators for PG movies (52.5%) versus PG-13 (56.3%).[29] While the MPAA provides four different levels of gradations for nudity and language, there are only really three distinguishable levels in violence. This makes it difficult for viewers to infer simply from a PG or PG-13 rating the level of violence in a film. The mean number of warning indicators reinforce the similarity of PG and PG-13 movies. The number of warning indicators by MPAA ratings is .1 for G, 1.9 for PG, 2.3 for PG-13, and 3.1 for R.[30]

For each of the content indicators, the percentage of films with a given content indicator declined as the number of stars increased. Whereas 66.7% of one-star films had a violence indicator, only 29.4% of the four-star films had violence indicators. Although debates about television violence often invoke the case of *Schindler's List* as an example of how violence can be part of a high-quality film, for the sample of over 11,000 early evening and prime-time films shown from February 1995 through March 1996 only 1.4% were four-star movies with violent indicators.[31] Of the movies with violent indicators that had star ratings, 20% were one-star, 50% two-star, 27% three-star, and 4% four-star. Use of nudity, adult language, and adult situations also declines consistently as the number of critical stars increases. One-star movies average 2.7 indicator warnings, whereas four-star films average .9 indicators. These figures do not suggest that high levels of violence, language, adult situations, or nudity are central to the creation of highly acclaimed films, at least for the sample of films on broadcast, basic cable, and premium channels analyzed here.

SCHEDULING STRATEGIES: ARE THE "SWEEPS" MONTHS MORE VIOLENT?

Channels clearly establish brand positions in their use of violent and sexual content in evening movies. This distribution could reflect a distribution in creative expression, so that violent content arises out of narrative needs. Broadcast officials often assert that violent programming is part of a creative rather than a commercial process. If this were true, then there would be no reason to expect that creative needs to use violence should be correlated with sweeps months, the periods during which local and national ratings are measured by Nielsen. This section uses scheduling changes between sweeps versus nonsweeps months to examine the commercial incentives involved in scheduling violent programming.

National television ratings for programs are available the day after their broadcast since the Nielsen company maintains a national sample of households whose televisions are continuously monitored electronically. In major television markets that account for over 52% of U.S. television households, Nielsen also provides overnight local market ratings from households whose televisions are electronically metered.[32] Four times a year, in February, May, July, and November, Nielsen develops estimates of local ratings for each of the 211 television markets in the United States by having viewers fill out diaries recording their viewing patterns. The ratings in these "sweeps" months help set local advertising rates. To aid their local affiliates (and the fortunes of the local stations they own), the broadcast networks often devote a great deal of attention and resources to scheduling programming during sweeps months that is designed to attract ratings. Basic cable networks also face incentives to increase ratings during sweeps months, since part of their revenues also depend on advertising. Premium channels are not dependent on advertiser responses to ratings, although they may face some incentives to respond to advertiser supported networks' sweeps scheduling if they felt these programming changes would affect their attempts to attract or retain subscribers.

At a broad level of analysis, there at first appear to be few differences in movie content when the full movie sample of 11,603 films is divided into sweeps versus nonsweeps month. Violent movies account for 55.8% of the evening films in sweeps months versus 57.1% in nonsweeps periods. In terms of comparing films with content indicators in sweeps versus nonsweeps periods, the percentages of the full sample of movies with violence indicators (46.4% vs. 46.6%), adult language (56.0% vs. 57.2%), adult situations (49.1% vs. 50.6%), and nudity (24.8% vs. 25.6%) are similar across these two sets of months.[33] For the three types of channels there again appear to be few differences in the net use of violent programming in sweeps months. The percentages of violent movies in sweeps versus nonsweeps periods are 41.6% versus 40.5% for broadcast networks, 48.2% versus 46.9% for basic cable, and 66.7% versus 65.4% for premium channels.

At the aggregate level, slightly stronger evidence that broadcast networks face incentives to use "controversial" content to attract ratings during sweeps periods comes from an analysis of the use of MPAA-rated films. In comparing the use of rated movies with four content indicators (i.e., one for violence, language, adult situations, and nudity), one finds that the use by the four broadcast networks of these movies with four warnings increases from 10.4% of the MPAA-rated films shown during nonsweeps periods to 19.3% scheduled during sweeps.[34] The use of rated films with four warnings remains the same for basic cable channels (8.1% nonsweeps vs. 8.3% sweeps) and for premium channels (25.4% nonsweeps vs. 27.0% sweeps).

Although the aggregate analysis provides little evidence of differences in sweeps programming, analysis of the programming decisions of individual channels clearly demonstrates how some networks increase and some networks decrease the use of violence and sexual content during the ratings races in sweeps periods. Tables 4.5 examines how the percentage of films that are violent and percentage of films that carry violent indicators (which are generally MPAA-rated films) vary during sweeps months by channel. One of the largest increases in the use of violent programming occurs for a basic cable channel, WGN. This Chicago station is also a local independent broadcast station, however, so it faces particularly high incentives to increase ratings during the sweeps period since these determine local ad rates. The percentage of violent movies on WGN increases from 70.1% to 88.7% during sweeps months, while the use of movies with violent indicators jumps from 59% to 84.9%.[35]

• C H A P T E R 4 •

TABLE 4.5
Sweeps Violent Programming Strategy, by Channel

Channel	% Violent		% Violent Indicator		No. of Films
	Nonsweeps	Sweeps	Nonsweeps	Sweeps	
Broadcast					
ABC	40.0	47.7	28.9	38.6	134
CBS	39.0	29.6	15.6	13.6	126
Fox	42.1	84.2	29.0	42.1	57
NBC	46.1	25.0	19.7	12.5	116
Basic Cable					
AMC	42.1	36.6	6.6	5.7	1,186
Bravo	41.0	34.8	35.2	32.1	724
Comedy Central	33.9	44.4	33.9	44.4	169
Disney Channel	32.1	26.7	20.4	19.2	736
Family Channel	59.2	53.7	14.2	17.9	187
Lifetime	24.3	28.8	8.4	13.0	460
Science Fiction	90.6	86.7	46.2	56.5	163
TBS	70.3	75.2	57.9	57.7	486
TNT	62.0	60.4	39.8	45.8	544
USA	62.3	64.4	48.0	53.4	370
WGN	70.1	88.7	59.0	84.9	170
Premium Cable					
Cinemax	74.0	76.3	73.7	74.9	1,361
Encore	45.4	39.4	40.2	35.1	1,106
HBO	71.8	75.0	71.3	75.0	996
Showtime	69.5	65.3	66.3	63.4	1,147
Movie Channel	71.1	69.8	70.7	68.5	1,174

Each of the major broadcast networks uses a different mix of violent films in sweeps programming, yet these programming moves can be in opposite directions. Fox and ABC both increased their percentage of violent films in sweeps months, while NBC and CBS decreased their use of violent movies. The most marked increase came on Fox, where the percentage of violent movies doubled during sweeps months from 42.1% to 84.2%. For ABC, the percentage of violent films increased but at a slower pace, from 40% to 47.7%. NBC dramatically reduced its reliance on violent films, from 46.1% in nonsweeps to 25.0%. CBS also dropped its percentage of violent films from 39% to 29.6%.[36]

While the "violent" film definition includes made-for-television movies in violent genres as well as MPAA-rated films that carry a violent indicator, the films with violent indicators (most of which were previously released in theaters) may be of special concern in terms of the intensity of violence. Table 4.5 demonstrates that the patterns of sweeps broadcasting of these films with violent indicators fell in line with the spatial positions established in the nonsweeps periods. Fox and ABC ranked first and second among the four major broadcast networks in nonsweeps programming use of movies with violent indicators, and both these networks increased their use of these films as ratings were measured in local markets. The use of movies with violent indicators increased from 29.0% to 42.1% on Fox, while ABC increased its use of these films from 28.9% to 38.6%.[37] From the standpoint of potential exposures of children, the Fox programming shifts during sweeps period are particularly problematic since all of its movies began airing before the 9 PM starting time generally used by the other networks.[38] NBC's use of films with violent indicators dropped from 19.7% to 12.5% during sweeps, while CBS used 15.6% during nonsweeps and 13.6% during sweeps. The sweeps period thus caused the "span" of brand positions to expand from a range of 15.6% to 29.0% in nonsweeps to 13.6% to 42.1% during the sweeps period.

Individual basic and premium channels generally showed smaller changes in the use of violence during the sweeps period than the individual broadcast channels. The use of violent movies decreased on a set of channels that market themselves as programmers of "quality" films: Bravo (41% to 34.8%); Disney (32.1% to 26.7%); Encore (45.4% to 39.4%); and the Family Channel (59.2% to 53.7%). Both TBS and HBO increased their use of violent movies (TBS from 70.3% to 75.2%, HBO from 71.8% to 75%). Comedy Central increased its use of violent movies from 33.9% to 44.4%, a pattern that also held for its use of films with violent indicators. In terms of the films with violent indicators, their use increased during sweeps months on TNT and the Science Fiction Channel, two channels with substantial programming aimed at male viewers. Note that the use of films with violent indicators also increased on the basic cable channel aimed primarily at women (Lifetime), although the percentage only increased from 8.4% to 13%.

Table 4.6 reveals that the many of the same channels which changed their use of violent content in sweeps programming also changed their use of films with indicators for adult situations and nudity. The use of violent and sexual content tended to be in the same direction. Just as WGN dramatically increased its use of violent programming in sweeps periods, this channel also increased its use of movies with indicators of adult situations (48.7% in nonsweeps, 60.4% in sweeps) and nudity (15.4% in nonsweeps, 26.4% in sweeps).[39] Among the broadcast networks, ABC increased its use of films with indicators of adult situations (from 23.3% to 38.6%) and nudity (7.8% to 25%) during sweeps. Fox actually dropped its use of movies with adult situations and nudity as it increased its dependence on violent programming during the sweeps. CBS reduced its use of movies with adult situations from 17.1% to 6.8%, while NBC reduced its use of movies with nudity indicators from 14.5% to 2.5%.[40] The channels with potentially the strongest interest in maintaining a family friendly brand identity, the Disney Channel and the Family Channel, continued to refrain from broadcasting movies with sexual content. The percentage of films with nudity indicators remained at 0 for the Family Channel for both sweeps and nonsweeps, while the adult situation indicator percentages were 10% and 13.4% for these periods. For Disney, nudity indicators were on 1.8% of films in nonsweeps versus 2.9 in sweeps, while the figures for adult situations were

TABLE 4.6
Sweeps Sexual Programming Strategy, by Channel

Channel	% Adult Situations		% Nudity		No. of Films
	Nonsweeps	Sweeps	Nonsweeps	Sweeps	
Broadcast					
ABC	23.3	38.6	7.8	25.0	134
CBS	17.1	6.8	6.1	6.8	126
Fox	47.4	36.8	15.8	10.5	57
NBC	19.7	15.0	14.5	2.5	116
Basic Cable					
AMC	8.0	7.1	1.6	1.3	1,186
Bravo	49.8	49.6	32.6	26.8	724
Comedy Central	73.9	77.8	30.4	27.8	169
Disney Channel	14.1	14.2	1.8	2.9	736
Family Channel	10.0	13.4	0.0	0.0	187
Lifetime	20.9	22.3	8.1	10.1	460
Science Fiction	25.6	32.6	17.1	17.4	163
TBS	45.4	43.6	18.1	20.1	486
TNT	32.3	43.1	11.8	18.8	544
USA	56.4	52.5	33.3	26.3	370
WGN	48.7	60.4	15.4	26.4	170
Premium Cable					
Cinemax	76.5	81.2	50.7	52.8	1,361
Encore	54.5	55.8	17.6	22.7	1,106
HBO	70.0	73.0	36.8	33.0	996
Showtime	66.6	64.7	33.9	34.7	1,147
Movie Channel	75.8	80.7	40.0	42.1	1,174

nearly identical (14.1% in nonsweeps, 14.2% in sweeps).[41] Two channels targeted strongly toward men that increased use of movies with violent indicators also increased their use of adult situations and nudity during the sweeps period. Nudity indicators went from 11.8% to 18.8% and adult situation figures grew from 32.3% to 43.1% for TNT during sweeps. For the Science Fiction Channel, adult situations also increased during sweeps, from 25.6% of films to 32.6%.

The variation in use of violence during sweeps is not unique to the 1995–96 sample period. The set of 2,295 movies shown on broadcast network television in prime time from September 1987 through September 1993 described in chapter 2 demonstrates that the broadcast networks used violent content as a competitive tool during sweeps months in those years. This dataset includes information on movies from May 1993, a month described by television critic Tom Shales as "the most violent sweeps month in TV history—a month in which movie after movie has dramatized ghastly true-life crimes and in which a deplorable ABC miniseries [*Murder in the Heartland*] about the killing spree of Charles Starkweather apparently inspired one young Canadian man to commit similar murders."[42] As another journalist described this movie in 1994, "the bloody docudrama, which aired during a May sweeps marked by wall-to-wall guns and gore, came to symbolize excessive television violence during hearings in Washington last spring and summer. In July, Ted Harbert, president of ABC's entertainment division, said it was a mistake to have aired the film."[43] The Chairman of Capital Cities/ABC later said that the airing of the film "was an economic disaster. All the advertisers left the show because it had the violence. It did not get particularly good ratings."[44] After the 1993 hearings in which the networks were publicly excoriated by legislators for their use of violent programming in sweeps, industry officials promised to reduce the level of violence in programming. Eventually, however, the networks began to assert again that legislators had unfairly characterized their programming. Six months after the May 1993 sweeps, ABC president Robert Iger said that, "I don't think the networks when it comes to violence have anything to be guilty about." He declared that, "'Murder in the Heartland' was a high-quality program that dealt with the subject of violent mass murder in a responsible fashion, in a quality fashion."[45]

Was the May 1993 sweeps month an aberration, or are the networks more likely to use violent content during sweeps to attract ratings? Table 4.7 indicates that from 1987 to 1993 the four broadcast networks did use violent content differently in sweeps versus nonsweeps months. Specifically, during sweeps months the networks were more likely to program movies with violent content (especially the type of violent content that appeals to female viewers), more likely to promote the presence of violence in advertising for these films, and less likely to use viewer discretion warnings on films that focus on murder. In

TABLE 4.7

Use of Violent Content in Prime-Time Broadcast Network Movies, Sweeps versus Nonsweeps Months, 1987–93 (%)

	Sweeps Months (N = 944)	Non-Sweeps Months (N = 1,723)	Difference of Proportions Test (Z Statistic)
Murder Theme	32.7	28.9	2.1**
Family Crime Theme	6.5	3.3	3.8***
True Story	23.2	16.5	4.2***
True Murder	10.7	4.6	5.9***
True Family Crime	4.2	1.6	4.2***
TV Guide Ad Features Homicide	13.9	9.5	3.4***
TV Guide Ad Features Dead Body	0.9	0.3	2.0**
TV Guide Indicates Film Is Particularly Violent	4.1	3.1	1.3
Warning Provided	2.8	3.3	−0.7
Murder Theme and Warning Provided	1.0	2.0	−2.0**

Note: *** = statistically significant at the .01 level; ** = significant at the .05 level.

sweeps months 32.7% of the films programmed by the networks dealt with murder, versus 28.9% for those in nonsweeps months. Family crime stories were offered at nearly twice their normal rate in sweeps programming (6.5% in sweeps vs. 3.3% in nonsweeps). True murder stories (10.7% sweeps vs. 4.6% nonsweeps) and true family crime stories (4.2% vs. 1.6%) were also more prevalent when ratings were being measured by Nielsen. The use of violence also extended to print ads taken in *TV Guide* by the networks. Movies during sweeps months were more likely to have ads that focused on homicide and more likely to have ads that showed dead bodies. Despite the use of violent content during sweeps, networks were not more likely to use viewer discretion warnings during sweeps months. In fact, the percentage of films that dealt with murder and had viewer discretion warnings was higher in nonsweeps months than in the sweeps periods. These results demonstrate that for the period from September 1987 through September 1993, the broadcast networks were more likely to use and promote violent programming in sweeps months.

COUNTERPROGRAMMING WITH VIOLENCE?

While the measurement of ratings clearly affects the incentives to use violent programming during different months of the year, violence may also be part of a strategy in countering programming offered on a particular evening. Consider the response of channels to ABC's airing of *NFL Monday Night Football* (*MNF*). This broadcast draws a large number of male viewers to ABC during the fall and early winter. Among adult demographic groups, the program draws ratings among men that are two times greater than those for women.[46]

Table 4.8 details how channels react that regularly program movies from 8 PM to midnight on Monday evenings. Many channels drop their use of violent movies on nights when *MNF* is being aired by ABC, in part ceding the likely audience for "violence" to ABC. When *MNF* goes off the air at the end of the regular football season, these channels increase their use of violent films to attract the former football audience to their programming. The percentage of violent movies drops appreciably when *MNF* is on for Cinemax (78.4% without *MNF* to 64.6% with) and also for Showtime (75.3% to 61.7%) and NBC (42.9% to 35.3%), although only the Cinemax difference is statistically significant at the .10 level. The largest response is the drop of violence on TBS. When *Monday Night Football* is on, TBS programs movies that are violent for 64.7% of the time. Once *Monday Night Football* is not shown, 91.9% of the films that TBS shows are violent. Some channels do not alter their mix of violence to counterprogram. The percentage of violent films is 81.3% with *MNF* and 81.7% without *MNF* on HBO, while it is 50% with and 51.5% without on Encore. Some channels actually increase their use of violent programming when *Monday Night Football* is on, perhaps to pry away marginal viewers from this ABC program. The percentage of violent movies increases from 25% to 44.1% on Bravo with the advent of *Monday Night Football*. TNT clearly engages in

TABLE 4.8

Counterprogramming against ABC's *NFL Monday Night Football*

| Channel | % of Violent Films, Full Sample | | | | Difference of Proportion Test (Z Statistic) |
	Mondays with Monday Night Football	N	Mondays without Monday Night Football	N	
Network					
NBC	35.3	17	42.9	35	−0.5
Basic Cable					
AMC	43.8	48	30.0	80	1.6
Bravo	44.1	34	25.0	60	1.9*
Disney Channel	38.1	21	28.6	49	0.8
Lifetime	50.0	20	27.8	36	1.7
TBS	64.7	17	91.9	37	−2.2**
TNT	76.5	17	39.2	51	3.0***
Premium Cable					
Cinemax	64.6	48	78.4	102	−1.7*
Encore	50.0	34	51.5	68	−0.1
HBO	81.3	32	81.7	71	−0.1
Showtime	61.7	47	75.3	73	−1.6
Movie Channel	76.5	34	71.4	70	0.6

Note: *** = statistically significant at the .01 level; ** = significant at the .05 level; * = significant at the .10 level.

counterprogramming against football, for the percentage of violent movies increases to 76.5% from 39.2% when *MNF* is shown. Note that TBS and TNT take opposite approaches to airing violent movies in response to *Monday Night Football*, consistent with models that indicate that ownership of multiple channels may lead to diverse programming responses.[47]

While sweeps programming and the concentration of viewers on evenings when *Monday Night Football* airs present channels with different incentives to change their use of violent programming, there are also returns to creating a brand name for consistently showing a given type of program at a given time on a given day each week. For the 11,603 movies shown over the course of 51 weeks on the thirty-two channels in the sample, I looked at how frequently films with particular types of content appeared on the same day, channel, and starting time. Table 4.9 shows the top ten combinations of day, channel, and starting time for three different types of content: violent movies, films with indicators for adult situations, and films with indicators for nudity. The results demonstrate that programmers clearly choose to broadcast particular types of movies in the same time and day slot over the course of a year. Out of the 51 weeks of programming in the sample, Cinemax broadcast a violent movie 51 times on Saturdays at 10 PM. Note seven of the top ten slots with violent movies are for films that start at 8 PM, which suggests the lack of a "family

TABLE 4.9
Top Ten Most Frequent Channel-Day-Time Combinations for
Particular Types of Movies

Type	Frequency within 51-Week Sample	Mean Star Rating
Violent		
Cinemax-Saturday-10 PM	51	1.6
Cinemax-Tuesday-8 PM	50	2.0
HBO-Friday-8 PM	48	1.9
Cinemax-Saturday-8 PM	47	2.0
HBO-Sunday-8 PM	46	2.1
Showtime-Tuesday-8 PM	44	1.8
Movie Channel-Saturday-8 PM	44	1.6
Cinemax-Friday-8 PM	43	1.9
HBO-Thursday-9 PM	43	1.4
Cinemax-Sunday-8 PM	42	2.0
Adult Situations		
Cinemax-Tuesday-8 PM	50	1.9
HBO-Friday-8 PM	45	1.9
Cinemax-Thursday-8 PM	44	2.2
Movie Channel-Thursday-9 PM	44	2.1
Cinemax-Friday-8 PM	43	1.9
Cinemax-Sunday-8 PM	42	1.9
Movie Channel-Friday-9 PM	42	2.2
Cinemax-Saturday-8 PM	41	2.0
Comedy Central-Wednesday-8 PM	41	2.3
Movie Channel-Tuesday-9 PM	41	2.2
Nudity		
Cinemax-Tuesday-8 PM	42	1.8
Cinemax-Friday-8 PM	33	1.9
Cinemax-Saturday-11:30 PM	33	1.4
Cinemax-Saturday-8 PM	32	1.8
HBO-Friday-8 PM	31	1.8
Cinemax-Saturday-10 PM	30	1.4
Movie Channel-Saturday-9 PM	30	1.4
USA-Saturday-11 PM	27	1.6
Bravo-Friday-8 PM	26	2.4
Cinemax-Thursday-8 PM	26	2.1

Note: Mean star ratings are for those films rated on the 1–4 star critics' scale.

hour" for premium channel programmers. There is a high overlap between the most frequent time slots for violent movies and those for adult situations and nudity. Seven of the top ten violent movie slots also appear on the top ten rankings for adult situations or nudity. For example, Tuesday at 8 PM on Cinemax ranks second in frequency of violent films, first in frequency of nudity, and first in adult situations. HBO's Friday at 8 PM slot ranks third in frequency of violence, second in adult situations, and fifth in nudity.

Programmers at times will publicly announce these strategies to heighten the expectation of violent programming at a given time. The most frequently occurring violent slot on basic cable is Sunday at 7 PM on TBS, which had a violent movie on 40 out of 51 weeks (which placed it thirteenth on the violent ranking). TNT, which like TBS was owned by Turner Broadcasting during this time period, frequently marketed its violent movie nights with titles. TNT's "Saturday Nitro," the scheduled programming of a violent movie at 10 PM on Saturdays, ranked thirtieth in terms of violence frequency. After the success of "Saturday Nitro," TNT introduced "Monday Nitro," a programming block featuring an action adventure program, professional wrestling, and two "Nitro" movies.[48] The first broadcast network time slot in the ranking appeared at thirty-eighth, with Fox's Tuesday at 8 PM slot involving at violent movie in 29 weeks in the sample.

Sometimes programmers will use violent movies to counterprogram against other channels without announcing the scheduling as a conscious policy. HBO adopted a strategy referred to internally during this time period as "Testosterone Thursday," which involved scheduling a low-quality violent film on Thursdays at 9 PM. The programmers believed that the movie would attract viewers among young males less interested in the type of comedy offered on NBC's *Seinfeld*. Table 4.9 indicates that among the top ten most violent time slots during this period, HBO's Thursday 9 PM slot had the lowest star ratings (1.4 stars). For the 43 out of 51 weeks when HBO showed a film with a violent indicator, 95% of the films also carried indicators for adult language, 74% for adult situations, 58% for nudity, and 51% had all four warnings for content in the viewing guide.

There are similar expectations of a given type of content at a given time period created by the scheduling of movies with adult situations. Seven of the top ten most frequently occurring movie slots with adult themes begin at 8 PM, including one time slot on basic cable (Comedy Central's Wednesday 8 PM movie). The first time slot in the adult situation rankings that appeared on a broadcast network was again Fox's Tuesday 8 PM movie, which had adult situations for 21 weeks. The frequency of movies with nudity indicators is lower than that for violence, perhaps because there are additional pay-per-view channels not included in this sample (such as Playboy and Spice) that have brand names established for nudity. The top four time slots are all on Cinemax, consistent with the earlier discussion of this channel's identification with films involving sexual content. A basic cable channel did make it into the top ten rankings for nudity indicators, although this USA slot is at Saturday night at 11 PM. The first broadcast network ranking for nudity does not occur until number 129, ABC's Sunday 9 PM movie (which aired films with nudity indicators seven times during the sample).

SCHEDULING AND POTENTIAL EXPOSURES OF CHILDREN

Concern about the violent and sexual content of movies on television arises primarily from the impact of these films on children. In defining the property rights of programmers and viewers, the government treats broadcasters differently than basic cable and premium cable in part on the argument that broadcast television is more accessible to children and more prevalent. This has given rise to pressure on broadcast networks to revive the "family hour" policy from the mid-1970s, in which the networks promised to air programs suitable for a family to watch together. This policy has parallels in the broadcast policies of other countries, such as Britain's watershed hour. Under this policy, British viewers can expect content to be family friendly until 9 PM, after which broadcasters may gradually increase the level of violence and sexual content in their programming.[49]

The sample of over 11,000 films allows one to explore how the movie content available on television changes over the course of the evening. Table 4.10 reports the characteristics of the films on network, basic, and premium cable during a particular time of day from 6 PM to midnight. These patterns are heavily influenced by basic cable (46% of the total movie programming hours in the sample) and premium channels (49%), since there are more of these

TABLE 4.10
Content by Programming Block

Content	% of Movies on during Evening Time Period, Monday–Friday, Full Sample							
	6–7	7–8	8–9	9–10	10–11	11–12
Violent	46.0	47.1	55.7	55.8	57.8	62.3
Violence Indicator	38.0	39.4	46.6	44.6	45.9	52.7
Adult Language	55.6	54.4	57.4	54.6	53.6	62.0
Adult Situations	44.6	46.3	49.3	47.2	48.1	55.7
Nudity	9.4	11.9	22.9	23.9	24.3	32.0
Total Warning Indicators						
0	29.9	30.4	28.6	32.7	34.7	27.2
1	16.6	15.3	13.1	11.3	9.1	8.0
2	32.3	31.4	24.2	21.7	20.4	20.3
3	17.3	17.6	21.4	21.0	20.6	23.3
4	3.3	5.3	12.8	13.3	15.3	21.2
MPAA Ratings						
Not Rated	30.8	28.4	27.8	32.5	36.3	30.6
G	1.9	4.9	4.7	3.3	2.5	1.9
PG	30.2	32.2	24.5	19.0	17.1	16.3
PG-13	32.9	27.1	13.2	11.7	10.9	8.1
R	4.2	7.5	29.9	33.5	33.1	42.9

Note: Sample consists of 13,780 hours of 1-hour programming blocks.

channels and they rely more heavily on movies than the four broadcast networks. Ratings data indicate that younger adult viewers (i.e., aged 18–34) begin to enter the viewing audience in larger numbers on Monday-Friday around 7 PM. Note that the percentage of violent movies increases from 47.1% for 7–8 PM to 55.7% for 8–9 PM. There is a similar jump in movies with nudity from 11.9% at 7–8 PM to 22.9% in 8–9 PM. The levels of violence and nudity remain relatively constant over the 8–11 PM period, at which point they increase again at 11 PM. Adult language and adult situations remain at the same level across prime time, and then increase too at 11 PM. Overall, these results indicate that cable programmers do not observe a "family hour" programming strategy. Instead, they increase the levels of both violence and sex at 8 PM, a time when nearly a third of all children 2–11 and teens 12–17 are watching television.[50]

The incidence of content warning indicators follows a similar pattern. The percentage of movies with one warning indicator on during the 6–7 PM hour is 16.6 %, a figure that gradually declines over the course of the evening to 8.0%. The number of movies with four indicators jumps from 5.3% at 7 PM to 12.8% at 8 PM. The MPAA-rating pattern similarly jumps at 8 PM. From 7 to 8 PM, R-rated films represent only 7.5% of the offerings on these 32 channels. At 8–9 PM, this figure jumps to 29.9%, and increases again to 42.9% from 11 PM to midnight. The percentage of PG films declines gradually from 30.2% at 6–7 PM to 24.5% at 8–9 PM. The sharpest decline emerges in programming of PG-13 films. As more adults enter the audience, the programmers drop PG-13 in favor of R-rated films. The percentage of PG-13 films declines from 27.1% at 7–8 PM to 13.2% at 8–9 PM.

Since basic and premium channels operate under different regulatory constraints and fewer advertiser considerations than broadcast networks, one would expect that the programming decisions made would focus more on the adult viewing patterns without great concern for the potential exposure of children to their offerings. Figure 4.2 provides evidence for this hypothesis by examining the content of movies shown throughout the entire programming day. This analysis is based on 24-hour movie schedules examined from April 1995 through January 1996, which yielded a set of 17,787 movies.[51] The movie schedules for broadcast, basic cable, and premium channels are analyzed in figure 4.2 in terms of movies starting within a given 2-hour time block. Note that the percentage of violent movies is nearly the same in the prime-time hours of 8–10 PM (61.5%) as in early morning hours (61.4% for 2–4 AM). The percentage of films with indicators for nudity jumps in the prime-time hours, and then jumps again in the early morning blocks (e.g., for midnight–2 AM and 2–4 AM). If programmers were concerned about the potential exposure of children to violence or nudity, they might alter their programming on Saturday and Sunday afternoons, time periods when more children are in the audience than is true when children are in school on Monday through Friday.[52] On the weekend, however, there are more young adult males and females in the television audience, so programmers face the incentive to increase content levels to attract these viewers. Figure 4.2 reveals that the potential to reach adults overrules

Monday - Friday

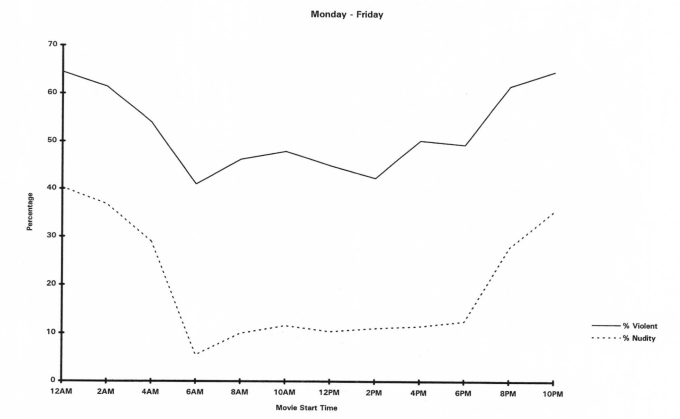

Figure 4.2. Patterns of Violence and Nudity, 24-Hour Programming

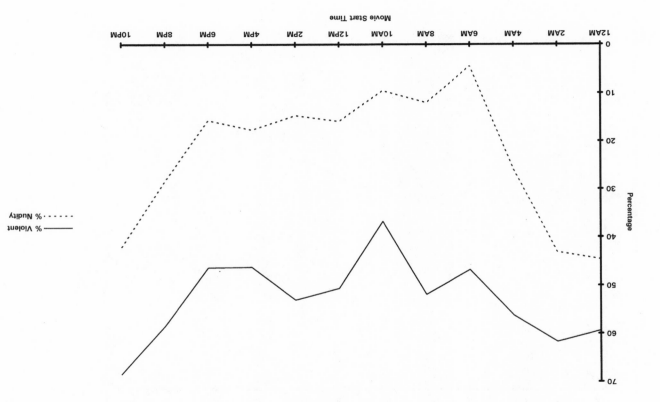

Movie Start Time

Percentage

% Nudity
% Violent

Saturday

10PM 8PM 6PM 4PM 2PM 12PM 10AM 8AM 6AM 4AM 2AM 12AM

0 10 20 30 40 50 60 70

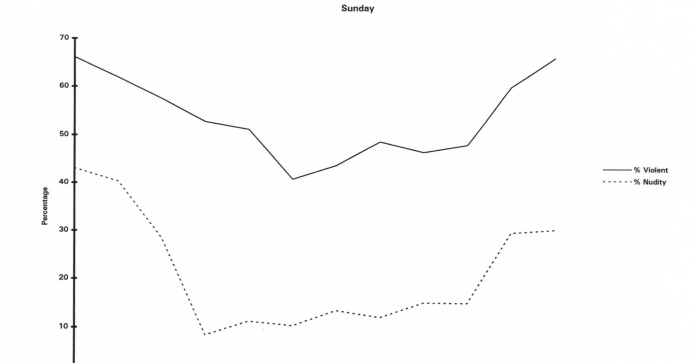

Sunday

Percentage

Movie Start Time

— % Violent
---- % Nudity

concerns (if any) of exposure to children on Saturdays and Sundays. For the noon–2 PM time slot, the percentage of violent films on Monday through Friday is 44.9% and for films with nudity is 10.4%. On Saturdays, this increases to 50.5% for violence and 15.8% for nudity. In the 2–4 PM slot, the percentage of violent films is 42.3% on Monday through Friday, 52.9% on Saturday, and 48.5% on Sunday. Similarly, the percentage of films with nudity is 11.1% on Monday through Friday for this afternoon time slot and 14.6% on Saturdays. Thus programmers take the opposite direction in using violence and sexual content during weekend programming than that predicted if they were taking the exposure of children into account.[53]

Channels do alter their weekend programming in response to reactions to violent content, but the incentives they face lead them to focus on how to use violence to attract particular adult audiences rather than reduce exposure to children. Consider the response to the concentration of male viewers during fall Sunday afternoons who watch football games. The percentage of films starting on Sunday afternoons from 2 to 4 PM that are violent is 42.9% in nonfootball weeks. This percentage increases to 54.3% during the Sundays when football is on.[54] On balance, programmers find it profitable to increase the use of violence to attract viewers on the Sundays when football dominates the ratings.

Another test of whether cable programmers alter their behavior in order to reduce exposure of children is to examine whether premium cable networks alter their programming during the summer months, when children may be more likely to be in the audience than during school months. During summer months, the percentage of films starting from noon to 2 PM that are violent is 50.7% and that carry adult situation indicators is 56.3%. In nonsummer months there is no statistical difference in these percentages for movies on from noon to 2 PM in terms of violence (51.9%) or adult situations (59.0%). There is no difference in the 2–4 PM slot in terms of summer use of violent movies (44.7%) and adult situations (55.3%) and nonsummer use of violence (50.8%) and adult situations (53.7%). There is even a slight (and statistically significant) increase in the use of R-rated films in the noon–2 PM slot from 4.2% of premium chan-nel offerings in nonsummer months to 9.2% in summer months (when young adults may be more likely to be in the audience).

CONCLUSIONS

The term "television violence" can be misleading, for the levels of violent pro-gramming will vary widely across different types of channels. The model in chapter 1 predicts that some channels will choose to develop brand identities for low levels of violence, others will use moderate amounts of violent pro-gramming in their schedules, and still other channels will seek to develop repu-tations for showing high levels of violence. The analysis of over 11,000 films shown on thirty-two channels from February 1995 to March 1996 indicates that channels clearly vary in their use of violent and sexual content. This variation in content could be explained by variations in the creative visions of writers, actors, producers, and networks. Some stories will have a violent narrative, others will contain little conflict.

While creative expression may explain part of the use of violent programming, this chapter sets forth several tests that rely on the premise that levels of violence are chosen strategically to build audiences to sell to advertisers or add to subscriber bases. Channels specifically schedule particular types of violent programming at given days and times, so that viewers will have an expectation that violence will be used in that programming. At times this is a publicly announced marketing campaign, such as TNT's "Saturday Nitro" programming of violent films at 10 PM on Saturdays. In other cases it is a programming strategy pursued privately without fanfare, such as HBO's counterprogramming of violent films on Thursdays at 9 PM to compete with *Seinfeld* in 1995. The changes in the use of violence and sexual content during sweeps months when ratings are measured provide strong evidence that these movie characteristics are strategically chosen to develop audiences. The changes in the use of violent programming in response to the concentration of male viewers on ABC during *Monday Night Football* further demonstrate how programmers increase or decrease violent content to attract viewers.

The scheduling of movies during the evening and daytime hours demonstrates how violent content is an externality, for the patterns follow the flow of adults in the viewing audience without a strong regard for the potential exposures of children. Monday through Friday the level of violence increases substantially from 7 to 8 PM as younger adults flow into the viewing audience. This is also a time, however, when significant numbers of children are in the potential viewing audience. The level of violent and sexual content is the same at 8 PM as it is at 10 PM, so that there is no evidence of a "family viewing hour" in terms of film scheduling on network, basic, and premium channels. The movies scheduled in the early afternoons on Saturday contain more violence and nudity than those scheduled from Monday through Friday, despite the fact that there are also more children in the audience at this time than during the week. Premium channels program the same level of violence in their afternoon movies during the summer months as they do during the school year, despite the added potential exposures to children. The next chapter uses a sample of violent movies to focus on decisions made by another set of participants in the market for violent programming: advertisers.

TABLE A4.1
Distribution of 11,603 Evening Movies, Full Sample (%)

Genre	
Action Adventure	10.7
Biography	1.5
Children	1.1
Comedy	20.9
Crime Mystery	2.0
Documentary	0.8
Drama	28.8
Horror	4.4
Miniseries	1.0
Musical	1.5
Romance	3.8
Science Fiction–Fantasy	7.8
Suspense	9.4
War	1.5
Western	4.8
Channel Type	
Broadcast	
ABC	1.2
CBS	1.1
Fox	0.5
NBC	1.0
Basic Cable	
A&E	0.5
AMC	10.2
Bravo	6.2
Comedy Central	1.5
Disney Channel	6.3
E!	0.5
Family Channel	1.6
Lifetime	4.0
Science Fiction	1.4
TBS	4.2
TNT	4.7
USA	3.2
WGN	1.5
Other	0.5
Premium Cable	
Cinemax	11.7
Encore	9.5
HBO	8.6
Showtime	9.9
Movie Channel	10.1
Release Year	
Through 1939	1.1

TABLE A4.1 (*Continued*)

1940s	3.9
1950s	6.9
1960s	7.9
1970s	9.7
1980s	20.9
1990	4.1
1991	4.6
1992	4.2
1993	12.9
1994	16.4
1995	6.3
1996	0.8

Note: Other included 12 films on the Discovery Channel, 14 on FX, 2 on MTV, 16 on PBS, 4 on the Learning Channel, 6 on UPN, 1 on VH1, 2 on WB, and 15 films on WOR. PBS was not included in later broadcast analysis totals.

TABLE A4.2
Content Characteristics of 7,984 Evening Movies, 1995–96, by Channel Type, Rated Only (%)

	Broadcast (N = 172)	Basic Cable (N = 2,707)	Premium Cable (N = 5,105)
Violent	57.6	55.1	67.4
Violence Indicator	57.6	55.1	67.4
Adult Language	73.3	62.5	87.2
Adult Situations	59.9	56.5	73.4
Nudity	27.3	25.7	38.4
Total Warnings			
0	7.0	11.6	1.8
1	23.8	19.9	11.2
2	26.2	33.4	30.3
3	29.7	26.9	30.8
4	13.4	8.1	25.9
Star Ratings			
Not Rated	2.3	2.1	4.4
1	8.1	15.0	19.9
2	44.8	40.8	49.9
3	42.4	36.8	24.1
4	2.3	5.2	1.6
MPAA Ratings			
G	4.7	11.1	1.6
PG	27.3	38.5	24.9
PG-13	27.3	12.2	23.0
R	40.7	38.1	50.4
NC-17	—	0.0	0.1

TABLE A4.3
Brand Positions of Television Channels, by Content, for 7,984 Rated Movies (%)

Channel	Violent	Violence Indicator	Adult Language	Adult Situations	Nudity
Broadcast					
ABC	61.4	61.4	65.7	54.3	25.7
CBS	60.7	60.7	78.6	60.7	28.6
Fox	55.9	55.9	85.3	73.5	23.5
NBC	51.4	51.4	70.3	54.1	29.7
Basic Cable					
A&E	83.3	83.3	60.0	76.7	50.0
AMC	41.3	41.3	56.5	55.8	10.1
Bravo	45.0	45.0	67.6	63.4	40.4
Comedy Central	37.0	37.0	85.2	77.2	29.0
Disney Channel	34.3	34.3	35.0	22.6	3.8
E!	81.8	81.8	60.6	69.7	42.4
Family Channel	62.8	62.8	34.9	44.2	0.0
Lifetime	37.1	37.1	76.7	82.8	34.5
Science Fiction	83.2	83.2	52.6	44.2	28.4
TBS	73.1	73.1	70.2	56.6	23.9
TNT	66.5	66.5	66.5	58.1	23.0
USA	61.4	61.4	68.3	67.9	37.2
WGN	81.3	81.3	66.2	63.3	22.3
Premium Cable					
Cinemax	75.1	75.1	93.3	77.9	50.3
Encore	46.5	46.5	71.3	65.9	23.9
HBO	71.9	71.9	93.1	72.4	36.5
Showtime	68.1	68.1	86.3	69.2	33.7
Movie Channel	70.8	70.8	89.2	78.8	42.0

• *CHAPTER 4* •

TABLE A4.4
Distribution of Movies, by MPAA Rating

Channel	NR	% Full Sample (N = 11,587)					% Rated Only (N = 7,984)				
		G	PG	PG-13	R	NC-17	G	PG	PG-13	R	NC-17
Broadcast											
ABC	47.8	3.7	17.2	13.4	17.9	0.0	7.1	32.9	25.7	34.3	0.0
CBS	77.8	0.0	6.3	5.6	10.3	0.0	0.0	28.6	25.0	46.4	0.0
Fox	40.4	0.0	8.8	10.5	40.4	0.0	0.0	14.7	17.6	67.6	0.0
NBC	68.1	2.6	9.5	12.9	6.9	0.0	8.1	29.7	40.5	21.6	0.0
Basic Cable											
A&E	44.4	0.0	24.1	1.9	29.6	0.0	0.0	43.3	3.3	53.3	0.0
AMC	88.4	2.7	7.7	0.0	1.3	0.0	23.2	65.9	0.0	10.9	0.0
Bravo	27.2	2.3	24.2	7.7	38.5	0.0	3.2	33.2	10.6	52.9	0.0
Comedy Central	4.1	0.6	35.5	17.2	42.6	0.0	0.6	37.0	17.9	44.4	0.0
Disney Channel	42.9	24.0	30.2	2.4	0.4	0.0	42.1	52.9	4.3	0.7	0.0
E!	45.0	0.0	1.7	18.3	35.0	0.0	0.0	3.0	33.3	63.6	0.0
Family Channel	77.0	4.8	18.2	0.0	0.0	0.0	20.9	79.1	0.0	0.0	0.0
Lifetime	74.8	0.0	4.8	8.5	12.0	0.0	0.0	19.0	33.6	47.4	0.0
Science Fiction	41.7	8.0	14.7	4.9	30.1	0.6	13.7	25.3	8.4	51.6	1.1
TBS	22.6	3.7	33.7	8.6	31.3	0.0	4.8	43.6	11.2	40.4	0.0
TNT	40.8	4.6	23.0	6.3	25.4	0.0	7.8	38.8	10.6	42.9	0.0
USA	20.5	0.3	20.5	18.9	39.5	0.0	0.3	25.9	23.9	49.4	0.0
WGN	18.2	4.1	19.4	11.8	46.5	0.0	5.0	23.7	14.4	56.8	0.0
Premium Cable											
Cinemax	8.3	0.1	11.5	22.5	57.1	0.4	0.2	12.6	24.5	62.3	0.4
Encore	20.5	5.4	44.8	8.5	20.7	0.0	6.8	56.4	10.7	26.1	0.0
HBO	11.2	0.9	16.3	27.0	44.6	0.0	1.0	18.3	30.4	50.2	0.0
Showtime	14.4	1.0	22.8	23.4	38.4	0.0	1.1	26.7	27.3	44.9	0.0
Movie Channel	5.2	0.2	16.7	20.0	57.9	0.0	0.2	17.6	21.1	61.1	0.0

• CHAPTER 5 •

Advertising: Who Supports Violent Programming?

TELEVISION NETWORKS sell audiences to advertisers by offering programs to viewers. While ratings data track who watches particular programs, commercials reveal which viewers are targeted by the firms that sponsor programs. This chapter focuses on how the products and firms that advertise on television programs differ between violent and nonviolent programs and vary across different types of violent shows.[1] The analysis also explores how broadcasters and sponsors react to the placement of viewer discretion warnings on programs, which may raise the probability that firms will become involved in controversy because of their sponsorship of violent shows. Drawing on a sample of more than 19,000 commercials, I find that placing a warning on violent theatrical movies does change the mix of advertisers willing to sponsor a movie on prime-time network television. Among the set of violent theatrical movies, products purchased by consumers less likely to be offended by television violence were more likely to advertise on movies with viewer warnings. Viewer warnings do not appear to change advertising sponsorship of movies on cable television, which is currently subject to much less scrutiny by advocacy groups. Controversy and scrutiny can have a significant impact on advertising rates on network television, which I explore through an analysis of advertising rates for the police drama *NYPD Blue.*

The exact impact of program content warnings on advertiser decisions is an open empirical question. When entertainment executives announced an agreement on February 29, 1996, to rate television programs for violence and sexual content, opinions varied widely on how advertisers would react to the content rating system. Ted Turner, president of Turner Broadcasting System, stated that the rating system would "cost us quite a bit of money because there are going to be a lot of advertisers, when the programs are rated, that consider themselves family-oriented companies that are not going to want to advertise in programs that carry parental guidance warnings." He predicted that "there will be more 'Brady Bunch'-type programming and less what we call cutting edge programming."[2] The president of ABC, Robert Iger, disagreed with the notion that warnings would cause an advertiser exodus, since companies already are sensitive to program content in their advertising decisions.[3]

Some in the entertainment industry felt that the warnings could spur more violent programming. As Dick Wolf, the producer of the crime drama *Law and Order,* put it, "If all these shows have warnings on them, you could have a situation where producers are saying to standards people at the networks, 'I've got a warning. I can say whatever I want. I can kill as many people as I want.'"[4] Advertisers explained that a warning such as an "R" rating on a program could have an additional impact on the decision whether to sponsor the program. The rating could make it more likely a company would be targeted by interest groups concerned about violence and sexual content. As Philip Guarascio, president of marketing and advertising at General Motors, described his belief that ratings could become "red flags" that drew interest group attention, "We want to sell our cars and trucks to a broad audience, but you cannot ignore external forces. We're a highly visible company, so we're under a magnifying glass."[5] Predictions about advertiser reactions to ratings thus include a massive migration of sponsors away from controversial programs, an increase in the violence levels on rated programs, and a marginal adjustment in sponsorship decisions to the additional information conveyed by warnings.

This chapter develops a theory of the reaction of broadcasters and advertisers to program warnings and tests explicit hypotheses about these reactions with a unique dataset of more than 19,000 commercials from a sample of 251 movies broadcast on prime-time network television from May 1995 through February 1996. The networks placed viewer discretion warnings on 14% of the prime-time films broadcast during this time period, which were often stated as, "Due to some violent content, parental discretion is advised." As chapter 3 indicates, program warnings on prime-time movies lower viewership by children 2–11 by approximately 14%. They have no net impact on the viewership of adults, perhaps because viewers drawn to violent programs are likely to know the content without the addition of a warning label. Even if the magnitudes of adult audiences for prime-time movies are not affected by warnings, however, advertisers may react to the labeling of a movie if they believe that this will increase the likelihood of companies being targeted by interest groups or increase the probability their brand images could be damaged by controversy.

Advertiser reactions to program warnings will vary depending on the audience for a broadcast film, the demographic makeup of a company's customer base, and the attitudes of viewers and consumers toward violent television. The prime adult consumers of violent television programming are men 18–34, followed by women 18–34 and men 35–49. These groups are less likely to view violent television as harmful to society or believe that it is a major cause of breakdown in law and order.[6] Companies that appeal primarily to these demographic groups may face little or no backlash from their customers from advertising on violent films.[7] Firms whose consumers include older viewers or whose products are aimed primarily at females (both groups which report higher frustration with violent programming) may face a greater risk of offending their customer base by advertising on labeled programs. If this theory of firm incentives is correct, then warning labels may cause the demographic mix of products to shift on violent films with warnings toward goods that have higher use among young or male consumers.

Broadcasters may also alter their programming decisions based on advertiser reactions. Viewer demand for a program determines the profit maximizing number of "nonprogram" (e.g., commercial) minutes per hour on prime-time movies. If a warning label is placed on a film, the supply of commercial minutes will remain the same but the demand for advertising sponsorship may drop because some firms may fear a consumer backlash from advertising on a show with warnings. The consequent drop in price means that networks may run more public service announcements and more promotions for their own programs on movies that carry viewer discretion warnings, since the cost in terms of forgone commercial prices will be lower on these films. Although in the longer run the networks' use of violent versus nonviolent films may also change as returns to programs change, this chapter investigates the short-run changes in the mix of advertisers and use of commercial time caused by program warnings.

The analysis here reveals that warnings on prime-time network movies do change broadcaster and advertiser incentives. Broadcasters run more network promotions and fewer general product ads on theatrical films with warnings, consistent with the theory that warnings cause advertiser pullouts that lower prices. Violent theatrical films with warnings are more likely to have products aimed at younger consumers, males, and households without children. Products in industries aimed at these consumers, such as sports and leisure and alcoholic beverages, are more likely to advertise on theatrical movies with warnings. Products from industries where "family" brand images are important, such as food or kitchen products, are less likely to sponsor ads on theatrical films with warnings. Advertisers also react to warnings on made-for-television movies, though not as strongly as to warnings placed on violent theatrical films. The results underscore the incentives that determine why broadcasters and advertisers support violent programming and how they react to providing information about television content to viewers.

The second set of results focuses on how the audiences targeted by advertisers on cable vary across different types of violent programming. The cable dataset consists of 5,700 commercials aired from noon to midnight on violent movies or series during the week of April 1–7, 1995, on TBS, TNT, USA, and WKFT (an independent broadcast station in the Raleigh-Durham television market). This yielded a set of 146 programs, which was supplemented with the addition of all movies (21) that carried viewer discretion warnings on these channels during the remainder of April. Analysis of the products advertised on these cable channels reveals that within the set of "violent" programs there are substantial differences in the audiences targeted by advertisers. Products advertised on crime series were more likely to be aimed at younger viewers than those on mystery series, consistent with the evidence from Nielsen ratings that the mystery genre attracts older viewers. Violent cable series are more likely to have products aimed at women than violent movies, consistent with the indications from syndicated violent series ratings data that young women view series programming in violent genres. Programs on the local independent station, WKFT, were more likely to have products aimed at men, consistent with the finding from the National Television Violence Study (1996a) that violent programs on independent stations are more likely to contain a higher number of violent interactions.[8] The differences between products advertised on violent cable movies with warnings and those without warnings are not as stark as those observed on broadcast network television movies. This may be due to the fact that advertising on cable channels or independent stations is not monitored by groups such as the American Family Association (AFA), so firms are less likely to experience a backlash for supporting violent programming on these channels. This underscores the role that anticipated scrutiny plays in the decision by firms to advertise on violent programs.

Controversy and scrutiny can also affect advertising decisions on network series programming. When the police drama NYPD Blue was first introduced by ABC in the fall of 1993, advocacy groups such as the AFA attacked the program's use of adult language and partial nudity. Using data on prime-time network advertising rates, I find that NYPD Blue initially generated advertising rates nearly 45% below levels predicted by the demographic audience attracted by the show. By November 1995, after interest group scrutiny subsided and the program had garnered critical acclaim, advertising on the program sold at a rate that fully reflected the makeup and size of the viewing audience. The "costs" of producing controversial material may thus drop over time as criticism and scrutiny subside.

VIEWER, ADVERTISER, AND BROADCASTER REACTIONS TO PROGRAM WARNINGS

Viewer Reactions

In 1993 broadcast networks and cable programmers voluntarily adopted a new policy of providing viewers with information about violent program content. Each network promised to provide parental advisories on a violent show, use audio and visual warnings when the program was broadcast, and include the warning in all promotions for the show. In theory, the provision of content information should lower the costs of parents to monitoring their children's viewing, so that audiences for violent programs will be reduced if they carry viewer discretion warnings. Chapter 3 indicates that for prime-time broadcast network movies, audiences for children 2–11 drop by 14% (approximately 222,000 children) when a warning is placed on the film.

Audiences for teens and adults remain the same, since the warnings are unlikely to provide new information to viewers in those groups who prefer to watch violent films. Nearly 35% of the movies shown on the four broadcast networks in prime time have previously been released in the theater, so that viewers may be familiar with reviews of the given film or the work of specific actors. Television reviews also provide data on story lines and genre so that viewers will develop assessments of likely content. Viewers most likely to be attracted to violent films (e.g., males and younger viewers) may be more likely to be familiar with the violent movies offered. The sparse amount of information conveyed in the warnings (e.g., "Due to some violent content, parental discretion is advised") may also mean that the information does not change assessments of content a great deal among those adults likely to view. While warnings may thus convey information to parents seeking to shield their children, viewers likely to watch violent programs may already know the content of the particular films likely to be shown on prime-time broadcast television.

Television warnings and ratings also provide information to individuals in their roles as consumers and citizens. Groups such as the American Family Association often target companies that sponsor violent programs for consumer boycotts. The AFA, led by the Reverend Donald Wildmon, mails updates each year to its members that track the top twelve sponsors of violence on prime-time network programming.[9] The group determines these ratings by monitoring a sample of programming and developing an index of a company's sponsorship of sex, violence, and profanity based on the number of commercials on shows with content perceived to be objectionable by the AFA. At times the group targets specific companies (such as Unilever) for boycotts, while at other times the threat of a boycott is used to sway company advertising policies. Some companies studiously attempt to avoid landing on the AFA list, while others take efforts to explain that their place on the ranking is due to support of controversial programming such as *NYPD Blue*.[10]

A person contemplating whether to boycott a product because she objected to the company's sponsorship of violent programming would trade off the benefits of this action with its costs. The net benefits of a boycott to an individual are captured by (Perceived benefits of reduced television violence brought about by a drop in corporate sponsorship)*(Probability a person's action will lead a company to change its advertising policies) + (Ideological satisfaction of participating in a boycott) − (Costs of learning about company sponsorship policies and costs of switching to another product to replace a boycotted item). Since the probability of influencing a company's policy is nearly zero for any individual, the returns to boycotting are negative unless a person derives a feeling of satisfaction from "doing the right thing" by participating in a boycott. This logic of collective action (Olson, 1971) explains why most people do not boycott companies, even though they feel that there is too much violence on television. Although the majority of viewers in a 1993 Roper poll said they had seen something "personally offensive or morally objectionable" on television within the previous few weeks, only 1% said they had stopped buying a product advertised on a program the last time they had been offended. Instead, 45% said they simply turned the channel (Roper Organization, 1993).

Though consumer boycotts are thus unlikely to attract large numbers of participants, companies may still fear being the targets of such efforts. Even a small percentage of customers participating may translate into lost sales. In addition, a company's brand identity may be damaged by the association with controversy. Consumers' reactions to a product could thus be negatively affected even if they were not consciously attempting to boycott a firm. Advertising on labeled films could thus appear less attractive to particular firms if they felt that the warnings made it more likely that they could be accused of supporting "violent television."

Advertiser Reactions

Nearly 70% of advertising spots on network prime-time are sold in the spring and early summer before the start of the television season. In this "upfront market," which totaled $5.6 billion in 1995, companies buy advertising on particular series and movies scheduled for the new season without knowing the exact content of the given episodes their ads will run on.[11] The networks reserve 30% of the ads for the scatter market, which allows them to provide companies with additional commercial time if ratings were not delivered on earlier shows and allows them to sell ads on a spot market closer to the airtime of the program. Once a prime-time program or movie is finished advertisers can learn the content of the episode through prescreening by a specialized firm or their advertising agency. Advertisers may then pullout of their sponsorship agreement if they have concerns about content or a warning label.

Research by Montgomery (1989) and Cowan (1979) details how advertisers often recoil from being associated with controversial television programming. For a company, an advertisement on a prime-time network movie represents a significant investment. Reported advertising prices for a 30-second slot on prime-time movies in November 1995 ranged from $90,000 to $150,000 depending on the evening and network.[12] To avoid sponsoring programs that may generate controversy for a particular product, firms often hire a company in New York (AIS) to prescreen prime-time network programs and alert them to content concerns, including violent and sexual content. Even without network warnings, major advertisers are thus apprised of the content of programs such as prime-time movies.

If firms find a program too controversial, they may pull their advertising from the show. Broadcasters may end up selling this advertising time at reduced rates or not selling it at all. The costs of controversy will vary by program and network. Robert Iger, president of Capital Cities/ABC, estimated that the network loses nearly $20 million in ad revenues each year because of decisions by sponsors to avoid controversial programs.[13] Statistical analysis later in this chapter of ad rates for the first season of *NYPD Blue* indicates that, relative to the demographics of the audience it was attracting, the program was selling at a discount of nearly 45%. Producer Dick Wolf estimates that NBC lost $800,000 in ad revenues on a single episode of *Law and Order* that focused on bombings at abortion clinics.[14] Industry estimates of the cost to a network of placing an advisory on prime-time movies run to $1 million in lost advertising per show (Federman, 1996).[15]

Firms advertising on prime-time broadcast movies explicitly face a decision of how much advertising time to buy on nonviolent versus violent programs. The prior theatrical runs for a third of prime-time movies and information from prescreening by advertising agencies and the networks provide companies with detailed information on the content of prime-time movies. The sales generated for a firm by advertising on violent programs are a function of how many ads the company purchases, what the ratings among different demographic groups are for these shows, and what the demographics of the purchasers of a company's products are.[16] If a program achieves a five rating among men 18–34, this translates into exposure of 1.6 million in this demographic group to a commercial sponsored by the firm.[17] The more men in this age group who use or potentially might use this product, the more likely these exposures would translate into additional sales. Sales revenues from nonviolent programs are similarly a function of the number of ads bought on these shows, the ratings for these programs, and the demographics of a company's customers. Total advertising costs are the sum of the price of the ads multiplied by the number of ads in each program category.

The potential for a backlash against a company advertising on violent television introduces another element for a firm to consider in advertising decisions. Advertising on a violent program may increase the likelihood a firm will be targeted for a boycott or increase the probability a firm's brand name will be damaged by association with controversy. Either of these effects translates into lower expected sales. The backlash will be higher the more ads bought on shows and the higher the ratings (and hence exposures to violence) of the programs. The amount of information available on whether a firm has advertised on violent programs will also influence the expected size of the backlash because it will raise the probability that people are aware of the firm's advertising practices. If the movie carries a warning, this will lower the cost to interest groups or individuals of linking a firm with violent programming and hence raise the potential backlash. The demographics of a firm's customers will also influence the expected loss in sales. If young consumers or males constitute a higher percentage of a firm's customers, the expected backlash from advertising on violent programs will be lower since these consumers are less likely to believe violent television is a serious public policy problem.

The firm's advertising decision can be modeled as follows. The firm chooses the amount of advertising time to purchase on violent programs (Q_v) and nonviolent shows (Q_{nv}), which have ratings R_v and R_{nv} and ad prices P_v and P_{nv}. Sales generated by these ads will in part be a function of the demographic characteristics α_i of a company's customers. For example, the higher the percentage of customers in the 18–34 age group, the more sales generated by advertising on violent shows (since these programs have a higher percentage of 18–34 viewers) and the lower the sales generated by nonviolent programs (which have a lower percentage of 18–34 viewers). Relevant demographic characteristics for this decision include the age and gender distribution of a company's customers. Sales from advertising on violent programs (VS) and nonviolent programs (NS) are thus $VS\,(Q_v,\,R_v,\,\alpha_i) + NS(Q_{nv},\,R_{nv},\,\alpha_i)$. If everyone were fully informed about the advertising practices of a firm, the backlash (BL) of lost sales from consumer reaction to the news that a firm advertises on violent programs would be a function of Q_v, R_v, α_i. The likelihood that this backlash will occur depends on the amount of information people have on the firm's advertising on violent programs. If a program carries a viewer discretion warning, for example, this makes targeting by interest groups more likely and thus press coverage more likely. The expected loss in sales is thus a product of the "fully informed" backlash BL and the function $A(I)$, which represents the probability the backlash will occur as a function of information available about the firm's advertising. The firm will maximize profits here by maximizing the expression

$VS(Q_v, R_v, \alpha_i) + NS(Q_{nv}, R_{nv}, \alpha_i) - A(I)BL(Q_v, R_v, \alpha_i) - P_v Q_v - P_{nv} Q_{nv}.$

Appendix 5.1 describes the solution to the model and comparative statics results. When the firm is maximizing profits, we find that

$$\frac{VS_{Q_v} - A(I)BL_{Q_v}}{P_v} = \frac{NS_{Q_{nv}}}{P_{nv}}.$$

This means that, when profits from advertising are maximized, the company will make advertising purchases $\underline{Q_v}$ and $\underline{Q_{nv}}$ so that the return per dollar spent on violent program ads equals the return per dollar spent on nonviolent program ads. Note that the returns to advertising on violent programs reflect both the increase in sales from additional ads and the decrease in sales from the expected backlash of advertising on violent programs. The amount of advertising time $\underline{Q_v}$ and $\underline{Q_{nv}}$ may change as company product demographics, information about advertising, ratings, and ad prices change. The results in the appendix reveal the following four points.

1. As the percentage of a firm's customers in the 18–34 demographic group or the percentage of customers that are male increases, the firm's purchase of advertising time on violent programs may increase or decrease depending on the relationship between sales increases and expected consumer backlash. Consider the increase in sales from the purchase of an additional ad versus the decrease in sales because of a backlash from the purchase of the additional ad. If the sales effect is larger than the backlash effect as the percentage of 18–34 consumers increases for a company (e.g., $VS_{Q_v \alpha_i} > A(I)BL_{Q_v \alpha_i}$), then the firm will purchase more ad time on violent programs as α_i increases. If the backlash effect dominates, the firm will purchase less time as α_i increases. In terms of the optimal purchase of ad time on nonviolent programs, $\underline{Q_{nv}}$ will decrease as the percentage of young consumers increases.

2. The placement of a warning on violent movies increases the information (I) about a company's advertising practices and thus increases the likelihood $A(I)$ that there will be a backlash from advertising on violent programs. As I increases, the amount of time purchased on nonviolent programs is unchanged but the amount of time purchased $(\underline{Q_v})$ on violent shows decreases. This decrease will be larger for firms with higher values of BL, such as companies with higher proportions of older consumers and higher proportions of female consumers.

3. As ratings for violent programs increase, the amount of advertising on nonviolent programs is unchanged but the amount of ad time purchased on violent shows will increase or decrease depending again on the relationship between additional sales and the expected backlash. If the increase in ratings increases the marginal impact of an additional ad on sales more than an increase in ratings increases the marginal impact of an additional ad on the expected backlash (e.g., $VS_{Q_v R_v} > A(I)BL_{Q_v R_v}$), then the amount of advertising time purchased on violent programs will increase. If the change in the expected backlash outweighs the change in sales, then purchases of ads on violent programs would decrease.

4. Increases in the price of ads on violent programs (P_v) would decrease purchases of $\overline{Q_v}$ and leave $\overline{Q_{nv}}$ unchanged, while increases in the price of ads on nonviolent programs (P_{nv}) will leave $\overline{Q_v}$ unchanged and decrease the purchase of ads on nonviolent programs $\overline{Q_{nv}}$.

This model of advertiser reaction suggests a series of hypotheses about the types of products that will be advertised on violent versus nonviolent prime-time broadcast movies and about how the mix of products on violent programs may change as warning labels are placed on violent programs. Specifically:

H_1. Products advertised on violent movies will be more likely to be used by younger consumers and male consumers than those on nonviolent movies. Products advertised on nonviolent movies will be more likely to be used by older consumers and female consumers than those on violent movies.

H_2. If a viewer warning is placed on a violent film, the mix of products advertised will change. Relative to a violent film without a viewer warning, a violent film with a warning will have a higher proportion of ads for products used by younger or male consumers.

H_3. Viewer discretion warnings will have a different impact depending on the type of company. Larger companies and those with "family" brand images are likely to face higher scrutiny for advertising on violent shows. Relative to violent programs without warnings, violent films with warnings should have fewer advertisements from larger companies and those with "family" brand identities.

Broadcaster Reactions

If warnings generate problems for some advertisers, then one would expect that broadcast networks would attempt to avoid placing advisories on shows that contain violence and that cable programmers would be more willing to use advisories since they are less reliant on advertisers for revenue. Recent research bears out both these predictions. For the 1994–95 television season, the UCLA Center for Communication Policy report (1995) found that of 161 made-for-television movies and miniseries on the four broadcast networks 23 raised issues of concern with respect to violence. Only 6 carried viewer warnings. Of 118 theatrical films shown on prime-time network television that were examined by the UCLA group, 50 were found to raise concerns about their use of violence. Yet only 28 of these films had viewer discretion warnings. Overall, the UCLA study demonstrates that for the 1994–95 television season the networks were placing advisories on less than half of the violent films that outside reviewers found raised issues of concern with their use of violence.

The National Television Violence Study (1996a) found that in its sample of 2,445 programs examined from broadcast and cable television, 4% carried viewer advisories. Nearly half of these advisories came from one premium channel, Showtime. Premium cable channels were much more likely to provide detailed information on content relating to violence and sex for the movies they aired than broadcast channels. Since premium channels rely on subscription rather than advertiser support, they do not face the same potential for backlash as broadcasters do in terms of labeling. Of the programs containing violence in this sample, 75% of those on premium cable had some type of viewer advisory before the program versus 3% for the violent programs aired on broadcast stations affiliated with the networks (Wilson et al., 1996).[18]

Fear of advertiser backlash may also have influenced the type of ratings system that broadcasters were willing to support (a point discussed more in chapter 8). During the drafting in 1996 of the television industry's TV Parental Guidelines rating system, the members of the executive committee charged with drawing up the rating system for programs indicated that one of the constraints on the development of the system was concern about the potential impact of program labels on advertisers.[19] Though survey evidence indicated that parents preferred a system that provided more information about program content, the age-based ratings implemented by the industry may have been less likely to generate advertiser backlash since they did not label a specific program as violent.[20] After substantial criticism, the drafters of the TV Parental Guidelines agreed in July 1997 to add specific content indicators such as a V for violence to the ratings system.

One impact of a program warning involves the amount of paid advertising carried on a program. Broadcast networks face a trade-off in determining the number of commercial minutes to include during a program. While additional ads bring the prospect of additional revenue, the inclusion of more ad time in a program may lead some viewers to select alternative shows. In this sense, viewing a television commercial represents the "price" individuals pay for viewing broadcast television. Figure 5.1, from Owen and Wildman's *Video Economics* (1992), conveys the decision broadcasters face in determining the amount of commercial time in a show.[21] As Owen and Wildman point out, if the advertising market is perfectly competitive the price per ad on a program will be constant. This means that the profit-maximizing amount of advertising will be the product of the number of ad minutes sold times the number of viewers of these ads (i.e., "audience and minutes"). If there were no commercials in a program, A_0 viewers would watch the program. As the number of commercial minutes climbs, the number of viewers willing to pay this "price" to watch a show drops. The demand curve D_a conveys the number of viewers willing to watch at a given amount of ad time. The curve MAM, the "marginal audience minutes" curve, represents the change in audience and minutes from the addition of another commercial. The broadcaster will add minutes of commercials until MAM equals zero, which is the point at which the gain in total audience and minutes from adding another commercial is just offset by the loss in total audience ad minutes from viewers fleeing the program because of the added commercial. Total audience ad minutes are maximized at this point. The broadcaster will choose to include $C*$ commercial minutes in the program, attract $A*$ viewers, and sell a total of ($C* \times A*$) audience minutes to advertisers.

If this model of advertising holds true, consider how a broadcaster will react to a system of voluntary warning labels on prime-time movies such as that

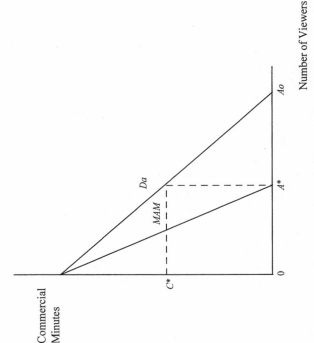

Figure 5.1. Broadcaster Determination of Commercial Minutes. *Source:* Owen and Wildman 1992.

adopted in 1993. If the value of advertising on a show is reduced for some advertisers because of the costs of controversy, the ad price a company can charge may drop.[22] The profit-maximizing amount of commercial minutes will remain the same (C^*), since this figure was independent of the price received for ads. In addition to running paid advertising from corporate sponsors, networks also run promotions for their own programs. These promos are essentially investments, which yield later returns in the form of additional viewers. The networks also run public service announcements, such as the commercials provided in campaigns sponsored by the Advertising Council.[23] As the price received for commercial ads drops, the networks will run more commercials promoting their own shows and more public service announcements since the "opportunity cost" of running these ads will have dropped. Since warning labels translate into lower ad prices and ultimately lower ad revenues, broadcasters will have an incentive to avoid placing warnings on programs even if they contain violent material that parents might consider objectionable or research might indicate is harmful. In the long run, the change in returns to programming may also affect the decision of which types of programs to air.[24]

This model of broadcaster incentives implies additional testable hypotheses:

H_4. Films with viewer discretion warnings will have the same number of "non-program" minutes per hour as those without warnings.

H_5. If the price of advertising drops on movies with warnings, broadcasters may run more promotions for their own shows and more public service announcements on these programs.

ANALYZING ADVERTISING ON PRIME-TIME BROADCAST MOVIES

Movies on prime-time broadcast network television were selected to test theories of advertiser reactions to viewer discretion warnings since there was a large enough fraction of films carrying these warnings (14%) to generate substantial data on sponsorship decisions. The results of both the UCLA Center for Communication Policy study (1995) and the National Television Violence Study (1996b) suggest that violence on broadcast television may be most problematic in prime-time movies. The UCLA study noted that for the 1994–95 season, "A large majority of the violence on broadcast television that raises concerns can be found in theatrical films."[25] As the study's principal investigator Jeffrey Cole put it,

of the 118 theatrical films we looked at this season, 50, or about 42 percent, would've raised concerns. The ones that raise the most concerns contextually were those action films that tended to have 40 to 60 scenes of violence. And what the networks are able to do is only remove the worst moments of the worst part. They can't do much more. And even though they do take the worst part of the worst moment, to say it better, they still have a film that has, really has nothing but scenes of violence.[26]

The National Television Violence Study (1996b) also found in its analysis of movies on cable and broadcast that

Movies as a genre have the highest percentage of programs with violence and the highest proportion of programs with numerous violent interactions. Movies portray violence in realistic settings much more than the norm and depict graphic blood and gore moderately above average. The positive features of movies are that long-term consequences are portrayed substantially more often, and that humorous violence and unrealistic harm are avoided.[27]

These findings suggest that studying advertising on movies allows one to analyze who sponsors some of the most violent programming on broadcast network television.

To analyze advertiser reaction to viewer discretion warnings on movies I collected information on program content, commercials aired, the consumer demographics of advertised products, and the demographics of program audiences. Information on movies aired on the four major networks during prime time from May 1, 1995, through February 29, 1996, was collected from TV Guide (e.g., movie airtime, genre) and from What's On Tonite!, an Internet source that had the MPAA ratings for movies and indicators (for theatrical movies) of whether the film contained violence, nudity, adult situations, and adult language. An attempt was made to record all prime-time broadcast network movies from May 1 through December 31, 1995. To expand the comparison sets of films all movies with warnings or violence indicators were recorded for January 1, 1996, through February 29, 1996. For each recorded movie, research assistants coded the commercial length and product advertised. All nonprogram segments were coded—for example, commercials for products, television show promotions during credits, public service announcements. This yielded a database of more than 19,000 commercials from 251 movies. For 151 films broadcast from May 1 through September 16, 1995, Nielsen information on ratings by demographic audience were also available.

The *1993 Simmons Study of Media and Markets* (Simmons Market Research Bureau 1994), based on a survey of 22,468 adults in the United States, provided data on the consumer demographics of products advertised on these films. This study gives a breakdown by age, income, education, and gender of product users.[28] Products were linked to parent companies through information from *Company Brand \$, 1993* (Leading National Advertisers 1994a). For each parent company total ad expenditures for 1993 were collected from *Ad \$ Summary, 1993* (Leading National Advertisers 1994b), which lists firm expenditures for advertising across ten media, including network television, syndication, spot, and cable television. Together these data link advertised products to particular programs, consumers, and parent companies.

Prime-Time Network Movies: The Impact of Viewer Warnings on Advertising

From May 1, 1995, through February 29, 1996, there were 357 movies scheduled for broadcast in prime time by ABC, CBS, Fox, and NBC. These movies were spread across a wide variety of genres: drama, 54%; comedy, 14%; crime drama, 10%; adventure, 4%; thriller, 4%; comedy drama, 4%; science fiction, 4%; fantasy, 3%; western, 2%; mystery, 1%; and other, 1%. This genre distribution is similar to that for prime-time network movies broadcast from 1987 to 1993 examined earlier in chapters 2 and 3.[29] Prime-time films broadcast during 1995–96 did differ in some dimensions from those broadcast in earlier seasons. The 1995–96 movies were more likely to be films first released in theaters (36% for 1995–96 vs. 29% for 1987–93), to deal with family crime (9% vs. 4%), and to be based on true stories (22% vs. 18%). In the 1995–96 sample, 23% of the films dealt with murder, a drop from 30% for the 1987–93 seasons.

Beyond the genre information and plot descriptions available in publications such as *TV Guide*, viewers had some additional indicators of the content of prime-time broadcast films. MPAA ratings were available for all the theatrical films.[30] The distribution of MPAA ratings for the films broadcast from May 1995 through February 1996 is 2% G, 12% PG, 10% PG-13, 15% R, and 62% unrated (nearly all of which are made-for-television movies).[31] Those films rated by the MPAA also carried program content indicators in the viewer guide *What's On Tonite!*, although the guide did not distinguish between the content of the theatrical release and the potentially edited version shown on network television. For the sample as a whole, 21% of the movies had a content indicator for violence, 9% for nudity, 21% for adult situations, and 25% for adult language. These figures may be lower bounds for the presence of these types of content, however, since made-for-television movies are not categorized by viewer guides on these dimensions. For the sample of theatrical movies shown in prime time by ABC, CBS, Fox, and NBC, 59% had an indicator for violence, 24% for nudity, 55% for adult situations, and 72% for adult language.

The broadcast networks placed viewer warnings on 18 out of the 230 made-for-television films and 33 out of the 127 theatrical films aired from May 1995 through February 1996. By MPAA rating, the breakdown of theatrical films that received warnings was 0 out of 5 G, 1 of 38 PG, 2 of 31 PG-13, and 30 out of 52 R films. Judging whether all movies that contained violence of concern (e.g., harmful to children) carried a viewer warning is difficult without a detailed examination of the content of each film. As discussed earlier, the UCLA Center for Communication Policy (1995) conducted such a study for the 1994–95 season and concluded that 50 out of 118 theatrical films and 23 out of 161 made-for-television films they examined had violence that raised concerns. For those films with problematic uses of violence, the networks placed warnings on 28 out of the 50 violent theatrical films and 6 of the 23 violent made-for-television films. By this measure, nearly half of the violent films that should have carried a viewer warning did not in the 1994–95 season. The use of warnings, though imperfect, has increased markedly from earlier eras. Between 1987 and 1993 only 2% of the films broadcast by the networks during prime time contained viewer discretion warnings.

Nielsen ratings for these prime-time films provide information on the demographic makeup of their audiences. For 151 films shown on broadcast television from May 1, 1995, through September 16, 1995 (a sample for which Nielsen data were available), the average rating for children 2–11 was 3.0. This translates into 1.4 million children on average viewing these prime-time network movies. As discussed in chapter 3, children in this age group had a 4.2 rating for prime-time network movies from 1987 to 1993. The increase in competition in the television market has thus lowered the number of children watching prime-time broadcast network movies. Note that 68% of these films started at 9 PM, so that concerns about content may lessen as the starting time of the film progresses. Teens 12–17 averaged a 4.2 rating for prime-time network films, which translated into 900,000 viewers in this age group.

Table 5.1 indicates that ratings for prime-time broadcast movies have also declined for adult demographic groups such as males 18+ and females 18+.[32] For some of these adult groups ratings for prime-time movies dropped by nearly a third from 1987–93 to the 1995–96 season. Competition from cable would be especially intense for movie viewers, since premium channels air recent releases more readily than broadcast networks. Overall, the films in the 1995–96 sample averaged a 15.3 share (down from 19.6 for 1987–93), which indicates that approximately one in six households watching television at the time the programs were aired were watching these movies. For each age group

TABLE 5.1

Broadcast Network Primetime Movie Audiences

Viewing Population	1987–93 Mean Ratings (N = 2,295)	1995 Mean Ratings (N = 151)	1995 Mean Viewers (Millions)
Children, 2–11	4.2 (2.8)	3.0 (1.8)	1.4
Teens, 12–17	5.5 (3.4)	4.2 (2.4)	0.9
Women, 18+	9.0 (3.7)	6.4 (2.8)	6.3
Women, 18–34	7.1 (3.4)	5.0 (2.7)	1.6
Women, 18–49	7.8 (3.3)	5.5 (2.6)	3.4
Women, 25–54	8.5 (3.5)	6.0 (2.8)	3.4
Women, 55+	11.2 (5.6)	8.0 (4.3)	2.4
Men, 18+	7.0 (3.0)	4.7 (2.3)	4.3
Men, 18–34	5.4 (2.9)	3.5 (2.3)	1.1
Men, 18–49	6.1 (3.3)	3.9 (2.5)	2.4
Men, 25–54	6.7 (3.0)	4.4 (2.5)	2.4
Men, 55+	9.3 (4.4)	6.6 (3.2)	1.5
Household Ratings	11.7 (3.9)	8.7 (3.2)	8.3

Note: Standard deviations are in parentheses.

women had higher ratings than men, which suggests that products aimed at women may be likely sponsors of these programs.[33] As is true for television in general, ratings among those 55+ were much higher than those for young adults. Since older consumers are less likely to be targeted by advertisers, however, the large number of elderly viewers may not translate into a significant number of commercials aimed at these consumers.

Differences in audiences across films will create different incentives for advertisers—for example, sponsors with products aimed primarily at males might find it more attractive to advertise on a movie with higher male ratings. Chapter 2 indicated that men in all age groups have higher ratings for movies that are particularly violent, that women are more likely to watch movies about family crime, and that women and men age 55+ have higher ratings for mystery films. Movie audiences and hence advertisers will vary by content. If there is a backlash among product customers from sponsoring violent television, there may be an independent impact of the warning label on the incentives of advertisers. Isolating this effect involves comparing commercials on movies that are similar in audience but differ in labeling. For 88 theatrical films, the analysis will focus on comparing the 28 violent theatrical films that received viewer warnings with the 25 violent theatrical films that did not receive a warning and the 35 films that did not have a violent content indicator.[34] Among the 164 made-for-television films, it is more difficult to identify a "violent" comparison set since the shows are not categorized by viewer guides as violent. For the 146 made-for-television films that did not carry warnings, I selected the films that were in a subset of violent genres (science fiction, thriller, westerns) or that had the words

TABLE 5.2
Nonprogram Minutes per Hour

	Mean	Standard Deviation	N	Difference of means Test (T statistic)	
				1 vs. 2	2 vs. 3
Theatrical Movies					
(1) Nonviolent	14.4	1.1	34		
(2) Violent, Warning	15.0	1.5	28		
(3) Violent, No Warning	15.1	1.6	25	−2.24**	−0.32
Made-for-television Movies					
(1) No Warning	14.6	1.0	140		
(2) Warning	14.4	1.2	17		
(3) "Violent," No Warning	14.7	0.6	18	0.69	−1.08

Note: *** = statistically significant at the .01 level; ** = significant at the .05 level; * = significant at the .10 level.

"dead" or "murder" in their titles. This resulted in a "violent" subset of 18 made-for-television movies to compare with the 17 that carried viewer discretion warnings.[35]

Broadcaster reactions to warning labels are initially analyzed in table 5.2. Even if the price of advertising were to drop on programs with warnings, broadcasters should still maintain the same number of "nonprogram" minutes per show. Table 5.2 indicates that for theatrical films broadcast in prime time by the networks, violent movies with warnings did have a higher number of nonprogram minutes (15.0) than nonviolent theatrical films (14.4). This may reflect the ability of broadcasters to charge audiences a higher "price" for the content of these films. Warnings do not, however, have an independent impact on nonprogram minutes. The number of nonprogram minutes on violent films without warnings (15.1) was nearly identical to the number of minutes on violent movies with warnings (15.0). Nonprogram minutes were also similar across the three made-for-television movie categories (e.g., 14.4 minutes for those with warnings, 14.6 for those without warnings, and 14.7 for the "violent," no-warning subset). Thus warnings do not have a separate impact on the number of nonprogram minutes broadcasters insert in prime-time movies.[36]

If the price of advertising drops for ads on movies with warnings, then broadcasters may substitute network promotions and public service announcements for commercial ads (H_5). In order to test this, each ad was assigned to a unique category: product ad (all commercial products and services, except for those broken down into finer categories noted later); commercials for movies showing in theaters; commercials for videos; health service, utility, military, or nonprofit ads; public service announcements; ads for television shows on the local stations (e.g., local news, syndicated programs); and ads for network pro-

TABLE 5.3
Percentage Distribution of Ads on Theatrical Movies

Ad Category	(1) Nonviolent Movies	(2) Violent Movies, Warning	(3) Violent Movies, No Warning	Difference of Proportion Test (Z Statistic)	
				1 vs. 2	2 vs. 3
Product	64.8	60.2	63.4	3.35***	−2.22**
Movie	1.4	4.3	1.8	−5.81***	4.68***
Video	1.3	0.6	1.4	2.32**	−2.36***
Health Services	0.2	0	0	1.46	0
Utility	0.1	0.1	0.3	0	−1.30
Military	0.2	0.6	0.1	−1.82*	2.30**
Nonprofit	0.1	0.1	0	0	0.98
Public Service	1.4	1.3	1.1	0.18	0.61
Network	20.8	24.1	22.0	−2.74***	1.64*
Local Station	9.6	8.5	9.6	1.31	−1.24
Total	99.9	99.7	99.7		
Network, Local Station, PSA	31.8	33.9	32.7	−1.55	0.76
Commercial Ads	68.1	65.8	67	1.69*	−0.83
Total number of ads	2,731	2,176	2,128		

Note: *** = statistically significant at the .01 level; ** = significant at .05; * = significant at .10.

grams.[37] Table 5.3 shows that for theatrical movies, programs with warnings had a lower proportion of general product ads (60.2%) than movies without warnings (64.8%) or movies that were violent but did not carry warnings (63.4%). Violent movies with warnings had a higher percentage of network promotions (24.1%) than violent movies without warnings (22%) or nonviolent movies (20.8%). These differences of proportion, which are all statistically significant, indicate that advertiser pullout may lead broadcasters to show less advertising for general products and substitute network promotions for the unsold advertising. Note that the percentage of ads devoted to public service announcements is very similar across the subsamples (1.4% for nonviolent films, 1.3% for violent films with warnings, and 1.1% for violent films without warnings). The broadcasters do not appear to respond to advertiser pullout by running more public service announcements on violent films with warnings.

The predicted pattern does not hold true for made-for-television movies that carry viewer warnings (see table A5.1). The percentage of general product ads on made-for-television movies with warnings (61.7%) is similar to that for movies without warnings (62.9%) and the "violent" made-for-television subset that did not carry warnings (62.3%). In difference-of-proportion tests, the difference between the made-for-television films with warnings and those in the other two samples is not statistically significant for general product ads or network promotions. This suggests that advertiser pullout may not be as great a problem for made-for-television films carrying warnings.

If warnings increase the probability for some firms that they will experience fewer sales, the model predicts that the products and firms advertising on movies with warnings should differ. Table A5.2 uses the industry classification system developed by the Simmons survey to detail the differences in consumer product demographics between nonviolent theatrical films and violent theatrical films with warnings. Movies with warnings had a higher percentage of products that did not fit into the Simmons classification system, consistent with newer products or products with a smaller audience having less to fear in terms of brand name backlash. The percentage of sports and leisure ads and alcohol ads was higher on movies with warnings, consistent with targeting younger consumers. Products with "family" brand identities, such as those in baking, cereals, and other food items, made up a lower percentage of ads on movies with warnings.

Table 5.4 attempts to isolate the independent impact of warnings by examining differences in advertiser mix between violent theatrical films with warnings and those without. Automobiles, trucks, and vans, sports and leisure products, and alcohol products constituted a higher percentage of ads on movies with warnings. Backlash may be lower for some of the firms in these industries because they are targeting younger or male consumers.[38] Products where firms may have family images, such as those in food industries (e.g., cereals, baking, condiments) and kitchen products, accounted for a lower percentage of ads on films with warnings relative to violent films without warnings.

Table A5.3 indicates that for made-for-television movies the difference between advertisers on movies with versus without warnings is consistent with the backlash theory. Sports and leisure and alcoholic beverage products constitute higher percentages of ads on films with warnings, while those associated with food industries constitute a lower percentage of ads on these films. When ad distributions are compared in Table A5.4 for made-for-television programs with warnings and made-for-television films without warnings that may be "violent," some patterns are consistent with the table 5.4 results for theatrical films. Sports and leisure products were more likely to be on programs with warnings, while cereals were less likely. Women's apparel and women's beauty aids, however, were more likely to be on made-for-television movies with warnings. This may be related to the fact that made-for-television movies in general have higher ratings among women, as do family crime movies. If backlash is lower for sponsoring these programs than for sponsoring the action adventure theatrical films, then advertiser reactions may differ to warnings on theatrical films versus warnings on made-for-television films.

Since violent films with warnings and nonviolent films attract different audiences, one expects that the products advertised on the two subsets of films will differ (e.g., by H_1 violent films should be more likely to have products aimed at younger viewers or men). If there is a backlash against advertising on films

TABLE 5.4

Percentage Distribution of Ads across Simmons Product Categories, Theatrical Movies

Product Category	Violent, Warning	Violent, No Warning	Difference Test (Z Statistic)
Product Unclassified	10.2	8.8	1.3
Automobiles, Cycles, Trucks, & Vans	13.4	10.4	2.5**
Automotive Products & Services	0.8	0.8	0.2
Travel	1.8	1.1	1.4
Banking, Investments, Insurance, Credit Cards & Contributions, Memberships & Public Activities	1.8	1.6	0.4
Games & Toys, Children's & Babies' Apparel & Specialty Products	0.9	1.5	−1.4
Computers, Books, Discs, Records, Tapes, Stereo, Telephones, TV, & Video	4.7	5.7	1.2
Appliances, Garden Care, Sewing, & Photography	3.6	4.9	−1.8*
Home Furnishings & Home Improvements	2.0	2.0	0.1
Sports & Leisure	3.6	2.0	2.5**
Restaurants, Stores, & Grocery Shopping	15.0	20.0	−3.5***
Direct Mail & Other In-Home Shopping, Yellow Pages, Florists, Telegrams, Faxes, & Greeting Cards	0.5	0.2	1.3
Jewelry, Watches, Luggage, Writing Tools, & Men's Apparel	0.8	0.6	0.5
Women's Apparel	1.1	1.1	−0.2
Distilled Spirits, Mixed Drinks, Malt Beverages, Wine, & Tobacco Products	2.7	1.6	1.9*
Coffee, Tea, Cocoa, Milk, Soft Drinks, Juices, & Bottled Water	4.2	2.9	1.8*
Dairy Products, Desserts, Baking, & Bread Products	0.6	1.8	−2.8***
Cereals & Spreads, Rice, Pasta, Pizza, Mexican Foods, Fruits & Vegetables	1.8	3.4	−2.7***
Soup, Meat, Fish, Poultry, Condiments, Dressings, & Sauces	1.6	2.9	−2.4**
Chewing Gum, Candy, Cookies, & Snacks	4.6	3.7	1.2
Soap, Laundry, Paper Products, & Kitchen Wraps	2.2	3.9	−2.6**
Household Cleaners, Room Deodorizers, Pest Controls, & Pet Foods	2.2	3.0	−1.3
Health Care Products & Remedies	7.6	6.0	1.7*
Oral Hygiene Products, Skin Care, Deodorants, & Drug Stores	5.9	4.7	1.4

TABLE 5.4 (Continued)

Product Category	Violent, Warning	Violent, No Warning	Difference Test (Z Statistic)
Fragrances, Hair Care, & Shaving Products			
Women's Beauty Aids, Cosmetics, & Personal Products	4.0	3.7	0.4
	2.5	1.8	1.3
Total	100.1	100.1	

Note: *** = Statistically significant at the .01 level, ** = significant at the .05 level, * = significant at the .10 level

with warnings, then within the set of violent theatrical films products with lower expected backlashes such as those aimed at men and younger consumers should be more likely to be advertised on films with warnings (H_2). Table 5.5 bears out both of these predictions for theatrical films. The numbers in the table represent the mean of the percentage of a product's customers made up by the consumers in a given category for the products advertised on a particular type of movie. For example, the figure 12.1 in the first cell in table 5.5 indicates that for products advertised on nonviolent movies, the average for the percentage of a product's adult consumers that were aged 18–24 was 12.1% for products sponsoring ads on these movies. For violent movies with warnings, the mean of the percentage of a product's adult consumers that were aged 18–24 was 13.0% for products advertising on these movies. Thus young adults account for a higher fraction of the consumers of products advertised on violent theatrical movies with warnings.

The differences in consumer product demographics across the three types of movies analyzed in table 5.5 are statistically significant but small in magnitude. This is what one would expect, however, for at least two reasons. Since advertising on broadcast network television is bought by companies seeking broad audiences, one may expect a degree of similarity across films in product target audiences. If advertiser pullout affects firms differentially, then only a small percentage of firms may pull out with a warning. The small number of ads affected by advertiser pullout would translate into small changes in the advertiser mix on films with warnings. A small number of advertiser pullouts on a movie would still translate into significant lost revenues given that 30-second commercials sell for between $90,000 and $150,000 for prime-time broadcast movies.

Relative to products sponsoring nonviolent theatrical films, table 5.5 reveals that products advertised on violent theatrical films with warnings were more likely to be used by individuals aged 18–24, males, households without children, and those with incomes of $40,000+.[39] Products advertised on violent theatrical films with warnings were less likely to be used by individuals age 55–64 or 65+, those with incomes $10,000–19,000, or high school graduates. These differences in product demographics may arise from differences in program audiences or advertiser reactions to viewer warnings. To isolate the inde-

TABLE 5.5
Consumer Demographics of Products Advertised on Theatrical Movies

Consumer Categories	Mean % of a Product's Consumers Accounted for by Consumers in a Particular Demographic Group			Difference of Means Test (T statistic)	
	(1) Ads on Nonviolent Movies	(2) Ads on Violent Movies, Warning	(3) Ads on Violent Movies, No Warning	1 vs. 2	2 vs. 3
Age					
18–24	12.1	13.0	12.4	-5.84***	3.66***
25–34	24.4	24.6	24.5	-1.42	0.62
35–44	24.6	24.5	24.6	1.04	-0.62
45–54	16.0	15.8	15.9	1.40	-0.86
55–64	10.4	10.1	10.3	3.63***	-2.24**
65+	12.6	12.1	12.4	3.47***	-2.0**
Male	49.2	49.6	49.1	-1.69*	1.96**
Female	50.8	50.5	50.9	1.60	-1.90*
Income					
< $10K	8.0	7.9	8.0	0.97	-1.26
$10K–19K	14.1	13.9	14.1	2.32**	-2.00**
$20K–29K	16.2	16.2	16.3	-0.20	-0.99
$30K–39K	15.1	15.0	15.1	2.58***	-2.04**
$40K+	46.7	47.1	46.6	-2.06**	2.29***
$50K+	34.2	34.5	34.0	-1.45	2.01**
$60K+	24.3	24.5	24.1	-0.88	1.67*
Education					
Not HS Graduate	16.1	16.0	16.1	1.13	-0.61
HS Graduate	35.7	35.3	35.7	3.08***	-2.75***
Attended College	25.9	26.2	26.0	-2.53***	1.38
College Graduate	22.3	22.6	22.3	-1.55	1.43
No Children in Household	55.4	56.1	55.7	-2.94***	1.88*
Mean % of Total Adults Using Product/Product Category	20.9	18.1	20.3	3.73***	-2.90***
Number of Total Ads	2,282	1,665	1,725		

Note: *** = statistically significant at the .01 level ; ** = significant at the .05 level; * = significant at the .10 level.

pendent impact of advertiser reactions to viewer discretion warnings, I compare the ads on violent theatrical films with warnings to ads on violent theatrical films without warnings (two subsets that may be relatively similar in audience). Products advertised on films with viewer discretion warnings were more likely to be used by those aged 18–24, by men, and by those in households with no children. Products on films with warnings were less likely to be used by those age 55–64 and 65+ and by women.

Each of these results is consistent with a backlash effect. Since younger consumers and males are less likely to view violent television as a problem, companies with products aimed at these consumers will be less likely to face a backlash. If other companies withdraw from advertising, the demographics of products advertising on movies with warnings will tilt more toward men and younger consumers. These firms may even be more likely to buy the ad time of those companies which pull out, which would accentuate this trend. Products with higher percentages of older consumers and women, two groups that report greater dissatisfaction with television violence, face greater backlash and hence are less likely to advertise on violent programs with warnings. If potential brand image damage from advertising on a film with a warning is greater for products with a "family" brand image, this would explain why products on violent movies with warnings had a higher percentage of consumers with no children in the household than those on violent films without warnings. Note that products on violent movies with warnings had a lower percentage of use by total adults (18.1%) than that for products on violent movies without warnings (20.3%). This too is consistent with companies trying to reach larger audiences facing a greater potential for backlash.[40]

The evidence of advertiser reactions to warnings is more mixed for made-for-television movies. There are statistically significant differences in the consumer demographics of products on made-for-television movies with warnings versus those without warnings. Table A5.5 indicates that products on these movies with warnings were more likely to be consumed by those aged 18–24 or 25–34 and by males. They were less likely to be consumed by those 45–54, 55–64, 65+, and by females. It is more difficult for the made-for-television movies to judge the independent impact of warnings since one needs to define an alternative set of movies without warnings that should be similar in audience. If one compares made-for-television movies with warnings with the subset of "violent" no-warning films, the predicted differences in product age do arise. Products advertised on the films with warnings were more likely to be used by those aged 18–24 or 25–34 and less likely to be used by those 45–54, 55–64, or 65+. Differences in use of the products by males and females are not statistically significant between the two subsamples. Products advertised on movies with warnings actually have a lower percentage of households without children as a percentage of customers than those on movies without warnings, which is the opposite pattern expected if "family" products faced a backlash from advertising on made-for-television films.

Another way to examine differences in program audiences is to examine advertising for products aimed directly at male consumers (e.g., Hair Club for Men) or female consumers (e.g., Maybelline Revitalizing Makeup). For each movie subsample, the percentage of these "gender-focused" products aimed at men was calculated. For nonviolent theatrical films, 29% of the gender-focused products were aimed at men, while for violent theatrical films with warnings the percentage was 39% and for violent theatrical films without warnings the percentage was 38%.[41] These figures suggest that even on violent films most gender-focused products are aimed at women. Made-for-television movies without warnings have a similar percentage of their gender-focused products aimed at men (32%) compared with those movies with warnings (31%).

The model of advertiser backlash predicts that, if one holds product level characteristics constant, larger firms may be more reluctant to advertise on violent programs with warnings because their actions may be more likely to be scrutinized by interest groups. The companies advertising on network prime-time broadcast movies are large firms with familiar brand identities. For theatrical movies, for example, the top three advertisers were Procter and Gamble, General Motors, and Pepsico for nonviolent films in the sample; Pepsico, Warner-Lambert, and Unilever for the violent films with warnings; and Sears, McDonald's, and Pepsico for violent films without warnings (see table A5.6). Although all of these companies are "large," the differences in firm size predicted in the backlash model do appear in the data. Table 5.6 defines firm size along two dimensions, advertising expenditures by the parent companies associ-

TABLE 5.6
Mean Company Media Expenditures and Products Advertised for Ads on Theatrical Movies

1993 Mean Parent Company Expenditures ($000s)	Ads on Violent Movies, Warning	Ads	Ads on Violent Movies, No Warning	Ads	Difference of Means Test (T Statistic)
Total Media	316,925	689	380,182	727	3.68***
Network Television	134,178	689	161,321	727	3.27***
Spot Television	73,080	689	78,699	727	1.44
Syndicated Television	16,321	689	21,700	727	2.34**
Cable Television	18,826	689	24,859	727	3.97***
Average No. of Products Advertised in Movie Sample by the Parent Company	19.7	727	22.6	765	2.52***

Note: Media expenditures information comes from Leading National Advertisers 1994b. Products were linked to parent company information using Leading National Advertisers 1994a. Total media expenditures are the sum of expenditures on network television, spot television, syndicated television, cable TV networks, network radio, national spot radio, magazines, Sunday magazines, newspapers, and outdoor advertising as reported in Leading National Advertisers 1994a. *** = statistically significant at the .01 level; ** = significant at the .05 level.

ated with the ads on particular types of movies and the number of products in the network ad sample associated with the parent companies sponsoring ads on these films. Companies that advertised on violent films with warnings did have lower average media expenditures ($316,925,000) than firms sponsoring ads on violent movies without warnings ($380,182,000). The difference of means tests for expenditures on network television, syndicated television, and cable television were also statistically significant for companies advertising on violent films with warnings versus those without warnings. Ads on violent movies with warnings came from companies with an average of 19.7 different products advertised on prime-time movies in the sample, versus a mean of 22.6 for ads on violent movies without warnings. As predicted by the backlash theory, products advertised on violent theatrical films with warnings are associated with parent companies with lower media expenditures and fewer advertised products. Larger firms may try to avoid theatrical films with warnings because of their greater potential to generate scrutiny of their advertising policies.

The analysis of the impact of advertiser backlash has rested in part on the assumption that violent movies with warnings and violent movies without warnings draw similar audiences and are similar in controversial content, so that firm incentives to advertise will relate to reputation effects caused primarily by the application of the warning label to the films. Ideally, one would like detailed information on movie content and audience composition so that one could control for these factors in analysis of advertising decisions. Table 5.7 addresses part of these concerns by using logistic analysis to analyze the factors that distinguish ads on movies with violence and analyze the factors that predict whether a product will be on a movie with a warning. The inclusion of the Nielsen ratings for women 18–49 and men 18–49 allows one to control for the nature of the audience captured by a film (and in part the nature of the content, since content and audience are related). The results indicate that products aimed at attracting men 18–49 will advertise on films with warnings, while those aimed at women 18–49 are less likely to advertise on films with warnings. In addition, products with a higher percentage of users 55–64 were less likely and products with a higher percentage of households with no children were more likely to advertise on theatrical films with warnings. If one controls for the rating of who shows up in the audience for a film, products with higher use among males were more likely to advertise on the films with warnings. These results are consistent with products facing different incentives to react to warnings based on the gender, age, and family status of their target customers. Products from firms with higher media expenditures were less likely to advertise on movies with warnings, consistent with the notion that these firms may try to avoid movies with warnings because they have a higher potential for attracting interest group scrutiny.

TABLE 5.7
Determinants of Advertising on Theatrical Movies with Warnings

Variable	(a)	(b)	(c)	(d)
Intercept	-2.90	1.12	-2.15	0.90
	(2.60)	(3.45)	(3.80)	(5.12)
% 18–24	-0.01	-0.03	-0.003	-0.04
	(0.02)	(0.02)	(0.03)	(0.04)
% 25–34	-0.03	-0.03	-0.03	-0.002
	(0.02)	(0.03)	(0.04)	(0.05)
% 45–54	0.02	0.03	0.38	0.05
	(0.03)	(0.03)	(0.04)	(0.05)
% 55–64	-0.12***	-0.18***	-0.11***	-0.13**
	(0.03)	(0.04)	(0.04)	(0.06)
% 65+	-0.02	-0.002	-0.03	-0.03
	(0.03)	(0.03)	(0.04)	(0.05)
% <$10K	0.06	0.04	0.07	-0.00001
	(0.04)	(0.05)	(0.06)	(0.07)
% $10–19K	0.05	0.02	0.05	0.06
	(0.04)	(0.04)	(0.05)	(0.07)
% $30–39K	-0.03	-0.10**	-0.07	-0.16***
	(0.04)	(0.05)	(0.05)	(0.06)
% $40K+	0.02	-0.02	-0.0009	-0.04
	(0.02)	(0.03)	(0.03)	(0.04)
% Male	0.01*	0.02	0.03**	0.03*
	(0.01)	(0.03)	(0.01)	(0.02)
% No Children	0.05***	0.04***	0.05***	0.05**
	(0.01)	(0.02)	(0.02)	(0.02)
Rating Men 18–49		0.36***		0.29***
		(0.04)		(0.06)
Rating Women 18–49		-0.23***		-0.19***
		(0.03)		(0.04)
Company Total Media Expenditures			-8.46e-7**	-1.46e-6***
			(3.56e-7)	(4.75e-7)
No. of Company Advertised Products			0.007	0.007
			(0.005)	(0.007)
Log likelihood	-1,708.9	-1,057.4	-914.3	-554.4
No. of Ads	2,499	1,647	1,356	865

Note: Dependent variable = 1 in logit analysis if ad was on a theatrical movie with a warning. Sample consists of all ads on theatrical violent movies (i.e., those with and without warnings). Standard errors are in parentheses. *** = Statistically significant at .01; ** = .05; * = .10.

MARKET SEGMENTATION IN ADVERTISING ON VIOLENT CABLE PROGRAMS

Cable television provides another avenue to examine advertiser support for violent programming. The NTVS research indicates that basic cable programming is more likely to contain violence than broadcast network programming and that, when it is violent, basic cable programming will be more likely than broadcast network programming to contain multiple violent interactions.[42] Ratings for cable networks are much lower than those for broadcast network programs, raising the possibility that programmers may adopt a strategy of niche programming to reach particularly narrow audiences through their violent shows. Basic cable channels are less likely than the industry average to provide advisories or content codes on violent programs, in part because, unlike the premium cable channels (which are the most likely to provide viewers with content information), these networks may be concerned about advertiser backlash. Advertising on cable is not monitored by interest groups such as the American Family Association, however, so the relative "anonymity" of cable sponsorship may mean that advertisers are less likely to believe that sponsoring shows with warnings on basic cable will lead to controversy.

To examine how advertising audiences vary across types of violent programming on cable, one first needs to select a sample of programs and adopt a definition of violent shows. Three basic cable channels were selected: TNT, USA, and TBS, which ranked first, second, and third in terms of Nielsen prime-time audience ratings for basic cable networks for June 1995.[43] In addition, a local independent broadcast station in the Raleigh-Durham market, WKFT, was selected. The shows from this outlet are included in the sample of basic cable programs since many viewers would (because of its weak broadcast signal on channel 40) only be able to see its programming through basic cable subscription. For the week of April 1–7, 1995, all programming from noon until midnight was taped for these four stations. Commercials were coded for all series programming in violent genres, defined as action adventure, science fiction, mystery, and dramas that dealt with crime, official police, or detectives. For movie programming, all movies in action adventure, horror, mystery, science fiction, thriller, and western genres were included in the commercial coding sample. Movies that were dramas were included if viewing guides indicated through content indicators or descriptions that the films were violent. To supplement the sample of movies from April 1–7 that contained viewer discretion warnings, all movies from April 8–30 on these four channels that contained viewer discretion warnings in viewer guides or were preceded by on air warnings were included. This added a total of twenty-one movies to the sample. The series programming on these cable channels consisted primarily of programs previously aired on broadcast network television. For analysis, these violent series were divided into three groups: "crime" series, which dealt with crime, science fiction, and western themes; mystery series; and children's series (i.e., *Tattooed Teenage Alien Fighters* and *VR Troopers*).[44] Overall, there were a total of 104 separate episodes of series programming and 63 movies that were coded, which yielded a sample of 5,700 commercials on "violent" cable programming.

One way to describe the audience segmentation across violent cable programming is to examine the variation across programs in the percentage of gender-focused products (i.e., those used primarily by one gender) that are aimed at males. Table 5.8 shows that there is no statistical difference in the percentage of gender-focused products aimed at males on violent movies with

TABLE 5.8

Percentage of Gender-Focused Products Aimed at Males, by Cable Subsample

	% Male Products	N	Difference Test (Z Statistic)
Violent Movies with Warnings	38.8	116	−1.2
Violent Movies without Warnings	46.1	165	
Violent Movies	48.9	262	1.4
Violent Series	43.1	281	
Crime Series	52.0	196	1.8*
Mystery Series	39.4	66	
TNT Programming	53.4	146	4.1***
TBS Programming	30.1	143	
USA Programming	42.1	178	−4.3***
WKFT Programming	69.7	76	

Note: Gender-focused products are those which Simmons presents data only for female use (e.g., Maybelline Revitalizing Makeup) or male use (e.g., Hair Club for Men). The table reports the fraction of these gender-focused products that are aimed only at males. N = number of ads for gender focused products in the program sample.

*** = statistically significant at the .01 level; * = significant at the .10 level.

warnings versus those without warnings, which may indicate that the backlash against advertising on labeled programs is not as significant a factor for movies on basic cable. The percentage of male products on crime series (52%) is much higher than that for mystery series (39.4%), consistent with women being a more likely target audience for the mystery programming. There is a wide range in the percentage of male products across channel outlets. TNT and TBS, both owned by Turner Broadcasting, had significantly different percentages of male products. TNT, which at the time had an established violent movie night on Saturdays that the channel advertised as "Saturday Nitro," had 53.4% of gender-focused products that were aimed at males.[45] In contrast, TBS had only 30.1% of its gender-focused product ads aimed at men. These differences are consistent with programming models that suggest that when channels are owned by the same firm, they will, other things being equal, be less likely to target the same audience at the same time.[46] The local independent broadcast station had a male product percentage of 69.7%, the highest of the four outlets. This accords with the evidence that programming on local independents tends to be more violent and, when violent, contains a greater number of violent interactions. As chapter 2 reveals, ratings data indicate that across all age groups men exhibit higher ratings for programs that critics describe as particularly violent.

The distribution of ads across product categories again provides another way to describe audience segmentation and test for advertiser reactions to the placement of program warnings on cable movies. Table 5.9 indicates that there are fewer changes in the pattern of advertisers when warnings are placed on cable movies than when warnings are placed on prime-time broadcast theatrical

TABLE 5.9
Percentage Distribution of Ads across Simmons Product Categories,
Violent Cable Movies

Product Category	Violent, with Warning	Violent, No Warning	Difference Test (Z Statistic)
Product Unclassified	19.4	20.0	−0.4
Automobiles, Cycles, Trucks, & Vans	10.3	9.9	0.3
Automotive Products & Services	0.9	2.3	−2.5**
Travel	1.4	1.4	−0.0
Banking, Investments, Insurance, Credit Cards & Contributions, Memberships, & Public Activities	4.1	2.9	1.5
Games & Toys, Children's & Babies' Apparel & Specialty Products	0.9	1.3	−0.9
Computers, Books, Discs, Records, Tapes, Stereo, Telephones, TV, & Video	3.0	2.0	1.4
Appliances, Garden Care, Sewing, & Photography	5.5	2.5	3.4***
Home Furnishings & Home Improvements	2.5	4.2	−2.2**
Sports & Leisure	2.3	0.8	2.7***
Restaurants, Stores, & Grocery Shopping	9.0	11.0	−1.5
Direct Mail & Other In-Home Shopping, Yellow Pages, Florists, Telegrams, Faxes, & Greeting Cards	2.7	4.0	−1.7*
Jewelry, Watches, Luggage, Writing Tools, & Men's Apparel	0.2	0.3	−0.3
Women's Apparel	0.5	0.8	−0.9
Distilled Spirits, Mixed Drinks, Malt Beverages, Wine, & Tobacco Products	1.9	1.3	1.1
Coffee, Tea, Cocoa, Milk, Soft Drinks, Juices, & Bottled Water	2.8	3.3	−0.6
Dairy Products, Desserts, Baking, & Bread Products	0.7	1.6	−2.1**
Cereals & Spreads, Rice, Pasta, Pizza, Mexican Foods, Fruits & Vegetables	4.0	4.5	−0.5
Soup, Meat, Fish, Poultry, Condiments, Dressings, & Sauces	1.6	1.7	−0.1
Chewing Gum, Candy, Cookies, & Snacks	4.0	4.1	−0.1
Soap, Laundry, Paper Products, & Kitchen Wraps	1.3	3.4	−3.3***
Household Cleaners, Room Deodorizers, Pest Controls, & Pet Foods	8.0	6.7	1.1
Health Care Products & Remedies	5.0	4.2	0.9
Oral Hygiene Products, Skin Care, Deodorants, & Drug Stores	4.0	4.5	—
Fragrances, Hair Care, & Shaving Products	2.7	2.2	0.7
Women's Beauty Aids, Cosmetics, & Personal Products	2.7	2.0	1.1
Total	99.7	100.2	0.9

Note: *** = statistically significant at the .01 level; ** = significant at the .05 level; * = significant at the .10 level.

movies (analyzed in table 5.4). Both cable movies with and without warnings had approximately 20% of product ads that did not fit into the general Simmons product categories, a figure that is double that for theatrical movies on broadcast television. This may be because products advertised on cable are less likely to be the traditional goods marketed to a mass audience through a mass medium such as broadcast network television. If one compares cable movies with and without warnings, there are fewer shifts in the distribution of products caused by the placement of the warnings on cable movies. For cable movies, there are a higher proportion of sports and leisure products advertised on films with warnings, consistent with these products having a lower potential backlash among target consumers for sponsoring violent programming. Unlike the case with broadcast network movies, movies with warnings on basic cable did not have a higher proportion of ads for alcoholic beverages. On broadcast network films those with warnings had a higher percentage of product ads for automobiles and trucks, yet this effect was not observed for the cable films with warnings. While products in four "family brand" categories (i.e., dairy products, cereals, soup, and soap) were less likely to advertise on broadcast theatrical network films with warnings, for the cable movies those with warnings only had lower percentages of ads from the dairy and soap industries. In sum, the product distribution of ads does change when warnings are placed on cable films, but these changes are less pronounced than those observed for broadcast network films. This is what would be predicted if advertising on cable and local independents was not likely to generate scrutiny, which in turn would mean that firms would be less likely to change their advertising decisions because of the addition of a warning to a movie.

Table 5.10 underscores that market segmentation for advertising on violent cable programming is evident from the distribution of products across industries. Cable series (crime, mystery, and children) contain ads that may be much more likely to be targeted to female viewers, who may be the principal shoppers for their families. Dairy products, soups, soap and laundry, health care products, and oral hygiene and skin care products accounted for a higher percentage of the ads on violent cable series. Cable movies, in contrast, had a higher percentage of ads from automobiles, travel, banking and insurance, home improvements, and men's apparel.

The target audience segmentation in advertising on violent cable programs is also evident in table 5.11, which details the consumer demographics of the products advertised on these shows. Relative to products advertised on violent cable movies, products advertised on violent cable series had a higher percentage of customers aged 55–64 or 65+, a higher percentage of female consumers, and a greater fraction of consumers with incomes less than $30,000. Products advertised on violent movies were more likely to have a higher percentage of users 18–24 or 35–44, a larger fraction of male consumers, and a greater percentage of consumers with incomes greater than $30,000. Products advertised on violent series were also used by a larger proportion of the adult population (21.4%) than those on violent movies (17.7%). These results are consistent with ads on violent cable series being more likely to be aimed at

TABLE 5.10

Percentage Distribution of Ads across Simmons Product Categories, Cable Series versus Movies

Product Category	Cable Series	Cable Movies	Difference Test (Z Statistic)
Product Unclassified	19.2	19.7	−0.4
Automobiles, Cycles, Trucks, & Vans	4.5	10.1	−6.9***
Automotive Products & Services	0.3	1.7	−4.9***
Travel	0.6	1.4	−2.6***
Banking, Investments, Insurance, Credit Cards & Contributions, Memberships, & Public Activities	1.9	3.4	−2.9***
Games & Toys, Children's & Babies' Apparel & Specialty Products	3.0	1.1	4.1***
Computers, Books, Discs, Records, Tapes, Stereo, Telephones, TV, & Video	2.3	2.4	−0.3
Appliances, Garden Care, Sewing, & Photography	3.4	3.7	−0.6
Home Furnishings & Home Improvements	1.5	3.5	−4.1***
Sports & Leisure	1.2	1.4	−0.6
Restaurants, Stores, & Grocery Shopping	11.3	10.2	1.2
Direct Mail & Other In-Home Shopping, Yellow Pages, Florists, Telegrams, Faxes, & Greeting Cards	3.2	3.5	−0.5
Jewelry, Watches, Luggage, Writing Tools, & Men's Apparel	0	0.3	−24.5***
Women's Apparel	0.6	0.7	−0.5
Distilled Spirits, Mixed Drinks, Malt Beverages, Wine, & Tobacco Products	1.9	1.5	1.1
Coffee, Tea, Cocoa, Milk, Soft Drinks, Juices, & Bottled Water	3.8	3.1	1.2
Dairy Products, Desserts, Baking, & Bread Products	2.6	1.3	3.2***
Cereals & Spreads, Rice, Pasta, Pizza, Mexican Foods, Fruits & Vegetables	4.7	4.3	0.6
Soup, Meat, Fish, Poultry, Condiments, Dressings, & Sauces	3.0	1.7	2.8***
Chewing Gum, Candy, Cookies, & Snacks	5.0	4.0	1.5
Soap, Laundry, Paper Products, & Kitchen Wraps	4.6	2.5	3.6***
Household Cleaners, Room Deodorizers, Pest Controls, & Pet Foods	6.7	7.2	0.6
Health Care Products & Remedies	6.1	4.6	2.2**
Oral Hygiene Products, Skin Care, Deodorants, & Drug Stores	4.3	2.4	3.4***
Fragrances, Hair Care, & Shaving Products	2.0	2.3	0.6
Women's Beauty Aids, Cosmetics, & Personal Products	2.1	2.0	
Total	99.8	100.0	0.3

Note: *** = statistically significant at the .01 level; ** = significant at the .05 level; * = significant at the .10 level.

TABLE 5.11

Consumer Demographics of Products Advertised on Cable Movies versus Cable Series

| Consumer Categories | Mean % of a Product's Consumers Accounted for by Consumers in a Particular Demographic Group | | Difference of Means Test (T Statistic) |
	(1) Ads on Violent Movies	(2) Ads on Violent Series	1 vs 2
Age			
18–24	10.9	10.6	2.13**
25–34	23.8	23.8	0.46
35–44	24.4	24.1	3.29***
45–54	16.6	16.1	5.84***
55–64	10.9	11.1	−1.87*
65+	13.4	14.3	−6.43***
Male	50.2	47.8	9.95***
Female	49.8	52.2	−9.91***
Income			
<$10K	8.0	8.7	−7.20***
$10K–19K	14.3	14.8	−5.00***
$20K–29K	16.0	16.2	−3.49***
$30K–39K	15.0	14.7	4.11***
$40.K+	46.8	45.6	5.42***
$50K+	34.2	33.2	5.04***
$60K+	24.5	23.7	5.05***
Education			
Not HS Graduate	16.1	16.7	−3.58***
HS Graduate	35.4	36.0	−4.36***
Attended College	26.1	25.6	4.59***
College Graduate	22.4	21.8	3.33***
No Children in Household	56.6	56.3	0.18
Mean % of Total Adults using Product/Product Category	17.7	21.4	−5.19***
Number of Total Ads	2,382	2,081	

Note: *** = statistically significant at the .01 level; ** = significant at the .05 level;* = significant at the .10 level.

TABLE 5.12
Comparing Media Expenditures, by Cable Programming Subsample

Ads Aired on	1993 Mean Parent Company Total Media Expenditures ($000)	Average No. of Parent Company Products	Difference of Means Test (T Statistic)	
			$	No.
Violent Movies with Warnings	315,528	18		
Violent Movies without Warnings	293,385	17	1.0	0.8
Violent Movies	307,967	18		
Violent Series	350,133	22	−2.7***	−3.5***
Crime Series	332,471	20		
Mystery Series	385,435	25	−1.8*	−2.4**
TNT Programming	277,963	17		
TBS Programming	298,072	16	−1.2	1.1
USA Programming	389,664	24		
WKFT Programming	364,332	20	0.9	2.4**

Note: Media expenditures information comes from Leading National Advertisers 1994b. Products were linked to parent company information using Leading National Advertisers 1994a. Total media expenditures are the sum of expenditures on network television, spot television, syndicated television, cable TV networks, network radio, national spot radio, magazines, Sunday magazines, newspapers, and outdoor advertising as reported in Leading National Advertisers 1994a. *** = statistically significant at the .01 level; ** = significant at the .05 level; * = significant at the .10 level.

older or female consumers, while ads on violent cable movies being aimed at younger or male consumers.[47]

Violent programs also may vary by the nature of the firms advertising on them. Table 5.12 reveals that the total company media expenditures and total number of products advertised in the sample of network programs are nearly identical for ads on cable movies with and without warnings. For broadcast theatrical films, products on movies with warnings came from firms with lower media expenditures and fewer products, consistent with the pullout of larger firms concerned about interest group scrutiny. For cable movies, however, the differences in company characteristics between products on movies with and without warnings are not statistically significant, providing further evidence that advertiser backlash may be less common on cable films because anticipated interest group scrutiny is lower.[48] Ads for products on violent series come from firms with larger media expenditures and more products advertised than those on violent cable movies, adding to the evidence that movies may be aimed at a narrower market segment than the series. Similarly, the products on mystery series come from firms with more media expenditures and advertised products than those on crime series, which may have a narrower audience. While there is no statistically significant difference in the figures for TNT and TBS in table

5.12, firms advertising on USA had more products advertised overall than those on the local independent WKFT.

CONTROVERSY AND ADVERTISING RATES

Although I lack information on how advertising rates change when warnings are placed on violent movies on broadcast or cable channels, in this section I am able to investigate how advertiser fears of being associated with a controversial network series can affect program rates. Specifically, prime-time ad data from November 1993 allow me to explore the initial reaction by companies to the introduction of *NYPD Blue*, a controversial police drama broadcast by ABC. The program's producer, Steve Bochco, announced that his goal for the program was to bring "R rated programming" to television. The American Family Association, led by the Reverend Donald Wildmon, announced a campaign to convince local affiliates not to carry the program and advertisers not to support the show. The program generated controversy more for its use of language and partial nudity rather than violence and generally carried a viewer discretion warning that emphasized adult content or language rather than violence.[49]

In the face of protest by groups such as the AFA about the content of *NYPD Blue*, fifty-seven ABC affiliates initially refused to carry the program when the show debuted in the fall of 1993.[50] In at least eight markets, the network arranged for other stations (generally Fox affiliates) to carry the program when the ABC affiliate refused to carry the show. The initial burst of publicity of the attempts by AFA to have advertisers refuse to sponsor the program did lead some companies to shy away from the program. As one assessment of the campaign against the program noted in November 1993, "The impact on 'NYPD Blue' has been that it has carried no spots from any of the mainstays of prime-time drama series advertising. No automobiles. No fast-food restaurants. No beers. No soft drinks."[51] Accounts of the early ad sales on the program noted that, although the show attracted high ratings, the controversy affected the ad revenues the network was able to generate from the show. The program was said to average fewer 30-second commercials per hour than most ABC shows, and the ad rates charged for these commercials were said to be lower than that suggested by the ratings levels.[52] Although some major advertisers did buy time on the program prior to the 1993–94 season, they reportedly stipulated that the ads run in the first, second, or third quarter of 1994, when the controversy surrounding the program would presumably have lessened.[53]

The ad data analyzed here allow one to test whether, as indicated in press accounts, the program was selling at a discount relative to the price one would expect, given the desirable demographics attracted by the program. Two months after its introduction, 30-second ads on *NYPD Blue* were selling for $89,800 according to Nielsen November 1993 data.[54] The show attracted a relatively high number of women 18–49 (an average of 6,590,000 per episode) and men 18–49 (5,990,000 per show), a set of viewers whose ratings generate higher advertising prices. To test the impact of controversy on *NYPD Blue* ad rates I used the full sample of 140 prime-time broadcast network shows to model ad prices as a function of the number of men 18–34, women 18–34, viewers 35–49, and viewers 50+ in the audience for a program.[55]

If the controversy surrounding the introduction of *NYPD Blue* caused some advertisers to avoid the show, one implication is that advertisers will not be willing to pay as much to sponsor the program because along with the benefits of exposure there are potential costs in terms of brand image damage. This could show up in lower than expected prices for *NYPD Blue* ads. The ad model predicts that, based on its audience of 2,740,000 men 18–34, 3,340,000 women 18–34, 6,500,000 viewers 35–49, and 6,380,000 viewers 50+, *NYPD Blue* should have commanded a 30-second ad price of $163,200. The difference between the expected ad price and the actual ad price, a difference of $73,400, represents the cost to ABC of the advertiser reaction to the controversy. The show thus sold at a discount of nearly 45% in November 1993 because of advertiser backlash.

The controversy surrounding *NYPD Blue* was unusual. The model provides additional confirmation for this, for the show had the largest negative prediction error (estimated price — actual ad price) for any program in prime time. The boycott efforts of AFA also extended to attempts to convince local ABC affiliates not to air the program. As of November 1993, the program was only being carried in 148 out of 211 television markets, though these were generally the largest markets in the United States.

Table A5.7 explores how the decision to carry *NYPD Blue* varied with the financial incentives for local stations. Stations should be more willing to show the program the larger the potential profits from local ads on the program and the smaller the potential adverse reaction from local residents. The logit results indicate the larger the number of television households in the market, the more likely an ABC affiliate was to air the program. This could be because ad prices are higher in larger markets and because viewers in these larger (urban) markets would be less likely to be offended by the program. The larger the percentage of residents in the market with cable television, the less likely the station was to carry *NYPD Blue*. This may relate to the relative competition faced by local broadcasters. In areas with low cable subscription rates, *NYPD Blue* may attract more viewers since they do not see programming with higher sexual content on cable. In areas with higher cable subscription rates, *NYPD Blue* may seem less distinctive because viewers have the option of viewing basic or premium cable channels.

Markets with a higher percentage of blue-collar workers were less likely to carry the show, which may relate to lower viewer interest in such programming in areas with high blue-collar concentrations. The percentage of residents subscribing to *Penthouse*, an adult entertainment magazine, was included to see if expressed consumer preferences for media with sexual content were related to local television programming decisions. The coefficient is positive, indicating that in areas where viewers were more likely to express a demand for media with sexual content the ABC affiliate (or, in some markets, another station such as the Fox affiliate) was more likely to carry *NYPD Blue*. However, the effect is only statistically significant at the .17 level.

Although controversy originally depressed advertising rates on *NYPD Blue*, prices for commercials on the program began to rise as the show garnered awards and the complaints about its contents dissipated. The president of sales and marketing at ABC stated that the honors won by *NYPD Blue* helped increase companies' willingness to advertise, noting, "It helped us make our case when the Emmys and the People's Choice awards started rolling in."[56] Assessing the show's marketability in the spring of 1995, an article in *Variety* noted:

A year ago, *NYPD Blue*'s proclivity for tough language and partial nudity prompted stations covering 20% of the country to drop this show and advertisers to stay away. That meant those with the courage to advertise on the controversial show bought commercials at bargain basement prices. Now *NYPD Blue* is on the air in 99% of the country, and advertisers who want in the hit cop show are paying close to market rates.[57]

By November 1995, a 30-second commercial on the program sold for $211,000. When I reran the model for prime-time ad prices using data from 146 prime-time shows in November 1995, *NYPD Blue* had a predicted ad price of $212,200 based on the demographics of its audience.[58] The residual for the program was thus only −$1,200, or .6% of its expected ad price. Although the initial controversy surrounding the program depressed its ad prices, 2 years later *NYPD Blue* was sold at a rate that indicated the show no longer paid a penalty for its content. Although ad prices eventually reached the level warranted by the program's audience, the lower net returns in the program's first year may have reduced the incentives for other producers to try to emulate the program's content.

CONCLUSIONS

Program warnings do change the mix of advertisers supporting prime-time movies in systematic ways. In response to program warnings, broadcasters do not change the number of "nonprogram" minutes in shows. They are more likely, however, to run promotions for network shows on theatrical films with warnings, consistent with a drop in price because of advertiser pullouts. For theatrical films, it is clear that warnings have an independent impact on which types of products are advertised on films. The placement of a warning on a violent theatrical film changes the incentives for particular products to advertise. Within the set of violent theatrical films, products aimed at younger consumers, males, and households without children are more likely to advertise on shows with warnings. Products from industries such as sports and leisure and alcoholic beverages play a larger role in supporting programs with warnings, while those products in industries with "family" images such as food or kitchen products are less likely to advertise on theatrical films with warnings. Some of these patterns are also present for warnings on made-for-television movies, although the reactions to these warnings are harder to measure because of the absence of a comparable made-for-television subset to compare the warning movies with. Reactions to warnings on made for television movies may differ because these films may be less violent than those theatrical films which receive viewer warnings.

The advertising differences identified as arising from viewer warnings are statistically significant and small in magnitude. In a market where a 30-second ad on a prime-time movie may cost $150,000, however, a small number of advertiser pullouts on a movie may translate into significant sums if multiplied across many broadcast movies. The results identified here such as the increase in network promotions on movies with warnings suggest that viewer advisories do translate into lost advertising revenues for prime-time broadcast networks. For example, the shift of 2% of ads on prime-time broadcast movies with warnings from paid advertising to network promotions could have cost networks approximately $8 million in lost revenues over the course of the sample period (May 1995–February 1996).[59]

These potential losses provide networks with multiple incentives. They will be less likely to place warnings on movies that are truly violent, as evidenced by the UCLA finding that networks had placed viewer advisories on less than half of the prime-time movies that raised issues of concern with respect to violence in the 1994–95 season. In a world of television rating systems, networks may be less likely to give viewers detailed information about violence that would raise the probability of advertiser backlash. This points to the importance of outside evaluation by interest groups, nonprofits (e.g., Federman 1996, Rideout 1996), and academics of the content of the television rating system and the implementation of these ratings.

In the long term, the reduction in advertising returns to violent programs may also affect the mix of programming offered. Evaluating this outcome from a social welfare perspective is difficult, in part because of the uncertainty of the magnitude of negative effects of violent programs on children and adults. Current policies such as the V-chip and ratings system are aimed at reducing consumption of violent programming by children. Yet research indicates that violent programming may affect both children and adults (Wilson et al. 1996). Advertiser reactions to warnings may reduce programming that is harmful to both groups, but this may also reduce the utility of adults who would like to consume the programming and are not affected by its content.

These results demonstrate that warnings on broadcast network films do change advertiser behavior. These changes in behavior are based not on the distribution of altruism among companies but on the distribution of incentives for firms to respond based on their consumer demographics. These results demonstrate the importance of recognizing the incentives for broadcasters and advertisers in supporting violent programming and of incorporating these incentives into assessments of the operation of policies such as the development of a program rating system by the television industry (discussed in more detail in chapter 8).

Analysis of cable advertising also confirms the model of advertiser decisions to sponsor violent programs. Ads on different types of violent cable programming are targeted at different consumer groups. Products on mystery series are aimed at older or female consumers relative to those on crime series. Ads on violent series in general are for products used more by females, older consumers, and those with lower incomes relative to ads for products on violent movies. The differences between products advertised on violent cable movies with and without warnings are much less stark, however, than those for movies with and without warnings on prime-time network broadcast television. This suggests that the prospects for advertiser backlash are less likely to influence firms' decisions about sponsoring violent cable programming since interest groups are much less likely to monitor these ads than those on prime-time broadcast television. This also indicates that firms' concerns about reputations for sponsoring violent programming may diminish if the division of the television audience into many different audiences makes monitoring of advertising by interest groups less likely.

The case of diminished advertising prices for *NYPD Blue* during its initial season demonstrates how controversy can lower returns. Although the advertising prices for the show climbed as the scrutiny of interest groups dissipated, the initial loss of potential advertising revenue in the first season of the police drama may have lessened the willingness of other producers to imitate such programming. The next chapter examines in more detail the incentives for producers to choose between violent and nonviolent program content.

A MODEL OF ADVERTISING ON VIOLENT VERSUS NONVIOLENT PROGRAMS

A FIRM considering the purchase of advertising time on violent and nonviolent programs will consider the sales generated by advertising, the possible consumer backlash from advertising on violent programs, and the costs of advertising. To model this decision, let

Q_v, Q_{nv}	=	Amount of minutes of ad time purchased on violent or non-violent programs
R_v, R_{nv}	=	Average ratings for the violent or nonviolent programs
P_v, P_{nv}	=	Average price per minute of advertising time on violent or nonviolent programs
α_i	=	Demographics of a product's consumers (this may include the percentage of a product's customers that are 18–34 or the percentage of a product's customers that are male)
I	=	Amount of information that people have on whether a firm advertises on violent programs
VS	=	Sales revenue generated by ads on violent programs
NS	=	Sales revenue generated by ads on nonviolent programs.
BL	=	Change in sales revenue if a product's consumers are fully informed about a firm's advertising purchases of violent programming
A	=	Probability that consumers will be fully informed about a firm's advertising purchases.

Note that $VS(Q_v, R_v, \alpha_i)$ and $NS(Q_{nv}, R_{nv}, \alpha_i)$. By assumption $VS_{Q_v}, NS_{Q_{nv}}, VS_{R_v}, NS_{R_{nv}} > 0$. The demographic characteristics α_i are defined so that as α_i increases VS increases and NS decreases. Thus as the proportion of a product's customers that are young increases, for a given level of other variables (such as program ratings) sales generated by violent programs will increase and those from nonviolent programs will decrease by violent programs will increase and those from nonviolent programs will decrease ($VS_{\alpha_i} > 0, NS_{\alpha_i} < 0$). Similarly, as the percentage of a product's customers that are male increases, sales from advertising on violent programs will increase. The expected value of the change in sales from advertising on violent programs is $A(I)BL(Q_v, R_v, \alpha_i)$, where $A_I, BL_{Q_v}, BL_{R_v} > 0$. Note that $BL_{\alpha_i} < 0$ since as the percentage of a product's users that are male increases the loss in sales will be lower since males are less likely to view television violence as a significant problem. Only advertising costs are considered (e.g., production costs are ignored here).

The firm will choose Q_v and Q_{nv} to maximize Z, where

$$Z = VS(Q_v, R_v, \alpha_i) + NS(Q_{nv}, R_{nv}, \alpha_i) - A(I)BL(Q_v, R_v, \alpha_i) - P_v Q_v - P_{nv} Q_{nv}.$$

The first order conditions are

$$Z_{Q_v} = VS_{Q_v} - A(I)BL_{Q_v} - P_v = 0$$

$$Z_{Q_{nv}} = NS_{Q_{nv}} - P_{nv} = 0,$$

which indicate that when the firm is maximizing profits from advertising that

$$\frac{VS_{Q_v} - A(I)BL_{Q_v}}{P_v} = \frac{NS_{Q_{nv}}}{P_{nv}}.$$

This means that the net return per dollar spent on advertising on violent programs will equal the return on a dollar spent on advertising on nonviolent programs. The Hessian is

$$|H| = \begin{vmatrix} VS_{Q_v Q_v} - A(I) BL_{Q_v Q_v} & 0 \\ 0 & NS_{Q_{nv} Q_{nv}} \end{vmatrix}.$$

The second-order sufficient condition for a maximum will be satisfied if we assume that $VS_{Q_v Q_v} - A(I) BL_{Q_v Q_v}$ is negative and $(VS_{Q_v Q_v} - A(I) BL_{Q_v Q_v})$ $(NS_{Q_{nv} Q_{nv}})$ is positive. This also implies that $NS_{Q_{nv} Q_{nv}}$ is negative.

We can explore how changes in the exogenous variables (α_i, R_v, R_{nv}, P_v, P_{nv}) affect a firm's selection of Q_v and Q_{nv} by using Cramer's rule. As α_i increases, we find that

$$\frac{\delta \overline{Q_v}}{\delta \alpha_i} = \frac{(-VS_{Q_v \alpha_i} + A(I) BL_{Q_v \alpha_i}) NS_{Q_{nv} Q_{nv}}}{|H|} \text{ and}$$

$$\frac{\delta \overline{Q_{nv}}}{\delta \alpha_i} = \frac{(VS_{Q_v Q_v} - A(I)BL_{Q_v Q_v})(-NS_{Q_v \alpha_i})}{|H|}.$$

Note that from the assumption that the second-order condition is satisfied we know that the denominator $|H|$ is positive. Since $NS_{Q_{nv} Q_{nv}}$ is negative from the second-order condition assumption, $\frac{\delta \overline{Q_v}}{\delta \alpha_i}$ will be positive if

$VS_{Q,\alpha_i} > A(I)BL_{Q,\alpha_i}$, and negative if $VS_{Q,\alpha_i} < A(I)BL_{Q,\alpha_i}$. Thus as the percentage of male consumers for a product increases, the purchase of advertising on violent programs will increase if the increase in sales caused by an additional ad as the male percentage increases is higher than the change in the expected value of the backlash from an additional ad as the male percentage increases.

$(VS_{Q,Q_v} - A(I)BL_{Q,Q_v})$ is negative from the second-order condition, and NS_{Q,α_i} is negative by assumption. This means that $\frac{\delta Q_{nv}}{\delta \alpha_i}$ is negative—that is, as the male percentage of product customers increases, fewer ads will be bought on nonviolent programs.

Use of Cramer's rule also demonstrates the changes in ad purchases as I increases, which would occur if warning labels were placed on violent films so consumers were more likely to be aware of firm's advertising actions:

$$\frac{\delta Q_v}{\delta I} = \frac{(A_I BL_{Q_v})NS_{Q_{nv},Q_{nv}}}{|H|} \text{ and}$$

$$\frac{\delta Q_{nv}}{\delta I} = 0.$$

A_I is positive, since by assumption the probability that people will associate a company with its advertising on violent programs increases if warning labels are placed on violent films. BL_{Q_v} is positive and $NS_{Q_{nv},Q_{nv}}$ negative, so $\frac{\delta Q_v}{\delta I}$ is negative. A firm will place fewer ads on violent programs as I increases. Note that this impact would be lower for firms with smaller backlash changes.

As ratings increase for violent programs, purchases of ads on the programs will depend on the relationship between sales increases and consumer backlash. Note that

$$\frac{\delta Q_v}{\delta R_v} = \frac{(-VS_{Q_v R_v} + A(I)BL_{Q_v,R_v})NS_{Q_{nv},Q_{nv}}}{|H|} \text{ and}$$

$$\frac{\delta Q_{nv}}{\delta R_v} = 0.$$

If the sales term outweighs the backlash term, the firm will purchase more ads on violent programs as ratings go up. If the backlash term is dominant, then the firm will purchase fewer ads on violent shows. The model also indicates that as the price of advertising on violent programs goes up, the firm will purchase fewer ads on these shows.

Table A5.1

Percentage Distribution of Ads on Made-for-Television Movies

	Movies Subsamples			Difference of Proportion Test (Z Statistic)		
Ad Category	(1) No Warning	(2) Warning	(3) "Violent" No Warning	1 vs. 2	2 vs. 3	
Product	62.9	61.7	62.3	0.86	−0.32	
Movie	1	2.8	1.4	−3.99***	2.50**	
Video	0.9	1	1.1	−0.41	−0.38	
Health Services	0.1	0.2	0	−1.14	1.63	
Utility	0.1	0.2	0.1	−0.19	0.66	
Military	0.2	0.4	0.3	−1.21	0.55	
Nonprofit	0.2	0.1	0.1	1.08	0.00	
Public Service	1.3	1.5	1.3	−0.48	0.37	
Network	21.6	22.7	22.2	−0.87	0.33	
Local Station	11.7	9.5	11.2	2.62***	−1.43	
Total	100	100	99.9			
Network, Local Station, PSA	34.6	33.7	34.7	0.65	−0.55	
Commercial Ads	65.4	66.3	65.2	−0.65	0.60	
Total number of Ads	10,700	1,318	1,408			

Note: *** = statistically significant at the .01 level; ** = significant at the .05 level; * = significant at the .10 level.

TABLE A5.2

Percentage Distribution of Ads across Simmons Product Categories, Theatrical Movies

Product Category	Nonviolent	Violent, Warning	Difference Test (Z Statistic)
Product Unclassified	8.5	10.2	−1.6
Automobiles, Cycles, Trucks, & Vans	12.2	13.4	−1.0
Automotive Products & Services	0.4	0.8	−1.6
Travel	1.3	1.8	−1.1
Banking, Investments, Insurance, Credit Cards & Contributions, Memberships, & Public Activities	2.0	1.8	0.4
Games & Toys, Children's & Babies' Apparel & Specialty Products	1.6	0.9	1.8*
Computers, Books, Discs, Records, Tapes, Stereo, Telephones, TV, & Video	5.6	4.7	1.1
Appliances, Garden Care, Sewing, & Photography	3.5	3.6	−0.1
Home Furnishings & Home Improvements	2.3	2.0	0.5
Sports & Leisure	0.8	3.6	−5.2***
Restaurants, Stores, & Grocery Shopping	17.8	15.0	2.1**
Direct Mail & Other In-Home Shopping, Yellow Pages, Florists, Telegrams, Faxes, & Greeting Cards	0.8	0.5	1.2
Jewelry, Watches, Luggage, Writing Tools, & Men's Apparel	1.3	0.8	1.4
Women's Apparel	1.2	1.1	0.3
Distilled Spirits, Mixed Drinks, Malt Beverages, Wine, & Tobacco Products	0.5	2.7	−4.7***
Coffee, Tea, Cocoa, Milk, Soft Drinks, Juices, & Bottled Water	3.7	4.2	−0.7
Dairy Products, Desserts, Baking, & Bread Products	2.0	0.6	3.5***
Cereals & Spreads, Rice, Pasta, Pizza, Mexican Foods, Fruits & Vegetables	3.4	1.8	2.9***
Soup, Meat, Fish, Poultry, Condiments, Dressings & Sauces	3.1	1.6	2.9***
Chewing Gum, Candy, Cookies, & Snacks	3.7	4.6	−1.3
Soap, Laundry, Paper Products, & Kitchen Wraps	2.7	2.2	0.9

TABLE A5.2 (Continued)

Product Category	Nonviolent	Violent, Warning	Difference Test (Z Statistic)
Household Cleaners, Room Deodorizers, Pest Controls, & Pet Foods	3.0	2.2	1.5
Health Care Products & Remedies	6.2	7.6	−1.6
Oral Hygiene Products, Skin Care, Deodorants, & Drug Stores	3.8	5.9	−2.7***
Fragrances, Hair Care, & Shaving Products	6.2	4.0	2.9***
Women's Beauty Aids, Cosmetics, & Personal Products	2.6	2.5	0.1
Total	99.9	100.1	

Note: *** = statistically significant at the .01 level; ** = significant at the .05 level; * = significant at the .10 level.

TABLE A5.3
Percentage Distribution of Ads across Simmons Product Categories,
Made-for-Television Movies

Product Category	No Warning	Warning	Difference Test (Z Statistic)
Product Unclassified	7.3	10.2	−2.7***
Automobiles, Cycles, Trucks, & Vans	13.2	10.0	2.9***
Automotive Products & Services	0.6	0.7	−0.3
Travel	1.1	0.2	4.4***
Banking, Investments, Insurance, Credit Cards & Contributions, Memberships, & Public Activities	1.7	1.3	1.0
Games & Toys, Children's & Babies' Apparel & Specialty Products	0.6	1.6	−2.4**
Computers, Books, Discs, Records, Tapes, Stereo, Telephones, TV, & Video	4.9	6.0	−1.3
Appliances, Garden Care, Sewing, & Photography	4.3	3.4	1.4
Home Furnishings & Home Improvements	2.6	1.0	3.9***
Sports & Leisure	0.8	2.7	−3.3***
Restaurants, Stores, & Grocery Shopping	16.7	16.6	0.1
Direct Mail & Other In-Home Shopping, Yellow Pages, Florists, Telegrams, Faxes, & Greeting Cards	0.7	0.1	3.6***
Jewelry, Watches, Luggage, Writing Tools, & Men's Apparel	0.9	0.9	−0.1
Women's Apparel	1.5	2.3	−1.6
Distilled Spirits, Mixed Drinks, Malt Beverages, Wine, & Tobacco Products	0.8	2.1	−2.7**
Coffee, Tea, Cocoa, Milk, Soft Drinks, Juices, & Bottled Water	3.3	3.4	−0.1
Dairy Products, Desserts, Baking, & Bread Products	2.5	1.3	2.9***
Cereals & Spreads, Rice, Pasta, Pizza, Mexican Foods, Fruits & Vegetables	4.0	0.7	8.9***
Soup, Meat, Fish, Poultry, Condiments, Dressings, & Sauces	3.0	2.0	2.1**
Chewing Gum, Candy, Cookies, & Snacks	3.3	3.5	−0.3
Soap, Laundry, Paper Products, & Kitchen Wraps	3.3	2.5	1.3
Household Cleaners, Room Deodorizers, Pest Controls, & Pet Foods	3.1	2.2	1.6
Health Care Products & Remedies	7.3	10.3	−2.8***
Oral Hygiene Products, Skin Care, Deodorants, & Drug Stores	4.5	5.8	−1.5
Fragrances, Hair Care, & Shaving Products	5.7	5.6	0.2
Women's Beauty Aids, Cosmetics, & Personal Products	2.5	3.7	−1.8*
Total	100.1	99.9	

Note: *** = statistically significant at the .01 level; ** = significant at the .05 level; * = significant at the .10 level.

TABLE A5.4

Percentage Distribution of Ads across Simmons Product Categories, Made-for-Television Movies

Product Category	Warning	"Violent," No Warning	Difference Test (Z stat)
Product Unclassified	10.2	9.2	0.7
Automobiles, Cycles, Trucks, & Vans	10.0	13.0	−2.0**
Automotive Products & Services	0.7	0.5	0.4
Travel	0.2	1.3	−2.6***
Banking, Investments, Insurance, Credit Cards & Contributions, Memberships, & Public Activities	1.3	1.3	−0.1
Games & Toys, Children's & Babies' Apparel & Specialty Products	1.6	0.5	2.2**
Computers, Books, Discs, Records, Tapes, Stereo, Telephones, TV, & Video	6.0	5.9	0.1
Appliances, Garden Care, Sewing, & Photography	3.4	4.4	−1.1
Home Furnishings & Home Improvements	1.0	2.2	−1.9*
Sports & Leisure	2.7	1.0	2.6**
Restaurants, Stores, & Grocery Shopping	16.6	17.1	−0.3
Direct Mail & Other In-Home Shopping, Yellow Pages, Florists, Telegrams, Faxes, & Greeting Cards	0.1	0.4	−1.3
Jewelry, Watches, Luggage, Writing Tools, & Men's Apparel	0.9	0.9	0.1
Women's Apparel	2.3	1.1	2.0*
Distilled Spirits, Mixed Drinks, Malt Beverages, Wine, & Tobacco Products	2.1	1.4	1.1
Coffee, Tea, Cocoa, Milk, Soft Drinks, Juices, & Bottled Water	3.4	4.1	−0.8
Dairy Products, Desserts, Baking, & Bread Products	1.3	2.1	−1.3
Cereals & Spreads, Rice, Pasta, Pizza, Mexican Foods, Fruits & Vegetables	0.7	3.3	−4.0***
Soup, Meat, Fish, Poultry, Condiments, Dressings, & Sauces	2.0	2.4	−0.6
Chewing Gum, Candy, Cookies, & Snacks	3.5	2.4	1.3
Soap, Laundry, Paper Products, & Kitchen Wraps	2.5	3.6	−1.3
Household Cleaners, Room Deodorizers, Pest Controls, & Pet Foods	2.2	2.7	−0.7
Health Care Products & Remedies	10.3	6.7	2.7***
Oral Hygiene Products, Skin Care, Deodorants, & Drug Stores	5.8	3.9	1.8*
Fragrances, Hair Care & Shaving Products	5.6	6.4	−0.7
Women's Beauty Aids, Cosmetics, & Personal Products	3.7	2.1	2.0**
Total	99.9	99.9	

Note: *** = statistically significant at the .01 level; ** = significant at the .05 level; * = significant at the .10 level.

TABLE A5.5
Consumer Demographics of Products Advertised on Made-for-Television Movies

Consumer Categories	Mean % of a Product's Consumers Accounted for by Consumers in a Particular Demographic Group			Difference of Means Test (T Statistic)	
	(1) Ads on Movies with No Warning	(2) Ads on Movies with Warning	(3) Ads on "Violent" Movies with No Warning	1 vs. 2	2 vs. 3
Age					
18–24	11.8	12.9	12.1	−6.56***	3.92***
25–34	23.9	24.6	24.1	−4.58***	2.92***
35–44	24.5	24.4	24.4	0.56	0.20
45–54	16.1	15.8	16.1	3.74***	−2.95***
55–64	10.6	10.2	10.6	5.32***	−3.62***
65 +	13.1	12.2	12.9	5.31***	−3.01***
Male	49.0	49.5	49.4	−1.84*	0.51
Female	51.0	50.5	50.7	1.86*	−0.55
Income					
< $10K	8.1	8.1	8.0	0.30	0.55
$10K–19K	14.1	14.0	14.0	1.77*	−0.05
$20K–29K	16.2	16.2	16.2	−0.76	−0.20
$30K–39K	15.0	15.1	15.0	−1.67*	1.56
$40K+	46.6	46.7	46.8	−0.38	−0.51
$50K+	34.1	34.0	34.2	0.40	−0.91
$60K +	24.2	24.1	24.3	0.61	−0.91
Education					
Not HS Graduate	16.1	16.2	16.0	−0.70	1.20
HS Graduate	35.7	35.8	35.5	−0.84	1.42
College Attended	25.8	26.1	26.0	−2.47**	0.78
College Graduate	22.5	22.0	22.6	2.17**	−1.97**
No Children in Household	56.2	55.4	56.3	3.49***	−3.41***
Mean % of Total Adults Using Product/Product Category	20.6	19.7	20.0	1.05	−0.30
Number of Total Ads	8,728	999	1,141		

Note: *** = statistically significant at the .01 level; ** = significant at the .05 level; * = significant at the .10 level.

TABLE A5.6
Top Ten Advertisers by Theatrical Movie Subsample

Advertiser	Total Ads
Nonviolent (N = 843 Matched Ads)	
1. Procter & Gamble	44
2. General Motors Corp.	42
3. Pepsico Inc.	38
4. Sears Roebuck & Co.	35
5. McDonald's Corp.	33
6. Chrysler Corp.	29
7. AT&T Corp.	23
8. Ford Motor Co.	21
9. Nissan Motor Co.	20
10. General Mills Inc.	19
Violent, Warning (N = 689 Matched Ads)	
1. Pepsico Inc.	45
2. Warner-Lambert Co.	28
3. Unilever PLC	24
4. General Motors Corp.	23
4. McDonald's Corp.	23
6. Procter & Gamble	18
7. Ford Motor Co.	17
7. Subway Franchising Co.	17
9. Wendy's International	16
10. Time Warner Inc.	15
Violent, No Warning (N = 727 Matched Ads)	
1. Sears Roebuck & Co.	48
2. McDonald's Corp.	41
3. Pepsico Inc.	39
4. Procter & Gamble	38
5. Walt Disney Co.	20
6. General Motors Co.	19
6. Wendy's International	19
8. AT&T Corp.	18
8. Warner-Lambert Co.	18
10. Philip Morris Co.	17

Note: Of the products advertised on theatrical movies in the sample, 2,259 matched with information in Leading National Advertisers 1994a that linked products with parent company information.

• *CHAPTER 5* •

TABLE A5.7
Determinants of Whether *NYPD Blue* Was Carried in a Market,
November 1993

	Parameter Estimate (Standard Error)
Intercept	4.50
	(6.50)
Number of Stations	0.03
	(0.14)
Total Television Households	7.8e−3***
	(2.49e−3)
% Cable TV	−0.05**
	(0.03)
% Multiset Households	−3.00e−4
	(0.05)
Buying Income per Household	2.76e−4
	(2.17e−4)
% Disposable Income $25K+	−0.13
	(0.12)
% Professional	−0.07
	(0.08)
% Blue Collar	−0.13**
	(0.07)
% Nonwhite	−0.02
	(0.02)
% of Women 18–49	8.93
	(17.00)
% of Men 18–49	−5.53
	(18.58)
% Subscribe to *Penthouse*	0.60
	(0.43)
Log Likelihood	−43.6

Note: Dependent variable in logit = 1 if the program was carried in
the market.
*** = statistically significant at the .01 level; ** = significant at the .05
level.

· C H A P T E R 6 ·

Producer Incentives

EACH VIEWING DAY the largest audience for television assembles during prime time, generally defined as the viewing hours between 8 and 11 PM on the East and West Coasts and 7 to 10 PM in the Midwest. For adult viewers, prime-time viewing accounts for nearly a third of their overall weekly television consumption.[1] Shows by the broadcast networks have traditionally garnered the largest share of viewers during these hours, though this dominance has declined with the proliferation of cable channels. In 1975, the three major broadcast networks' share of prime-time viewers was 91%, while in 1992 the three major broadcast networks' share of this audience was 61%.[2] Thus for many viewers for many years, television has been prime-time broadcast television. For producers of violent programming, however, prime-time broadcast network television is just one of the distribution avenues or "windows" where their programming can be viewed. Today, budget and content decisions for television programming are made with consideration of the prospects for multiple viewing windows: broadcast networks, cable channels, broadcast syndication to local stations, and export to foreign television markets.

This chapter analyzes economic decisions and trends that affect producer estimates of the returns to violent programming across different programming markets. During the mid-1980s, shows in violent genres accounted for as much as 51% of all prime-time broadcast network series programming hours. As the most violent programming shifted to cable, violent shows accounted for an increasingly smaller percentage of prime-time broadcast offerings. By 1993, only 23% of prime-time broadcast network series programming hours were in violent genres. Ratings data for programs in violent genres contradict one of the stylized facts in the debate over television violence, that violent shows enjoy higher ratings. Historically, shows in violent genres have earned lower household ratings than those in nonviolent genres. Violent programs are valued by advertisers, however, for their ability to attract younger viewers (e.g., those in the 18–49 demographic group). The analysis also demonstrates that overall violent shows are slightly cheaper for the networks to purchase.

While violent series programming has declined as an element of broadcast network programming, producers have gained another outlet for violent content through the expansion of cable programming. The content analysis in chapter 4 emphasized the large role that violent movies played in the scheduling lineups of basic and premium channels. The analysis in this chapter reveals that demand for violent programming increases the likelihood that an individual will make the decision to subscribe to cable. Among the top-rated shows on premium cable channels, the ratings data examined in this chapter show that over half are movies that carry indicators of violent content.

Economic considerations from other programming windows also influence the likelihood that a producer will choose to use violent content. Prospects for syndication of violent programming in part depend on the likely audience composition in a local television market. The greater the percentage of women in a market that are 18–49, the higher the probability that violent syndication series will be shown in the market. This provides additional confirmation that viewing by young women, a group highly valued by advertisers, accounts for part of the prevalence of violent programming. The analysis here reveals that violent programs are more likely to be exported, so that considerations of foreign markets will also affect the decisions by producers to invest in violent programs. The chapter also indicates that government activity in the debate over television violence appears to influence the mix of violent and nonviolent programs offered over time on broadcast networks. Higher scrutiny of violent content by the government results in higher probabilities that new nonviolent programs will be renewed by the networks. Overall, the analysis in this chapter confirms that the returns to producing violent content will vary with economic incentives offered in many different programming windows.

THE IMPACTS OF MULTIPLE VIEWING WINDOWS

A television program produced in the United States may be shown eventually through many different distribution channels: prime-time broadcast, broadcast syndication, cable syndication, and foreign television markets. Films similarly are shown across multiple viewing windows: theaters, pay-per-view, video-cassette, premium cable television, network broadcast, and independent broadcast television. The existence of multiple revenue streams affects both initial investment in a program and the ultimate number of viewers for a show.

Owen and Wildman (1992) have analyzed how different distribution channels affect investment in program budgets. Consider figure 6.1, which is based on their analysis of program supply.[3] Assume that the production market for television programs is competitive, so the suppliers earn zero economic profits and those who control distribution channels may earn positive profits. A program could be distributed through two separate windows. The first window might be American network broadcast television, and the second window could be syndication in the U.S. market (or export to foreign television markets). Let the distribution costs for the program be the same (D) in each market. Revenues are assumed to increase with the production budget. This is because higher budgets are assumed to purchase higher-quality actors, writers, or production qualities, which generate increased viewer interest. Revenues increase at a decreasing rate, since the additional attractions of added stars or production quality are assumed to diminish gradually. The higher the budget, the greater the number

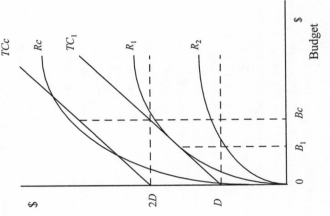

Figure 6.1. Programming Windows and Program Budgets. *Source:* Owen and Wildman 1992.

of viewers and hence revenues. Total costs are the sum of the production budget and distribution costs.

If there were only one market for a program, say broadcast network television, profits would be maximized at budget B_1, the point where the slopes of the total costs and revenue curves are equal. In this example, profits of the producer and distributor are zero. The existence of a second programming window, for example, the broadcast syndication market, means that a producer will view the additional revenue generated by a dollar increase in the production budget as a function of viewers attracted in the prime-time market and the syndication market. The total revenue from a program is thus R_c, which is the sum of the prime-time revenues R_1 and the syndication revenues R_2. The profit-maximizing budget is B_c. Revenues from the first window no longer cover the cost of program production and first-window distribution, so the program will show a deficit based only on the production costs, distribution costs, and revenues from the first window. Revenues from the second window are necessary for the producer to break even on the program. Note that the existence of the second window results in a larger budget and more viewers in the first window than in the single window case.[4]

These windowing results from the Owen and Wildman model have clear implications for the market for violent programming. If violent shows are more likely to survive in syndication than other types of genres, then one would expect them to have larger program deficits in the first window (e.g., producers would sell their programs to network television for fees that generated larger deficits). If violence sells better abroad than other genres (which may lose viewer interest in translation), then this will also generate greater program deficits. Although producers of violent programs are often described as having to go to the world market to cover their losses, these deficits actually arise because suppliers make their program investment decisions based on the fees they anticipate negotiating in multiple programming windows. Debates about violent programming frequently emphasize that it is "cheaper" and "exports well." While both these facts could be true, a greater export market for violent programs means higher production budgets than otherwise. The boost to production budgets from syndication and export opportunities means that violent shows may generate higher ratings in prime time than they otherwise would because their budgets (e.g., production quality) are higher. Thus the syndication and world markets have an indirect influence on viewership in the first-window market.

Similar logic explains investment in violent movies. If these pictures have wider audiences overseas, then producers will invest more in their budgets. Movies may thus appear to lose money if one focuses only on the domestic theater market, but this ignores the additional revenues provided through video-cassettes, cable and broadcast television, and foreign film and television markets. The incentives created by export markets may make violent films more desirable investments, which affects the type of theatrical films available for broadcast on network television. In addition, the preferences of women may carry greater weight than those of men in the calculus of broadcast programmers because of the value of female demographic groups to advertisers. This may create incentives for networks to generate made-for-television films that focus on different topics (e.g., family crime stories that attract female viewers) than the theatrical films they offer. The ratings evidence from chapter 2 indicates that ratings for family crime movies are higher across all female demographic groups.[5]

VIOLENCE IN PRIME TIME: BROADCAST NETWORK PROGRAMS

Debates over the role of violent programming in broadcast network schedules often falter over the apparent difficulty of defining what constitutes violence. The definitions used by communications researchers vary. George Gerbner's Cultural Indicators' Project, which tracked the content of a sample of prime-time broadcast programs yearly from 1967 to 1992, defined violence in television programs "based on the reliable observation of clear-cut, unambiguous, and overt episodes of physical violence—hurting or killing or the threat of hurting and/or killing in any context."[6] The National Television Violence Study (1996a) primarily defined violence as "any overt depiction of the use of physical force—or credible threat of such force—intended to physically harm an animate being or group of beings. Violence also includes certain depictions of physically harmful consequences against an animate being or group that occur as a result of unseen violent means."[7] The NTVS emphasizes that the context of violence, not just its frequency, is an important determinant of what types of violent programs may be harmful to children. The NTVS analysis of the 1994–95 television season, however, is the first in-depth content study to develop statistics on context. Although detailed evidence on the violent content of specific programs has not been published by academic researchers, the National Coalition on Television Violence has compiled counts of the frequency of violent acts per hour for prime time shows from 1980 through 1991. In this chapter I use this rough measure of violent content to classify particular prime-time genres as violent, which then allows me to analyze how ratings and costs vary based on violent content.[8]

As described in chapter 1, the National Coalition on Television Violence derived a measure of the number of violent acts per hour by counting the number of "physically violent acts" and using a weighting system that weights minor acts of violence such as shoves differently than major acts of violence such as murder and rape. From 1981 through 1993 the group released counts of violent acts per hour for television shows, movies, music videos, and cartoons, all in an effort to focus attention on the negative impacts associated with violent content. For the set of 770 prime-time series on which the NCTV reported data, the mean number of violent acts per hour was 8.4. As chapter 1 indicated, this number varies widely across genres. If one defines "violent" genres as those with a mean number of violent acts per hour greater than the prime-time average of 8.4, then the following genres of prime-time series are classified as violent series: action adventure (an average of 27.6 violent acts per hour), comic book (12.0), crime (20.2), documentary (18.3), horror (12.3), journalism (9.9), military (21.6), mystery (25.3), police–real people (26.6), science fiction (22.8), and western (22.5). Within these violent genres, there are statistically significant differences in the level of violence. For example, action adventure shows are nearly one-third more violent than crime shows.[9] Programming genres with less than 8.4 violent acts per hour were defined as nonviolent: animation, animal shows, child actor, comedy variety, drama, family or family drama, family situation comedy, legal, lawyers, medical, musical variety, news, occupational comedy, spinoffs, real people, romance, and soap opera.

Within the sample of 770 programs, the mean number of violent acts per hour in the violent program genres (21.6 acts per hour) is nearly nine times higher than the level in the nonviolent (2.6).[10] From 1981 through 1991 the level of violence in violent prime-time broadcast programs remained relatively stable. In 1985 the mean for violent program genres was 22.3, while in 1991 this figure was 22.4. Nonviolent program genres became slightly more violent over this period. In 1985 the mean number of violent acts per hour was 2.1, whereas in 1991 this figure was 4.2.

In discussions of rating television shows for violence, program producers often argue that it is difficult to determine whether a given show is "violent." As one entertainment executive involved in discussions about television violence put it, "it's always, at bottom, a dispute about what constitutes violence and what kinds of programming ought we be concerned about."[11] Another difficulty that arises with simple classifications of shows is that particular episodes of a given series may vary in violence depending on the story line. Within a show such as *NYPD Blue* there is often variation across episodes in the sexual and violent content. As the show's executive producer indicated in discussions about program ratings, "If 'R' is as adult as it gets, we would want it to be labeled that simply to keep our options open in terms of storytelling. But episode to episode, there will certainly be 'PG' episodes."[12]

The NCTV figures overall indicate that it is possible to predict accurately whether a program is violent or nonviolent based on its genre, as one would expect in a market where products are differentiated in part on violent content.[13] Consider the definition of violent programming used in this chapter—that is, a program is violent if it is in a genre that has an average number of violent acts per hour greater than the mean historical figure (8.4) for prime-time broadcast network series. Any classification of programs, whether it is based on genre definitions or more detailed analysis, will inherently give rise to complaints about false positives (i.e., shows that are labeled as violent but are not) and false negatives (i.e., shows that are classified as nonviolent but are actually violent). Of the 534 programs classified as nonviolent based on genre, 34 had counts of violent acts per hour higher than the sample mean of 8.4. These can be viewed as false negatives. Of the 233 shows in violent genres, 34 had violence counts less than the sample mean (i.e., were false positives). Overall a sorting of prime-time series into violent versus nonviolent programs based only on genre was correct nearly 89% of the time. While this classification scheme misses differences in the context of how violence is portrayed, the analysis of programs based on the frequency of violence associated with the show's genre does appear to offer a way to test general theories about the market for "violent" shows.

While legislators and interest groups concerned with violent programming often say that television is too violent, network officials and other industry participants often reply that prime-time *broadcast network* programming has become much less violent in the 1990s.[14] Classification of programs by genre provides one way to analyze these claims. Figure 6.2 shows that the percentage of prime-time broadcast network hours devoted to programs in violent genres was near historic lows in the 1993–94 television season.[15] The percentage of prime-time broadcast network hours devoted to violent series reveals a cyclical pattern. Two peaks occur in 1974 and 1984. In each of these years, violent series accounted for 50% of the total hours of prime-time network broadcast series programming. Note that this does not take into account that some of the network broadcast movie hours would inevitably include violent films, so the figures in figure 6.2 are a lower bound on violent network content. At each of the peaks in 1974 and 1984, there was a flurry of government

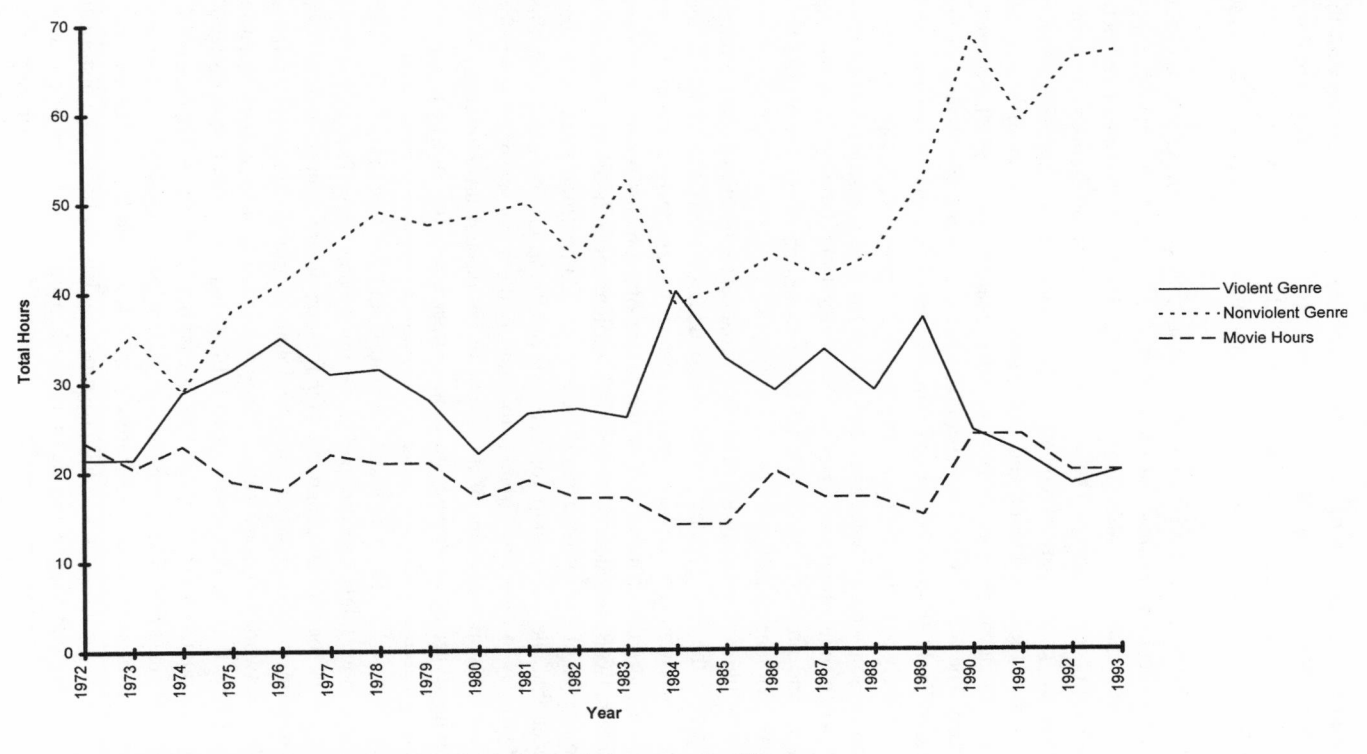

Figure 6.2. Distribution of Prime-time Broadcast Network Programming Hours

activity and critical scrutiny of violent programming. In addition, ratings for the increasing number of violent shows were declining as more violent programs competed for the audience for violent shows. Both these forces may have contributed to the evident decline in violent prime-time programming after these years.

By the mid-1980s a third factor also came into play in determining the amount of violence in prime-time broadcasts, the competition from basic and premium cable channels. Cable stations have an advantage in content competition against broadcast stations. The accessibility of broadcast stations' programs to children, the greater pervasiveness of their broadcasts, the licensing of local broadcasters by the government, and their greater dependence on advertisers all make these broadcasters less likely than cable channels to program extremely violent fare. The NTVS found, for example, that premium cable channels were much more likely to show programs with numerous violent interactions and were more likely to show programs with blood and gore.[16] This may provide an additional reason why violent series accounted for a near historic low of only 23% of prime-time broadcast series hours in the 1993–94 television season, since basic and premium cable series offered those in search of violence programs with greater violent content.

Analyzing the composition of prime-time broadcast schedules is only a rough way to proxy the key variable in an assessment of television violence, the exposure of viewers (i.e., children and adults) to violent programming. Figure 6.3 offers a more direct indication of the extent of problems posed by violent prime-time network broadcasts. Since 1984, violent series hours have declined as a percentage of broadcast network schedules. Competition from cable has also meant that the viewership for network programs has declined over this period. One way to reflect this trend is to multiply the mean season's ratings for a broadcast network program by its length in hours, add up these figures by programming type, and compare the total ratings hours for violent programs, nonviolent programs, and movies. In 1972, these ratings hour totals were 355 for violent series, 923 for nonviolent programs, and 386 for movies. By 1993 these ratings hour totals had dropped in all three categories. The ratings hour totals were 198 for violent programs, 869 for nonviolent genres, and 202 for movies. In terms of household viewing of violent programs, figure 6.3 confirms that violent network broadcast series generated much smaller ratings totals in the early 1990s than in the peak years of 1974 and 1984. Violent series programming accounted for 21% of total broadcast network ratings hours in 1972 but only 16% in 1993. The migration of violent programming to cable and independent stations prevents one from claiming that overall levels of violence on television or consumption of such programming has declined. The historical data do indicate that violent broadcast network prime-time series hours were near historic lows in the early 1990s and accounted for a smaller percentage of overall prime-time broadcast network viewing.[17]

One of the most frequently repeated observations by those critical of the level of television violence is that violence increases ratings, a statement that

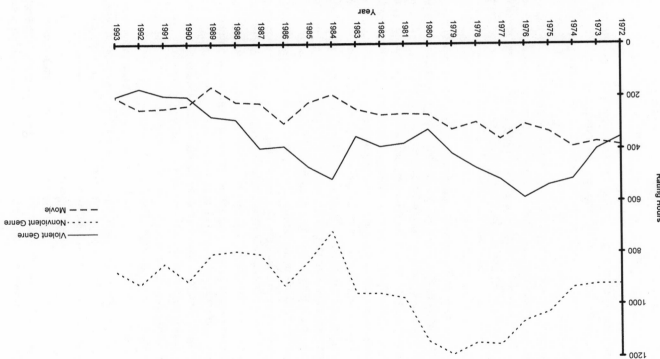

Figure 6.3. Distribution of Prime-time Broadcast Network "Rating Hours"

sometimes is transformed into the assertion that violent shows earn higher ratings in absolute terms. The model in chapter 1 emphasized that, in equilibrium, ratings for violent programs may be greater than, equal to, or less than those for nonviolent shows and that this relationship will depend on factors such as programming costs and advertiser values for particular types of viewers. If one analyzes prime-time broadcast network programs aired from the 1972–73 television season through the 1993–94 season, the evidence is clear that violent shows earned lower household ratings. The mean season household rating (i.e., the percentage of households viewing a particular program) was 14.2 for the 613 programs in violent genres aired on broadcast networks during prime time from 1972–93. For the 1,409 prime-time network programs in nonviolent genres, the mean rating was 15.0, a difference statistically significant at the .01 level. For twelve of the television seasons from 1972 through 1993, nonviolent shows had statistically significant higher ratings than violent series (see table A6.1). Overall, among prime-time broadcast programs violent series have consistently earned lower household ratings than nonviolent shows.

Violent content is just one of the factors that will influence a program's ratings. Prime-time broadcast ratings also vary with the year the program aired (since ratings for network shows have declined with competition from cable), the starting time of the program, and the network (which may affect the rating for the lead-in show and hence the size of the audience that remains to watch the following program). Regression analyses in table A6.2 and table A6.3 reveal that even controlling for many other factors, violent content still results in lower household ratings. Table A6.2 models ratings for the sample of 595 shows (1981–91) for which NCTV violent counts are available. After controlling for network, genre, time of showing, year, and network fee paid for a program, the higher the NCTV violence count, the lower household rating. In the regression model, an additional violent act translates into a slight drop of .03 ratings points.

For the 1991–93 seasons, data are available on total production costs for a program (the sum of the network fee paid to producers and the deficit run by the producers of the program).[18] Table A6.3 shows that as total production expenditures on a program increase, household ratings for the program also increase, which is consistent with a model where expenditures increase the attractiveness of a show to viewers. The magnitude of this impact is relatively small, however. A $100,000 increase in a program budget translates into a .14 increase in ratings points. Note that controlling for total program costs, shows with higher deficits had slightly lower ratings ($T = 1.5$). This would be consistent with the notion that producers would accept lower network fees (and hence higher deficits, for a given program cost) for shows where audiences exist in other programming windows. Controlling for network, program cost, and the time a show aired, one finds in table A6.3 that a program in a violent genre had an audience that was 2.4 ratings points smaller than a nonviolent show. Thus whether one defines violence in terms of program genre or violent acts per hour, violent shows earn lower household ratings.

Another frequent argument for the prevalence of violent programming in prime time is that it is cheaper to produce. An often expressed view is that violence entails less imaginative acting or writing and hence less expensive talent. The opposite argument is made, however, in the discussion of action adventure films, whose large-scale budgets are seen as an investment in generating an audience through special effects. An economic analysis of program costs involves recognizing the difference between the fees paid by network shows and the total costs to produce these programs, the variation in the average costs of producing shows across different genres, and the question of whether an additional act of violence lowers overall production costs for particular types of programs.

Estimates of program production costs are often private information, that is, calculations not released to the public. Controversy over the methodology of estimating movie costs has generated labor disputes and court cases.[19] Since networks will calculate their profits from airing programs on the basis in part of the fees that they pay producers for the right to air the shows, network production fees are one measure of "costs." The amount that program producers are willing to invest in a show will in turn in part depend on the revenue streams available from exhibition other than prime-time broadcast, for example, future syndication in the United States or export abroad. In this case, program deficits (defined as the actual cost of making a program minus the production fee paid by the network) should be related to the likelihood that a program will be syndicated or sold abroad. In more intricate models of programming, the number of viewers attracted to a particular program may be related to the quality of the production, which is assumed to be related to the costs of production. This would imply that programs with higher production costs should, other things being equal, earn higher ratings.

Each year *Variety* releases estimates of the production fee paid by the networks for prime-time broadcast shows, that is, the amount per episode that the network pays program producers for the right to air a particular episode.[20] This fee is the cost from the network's point of view of the program. I assembled these data on 1,656 shows for the period 1970–93. For 1,166 programs in nonviolent genres, the average network production fee per hour of programming was $960,100 (1994$). For the 490 programs in violent genres, the average network production figure was $935,600.[21] This means that shows in violent genres are slightly cheaper (2.6%) than other programs from the perspective of networks purchasing episodes of prime-time broadcast series.

For 1991–93, *Variety* published information per program on the network production fee and the size of the program deficit. Together, these two figures add to the total cost of producing a given episode of a program. The mean network production fee per hour for violent programs from 1991–93 was $997,700, versus $1,093,800 for nonviolent series. The average program deficit per hour for the 164 nonviolent programs was $210,900, while the average program deficit per hour for the 34 violent genre programs was $318,900.[22] This is consistent with the theory that producers would be willing to run larger deficits on programs where revenue streams outside of those provided by the networks are higher. If violent shows are more likely to be exported or sold into syndication, then producers would be willing to run larger program deficits. In terms of total production costs per hour, there was no statistically significant difference in the amount of money spent on the production of an hour of violent series programming (mean $1,228,400) and the average amount spent on producing an hour of nonviolent programming ($1,229,400).

More evidence on whether violent shows may be cheaper for networks to purchase comes from the combination of the *Variety* data with the information on violent acts per hour collected by the NCTV. Table A6.4 indicates that for the years 1981–91 the average number of violent acts per hour does not have a statistically significant impact on the production fees per hour paid by networks for either violent shows or nonviolent shows. It may be, however, that one needs to control for different levels of violence and then examine the marginal impact of an additional act of violence on production fees. This would be necessary if there were differences in the fixed costs of producing certain types of programming and marginal trade-offs of using violence or some other type of content once the overall genre context of programming had been set. For the shows in "violent genres," specification (3) in table A6.4 controls for whether the program actually did contain more than the sample mean number of violent acts per hour (8.4). Once one controls for whether a show in a violent genre does contain more than average levels of violence, it appears that an additional act of violence lowers the fee paid by the network by $1,500. Networks thus face lower "costs" of violent programming in the sense that the production fee they pay for violent episodes declines with the number of violent acts.

CABLE AUDIENCES FOR VIOLENCE

The key role that violence plays in building audiences for cable programming is evident from the fact that viewers who watch more violent programming are also more likely to subscribe to cable television. A moderate increase in consumption of violent programming is associated with an increase in cable subscription probability from .74 to .81.[23] This effect is similar in magnitude to the difference in cable subscription probability between low viewers of television (.70 cable probability) and high television viewers (.76 probability). The NTVS (1996b) study found that 85% of all premium cable shows and 59% of basic cable programs had violent acts in them, versus 55% for independent stations, 44% for broadcast network channels, and 18% for public broadcasting programs.[24] Premium cable programs were also much more likely to contain a high number of violent interactions (9+) than programs on broadcast network channels. Cable operators and cable channels in search of subscribers may thus offer violent programming in an attempt to land marginal viewers attracted by the frequency and nature of violent programming on cable.

The analysis of basic and premium movie schedules in chapter 4 also underscores that violent content is a key component of the brand identities established by cable channels. Movie or series producers considering the potential audiences for their productions will thus factor in the returns to violent content from this programming window. It is difficult for an analyst outside the industry to estimate the magnitudes of cable audiences, since ratings data for premium channels are rarely released because they do not rely on advertising. *Broadcasting and Cable*, however, has published a weekly listing of ratings for the top five premium cable programs. Examining the top five most popular programs provides only a small snapshot of the relationship between premium cable content and ratings. Yet, with the general lack of data on premium cable audiences, these figures provide the best evidence on the nature of the audiences for premium cable programs.

Table 6.1 contains information on the content and ratings of the top five rated programs on premium cable for a sample of 57 weeks from December 1994 through February 1996. For this sample of 285 shows (all of which were on HBO), movies comprised 79.3% of the most popular programs. Violent movies constituted 55.1% of the top five programs on premium cable. While broadcast networks often point out that the top ten network broadcast programs are rarely violent, the same claim cannot be made for premium cable programs. One of the comparative advantages of premium cable is its ability to use programming that might not survive the constraints of advertiser approval or indecency regulation on broadcast television. Movies with adult language constitute 66.7%, with adult situations 55.8%, and with nudity 28.8% of the top premium cable programs. If one broadens the definition of violent programming to include athletic violence such as boxing, the fact that 9.5% of the top five premium cable shows are boxing events underscores the importance of violent programming to building cable audiences.

Note that 3.5% of the top five programs are part of the HBO series of programs called *Real Sex*, which adopt a documentary or newsmagazine approach

TABLE 6.1
Content of Weekly "Top 5" Premium Cable Shows, 1994–96 ($N = 285$)

Program Type	% Total Top 5 Premium Cable Shows
Movies	79.3
Boxing Event	9.5
Comedy Program	4.6
Sex Program	3.5
Other	1.4
Movies with Indicators for	
Violence	55.1
Adult Language	66.7
Adult Situations	55.8
Nudity	28.8

to presenting stories focused on sex. According to one assessment of these sexually explicit programs, "Real Sex . . . gets no publicity push whatsoever. Still, HBO acknowledges that the company's research indicates it is a subscriber favorite. The fact that it continues to appear is evidence of its customer support. Because a bill arrives in HBO homes every month, the cable channel is particularly sensitive to consumer preferences."[25] Describing how adult programming fits into the HBO strategy, Chris Albrecht, HBO senior vice president for original programming explains, "Subscribers view us as a complete service. There are things for family-type viewing, things for teens, things for adults only. We're careful how we schedule all of them."[26] The *Real Sex* programs are generally scheduled to run on Fridays after 11 PM, which would reduce the risk of exposure to children 2–11 since they are less likely to be in the viewing audience at this hour. The fact that these programs rank in the top five of all shows on cable emphasizes the important role that sexual, as well as violent, content plays in distinguishing cable from broadcast programming.

The published audience figures for premium channels relate to television households, so one cannot breakdown the viewing figures by age group. These audience numbers do provide a rough indication of how the audiences for premium cable programs compare to network broadcast shows. The U.S. household ratings for the top five premium cable programs ranged from 1.7 to 5.5, with a mean of 2.5. For comparison, the mean household ratings for 151 prime-time broadcast network television films in 1995 was 8.7. The top premium cable programs thus garner household audiences that are only a third of the average network broadcast movie. These audience figures raise again the issue discussed in chapter 1 of how to assess the likely impact on society of violence in broadcast versus cable programming. While broadcast networks may edit out particular violent scenes from theatrical films that premium cable channels run intact, the number of children exposed to the acts of violence that remain in broadcast programs will outnumber the audiences of children exposed to unedited theatrical films on premium cable.[27]

MARKETS FOR VIOLENT SYNDICATED PROGRAMS

Local independent stations and network affiliates seeking to fill programming gaps both rely on syndicated programs, shows provided to individual stations in a market by program distributors whom stations pay to run the programs by providing them with cash payments and/or ad time to market during the programs. While debates about television violence often center on network broadcast shows, content studies suggest that syndicated original programming may be more violent than prime-time broadcast network programming. The 1995 UCLA study concluded that "A much higher percentage of original syndicated programs raises concerns about the use of violence when compared to the programs on the broadcast networks."[28] The National Television Violence Study analysis of the 1994–95 television season concluded that programming on independent broadcast stations, which draw heavily on syndicated programs and movies, is much more likely, when violent, to contain a high number of violent interactions.[29] The Center for Media and Public Affairs study of program content in 1993 compared prime-time network and syndicated programs and concluded that "not only is there more violence in syndicated shows, but it also tends to be more serious."[30] Network executives pressed on the television violence issue are also quick to point out that syndicated violent programs are a problem too. Discussing the problem of television violence, then CBS Entertainment President Jeff Sagansky said, "I see the problem everywhere. In first run syndication, 'The Untouchables,' for one. We would never let that air over our network."[31]

Unlike broadcast network programs, which are generally carried by all a network's affiliates, the distribution of violent syndicated programs will vary across different markets. Analysis of which markets have a station sign up to carry a syndicated violent program offers a natural way to test how returns to violent programming in the syndication market will vary as predicted by the programming model developed in chapter 1. This model emphasized that the number of violent programs offered will depend on the number of stations in a market, the number of viewers and their preferences for program types, the value of different demographic groups to advertisers, and programming costs. For four of the violent syndication programs available in November 1993 (*Acapulco H.E.A.T.*, *Cobra*, *Highlander*, and *Real Stories of the Highway Patrol*), I developed a logit equation which estimated the likelihood that a particular program was carried in the 211 local television markets defined by Nielsen.[32]

The results in table 6.2 indicate that for three of these four syndicated shows the number of stations was statistically significant in explaining whether a program was carried. The larger the number of broadcast stations in a market, the more likely that a station in the market would sign up to carry a program. The larger the number of television households in the market, the greater the chances that crime or action adventure programs such as *Acapulco H.E.A.T.*, *Cobra*, and *Highlander* were carried. The model in chapter 1 emphasized that increases in the value of violent viewers to advertisers and the size of the viewing segment that prefers violent programs to other offerings would increase the number of violent programs in a market. Increases in the mean buying income per household, a measure of attractiveness of households for some advertisers, lead to increased odds that *Acapulco H.E.A.T* and *Highlander* were carried in a market. Increases in the percentage of households with disposable incomes of greater than $25,000 increased. The individual survey data from chapter 2 indicated that high-income viewers were slightly less likely to watch particular types of violent programming. The results on disposable income suggest that the potential viewing audience for a violent program may drop in markets where there is a higher percentage of households with incomes greater than $25,000.

For three of the programs, *Acapulco H.E.A.T.*, *Highlander*, and *Real Stories*

TABLE 6.2
Determinants of Whether a Syndicated Program Is Carried in a Local Television Market

	Acapulco H.E.A.T.	Cobra	Real Stories of the Highway Patrol	Highlander
No. of Broadcast Stations	0.07 (0.11)	0.26** (0.13)	0.31** (0.14)	0.45*** (0.16)
Total Television Households	5.76e−3*** (1.77e−3)	4.34e−3*** (1.58e−3)	1.14e−3 (1.38e−3)	3.36e−3* (1.88e−3)
% with Cable TV	−0.02 (0.03)	−0.02 (0.02)	5.73e−3 (0.02)	4.94e−3 (0.03)
% Multiset Households	6.94e−3 (0.05)	9.1e−3 (0.05)	0.05 (0.05)	0.06 (0.05)
Buying Income per Household ($)	4.9e−4** (2.13e−4)	2.35e−4 (1.77e−4)	3.29e−4 (2.01e−4)	4.09e−4** (2.07e−4)
% Households with Disposable Income $25K+	−0.25** (0.11)	−0.14 (0.10)	−0.15 (0.10)	−0.28** (0.12)
% Professional	−0.17** (0.09)	−0.12 (0.10)	−0.19** (0.09)	−0.08 (0.09)
% Blue Collar	−0.13 (0.09)	−0.11 (0.09)	−0.11 (0.09)	−0.05 (0.09)
% Service	−0.02 (0.09)	−0.10 (0.08)	0.06 (0.09)	−0.03 (0.09)
% Nonwhite	2.21e−3 (0.16)	0.02 (0.14)	7.56e−3 (0.17)	−0.03 (0.16)
	(0.02)	(0.02)	(0.02)	(0.02)
% of Women 18–49	41.72** (18.17)	23.81 (17.31)	41.86** (18.35)	62.14*** (20.64)
% of Men 18–49	−30.11 (18.70)	−15.67 (18.61)	−33.36* (18.89)	−53.70*** (21.04)
Log Likelihood	−97.1	−94.6	−102.8	−90.0
No. of Markets Carrying Program	121	100	140	127

Note: For each program, a logit analysis was run to specify the determinants of which of the 211 television markets carried the syndicated program. Each logit contained an intercept term. *** = statistically significant at the .01 level; ** = significant at the .05 level; * = significant at the .10 level.

of the Highway Patrol, markets were more likely to carry these shows as the percentage of total adult women accounted for by women 18–49 increased. For the last two shows, the likelihood decreased as the percentage of total men accounted for by men 18–49 increased. This provides strong evidence that the combination of the value that advertisers place on younger women as consumers and the viewership of women 18–34 for violent programming helps explain the prevalence of some types of shows. Television critics attribute part of the content of syndicated action adventure programs to attempts to attract young female viewers.[33] *Acapulco H.E.A.T.*, for example, featured male models who acted in the program as secret government agents posing as fashion models. Critics also attribute the high frequency of scenes exposing male and female bodies in action adventure syndicated programming as an (often successful) attempt to attract young adult viewers of both genders to these programs. Overall, these results show that the ability of producers to distribute violent programming across markets will depend in part on the local demographics of the viewing audience in each locality and the number of broadcast outlets in the local market.

EXPORT MARKET FOR VIOLENT CONTENT

One of the stylized facts about violent programming is that it is more likely to be exported to foreign broadcast markets. The notion is that violence loses less in translation than, for example, situation comedies that rely on knowledge of popular culture. The ability of producers to export a show abroad adds another revenue stream to a show's valuation. As the programming window model indicates, this may affect the willingness of producers to invest more money in a show (because of the prospect of foreign viewers) and affect the program's deficit (the difference between the total production cost and the fee paid by the network). If violent shows export more easily, then foreign viewers may be more likely to associate American television with violence.[34] The existence of these foreign viewers will also have a feedback impact on the American market. Greater investment in budgets of violent shows may result in higher viewership in the United States because of the higher production values.

Violent shows did have higher program deficits than nonviolent shows, consistent with a greater likelihood that they will succeed in U.S. syndication or world export markets. Analysis of whether violent shows from the United States are more likely to be exported is hampered by the lack of a central listing of what programs are exported. Gerbner, Morgan, and Signorielli (1994) stress that violent shows play a large role in the export of U.S. programs, concluding:

An analysis of international data from 1987 in the Cultural Indicators database shows that violence dominated U.S. exports. We compared our sample of 250 U.S. programs exported to 10 countries with 111 programs shown in the U.S. during the same year. Violence was the main theme of 40 percent of home-shown and 49 percent of exported programs. Crime/action series comprised 17 percent of home-shown and 46% of exported programs. The tendency to produce violence for the world market and the pressure to exhibit at home whatever global economies of scale make most profitable . . . has accelerated since.[35]

To investigate further the role violent content plays in the export of U.S. programs, I gathered information from *BIB Television Programming Source Books, 1994–95*, volume 4: *Series* (Broadcast Information Bureau 1994), an industry publication that lists the titles and series distributors of programs that have been translated into foreign languages. Since the publication is used as a guide to what programs can be easily shown abroad because they have already been translated, I use this as a sample of U.S. shows that have been exported.[36] I then matched this set of exported programs with the 1,201 unique program titles in the set of network prime-time shows broadcast from 1970 to 1993 analyzed earlier. This allows me to answer the question, Among shows broadcast on prime-time network television in the United States, are programs in violent genres more likely to be exported?

Of the 1,201 primetime broadcast shows, 19.7% were listed in the industry program guide as having been translated into a foreign language (my measure of program export). The percentage of shows exported varies, however, by genre. Of the 807 programs in nonviolent genres, 14.5 % (117 shows) had been exported. For the 317 programs in violent genres, 30.5% (120 programs) had been exported. For the set of prime-time network broadcast programs, violent shows have been exported at twice the rate of nonviolent programs.

Table A6.5 offers an additional way to view program export. The likelihood that a prime-time show had been translated into a foreign language may vary with how old the program is (e.g., when did the program first air?) and how popular the program was (e.g., what was the average household rating for the show over the time it was aired?). Relative to shows first aired after 1988, shows first aired in earlier eras were more likely to have been exported (which may indicate a lag for translation). The higher a show's average rating, the more likely it was exported abroad. This shows that success in the U.S. market is related to the probability a show will be seen abroad. If one controls for these factors, programs in violent genres were still more likely to be exported. The coefficient on the violent genre variable implies that for the mean show the probability of export increases by .16 if the program is in a violent genre.

IMPACT OF GOVERNMENT SCRUTINY

Although broadcasters enjoy protection under the First Amendment, the potential influence of government activity on their content may be greater than that of print media (or even cable television) because local broadcast stations operate under licenses renewed by the Federal Communications Commission (FCC). Several times over the past three decades the question has arisen over whether the FCC would become involved in scrutinizing the level of violent content in broadcast television through the license renewal process. In 1974, Chairman Richard Wiley considered whether to add this explicitly to the renewal process.[37] The networks resisted this suggestion. In part through the persuasive efforts of FCC Chairman Wiley, the networks led the National Association of Broadcasters Television Code Review Board to adopt a "Family Viewing Policy," which called for warnings on certain types of programs and stated that from 7 to 9 PM "entertainment programming inappropriate for viewing by a general family audience should not be broadcast."[38] The policy was declared invalid by a federal court, which ruled that this "voluntary" industry program had actually been formulated as part of a government policy, which should have followed a formalized rulemaking process.[39]

Government scrutiny in the form of congressional hearings, speeches by legislators, and statements by the chairman of the FCC and the president can indirectly influence the content of violent programming. If these statements increase the attention paid to which companies sponsor violent and sexual content on television, then they raise the probability that advertising on a program will associate a company's brand identity with controversy. This in effect may lower the expected return to a firm of advertising on a violent program, which will lower the willingness of a set of firms to sponsor such programs.[40] The result from the network's perspective may be a drop in the expected price per thousand that advertisers will pay for audiences on violent programs (overall audiences are assumed not to drop for violent programs in the short run, in part because viewers of these shows may not be as likely to agree that violent programming adversely affects society). In terms of the programming model in chapter 1, the drop in P_h would eventually result in fewer channels (N_h) offering violent shows.

In a more complex model, a network would consider the present value of the stream of profits from a program in its decision of whether to place a program on its schedule or renew the show. The net present value of a prime-time violent show can thus be thought of as the sum of $i = 0$ to n of $(P_iQ_i - C_i)/(1 + r_i)^i$, where P_i represents the average price per thousand viewers paid by advertisers in year i, Q_i is the number of thousands of viewers attracted to the program over the course of the year, C_i is the cost of the program to the network over the course of the year, and r_i is the interest rate.[41] Additional scrutiny by the government may lower the expected price per thousand viewers advertisers will pay to advertise on a violent program. This could cause the number of channels offering violent programming to drop, which in turn could mean that the expected number of viewers for a remaining violent program Q_i could actually increase. Overall, the possibility exists that additional scrutiny could lower the net present value of the profit stream from a particular violent program, so that the program was not placed on the schedule or its cancellation was hastened.

Has this cycle of government scrutiny of violent programs affected which programs networks have chosen to air in prime time? Networks will consider the net present value of the profits from a program in decisions to offer a new program or continue an existing program. Government scrutiny of violent programming could lower the returns to this genre if it translated into greater controversy associated with sponsoring such programs and hence lower ad rates (as in the *NYPD Blue* example, where private protest lowered initial programming returns). One way to examine this is to ask whether the level of government activity in a given year affects the renewal decisions for newly introduced shows.

From the historical network prime-time set of shows, I have information on the renewal decision for new programs (i.e., the decision at the end of the year of the introduction of a show) for 1,132 shows over 1971–93.[42] For the 780 nonviolent shows in this time period, 234 (30%) were renewed after their first year. For the 352 programs in violent genres, 25.6% were renewed after their first year. Thus there is no statistically significant difference in the proportion of shows initially renewed for violent versus nonviolent shows.

For each year from 1972 to 1993 I created a dummy variable indicating whether there was a House or Senate Committee hearing, congressional report, or executive agency report issued on violent programming. Over this dataset, there were 14 years in which this government scrutiny variable was set equal to 1. From the data assembled by Adams (1993), I created a logit model of program renewal for new shows. The decision to renew is modeled in table A6.6 as a function of the rating for the show (higher ratings leading to higher expectations for future success), the change in the rating for the time slot for this program over the rating for the previous year (increases in ratings again leading to increases in expected profits), the network, day of the week, and year. In addition, a dummy variable is included for whether violent television was a topic of government scrutiny during the year the program was first offered.

Table A6.6 demonstrates that the scrutiny variable was not statistically significant in the renewal process for violent programs. For nonviolent programs, however, a program was much more likely to be renewed if government was focusing attention on violent programming. If all variables are evaluated at their means, a nonviolent program's probability of being renewed increases by .31 in years in which the government has focused attention on violent television. There are many avenues through which government activity could affect the violent content of prime time. The controversy associated with violent programming might, for example, lead broadcasters to be less likely to start new violent programs if they expected advertiser backlash to these shows. This section has tested for such an indirect effect and found that, in the program renewal process, greater government activity on violent programs leads to higher renewal rates for nonviolent shows.

CONCLUSIONS

Although legislators and advocacy groups often focus on violent programming on prime-time broadcast television, a producer of a violent program will consider the returns from showing a movie or program in many different venues in making content decisions. This chapter has reviewed some of the evidence on what factors and trends will influence the returns to using violent content to attract audiences across various programming windows. On broadcast network programming, violent shows have declined as a percentage of series hours from a high point of 51% in the mid-1980s to 23% in 1993. Much violent programming has migrated to cable channels, where violent movies play a prominent role in scheduling strategies. A demand for violent content, for example, increases the probability that a person will subscribe to cable at all. For premium cable channels, violent movies account for over half of the weekly top five programs in terms of total audiences. The ability of producers to sell violent series in syndication will depend in part on economic factors such as the demographics of the local markets. For shows such as *Acapulco H.E.A.T.* or *Highlander*, the program was more likely to be carried in a local market as the percentage of women that were 18–49 increased, a testament to the importance of female audiences in this programming window.

Violent programs are more likely to be exported, which in turn may influence the audience size for these programs in the United States. If producers are able to count on revenues from abroad, then they may increase the budget for programming in the United States, which in turn may increase the audience attracted to the quality of violent programming produced here. The government attention attracted by violent programming may also alter the mix of programs offered here. I find that when scrutiny by the government increased, networks were more likely to renew nonviolent programs for a second season. While government attention did not lead to a chilling effect on the renewal of violent series, it did lead to a "warming effect" for network attitudes to continuance of nonviolent shows. Chapter 8 explores in more detail the possible impact of government policies on violent programming. The next chapter first focuses on a different genre of programming criticized for violent content, local news shows.

TABLE A6.1

Ratings per Year from 1972 to 1993 for Prime-time Broadcast Network Programs

	Mean Violent Program Rating	Mean Nonviolent Program Rating
1972	17.9	18.1
1973	18.5	17.7
1974	17.4	19.5
1975	17.0	18.4
1976	17.2	18.5
1977	17.8	17.6
1978	16.3	17.9*
1979	16.0	18.8**
1980	16.2	18.2**
1981	15.4	17.3**
1982	14.4	16.2**
1983	15.3	14.9
1984	14.5	15.4
1985	14.2	15.8
1986	13.5	15.4*
1987	11.9	14.7***
1988	11.2	13.9***
1989	10.8	13.7***
1990	8.8	11.2***
1991	8.7	11.1***
1992	8.8	9.9*
1993	9.6	10.6
Overall	14.2	15.0***

Note: *** = difference statistically significant at .01 level; ** = significant at the .05 level; * = significant at .10 level.

TABLE A6.2
Determinants of Prime-time Household Ratings, 1981–91, (N = 595 Programs)

	Parameter Estimate
Intercept	6.02***
	(1.99)
Network Program Fee	1.41e − 6***
	(5.80e − 8)
Average Violent Acts per Hour	−0.03*
	(0.02)
Season	
1981	4.78**
	(0.80)
1982	2.04***
	(0.74)
1983	2.07***
	(0.77)
1984	1.85***
	(0.75)
1985	2.05***
	(0.72)
1987	−0.31
	(0.71)
1988	−0.11
	(0.75)
1989	1.13
	(0.71)
1990	2.58***
	(0.68)
Network	
ABC	4.95***
	(1.07)
CBS	6.20***
	(1.07)
NBC	6.17***
	(1.07)
Genre	
Action Adventure	0.16
	(1.75)
Drama	0.98
	(1.72)
Fantasy–Science Fiction	−1.39
	(1.89)
News	2.50
	(1.73)
Situation Comedy	1.84
	(1.69)
Mystery	2.41
	(1.91)

TABLE A6.2 (Continued)

Time Program Aired	Parameter Estimate
7:30	−3.82*
	(2.25)
8:00	0.25
	(0.93)
8:30	0.16
	(1.05)
9:00	0.84
	(0.97)
9:30	0.29
	(1.08)
10:00	0.09
	(0.95)
10:30	−2.46
	(4.10)
Adjusted R^2	0.29

Note: Dependent variable is the season household rating for a program on prime-time broadcast network television. Standard errors are in parentheses. *** = statistically significant at .01 level; ** = significant at the .05 level; * = significant at the .10 level.

TABLE A6.3
Impact of Program Production Costs on Ratings, 1991–93

	(1)	(2)
Intercept	7.79***	0.64
	(1.14)	(2.28)
Program Production Cost per Hour	1.43e−6***	4.04e−6***
	(5e−7)	(1e−6)
Program Deficit per Hour		−9.45e−7
		(6.30e−7)
1992 Season	−0.91**	−0.79
	(0.47)	(0.60)
1993 Season	−0.43	−0.24
	(0.47)	(0.59)
ABC	3.83***	3.65***
	(0.58)	(0.59)
CBS	4.07***	3.34***
	(0.58)	(0.75)
NBC	2.38***	1.98***
	(0.60)	(0.78)
Violent Genre	−2.38***	−1.79***
	(0.53)	(0.65)
Adjusted R^2	0.28	0.31

Note: Dependent variable in the OLS regression is average season program rating. Regressions also included dummy variables for program starting times. Standard errors in parentheses. *** = statistically significant at the .01 level; ** = significant at the .05 level.

TABLE A6.4
Network Production Fees per Hour, 1981–91 (1994 $)

	(1) Nonviolent Genre Programs (N = 437)	(2) Violent Genre Programs (N = 191)	(3) Violent Genre Programs (N = 191)
Intercept	1.21e6***	1.07e6***	1.05e6***
	(5.2e4)	(5.16e4)	(4.36e4)
1981	−2.34e5***	−9.59e4*	−9.42e4*
	(8.09e4)	(5.16e4)	(5.15e4)
1982	−2.49e5***	−9.63e4**	−9.41e4**
	(7.51e4)	(4.69e4)	(4.69e4)
1983	−1.67e5**	−8.42e4*	−7.75*
	(7.83e4)	(5.12e4)	(5.13e4)
1984	−1.57e5**	−7.64e3	−3.61e3
	(7.56e4)	(4.38e4)	(4.39e4)
1985	−1.93e5***	3.45e4	3.47e4
	(7.79e4)	(4.32e4)	(4.32e4)
1987	−9.82e4	1.65e4	2.15e4
	(7.44e4)	(4.44e4)	(4.45e4)
1988	−1.27e5*	5.34e4	5.29e4
	(7.51e4)	(5.03e4)	(5.02e4)
1989	−1.37e5**	3.01e4	3.45e4
	(7.08e4)	(4.67e4)	(4.67e4)
1990	−9.50e4	−4.06e4	−3.33e4
	(6.61e4)	(4.62e4)	(4.65e4)
Average Violent Acts per Hour	−5.87e3	−9.34e2	−1.49e3*
	(4.41e3)	(7.62e2)	(8.80e2)
"Very Violent" Program			4.05e4
			(3.21e4)
Adjusted R^2	0.02	0.08	0.08

Note: Dependent variable in each OLS regression is the network production fee per hour (1994 $). Average violent acts per hour were calculated by the NCTV. "Very Violent" programs are those whose violent acts per hour are greater than 8.4, the average for programs coded by NCTV from 1980 to 1991. Standard errors are in parentheses. *** = statistically significant at the .01 level; ** = significant at the .05 level; * = significant at the .10 level.

TABLE A6.5
Determinants of Whether a U.S. Prime-time Network Program Was Exported

	Parameter Estimate
Intercept	−5.23***
	(0.46)
Average Program Rating	0.11***
	(0.03)
First Aired 1970–75	2.81***
	(0.42)
First Aired 1976–81	1.82***
	(0.40)
First Aired 1982–87	0.46
	(0.43)
Violent Program Genre	1.41***
	(0.19)
Log Likelihood	−366.09

Note: Dependent variable in logit = 1 if the program was exported. Of the 1,091 U.S. prime-time network programs in the logit sample, 186 (17%) were exported. Standard errors in parentheses. *** = statistically significant at the .01 level.

TABLE A6.6
Determinants of Network Program Renewal

	Nonviolent Programs (N = 729)	Violent Programs (N = 351)
Intercept	-7.67***	-10.50***
	(1.05)	(1.92)
Average Program Rating	0.40***	0.60***
	(0.04)	(0.09)
Change in Time Slot Rating from Previous Year	0.14***	0.10
	(0.04)	(0.07)
Government Scrutiny of TV Violence during Current Year?	1.94**	1.65
	(0.93)	(1.40)
Networks		
ABC	-0.98*	-1.79
	(0.52)	(1.32)
CBS	-0.77	-1.83
	(0.52)	(1.30)
NBC	-0.39	-1.90
	(0.51)	(1.32)
Season		
1974	-1.23	-0.15
	(0.83)	(1.30)
1975	0.88	1.89
	(0.85)	(1.36)
1976	-1.14	-1.84
	(0.78)	(1.29)
1977	-1.55**	-0.78
	(0.76)	(1.25)
1978	0.05	2.13*
	(0.83)	(1.26)
1979	-1.58**	-0.65
	(0.77)	(1.32)
1980	1.51*	1.95
	(0.82)	(1.41)
1981	-0.33	0.96
	(0.78)	(1.28)
1982	2.00**	3.33***
	(0.83)	(1.30)
1983	-0.54	1.77
	(0.79)	(1.25)
1984	-0.16	2.01*
	(0.86)	(1.22)
1985	1.76*	3.77***
	(0.93)	(1.24)
1986	0.28	2.88**
	(0.76)	(1.31)

TABLE A6.6 (Continued)

	Nonviolent Programs (N = 729)	Violent Programs (N = 351)
1987	0.80 (0.80)	3.18*** (1.25)
1988	1.04 (0.80)	3.75*** (1.33)
1989	1.07 (0.76)	2.90** (1.42)
1990	3.59*** (0.82)	4.77*** (1.63)
1991	3.42*** (0.83)	5.16*** (1.36)
1992	2.10*** (0.75)	3.78*** (1.55)
1993	0.96 (0.77)	4.14*** (1.34)
Day of Week Sunday	0.59* (0.36)	0.06 (0.63)
Monday	0.13 (0.37)	−0.70 (0.87)
Tuesday	1.06** (0.46)	0.16 (0.68)
Wednesday	−0.54 (0.33)	−0.14 (0.57)
Thursday	0.07 (0.34)	0.54 (0.56)
Friday	0.50 (0.33)	−0.18 (0.52)
Log Likelihood	−146.35	−128.23

Note: Dependent variable in logit = 1 if the program was renewed. Standard errors in parentheses. *** = statistically significant at the .01 level; ** = significant at the .05 level; * = significant at the .10 level.

Local News as (Violent) Entertainment?

"IF IT BLEEDS, it leads" is a frequent assessment of the role that crime coverage plays in local television news programming. Media monitoring groups document the high percentage of stories in local evening newscasts that focus on crime. Television critics often write during sweeps periods about the use of violence to attract ratings. Researchers confirm that crime is a major staple in local television news. Broadcasters respond that "high" levels of crime coverage reflect high levels of crime, and that covering crime is part of a responsible attempt to provide public affairs programming that informs citizens about their communities.

In this chapter, I demonstrate that the same economic model that explains variations in channel selections of entertainment programming also explains variations in the content decisions of local news programmers. News programs, like sitcoms and dramas, are fashioned to respond to the interests of particular demographic audiences. Using a November 1993 sample of 16,000 local news stories from fifty-seven stations in nineteen different markets, I find that the amount of crime coverage in local news varies not with the amount of crime in the local market but with viewer interest in violent programming. Coverage of government and business topics within local news shows similarly varies with expressed viewer interest in "hard news" programming. Within a given local market stations segment themselves by the amount of crime coverage. Stations offering high amounts of crime are more likely to focus on the details of crime, less likely to provide context through coverage of trials or crime statistics, and more likely to use styles aimed at younger viewers such as shorter stories and more use of video clips. Survey data confirm the relation between interest in violence and news coverage. Controlling for many demographic factors, I find that viewers who report higher consumption of violent entertainment programming are more likely to watch local news and more likely to follow issues involving violence, such as U.S. involvement in Somalia and Bosnia. Overall, the results demonstrate how modeling news as a commercial product can explain much of the way that crime is covered in local news programs.

PUBLIC INTEREST IN THE PUBLIC INTEREST?

The market for public affairs reporting operates differently than the market for pure entertainment, a point first made by Anthony Downs in *An Economic Theory of Democracy* (1957). Downs notes that there are four different types of information that people demand: information that helps people in their roles as consumers (e.g., price data) or producers (e.g., knowledge that helps in business decisions); information that is consumed for its entertainment value (e.g., a prime-time situation comedy); and information that helps a person make a decision in public affairs, such as voting. The markets for the first three types of information work relatively well, since people will generally not gain all the benefits of consumer, producer, or entertainment data unless they search out the information and "consume" it themselves. Shoppers may not find sales unless they search out ads, stockbrokers may not find out about a company's liabilities unless they read about the company's past investments, and viewers may not gain utility from a situation comedy such as *Home Improvement* unless they watch the program. When it comes to expressing a demand for information that might help them make more informed decisions about voting, however, viewers have an incentive to free-ride on the efforts of others and remain "rationally ignorant" of the details of policy. This means that the viewers will not turn out in optimal audiences for public affairs programming, despite the potential benefits of the information to themselves and society.[1]

Downs emphasizes that a viewer in search of information about the details of public affairs issues will trade off the costs and benefits of becoming informed. For an individual, there may be a large difference in the value of the policies supported by candidate A versus candidate B, and there may also be information that would help the viewer make the correct decision (from the voter's perspective) about which candidate to support. Yet the probability that the voter's decision will influence whether candidate A or B is elected is so small that the gross benefits of public affairs information will be minuscule. The costs of becoming informed, however, are not negligible, because they involve the opportunity costs of viewing time and the additional costs of charges that may be imposed to obtain the viewing material. The net benefits of becoming informed about the details of policies, defined as (Benefit of candidate A vs. candidate B) × (Increase in probability that voter makes the correct decision) × (Probability vote is decisive) - (Costs of becoming informed), is negative for nearly all individuals. Thus, individuals "rationally" choose to remain ignorant of the details of policy, which translates into lower incentives for broadcast and cable coverage of public affairs issues.[2]

The same logic of collective action that leads some people not to vote (e.g., why vote if my influence is nearly zero?) will lead some people to remain rationally ignorant (e.g., why should I formulate my own policy on Bosnia? on acid rain?). Yet millions do vote, and millions will watch public affairs programming. For some individuals, the ideological satisfaction of "doing the right thing" may lead them to the voting booth. To the extent that people feel a duty to become informed about their votes, there will also be an expressed demand for public affairs reporting. Some find the details of policy interesting, so they will view pure public affairs reporting as entertainment (e.g., information consumed simply for its own sake). Moreover, the human elements and sporting nature of politics lead many people to view political news as entertainment. This means that the private market for entertainment will provide coverage of politics as human drama (thus the prevalence of character issues) or as a horse race (which focuses attention on "who's ahead").[3] Voters are likely to remain rationally ignorant about the details of many public policies even as they express a demand for politics as theater and sport. To the extent that viewers learn detailed information about policies that help them make informed voting decisions, this learning will arise as a positive externality generated by the pursuit of information sought for private ends (e.g., entertainment, or consumption or production decisions).[4]

In a world of rational political ignorance, the programming model presented in chapter 1 captures the incentives that stations face in determining what type of local news program to offer. The same factors that influence a station's decision of what type of entertainment programming to offer at 3 PM or 7 PM influence the decision of what type of local news programming (if any) to offer during the dinner hour. Local news content decisions will be driven by the distribution of viewing audience tastes, the cost of different types of local news programming, the values of different demographic audiences to advertisers, and the number of channels competing in the marketplace (some of which may choose to offer sitcoms or drama programs during the local news dinner hour). Channels face the decision of where to locate along a spectrum of low violence to high violence, a spectrum that may be correlated with coverage of hard news (e.g., high public affairs content) versus soft news (e.g., high crime, accident coverage). Stations with high crime coverage may generate negative externalities in the form of an increased probability that viewers will develop the "mean world" syndrome (e.g., come to view the world as a more fearful or hostile place).[5] Stations with low violence content may generate positive externalities, in the form of increasing understanding of the issues of concern to viewers in their roles as citizens and voters. The content of the local news will be driven by the returns to capturing different types of audiences, however, since broadcasters will not be led to internalize the externalities they generate.

In balancing the private information demanded by viewers for personally useful or entertaining information with the possible benefits to society of coverage with a "hard news" focus, stations are often described as "giving viewers what they want, rather than what they need."[6] Ignoring the positive externalities of news coverage goes against the trustee model of local broadcasting, under which stations receive their broadcast licenses for free in return for a promise to broadcast in the "public interest, convenience, and necessity." Historically, the areas of programming the FCC examined in determining "public interest" broadcast requirements included those types of programming which generate positive externalities, such as public affairs programming and children's educational shows. The agency at one time required local stations to report to the FCC the number of hours of public affairs programming they broadcast and required them to conduct "ascertainment surveys" in their local communities.[7] In this manner, the licensing system would function as a way to remedy in part the market failures inherent in the private incentives broadcasters face in providing public affairs programming.[8]

Gradually, the FCC's approach of informal content regulation gave way during the 1980s to a laissez-faire attitude toward public interest requirements. FCC Chairman Mark Fowler argued that television was simply a "toaster with pictures," so that the same market mechanisms that work in the market for private goods (such as toasters) would also work in the broader information marketplace of television broadcasting.[9] Under this model, content is driven by viewer interests. Local stations will provide local news programming with a content and style that respond to viewers who vary in their interest in consumer, producer, entertainment, and voter information. To those who objected that public affairs programming was offered in insufficient amounts, Fowler pointed out that the market determines which programs were offered and that a lack of programming reflects a lack of viewer demand. Summing up this result, he noted, "The public's interest, then, defines the public interest."[10]

If broadcasters offer public affairs programming to educate and inform the public, then the coverage of crime in local news should reflect assessments about crime as a policy issue. Variations in crime coverage across stations should reflect variations in news judgments about the reality and relevance of different types of local crimes. If content is driven by profit maximization, however, stations will choose local news content based on audience interest, story costs, advertiser values, the number of competitors in the marketplace, and the relative brand positions established by these competitors. The reality of the incidence of crimes in the local market will affect a profit maximizing station's crime coverage, but this effect will be depend on the extent that viewers are interested in crime, the relative costs of covering crime, and the extent that other stations are covering crime.

If profits drive local news coverage, then the model in chapter 1 can be readily applied to station decisions about this type of programming. Assume that viewers vary in their interest in crime, so that there are three types of audiences for local news: those interested in low, moderate, or high levels of crime stories. Interest in crime stories may be correlated with viewers' interest in "soft" versus "hard news," so that viewers who prefer high amounts of crime coverage may not express a strong interest in detailed public affairs programming while those with a low interest in crime coverage prefer more information about hard news topics such as the actions of state or local governments. To simplify the discussion of station decisions, assume that programmers face the decision of whether to offer a program with a low, medium, or high amount of crime coverage. The content the news director will choose depends on the relative number of viewers in the different viewing interest segments, the value of these viewers to advertisers, the costs of developing newscasts with different levels of violent content, the number of competitors in the marketplace, and the relative positions chosen by these competitors along the crime coverage spectrum. Five specific hypotheses about news content follow from the chapter 1 model:

Stations within a given television market will vary in the amount of crime coverage. Although journalistic accounts describe local news programming as following the motto "if it bleeds, it leads," market segmentation means that some stations will choose higher rates of crime coverage to attract a given viewing audience while other stations will opt for programming that emphasizes a different set of topics. Variations in viewer interests will generate different amounts of crime coverage across stations within a given viewing area.

Crime coverage will be positively correlated with some news topics and negatively correlated with others, depending on the viewing interests of the station's target audience. If ratings drive local news judgments, then a station's newscast should vary in its treatment of topics depending on the strategy adopted by its programmer in assembling an audience. The Times Mirror survey described in chapter 2 indicates that younger viewers are more interested in violent entertainment programming, that men turn out in higher numbers for fictional crime programs, and that older viewers express higher levels of interest in public affairs programs. High-crime stations (targeted at younger viewers) may be more likely to cover topics such as accidents and entertainment stories, topics that have less public affairs content. Low-crime stations may be more likely to cover "hard news" topics such as state or local government.

Since content and style together establish a station's brand position, high crime stations will differ in their overall newscast style and in the way that they treat crime stories. If viewers for high-crime stations are more entertainment oriented, these stations will respond by offering a product that differs in style as well as content. High-crime stations should have more stories, a faster pace, and focus on different types of crime stories. High-crime stations, for example, may be more likely to show the details of a crime and arrests rather than offer stories that involve less action, such as trials or crime statistics.

In equilibrium, there is no reason to expect that high-crime stations will necessarily have higher, lower, or equal ratings; higher-crime stations may, however, draw more males relative to the lead-in program. The model in chapter 1 indicates that profits are driven by a combination of ratings, program costs, advertiser values, and competitors trying to target a given set of viewers. Competition for viewers means that, in equilibrium, high-crime stations may have higher, lower, or equal ratings to those that choose other brand identities within a market. Although journalists sometimes assume that violence increases ratings, competition in the market for local news programming means that there is no a priori reason to expect that high-crime stations will have higher ratings. The model does suggest, however, that as stations shift to local news programming at the dinner hour the rearrangement of audiences will mean that high-crime stations will experience a greater change in male viewers, who may migrate to the more violent local news programs.

Local news content and style will vary across markets depending on audience interests in news topics, styles of presentation, and particular stories. Viewing audiences vary across markets in their interest in "hard news," melodrama, and violent crime, differences that in turn may shape the incentives for local news programmers. This chapter will use ratings in a market for the evening network news, Melrose Place, and Cops to capture these variations in expressed viewer preferences. If programming follows viewer interest, the topics and style chosen by stations across different television markets should vary with these measures of viewer interest. Even after controlling for the underlying nature of crime in a city, stations across different markets should vary in their handling of crime stories depending on the viewing interests of their target audiences.

These hypotheses are tested in the following sections using data on local television news programs from nineteen different markets. This analysis does not allow me to make claims about how local news content in aggregate affects public opinion about crime or what an "ideal" news broadcast would look like if provision of information rather than profit maximization were the goal of a news director. Adding crime stories to attract viewers could even have some positive impacts on consumption of other information about public affairs, if viewers attracted to the programs carried away more public affairs information. My goal in the following analysis is rather to show that variations in both style and content of news programming, including a focus on crime, can be explained by the same product model that explains the variation in entertainment programming decisions.

A SNAPSHOT OF LOCAL NEWS COVERAGE: NOVEMBER 1993

The private market for media information makes analysis of local news content feasible, since abstracts that detail each story on the local evening news are available on Lexis. For coverage in November 1993, Lexis had transcript information for weekday dinner hour newscasts for fifty-seven different stations in nineteen local television markets.[11] Each story, except those dealing with sports and weather, was coded according to a list of general topics (see table 7.1). Story style is noted, including use of video graphics, clips (i.e., video scenes accompanied by voice-overs from anchors or reporters), and soundbites (i.e., video scenes that include clips of individuals talking, generally in response to reporter questions). Crime stories were coded in more detail to capture the type of crime, identity of the principals involved, point in the chain of events covered by the story (e.g., arrest, trial), and contents of the video graphic, clip, or soundbite accompanying the story (e.g., did the clip focus on the perpetrator, the crime scene?). The 22 weekdays of newscasts coded across the nineteen markets yielded a sample of 16,079 stories. Summary statistics for each station were calculated to yield a snapshot of the content and styles chosen within and across markets in local news programming.

TABLE 7.1
Mean Percentage Story Distribution, Local News Broadcasts

Topic	Mean % Stories	Minimum %	Maximum %
Accident	10.3	2.0	24.8
Art	0.2	0.0	1.5
Business	11.1	2.1	29.6
Crime	29.4	17.7	42.4
Crime Prevention	2.4	0.4	9.2
Education	3.0	0.0	8.3
Entertainment	3.8	0.0	16.2
Environment	0.5	0.0	3.9
Government/Human Interest	2.1	0.0	4.2
Government/International with U.S Involvement	3.2	0.0	8.9
Government/International without U.S. Involvement	0.4	0.0	4.0
Government-Local	4.2	0.5	8.7
Government-Military	0.4	0.0	3.1
Government-National	2.1	0.0	6.4
Government-Other	0.0	0.0	0.2
Government-State	4.1	0.0	13.5
Gun Control	1.0	0.0	3.0
Health	4.3	0.0	15.4
Homeless	0.6	0.0	3.2
Human Interest	11.6	3.7	28.9
Labor	2.8	0.4	14.9
Other	0.4	0.0	9.4
Recaps	0.4	0.0	7.4
Religion	0.3	0.0	2.1
Science	0.8	0.0	9.9
Traffic	0.7	0.0	5.9

Note: Story percentages were calculated for fifty-seven stations' local news broadcasts for November 1993.

Table 7.1 reports means for the percentage of stories for each station dealing with particular news topics. Crime coverage accounts for nearly a third of the local evening news stories. There was wide variation in the percentage of news programming devoted to crime, ranging from a minimum percentage of 17.7 % of a station's stories to a maximum of 42.4%. These crime stories dealt with the commission or aftermath of crimes, rather than crime prevention (which accounted for an average of 2.4% of a station's stories). The next three most prevalent story topics were business stories (11.1%), accidents (10.3%), and human interest stories (11.6%), with the latter two categories demonstrating the role that "soft news" plays in dinner hour news. There were also wide ranges in these areas of programming, with human interest percentages ranging from 3.7% to 28.9% and business stories accounting for between 2.1% to 29.6% of a station's news items. Public affairs stories were spread across many different levels of government, with state government (4.1%) and local government (4.2%) accounting for the largest share of the local news stories dealing explicitly with government.

Each crime story was assigned to a specific category, so the percentage of a station's crime stories dealing with particular types of crime could be calculated. Table 7.2 reveals that on average 30% of a station's crime stories deal with murder. The percentage varied widely, with murder accounting for a minimum of 6.9% to a maximum of 69.8% of a station's total crime stories for November 1993. Violent crimes other than murder played a large role in crime coverage. Nonfatal shootings (8.7%), rape (8.6%), and robbery (7.9%) attracted significant attention in local news crime programming. White-collar crimes

TABLE 7.2
Mean Percentage Crime Story Categories

Crime Category	Mean % of Crime Stories	Minimum %	Maximum %
Murder	30.0	6.9	69.8
Nonfatal Shooting/Stabbing	8.7	0.0	17.3
Rape	8.6	0.0	34.4
Robbery	7.9	0.0	20.0
Child Abuse	7.9	0.0	26.0
Assault	6.8	1.5	24.1
Vehicular Crime	4.9	0.0	13.6
Drug Offense	4.7	0.0	14.5
Unknown Crime	4.0	0.0	13.4
Nonviolent Crime	4.0	0.0	10.1
Abduction	3.4	0.0	24.5
Arson	3.1	0.0	30.1
Theft	2.6	0.0	9.6
Missing Persons	2.6	0.0	13.6
Assisted Suicide	1.8	0.0	12.9
Fraud/Counterfeit	1.7	0.0	7.1
Death Threat/Hate Crime	1.4	0.0	23.3
Bombing/Bomb Threat	1.3	0.0	6.5
Business Crime	1.2	0.0	7.8
Suicide	1.1	0.0	6.1
Assassination	0.9	0.0	4.4
Harassment	0.8	0.0	4.5
Animal Abuse	0.8	0.0	4.0
Bribery	0.7	0.0	6.8
Sports Fighting	0.5	0.0	5.4
Discrimination	0.4	0.0	4.3
Noncriminal Missing Persons	0.1	0.0	2.7
Extortion	0.1	0.0	2.7
Abortion	0.1	0.0	1.7

such as tax evasion, bribery, extortion, and business crimes accounted for a relatively small amount of crime stories. When local news focuses on crime, it is generally on crimes relating to violence. These results are consistent with other research that indicates that crimes such as murder account for a much higher percentage of crime stories than their percentage of overall crimes.[12]

Table 7.3 summarizes how stations treat the details of crime in their local

TABLE 7.3
Crime Details

	Mean %
Mean % of Crime Story Event	
Under Investigation	28.9
Crime Details	21.1
Trial	16.6
Pretrial	11.0
Arrest	9.0
Posttrial	7.3
Other News	3.4
Crime Statistics	2.6
Mean % of Crime Story Principals	
Nonfamous Principals	55.2
Minor Victims	22.1
Government Officials	11.4
Minor Suspects	9.2
Entertainment Figures	3.8
Sports Figures	2.5
Gangs	1.8
Religious Leaders	1.0
Mean % of Crime Story Clips	
Perpetrator	13.7
Law Enforcement Officials	10.5
Crime Scene	9.4
Crime Victim	8.4
Family of Victim	4.8
Courtroom	4.2
Prosecutor	3.6
Defense Attorney	3.2
Neighbor	3.2
Actual Crime	1.9
Witness	1.8
Family of Perpetrator	1.3
Judge	0.7
Funeral	0.6
Arrest	0.5
Body	0.4
Other	0.4

Note: A given crime story could feature more than one type of principal or story clip.

news programming. If one divides crime stories into a chain of events from commission to (possible) conviction, it becomes clear that most stories focus on the more visually entertaining aspects of the crime chain. On average stories about the details of a crime account for 21.1% and investigation stories another 28.9% of crime stories. Trials account for 16.6% of crime stories. Stations rarely provide a context for the large amount of crime coverage they offer. Stories dealing with crime statistics account for just 2.6% of crime coverage.[13] There are large differences on which parts of the crime chain stations choose to focus, with the details of crime accounting for a minimum of 8.5% and a maximum of 44.6% of crime stories. Stories about crimes under investigation similarly ranged from 14.0% to 49.4% of a station's crime stories.

On average over half of the crime stories dealt with "nonfamous" adults, individuals who did not fit into the other categories outlined in table 7.3. For a third of the crime stories minors were either victims (22.1%) or suspects (9.2%). Gangs were involved on average with only 1.8% of the crime stories covered in these local news broadcasts. Government officials accounted for 11.4% of crime stories, a much higher percentage than sports figures (2.5%) or entertainers (3.8%). There were also wide variations in the percentages of crime stories devoted to different principals, with stories featuring sports figures ranging from 0% to 12.2% and those relating to entertainers accounting for 0% to 16.3%.

Although crime coverage is often criticized during the debate over television violence, table 7.3 emphasizes that actual crimes are rarely shown on local evening news programs. Actual crimes accounted for a mean percentage of 1.9% of the crime clips shown, with a minimum of 0% and a maximum of 6.4%. The most prevalent types of clips on average are those that show the alleged perpetrator (13.7%), or the crime victim (8.4%). Bodies of crime victims were shown on twenty-one of the fifty-seven stations, although they account on average for only a small percentage (.4% of crime clips) of video coverage. Stations were much less likely to run clips dealing with the later judicial outcomes of crimes, such as courtroom clips (4.2%) or judge clips (.7%). Stations varied greatly in what aspects they highlighted in crime video coverage, with clips of perpetrators accounting for between 0% and 32.5% on average of crime clips and law officials accounting for between 1.3% and 19.6% of clips. Although clips of the family of victims were more frequent (4.8%) than those of the family of the perpetrator (1.3%), video coverage of defense attorneys (3.2%) and prosecutors (3.6%) was roughly equivalent.

These overview figures confirm that on many stations local news is crime news. Crime stories accounted for nearly a third of a station's stories on average, with nearly a third of these crime stories focused on murder. The results are consistent with earlier research on crime coverage. Rocky Mountain Media Watch (1995) found in an analysis of evening local news broadcasts for a single day (September 29, 1995) at 100 stations that crime accounted for 30.2% of the average news time on a station and that violent crimes were the most frequent types of crime covered. Graber (1980) found that in print and broadcast media outlets in Chicago violent crimes such as murder accounted for a higher percentage of media crime stories than their percentage in police data on crimes. McManus (1994) found in case studies of local news decisions that editors favored using a high percentage of crime stories because they were low cost to discover and report.[14] More can be learned from these patterns in coverage, however, when the model in chapter 1 is applied.

Content, Style, and Correlations

If local news programs are shaped by competition for viewers, then a station's selection of news topics and style of presentation will be related parts of establishing a brand position for the local newscast. Since news decisions will vary depending on a program's time constraints, this section will analyze the content and style correlations for a subset of the November 1993 data, the thirty-eight stations that had half-hour (as opposed to an hour) dinner evening news programs. The analysis demonstrates that stations high in crime coverage do differ from other broadcasters along dimensions predicted by the market model. High-crime stations were more likely to carry topics with a "soft" news content, had a quicker pace and greater use of video clips, teased crime stories more throughout the broadcast, and were more likely to carry crime as the top story. High-crime stations also focused on different parts of the chain of crime events, with stories and clips that dwelled more on the crime commission parts (e.g., scene, bodies) and less on the later workings of the criminal justice system. Overall, stations that choose to emphasize crime offer content and style associated more with entertainment.

Table 7.4 reports sample means for the half-hour local news broadcasts. One decision that news directors face in developing a broadcast is the relative positioning of stories. Top stories play a prominent role in anchoring viewers to a program and emphasizing the relative importance of stories. While crime accounted for a mean of 31.3% of a station's stories, crime stories accounted for nearly half of the top stories (47.5%) or top five stories (46.4%) on a broadcast. The emphasis on leading with a crime story varied across stations, from a low of 15.8% to a high of 76.2%. These crime stories dealt primarily with murder, which made up a mean of 17.5% of the lead stories for these stations. The station with the lowest percentage of top stories dealing with murder had 0%, while one station had over half of its lead stories for the month (56.3%) focusing on murder. Stations had similarly wide ranges for the percentage of top five stories dealing with crime (24.5% to 73.3%) and total stories dealing with crime (17.8% to 42.4%).

Another decision that programmers face is what stories to promote in the teasers that local newscasts use to retain audiences across commercial breaks. The most popular stories in teasers are those that come later in the broadcasts, such as sports (17.9%), human interest (14.9%), and weather (13.5%).[15] Even though crime stories play a prominent role early in the broadcasts, crime stories

TABLE 7.4

Half-Hour News Broadcasts: Style and Content

Mean % of Topics Covered	
Top Story	
Crime	47.5
Accidents	14.6
Labor	6.4
Business	5.7
State Government	3.5
Top 5 Stories	
Crime	46.4
Accidents	8.2
Business	6.7
Labor	4.7
State Government	4.5
Total Stories	
Crime	31.3
Human Interest	12.1
Business	11.3
Accident	10.8
State Government	4.3
Mean % of Story Teasers	
Sports	17.9
Human Interest	14.9
Weather	13.5
Business	12
Crime	8.1
Program Elements per Daily Broadcast	
Stories	11.2
Crime Stories	3.5
Murder Stories	1.2
Graphics	1.9
Clips	8.2
Soundbites	10.6

still account for the fifth largest topic of teasers (8.1% of story teasers). The use of crime teasers varies from a minimum of 0% to a maximum of 26.1% of a station's story promotions. Of the teasers that deal with crime, murder accounted for a mean of 19.2% of a station's crime teasers. The next most prevalent crime types in crime teasers were assault (7.9%), child abuse (7.6%), and robbery (6.9%).

If one excludes sports and weather coverage, these half-hour broadcasts averaged 11.2 stories. Crime coverage accounted for 3.5 stories per day, including an average of 1.2 murder stories daily on each broadcast. Visuals played a large role in these programs, with a daily average of 1.9 graphics, 8.2 clips (e.g., video segments that generally had voice-overs from reporters or anchors), and

10.6 soundbite segments where individuals are both seen and heard responding to questions or talking. Table 7.4 thus offers multiple ways to measure the role of crime coverage in a station's broadcast, including the percentage of total stories devoted to crime, percentage of teasers that focus on crime, and the daily number of crime stories. These indicators, which are highly correlated, will be used to explore how "high crime" stations vary in content and style.[16]

Greater coverage of crime stories is associated with newscast decisions to emphasize topics with higher entertainment value and downplay public affairs content, create a faster-paced program through the use of more stories, and use more visuals and rely less on explanations of events. Table 7.5 reveals that coverage of crime moves together with coverage of accidents and military stories, two topics that may also share an appeal to those interested in violence. Stations with more crime stories are also more likely to cover health issues,

TABLE 7.5

Content and Style Correlations, Half-Hour Evening News Broadcasts

Correlation of Station Crime Indicators with % Total Story Types	
Daily Average Crime Stories	
% Accident	.41***
% Government-Military	.29*
% Health	.29*
% Government-State	-.27*
% Education	-.41**
% Business	-.49***
% Crime Stories	
% Entertainment	.39**
% Government-Local	-.34**
% Recaps	-.35**
% Business	-.43***
% Education	-.44***
% Crime Teasers	
% Accident	.44**
% Crime Prevention	-.32**
% Education	-.32**
% Government-Local	-.33**
% Business	-.44***
Correlation of Station Crime Indicators with Newscast Styles	
Daily Average Crime Stories	
Stories per Day	.83***
Teasers per Day	.40***
Clips per Day	.57***
Soundbites per Day	.31*
Soundbites per Story	-.31**
% Crime Teasers	.60***

Note: *** = statistically significant at the .01 level; ** = significant at the .05 level; * = significant at the .10 level.

stories that are often framed as "news you can use" (e.g., that satisfies viewer demand for practically useful information). The higher the percentage of stories devoted to crime, the larger percentage of stories devoted explicitly to entertainment issues. Stations that choose to promote crime stories through teasers are also those more likely to devote more attention to accident coverage.

Crime coverage is negatively correlated with coverage of issues with a hard news or public affairs content. The greater the number of daily crime stories aired by a station, the lower the chance that the station will focus attention on state government stories, education, or business topics. Stations with higher percentages of their total stories devoted to crime have lower percentages devoted to local government, business, or education. These stations are also less likely to use recaps in their broadcasts, narratives that summarize stories covered in the broadcast.[17] Coverage of issues such as education and local government is negatively correlated with the percentage of story teasers relating to crime. Broadcasts that promote upcoming crime stories in their teasers are actually less likely to have stories that deal with crime prevention.

News directors may vary in their assessment of the relative importance of news topics, so even if stations were attempting to broadcast according to a trustee model, there might be correlations in story type selection. The connection between crime coverage and broadcast style, however, is strong additional evidence that concern for viewer interests shapes local news programs. Table 7.5 reveals that broadcasts that use more crime stories per broadcast are also more likely to use a style that emphasizes entertainment. Broadcasts with more crime stories are faster paced since they have more stories per program. Stations with more daily crime stories use more teasers during their programs, which reflects a greater attempt to attract and retain viewers through internal promotions. Stations with more crime stories also use more clips and more soundbites per broadcast, though this correlation is stronger for the use of clips (i.e., video that uses voice-overs from anchors or reporters). Higher crime coverage is associated with fewer soundbites per story, which means that these stations are less likely to allow the individuals involved in stories to explain events (which may slow down the pace of a broadcast). Stations with higher daily crime stories are also much more likely to devote their teasers to crime, consistent with an attempt to use crime to spark and retain viewer interest.

Stations with higher crime coverage also cover crime in a different way, primarily by focusing on the more visually arresting or entertaining parts of the criminal process. Table 7.6 reveals that within the chain of events involved with a crime, stations with more crime stories per day devoted a higher percentage of their crime stories to the details of the crime. These stations devoted smaller percentages of their crime stories to trials or crime statistics, two areas that help place individual crimes in context within the criminal justice system. Stations that devoted a higher fraction of teasers to crime were also more likely to focus on arrests of alleged criminals, which again may provide more visual entertainment than stories about investigations or trials.

In terms of crime clip contents, stations with more crime stories were more

TABLE 7.6

Crime Coverage Styles and Correlations

Chain of Crime	
Daily Average Crime Stories	
% Crime Details	.31*
% Trial	−.31*
% Crime Statistics	−.35**
% Crime Stories	
% Crime Statistics	−.44***
% Trial	−.30*
% Crime Teasers	
% Arrest	.37**
Clip Content	
Daily Average Crime Stories	
% Actual Crime	.29*
Average body clips per crime story	.35**
% Crime Stories	
% Witness	.35**
% Family alleged Perpetrator	.36**
% Actual Crime	.31*
% Funeral	−.32**
% Crime Teasers	
% Witness	.34**
% Actual Crime	.32**
% Arrest	.28*
Crime Principals	
% Crime Stories	
% Entertainers	.35**
% Crime Teasers	
% Entertainers	.42***
Crime Categories	
Daily Average Crime Stories	
% Theft	.39**
% Robbery	.30*
% Crime Stories	
% Suicide	.33**
% Theft	.29*
% Robbery	.28*
% Hate Crime	−.31*
% Murder	−.43***
% Crime Teasers	
% Suicide	.49***
% Theft	.35***
% Arson	.34***
% Sexual Harrassment	.31*

Note: *** = statistically significant at the .01 level; ** = significant at the .05 level; * = significant at the .10 level.

likely to show clips of the actual commission of crimes. The average body clip per crime story was also higher for these stations. Both of these events were rare in local television news. For the sample of thirty-eight half-hour broadcasts, on average 1.9% of a station's crime clips had footage of the actual crime. For this sample there were only thirty-eight clips showing the actual crime. Only fifteen out of the thirty-eight stations aired a crime clip of an actual body, with one station (WSVN, discussed later) showing fifteen in the month of November. The clips shown by stations with a higher percentage of crime stories focused more on the actual crime, interviews with witnesses, and clips of the family of the alleged perpetrator. Stations that teased crime stories more also focused more on the early stages of the criminal process in their clip selection. They had a higher percentage of their crime clips focused on the actual crime, arrests, and witnesses. Stations with a higher percentage of crime stories or crime teasers were also more likely to focus on crimes that involved entertainers. In sum, stations with a higher crime focus were more likely to cover the details associated with the commission of a crime and less likely to report on the resolution of crime cases through the criminal justice system.

Stations with a greater focus on crime also covered a different mix of crime stories. Stations with a higher percentage of stories devoted to crime were more likely to have a larger proportion of their crime stories devoted to suicides, thefts, and robberies. These stations had a lower percentage of crime stories covering murder. This pattern may indicate that, when low crime stations focus on crime, the stories they report are more likely to deal with murders. High-crime stations cover murders too, but they also add other types of stories that aggregate to a higher level of crime coverage. These stories may be those such as thefts and robberies, crimes that are not judged as "newsworthy" on low-crime stations but are added on stations that feature crime. Note that stations with a higher proportion of crime stories were less likely to cover hate crimes, which would be consistent with their larger failure to cover news with greater public affairs or hard news content. Stations that devoted a larger fraction of their teasers to crime also chose to emphasize a different mix of crimes. These stations devoted a higher proportion of their crime stories to suicide, theft, arson, and sexual harassment. These were the types of crimes added to cover-age by stations that used crime to build audiences.

One way to see how content helps build audiences is to examine the relation-ship between news topics focused on by stations and the change in ratings among different demographic groups between the lead-in show (i.e., the prior program on the channel) and the local dinner hour newscast coded. For the fifty-six stations with both Nielsen data and coded content available, it is clear that there is a relationship between ratings changes and the type of news offered by a particular station. The percentage of stories devoted to crime is positively correlated for the change in ratings (e.g., local news ratings - lead-in program ratings) for men 18–34 (correlation, .39***), men 18–49 (.25*), and men 18 + (.34***). There was no statistically significant correlation between these ratings changes for men and the percentage of the newscast devoted to entertainment stories. For women, however, the reverse pattern appeared. There was a positive correlation between the percentage of entertainment stories and the lead-in ratings differences for women 18–34 (.32***), women 18–49 (.35***), and women 18+ (.25*). There was no statistically significant correlation between the percentage of stories devoted to crime and the change in ratings for female demographic groups. The survey results in chapter 2 suggested that men had higher expressed preferences for violent content and that women were more likely to watch programs which focused on entertainment figures. These local news patterns suggest that violent content may similarly be used to attract male viewers to these programs. The relation between content and audience is more readily explored through analysis of interactions within individual markets, the topic pursued next.

Within Market Brand Positions

If competition for ratings drives the content of local news programs, the model in chapter 1 yields a set of testable predictions about how stations will position their newscasts within a local market. There should be variation in the use of crime stories across stations, which should be correlated with the other topics programmers decide to package with crime news. Since content and style are part of a brand position, a station's selection of crime news should be correlated with its overall style and its manner of treating crime stories. In equilibrium there is no reason to expect that focusing on crime news will lead to higher or lower overall household ratings, although stations with high crime may be targeted more at younger or male audiences. This section confirms these hypotheses, first through an examination of spatial competition in one market (Miami–Fort Lauderdale) and then in a statistical analysis of the brand position patterns in the nineteen local markets with data coded for November 1993.

If stations develop brand identities for their coverage of crime, these positions should be evident in local reviews of the television market. The Miami–Fort Lauderdale market offers one example of distinct segmentation in the local news market, with one station (WSVN) perceived as providing high-crime coverage and another station (WCIX) offering coverage with distinctly less crime news. When WSVN lost its affiliation with NBC in 1989, the station began to offer extensive news coverage as a way to create its own programming, although the station eventually went on to become affiliated with Fox. As one analyst described the change in WSVN's news style,

Word-based, informational news was out. In came video feeds on crime, sex, disaster. WSVN cameramen jerked the camera around, to increase the perception of action. Watch any WSVN newscast. Sharp graphics and dramatic music introduce each segment. . . . WSVN will often cut live to whatever news is most gripping, regardless of its local news value. The station's "world news" segment details floods in England, an auto accident in France, a bus crash in South Africa.[18]

Critics noted that the station not only devoted a large percentage of its coverage to crime but that it covered crime in a different way than other stations. As one spokesperson for a group of hotels that stopped providing WSVN in their rooms because of its crime coverage explained: "Channel 7 [WSVN] sensationalizes the crime. It's the way they take a crime story . . . the way they follow a trail of blood up to the body."[19] Reviewers also noted that in addition to providing crime coverage, WSVN offers other news topics geared to appeal to younger viewers. One reviewer indicated that WSVN provides "a lot of medical news for the health-obsessed, many of whom are young. And entertainment news, the mind foof of the MTV generation, is ubiquitous."[20] Summing up the image that viewers have of WSVN, a local television critic in the city stated: "Most stations have policies against showing dead bodies, except in special circumstances. And those who tune to stations such as WSVN know what to expect. The promise of ghoulish titilation might be the reason for their viewing choice."[21]

The owner of WSVN, Ed Ansin, states explicitly that the station's content and style are aimed at attracting younger viewers. Responding to criticism of its crime coverage, he noted that "The controversy surrounding our news is that our news is really targeted to younger adults. Some people want a more traditional and stylized newscast. A lot of complaints come from people who don't watch us. Which is fine. In a perfect world maybe everyone will be watching the MacNeil-Lehrer Report."[22] The supervisor of news operations at the station, Joel Cheatwood, argues that the style of coverage draws people to the broadcast, which he says may ultimately leave them better informed (a point disputed by reviewers). Defending the station's approach, he said:

We're going to make ourselves as aesthetically pleasing as we can as well, so if somebody looks at my newscast in Miami . . . and says, "You know what, they look like Entertainment Tonight, they have graphics like Entertainment Tonight," well, great. If that's going to draw them in and make them watch our news and become better informed, then I say more power to us.[23]

The article went on to conclude, however, that "Cheatwood's critics say nobody becomes a better citizen by watching WSVN. To the contrary, detractors say WSVN distorts people's view of their community by focusing on crime and disaster to the exclusion of more important kinds of news."[24]

The station's news content has been successful in attracting younger viewers, who also turn out for the affiliate's Fox programming. The WSVN dinner hour (6 PM) newscast was generally the second highest rated in the market during 1993, after station WPLG. WSVN was said to be the most profitable station in the market, with revenues jumping "by more than 40 percent since adopting 'if it bleeds, it leads' as its news philosophy."[25] The station's owner links the news programming profitability directly to the younger viewers attracted, noting that "We are an advertiser-supported medium. We excel in the demographic group with younger adults. This is the group advertisers want. That's where they spend the bulk of their money."[26]

The number one news broadcast among the four dinner hour broadcasts in the Miami market was WPLG, which also offered extensive crime coverage but attracted less criticism for its manner of coverage.[27] The least watched newscast, WCIX, had a market reputation for showing less violent crime. It adopted an explicit strategy of "family sensitive programming," a label applied to newscasts that promise not to use violent images such as "bodies or blood on the pavement," in reporting on crime.[28] The station reportedly suffered a ratings drop, however, when it officially adopted this programming policy.[29]

The critical reviews of local news programming in Miami portray a market consistent with the model in chapter 1. WSVN targets younger viewers through focusing on violence, accidents, health, and entertainment issues. Crime is covered in a more "entertaining" way, so that the viewers may be more likely to see details at the crime scene, such as bodies or blood. The programmers use a faster pace (e.g., more stories per broadcast), more graphics, and live coverage to retain these younger viewers. The station's owner explicitly notes that an advantage to bringing in younger viewers is their high values to advertisers. WPLG also provides a high proportion of crime, but covers violent incidents in a less sensationalistic manner. WCIX offers a news broadcast with less crime and less focus on potentially offensive details. If the data in the November 1993 snapshot are accurate indicators of coverage patterns and if these perceived brand positions are true, then statistical analysis of the Miami shows should confirm the reviewers' assessments.

Table 7.7 bears out reviewers' assessments of the local news market in Miami. WSVN has the highest percentage of its stories devoted to crime (35.0%), followed next by WPLG (30.1%), WTVJ (25.6%), and WCIX (17.8%). On average there were 7.8 crime stories per half-hour broadcast on WSVN versus 2.5 on WCIX. WSVN had three times the number of murder stories per day (2.7) as WCIX (.9). Although WPLG had a similar percentage of crime stories to WSVN, the emphasis that WSVN gives to crime stories and the way the station covers crime sets it apart. Two-thirds of the top five stories on WSVN dealt with crime, versus 46.0% for WPLG and 30.1% for WCIX. The stations in Miami had a similar percentage of their crime stories dealing with murder (c. 35% of all crime stories), but WSVN emphasized these stories more. Murder stories accounted for 21.1% of the top stories on WSVN versus 0% for WCIX, the station that eventually adopted the "family sensitive news" brand name. The WSVN crime style is also evident in table 7.7. The station was much more likely to cover the details of crime (31.8% of its crime stories) than other stations (20.9% for WPLG and 18.9% for WCIX). WSVN was less likely to provide coverage of trials (5.4% of its crime stories) or crime statistics (1.4%). WCIX was more likely to emphasize trials (9.4%) and crime statistics (5.7% of its crime news). For November 1993, WSVN had fifteen stories in which bodies were shown in crime stories, a practice frequently criticized in reviews of the station. In the other three stations combined there was only one crime story during the month that showed a body.

TABLE 7.7
Spatial Competition: Miami 6 PM Local News Broadcasts

	WSVN	WPLG	WTVJ	WCIX
Crime				
% Crime Stories	35.0	30.1	25.6	17.8
Daily Average Crime Stories	7.8	3.4	3.2	2.5
% Crime Teasers	16.2	5.2	1.9	1.0
% Top 5 Stories Crime	63.2	46.0	43.8	30.1
Daily Average Murder Stories	2.7	1.3	0.8	0.9
% Top Stories Dealing with Murder	21.1	15.0	10.5	0.0
% Crime Stories Dealing with Murder	35.1	37.3	25.0	35.8
% Crime Stories Focusing on Murder	31.8	20.9	31.7	18.9
% Crime Stories Focusing on Crime Details	5.4	13.4	15.0	9.4
% Crime Stories Focusing on Trial	1.4	0.0	6.7	5.7
% Crime Stories Focusing on Statistics	0.0	0.0	0.0	1.0
Total Stories with Body Shots, Nov. 1993	15.0	0.0	0.0	1.0
News Topics				
% Human Interest	6.4	12.8	7.3	20.1
% Local Government	3.1	6.0	6.4	6.4
% Business	2.1	5.5	7.3	9.7
% Accident	13.5	11.0	9.8	6.4
% Health	15.4	6.9	10.7	5.0
% Government-Military	3.1	0.0	0.9	0.3
Style				
Daily Stories	22.3	10.9	12.3	14.2
Daily Clips	29.2	0.2	2.2	12.5
Daily Soundbites	17.1	14.5	13.1	9.1
% Accident Teasers	12.4	6.5	3.8	6.9
% Health Teasers	25.5	9.0	21.7	7.9

The distribution of story topics in the November 1993 data is consistent with the notion that stations are making story selections to appeal to particular audiences. WSVN combined high crime coverage with accident coverage (13.5% of total stories, vs. 6.4% for WCIX). WSVN also provided more health coverage, which was designed to appeal to younger viewers. The station carried 15.4% health stories, versus 5% for WCIX. WSVN carried a higher percentage of government military stories (3.1%, vs. .3% on WCIX), which survey evidence discussed later indicates were of interest to younger viewers and those with an interest in violent entertainment. In developing a brand position for "nonviolent" news programming, WCIX carried a much higher percentage of human interest stories (20.1%) than WSVN (6.4%) or WTVJ (7.3%). While WSVN devoted 3.1% of its stories to local government, each of the other stations carried twice that percentage of local government stories. WSVN also carried a lower percentage of business stories (2.1%, vs. 9.7% for WCIX).

The correlation between soft news content and entertaining styles is also evident in table 7.7. WSVN carried 22.3 stories per broadcast, twice the number

(10.9) shown by WPLG in the same amount of time. On average, WSVN had 29.2 video clips per day, versus 12.5 for WCIX. WSVN also used more sound-bites per day (17.1) than WCIX (9.1). The WSVN broadcast thus had shorter stories and more audiovisual stimulation for viewers. The station's marketing emphasis was also evident in the use of teasers. Of the total teasers on WSVN, 16.2% dealt with crime stories, versus 1.0% on WCIX. WSVN also emphasized health (25.5% of total teasers) and accidents (12.4%) more than WCIX (6.9% accident teasers, 7.9% health teasers).

The ratings for November 1993 confirm that WSVN does better with younger viewers than older demographic groups. WSVN was the only station where ratings declined among women with age (WSVN's ratings for women were a four rating for 18–34, a three for 18–49, and a five for 18+). WSVN's ratings for men were four for 18–34, 18–49, and 18+. By contrast, the ratings for the top station WPLG increased with age. For women the ratings were three for women 18–34, five for 18–49, and nine for women 18+. For men the ratings were two for men 18–34, three for men 18–49, and seven for men 18+. Thus violent news programming allowed WSVN to win the ratings race among younger viewers, while WPLG gained higher ratings overall because of its popularity with older viewers.[30] WPLG also had a higher rating of two among children 2–11, versus a rating of one for WSVN and WTVJ.

Television reviews and content analysis demonstrate that local news programs in Miami do reflect the hypotheses generated in chapter 1: market segmentation based on crime content; the movement of crime news with coverage of topics of concern to younger viewers, such as health issues; and a correlation between "soft news" content and a faster-paced style that emphasized entertainment. To test whether these within market patterns held across the sample of nineteen local television markets, I analyzed differences in content and style between the high-crime and low-crime station in each market, with high or low-crime stations defined on the basis of daily average crime stories or the percentage of total stories devoted to crime. For example, the model in chapter 1 suggests that if stations choose high crime coverage to attract younger viewers, then these stations may also use a faster-paced style (i.e., more stories per half hour) to build a younger audience. Within each market I calculated the difference between the average number of total stories on the high-crime station and the average number on the low-crime station in the market. The null hypothesis is that there is a .5 probability that this difference will be positive (i.e., if there is no relation between crime content and story style, then this difference is equally likely to be positive or negative across markets). The alternative hypothesis is that high-crime stations will have more stories since they are faster paced, which means the probability that the difference is positive should be greater than .5. The greater the number of markets in which the difference is positive, the more confidence one has in accepting the alternative hypothesis that high-crime stations carry more stories per broadcast.[31]

Table 7.8 demonstrates that across the nineteen markets monitored in November 1993 the station with the highest amount of crime coverage in each area

TABLE 7.8
Within-Market Brand Positions

	No. of Markets Positive	No. of Markets Negative	Statistical Significance
High Daily Average Crime Station—Low Daily Average Crime Station			
Daily Average Robbery	14	5	**
Daily Average Assault	14	5	**
Daily Average Child Abuse	15	4	***
Daily Average Murder	18	1	***
% Top 5 Stories, Crime	13	6	*
Soundbite per Crime Story	5	14	**
% Crime Teasers	15	4	***
% Crime Clips and Perpetrator	13	6	*
Sum of Bobbitt Stories, Nov. 1993	12	0	***
% Health Stories	14	5	**
% Human Interest Stories	5	14	**
Daily Stories	19	0	***
Daily Clips	14	5	**
Soundbites per Story	4	15	***
Ratings			
Women 18–34	7	7	
Men 18–34	8	9	
Households	8	11	
High Crime % Station—Low Crime % Station			
Local News – Lead-In Rating			
Men 18–34	13	1	***
Men 18+	11	2	***
% Crime Stories, Details	13	6	*
% Crime Principals, Government Officials	6	13	*
% Top 5 Stories, Theft	11	3	**
% Top 5 Stories, Rape	10	4	**
Daily Average Soundbites	5	14	**

Note: *** = statistically significant at the .01 level; ** = significant at the .05 level; * = significant at the .10 level.

offered a very different newscast from the station that offered the least amount of crime coverage in the market. The station with the highest number of crime stories per day broadcast higher daily averages of many types of crime stories: robbery, assault, child abuse, and murder. This is consistent with the notion that high-crime stations generate more crime stories per day by focusing more on robberies and assaults and by running more murder stories, perhaps by running murder stories on crimes committed outside the local jurisdiction. Table 7.8 indicates that the high-crime stations ran more stories over the course of November about the case of Lorena Bobbitt, who was accused of "malicious wounding" of her husband after he allegedly raped her.[32] High-crime stations also gave crime stories more emphasis, evident from the fact that they had a higher percentage of top five stories that dealt with crime and a higher percentage of story teasers devoted to crime. The high-crime station in the market was more likely to focus on clips of the alleged perpetrators of a crime. The high-crime station in each market had a lower number of soundbites per crime story than the low crime station. Soundbites may provide more background on a story, since the viewer can hear a principal in a case explain something. Video clips may add to a faster pace than soundbites, since the picture retains the viewer's interest while reporters or anchors do the voice-over for the story. These results indicate that low-crime stations were more likely to provide context through using soundbites on crime stories.

Television reviews and statistical analysis from the Miami market indicated that high-crime stations also differed from low-crime stations in their overall story selection and general broadcast style. If a station chooses to use crime coverage to attract younger viewers, one would predict that this would be correlated with the use of other stories to attract these viewers. Table 7.8 confirms that within each market the high-crime station carried a higher percentage of health stories popular with younger viewers than the low-crime station. In contrast, low-crime stations use human interest stories more than high-crime stations. In each of the nineteen markets studied, the station with the greatest number of daily crime stories had a faster paced broadcast (i.e., more stories overall). High crime content also meant more daily video clips. Low-crime stations were more likely to provide explanations with their stories in the words of those involved, as evident from their higher soundbite per story average across these markets.

The model in chapter 1 indicates that there is no reason in equilibrium to expect high-crime stations to have higher, lower, or equal ratings in a market. The sign tests are not statistically significant for any of the November 1993 ratings data differences between high-crime and low-crime stations. In eight markets the high-crime station had higher household ratings than the low crime station, while in eleven other markets the reverse is true. Even among younger viewers in the markets examined overall the high-crime station did not have higher ratings than the low-crime station among women 18–34 (7 positive, 7 negative differences) or men 18–34 (8 positive, 9 negative differences).

Additional evidence on content, style, and audience differences can be seen if one defines station brand positions on the basis of the percentage of total stories devoted to crime. The station with a higher crime story percentage did approach crime stories differently than the station with the lowest crime story percentage. The high-crime station was more likely to focus on the details of the crime, consistent with earlier suggestions that focusing on events earlier in the chain of a crime is more prevalent among high-crime broadcasts. Low-crime stations had a higher percentage of crime stories about government officials, which may be because high-crime stations are aimed at younger audiences with less interest in government or public officials. The high-crime station in each market had a higher percentage of top stories devoted to rape than the low-crime station, reflecting a decision about what type of story to use to grab a viewer's attention. High-crime stations were more likely to put theft stories in the top five news items, again emphasizing a difference in assessments of news values. Low-crime stations had more soundbites per day than high crime stations, providing viewers with more information directly from principals involved with stories.

While there is no statistically significant relation between ratings for high-crime stations versus those for low-crime stations in these markets, there is evidence that high-crime stations attract more male viewers relative to the number of males watching the lead-in programming on these channels. For Nielsen demographic groups based on age and gender, I calculated the difference between the rating for the local news program among that group and the rating for the preceding programming. For men 18–34 this difference was greater for high-crime stations than for low-crime stations in thirteen markets, while the reverse was true in only one market. For men 18+ it was also true that the change in ratings was greater for high-crime stations than for low-crime stations. This is consistent with the notion that violent content may be used especially to attract male viewers.

Content across Markets: The Impact of Audience Interests

If the selection of content and style in local news is driven by profits, these choices should respond to the level of audience interests in particular types of programming. For a given market size, the larger the proportion of viewers interested in high-violence entertainment programming, the greater the number of stations that will choose to offer high-violence entertainment shows. The same reasoning extends to brand positions in local news broadcasts. Since the nineteen markets with local news programs coded for November 1993 vary widely in their demographic makeup, the comparison of station decisions across markets offers the opportunity to test the impact of audience interest on news decisions. In this section I model station choices in local news programming as a function of eight variables: total television households and local broadcast stations in the market; the number of potential viewers aged 18–49 and females 18+ in the area; Nielsen ratings in the market for the network evening news broadcasts (i.e., the sum of ratings for the ABC, CBS, and NBC network nightly news programs), *Melrose Place*, and *Cops*; and whether the broadcast is an hour long rather than a half hour.

Opinion surveys and Nielsen data reveal that younger viewers express more interest in violent programming and faster-paced shows. If news programmers explicitly calibrate content to audience demand, the higher the number of viewers 18–49 in the market (controlling for market size) the more likely that a station will fashion its news content to meet these demands for entertainment.

The larger the number of women in a given size market, the less likely a station will be to offer violent programming. Nielsen data on household viewing within the market offer an even finer way to gauge the likely size of audiences interested in particular types of programming. To measure the interest in "hard news" in a local television market, I summed the Nielsen household ratings for the three broadcast network nightly news programs (i.e., *ABC World News Tonight, CBS Evening News,* and *NBC Nightly News*). Ratings for the prime-time Fox soap opera *Melrose Place* are used to capture interest in melodrama, while viewer interest in crime and violence are captured by ratings for the reality police program *Cops.* The higher the ratings for these programs, the greater the incentive that local news programmers will face to offer programs to meet these audience interests.[33]

News judgments will vary with the time constraints faced by the programmer, so that the style and content models control for whether the broadcast is an hour or half-hour program. The number of broadcast stations in the market is included in the model, since the nature of competition will affect brand position decisions. The model in chapter 1 indicates that an increase in the overall number of stations in a market can lead to an increase in all types of programming, so that one genre of programming is not necessarily more likely in a market with more broadcasters. But consider that as the number of local broadcast stations in a market grows, the number of nonnetwork affiliated stations will increase, which are outlets that are less likely to have their own local news broadcasts. If these stations program entertainment shows at the dinner hour, then the local news programs that are offered may be aimed at a remaining segment of the audience that has more "hard news" interests. Thus an increase in total broadcast stations may mean an increase in "hard news" content for those stations that choose to broadcast local news. In smaller markets local news programs may be more likely to offer a mix with "softer" news since they may be competing for more entertainment driven viewers.[34]

The model also controls for the total number of television households in the market. This variable may represent at least two different factors. City size in part may capture additional variations in viewer interests, since people in larger cities may have different viewing tastes that are not captured by the ratings, age, and gender variables in the model. The underlying reality that news directors are faced with in deciding what to report will also vary with city size. Variations in crimes across cities may thus leave news directors with different events to cover. The costs of covering crime and audience interest in crime may also vary with the crime rate. Later in this section I explicitly add measures of the number and types of crimes committed in the city during November 1993 as another control for the variation of the nature of events across markets.

The results of this model confirm that the public's interests do shape both the content and style of public affairs programming. Analysis of the more than 16,000 stories covered by fifty-seven stations across nineteen different markets demonstrates that programming decisions explicitly respond to variations in viewer interests. The topics selected for inclusion in the dinner hour news broadcasts, the stories selected to lead these programs, the pace and style of the programs, and the way that crime is covered all vary with the profit incentives generated by audience interests in different markets.

Consider first the selection of which stories to include in local news broadcasts (see table 7.9). The larger the rating for *Cops* in a market, the higher the percentage of stories devoted to crime. For the broadcasts in the regression sample the mean percentage of a station's stories devoted to crime was 29.7%. A ratings point increase in viewership for *Cops* translates into an increase of 1.8% points in the share of a station's stories that focus on crime. An increase in the number of potential viewers 18–49 in the market results in a greater focus on crime, consistent with the earlier indication that news programmers use crime stories to attract younger viewers and with the survey evidence that reveals a higher interest in violence among these viewers. The larger the number of adult women in the market, however, the lower the fraction of news devoted to crime coverage. Hour-long broadcasts have a lower percentage of crime stories (by 6% points) than half-hour shows, which one would expect if programmers use the expanded time to cover topics other than breaking crime stories. Note that the percentage of crime stories is higher in larger markets.

TABLE 7.9
Viewer Interest and Topic Coverage

	% Crime Stories	% Human Interest Stories	% Business Stories	% Government Stories
Total Television Households (000)	0.06***	−0.02	−1.36e−3	−0.02
	(0.03)	(0.02)	(0.03)	(0.02)
No. of Broadcast Stations	−0.41	−0.78**	0.54	1.27***
	(0.40)	(0.38)	(0.52)	(0.28)
Broadcast Length 1 Hour	−5.95***	−0.78	0.14	1.29
	(1.40)	(1.36)	(1.83)	(1.01)
Network Evening News Ratings	−0.07	−0.38*	0.50*	0.74***
	(0.22)	(0.22)	(0.29)	(0.16)
Melrose Place Ratings	−0.35	−0.57*	−0.09	0.30
	(0.33)	(0.32)	(0.43)	(0.24)
Cops Ratings	1.80***	1.51**	−1.60*	−1.80***
	(0.62)	(0.60)	(0.81)	(0.45)
Total 18–49 (000)	5.26e−3*	2.75e−3	2.0e−3	5.59e−3*
	(3.13e−3)	(3.05e−3)	(4.1e−3)	(2.26e−3)
Total Women 18+ (000)	−0.06***	0.02	−2.15e−3	0.03**
	(0.02)	(0.02)	(0.03)	(0.02)
Adjusted R^2	0.47	0.05	0.14	0.44

Note: Standard errors in parentheses. *** = statistically significant at the .01 level; ** = significant at the .05 level; * = significant at the .10 level. Each specification also included an intercept term.

This may be because the underlying crime rate is higher in these areas, which may translate into lower coverage costs or greater audience interests.

Human interest coverage in markets also responds strongly to audience interests. In markets where viewers express a preference for "hard news" via their ratings for network evening news programs, local news directors choose lower amounts of human interest stories. A one-point ratings increase in the evening news total translates into a .4% point drop in human interest coverage. An increase in the rating for *Melrose Place*, a program favored by the 18–34 demographic, was associated with a .6% point drop in human interest news. Markets with stronger viewership for *Cops*, however, had much higher human interest story content. A one-ratings point increase for *Cops* translated into 1.5% points more coverage of human interest stories in local news broadcasts. The greater the number of broadcast stations in the local market, the lower the human interest content in the station's broadcast, an outcome consistent with the earlier prediction that more stations overall may translate into a harder-news focus for those channels that choose to offer local news.

The selection of stories associated with "hard news" content also varies by potential viewer interest. Table 7.9 indicates that the percentage of stories devoted to business coverage is higher in markets where ratings are greater for the network evening news and lower in areas where *Cops* attracts higher ratings. The percentage of government stories, defined as the sum of local, state, and national government stories, also increases systematically with market characteristics. Programmers in markets with audiences more interested in public affairs will include a higher proportion of government stories. A one-point increase in the ratings for the national network news is associated with a .7% point increase in government coverage. An increase in the number of younger viewers, defined as those 18–49, results in a drop in government coverage, consistent with the lower expressed interest by these viewers in public affairs issues. An increase in the number of adult women in the viewing audience translates into more government coverage. Programmers are much less likely to include government stories in areas where "reality" police programs are popular. Government coverage drops by 1.8% points with an increase of one rating point for *Cops*. Government coverage is also more prevalent in markets with more stations, with an additional station resulting in 1.3% points more coverage of local, state, and national government stories.

Local news programmers use the top story of the broadcast to attract viewer interest.[35] Table 7.10 confirms that the selection of which stories will lead the news depends strongly on audience interest levels. The mean percentage of a station's top stories that focused on crime was 48% for the stations in the regression sample for November 1993. In areas where viewers express a stronger interest in crime programs, local news stations respond by placing crime stories at the head of the newscast more frequently. A one-point rating increase in household ratings for *Cops* in a market leads to a 5.6% point increase in the percentage of lead stories devoted to crime. In areas where viewers evince interest in hard-news coverage, stations are less likely to use a crime story as

TABLE 7.10
Viewer Interest and Story Placement

	% Top Stories, Crime	% Top Stories, Accident	% Top Stories, Business	% Top Stories, Government
Total Television Households (000)	0.13* (0.07)	−7.62e−3 (0.05)	0.02 (0.04)	−0.04 (0.03)
No. of Broadcast Stations	−4.07*** (1.10)	−1.79** (0.80)	1.91*** (0.57)	1.63*** (0.51)
Broadcast Length 1 Hour	1.96 (3.89)	0.26 (2.82)	−3.45* (2.03)	0.14 (1.79)
Network Evening News Ratings	−1.46** (0.61)	−1.12** (0.45)	1.72*** (0.32)	1.45*** (0.28)
Melrose Place Ratings	−2.11** (0.92)	−0.49 (0.66)	1.23*** (0.48)	1.09*** (0.42)
Cops Ratings	5.60*** (1.72)	2.07* (1.25)	−3.50*** (0.90)	−3.20*** (0.79)
Total 18–49 (000)	−4.23e−4 (8.7e−3)	0.02*** (6.32e−3)	−1.14e−3 (4.54e−3)	−9.4e−3** (4.0e−3)
Total Women 18+ (000)	−0.12* (0.06)	−0.01 (0.04)	−0.02 (0.03)	0.05* (0.03)
Adjusted R^2	0.28	0.19	0.33	0.48

Note: Standard errors in parentheses. *** = statistically significant at the .01 level; ** = significant at the .05 level; * = significant at the .10 level. Each specification also included an intercept term.

the top story. An increase of ratings for the network evening news by one point is associated with a 1.5% point drop in the percentage of lead crime stories. Areas where viewers turn out more for *Melrose Place* evoke less emphasis on lead crime stories. The greater the number of adult women in the market, the less likely stations will be to lead with crime, consistent with the fact that female viewers express less interest in and satisfaction with crime coverage in news. The greater the number of stations in the market, the less emphasis on crime as the lead story. Here again the competition among broadcast stations leads overall to less emphasis on crime for those stations offering local news in a market.

Leading broadcasts with accident coverage is also a function of viewer interests. The average percentage of top stories devoted to accidents in the sample was 15.0%. Areas with more viewers aged 18–49 were more likely to have stations use accidents as the lead news item. A one-point increase in the ratings for *Cops* is associated with a 2.1% point increase in top stories devoted to accidents. Where viewers express a greater preference for hard news via ratings for the network news, stations are less likely to emphasize accidents. An increase in the number of broadcast stations in the market also reduces the likelihood that a broadcast will lead with a story in this soft-news category.

Stations that lead with hard-news stories such as those relating to government or business are also responding to audience interest. The percentage of top stories devoted to business increased with network evening news ratings and in areas with more broadcast outlets. In markets with higher rates for *Cops*, however, stations were less likely to use a business story as the lead topic. Government stories accounted on average for 8% of the lead stories on local news broadcasts in the sample. In areas with higher viewer interest in the network evening news, stations were more likely to lead with stories about local, state, and national government. In areas with higher viewership for the type of violent reality programming embodied by *Cops*, however, stations were much less likely to begin newscasts with a focus on traditional public affairs stories. Stations in markets with more viewers 18–49, who indicated in survey data less interest in government topics than did older viewers, are less likely to offer lead stories dealing with government. The greater the number of broadcast outlets in the market, the larger the chance that a station will start the program with a government story.

Television critics' reviews and the statements of programmers in their articles clearly indicate that broadcast styles are part of a station's brand position for its local news show. Since a station's choice of position in the continuum of broadcast types depends ultimately on profits, broadcast styles should respond to audience interests in the same way that content selection does. Table 7.11 shows that the same considerations that programmers take into account when picking news topics also affect how they decide to convey the news. The number of stories per broadcast is lower, for example, in areas where viewers express a greater interest in hard news (and hence the details of news stories). The greater the rating for network evening news, the fewer the stories and hence the greater time per story the local news station devotes to the topics it covers. More broadcast outlets also lead to fewer stories in the local news broadcasts in a market, again consistent with the notion that more outlets means more entertainment programs and hence a focus on hard news for those stations that choose to offer local news. Hour-long broadcasts carry more stories (11.8 more) than the half-hour programs in the sample.

Story teasers, the promotions within a show that highlight upcoming stories, are a way to differentiate the degree that stations treat the news as a product to be promoted. Stations use teasers to try and retain viewers across commercial breaks. Table 7.11 reveals that the use of teasers varies with audience interest in entertainment. The higher the ratings for the network news, the lower the number of teasers used by stations in a market. The greater the number of stations broadcasting, the fewer teasers used per broadcast. Longer programs use more teasers. The strongest evidence that teasers are related to entertainment comes from the fact that in areas where viewers have higher ratings for *Cops* stations are more likely to fashion the news as entertainment and include internal story promotions.

The audiovisual style of a news broadcast is also an outcome of audience interests. Video clips, which are video segments with a voice-over by an anchor

TABLE 7.11
Viewer Interest and Broadcast Style

	Average Daily Stories	Average Daily Teasers	Average Daily Clips	Average Daily Soundbites
Total Television Households (000)	0.02	−5.6e−3	−8.2e−3	−0.04
	(0.02)	(0.01)	(0.03)	(0.03)
No. of Broadcast Stations	−0.74**	−0.42**	−0.91*	−0.07
	(0.34)	(0.19)	(0.51)	(0.41)
Broadcast Length 1 Hour	11.85***	3.37***	6.58***	7.92***
	(1.19)	(0.67)	(1.82)	(1.43)
Network Evening News Ratings	−0.34*	−0.29***	−0.53*	0.10
	(0.19)	(0.10)	(0.29)	(0.23)
Melrose Place Ratings	0.35	−0.16	−0.09	−0.26
	(0.28)	(0.15)	(0.43)	(0.34)
Cops Ratings	0.10	0.59**	0.46	0.25
	(0.53)	(0.29)	(0.80)	(0.63)
Total 18–49 (000)	−3.18e−3	−1.59e−3	−2.05e−3	−6.02e−3*
	(2.67e−3)	(1.47e−3)	(4.06e−3)	(3.21e−3)
Total Women 18+ (000)	−0.02	7.12e−3	0.01	0.04*
	(0.02)	(0.01)	(0.03)	(0.02)
Adjusted R^2	0.69	0.39	0.22	0.53

Note: Standard errors in parentheses. *** = statistically significant at the .01 level; ** = significant at the .05 level; * = significant at the .10 level. Each specification also included an intercept term.

or reporter, are less prevalent in markets where ratings for network news are higher. Audiences for network news programs may demonstrate through their viewing a greater preference for news details. Broadcasts that rely on clips rather than using the words of the principals involved in a story, however, may provide a viewer with less information about a topic. Soundbites, video segments where viewers see and hear the principals involved in a story, are used in lower numbers in areas where there are more viewers 18–49, who may prefer visual entertainment to the details of stories. Note that soundbites are used in greater numbers in areas with larger numbers of women, which may reflect a stronger interest in hearing the details of stories from participants themselves.

Crime stories vary in terms of the principals involved, for example, minor victims, gangs, sports figures, "nonfamous" individuals. The mix of principals in crime stories that stations choose to focus on is also a product of audience interests (see table 7.12). Stories with minors as victims had greater interest in crime stories in areas where viewers had greater interest in hard news (e.g., higher ratings for the nightly network news) and where competition leads to a greater focus on hard news (e.g., markets with more broadcast outlets). Crime stories involving government officials, which are often white-collar crimes, account for a larger share of crime stories in markets where

TABLE 7.12
Viewer Interest and Focus on Crime

	% Minor Victims	% Government Officials	% Sports Figures	% Entertainment Figures
Total Television Households (000)	0.04	−0.03	1.87e−3	−6.11e−3
	(0.04)	(0.02)	(0.01)	(0.02)
No. of Broadcast Stations	−1.31**	1.23***	−0.27	−0.53**
	(0.58)	(0.38)	(0.21)	(0.24)
Broadcast Length 1 Hour	1.77	1.35	−1.29*	1.57*
	(2.06)	(1.36)	(0.74)	(0.86)
Network Evening News Ratings	−0.65**	0.79**	−0.28**	−0.23*
	(0.33)	(0.21)	(0.12)	(0.14)
Melrose Place Ratings	−0.19	0.46	−0.29*	0.05
	(0.49)	(0.32)	(0.18)	(0.20)
Cops Ratings	1.42	−1.40**	0.29	0.83**
	(0.91)	(0.60)	(0.33)	(0.38)
Total 18–49 (000)	4.08e−3	−3.63e−3	−3.28e−3*	0.01***
	(4.62e−3)	(3.04e−3)	(1.67e−3)	(1.92e−3)
Total Women 18+ (000)	−0.04	0.03	2.68e−3	−6.34e−3
	(0.03)	(0.02)	(0.01)	(0.01)
Adjusted R^2	0.24	0.26	0.20	0.72

Note: Standard errors in parentheses. *** = statistically significant at the .01 level; ** = significant at the .05 level; * = significant at the .10 level. Each specification also included an intercept term.

viewers have higher ratings for network news and in markets with more broadcast outlets. An increase in ratings for Cops, however, is associated with a lower tendency to focus on the crime stories involving government officials. Stations chose to use crimes involving sports figures less frequently in markets where ratings were higher for the network evening news or Melrose Place. Stations chose to use crimes involving entertainers in higher percentages in markets with a greater interest in soft news. The greater the rating for Cops or the larger the number of viewers 18–49, the higher the percentage of crime stories dealing with entertainment figures. This is consistent with the earlier descriptions of WSVN's use of entertainment stories to attract younger viewers. The higher the ratings for the network evening news, the less likely stations were to use crime stories involving entertainment figures.

During November 1993 a crime story involving pop singer Michael Jackson offered a natural experiment to test how stations are influenced in their story selection by audience interests. In November 1993 there were widely reported stories about criminal investigations in Los Angeles and Santa Barbara counties into possible molestation by Jackson of a 13-year-old boy, who also filed a civil suit against Jackson.[36] Table 7.13 shows that a station's decision of whether to include this "national" crime story in its local news program can be modeled as

270

• *CHAPTER 7* •

TABLE 7.13
Michael Jackson Coverage

Intercept	3.53
	(5.38)
Total Television Households (000)	1.19e–3*
	(6.98e–4)
No. of Broadcast Stations	–0.68**
	(0.31)
Broadcast Length 1 Hour	2.76**
	(1.27)
Network Evening News Ratings	–0.08
	(0.12)
Melrose Place Ratings	0.29*
	(0.17)
Cops Ratings	–0.05
	(0.35)
% Teasers Devoted to Crime	0.12*
	(0.07)
Log Likelihood	–20.2

Note: Dependent variable in logit = 1 if station carried a crime story about Michael Jackson during November 1993. Standard errors are in parentheses.
** = statistically significant at the .05 level; * = significant at the .10 level.

a function of audience interests in different types of programming. The model also includes a variable for the percentage of a station's teasers devoted to crime as an indicator of whether the station uses crime to attract viewers. Of fifty-one stations in the sample, thirty covered the Jackson criminal story at some point during November 1993. The larger the number of broadcast outlets in the market, the less likely the station was to cover the Jackson story, which may be because the additional outlets in larger markets are capturing viewers interested primarily in entertaining information. The higher the rating for *Melrose Place* in the market, the more likely the station was to cover the case, support for the notion that stations choose content in part based on audience interest in melodramatic figures. The higher the percentage of a station's teasers devoted to crime, the higher the probability that the station chose to cover the story. The impacts of these incentives to entertain on the probability of covering the Jackson story were substantial. An increase from one standard deviation below the mean *Melrose Place* rating to one standard deviation above (e.g., from an 8 rating to 15) increased the probability of a station's covering the Michael Jackson story from .41 to .84. Similarly, an increase in the percentage of a station's teasers devoted to crime from 2% to 17% increased the probability of coverage from .48 to .85.[37] For stations using crime to attract and retain viewers, covering the sexual charges against Michael Jackson as part of their local news programming was consistent with their brand position for crime and entertainment.

While all local news programs faced the decision of whether to include a crime story about Michael Jackson, stations will vary in the amount of crime in their local markets that they can choose to cover or ignore. In table 7.14 I explicitly control for the general amount of crime and incidence of specific crimes in each city in November 1993 to see how the underlying level of crime in a city influences story decisions. The crime figures used come from the FBI's Uniform Crime reporting system. Previous research such as Graber (1980) and Surrette (1984) indicates that crime coverage may not bear a strong relation to

TABLE 7.14
Crime Coverage and Crime Statistics

	Total Stories		Crime Stories		
	Lead Stories, Crime	% Crime Stories	% Murder	% Nonfatal Attacks	% Rape
Total Television Households (000)	0.17*	0.03	-0.10*	-0.02	-0.02
	(0.09)	(0.03)	(0.06)	(0.02)	(0.02)
No. of Broadcast Stations	-3.27**	-0.57	0.47	-0.92**	-0.56
	(1.47)	(0.53)	(1.03)	(0.40)	(0.45)
Broadcast Length 1 Hour	3.18	-6.57***	-2.87	-0.10	4.11***
	(4.25)	(1.54)	(3.12)	(1.25)	(1.16)
Network Evening News Ratings	-0.91	-0.23	-0.28	-0.47**	0.30
	(0.76)	(0.28)	(0.51)	(0.21)	(0.20)
Melrose Place Ratings	-1.52	-0.61	-1.06	-0.26	-0.41
	(1.04)	(0.38)	(0.73)	(0.29)	(0.31)
Cops Ratings	4.94***	1.80***	-0.58	-0.20	-0.39
	(1.83)	(0.66)	(1.28)	(0.52)	(0.51)
Total 18–49 (000)	5.9e−4	4.03e−3	1.33e−3	−6.91e−3***	3.14e−3
	(9.53e−3)	(3.47e−3)	(6.4e−3)	(2.54e−3)	(2.39e−3)
Total Women 18+ (000)	-0.15*	-0.03	0.09	0.02	0.02
	(0.08)	(0.03)	(0.05)	(0.02)	(0.02)
November Crime	1.22e−4	−3.88e−4			
	(7.89e−4)	(2.87e−4)			
November Murders			0.02		
			(0.13)		
November Aggravated Assaults				−2.73e−3**	
				(1.31e−3)	
November Rapes					-0.05
					(0.06)
Adjusted R^2	0.17	0.45	0.29	0.32	0.52

Note: Standard errors in parentheses. *** = statistically significant at the .01 level; ** = significant at the .05 level; * = significant at the .10 level. Each specification also included an intercept term.

the actual level of crime, a point confirmed by the models in table 7.14. On average, nearly half of a station's lead stories in November 1993 dealt with crime. The number of crimes in the city during that month, defined as the sum of aggravated assaults, burglaries, larcenies, motor vehicle thefts, and murders tracked in the FBI data for November 1993, did not have a statistically significant impact on a station's proportion of crime lead stories. Market characteristics rather than the crime level determined whether a local news station would choose crime as the top story. An increase by one ratings point for *Cops* is associated with a 5% point increase in the proportion of lead stories dealing with crime, a strong testament to the impact of audience interest on this editorial decision. The larger the number of female viewers in the area, the less likely the station was to focus on crime as the top story. More broadcast outlets in the market lead to less emphasis on crime as the lead news story. The overall percentage of stories devoted to crime by a station is also independent of the total number of crimes in the city during November 1993. Audience interest in crime again determines the proportion of coverage, with a one ratings point increase in *Cops* leading to a 1.8% point increase in the percentage of stories that focus on crime.

Table 7.14 also explores whether the incidence of specific types of crime influences the mix of crime stories selected by a station. The number of reported murders in a city did not influence the percentage of crime stories devoted to murder, nor did the number of reported rapes affect the percentage of crime stories devoted to rape. The percentage of nonfatal shootings and attacks did influence the percentage of crime stories devoted to these attacks, but in the opposite direction one might expect. The higher the number of aggravated assaults in the city, the lower the percentage of crime stories devoted to nonfatal attacks. This may indicate that in a city with a large number of such incidents they are deemed less newsworthy. Market characteristics also play a role in the attention devoted to these nonfatal incidents. The higher the ratings for network evening news, the less likely that a station will cover such attacks in the local news broadcast. The greater the number of broadcast outlets, the lower the attention focused on such stories.

SURVEY EVIDENCE ON CRIME COVERAGE

The analysis of local news programs here reveals that news coverage of crime and violence is chosen strategically to attract particular viewing audiences. If this were true, one would expect decisions about whether to watch local news and levels of interest in stories to be correlated with viewer interest in violence. Evidence from the 1993 Times Mirror survey confirms both these predictions.

A taste for violent programming will lead some viewers to watch local news because of this crime coverage. Table A7.1 examines the factors that influence whether an individual regularly watches the local news or the national news. Older viewers (50+) are more likely to watch local news than younger viewers. Those with less income (annual income less than $20,000) are less likely to choose to watch local news. Moderate and heavy television viewers are also more likely to watch local news, as are viewers with higher political interests. Controlling for these and many other factors, one finds that people are also more likely to watch local news if they are higher consumers of violent entertainment programming. This effect is statistically significant but small in magnitude for local news. For the average viewer, a moderate increase in the index that measures consumption of violent television programming causes the probability of viewing local television regularly to go from .79 to .81.[38] This impact is similar, however, to the increase in viewing associated with a moderate increase in the political interest index, which causes the estimated probability of local news viewing to go from .79 to .83. Local programmers cannot change the overall demographic mix of the total viewing audience in their city. They do have control over the content of their programs, however, so that story content can be changed to appeal to the interests of marginal viewers. For local news, Table A7.1 shows that individuals who have demonstrated a greater interest in violent entertainment programming are also more likely to watch local news.

Another way to examine the incentives of local news programmers is to estimate which respondents are likely to be viewed as the "marginal" local news watchers, the viewers on whom local stations might be focusing to lure to their newscasts. The definition of marginal viewers may vary across stations, since stations may be trying to attract viewers away from other news programs, from nonnews programs, or from nonviewing activities. A high fraction of the sample (77%) claims to watch local news broadcasts either at the dinner hour or at 10 or 11 PM. One could consider the proportion of the sample (241 out of 1,516 respondents) who say they "sometimes" watch local news as the marginal viewers whose preferences would especially influence the decisions of news directors. These marginal viewers are less likely to say that television news is too full of violence than regular viewers. Of regular viewers, 53% agreed with this statement, versus 47% of the marginal viewers—a difference of proportions statistically significant ($Z = 1.9$) at the .10 level. The marginal viewers were also more likely to say that violence on television does not bother them. Only 38% of the regular local news viewers said they were not bothered by violence on television, versus 46% for the marginal viewers ($Z = -2.3$, statistically significant at the .05 level). Local news programmers may have the incentive to use crime coverage to attract marginal viewers since these viewers are less likely to see violence on television as bothersome.

This influence of a taste for violent content on viewership does not appear as strong for national news. Older viewers, those who watch moderate to heavy amounts of television, and viewers with higher levels of political interest are all more likely to watch national news programs. The viewing of violent entertainment programming is not associated with the decision to watch national news. This is consistent with the perceived brand identities of these two programs. Respondents were a bit more likely to report dissatisfaction with the levels of violence on local news than national news. Of those respondents who said that television news gives "too much attention to stories about violent crimes," 71% said this applied to both local and national news, 16% said it applied to local news only, and 12% said it applied to national news only. National news may have a higher hard-news content than local news, so its consumption could be less likely to be driven by factors such as crime coverage. A moderate increase in political interest results in a higher increase in probability of viewing for national news (an increase from .60 to .70) than it did for local news, consistent with a higher political news content for national news. Viewers who said they were very or somewhat interested in the personal lives of famous people were less likely to watch the national news, which would indicate that these viewers interested in softer news find programs other than the national news to watch.

Interest in violence does appear related to the degree that individuals follow particular issues in politics. The Times Mirror survey asked respondents the degree that they were following seven stories in the news during February 1993. The percentage of respondents who said they were following an issue very closely varied greatly across topics: civil war in Bosnia (16%), U.S. troops in Somalia (29%), attempts to lift the ban on gays in the military (47%), condition of the U.S. economy (52%), President Clinton's economic plan (51%), the controversy over hiring of illegal aliens by Zoe Baird and Kimba Wood (two potential nominees for U.S. attorney general) (25%), and the creation of a health care reform task force headed by Hillary Clinton (28%). Local and national television news programmers face a decision nightly about which stories merit inclusion in the 22 noncommercial minutes in a half-hour broadcast. Table A7.2 offers another way to analyze broadcaster incentives created by viewer interest in violence. Overall, interest in these particular issues varied greatly with demographic characteristics. Older respondents and those with annual incomes that exceed $50,000 were more likely to follow each of these issues very closely.

Table 7.15 reveals how demographic factors affected interests in the two policy issues (Bosnia and Somalia) that involve potential coverage of violence. For nonviolent issues, viewers with the lowest incomes are consistently less likely to follow an issue very closely. For Bosnia and Somalia, however, the pattern is reversed. Relative to those with annual incomes greater than $50,000, the probability a person with an annual incomes less than $20,000 is likely to follow the civil war in Bosnia is higher by .09 and higher for the issue of U.S. troops in Somalia by .09. Women were less likely to follow the civil war in Bosnia by .10, just as women were less likely to express interest in violent entertainment programming.[39] Controlling for many demographic factors, one finds that respondents classified as "heavy consumers" of violent entertainment programming were much more likely to say they were following the civil war in Bosnia and following the two policy issues related to violence. The probability of following the civil war in Bosnia increased from .12 to .17 if a person was a heavy consumer of entertainment violence, while the probability of following very closely the story of U.S.

TABLE 7.15

Change in Probability of Following Very Closely the Civil War in Bosnia or U.S. Troops in Somalia

Variable	Change in Probability	
	Bosnia	Somalia
Female vs. Male	−.10	−.13
Age 18–34 vs. Age 50+	−.14	−.13
Age 35–49 vs. Age 50+	−.09	−.13
Less Than HS vs. College Graduate	−.10	−.05
HS vs. College Graduate	−.06	.09
Annual Income < $20K vs. $50K+	.09	
Annual Income $20K–29K vs. $50K+	.06	
Annual Income $30K–49K vs. $50K+	.05	
Don't Know/Refused to Give vs. Annual Income $50K+	.08	.08
Town vs. Rural	−.04	−.06
Suburb vs. Rural	−.05	−.06
Heavy Consumer of Violent Entertainment Programming vs. Not	.06	.11

Note: See table A7.2. The probability of following the civil war in Bosnia based on mean sample characteristics was .14, while for U.S. troops in Somalia it was .27.

troops in Somalia increased from .23 to .34 with heavy violent entertainment viewing.

Even at the level of foreign policy coverage, interests in violence may influence the quantity or manner of coverage of issues such as Bosnia and Somalia. The results presented earlier in the chapter indicate that local news programmers act on these incentives, since local stations that have a brand identity for high crime coverage are also more likely to include war coverage. During the month of February 1993, violent footage was a part of the coverage of both Bosnia and Somalia on the broadcast network nightly newscasts. Bosnia was covered on 23 nights on ABC, 22 on CBS, and 13 on NBC, while Somalia was covered on 8 nights on ABC and CBS and 4 nights on NBC. These stories were accompanied by approximately 128 "visual segments" of Bosnia and 28 for Somalia. If one defines violent clips as those containing shelling by artillery, weapons, assaults, scenes of small-arms fire in the streets, or the aftermath of violence in terms of property or human life (e.g., destroyed building, mourning over dead bodies), then approximately 21% of the Bosnia visuals were violent versus 50% of those from Somalia. The finding that interest in violent entertainment programming had a greater impact on following Somalia coverage than on following Bosnia coverage is consistent with the fact that network coverage of Somalia was more likely to focus on violent scenes and images.[40] On stories from Bosnia 54% of the visuals dealt with political or diplomatic issues (e.g., visuals of government officials, UN officials, relief efforts, diplomatic meetings), while only 14% of the clips from Somalia dealt with these "nonviolent" issues.[41]

CONCLUSIONS

The analysis of local news content in November 1993 across nineteen different markets suggests that crime coverage may be better summarized as, "If it bleeds, it leads, where profitable." Nearly a third of a station's stories on average dealt with crime, and nearly a third of the crime stories dealt with murder. A focus on these average figures, however, misses the wide variation in crime content and styles. There is a clear segmentation of stations in their approach to crime coverage in local news. Stations that offer broadcasts with a high percentage of crime stories were more likely to offer other stories geared toward younger viewers such as health segments or accident stories. High-crime stations were more likely to focus on the details of crime and less likely to provide context through coverage of trials or crime statistics. High-crime stations chose styles aimed at younger viewers. Their broadcasts were faster paced (covered more stories per broadcast) and more visual (more clips per day). They were less likely to use soundbites in covering a story, in part because this type of coverage could slow down the broadcast pace.

Across markets, stations responded to the size of likely viewing audiences in their selection of story topics. Stations were more likely to cover crime stories or lead broadcasts with a focus on crime as the likely audience for crime coverage increased (as measured by ratings for *Cops* or the number of potential viewers 18–49). Broadcasts were more likely to offer coverage of government or business as the likely audience for hard news increased (as measured by the ratings for network evening news). Broadcasters offered "more entertaining" styles in markets with less expressed interest in hard news. Overall, the predictions derived from a model where stations fashion broadcasts in search of profits were confirmed in this analysis: spatial segmentation; a packaging of story topics aimed at particular audiences; a correlation between content and style; and the selection of brand positions on the basis of audience interests. Crime coverage in local news has attracted attention for at least four reasons: potential exposure of children to objectionable content; the impact of television on adult perceptions of reality, especially levels of fear; the influence of crime coverage on political assessments; and the relation between the licensing system and broadcaster responsibilities to program public affairs shows. This section explores the implications of the market model for each of these areas of concern.

The exposure of children to local news broadcasts is clearly an externality, for viewers aged 2–11 are not the target audience for advertisers on dinner hour local news broadcasts. Chapter 1 indicates that the mean children's rating for local news broadcasts in the nineteen sample markets was a 1.3 rating. Children were much more likely to register higher viewing during the dinner hour for situation comedies (mean children's rating, 6.1), children's cartoons (6.1), or children's nonanimated shows (4.3). The content analysis reveals that local news crime coverage, while focusing on violent acts such as murder, was unlikely to expose children to actual scenes of violent acts. On average only 1.9% of the crime clips shown on local news showed the actual crime, and only .4% showed a body. The lack of actual crime footage reduces the likelihood of harm to children. Note that lab research indicates that children are more likely to be affected by fight scenes viewed as part of a newscast since they identify with these incidents as more realistic.[42]

A second concern about local news coverage arises from the cultivation hypothesis developed by Gerbner, who posited that individuals who consume more television are more likely to come to believe the messages and themes inherent in its content.[43] Gerbner and colleagues found that individuals who consumed more television were more likely to be fearful about their safety and pessimistic about society, a finding summarized by the notion that higher television consumption leads to a "mean world" syndrome. The magnitude of this effect is controversial, since the impact of hours of television viewing varies when one introduces statistical controls that relate to demographic characteristics. There is evidence that the impact on views varies with the type of programming consumed, with cultivation of "mean world" beliefs being associated more strongly with viewing of entertainment crime programming and the news rather than measures of television in general. Research also indicates that, although exposure to crime media stories affected individuals' beliefs about the general crime rate, this did not influence their assessment of their personal risk of crime.

The findings in this chapter are relevant to the debate over the "mean world" syndrome since they indicate that there is a clear delineation within markets in the coverage of crime. Those made fearful or otherwise dissatisfied by crime do have options within a given viewing market about the type of local news to consume. Within each market a high-crime station may offer more coverage of crime, more focus on details of crimes, and a faster-paced, more visual style of presentation. Viewers who prefer less emphasis may choose to consume low-crime stations, which often have a greater focus on hard news and present stories more in depth in terms of story length and use of soundbites. Programmers' incentives to focus on crime more than some sets of viewers would prefer, but spatial competition within markets should provide viewers with options about the amount of crime coverage they choose to consume.

A third potential influence of crime coverage in local news is its impact on political beliefs.[44] Iyengar (1991) has conducted extensive lab research on how the manner of presentation of news affects the willingness of individuals to attribute the source of policy problems to individuals or broader social forces (e.g., "framing effects") and affects their evaluation of the performance of politicians.[45] In coverage of public affairs topics, news organizations often select "episodic" stories that focus on individuals that illustrate a policy dilemma rather than presenting "thematic" stories that place an issue in a broader social context. This tilt toward focusing on individuals is consistent with the drive for entertainment. Iyengar found in lab experiments that people who saw episodic coverage of crime (e.g., crime stories that focused on individuals) were more likely to view crime as emerging from individual rather than broader social circumstances. This effect emerged in stories dealing with white perpetrators and the criminal justice system as a whole. In stories featuring black perpetrators, viewers were less likely to cite social forces as responsible for crime when they saw episodic coverage.[46] Those viewers who attributed crime to social phenomena were less likely to evaluate the president favorably. Thus the drive for entertainment in news programming can lead to a focus on individuals in stories, which in turn can influence viewer attributions for the source of policy problems and evaluations of politicians dealing with these issues. Entman (1990, 1993) argues that crime coverage in local news and national network news may also foster antiblack feelings and racial resentment because of the manner in which blacks are portrayed in news stories dealing with crime.

The analysis of local news content from November 1993 confirms that programmers face incentives to use crime stories to entertain rather than inform. Only an average of 2.6% of a station's crime stories dealt with statistics, while half focused on the details or investigation of specific crimes. The use of crime stories varied with audience interest, so that stations were more likely to program crime stories or lead their broadcasts with crime news items in areas where viewers expressed more interest in crime (as measured by ratings for *Cops*). The focus on crime and entertainment is negatively related to viewer interests in hard news topics. In areas with higher ratings for network evening news, programs are less likely to emphasize crime and more likely to program stories about local, state, and national government. Spatial competition may thus affect the amount and manner of coverage, which in turn may influence opinions about crime and politicians. The degree that this is a policy concern for government action, however, would depend on whether government should attempt to influence the distribution of opinions about crime (a topic discussed more in the next chapter). The closer the impacts of local news relate to political opinions, the greater the concern about First Amendment issues involved in content.[47]

A final issue raised by crime coverage in local news programming is the extent that broadcasters are serving their "public interest" requirements through public affairs programming. In championing the effective deregulation of public affairs content in the 1980s, FCC Chairman Fowler indicated that market interests defined the "public interest" so that stations would be led to satisfy their license requirements through profit motives. In the 1990s, FCC Chairman Hundt took the opposite position, noting that following the dictates of the market is not enough to satisfy the FCC's public interest requirements.[48] If one views the free spectrum license granted to a broadcaster as a contract, then the "public interest" requirement can be seen as part of a price that a station pays for spectrum use. If profit maximization alone equals the public interest, then the requirement is basically an empty constraint and broadcasters are in effect paying a zero price for spectrum licenses.

The analysis here does not indicate what the ideal distribution of local news programming content should look like, or what the aggregate impacts of the levels of crime coverage are.[49] The chapter does indicate that profit maximization explains a great deal of the variation in local news content. Stations often defend their free use of the spectrum by pointing to their public affairs programming, specifically local news, as evidence that they provide programming focused on informing the public. The analysis here suggests, however, that the content and style of local news programs are selected based on audience interests and market competition. Stations provide given types of news because they are profitable. Stations may provide a measure of hard news that relates to political affairs, but this will depend again on the degree that viewers in the particular market are interested in public affairs. The response of producers to audience preferences in general leads to optimal outcomes in many markets. In a world where news coverage generates both positive and negative externalities, however, the market-driven nature of local news may be an argument for reexamination of what the "public interest" responsibilities of broadcasters should be.[50] In the next chapter, I examine a range of policies designed to deal with programming externalities.

• *C H A P T E R   7* •

TABLE A7.1

The Impact of Preferences for Violent Television on Viewing

Variable	Coefficient (Standard Error)	
	(1) Watch Local News?	(2) Watch National News?
Intercept	0.79**	−0.15
	(0.39)	(0.34)
Female	0.12	0.01
	(0.14)	(0.12)
White	0.07	−0.03
	(0.20)	(0.18)
Age 18–34	−0.89***	−1.06***
	(0.19)	(0.17)
Age 35–49	−0.60***	−0.58***
	(0.19)	(0.16)
Less Than HS Education	−0.14	−0.15
	(0.25)	(0.23)
HS Education	0.01	0.12
	(0.18)	(0.16)
Some College/Post-HS Education	0.23	0.06
	(0.18)	(0.16)
East	−0.01	0.34*
	(0.21)	(0.19)
Midwest	0.18	0.08
	(0.20)	(0.17)
South	0.03	0.19
	(0.19)	(0.16)
Annual Income < $20K	−0.45**	−0.27
	(0.22)	(0.19)
Annual Income $20K–29K	0.11	−0.01
	(0.23)	(0.19)
Annual Income $30K–49K	−0.07	−0.13
	(0.19)	(0.17)
Don't Know/Refused to Give Income	−0.45*	−0.39*
	(0.25)	(0.23)
City	−0.21	0.02
	(0.20)	(0.17)
Town	−0.27	−0.004
	(0.20)	(0.17)
Suburb	−0.05	0.35*
	(0.22)	(0.19)
Watch 2–3.5 Hours of TV per Day	0.66***	0.81***
	(0.15)	(0.14)
Watch 4+ Hours of TV per day	0.79***	0.62***
	(0.17)	(0.15)

TABLE A7.1 (*Continued*)

Variable	Coefficient (Standard Error)	
	(1) Watch Local News?	*(2)* Watch National News?
Political Interest Index	0.14***	0.23***
	(0.04)	(0.03)
Violent Viewership Index	0.07**	−0.002
	(0.03)	(0.03)
Interest in Personal Lives of Real People[a]	0.13	0.11
	(0.16)	(0.14)
Interest in Famous People[b]	−0.02	−0.20*
	(0.14)	(0.12)
Log Likelihood	−748.4	−901.4

Note: Dependent variable in logit analysis = 1 in (1) if respondent was a regular viewer of local news and in (2) if watched national news regularly. *** = statistically significant at the .01 level; ** = significant at the .05 level; * = significant at the .10 level.

[a]Based on respondents who were "very" or "somewhat" interested in shows in which real people tell the intimate details of their personal lives.

[b]Based on respondents who were "very" or "somewhat" interested in shows about the personal lives of famous people.

The Market Demand for Policy Issues

Variable	Civil War in Bosnia	U.S. Troops in Somalia	Attempts to Lift the Ban on Gays in the Military	Coefficient (Standard Error) Condition of the U.S. Economy	President Clinton's Economic Plan	Controversy over Zoe Baird and Kimba Wood Hiring Illegal Aliens	Creation of Health Care Reform Task Force
Intercept	−0.86*	−0.75*	0.19	0.14	0.16	−0.90**	−0.54
	(0.48)	(0.41)	(0.37)	(0.38)	(0.38)	(0.46)	(0.41)
Female	−0.83***	−0.06	−0.09	−0.04	−0.10	−0.05	0.20*
	(0.16)	(0.12)	(0.11)	(0.11)	(0.11)	(0.13)	(0.13)
Age 18–34	−1.12***	−0.61***	−0.47***	−0.83***	−0.69***	−1.23***	−1.26***
	(0.21)	(0.16)	(0.15)	(0.15)	(0.15)	(0.18)	(0.17)
Age 35–49	−0.64***	−0.61***	−0.32**	−0.48***	−0.38***	−0.47***	−0.68***
	(0.19)	(0.16)	(0.14)	(0.15)	(0.15)	(0.16)	(0.15)
Less Than HS Education	−0.87***	−0.67***	−0.44**	−1.05***	−1.14***	−0.77***	−0.47*
	(0.31)	(0.24)	(0.22)	(0.22)	(0.22)	(0.26)	(0.25)
HS Education	−0.46**	−0.17	−0.29**	−0.42***	−0.52***	−0.77***	−0.22
	(0.20)	(0.16)	(0.15)	(0.15)	(0.15)	(0.17)	(0.17)

Some College/Post-HS Education	−0.25	−0.27*	0.17	−0.13	−0.24*	−0.51***	−0.07
	(0.20)	(0.17)	(0.15)	(0.15)	(0.15)	(0.17)	(0.17)
Annual Income < $20K	0.79***	0.47**	−0.36**	−0.64***	−0.49***	−0.35*	−0.34*
	(0.26)	(0.20)	(0.18)	(0.19)	(0.18)	(0.22)	(0.21)
Annual Income $20K–29K	0.54**	0.10	−0.06	−0.55***	−0.60***	−0.14	−0.46**
	(0.26)	(0.21)	(0.18)	(0.18)	(0.18)	(0.21)	(0.21)
Annual Income $30K–$49K	0.49**	0.19	−0.07	−0.30*	−0.26*	−0.08	−0.07
	(0.23)	(0.18)	(0.18)	(0.16)	(0.16)	(0.18)	(0.18)
Don't Know/Refused to Give Income	0.71***	0.39*	−0.11	−0.55**	−0.45**	0.10	−0.06
	(0.29)	(0.23)	(0.21)	(0.21)	(0.21)	(0.24)	(0.23)
East	0.34	−0.02	−0.24	−0.06	−0.06	0.05	0.17
	(0.25)	(0.19)	(0.18)	(0.18)	(0.18)	(0.20)	(0.20)
Midwest	0.12	−0.16	0.09	0.04	0.002	−0.25	0.20
	(0.23)	(0.18)	(0.16)	(0.16)	(0.16)	(0.19)	(0.19)
South	0.26	−0.01	0.07	0.12	0.05	−0.08	0.30*
	(0.22)	(0.17)	(0.15)	(0.16)	(0.16)	(0.18)	(0.18)
City	0.03	−0.09	0.28*	0.19	0.08	0.40**	0.08
	(0.21)	(0.17)	(0.16)	(0.16)	(0.16)	(0.19)	(0.17)
Town	−0.31*	−0.28*	0.25*	0.02	0.06	0.26	−0.23
	(0.22)	(0.18)	(0.16)	(0.16)	(0.16)	(0.19)	(0.18)
Suburb	−0.44*	−0.30*	−0.10	−0.09	−0.04	0.27	−0.33*
	(0.24)	(0.19)	(0.18)	(0.18)	(0.18)	(0.21)	(0.20)
Republican	−0.44	−0.07	0.04	0.63**	0.63**	0.55*	−0.30
	(0.36)	(0.32)	(0.29)	(0.30)	(0.31)	(0.38)	(0.33)
Democrat	−0.41	0.14	−0.17	0.73***	0.88***	0.60*	0.01
	(0.35)	(0.32)	(0.28)	(0.30)	(0.30)	(0.38)	(0.32)

Variable	Civil War in Bosnia	U.S. Troops in Somalia	Attempts to Lift the Ban on Gays in the Military	Condition of the U.S. Economy	President Clinton's Economic Plan	Controversy over Zoe Baird and Kimba Wood Hiring Illegal Aliens	Creation of Health Care Reform Task Force
			Coefficient (Standard Error)				
Independent	−0.34	0.07	−0.17	0.65**	0.62**	0.35	0.17
	(0.36)	(0.32)	(0.29)	(0.30)	(0.30)	(0.38)	(0.32)
Watch 2–3.5 Hours of TV per Day	0.18	−0.02	0.08	0.21*	0.15	0.30*	0.32**
	(0.18)	(0.15)	(0.13)	(0.13)	(0.13)	(0.16)	(0.15)
Watch 4+ Hours of TV per Day	0.16	0.13	0.24*	0.30**	0.28**	0.44***	0.41***
	(0.20)	(0.16)	(0.14)	(0.15)	(0.15)	(0.17)	(0.16)
Interest in Personal Lives of Real People[a]	−0.15	0.16	−0.12	−0.18	−0.06	0.03	−0.0002
	(0.18)	(0.14)	(0.13)	(0.13)	(0.13)	(0.15)	(0.15)
Interest in Famous People[b]	−0.07	0.10	0.21*	0.24**	0.14	0.13	0.11
	(0.16)	(0.13)	(0.11)	(0.12)	(0.11)	(0.13)	(0.13)
Heavy Violent Entertainment Viewing	0.46***	0.58***	0.17	0.22*	0.15	−0.16	0.13
	(0.17)	(0.14)	(0.12)	(0.12)	(0.12)	(0.15)	(0.14)
Log Likelihood	−609.7	−854.4	−993.1	−972.0	−979.2	−772.5	−829.1

Note: Dependent variable in logit analysis equals 1 if viewer reported following policy issue "very closely." *** = statistically significant at the .01 level; ** = significant at the .05 level; * = significant at the .10 level.

[a]Based on respondents who were "very" or "somewhat" interested in shows in which real people tell the intimate details of their personal lives.
[b]Based on respondents who were "very" or "somewhat" interested in shows about the personal lives of famous people.

Dealing with Television Violence: Politics and Policies

THE DEBATE over television violence often centers on questions about motivations, with a focus on the motivations of government officials trying to reduce the effects of violent television. Broadcast network officials portray television violence as an issue raised by politicians primarily because of its appeal to voters. This reaction reached a peak during the 1996 presidential elections, when President Clinton and Senator Dole attacked Hollywood for its use of violent and sexual content. Capturing the beleaguered feeling of broadcasters, an industry article entitled "Campaign against Television—Candidates Put Heat on Media: It's TV-Bashing Season" described the assessments of broadcasters. Martin Franks, CBS Washington vice-president, noted that, for politicians attacking violence on television, "No doubt the polling is telling all of them that it's a good issue. I'm told that last summer the House Democrats were looking at polling and were told that introducing the v-chip was one way to restore themselves on family values."[1] Another industry official, NBC West Coast President Don Ohlmeyer, told a meeting of network affiliates:

We've become one of their favorite whipping boys because we take it so well. We're allowing ourselves to be pummeled by a group of people who can't balance the budget, get the guns off the street, solve welfare, cut corruption, but they can get their picture on the cover of *The New York Times* by coming out against violence on television.[2]

During the summer of 1996, Vice President Gore criticized children's television for its violence, noting:

Shows like the "Mighty Morphin Power Rangers" are just not good for children. Like those tobacco ads, these programs teach children precisely the opposite lesson their parents want them to learn. Shows like "Power Rangers" tell children that the best way to solve a problem or win an argument is to get violent—to kick, to karate-chop, sometimes to launch a missile.[3]

Responding to the frequent criticisms of the *Power Rangers*, the show's producer Saban Entertainment released a statement that declared: "We submit that some people criticizing the Power Rangers are trying to ride a political bandwagon utilizing our property as a lightening rod, and suspect that those critics may have never screened an episode of the show."[4]

Broadcasters may be correct in their analysis that some politicians focus on television violence out of concern for their own election rather than concern for the impacts of television on children. Opposing television violence involves popular political dimensions such as protection of children, reduction in violence, and resistance to moral decline. Championing these dimensions may be attractive to candidates from all parties because of returns at the ballot box. The difference between the marginal voters courted by politicians and the marginal viewers targeted by television programmers sets up an inevitable conflict between Hollywood and Washington. Television programmers use violent television to reach male and female viewers 18–34, a group highly valued by advertisers but a group less likely to vote. Politicians use the issue of violent television to reach many sets of voters, ranging from parents concerned about children's exposure to older voters concerned about crime and morality. The political economy of why candidates respond to public concern about television violence, however, does not negate the fact that a large body of research indicates violence on television causes violence in society. While producers such as Saban Entertainment may claim that the *Power Rangers* is unfairly singled out for criticism, research (Boyatzis, Matillo, and Nesbitt 1995) still indicates that the show increases aggression among children.

Discussion of incentives should play a role in the debate over television violence, since economics drives the production and distribution decisions that determine the frequency and intensity of violent images on television screens. The analysis presented here demonstrates that television violence is fundamentally a problem of pollution. Violent television programs potentially lead to a number of harmful outcomes for society: increases in aggression and crime; heightened desensitization to violence; and elevated levels of fear and insecurity, as in the "mean world" syndrome. In addition, some people experience disutility simply knowing that society produces a culture where violence plays such a central role in entertainment. These impacts are truly external, however, to the choices made by television executives. In deciding whether to provide violent or nonviolent content at a given time, broadcast or cable programmers will consider the number of people with particular viewing preferences, their values to advertisers or willingness to pay for programming, the cost of securing different types of shows, and the number of competitors offering various types of fare. Broader social costs engendered by violent programming do not explicitly enter the content calculus unless they affect variables that determine programming profits. This chapter will analyze how different policy proposals could lead viewers and producers to consider more directly the costs associated with violent programming.

If television violence is akin to pollution, then the policies designed to deal with the negative externalities generated by pollution are an obvious place to start in considering how to deal with television violence.[5] Key differences should be acknowledged, however, before pollution policies are analyzed. The First Amendment declaration, "Congress shall make no law . . . abridging the freedom of speech, or of the press," places an additional restraint on government policies dealing with the media. Legal scholars have explored in depth the implications of the First Amendment for government attempts to influence the distribution and consumption of violent media content.[6] These writers (e.g., Edwards and Berman 1995, Spitzer 1996) stress that the constitutionality of government action on media violence will depend on questions such as whether the state has a compelling interest involved, if the policy is likely to achieve its goal, and whether the remedy is narrowly tailored. In the sections that follow I will generally focus on a single goal, the protection of children from exposure to violent television, and analyze whether a proposed policy is likely to achieve this. A second difficulty in applying the pollution framework is that the magnitude of the impacts of media violence is even harder to measure directly than the (sometimes controversial) impacts of pollution.[7] While both television violence and environmental pollution present difficulties because their impacts can be indirect and long-term, some policies aimed at reducing pollution are easier to fashion because acute, immediate reactions to toxic contamination implicate the source of the problem. Applying a cost-benefit framework to efforts to deal with media violence can be made difficult because of the uncertainty surrounding the magnitude of harms.[8] Finally, the benefits of television violence, such as the utility derived by adult consumers of violent films and programs, are also hard to measure in dollar terms because distribution often occurs either through free, over-the-air television or as part of a bundling of program services in cable packages. The satisfaction adult consumers derive from programming should be factored into a complete analysis of policies that affect violent programming, although they are difficult to monetize. With these caveats in mind, I explore how policies designed to deal with negative externalities would help mitigate the negative impacts of television violence.[9] Before analyzing the merits of different policies to deal with television violence, I first analyze the political incentives for government officials to focus on this issue.

The Political Appeal of Television Violence

The debate over violence on American television spans 4 decades of congressional hearings, hundreds of scientific studies, and numerous commission reports. Media violence is a public policy issue in part because of the costs to society associated with its impact. Yet media violence is also a public policy issue because of the political benefits for legislators and other politicians associated with addressing public concern about its impacts. This section briefly analyzes the politics of television violence by examining the vote on the V-chip in 1995 and the incentives for presidential candidates in 1996 to address television violence.

Most government policies proposed to deal with television violence have concentrated costs and diffuse benefits. If the government were to publish information on the amount of violence in shows and their advertising sponsors, for example, the costs of this policy would be concentrated in the entertainment and marketing industries. If this information were released, some advertisers would be less willing to be associated with a violent show and broadcasters might ultimately be less willing to offer violent programming.[10] Producers, writers, and actors who specialized in violent programs could see the returns to their work drop. Network broadcasters might lose viewers to cable networks, which would be less likely to reduce their violence because they are less dependent on advertising. Some companies could end up paying higher premiums to advertise on nonviolent shows to reach viewers that were targeted more cheaply on violent programs. Broadcast networks will thus be active opponents of efforts to restrict television violence, supported by associations representing stations, writers, and actors. Cable networks may actually follow a strategy of raising their rivals' costs and support efforts that affect broadcast networks more than cable programmers (who rely less on advertisers). The National Cable Television Association historically has been more supportive than the National Association of Broadcasters of a ratings system for programs and technologies within television to block violent programming. Since their customers are more likely to be viewers that like violent programs and since they are less dependent on advertisers, cable channels may support efforts to restrict violent programming that have a greater impact on broadcast networks.

There are also diffuse costs to government policies that try to influence the violent content of television programming. Some individuals may see violence on television as creative expression and view any attempt by government to influence it as a violation of the First Amendment. In *Democracy and the Problem of Free Speech*, Cass Sunstein (1993) identifies five beliefs that define the position of those who hold freedom of speech as an absolute value: any attempt by government to regulate speech threatens free expression; the First Amendment means that government must exhibit neutrality in speech, so that it should not distinguish between expression it favors and disfavors; free expression is not limited to just "political speech"; restrictions on speech tend to expand; and judges should not attempt to "balance" competing interests when ruling on cases involving freedom of expression. For voters that hold these views, if the government did try to influence television content they would be dissatisfied with such policies. In addition, voters who view government intervention into the marketplace in general as undesirable could view efforts to regulate television violence as misdirected.

The benefits of reducing violence on television are spread diffusely throughout society. If violence on television adds to violence in society, then the reduction of consumption of television violence by children would ultimately lead to the reduction of violent crime. The benefits of government action in this area would be difficult to trace directly, however, since people who did not become criminals or victims because of the government efforts to reduce television violence would not tie their good fortune to these policies.[11] Voters concerned about media violence, however, might gain satisfaction from government efforts to reduce the impact of television violence.

The beneficiaries of reductions in television violence are unlikely to be active in lobbying for legislation, since the costs of such action will for most people outweigh the expected benefits of their political activity (since an individual is unlikely to have an impact on policy). Some people may gain ideological satisfaction from acting on their principles, so they may end up supporting interest group activity by groups such as the American Family Association. Viewers in general will not be active on this issue. Broadcasters, entertainment industry participants, and advertisers are more likely to lobby since the costs of their political activity are small relative to the possible gains from halting legislation and since there is a greater likelihood that their concerted efforts will influence policy. Those who oppose on First Amendment grounds government efforts to influence television content face the same logic of collective action as viewers supporting the bills, so they are not likely to organize specifically to lobby on this issue. Viewers with First Amendment concerns may be represented, however, by a lobbying group active on freedom of expression issues such as the American Civil Liberties Union.

In a world where broadcasters and advertisers may be politically active to oppose government efforts to regulate television violence, the interests of viewers may be represented by political entrepreneurs, individuals who act without being lobbied by organized groups to take action.[12] Legislators may gain at the ballot from representing the interests of viewers, even if they are not directly contacted by an organized viewer group. Legislators may offer proposals because they believe in the policies, because the measures further their reelection goals, or some combination of these motives. Efforts to restrain violence on television have been championed both by legislators seen as attempting to address serious policy problems and by representatives seen as searching for political gain by being associated with the issue. Polling data indicate that both Democrats and Republicans view television violence as a source of violence in society, which makes the issue attractive to candidates from both parties. A representative's vote on legislation dealing with television violence will thus involve a calculus involving lobbying by interest groups, potential support from viewers concerned about a negative impact of television violence, and the preferences of voters who view government action here as a violation of the First Amendment or another example of an intrusive regulatory state. Analysis of the votes surrounding the passage of the V-chip in August 1995 offers an indication of the returns to both Republicans and Democrats of addressing the issue of violence on television.

During July and August 1995 Representative Edward Markey (D-Mass.) worked to gain passage of an amendment to the Telecommunications Act that would require television sets with screens 13 inches or larger to have V-chip circuitry that would enable viewers to block programs carrying ratings, which the measure encouraged the industry to develop. Markey noted that Republicans felt pressure to do something about television violence because Republican presidential candidate Bob Dole "catapulted this to the front pages of newspapers" by attacking the entertainment industry for its use of violence and sex.[13] As one observer noted:

Rep. Chris Cox (R-Calif.) . . . conceded that GOP leadership needs to "develop new alternatives" to the V-chip idea to prevent it from becoming law. . . . Cox lamented the "explosiveness of the subject matter" is a sign that Republicans may be ceding the issue to Democrats. One GOP staff aide said Republicans "are scared of the politics of this. It's poison" to be against V-chips, he said.[14]

The Republican counterproposal offered, the Coburn amendment, called upon the industry to develop voluntarily the technology that would help parents block programs and required the General Accounting Office to report to Congress in 18 months on the availability of such technology. The four broadcast networks announced on August 1 (3 days before the votes) that they would devote $2 million to the development of blocking devices, although V-chip supporters noted that the stand-alone blocking devices would be more expensive than the V-chip and thus less likely to be widely used.[15] The Republican House leadership structured the rule on amendment voting so that if the Coburn amendment passed it would substitute the rule for the Markey amendment, thereby allowing Republicans to demonstrate action on television violence and kill the V-chip without having to vote explicitly against it.[16] The (broadcaster-supported) Coburn amendment calling for a technology study passed 222–201. Rep. Markey was able to use a parliamentary procedure to engineer a direct vote on the V-chip immediately afterward, which passed 224–199.[17] The high profile nature of the issue made it difficult for some legislators to vote against the V-chip on the direct vote, since "Markey said many members reversed their votes once they realized that they would be held accountable for a vote against television violence."[18]

There were multiple political dimensions involved in the vote on the V-chip, including protection of children, freedom of expression, and the desirability of government intervention in the marketplace. To capture representatives' general stands on civil liberties issues, I analyze their scores on the voting index compiled by the American Civil Liberties Union (ACLU).[19] I use the Christian Coalition voting index as a measure of support for conservative values, which include preservation of "family values" and opposition to government regulation. Note that for some Republicans these dimensions pulled them in different directions, since some viewed the V-chip as unnecessary government intervention in private actions. Representative Bill Paxon (R-N.Y.) led the fight against the V-chip by proclaiming "it's a major example of government paternalism and an area that government should not be involved in."[20] Paxon indicated that conservative groups such as the Christian Coalition and Eagle Forum opposed the V-chip.

Only twelve representatives voted against both television violence measures, consistent with the reported incentives both Democrats and Republicans had to signal they were doing "something" about television violence. The vast majority of Democrats voted no on the technology study and yes on the V-chip.[21] A vote against the technology study could be more costly for representatives with conservative constituents. The Democrats who voted yes on the technology study and then yes on the V-chip had higher Christian Coalition scores (by approximately 20 percentage points) than those Democrats who voted no, then yes.[22] The Republicans who broke ranks on the amendments and voted no on

TABLE 8.1
Predicting V-Chip Votes

Parameter	Estimate (Standard Error)
% Female	0.19
	(0.16)
% Nonwhite	−0.04***
	(0.01)
% < 18	0.02
	(0.06)
% 18–49	0.03
	(0.06)
% College Educated	−0.08*
	(0.05)
Mean Household Income	$5.2e-5$*
	$(2.8e-5)$
Democrat	2.64***
	(0.63)
ACLU Voting Index	$-3.3e-3$
	(0.01)
Christian Coalition Index	−0.03**
	(0.01)
Log Likelihood	−167.98

Note: Dependent variable in logit = 1 if the Congress member voted in favor of the V-chip. Congressional district characteristics based on 1990 Census. Logit includes an intercept term. ACLU Voting Index does not include V-chip vote. *** = statistically significant at the .01 level; ** = significant at the .05 level; * = significant at the .10 level.

the technology study and yes on the V-chip had only slightly lower Christian Coalition vote ratings than the Republicans who voted yes, then no.

Table 8.1 models the decision to vote for the V-chip amendment as a function of congressional district demographic characteristics, representative's party affiliation, and support for ACLU and Christian Coalition positions. Survey data in chapter 3 indicated that in response to questions about whether they have switched channels during local news broadcasts because of objectionable material, women, whites, those with less than a college education, and those with relatively higher incomes are more likely to act to shield their children. The congressional district level data indicate that Congress members were generally more likely to vote for the V-chip as demographic characteristics of their constituents fit the profile of those parents likely to intervene in viewing. The higher the nonwhite population percentage and higher the percentage of residents with a college degree or higher, the less likely the representative was to vote for the V-chip. The higher the mean household income in the district, the more likely the representative was to favor the measure. The ACLU index was not statistically significant, while the Christian Coalition index had a negative coefficient. Conservative groups such as the Christian Coalition did oppose the V-chip as intrusive government regulation. Opposition to government regulation may have thus won out over concern for "family values" in the influence of conservative ideology on the V-chip vote. Democrats were, as expected, much more likely to support the V-chip.

In the aftermath of the V-chip vote in the House, Senator Hollings brought an even stricter measure to a vote in the Senate Commerce Committee. Hollings proposed that the FCC define "violent" television programming and limit its broadcast to hours when children were less likely to be in the audience, with fines and loss of license possible for broadcast stations that violated the regulations. The measure passed 16–1, despite the fact that many senators privately opposed the bill and felt it was unconstitutional. Capturing the influence of public opinion on Senators from both parties, a media publication described the committee vote:

> GOP Senators and conservative Democrats had vociferously complained that Hollings was "grandstanding" with a bill that would not survive its first legal challenge. McCain said that if the bill was shot down in court, as he anticipated, the Committee would not have solved the TV violence problem, just gotten itself good press for "feel-good" politics. . . . Afterwards, several GOP members privately promised they would put a hold on the bill they'd just passed, to keep it from going to the full Senate.[23]

Public interest in media violence and potential scrutiny of legislators' votes thus made television violence a public policy issue championed by both Democrats and Republicans in the House and Senate during 1995 and 1996.

The Times Mirror data described in chapter 2 indicate that respondents who identify themselves as Democrats, Republicans, or Independents hold very similar views about violent programming. When asked whether there was too much violence in nonnews programming, there was no statistical difference in the replies of Democrats (73% said yes), Republicans (74%), or Independents (70%). When asked about the degree that violence on television bothered them, similar percentages of Democrats (40%), Republicans (38%), and Independents (40%) said it did not bother them. There was a statistically significant difference in response to the question, "What would you say bothers you more: the amount of violence on TV or the amount of sex on TV?" Republicans (33%) were slightly more likely to say they were more bothered by the amount of sex on television than were Democrats (30%) or Independents (26%), a statistically significant difference from the Republican proportion at the .05 level). This may create marginally higher returns for Republican politicians to focus on sexual content on television. Republicans were also more likely (44% vs. 37% for Democrats and 36% for Independents) to view violence on television and in the movies as a "major cause" of "breakdown in law and order." Republicans were also more likely than Democrats (80% vs. 73%) to agree with the statement that "TV news should run more stories about 'good news' and fewer stories about violence." Both these elements may create slightly stronger incentives for Republicans to criticize the media based on these political dimensions. While these figures represent the average of opinions among different sets of voters, candidates in the presidential and congressional elections often focus on using issues to sway marginal voters to support them. Candidates concerned about reelection will choose the set of issues to discuss in a campaign based on the positions of opponents and the likelihood of creating particular voting coalitions when particular issues are raised (Riker 1986; Hinich and Munger 1994). Political theory has less to say about why particular issues move a given set of voters, which makes it difficult to derive hypotheses about which voters are the exact targets of an issue raised by a candidate. Table 8.2 uses four different possible definitions of a "marginal voter" in the 1996 presidential race and examines opinions among these voters in 1993 about television violence.

Early in the Clinton presidency individuals who voted for Ross Perot in 1992 were described as a targeted demographic by the president's advisors and Republican strategists.[24] Table 8.2 reveals that there was too much violence in nonnews programming. When asked whether they were more bothered by violence or sex on television, Perot voters were similar to Clinton voters in saying that they were more bothered by violence than by sex on television. The conflict between marginal voters and marginal viewers is also evident in this table from the opinions of those who did not vote in 1992 presidential race. Nearly two-thirds of those who did not vote (62.3%) were heavy consumers of violent programming, versus 44.5% of Clinton voters, 36.2% of Bush voters, and 46.0% of Perot voters. Of the respondents who were both heavy consumers of violent programming and nonvoters in the 1992 presidential election, 67.4% were 18–34 and 91.3% were 18–49, the two demographic groups sought after heavily by advertisers. While programmers may try and reach these heavy violence consumers who did not vote, candidates are less constrained by their opinions since they do not participate in elections.

Another way to identify "marginal voters" at the presidential level is to break down survey respondents based on their evaluation of President Clinton in February 1993. When asked whether they "approve or disapprove of the way Bill Clinton is handling his job as President," 55% said they approved, 27% said disapproved, and 18% said they had no opinion. If one focuses on the "no opinion" voters as part of those in contention among Democrats and Republicans, table 8.2 demonstrates that 73% of these respondents believe there is too much violence in nonnews programming on television. Those without an opinion on the presidential approval question were also more likely to be bothered by violent content than sexual content on television, the same pattern as those who approve of the president's job handling. Note that those who disapprove of the president's performance were more likely to be offended by sexual content than violent content. Those without an opinion on the president's job performance were also (relative to those who approved of the president's performance) less likely to be heavy violence consumers and more likely to be light viewers of violent content.

Another set of voters identified in electoral strategies as swing voters in congressional battles and the presidential race are suburban voters.[25] Again, these

TABLE 8.2
Marginal Voters and Marginal Viewers (% of Column Respondents)

Survey Response	In 1992 Voted for				Approve Clinton Job Handling?			Live in Suburbs?		Women (18–34)		Men (18–34)	
	Clinton (N = 515)	Bush (N = 381)	Perot (N = 187)	Did Not Vote (N = 297)	Approve (N = 835)	Disapprove (N = 403)	No Opinion (N = 278)	Yes (N = 304)	No (N = 1,200)	Married (N = 108)	Never Married (N = 93)	Married (N = 126)	Never Married (N = 149)
Too much violence in nonnews programming	74.4	76.9	67.4	62.0	70.9	73.2	73.0	74.3	71.5	65.7	62.4	61.9	47.7
Bothered more by amount of violence or sex on TV?													
Violence	47.0	32.3	42.3	32.7	44.6	31.8	32.7	51.0	36.0				
Sex	22.9	36.2	23.0	36.4	27.1	35.5	25.2	21.7	30.8				
Both equally	24.9	25.5	23.5	20.5	22.0	25.1	30.2	20.0	25.3				
TV Violence Viewing?													
Heavy	44.5	36.2	46.0	62.3	47.0	44.4	38.5	43.1	45.3				
Medium	34.6	37.3	42.8	27.6	35.3	33.3	38.9	36.8	35.0				
Light	21.0	26.5	11.2	10.1	17.7	22.3	22.7	20.0	19.7				

voters report that they too believe that there is too much violence in nonnews shows on television. Among suburban respondents, 51.0% said they were more likely to be offended by violence than by sex (21.7%) on television, while for nonsuburban respondents these figures were 36.0% and 30.8%. The results also suggest that television violence is an issue that resonates with young women, confirming the statements of Clinton strategists. Among those women aged 18–34, 65.7% of married women and 62.4% of those who had never been married agreed that there was too much violence in entertainment programming on television. Among men 18–34 there was a statistically significant difference of opinion on this issue based on marriage status, with 61.9% of married men agreeing with this statement versus 47.7% for those who had never been married. Overall, table 8.2 reveals that among voters identified as potential targets of President Clinton's and Senator Dole's campaign messages there was a high level of dissatisfaction with violence on television.[26] Though politics helps explain why politicians focus on policies to deal with television violence, a separate question remains of what policies one would favor if protection of children from violent content were the goal of these policies. In the following section, I examine how different types of policies designed to deal with negative externalities such as pollution could be applied to deal with television violence.

Property Rights and Liability

If information and negotiations were costless, the definition of property rights and functioning of liability law would offer a way to deal efficiently with the damages arising from television violence. Consider a world where the instigation of violence could be traced to a particular television program. If people enjoy the right to be free from criminal attack, then a person injured as a result of a crime inspired by television violence could sue a broadcast or cable network for damages. This would cause programmers to face the full social costs of their shows, which would result in a reduction of the amount of television violence and an alteration of the way violence is portrayed to lessen its harmful effects. Alternatively, programmers could enjoy the right to broadcast any type of violent programming they chose. Individuals potentially harmed by television violence would under this scenario band together and pay the industry to reduce its level and manner of violent programming.

Ronald Coase (1960) first noted that in a world of zero "transaction costs" the definition of property rights would lead individual decision makers to internalize externalities, so that firms would be led to consider the costs of their pollution either through potential lawsuits demanding damages or compensation offers for reductions. He proposed this solution not because he believed that markets work in this manner but because he wanted to stimulate economists to reason why the world observed diverges from this zero transaction cost society (1988). For the issue of television violence, at least three problems cause a liability system to break down. The impacts of television violence are often manifested years after consumption, so that it is difficult to determine which crimes are caused by television violence. If television violence influences children by teaching them scripts of behavior acted upon in later life, how can one trace a shooting by a 20-year-old perpetrator to television consumption at age 10? Similarly, even if one identifies a set of crimes as inspired by television violence, the question remains of which particular shows contributed to the crime. Individuals making their own assessments of the likely dangers of particular types of programming could offer networks or cable operators compensation to remove or alter their use of television violence. Yet the logic of collective action predicts that few individuals would participate in such an effort. Why contribute money to eliminate television violence if you can enjoy the potential benefits even if you do not contribute?

It is not difficult to define television violence. The National Television Violence Study (1996b) offers a clear definition:

> Violence is defined as any overt depiction of a credible threat of physical force or the actual use of such force intended to physically harm an animate being or group of beings. Violence also includes certain depictions of physically harmful consequences against an animate being or group that occur as a result of unseen violent means.[27]

The review of the effects literature by the NTVS researchers also identifies the contextual factors that influence the degree of harm generated by a violent act on television: attractiveness of the perpetrator or target, whether the violence was portrayed as justified, use of a weapon, graphic violence, realism of the violence, whether the act was rewarded or punished, use of pain or harm cues, and use of humor. Research thus provides a basis for indicating the direction of harm (e.g., is a given scene more or less likely to stimulate aggression if a certain context is used?), but the exact magnitude of the harm remains uncertain and probably unknowable. The interactive effects of these contextual factors have not been explored. The probabilities that particular acts will be stimulated by a given show have not been established, in part because what is measurable in the lab (aggression, statements of hostility) does not always correspond to the real-world outcome of concern (criminal behavior). Since information is costly, one cannot today state what the exact harms will be from the showing of a given television program.

Many of these same difficulties in measuring damage and establishing causation arise in mitigating the effects of pollution. The onset of cancer may come many years after exposure, the interactive effects of most pollutants remain unmeasured, and for many noncancer effects the probability that the harm will arise from a given level of chemical exposure is unknown. Liability law works best when the damage can be directly linked to exposure. Litigation over worker exposure to asbestos, for example, was successful since some of the diseases generated by asbestos have unique characteristics that make their cause readily identifiable.[28] For many other types of cancers, however, the fact that Americans on average face a one in three chance of contracting cancer means that it is difficult to identify the excess cancers arising from a particular chemical exposure. Isolating the additional crime caused by television remains similarly difficult, since this is one of many factors (e.g., biological, psychosocial, situational, and social) that contribute to crime.[29]

The strongest candidates for the use of liability law as a constraint on programming are the so-called copycat crimes, where the harm allegedly arises from direct imitation of media violence.[30] Attempts have been made by injured individuals to sue media outlets for damages when a particular media product appears linked to a harmful action.[31] NBC was sued for its September 10, 1974, 8 PM broadcast of *Born Innocent*, which contained a scene where a young girl is raped with a plunger handle by a group of adolescent girls. The network was sued because according to a court decision in the case:

It is alleged that on September 14, 1974, appellant, aged 9, was attacked and forcibly "artificially raped" with a bottle by minors at a San Francisco beach. . . . The assailants had viewed and discussed the "artificial rape" scene in "Born Innocent," and the film allegedly caused the assailants to decide to commit a similar act on appellant. Appellant offered to show that NBC had knowledge of studies on child violence and should have known that susceptible persons might imitate the crime enacted in the film. Appellant alleged that "Born Innocent" was particularly likely to cause imitation and that NBC televised the film without proper warning in an effort to obtain the largest possible audience.[32]

The California court of appeals held that if broadcasters were held liable for acts allegedly arising from consumption of programming that this would drastically alter the content they would choose to offer. The appeals court upheld the dismissal of the case in part based on this prospect of inhibition. The court held:

Realistically, television networks would become significantly more inhibited in the selection of controversial materials if liability were to be imposed on a simple negligence theory. . . . The deterrent effect of subjecting the television networks to negligence liability because of their programming choices would lead to self-censorship which would dampen the vigor and limit variety of public debate. . . . the effect of the imposition of liability could reduce the U.S. adult population to viewing only what is fit for children.[33]

While research on media effects can indicate relative harms of different types of violent programming, the inability to specify exact causation linking particular programs with given adverse outcomes makes it unlikely that a liability system would effectively and efficiently deal with the problem of television violence.

Programming Taxes

Taxes are another policy instrument that could lead programmers to incorporate the negative impacts on society of their shows. Economists propose pollution taxes as a way to make firms face the costs of their emissions. Companies that find it costly to reduce pollution may pay the tax rather than reduce emissions greatly, while firms who can reduce pollutants at a relatively lower cost would engage in pollution prevention or control rather than pay the pollution fee. The system economizes on information, for regulators do not have to determine which firms face high or low costs of pollution prevention or control. The government simply announces the pollution tax level and then monitors emissions and collections to insure that rules are adhered to. Pollution taxes are popular in theory with some, who believe that the market mechanism increases efficiency of pollution control, and unpopular with others, who reject the implicit notion of allowing firms to pollute natural resources or endanger human health for a price. In practice pollution taxes are difficult to implement because of the amount of knowledge required in "getting the prices right." If the fees are designed to encourage efficient reduction, the level should in part depend on the harm to society generated by the release of dangerous emissions. This information requirement is similar to that which makes a liability system difficult to rely on for control of many types of pollution.

In theory, violence taxes could operate as pollution taxes. Firms may vary in their ability to "reduce" violent content in programming. Some genres could substitute slightly more costly nonviolent inputs (e.g., better dialogue, more recognizable actors) to retain an audience, and thereby avoid extensive violence "fees." Other genres might find it difficult to reduce reliance on violence and might end up maintaining a relatively high level of violent content while paying a tax. Knowing where to set the tax again brings the debate back to the difficulty in determining the impacts of particular types of programming.

Missouri enacted a form of a violent media tax in September 1996 by placing a 25% tax on "gross receipts . . . derived from the sale, lease or other exploitation in this state of broadcasting, television, closed-circuit telecast and motion picture rights for any ultimate fighting contest."[34] Live "ultimate fighting championships," which feature "no-holds-barred, bare-knuckle fighting," were already banned in the state. Dangers from these events include the possibility of death for participants, as happened with the death of a boxer in a 1995 Kansas City ultimate contest. Independent of these physical harms, individuals also express dissatisfaction with the knowledge that the events are allowed to transpire. As the executive director of the Missouri Cable Television Association put it, "Some people have a general dislike and distaste for these events." The 25% tax on pay-per-view telecast of ultimate fighting events compares with a 5% tax for other pay-per-view events in Missouri. The state legislature instituted the tax according to observers "to discourage the events . . . from airing on cable television." No court challenge was immediately mounted to the measure, although one promoter said that "if a lot of other states jumped on this bandwagon, it will put a lot of people out of business." The difficulty of calibrating violence taxes in other entertainment programming and the fact that there are much less restrictive ways to reduce exposure of children to violent programs (the state interest most often cited in debates over television violence) make it unlikely that broad violence taxes would survive legal challenge.

Zoning Violent Programming

While liability and tax provisions aim at reducing the level of externalities generated, zoning provisions offer a way to reduce the harms created by a given level of externalities. Local governments frequently restrict polluting enterprises to certain zones within a community, which serves to lessen the impact of their emissions by reducing the probability that there will be residences nearby threatened by the pollution. Shifting violent television programs to later evening hours is similar to zoning, for it would reduce the likelihood that children consume these images since they are less likely to be in the late night viewing audience. In 1995 Senator Fritz Hollings introduced a bill, S 470: The Children's Protection from Violent Programming Act, that would have required the FCC to define violent programming and develop rules requiring network and cable programmers to channel violent shows to times when children were not likely to be a substantial part of the audience, and would have provided for fines and the potential loss of broadcaster licenses for repeated violations of these programming rules.[35] In October 1993 Attorney General Janet Reno had testified that this "safe harbor" approach to dealing with television violence was "constitutionally permissible." The June 1995 decision by the U.S. Court of Appeals upholding a FCC rule that prohibits indecent programming broadcasts between 6 AM and 10 PM because of the government's compelling interest in protecting children bolstered the case that zoning might be a permissible approach to curbing the exposure of children to violent programming.

Currently, the market provides only a modicum of zoning of violent programming on broadcast and cable television. The results from chapter 4 indicate that Fox is the most violent broadcast network in terms of its use of movies (e.g., 56% of its prime-time films are violent), yet these films generally start at 8 PM. Basic cable and premium channels increase violence levels as the 18–49 demographic group enters the viewing audience in greater numbers, between 7 and 8 PM each weeknight. These channels thus end up broadcasting violent films at the time (8 PM) when a sizable fraction of all children 2–11 (e.g., 30%) are in the viewing audience. Syndicated action adventure shows are often shown in the pre-prime-time slots or on weekend days, a time when chapter 3 indicates a large number of children end up viewing these shows. Networks do not segregate advertising that uses violence away from shows where children are likely to be in the audience, so young viewers are often exposed to short strings of episodic violence during nonviolent programs.[36] TBS, which chapter 4 indicates offers 72% violent movies on the West Coast, which means that violent movies playing at 10 PM on the East Coast on TBS are playing simultaneously at 7 PM on the West Coast.

NBC

	Nonviolent	Violent
Nonviolent	X, X	$X-B, X+B$
Violent	$X+B, X-B$	$X-C, X-C$

ABC

Figure 8.1. Industry Restraint as a Prisoners' Dilemma

Why don't networks voluntarily restrict the use of violent programming until later hours? The logic of the prisoners' dilemma helps explain why individual networks pursuing rational self-interests may adopt programming strategies that leave the industry as a whole collectively worse off.[37] Consider a world with two broadcast networks, ABC and NBC. Their programming payoffs are represented in figure 8.1. If both broadcast nonviolent programming, they each gain an audience worth $X. If one network includes violent programming in its schedule while the other broadcasts only nonviolent programming, the broadcaster that incorporates violence is assumed to gain an audience worth $B at the expense of the nonviolent network. If only one network is using violent programming as part of its schedule, there is no government backlash. If both networks use violent programming, neither gains a commercial advantage because violent viewers are not attracted away from the other network. Yet if both networks use violent programming, government may increase scrutiny because of public concern that there is "too much" violence on television. Each network may face costs of $C from the government reaction, loss of goodwill, and advertiser backlash that may arise with the perception that all broadcasters are "violent."

If these are the payoffs, what strategy should NBC follow? If NBC assumes that ABC will be offering nonviolent programming, then the highest payoff for NBC is to offer violent programming ($X + B$, its payoff for violent programming, is greater than X, its payoff for nonviolent programming). If ABC is offering violent programming, then NBC must choose between a payoff of $X -

B if it offers nonviolent shows only or *X* − *C* if it offers violent shows. Assume that the commercial losses (*B*) are greater than the additional costs of government scrutiny and advertiser backlash (*C*). This means that NBC would choose to air violent programming and earn *X* − *C*. Thus regardless of the strategy adopted by ABC, NBC's best strategy is to offer programming that contains some violence. ABC faces the same payoffs: no matter what NBC does, its best strategy is to offer violent programming. Self-interest thus leads both broadcasters to choose violent programming, which yields each a payoff of *X* − *C*. This logic of individual rationality leading to outcomes that are collectively inferior is referred to as the prisoners' dilemma.

Both networks would be better off if they could reach the world where each offers nonviolent programming (where each would receive *X*). If they play this game only once, then no matter what they may promise each other each will have the incentive to broadcast violent programming. If they are viewed as interacting multiple times, then their behavior may change. The ability to make credible commitments or to have a third party (e.g., government?) coordinate agreements also increases the probability that networks may be able to agree to reduce violent programming. In general, however, the logic of competition causes each network to select programming that results in inferior outcomes for the industry as a whole and each network individually.[38]

The logic of the prisoners' dilemma thus prevents a broadcast network from unilaterally renouncing the use of violence until 9 PM, since competitive pressures point to an outcome where networks use violence to attract audiences. When FCC Chairman Wiley in the mid-1970s coordinated the joint adoption of such a "family viewing" policy as part of the National Association of Broadcaster's Television Code Review Board standards, the action was struck down as improperly adopted. If the Hollings legislation passed, however, the FCC would be required to go through the notice and comment rule-making process to develop a definition of violent programming and a determination of when children were likely to be in the audience and thus in need of protection from violent programming.

How these two questions of definition and timing were answered would likely determine whether the zoning of violent programs would pass a cost-benefit analysis test. The agency could try to delineate different types of violent images based on the media effects literature, as the NTVS researchers did in their focus on the importance of context. This would shift more harmful violence to later hours and thus reduce the likelihood that children would be exposed to these images. Forcing harmful types of violent programming to later hours also may reduce the utility of adult consumers who enjoy this type of programming and who may not be affected by its content in an adverse way. Shifting violence to later hours runs the risk of reducing the adult audience available to consume such programs, which in turn may reduce advertiser support for these shows. If one assumes that heavy violence consumers will consume the "moderately violent" programs before 10 PM and then search out the heavily violent programming after 10 PM if such programming were not allowed until later hours, then the loss to society from zoning involves the degree that these consumers would have gained more utility from viewing "gratuitous violence" at 8 PM. Assessing the magnitudes of these gains and losses is difficult. Legislators and regulators are faced with trading off reducing the exposure of children, which reduces crime and aggression, with reducing the viewing utility of adults forced to wait until an hour such as 10 PM to view extremely violent shows. In application, however, this policy involves potentially lower information, negotiation, and enforcement costs than the liability or tax solutions.

Information Provision

Government increasingly uses information provision as a regulatory tool to change behavior in private markets. To lead firms to reduce their emissions, the Environmental Protection Agency (EPA) publishes each year pollution data on the releases of over 300 chemicals from more than 20,000 facilities. The figures have been used by investors as a measure of firms' potential liabilities, by environmental groups as an indicator of human health threats, and by regulators as a yardstick to measure pollution reduction progress across firms.[39] In part because of the scrutiny attracted by these data, the pollution totals tracked under the EPA's Toxics Release Inventory dropped by one-third between 1988 and 1992.[40] The impact of information will vary depending on the property rights enjoyed by those generating the negative externalities tracked, the degree that the data attract scrutiny, and the likelihood that individuals affected by the externalities will use the data in collective action efforts or individual decisions.

Congress members have proposed several different types of information provision policies to deal with the problem of television violence. In August 1995, the Senate Commerce Committee voted in favor of a bill proposed by Senator Byron Dorgan that required the Commerce secretary to hire a nonprofit group to devise a quarterly report on television violence. The information provided would grade programming based on violent content and provide information on which advertisers bought times on violent programs.[41] The Telecommunications Act of 1996 also dealt with television violence through information provision. The bill required television manufacturers to place within 2 years technology capable of reading a program rating in newly manufactured sets, required the FCC to develop a committee to create a ratings methodology if the industry had not generated an acceptable ratings plan within 1 year, and mandated that broadcasters include a rating in their signals if a program were rated. Spitzer (1996) demonstrates that from a legal perspective the requirements are likely to survive a court challenge because they serve a compelling government interest of protecting children and are narrowly tailored to achieve this goal.

The theories and empirical analyses in chapters 2 and 3 indicate that a system of ratings and the V-chip technology should reduce the exposure of some children to violent programming. The rating system reduces the transaction cost to parents of determining program content, so that they do not have to bear extensive costs of investigating the content of unfamiliar programs or movies. The V-chip technology dramatically lowers the costs of acting upon the ratings information. Rather than having to monitor what programs are on at what hours and whether the set is turned to these channels, parents can choose a level of content they believe is appropriate for their children and set the chip to block out programs with content that does not satisfy their own chosen specifications.

With the V-chip embedded in a newly purchased set and ratings that make it possible to block programs, parents will face the choice of whether to invest the time to program the set to shield their children. The ratings data on prime-time broadcast network television movies indicate that when the networks lowered the cost of information gathering by providing viewer discretion warnings, parents and children acted upon this information. Ratings among children 2–11 dropped by 14% on movies that carried warnings from 1987 to 1993, which translated into a substantial number of children. On average, the placement of a warning on a prime-time broadcast network film resulted in 222,000 fewer children in the audience. The audiences for teens and adults for these films were not affected by the warnings. Thus unlike the zoning or liability proposals, information provision offers the ability to change children's exposure without directly affecting the ability of adults to consume violent programming. The value placed on this distinction depends in part on the degree that one is concerned about the negative externalities generated by consumption of such programming by adults.

The ratings system could indirectly affect the type of programming offered in the long run. Chapter 5 indicates that the controversy surrounding *NYPD Blue* caused the program to sell for a 45% discount early in its first season. Within 2 years the controversy surrounding the program declined, so that the program's ads commanded a "full" market price based on the show's highly desirable demographics. The prospect of controversy generating advertiser backlash and the attendant initial drop in ad prices may influence decisions about what projects get approved initially or what programs are renewed. Chapter 6 indicates, for example, that nonviolent programs are more likely to be renewed when government attention is turned toward television violence. Chapter 5 demonstrates that warnings on theatrical films shown on prime time do change the mix of advertisers willing to support a program. Theatrical films with warnings carried slightly lower amounts of general product commercials, which over time may translate into a lower willingness to pay by networks for violent offerings. The composition of advertisers changed too, so that products aimed at consumers less likely to be offended by television violence (e.g., younger consumers, males, those without children) accounted for a greater percentage of ads. Spitzer (1996) points out the precise impacts of the rating system on content offerings are hard to anticipate, which ironically may make the Telecommunications Act provisions more likely to survive. He notes that if the legislators had explicitly stated that the purpose of the bill was to reduce the number of hours of violent programming offered, then the courts might be less likely to view the legislative remedy as narrowly tailored.

The prospect of advertiser backlash explains why broadcast networks have historically been reluctant to place ratings or content descriptions on their movies.[42] For broadcast network films for 1987–93, the placement of warnings did not affect the ratings for these films among any of the teen or adult demographic groups based on age or gender. Although warnings drop the number of children 2–11 who will view these films, these are not the target audience of advertisers in prime time and thus their numbers do not add to the ability of networks to charge a given price for ads on movies. Broadcasters are leery of warnings not because they affect the calculus of the set of advertisers worried about consumer backlash. Companies that sell products aimed at groups that express higher dissatisfaction with television violence, such as older or female consumers, may be less likely to support a movie with a warning. Since basic and premium channels rely less or not at all on advertiser support, they are much more likely to provide content descriptions voluntarily.

If warnings have the potential to reduce broadcast network advertising revenues, why would the networks choose to label some of their programs? In February 1996 MPAA President Jack Valenti announced the formation of a group that would develop ratings for television programs. The effort, led by Valenti and the heads of the National Cable Television Association and National Association of Broadcasters, came in response to the Telecommunications Act provision that gave the industry 1 year to develop a rating system, after which the FCC could appoint an advisory committee to formulate a methodology.[43] The voluntary efforts taken by the industry can thus be seen in part as attempts to head off potentially more costly actions by the government. Some analysts have noted that such "regulation by raised eyebrow" means that industry actions are not voluntary and that government attempts at moral suasion are actually violations of the First Amendment.[44] In this view, broadcaster concerns about issues such as the potential auction of the spectrum, which would require them to pay for their currently free licenses, cause them to trade off some control over content for favorable government policies or treatment.

If broadcasters, cable executives, and program producers view reduction of political pressure rather than reduction of the exposure of children to violent television as the goal of a ratings system, this will have an impact on the design and efficacy of the rating system. Age-based ratings akin to those established for motion pictures by the MPAA may allow the industry to label programs without providing information on specific types of content. An alternative rating system, such as that initially proposed for Canadian television, would provide viewers with a shorthand summary of content. The Canadian system rated each program on a 0–5 scale in terms of violence, sexual content, language, and overall audience level.[45] Premium cable channels in the United States such as HBO and Showtime currently use content indicators, so that violent content may be conveyed by icons before the start of a film to indicate mild violence (MV), violence (V), or graphic violence (GV).[46] Content ratings would provide parents with information on exactly what types of potentially objectionable material are in a show. The same information would be available to interest groups targeting companies for their sponsorships, however, so that content-based warnings may give rise to more advertiser backlash. Pepsico, the top prime-time network advertiser on the violent theatrical films tracked in chapter 5, might face greater consumer backlash for advertising on programs labeled as "graphic violence" than on programs labeled as inappropriate for those under 14. Age-based ratings may cloak the specific types of content that could give rise to parental objections. Under the current MPAA system, for example, that chapter 4 underscores, it is difficult to distinguish between a PG versus a PG-13 movie on the basis of violence.[47]

The development and implementation of the TV Parental Guidelines, the rating system put into place by the television industry in 1997 in response to the Telecommunications Act of 1996, reveals how economic incentives may influence the success of information provision programs. The initial industry guidelines implemented in January 1997 classify shows other than news or sports programming into one of two categories for children's programming (TV-Y, all children, or TV-Y7, directed at older children) or one of four categories for general audience programs (TV-G, general audience; TV-PG, parental guidance suggested; TV-14, parents strongly cautioned; and TV-MA, mature audience only). The ratings are assigned by broadcast and cable networks and program producers, although a local station could choose to assign a different rating in a particular market.[48] Table 8.3 provides the definitions of these categories provided by the industry to viewers. The categories are similar to the MPAA rating system in that both systems are age-based and both systems fail to specify in the rating the exact type of content in the program (e.g., adult language, violence, sexual content) that may be of concern to parents.

Interest groups and researchers criticized the industry guidelines for their failure to provide parents with specific content information. A survey conducted by Cantor, Stutman, and Duran (1996) with the support of the National PTA found that when given the choice between a rating system indicating "what age of child the program is appropriate for" or a system indicating "what the content of the program is (i.e., amount or type of sex, violence, and language)," 80 percent of parents chose the content-based system. The industry responded with its own survey data, which indicated that "90 percent of America's parents favored the TV Parental Guidelines system" and "83 percent of parents said a television rating system like the one used for movies would be helpful."[49] Part of the difference in survey responses from parents lies in the fact that the industry survey framed the questions as evaluating whether the TV Parental Guidelines were an improvement over a status quo of no ratings for most programs. The National PTA survey chose a methodology that evaluated an age-based system by comparing it with other possible types of programs classification, including content ratings. Six weeks into the implementation of the industry rating system, a survey by the New York Times found that, although 86% of parents approved of the idea of program ratings, only 37% reported using the TV Parental Guidelines in their viewing decisions.[50]

TABLE 8.3
TV Parental Guidelines, Spring 1997

The following categories apply to programs designed solely for children:

TV-Y. All Children. *This program is designed to be appropriate for all children.* Whether animated or live-action, the themes and elements in this program are specifically designed for a very young audience, including children from ages 2–6. This program is not expected to frighten younger children.

TV-Y7. Directed to Older Children. *This program is designed for children age 7 and above.* It may be more appropriate for children who have acquired the developmental skills needed to distinguish between make-believe and reality. Themes and elements in this program may include mild physical or comedic violence, or may frighten children under the age of 7. Therefore, parents may wish to consider the suitability of this program for their very young children.

The following categories apply to programs designed for the entire audience:

TV-G. General Audience. *Most parents would find this program suitable for all ages.* Although this rating does not signify a program designed specifically for children, most parents may let younger children watch this program unattended. It contains little or no violence, no strong language, and little or no sexual dialogue or situations.

TV-PG. Parental Guidance Suggested. *This program may contain some material that some parents would find unsuitable for younger children.* Many parents may want to watch it with their younger children. The program may contain infrequent coarse language, limited violence, some suggestive sexual dialogue and situations.

TV-14. Parents Strongly Cautioned. *This program may contain some material that many parents would find unsuitable for children under 14 years of age.* Parents are strongly urged to exercise greater care in monitoring this program and are cautioned against letting children under the age of 14 watch unattended. This program may contain sophisticated themes, sexual content, strong language, and more intense violence.

TV-MA. Mature Audience Only. *This program is specifically designed to be viewed by adults and therefore may be unsuitable for children under 17.* This program may contain mature themes, profane language, graphic violence, and explicit sexual content.

Source: Descriptions of program ratings are from TV Guidelines Oversight Monitoring Board 1997.

Research from the second year of the National Television Violence Study (1997a, 1997b) indicates that the format of age-based ratings may actually serve to increase interest in violent programming among some children. Researchers from the University of Wisconsin provided children with program descriptions using eight different types of program ratings, including the MPAA ratings, the HBO-Showtime content codes (i.e., None, "MV: Mild Violence," "V:Violence," or "GV: Graphic Violence"), and parental advisories (e.g., "Parental discretion advised"). Only the age-based MPAA ratings significantly attracted older children to programs, with children aged 10–15 being more interested in movies with PG-13 or R ratings.[51] Among younger children (aged 5–9), the study found that the most aggressive children and those who watched television the most were the most attracted to watch programs with higher MPAA ratings. The study concluded that ratings or advisories "that urge parental control based on age considerations seem the most likely to produce the 'forbidden fruit' effect," where the perceived limitation of viewing elicits higher interest among children.[52]

If providing information to parents about program content were the top priority in the design of a rating system, then one would expect programs to carry content codes with more information for parents rather than age-based indicators. If consideration of advertiser reactions were a significant factor in the design of a rating system, however, one might expect program categories to be less explicit about program content. A full evaluation of the TV Parental Guidelines would examine how the ratings used by the industry match up with the actual types of violence or sexual content used in shows. Table 8.4 presents preliminary evidence from the implementation of the TV Parental Guidelines that indicates that the application of the ratings is affected by potential advertiser reactions.

For the period January 25 through April 18, 1997, 65.7% of the prime-time, rated program episodes (excluding movies) on the six broadcast networks carried TV-PG ratings, 22.9% were TV-G, and 11.4% were rated TV-14.[53] *Advertising Age* published an estimated ad price figure for each prime-time show in the fall 1996 schedule for ABC, CBS, Fox, and NBC.[54] These ad price estimates, which reflect prices *before* the implementation of the rating system, appear to indicate that controversial programming (i.e., shows rated TV-14 in 1997) had lower ad prices (mean $159,000 per 30-second commercial) than TV-PG programming (mean $200,000 ad price).

Yet were broadcasters actually rating all programs containing "some material that many parents would find unsuitable for children under 14 years of age," the definition of TV-14 programming, as TV-14? One approach to answering this question is to compare the episode ratings for prime-time network programs developed under the TV Parental Guidelines with the program rating system developed by the Parents Television Council (PTC), a group that published its own guide at the start of the 1996 season rating the six broadcast network prime-time shows on a program basis rather than episode basis.[55] The PTC guide rated programs using a stoplight icon, with a green show defined as a "family-friendly show promoting responsible themes and traditional values," a yellow show as one where the "series' adult-oriented themes and dialogue may be inappropriate for youngsters," and a red program as one that "may include gratuitous sex, explicit dialogue, violent content, or obscene language, and is unsuitable for children." Of the episodes of the prime-time programs rated by

TABLE 8.4
Rating Television Programs, Spring 1997

TV Parental Guidelines Rating	% Episodes	Average Ad Price, Fall 1996
	(N = 1,039)	(N = 635)
TV-G	22.9	$174,000
TV-PG	65.7	$200,000
TV-14	11.4	$159,000
Parents Television Council Rating	(N = 904)	(N = 665)
Green	25.3	$190,000
Yellow	50.9	$162,000
Red	23.8	$242,000

Average Ad Price of Programs Rated Yellow That Are . . .

Rated TV-PG	Rated TV-14	Difference of Means Test
(N = 269)	(N = 43)	(T Statistic)
$173,000	$125,000	4.9***

Average Ad Price of Programs Rated Red That Are

Rated TV-PG	Rated TV-14	Difference of Means Test
(N = 131)	(N = 39)	(T Statistic)
$253,000	$198,000	3.5***

Average Ad Price of Programs Rated TV-PG That Are

Rated Yellow	Rated Red	Difference of Means Test
(N = 269)	(N = 131)	(T Statistic)
$173,000	$253,000	−6.0***

Note: Data for TV Parental Guidelines for all rated prime-time program episodes (except movies) shown on the six broadcast networks are from January 25 through April 18, 1997. Parents Television Council data are overall program ratings for the 1996–97 season. Ad prices are from *Advertising Age* September 1996 estimates for 30-second commercial spots on the four major broadcast networks and are meant to reflect prices prior to advertiser reactions to the TV Parental Guidelines ratings. *** = statistically significant at the .01 level.

the Parents Television Council, 23.8% were rated "red," the highest content category for this group. Within the PTC system, nearly twice as many program episodes were in the most controversial program rating (i.e., red) as in the TV Parental Guidelines category of TV-14.[56] The mean 30-second advertising price for programs in the red category was $242,000, nearly 50% more than the mean of $162,000 for programs in the yellow category. Thus according to the ratings by the PTC, programs with the greatest cause for parental concern had the highest fall 1996 advertising rates.

Groups developing content codes may obviously differ in how they categorize particular shows. If programmers feared that a TV-14 rating would discourage some advertisers from sponsoring a program and would thereby lower ad rates, networks might be less willing to label potentially controversial programs as "TV-14" if ad prices on the program (prior to program rating) were high. Table 8.4 confirms this hypothesis. Among the 174 episodes of programs with ad price data that were rated as "red" by the Parents Television Council, the industry was willing to place a TV-14 rating on only 39 episodes, with a mean ad price of $198,000. For the vast majority (131 out of 174) of "red" episodes, the networks placed a TV-PG rating on these programs, which had an average ad price of $253,000. For those programs labeled as TV-PG by the industry, the mean ad price was $173,000 for shows in the yellow category and $253,000 for those in the red.[57] This is consistent with networks being less willing to use the TV-14 rating on programs with higher advertising rates, for fear of generating advertiser backlash.[58] The mean ad price of episodes where the Parents Television Council and the TV Parental Guidelines "agreed" on ratings (e.g., green programs were rated TV-G, yellow were rated TV-PG, and red were rated TV-14) was $178,000. For episodes where the TV Parental Guidelines rating was higher than that of the PTC, the mean ad price was $144,000. For episodes where the TV Parental Guidelines rating was lower (e.g., TV-PG when the program was rated red), the mean ad price was $235,000. These data suggest that the industry "underrates" potentially controversial programs that carry higher ad prices.

Faced with criticism of the age-based ratings, the drafters of the TV Parental Guidelines announced in July 1997 that content indicators would be added to program ratings. For children's shows in the TV-Y7 category, those "programs where fantasy violence may be more intense or more combative" would carry a FV designation (PR Newswire Association 1997). Programs in the TV-PG, TV-14, or TV-MA categories would also be supplemented with content indicators V, S, L, or D. The exact definitions of what levels of content these indicators are meant to convey vary with the age-based ratings. For programs classified as TV-PG, the indicators are used to denote "moderate violence (V), some sexual situations (S), infrequent coarse language (L), or some suggestive dialogue (D)." For programs in the TV-14 range, the indicators denote "intense violence (V), intense sexual situations (S), strong coarse language (L), or intensely suggestive dialogue (D)." For programs in the TV-MA category, the signs indicate "graphic violence (V), explicit sexual activity (S), or crude indecent language (L)." The revised guidelines thus give some indication of the intensity of violence, although the drafters avoided explicit intensity labels such as the GV for graphic violence used by premium channels.

Industry officials involved in negotiations with advocacy groups about the content ratings agreed to implement this revised guidelines system by October 1997 in order to avoid antagonizing members of Congress considering proposals dealing with issues such as spectrum auctions, copyright treaties, and violent programming. MPPA president Jack Valenti said of the revised plan, "This is not what I would've done if I didn't think I had to. We went into these negotiations for one reason, and that was to shut the flow of legislation that we thought was inimical to our future and that may trespass on the First Amendment. I don't think it's as good as the rating system we have now [in July 1997]" (Pottinger 1997). The major broadcast networks announced that they would adopt the new content indicators, except for NBC. In a statement issued when the revised guidelines were announced, the company declared, "The ultimate aim of the current system's critics is to dictate programming content. NBC is disappointed that the industry capitulated to political and special-interest pressure and did not look more seriously at the implications of the flawed process in which they engaged. Therefore, NBC will not be a part of the new agreement" (Albiniak 1997, p. 6).

NBC's refusal in July 1997 to adopt the content indicators may in part stem from the potential losses it might face if more content indicators lead to more advertiser backlash. In terms of data analyzed in Table 8.4, NBC had the highest average price per 30-second advertisement on shows with the Parents Television Council red classification. Mean 1996 ad prices for episodes in the sample of programs rated as red by the PTC were $239,000 for ABC, $223,000 for CBS, $178,000 for Fox, and $340,000 for NBC. From the perspective of the PTC ratings, NBC thus had the highest mean advertising price on programs the group felt contained "gratuitous sex, explicit dialogue, violent content, or obscene language." One can also look at the content indicators as making it more difficult to underrate "controversial" content, since the revised system would require networks to indicate their assessment of the particular levels of sex, violence, language, and suggestive dialogue in programs. NBC may also have had much to lose by greater specificity, since it had the highest mean ad prices on programs "underrated" in the initial implementation of the TV Parental Guidelines system. If one defines "underrated" programs as those where the TV Parental Guidelines rating for an episode is lower than the PTC program rating (e.g., a program rated as red by PTC but TV-PG by the network), the mean ad price per episode for underrated programs was $215,000 for ABC, $207,000 for CBS, $159,000 for Fox, and $300,000 for NBC. The difference of means tests between the ad price on underrated episodes on NBC and the ad price on each other major broadcast network is statistically significant at the .01 level. NBC's reluctance to provide more detailed program information may thus stem from potential advertising losses on programs likely to attract content indicators for sex, violence, language, or suggestive dialogue.

In sum, information provision offers a way to reduce exposure of children to violent programming while allowing adult viewers to consume what they wish. The private market does generate information and technology aimed at helping parents shield their children from objectionable content, including devices that block channels or day parts or specific programs.[59] Currently, however, the industry's rating code provides less than ideal amounts of information about program content, and programmers face incentives to avoid using a rating such as TV-14 because of fear of advertiser backlash. As the number of channels expands to the point that software will be required to navigate viewing options, content information can be easily incorporated into program selection software.[60] Different interest groups may develop their own content codes, since the cost to a group of assessing program brand types would not be prohibitive. For example, the analysis of the NCTV data reveals that based simply on genre one can correctly predict nearly 90% of the time whether a prime-time network series program will contain more than the average number of violent acts per hour. Classification schemes always run the risk of false negatives and positives. Some violent movies may contain other messages or values that parents wish their children to become exposed to at some age. *Schindler's List*, for example, might be rated as containing objectionable material because of its violent incidents. A V-chip system can be turned off, however, so that if parents want their children to see a movie such as *Schindler's List*, then they can override the rating. Chapter 5 indicates that the question of high-quality violent films may not be a large problem, in that only 1.4% of the evening movies shown on broadcast and cable television are four-star movies with indicators for violence.

Though some parents are willing today to pay for technology to shield their children from violent images on television, the failure of parents to take into account the additional benefits to society of their children being protected means that parents will not engage in the optimal amount of effort to monitor the viewing of their children. The government inducements of the V-chip and rating system can thus be viewed as attempts to intervene in the programming market to lower the costs to parents of protecting their children. Even with this technology available, a process that may take years as it relies in part on the purchase of newly equipped television sets, adults will still not fully consider the broader benefits of influencing the television consumption of their children. Reducing the costs of monitoring will, however, result in more children being protected from objectionable material.[61]

Norm Creation

The creation and consumption of norms offers another way to overcome the problems created by negative externalities. Consider a person deciding whether to recycle newspapers at her home. The personal costs of recycling involve stacking and sorting newspapers and taking them to the curb for collection. The benefits of newspaper recycling may include the value that a person places on a world without another local landfill. The probability that a person's recycling affects whether another landfill is built, however, is so small that the net calculation of expected benefits minus costs will be negative. Individuals do recycle, however, because they gain satisfaction from ideological consumption, from feeling that they are "doing the right thing" by recycling. One policy to encourage recycling is to encourage the spread of beliefs that recycling makes a statement and that recycling is the proper thing to do. Sunstein provides a definition of the broader class of these beliefs, called social norms:

We might, very roughly, understand "norms" to be social attitudes of approval and disapproval, specifying what ought to be done and what ought not to be done. Some norms set good manners, for example, about how to hold one's fork; others reflect morally abhorrent views, as in the taboo on interracial relations; others reflect hard-won moral commitments, as in the norm against racial epithets.[62]

At least five groups of people involved in the negative externalities arising from violent television could be affected by norm creation: owners or boards of directors of media companies, managers in the entertainment industry, parents, and children.

For an individual who owns a sufficient stake in a media property to become identified with its programming, there are great potential returns for influencing the content produced. Analysis of ownership across different industries suggests that historically media properties have had ownership concentrated among individuals (as opposed to ownership being widely dispersed through publicly traded stock) because they afford the opportunity for psychic benefits.[63] For many years after its founding, for example, CBS was identified with its founder William Paley. The high quality of the "Tiffany" network's public affairs programming was traced in part to Paley's satisfaction from providing a public service.[64] If owners came to believe that it was their duty to reduce the influence of violent programming on children, then they might be willing to trade off a measure of profits for the knowledge or acknowledgment that they were protecting society as a whole. Ironically, the two owners most identified with current programming, Rupert Murdoch with Fox and Ted Turner with TBS and TNT, control channels with brand identities for violence.

The analysis in chapter 4 indicates that Fox has the highest percentage of films with violent content among the four major broadcast networks. Because Fox offers weeknight programming from 8 to 10 PM, these violent movies start earlier than those on the other broadcast networks. The movie data and critics' reviews noted in chapter 4 also indicate that the Fox network has a brand name for using more adult language and sexual content. When Ken Auletta asked Rupert Murdoch in a famous *New Yorker* article "What won't you do?" Murdoch's replies indicate the difficulty for some of articulating what is harmful and damaging to society about different types of media content:

If you thought you were doing something that was having a malevolent effect, as you saw it, on society, you would not do it. We would never do violence such as you see in a Nintendo game. . . . There has been violence in movies that we put out. Some of it I disliked. . . . But is violence justified? Is the violence of "Lethal Weapon" O.K.? I think so. If it involves personal cruelty, sadism—obviously, you would never do that.[65]

Murdoch indicated that he would not have made the picture *Basic Instinct*, which he described as using violence for shock effect and as being "a film of no redeeming moral values." He also indicated that the publishing arm (Harper Collins) of his company (Twentieth Century Fox) "would never have published the Salman Rushdie book. It clearly went out of its way to give great offense to a lot of people. Now obviously, I'm not supporting anyone saying, 'Let's kill him for it,' but I think it went to the point of being an abuse of free speech."

Ted Turner has long publicly campaigned against the levels of violence on television. In describing his original goals in running the independent station WTCG in Atlanta, Turner noted:

I felt the people of Atlanta were entitled to something different from a whole lot of police and crime shows with murders and rapes going on all over the place. I believed, and still believe, that people are tired of violence and psychological problems and all the negative things they see on TV every night. I wanted to put on something different and give them a choice.[66]

In voicing his support for the V-chip, Turner noted that television is "definitely a contributing factor" to violence in society.[67] Despite these opinions, the data in chapter 4 indicate that the cable stations identified with Turner, TNT and TBS, in 1995 programmed high levels of violent movies during the evening hours. This was true even during the "Voices against Violence Week," a weeklong campaign in March 1995 organized by cable television channels "to raise awareness about violence in society." The contradictions in Turner's programming did not go unremarked, for as critic Robert Laurence noted:

The other major offenders have been Ted Turner's TBS and TNT channels. On TBS Saturday, March 11, the day began with two hours of pro wrestling at 6 a.m. (prime time for many small children who don't know wrestling is fake violence), and continued through the day with "Kickboxer 2: the Road Back" and "The Octagon," starring Chuck Norris. You might think the cable programmers would staunch the flow of blood during nonviolence week. . . . This Thursday, TBS fills prime-time hours with three more Chuck Norris karate kick-flicks, beginning with "Invasion, U.S.A.," described by film critic Leonard Maltin as "repellent in the extreme."[68]

Turner is noted for forsaking some profits to program shows devoted to the environment or Native Americans. Despite his political statements against violent television and expressed distaste for some TNT programming, violence remains a staple of the movies broadcast on TNT and TBS.[69]

Many entertainment industry businesses are publicly traded stock companies rather than firms with ownership concentrated among a few individuals, which means that the board of directors is the group that might exercise moral judgment in defining what products the company will not produce. Senator Joseph Lieberman, William Bennett of the conservative lobbying group Empower America, and C. DeLores Tucker of the National Political Congress of Black Women have attempted to induce entertainment industry companies to demonstrate corporate responsibility by refusing to promote music with graphically violent and sexually explicit lyrics.[70] The group specifically brought its arguments urging restraint on the types of music the company will produce to boards such as that governing Time Warner. Senator Lieberman noted that "The obvious fact is that these companies have no effective standards in place governing what they will or will not distribute. You cannot put out this pornographic junk and pretend that you have any lines that you will not cross."[71] The Empower America effort directly identified the negative impacts generated by harmful and degrading lyrics as "pollution of our culture." William Bennett asserted that the distribution of such offensive material was hypocritical, as he announced that one thing we will not take is these companies standing up, telling us they are first class corporate citizens—that they contribute to the well being of American international life. These people being honored and knighted and saluted at dinners for their company's brand image. Board members may also be affected by appeals based foundations and pouring this filth into the minds of children. Put this stuff back behind the red light districts, let the low-ball companies do this stuff. Every society has red light districts. What these companies do is legitimate it by their entry into the mainstream. The standing of these companies gives this music respectability."[72]

If a firm is targeted for scrutiny because of the negative externalities generated by its products, the board may decide to alter policies if there is a threat to the company's brand image. Board members may also be affected by appeals based on morality. Some board members, however, may be reluctant to forsake profit opportunities for moral considerations because they feel they have a fiduciary responsibility to maximize profits for shareholders.

Executives and managers in the entertainment industry are another set of individuals whose decisions could be influenced by social norms.[73] For these individuals to trade off profits for the notion of doing good, however, another market imperfection needs to exist. If stockholders direct managers to maximize profits and executives fail to do this because they wish to avoid using excessively violent programming, then if these actions were fully observable companies that were not maximizing profits could be taken over or managers failing to maximize returns could be fired by the board. Yet information is costly to obtain, takeovers have transaction costs too, and detecting manager behavior can be difficult. This creates a margin for managers to avoid some uses of violent programming if they believed there were a social norm against using such images or exposing children to them. In Ken Auletta's discussions with industry officials about television and movie content, most indicated that profits pressure executives into making the decisions which result in levels of sex and violence in programming that they say they would not let their own children watch. As one agent put it, "one of the things that have hurt our business the most is the lack of people who have the ability to work through their convictions over long periods of time. They're always worried about quarterly reports, and about getting thrown out of their jobs. That instability creates bad product."[74] The former chairman of NBC, Grant Tinker, described entertainment industry officials as separating personal and business ethics in this way: "They give generously. They're good parents. Then, on the lot, they make creative decisions for the wrong reason—to save their jobs. They are schizophrenics."[75]

Parents are an obvious group potentially subject to norms about the consumption of violent television. A high percentage of parents believe that television contains too much violent programming. Concern for their children's development in part will motivate some parents to shield their children from potentially harmful programs. This action might become more frequent if parents also came to believe that it is a social obligation rather than a matter of taste to direct children away from violent programming. If physicians treated television violence as a public health issue and teachers emphasized media literacy as a skill necessary for children to have, parents might come to appreciate the broader benefits to society from monitoring their children's viewing.[76] Information on the harms associated with exposure to television violence would thus reinforce parent's private interests in protecting their children and broader interest in protecting society from the harmful effects of violent programming.

If protecting children is the ultimate goal of attempts to reduce the harms of media violence, creating a norm among children against the consumption of violence is a possible policy lever. Currently, industry officials often insist that cartoon violence is not harmful to children, a position that undercuts efforts to develop the norm that children should not watch violent cartoon programs. Advertisers of toys based on violent imagery often use violent children's shows to reach their target audience, so these companies may also resist the notion that such shows are harmful. The creation of a norm among children against consumption of violent programs may be difficult in a society that often appears to reward or glorify violence in entertainment programming. Yet norms can make a difference in children's and teen's behavior, as evident by the apparent impact of norms among black youths against smoking cigarettes. In 1993, for example, 22.9% of white teenagers reported smoking versus 4.4% of black teenagers.[77]

Norms, like ideas in general, are public goods. This raises the question of who will reinforce norms against the production and viewing of violent programming, and who will generate the public scrutiny that helps set up incentives to comply with these norms. If violence is viewed as a public health issue, government activity in information provision may help sustain the notion of the dangers to society from violent media. Politicians as speakers themselves enjoy the right to speak out against firms whose production or programming practices lead to greater exposures of children to objectionable material. The idea of government as a source of moral values, however, runs up against a basic difficulty in liberalism, namely that government is designed to be silent on the "nature of the good life," a topic left open for contention in civil society. In this sense it becomes the role of nonprofit organizations and professionals such as teachers and physicians to identify the importance of protecting children from media violence. In an era of declining costs to collecting and disseminating information, interest groups may be able to distribute data on corporate responsibility so that programmers and advertisers face greater incentives to follow norms about media violence.

License System

Broadcasters currently receive licenses from the Federal Communications Commission for free, in exchange for a promise to broadcast in the "public interest, convenience, and necessity."[78] Another way to reduce the damages from violence on television would be to use the license system as a way to influence explicitly the content of broadcast television. The analysis in this book emphasizes how programmers use violence as part of a profit-maximizing attempt to garner particular viewing audiences. The FCC could in effect increase the implicit "price" that broadcasters pay for licenses by requiring them to adopt broadcast policies that diverge from those suggested by profit maximization. The agency could stipulate that in order to reduce the exposure of children to violent programming, a broadcast station would have to refrain from using violent advertisements during hours when children are in the viewing audience in substantial numbers, place ratings or warnings on violent programs, and shift excessively violent programming (defined along the lines of the NTVS methodology) to later hours (such as 9 PM).[79] Stations that failed to certify that they met these criteria at license renewal time could face greater scrutiny during the process, shorter grants of license renewal periods, or eventual loss of license for repeated violations.

Outside intervenors and FCC officials have historically considered making violence part of the license renewal process. FCC Chairman Wiley, for example, suggested adding a question about violent programming to the license renewal process, which broadcasters strongly opposed.[80] Courts might be less likely to approve these license requirements if they believed there were less restrictive means (such as the V-chip) of reducing the exposure of children.

The FCC currently "requires" broadcasters to program a specific type of content, a minimum of 3 hours of children's educational programming per week, as part of license requirements. Chapter 3 indicates, however, that compliance in the early 1990s with the spirit of the Children's Television Act of 1990 followed the predictions of traditional regulation models. Stations attempted to comply with the provisions of the bill at the lowest possible cost, a strategy that often would lead to a lower level of positive externalities being generated since educational shows were shifted to early morning hours. A possible remedy here lies in the auctioning of the broadcast spectrum.[81] This would free broadcasters of the requirement to provide "public interest programming," such as public affairs or children's educational shows. Broadcasters would still program shows with these elements, for there are markets for programs that provide a measure of public affairs or children's educational information in an entertaining manner. The funds from the auction could be used to provide funding for public broadcasting, whose programmers explicitly try to take into account positive externalities in their design of shows. Enhanced funding leading to increased quality would also increase audiences for these shows. The spectrum auction thus offers an alternative that would increase the positive externalities generated by broadcasting.

WHAT CAN ECONOMICS CONTRIBUTE TO THE POLICY DEBATE?

Television violence, like real-world violence, is governed by decisions about individual incentives. The theories and evidence presented here underscore that violent content in entertainment and news programming is an information product strategically chosen by channels in search of audiences and advertiser support. Although research demonstrates that violence on television harms children, the programmers who use violence are not led to consider the increases in aggression and fear that their shows engender. Television violence is thus an externality problem similar to pollution, since the choices of private actors will not reflect the full costs to society of their actions. The uncertainty surrounding the exact impacts of particular programs suggests that the same cost-benefit framework used to analyze environmental pollution will be difficult to apply in practice to television violence. Reasoning about individual incentives and the empirical evidence developed here suggest at least two policies, information provision and norm creation, may help reduce the damage to society arising from violent programming.

The audience for violent programming is well defined and highly valued by advertisers. Men 18–34 are the top consumers of violent content, with nearly 73% defined as heavy viewers of violent programming. Women 18–34, a group valued by advertisers for their influence on purchase decisions, are the second highest consumers. Violent shows are aimed at attracting these younger demographics. While broadcast networks gain advertising revenues for attracting viewers 18–49 and 50+ to nonviolent shows, ad prices increase only for increases in the 18–49 demographic for violent programs. Though violent programs attract substantial numbers of children 2–11, their viewership has no impact on ad rates since they are not the target audience for the products advertised on violent programs. This underscores that their exposure is truly external to the calculations of network programmers.

The scheduling of movies on broadcast, basic cable, and premium channels underscores how violence is chosen strategically by programmers. As predicted by a model of product differentiation, channels develop brand identities for their use of violent or sexual content. Within each distribution system there is a span of violent content, ranging from Fox (56% violent movies) to CBS (36%) for the broadcast networks, WGN (76%) to Disney (30%) on basic cable, and Cinemax (75%) to Encore (44%) on premium channels. Programmers establish viewer expectations for violence by consistent scheduling of this content on particular days and times, such as the use of a low-quality (average 1.6 stars) violent movie at 10 PM on Saturday by Cinemax for each of the 51 weeks in the sample studied. The pattern of violence follows the flow of young adult viewers into the viewing audience, so that on basic cable the percentage of violent films increases during weekdays from 53% at 7 PM to 63% at 8 PM. The use of violence clearly varies with likely competition. The use of violent movies by TBS on Mondays drops from 92% to 65% when ABC airs *Monday Night Football*. The measurement of ratings during sweeps periods causes some channels to alter their mix of movie programming. The broadcast networks are more likely to use family crime stories (6.5% of sweeps movies vs. 3.3% nonsweeps) and true murder stories (10.7% sweeps vs. 4.6% nonsweeps). WGN, a broadcast "superstation" carried nationally on cable, increases its use of violent movies from 70% to 89% and use of movies with adult situations from 49% to 60% during sweeps.

The same economic factors that govern the content of entertainment programming influence the composition of news programming. The analysis of local news programs reveals that within a given market there is product differentiation among stations in how they cover crime, their mix of news stories, and their style of coverage. High-crime stations were more likely to focus on the details of crime, less likely to provide context through coverage of trials or crime statistics, and more likely to cover topics of interest to younger viewers. These stations chose styles aimed at younger viewers, devising broadcasts that were faster paced and more visual (e.g., more clips per day). Across markets, the amount of crime coverage did not vary with the amount of crime committed during the sample period. Stations rather chose levels of crime coverage depending on potential audience interest in violence (as measured by ratings for *Cops*) and chose levels of government news coverage depending on interest in hard news content (as measured by market ratings for the network nightly news programs).

Broadcasters stress that their business is selling audiences to advertisers, not raising or educating children. Even when the interests of children are clearly identified and the request is made part of the condition for licensing, broadcasters naturally seeking to maximize profits will attempt to evade program strategies that might benefit children but reduce profits. The analysis of children's television programs here demonstrates that educational shows earn lower ratings and lower advertising rates than other children's shows. Although the Children's Television Act required stations to air programs aimed at the educational and informational needs of children, broadcasters tried to comply with these measures at the lowest cost. They claimed entertainment programs were educational, such as *Geraldo* and *Beverly Hills, 90210*. The network affiliates shifted educational programs on Saturday mornings to different times at twice the rate for noneducational programs. In the top 25 markets, for example, 28% of the airings of network educational programs were shifted to other times. Ratings for *Beakman's World* in the top 100 markets reveal how these deviations can alter the audience for educational programs. Though the program was scheduled to run at noon on Saturdays, in 41 of the top 100 markets stations chose to deviate and air the program at another time. For those stations that shifted the program to air at 7:30 AM or earlier, ratings among children 2–11 for the program dropped by over half the average viewing level.

Overall, these results demonstrate that the negative impacts on society that arise from violent programming and the positive impacts that arise from children's educational programs or public affairs coverage are both external to the decisions that programmers make. Television programmers will not take into account the harmful effects of content on children watching adult-oriented shows, just as manufacturers will not take into account (absent policy interventions) the impact of their pollutants on society. The existence of a market failure, however, does not imply the existence of a remedy guaranteed to leave society better off if implemented. The nature of the damages arising from violent television programming are clear: increased probabilities of aggression, crime, fear, and desensitization. Added to these are the dissatisfaction of those who dislike the mere existence of certain types of programming and the knowledge that it is being consumed, independent of its impacts. A formal cost-benefit analysis of policies to deal with television violence, however, is hampered by the fact that the magnitude of these harms and their links to specific programs remain uncertain. The inability to specify what fraction of child viewers will be motivated after viewing violent shows to commit particular types of crime make it hard to use liability or tax schemes, since these are linked to the ability to articulate the particular harms from a show. Assessing attempts to shift programming to later hours such as 10 PM is also made difficult, since the difficulty in valuing the reduction in children's exposure makes it hard to trade off against the reduction in utility for adult viewers less likely to watch at later hours.

The arguments against government attempts to influence the production or consumption of television violence are many. Some believe that efforts to restrict violent programming will inevitably harm the rights of adult viewers or the freedoms of producers. Others place an existence value on freedom of expression, so that any attempt to channel expression generates harms regardless of its outcomes. The application of the First Amendment can be viewed as a policy that means the dangers of government intervention are so great that it is prohibited. The damages arising from the exposure of children to television violence would be seen as part of the cost of creative freedom.

Although uncertainty about the exact magnitude of harms does not preclude action, it does suggest caution in the goals sought and policy instruments chosen in dealing with media violence. Reducing the exposure of children may be the policy goal with the least danger of restricting First Amendment rights of adults. Even though lab and survey evidence indicate that adults are stimulated to aggression (though less so than children), fear, and desensitization by violent programming, their sovereignty as rational consumers and the involvement of news programming in some of these problems suggest that attempts to limit adult consumption might be more problematic. Prime-time ad rates are not affected by reduction in viewers 2–11, so advertisers and broadcasters would not be affected by a loss of this audience.

The economic theories and evidence developed in this book suggest that information provision and norm creation may be the most attractive policy tools for dealing with media violence. These policies have the ability to protect children from exposure while leaving open the possibility that adults may freely choose to consume violent programming. There are clear roles for the government, nonprofit, and private sectors in these policies in both the creation of information (such as a rating system) and the dissemination of ideas about the influence of media violence.

The results developed here demonstrate that information provision about content affects the decisions of parents, programmers, and advertisers. When viewer discretion warnings were placed on prime-time broadcast network films, audiences for children 2–11 dropped by 14% (approximately 222,000 viewers) and viewership among teens and adults remained unchanged. Even though the sizes of adult viewing audiences are not affected by the warnings, the placement of warnings on violent theatrical films on broadcast television changed the mix of advertisers willing to sponsor a show and slightly lowered the amount of general product ads aired. Products aimed at those less likely to be offended by television violence, such as those targeted at younger consumers, males, and households without children, were more likely to sponsor these movies with warnings. Products from industries where "family" brand images are important, such as food or kitchen products, are less likely to sponsor ads on these theatrical films with warnings. These changes are linked to company concerns about backlashes among consumers and targeting by interest groups.

The desire by advertisers to avoid association with controversy can cause advertising prices to drop, as evidenced by the 45% discount at which spots on *NYPD Blue* sold during its first season. The case of *NYPD Blue* demonstrates that when controversy and scrutiny subside, advertisers return and ad prices increase to reflect the demographic audience captured by a program. Advertiser reaction obviously depends on anticipated scrutiny. The placement of a warning on violent movies on basic cable, for example, did not change the mix of advertisers in the same way that this action affected advertisers on broadcast television. Since interest groups such as the American Family Association currently do not monitor cable programming, companies face lower expected backlash from supporting violence on these channels. The scrutiny attracted by government attention to television violence can ultimately affect the mix of programming that broadcasters choose to offer, as evidenced by the finding that the networks were much more willing to renew a new nonviolent show during times when the government was focused on television violence.

If information provision about content would help parents, why doesn't the market provide detailed content information in a readily usable format? One reason lies in the demand for information by parents. Consider the information that parents might want to know about a program. The results of the NTVS study (1996a) demonstrate that one can define what violent programming is and what types of violent programming are more likely to be harmful to children. Parents would want to know what programs contain particular types of content, when these programs air, and would want a low-cost way to prevent their children from consuming these programs. In calculating the effort they will expend to monitor their children's viewing, parents will not factor in the added benefits to society of shielding their children from objectionable content. This means that they will demand less than the optimal amount of information about program content.

Broadcasters may be less likely to provide detailed content information for parents, since the same information may make it easier for interest groups to target advertisers. Pepsico, the top advertiser on violent theatrical films in the sample of network movies analyzed, may face less consumer backlash for sponsoring a movie labeled inappropriate for children under 14 than for advertising on the same movie labeled as "graphic violence." The TV Parental Guidelines initially developed by the industry did not provide detailed content information in part because of advertiser fears. Survey data indicate, however, that parents prefer content-based ratings rather than the age-based system first adopted by the industry. The revised guidelines may provide more content information on broadcast and cable programming, although this will depend on how the content ratings are implemented. Uncertainties surrounding the implementation of the revised TV Parental Guidelines include the possibility of legal challenge by the writers' or directors' guilds, the likelihood that NBC or program syndicators will eventually provide content indicators, and the manner in which programmers will decide to apply these indicators to types of programming content.

As the number of channels available to viewers increases, the ability of interest groups to monitor sponsorship of programming may decline. Ironically, however, the profusion of channels will also create a demand for software to help viewers navigate among shows. As this demand develops, software will evolve that shields children from content. Predicting which shows are violent, for instance, can be done rather easily right now given information about program genre. If one knows the genre of a program, then nearly 90% of the time one can correctly predict whether a program is above or below average in the use of violent acts per hour. Any system will have false negatives and positives. A system screening out movies that carried indicators for violence would catch, for example, *Schindler's List*. Among movies the magnitude of such false positives may be small, since only 1.4% of the films on broadcast and cable television are four star violent films.

The government may encourage the development of alternative ratings systems in several ways. In specifying the technology of the V-chip, the FCC may strive to choose a technology that would allow the V-chip to operate with rating systems in addition to the age-based one chosen by the industry.[82] As digital broadcasting spreads, stations will have the ability to broadcast data to television sets. Public broadcasting stations could broadcast content ratings from many different groups to parents, who could then choose which system to use in their television. Ultimately, the complexity and profusion of information options may generate the technologies to make the protection of children from violent programming easier.

The creation of a norm to protect children from television violence is another policy tool. The private returns to programmers indicate that commercial pressures will make it unlikely for broadcasters to reduce violence out of altruism. Even in an area where there are clear psychic rewards to helping children—for example, the provision of educational programming—stations attempt to comply with regulations at the lowest possible private cost. Norms may have a higher degree of success among parents, physicians and teachers. Chapter 3 indicates that parents who are bothered by television violence are 20% more likely to switch channels when something objectionable comes on the news. The Nielsen ratings also indicate that both men and women with children 2–11 in the household have lower ratings for violent prime-time programs, evidence of potential attempts to alter viewing to shield children. If parents were given more information about the dangers of violent programming and if the costs of shielding their children were reduced (through ratings and a V-chip), then parents might act more on desires to protect their children (and thus society) from violent content.

Professions by definition involve adherence to a set of beliefs about responsible conduct. Educators and physicians who come into contact with children also have the potential to influence viewing. Professional associations such as the American Medical Association have the resources to develop and distribute to doctors information about television viewing. Since children on average watch over 20 hours per week, helping parents understand the benefits of avoiding television violence could come to be seen as part of a doctor's assessment of a child's health.[83] Associations such as the National PTA and the National Education Association could also recognize more the role that television plays in influencing children. In this way teachers would come to focus on television viewing in discussing behavior with parents. In addition, insights from media literacy could be brought into the classroom, so that children become more aware of the dangers and drawbacks associated with some types of program content.

The ultimate success of these policies will depend on the degree that people truly believe violent television programming is harmful to children and the broader society. If programs carry ratings and televisions contain V-chips, this will lower the costs to parents of acting on their desires to shield children from objectionable material. If politicians, doctors, entertainment industry officials, and parents discuss the potential harms of violent television, then the norm will be reinforced that parents have a responsibility to act to shield their children. Information and norms will also influence industry decisions about the context of violence used in shows, the scheduling of programs, and the promotion of violent shows.[84] The scrutiny generated on broadcasters and advertisers creates the potential for more consumer backlash against companies that sponsor programming harmful to children.

Information about violent content and norms about viewing and producing can be freely consumed once they are generated, but the question remains of who will bear the costs of producing them. Left on its own, the market for television programming will generate significant externalities through the exposure of children to violent programs generally targeted at a segment of adult viewers. The model in chapter 1 indicates that as channels proliferate there will be an increase in the amount of violent programming offered. Currently, information about the content of programming comes partly from an entertainment industry willing to bear these costs because of the threat of other government actions, such as the auction of the spectrum or change in cable competition regulations. In the future, information and norms may be produced by an industry fearful of more regulation, by a government willing to subsidize or require content information, or by interest groups able to collect and distribute data on programming to generate scrutiny. In this manner, information and ideas may ultimately hold the key to limiting the dangers associated with another information product, violent television programming.

CHAPTER 1

WHY IS TELEVISION VIOLENCE A PUBLIC POLICY ISSUE?

1. Formally, an externality is defined by two conditions (Baumol and Oates 1988, p. 17):

Condition 1. An externality is present whenever some individual's (say A's) utility or production relationships include real (that is, nonmonetary) variables, whose values are chosen by others (persons, corporations, governments) without particular attention to the effects on A's welfare.

Condition 2. The decisionmaker, whose activity affects others' utility levels or enters their production function, does not receive (pay) in compensation for this activity an amount equal in value to the resulting benefits (or costs) to others.

2. For recent overviews of the impact of violence on television, see Spitzer 1986, Comstock and Paik 1991, Paik and Comstock 1994, Gunther 1994, and the National Television Violence Study (NTVS) 1996a, 1996b.

The NTVS and UCLA Center for Communication Policy 1995 studies provide information on the violent content of television programming. The NTVS, which I refer to frequently for evidence on statistical measures of violent content, was a joint study involving researchers from four different universities. At the University of California, Santa Barbara, Dale Kunkel, Barbara Wilson, Dan Linz, James Potter, Ed Donnerstein, Stacy L. Smith, Eva Blumenthal, and Timothy Gray studied the content of violent entertainment programming. At the University of Texas, Austin, Wayne Danielson, Dominic Lasora, Ellen Wartella, Charles Whitney, Shannon Campbell, Saam Haddad, Marlies Klijn, Rafael Lopez, and Adriana Olivarez monitored the violent content of "reality programming." At the University of Wisconsin, Madison, Joanne Cantor, Kristen Harrison, and Marina Krcmar analyzed the reactions of children and parents to viewer advisories. At the University of North Carolina, Chapel Hill, Frank Biocca, Jane Brown, Fuyuan Shen, Jay M. Bernhardt, Leandro Batista, Karen Kemp, Greg Makris, Mark West, James Lee, Howard Straker, Henry Hsiao, and Elena Carbone assessed the impact of television antiviolence messages. I will generally refer to the work of these multiple research teams as the NTVS work. The UCLA Center for Communication Policy monitoring report had as its principal investigator the center's director, Jeffrey Cole.

For an overview of the legal issues involved with restrictions on media content such as television violence, see Sunstein 1993, Corn-Revere 1995, Edwards and Berman 1995, Minow and Lamay 1995, and Spitzer 1996 (which uses an economic model to assess the impact of the V-chip).

3. For a discussion of risk assessment techniques at Superfund sites and evidence on the cost and benefits of site remediations, see Hamilton and Viscusi 1994, 1996.

4. A television show's rating in a given demographic group is defined as the percentage of the potential viewing audience tuned to the show. A program's share refers to the percentage of viewers watching television that are tuned to the program. Ratings data used in this book come from Nielsen Media Research (1993a–d, 1994a–h, 1996a–b),

which I generally refer to as Nielsen. Ratings data for children and teens for November 1993 are from Nielsen 1994b.

5. Data for network children's programs and prime-time programs came from Nielsen 1994b. I define violent television genres as those that had mean violent acts per hour as calculated by the National Coalition on Television Violence greater than the network prime-time mean of 8.4 violent acts per hour that I calculated from NCTV data for network television programs from 1980 to 1991. See table 1.2 and chapter 6 for more on the NCTV counts. Ratings for syndicated children's programs are from Nielsen, 1994d. Ratings for dinner hour and late night programming genres were compiled for the nineteen markets analyzed in chapter 7, with the ratings data from Nielsen 1994f reports for the 1992–93 television season and is derived from information in Nielsen 1996a.

6. Note that another source of variation in estimates of television consumption is sampling variability. For a description of sampling techniques used by Nielsen, see Nielsen 1993d.

7. Signorielli, Gross, and Morgan 1982 offers a review of violence ratings.

8. Gerbner et al. 1978, p. 179.

9. See Signorielli, Gross, and Morgan 1982.

10. Gerbner and Signorielli 1990 presents data on patterns from 1967 to 1989.

11. Seigel 1993, p. 1.

12. Lichter and Amundson 1992, p. 6.

13. Center for Media and Public Affairs 1994, p. 4.

14. Cowan (1979) and Montgomery (1989) describe how the NCCB used Gerbner's definition of violence and developed their own narrower measure of "murder-mayhem" that focused on "aggressive personal violence." The NCCB, led by former FCC Commissioner Nicholas Johnson, published rankings of the use of violence in programming and determined which companies sponsored violent programming. For the fall 1976 rankings the top ten sponsors of violent programming were "(1) Chevrolet, (2) Whitehall Labs' Anacin, (3) American Motors, (4) Sears, Roebuck, (5) Eastman Kodak, (6) Schlitz beer, (7) Procter & Gamble soaps, (8) General Foods, (9) Burger King, and (10) Frito-Lay" (Cowan 1979, p. 248). Assessing the impact of these ratings, Cowan (p. 249) notes:

Though no formal consumer boycott had been organized, the threat, or possibility, that one might be forthcoming, had had a profound effect on advertisers. And the advertisers, by pulling their spots from action shows, made their muscle felt at the networks. When the networks announced their fall schedules that May [1977], the new lineups had been drastically changed. Police shows were out.

Montgomery (1989) describes how the scrutiny attracted by the NCCB efforts led many advertisers to develop policies against advertising on violent programs. In the wake of declining violence levels on television, the NCCB eventually stopped monitoring advertiser support of violent programs.

15. See chapter 5 for a fuller description of the AFA.

16. National Coalition on Television Violence 1991, p. 7. For the use of NCTV violence counts to study the application of movie ratings, see White 1994.

17. The difference of means T statistic for violent acts per hour in PG versus PG-13 is -1, while the T statistic for the difference in the sexual content index for PG versus PG-13 movies is -2.6 (statistically significant at .01). Note that Cantor, Harrison, and Krcmar (1996, p. 35) find that

when a parent sees a "PG" rating for a movie, he or she does not know if that rating was assigned because of language, violence, sex, or a combination of these things. Our analysis of the NTVS sample of movies revealed that "PG" and "PG-13" movies have considerable overlap in contents, and that "PG"-rated movies issued before 1984 are misleading because they often are as full of objectionable content as current "PG-13" movies.

18. See UCLA Center for Communication Policy 1995.

19. The broadcast series that raised "frequent issues" with regard to their presentation of violence were *Walker, Texas Ranger; Mantis, X-Files, Due South, Lois and Clark, Fortune Hunter, Tales from the Crypt, VR-5, Marker,* and *American's Funniest Home Videos.* Shows with "occasional issues" were *America's Most Wanted, SeaQuest, Unsolved Mysteries, The Watcher, Rescue 911, Earth2, The Simpsons,* and *The Marshall.*

20. National Television Violence Study 1996b, p. 1-36.

21. Note that the NTVS study also tracked "talk about violence" in reality programming, thus providing an additional measure of content that may be potentially harmful to children.

22. National Television Violence Study 1996b, p. 1-29.

23. Ibid., 1996a, p. x.

24. Paik and Comstock (1994, p. 535) concluded based on their metaanalysis that the r value of .31 found for the overall magnitude of effect in this study is a medium effect size, and the r value of .10 for criminal violence is a small effect size. Although small r values may be dismissed as negligible effect sizes, evaluating the same effect size in terms of the binomial effect size display (BESD) leads to a different conclusion. For example, an r value of .10 corresponds to an increase in success rate from 45% to 55%. This 10% increase in success rate, or 10 viewers out of 100 being affected by television violence, cannot be dismissed as an insignificant effect.

25. Spitzer 1986, p. 97.

26. Comstock and Paik 1991, p. 241.

27. Belson 1978, p. 15.

28. Milavsky et al. 1982, p. 487.

29. Comstock and Paik 1991, p. 253. For assessments of the impact of television violence that argue against prevailing conclusions, see Freedman 1984, 1986, 1988. McGuire 1986, and Committee on Communications and Media Law 1997.

30. Eron and Huesmann 1987, p. 196.

31. Ibid., p. 198.

32. Comstock and Paik 1991, p. 260.

33. Pearl, Bouthilet, and Lazar 1982, p. 6.

34. Comstock and Paik 1991, p. 287.

35. See Hawkins and Pingree 1982, Comstock and Paik 1991, and National Television Violence Study 1996b, for reviews of these effects.

36. For debates about the "mean world" syndrome, see Hirsch 1980, 1981, Hughes 1980, and Gerbner and Signorielli 1990.

37. Gerbner, Morgan, and Signorielli 1994, p. 13.

38. Comstock and Paik 1991.

39. Existence and bequest values in environmental economics are elicited through the survey methodology of contingent valuation, in which respondents are asked to state

their willingness to pay for different environmental states. See National Oceanic and Atmospheric Administration, 1993, for a discussion of the difficulties inherent in this methodology.

40. This is an example of what Amartya Sen terms the "Impossibility of a Paretian Liberal." Sen (1970, p. 157) noted:

If someone takes the Pareto principle seriously, as economists seem to do, then he has to face problems of consistency in cherishing liberal values, even very mild ones. Or, to look at it in another way, if someone does have certain liberal values, then he may have to eschew his adherence to Pareto optimality. While the Pareto criterion has been thought to be an expression of individual liberty, it appears that in choices involving more than two alternatives, it can have consequences that are, in fact, deeply illiberal.

41. See Viscusi 1992, p. 73. This is a comprehensive treatment of the empirical and theoretical issues raised in value of life literature, issues which would arise in a full cost-benefit treatment of policies dealing with media violence.

42. The evidence in chapter 5 suggests that the net impact of a parental discretion warning placed on a violent theatrical film may be the replacement of two paid ads with two network promotions. If one values the ads' information content by their market price (c. $100,000) and assumes that the promotions for the networks have zero value (e.g., they simply redistribute viewers from one channel to another), then the net loss to society in terms of advertising changes is $200,000.

43. This calculation assumes that the utility of adult viewing audiences for the movie is not affected by the knowledge that the movie carries a warning label. It also assumes that children who are led by their parents to engage in an alternative activity instead of viewing the violent film do not experience a change in overall utility.

44. The regulatory reform bill passed the House but stalled in the Senate in 1995. See Mayberry 1995.

45. For descriptions of proposals affecting television violence offered in Congress during 1995, see Stern 1995a, 1995b.

46. Oldenburg 1992.

47. If physiological responses in viewers to violent programming are identified, one would be able to quantify the specific adverse health outcomes from programming in the form of increased chances of high blood pressure or heart disease. "Copycat crimes," in which viewers are said to imitate specific violent acts, periodically attract significant media attention as evidence of the direct harms of a particular program. Yet even here it is difficult to establish whether a program generated the violence, whether the program simply influenced the form of violence chosen, or whether the program drew media attention to violence that would sometimes go uncovered by the press.

48. Centerwall (1992, 1993) estimates that half of homicides in the United States are due to media violence. He argues that the delay of between 10 to 15 years between the introduction of television and a doubling in the murder rate in the United States, Canada, and South Africa is consistent with children learning scripts of behavior from television and then acting upon them once they reach adolescence and adulthood. He underscores that only a relatively small number of individuals need to be affected to generate a large increase in the homicide rate. This research points to the effect of television in general, rather than the impact of specific violent shows.

49. Kushman 1994, p. C1.

50. Simon 1994, S5199.

51. U.S. House Committee on the Judiciary 1989, p. 111.

52. Gerbner 1994a, p. 2.

53. Kim 1994, p. 1431.

54. Simon 1989, S5793.

55. Nyhan 1994, p. 71.

56. Gerbner 1994a, p. 2.

57. Glickman 1988, H10. This was part of the debate over the Television Violence Act of 1988.

58. Simon 1989, S5793.

59. This statement was made by Arthur Taylor, then president of CBS, to FCC Chairman Richard Wiley in a 1974 meeting of network presidents at the FCC. See Cowan 1979, p. 97. Since that time, cable television has replaced broadcast independent stations as the target of broadcast network complaints about competitors using violence to attract audiences.

60. Schlegel 1993, pp. 214–15.

61. Nossiter 1985, p. 402.

62. Owen and Wildman (1992) provide the best review of the development of models of television programming, including those by Steiner (1952), Beebe (1977), Spence and Owen (1977), Wildman and Owen (1985), Noam (1987), Waterman (1990), Wildman and Lee (1989), and Spitzer (1991). Additional works that focus in part on empirical assessments of broadcast outcomes include Noll, Peck, and McGowan 1973, Owen, Beebe, and Manning 1974, Owen 1975, Levin 1980, Noam 1991, Waterman 1992, Wildman and Robinson 1995, Shachar and Anand 1996, and Shachar and Emerson 1996. Many of these models focus on questions of the impact of market structure on program diversity and social welfare. Spitzer (1996) uses a spatial model in the manner of Hotelling (1929) to examine explicitly the market for violent television programming and the potential impacts of the V-chip on that market. What distinguishes the model I develop in this section is the combination of assumptions that viewers fall within discrete viewing groups, that advertisers may value these viewers differently, that costs of programming vary by genre, and that externalities arise from consumption. This new combination of assumptions yields a set of testable hypotheses about the market for violent programming.

63. The model makes a number of simplifying assumptions:

A. Programming is portrayed in terms of a single dimension, the amount of violence contained in the show. Particular viewers are assumed to watch only a given type of programming, rather than choosing among different genres. For spatial models in which a given viewer may consume many different types of programming (depending of the location of programming alternatives), see Noam 1987 and Spitzer 1996. One difficulty with spatial models is that results are highly sensitive to assumptions made about the shape of the distribution of viewer preferences and the number of competitors.

B. Advertising values are taken as determined outside the interactions of the television market, that is, the value placed by advertisers on particular viewers is assumed to emerge from a larger market for advertising across different media. For a discussion of models of advertising purchases, see Rust 1986. Baker 1994 details how advertising values may influence the content of the print media.

C. The costs of programming are assumed to be given, so that if a channel wants to show a low-violence program it faces a set cost of C_l for the show. Channels competing for viewers within a genre are all assumed to offer shows with the same cost and to split viewers evenly. The number of viewers attracted to a given show is not assumed to vary with the (production) cost of the program.

D. An equilibrium where profits are equal across all three programming genres may, depending in part on the value of N, imply fractional values for the number of channels that choose to program within a given genre such as N_1. One can think of the channel divided up into fractions as providing part of its programming in each of these genres (which also entails assumptions about the programming costs faced by this fractional channel).

64. In describing the current calculus in the entertainment industry, film critic Michael Medved notes, "In deciding which few of these projects will get made and which won't, the studios appropriately ask two basic questions: Will it make money? Does it have artistic value? Executives should add a third fundamental question to the equation: What will be the impact of this proposed entertainment on the society in which we live?" See Medved 1995, p. E2.

65. While television violence generates negative externalities for children, some types of programming (e.g., children's educational programs) will generate positive externalities for this demographic group. See chapter 3 for a discussion of the market for children's educational programs.

APPENDIX 1.2
SOCIAL WELFARE

1. In their analysis of a competitive pay cable industry (which is a model of monopolistic competition), Owen and Wildman lay out a number of assumptions that their analysis is based on, including that "new programs are introduced as long as it is profitable to do so (that is, as long as they generate revenues large enough to cover production costs)" and that "in deciding whether to offer a program and how to price it, each programmer assumes that its competitors will respond by adjusting their prices to avoid any loss of audience" (Owen and Wildman 1992, p. 109). Their general analysis is based on the Spence-Owen model of programming. They develop in their analysis the general result that competitive pay television will be biased against shows "highly valued by a few viewers" and against "expensive programs" (Owen and Wildman, 1992 p. 111).

2. The figures without externalities in figures A1.1 and A1.3 are based on graphs from Owen and Wildman 1992 , pp. 110, 117. Reprinted by permission of the publisher from *Video Economics*, Bruce M. Owen and Steven S. Wildman, Cambridge, Mass.: Harvard University Press, Copyright 1992 by the President and Fellows of Harvard College.

3. Note that area b stops at the point that D equals zero on the assumption that viewers are not paid to watch programs. If viewers were paid to watch programs, then b would extend to the point that $D + E$ equals 0. In the last section of this triangle, private valuation of the program by the marginal viewers would be negative (e.g., one would have to pay them to watch), but the net benefit to society could be positive because of the externality value per viewer E.

4. The majority of viewers of a violent program may not experience increases in aggression, fear, or desensitization after viewing a violent show. The impacts will vary with many demographic factors, especially age (e.g., children are thought to be particularly susceptible to adverse effects). E should therefore be thought of as an expected value of the costs to society. Consider a hypothetical example. If there are 1,000 viewers of a program and 5 are led by the consumption of a violent program to commit aggres-

sive acts that impose a cost on society of $1,000 each, the expected value of E for each viewer would be $(5/1000) * \$1,000 = \$5$ per viewer.

Chapter 2
Adult Audiences

1. See Webster and Lichty, 1991, for a description of how ratings data are collected and for information on the evolution of Nielsen ratings. The figures collected by Nielsen Media Research form the basis of advertising and programming decisions in the television industry.

2. Washington Post media critic Howard Kurtz discussed the interplay between ratings and content on newsmagazines in "Sex! Mayhem! 'NOW'!: In the *Newsmagazine Derby,* NBC's Star-Driven Vehicle Puts a Sheen on Sensationalism," *Washington Post,* March 14, 1994, p. D1. NOW was a prime-time newsmagazine program on NBC during 1994 featuring Tom Brokaw and Katie Couric. The program was criticized for doing thirty-nine out of eighty-nine stories during one period on crime and violence. The show's executive producer Jeff Zucker commented on the focus on violence by saying that, "It's not something I'm overjoyed about. . . . Everyone's now doing these violent stories and it's become a staple of newsmagazines. We're doing well and it's worked for us." During the coverage of the Tonya Harding scandal following the attack on figure skater Nancy Kerrigan, Zucker discussed the impact of minute-by-minute Nielsen ratings on his story selection for the newsmagazine. "When I looked at the minute-by-minute stuff on Tonya, it went up a lot. That's how we knew to keep doing it."

3. The Times Mirror survey was a national sample of adults age 18+, so it does not provide information on viewing consumption by teens and children. In the sample overall, 31% of the respondents were defined as heavy viewers of television (4 or more hours of viewing in the previous day), 39% were moderate viewers (2–3.5 hours of daily television), and 31% were light viewers (0–1.5 hours of viewing the previous day). See Times Mirror Center for the People and the Press 1993.

4. Per capita spending is $10,212 for those 26–34, $14,650 for those 45–54, and $12,477 for those 65–74. See Thomas and Wolfe 1995, p. 27.

5. See ibid., p. 29.

6. Ibid., p. 27.

7. See Simmons Market Research Bureau 1994, for information on the relative volume of consumption of individual products. All text figures on relative consumption by gender come from this source.

8. See Nielsen 1994a. The percentage breakdown of the adult population in television households by age-gender category is thus females 18–34, 17.7%; females 35–49, 15.5%; females 50+, 19.0%; males 18–34, 17.4%; males 35–49, 15.0%; and males 50+, 15.4%. For the February 1993 Times Mirror survey the percentage breakdown of the sample is females 18–34, 15.8%; females 35–49, 15.4%; females 50+, 18.6%; males 18–34, 20.0%; males 35–49, 16.5%; and males 50+, 13.6%. The survey sample demographics are thus close to the percentages for the U.S. television household population as a whole.

9. See Nielsen 1993c.

10. The ten-question index included the nine questions used by the Times Mirror survey to classify respondents into light, medium, and heavy consumers of violent programming, plus a separate survey question on the viewing of *Terminator 2.*

11. The overlap of viewing audiences for violent programs allows advertisers to reach the same viewers with multiple exposures to a given message. While 33% of the survey respondents said they regularly watched reality crime and emergency programs such as *Cops* and *Rescue 911* and 21% regularly watched fictional crime dramas, 14% of the sample reported watching both programs. Of the reality crime viewers 42% also watched fictional crime programs, while 65% of the fictional crime viewers also were regular watchers of shows such as *Cops*.

12. The logit model in table A2.1 was run to yield an estimated probability of heavy violence viewing. If all variables are set to their sample means, the predicted probability is .44. The change in probabilities in table 2.3 was estimated by setting all demographic variables to their sample means, except for the two indicated in the row. These were all dummy variables. The probability was estimated with the value represented by the first demographic characteristic and then the value represented by the second characteristic. For example, for a female viewer the female dummy variable was set to 1 and then run with the other sample means, which yielded a probability of .36. The model was then run for a male viewer (i.e., female dummy = 0), which yielded a predicted probability of .51. The change in the probability of being a heavy consumer of violent television programming for a female versus a male viewer in the sample is thus $(.36 - .51) = -.15$. This methodology was used to derive probability changes in logit models throughout the book.

13. The UCLA Center for Communication Policy report (1995) found that *Walker, Texas Ranger* was one of the 10 prime-time broadcast network shows (out of 121 monitored during the 1994–95 season) that frequently raised issues of concern because of violent content. The report noted, "Violence is completely integral to the concept of this series. Chuck Norris plays a laconic ranger who uses his martial arts skills to catch Texas bad guys. . . . The show seems to be simply a vehicle for Norris to demonstrate his physical abilities. While the fight scenes are always a part of the story, they are excessively long and graphic only to showcase Norris' impressive fighting skills and have little to do with character or plot" (UCLA Center for Communication Policy 1995, p. 40). *Murder, She Wrote* did not raise issues of concern about violence in the UCLA monitoring. For the fall 1993 sweeps period, *Walker, Texas Ranger* drew a 5.2 rating among males 18–34 and 5.1 among females 18–34, versus 3.1 for males and 4.0 for females in this age group for *Murder, She Wrote*. *Murder, She Wrote* drew a 32.0 rating for females 55+ and 22.5 for males 55+, compared to a rating of 12.7 for women 55+ and 12.0 for men 55+ for *Walker, Texas Ranger* (Nielsen 1994b). Although *Murder, She Wrote* often was the most watched show in its time period in terms of total households, its failure to attract younger viewers resulted in lower ad rates. As one assessment of advertising rates noted, "Advertisers have shown that they don't recognize these (older appeal) shows,' [CBS executive David] Poltrack acknowledges, while maintaining that a show like 'Murder, She Wrote'—which boasts an educated, affluent and yes, older audience profile—is perhaps 'the most undervalued program on network television.' Per-unit advertising prices for the veteran drama run fourth in its time period despite a slot-winning household rating." See Lowry 1995, p. 19.

14. The NCTV used the same definition to count violent acts per hour in television shows and in movies shown in theaters (National Coalition on Television Violence 1991, p. 7):

NCTV's violence scores are actual counts of physically violent acts, hostile acts committed with the intention of hurting another person. NCTV uses a weighting system so the minor acts of violence, such as an angry push or shove, count very little (1/3 of an act of violence), and violence with serious consequences such as an attempted murder, murder, rape or suicide count as somewhat more than a standard act of violence (1 2/3 acts of violence).

15. Note that teens and children were not included in the Times Mirror survey, so their moviegoing is not reflected in table 2.5 or 2.6. The survey question asked whether the respondents had seen the movie "at home or in a theater," so the figures may reflect viewing in different viewing windows (e.g., in the theater or television).

16. Simmons Market Research Bureau tracks consumption of products by demo-graphic group, including movie consumption. While Simmons estimated that those 18–34 were 45.8% of the male population, they were 36.9% of the male population that reported that they had attended a movie within the last 30 days (a ratio of 1.24). The ratio of percentage of male movie population to percentage of male total population was 1.03 for males 35–49 and .7 for males 50+. Among females, those 18–34 were also more likely to have attended movies in the last 30 days. For females, those 18–34 accounted for 35.1% of the female total population and 45.3% of those females who had attended a movie within the last 30 days (a ratio of 1.29). For females 35–49 the ratio was 1.08 and for females 50+ the ratio was 65. See Simmons Market Research Bureau 1994.

17. The movies with warnings were more likely than other films to be from violent genres (such as crime dramas, science fiction, and adventure), involve murder or at-tempted murder, and be described by *TV Guide* in its write-ups as involving violence. Note that not all movies whose descriptions mention murder or attempted murder or that are labeled as crime dramas are violent. The viewer discretion warnings printed in the television listings are used to denote which movies carried warnings, though additional programs could also have carried audiovisual warnings from the networks.

18. See Comstock et al. 1978. A movie's rating for a given demographic group is defined as the percentage of the potential television audience among that group estimated to have viewed the film. See Webster and Lichty 1991, for a description of how ratings are measured.

19. Shales 1994.

20. The overall rating referred to in table 2.7 is the percentage of potential households that watched the film, while share refers to the percentage of households actually view-ing television at that time that watched the film.

21. Note that these regressions rely on limited descriptions of movies to code film content indicators that may be associated with violence (e.g., murder or family crime themes, genre indicators such as crime drama, mystery, adventure, and reviewer refer-ences to violence) rather than a visual assessment of the violent acts in each film.

22. Shows in violent genres, that is, those in genres with violent acts per hour greater than the average for prime-time programs as calculated with the NCTV data, were de-fined as "violent" for this analysis. See chapter 6 for discussion of the NCTV data. The breakdown of violent shows included 3 mysteries (*Unsolved Mysteries, NBC Friday Night Mystery, Murder, She Wrote*), 8 reality programs (*Top Cops Special, I Witness Video, Cops 2, America's Most Wanted, Cops, Rescue: 911, Code 3 Special, I Witness Video Special*), and 16 violent dramas (*X-Files, Seaquest DSV, Lois and Clark, NYPD Blue, Brisco County, Walker, Texas Ranger, Moon over Miami, Law and Order, Matlock Specials, South of Sunset, Commish, Matlock, In the Heat of the Night, In the Heat of the Night Special, Missing Persons*). If programs were aired at different times during the

month they often had several entries in this dataset since Nielsen (1994e) reported ratings and ad prices for each of the different showing times separately. For example, there were three entries for *Matlock* since the program aired on both Thursday and Saturday during the November 1993 sweeps period. The total of 140 prime-time programs analyzed includes ratings averages for the movie slots in the network schedules, such as the *ABC Sunday Night Movie*. These movie slots are not treated as violent programs in the analysis, even though they sometimes contain violent programming such as violent theatrical films.

23. There is also a gender gap in reactions to news coverage. While 52% of the sample agreed that television news is too full of violence, 44% of males versus 60% of females agreed with this assessment. While 38% of the respondents overall agreed that television news reporting does "exaggerate the amount of violence in our country," 43% of men versus 33% of women agreed with this statement. This may relate to the fact that women perceive higher risks of crime and hence view a given amount of coverage of violence as less exaggerated. For evidence that women report higher estimated risks than men in many different settings, see Flynn, Slovic, and Mertz 1994.

24. Note that 56% of men versus 23% of women said that violence on television shows did not bother them. Controlling for the amount of violent television consumed, women were more likely to see entertainment programming as too full of violence and less likely to report that they were not bothered by violent television programs. For example, among male 18–34 heavy consumers of violent programming 50% said there was "too much violence" in nonnews programming and 47% said there was a "reasonable amount." Among female 18–34 heavy consumers of violent programming, 60% said there was "too much violence" and 36% said there was a "reasonable amount." When asked whether the amount of violence or the amount of sex on television bothered them more (or if both bothered equally), a higher percentage of women (32%) than men (26%) said they were bothered more by the amount of sex than the amount of violence on television. The fact that women who are heavy viewers of television violence are more likely to be critical than men of the amount of violence has led some to posit that part of the heavy viewing by women may come about from joint viewing decisions with men who prefer to watch heavy amounts of violent programming. However in logit analyses similar to that in table A2.1 run for the full sample of women and for women 18–34, being married was associated with a lower probability of being a heavy consumer of television violence.

25. With respect to news programming, light viewers of violent programming were much more likely to agree that "TV news should run more stories about 'good news'" and fewer stories about violence" (87% agreed with this) than heavy viewers (70%). The overwhelming majority of light viewers (78%) and heavy viewers (68%) said that they felt graphic violence was on television to "attract viewers," although heavy viewers were more likely (25% vs. 14% for light viewers) to agree with the alternative explanation presented that graphic violence is shown on television "because it is necessary to make a point."

1. Nielsen 1993c indicates that in November 1992 children 2–11 in television households averaged 23:01 hours of television viewing per week, with 5:42 hours of viewing concentrated in prime time.

2. November 1993 ratings figures are from Nielsen 1994a.

3. For a discussion of the Children's Television Act, see Federal Communications Commission 1996.

4. The Center for Media Education's *Report on Station Compliance with the Children's Television Act*, September 1992, found that stations were often claiming entertainment-oriented cartoons as educational and shifting the programs that were clearly educational to early morning viewing slots such as 5:30–7:00 AM. Describing the plot summaries offered in station license renewal applications that explain why a station considers a program to be educational, the center found (p. 6) that the renewal application for New Orleans station WGNO contained summaries such as:

Chip'n Dale Rescue Rangers: "The Rescue Rangers stop Chedderhead Charlie from an evil Plot. The rewards of team efforts are the focus in this episode."

Bucky O'Hare: "Good-doer Bucky fights off the evil toads from aboard his ship. Issues of social consciousness and responsibility are central themes of program."

GI Joe: "The Joes fight against an evil that has the capabilities of mass destruction of society. Issues of social consciousness and responsibility are show themes."

In a separate study of license renewal applications, Dale Kunkel found that many entertainment-oriented shows such as *GI Joe, Teenage Mutant Ninja Turtles,* and *The Jetsons* were being cited as educational programming and that 29% of the stations in the sample that he examined had failed to provide in the license renewal application the minimal amount of information (day, time, duration, and brief content description) required by the FCC for programming the stations claimed served the educational and informational needs of children. See Kunkel 1993.

5. See chapter 2 for a list of the violent programs.

6. For teens, the first violent program to appear in the percentage ranking was a *Code 3* special, which ranked thirty-eighth with an audience percentage of 10% teen viewers. The show with the lowest percentage of teen viewers overall was *Murder, She Wrote,* where only 1% of the audience was aged 12–17. The first violent show in terms of absolute number of teen viewers was *Seaquest,* ranking forty-second with 1,470,000 teen viewers. For children 2–11, the first violent program to show up in terms of audience percentage was *Lois and Clark,* which ranked twenty-eighth with an audience comprised of 19% children 2–11. The show with the lowest audience percentage comprised of children was *Law and Order* (2% of whose audience was comprised of children 2–11). *Lois and Clark* was also the first violent program to turn up on the ranking of shows by absolute number of children viewing (twenty-seventh, with 3,060,000 viewers aged 2–11).

7. UCLA Center for Communication Policy 1995, pp. 111–12.

8. Lasorsa et al. 1996, p. 13.

9. UCLA Center for Communication Policy 1995, p. 112.

10. See Thomas 1992, p. 7, and Press Association Limited 1994.

11. Lieberman and Bennett wrote letters to the parent companies that own talk shows to urge executives to "clean up the programming you are putting on the air . . . set some basic standards that your production company will not violate, and put an end to the deceptive tactics that have humiliated many talk show guests and given the industry a black eye." The letter stated, "The parade of pathologies and dysfunctions seen on talk TV offers our children a warped view of the world, making the abnormal appear normal, and is teaching them that emotional violence is the best way to resolve conflict." Shows cited in this campaign included *Geraldo, Jenny Jones,* and *Ricki Lake.* See *U.S. News-wire* 1995.

12. Lasorsa et al. 1996, p. 13.

13. UCLA Center for Communication Policy 1995, p. 113.

14. The twenty-eight violent crime programs in syndication included in table 3.4 are *Kung Fu: The Legend Continues, Renegade, Highlander, Acapulco H.E.A.T., Cobra, The Untouchables- AS* (twice), *21 Jump Street, Matlock, The A Team, Hunter, Knight Rider, Acapulco H.E.A.T. Repeat, Magnum, Kojak, Gunsmoke, Bonanza, Airwolf, Wise Guy, Simon and Simon, Remington Steele, The Untouchables, Wild, Wild West, Rifleman, Barnaby Jones, Hill Street Blues, Cannon,* and *Streets of San Francisco.*

15. The additional shows included in this definition of violent programs are *Star Trek: The Next Generation* (three times), *Rescue 911* (twice), *Cops, Star Trek: Deep Space Nine* (twice), *Twilight Zone, Time Trax, Real Stories of the Highway Patrol, Emergency Call, On Scene: Emergency Response, Prime Suspect, Star Trek,* and *Real Stories of the Highway Patrol Weekend.*

16. See U.S. House Committee on Energy and Commerce 1994.

17. See UCLA Center for Communication Policy 1995.

18. See chapter 8 for an extensive discussion of the TV Parental Guidelines.

19. Federman 1996 summarizes the types of "consumer discretion technologies" available that allow parents to screen or block certain channels or programs.

20. Figure 3.1 does not reflect the costs to industry of developing and implementing the rating system or the initial cost to the parent of purchasing the V-chip. A cost-benefit analysis of the ratings and V-chip system would balance these costs with the benefits to society of reduced exposure of children to violent programming.

21. A comparison between the opinions of the general public and entertainment industry participants found that industry figures, while concerned about media violence, were less likely to view violence on television and movies as a serious or very serious problem (Guttman 1994). A majority of the public surveyed said that violence in entertainment media is a "major factor" that contributes to the level of violence in America, while a majority of industry figures viewed it as a minor factor.

22. Bower 1985. For a review of recent laboratory evidence on the use of content information by children, parents, and other viewers, see Cantor and Harrison 1996, Cantor and Krcmar 1996, and Bushman and Stack 1996.

23. Comstock and Paik 1991, p. 51.

24. Opinion Research Corporation 1993.

25. See Greenberg, Abelman, and Cohen 1990, as cited in Comstock and Paik 1991.

26. Roper and TVSM 1993.

27. U.S. House Committee on Energy and Commerce 1994. The four broadcast networks had proposed in June 1993 to use an advance parental advisory stating, "Due to some violent content, parental discretion is advised."

28. For a comprehensive review of the rating of television and movie content across different countries, see Federman 1996.

29. Cantor and Harrison 1996, p. III-14.

30. See McDonald 1986.

31. Parents theoretically might switch channels not only because of the benefit to their child of shielding him or her from objectionable content but also because of the broader benefits to society, as discussed in chapter 2. The logic of collective action, however, would predict that parents would not act to shield a child because of broader social benefits unless the parents were strongly altruistic toward society. Whether a parent voted in the 1992 election was included as a proxy for a parent's "civic mindedness," but this was not statistically significant in predicting intervention. The degree that parents

intervene in shielding their children from violent or otherwise objectionable material on television will likely depend on private benefits (e.g., concern for their child) rather than broader benefits to society, unless they are encouraged to consider the broader social benefits through the creation of a social norm to do this.

32. Note that some children report that they do perceive the *Roadrunner* as violent programming. As Comstock and Paik (1991, p. 152) note, "Snow (1974) interviewed 50 children between the ages of 4 and 12 as to whether certain portrayals were violent. About one-fourth so described a 'Road Runner' cartoon; about one-half, a fighting clown sequence; about two-thirds, a scene from a western; and all, news footage of battle action. Younger children somewhat more frequently described the cartoon and fighting clowns as violent."

33. Cable News Network 1993.

34. See NTVS 1996b, "Chapter 2: The Effects of Exposure to Media Violence." This section draws heavily on the NTVS summary of media effects.

35. Ibid., p. I-28.

36. Ibid., p. I-29.

37. Rideout 1996.

38. Ibid., p. 6.

39. Examples of children's shows and their network or station in the NTVS sample include *Auggie Doggie* (CAR), *Muppet Babies* (NIK), *Heathcliff* (CAR), *Daisy-Head Mayzie* (TNT), *Under the Umbrella Tree* (DIS), *Captain Planet* (KCAL), *Gumby* (NIK), *Beetlejuice* (NIK), and *Cartoon Express* (USA). See NTVS 1996b, p. I-78.

40. Ibid., p. I-86.

41. NTVS 1996a, p. 21.

42. NTVS 1997a, p. 28. The researchers called depictions a "high risk" for stimulating aggression if they combined in one scene an attractive perpetrator, violence that appeared justified, unpunished violence, violence with few consequences for the victim, and violence that "seems" realistic. Many of the "high-risk" portrayals for children under 7 involve cartoons since for these young viewers cartoons may seem "realistic."

43. In the NCTV newsletter (NCTV 1991, p. 7) the organization noted:

NCTV's violence scores are actual counts of physically violent acts, hostile acts committed with the intention of hurting another person. NCTV uses a weighting system so the minor acts of violence, such as an angry push or shove, count very little (1/3 of an act of violence), and violence with serious consequences such as an attempted murder, murder, rape or suicide count as somewhat more than a standard act of violence (1 2/3 acts of violence).

44. The NCTV data covered broadcast network children's programs for 1982–87 and 1989–91 and syndicated and cable programs for 1985 and 1989–91.

45. Neither of these differences is statistically significant at the .1 level. The broadcast network average does not include violence counts for the PBS shows in the NCTV data, which had low violence counts. For example, in the March, 1985 NCTV monitoring *Sesame Street* and *Mr. Roger's Neighborhood* both had zero acts of violence per hour.

46. During the debate over the development of the television rating system, the president of Nickelodeon Herb Scannell noted (see Walley 1996):

The truth about cartoons is that they are doing what live-action can't do. They are doing the fantastic, exaggerated beyond what humans can do. . . . In animation, we do the squash and squish like "Ren and Stimpy." The squash and squish is a tradition in cartooning and if that becomes a problem, then that's over the top.

47. Federal Communications Commission 1996, p. 15.

48. Owen and Wildman 1992, p. 148.

49. See Federal Communications Commission 1996, p. 5, for a discussion of the studies of the benefits of educational programming for children.

50. Fay et al. 1995, p. ii.

51. Ibid. p. viii.

52. One preview of the fall 1993 programming lineups opened with the assessment, "When it comes to the battle over quality children's programming, cable networks such as Showtime, The Disney Channel and Nickelodeon are stomping all over the networks." See Holbert 1993. In describing the marketing of its program *Nick News* in the broadcast syndication market, the chairman of the Viacom Entertainment Group noted that "'Nick News' is the ideal vehicle for stations looking to acquire quality, pro-social children's programming that also can generate ratings. Kids recognize that the Nickelodeon names mean fun even as they're informed." See Layne 1993.

53. See Federal Communications Commission 1996, for details about the debate over rules implementing the CTA.

54. In describing one educational program (*Frog*) an industry participant noted (Newsbytes, News Network 1994): "It's an ensemble group of multicultural kids who have a clubhouse in an attic. They find objects, create inventions, and solve problems involving science. It's the story line that engages, not the learning. It's that kind of engaging program—you have to reach before you teach."

55. Margaret Loesch, President of the Fox Children's Network, told an en banc FCC hearing that:

Although the Commission has stressed the importance of long-form educational programming, our experience has been that attractive short-segment interstitial material, embedded throughout the entertainment programming that we know children are watching, is a most compelling means of conveying information to our audience, perhaps more effective than standard-length programming. Indeed, the standard program lengths were not designed to best take advantage of the developing cognitive abilities of young children. Rather, short segments, which grab children's attention immediately and hold it briefly, have been shown to be a much more effective didactic tool for the electronic media.

See Loesch 1994, p. 5.

56. The Nielsen data come from Nielsen 1994e. If a show appeared in different time slots during November 1993, the Nielsen data treat this as a different show, so that some programs appear in the data twice. The programs termed educational were *Name Your Adventure, Beckman's World, Citykids* (twice), *Schoolhouse Rock, California Dreams, Saved by the Bell, Dog City, CBS Storybreak Special, Disney's Little Mermaid, Bobby's World* (twice), *CRO,* and *ABC Weekend Specials*. All other children's programs were defined as noneducational in the analysis.

57. Prime-time ratings data are from Nielsen 1994b.

58. Educational programs "broadly defined" included *Adventures in Wonderland, Biker Mice from Mars, Bill Nye—The Science Guy, Captain Planet and the Planteers, Energy Express, Exosquad, Hallo Spencer, Mad Scientist I, Mad Scientist II, New Adventures—Captain Planet, Nick News, Pick Your Brain, Scramble, Widget, Xuxa*. Educational programs narrowly defined were *Adventures in Wonderland, Bill Nye—The Science Guy, Energy Express, Hallo Spencer, Nick News, Pick Your Brain, Scramble,* and *Xuxa*. Ratings data are from Nielsen 1994d.

59. Children in low-income households or in households headed by those without a college education consume more children's television programming, including educational programming. The positive externalities associated with educational programming may benefit these children more if they are not receiving as many educational benefits at home or in the classroom.

60. Linda Mancuso, vice-president, Saturday Morning and Family Programs, NBC, described the network's teen-targeting strategy to a congressional hearing in 1994 on the CTA (see Federal Document Clearing House 1994):

NBC looked around and noticed that our competitors—the other networks, syndication, cable and PBS—were all providing programs for young children. But no one was consistently offering programs targeted to teens, even though these kids want and need programming created specifically for them. As we have learned, teens can be influenced in a very positive way by entertaining programs that present positive role models and deal with the issues they confront as adolescents . . . . So, in 1992 NBC decided to build on the strength of *Saved by the Bell*. We completely abandoned animated cartoons in favor of an entire two-hour block of live-action programs for the most underserved segment of the television audience—teens.

In describing the younger audience aimed at by ABC in the fall 1994 children's schedule, Jennie Trias, president of ABC's children entertainment noted (see Littlefield 1994): "We're concentrating on 6- to 11-year-olds as a primary target, with real emphasis on 7- to 10-year-olds. . . . It's a little harder to produce for the under-4 set, because there are still a lot of concepts they have to grasp."

61. Note that the data in this section demonstrate that ad revenues for educational programs are lower for broadcast networks. I do not have information on net profits, which would combine data on revenue with network program costs.

62. Center for Media Education 1992. The station description for the claim that *Yo Yogi!* was educational read (p. 6), "Snag learns that he can capture the bank-robbing cockroach more successfully by using his head, rather than his muscles." A station's claim (p. 7) that a weekday 1:30 PM airing of *Leave It to Beaver* was educational claimed that in the episode, "Eddie misunderstands Wally's help to girlfriend, Cindy, and confronts Wally with his fist. Communication and trust are shown in this episode."

63. See Federal Communications Commission 1996, p. 20.

64. This statement is from WLFL-TV 22, *Children's Educational/Informational Programming Report (3rd Quarter 1993)*, submitted by Gayle Hurd, Public Affairs Director, WLFL, Raleigh, North Carolina. The report is contained in the public inspection file at the station.

65. See WLFL-TV 22, *Children's Educational/Informational Programming Report (3rd Quarter 1992)*. The report is contained in the public inspection file at the station.

66. Nielsen 1994c contains information on which stations aired a network program at a time other than that regularly scheduled by the network.

67. Nielsen 1994c contains data on scheduling deviations for the 4 program weeks during the November 1993 sweeps period. A show is counted as having a deviation if it is shown at a time other than the network scheduled time for any of these 4 weeks. Note that for the majority of stations that deviate they will "deviate" for all 4 weeks, that is, they will shift the program to a time other than the network scheduled time for all 4 weeks.

68. Difference of proportion tests for figures in this section are: 20.2 versus 10.3, $Z = 3.9$, .01 level; 9.7 versus 3.5, $Z = 2.3$, .05 level; 27.6 versus 16.9, $Z = 1.8$, .1 level; 12.3

versus 8.7, $Z = 0.4$; 23.3 versus 20.1, $Z = 0.3$; 5.0 versus 3.6, $Z = 0.1$; 9.9 versus 3.5, $Z = 2.4$, .05 level.

69. See Media Dynamics 1994, pp. 57–63, for May 1993 cost per household ratings point estimates for 30-second television spots in each local television market. These figures are much higher in larger markets.

70. The largest shift of an educational program detected in the November 1993 data was the airing of *Saved by the Bell* by KVBC in Las Vegas at 1 AM during all four weeks of November.

71. The networks do schedule children's programs to air at different times on the two coasts, which means that ABC will schedule a show such as *Bugs Bunny/Tweety Show* to air at 10:30 AM in the eastern time zone and 9:30 AM in the western time zone.

72. Changes in probabilities in the logit specifications for dummy variables involve setting all variables to their mean values and then calculating the change in probability from shifting the dummy variable value from a 0 to 1. To calculate the impact of a continuous variable, all variables are set at their means and the continuous variable is set at one standard deviation below the mean and then one standard deviation above the mean.

73. There are many reasons why a larger number of broadcast stations may lead to greater incentives to deviate on the scheduling of network children's shows. More stations may mean more independent stations that are airing cartoons, which could reduce the returns to a network affiliate's airing of a network children's show. More competition may also mean lower profits, which could reduce the likelihood that a network affiliate would be willing to forsake some marginal revenues by keeping a children's show in a desirable time slot. The change in probability of deviation is based on a shift from four to ten stations since the mean number of stations is seven and the standard deviation is three stations.

74. See Hamilton 1996 for a discussion of the types of externalities generated by broadcasters. Ironically, sometimes the programming that stations will decide to air when they shift Saturday morning children's programming is local news. For example, WFMY, the CBS affiliate in Greensboro, announced in 1994 that it would air a local news program on Saturdays from 7–10 AM. The article describing the programming change noted, "WFMY tested the idea of a Saturday morning news show in March 1993 when it covered the effects of the Triad's severe ice storms. The response was phenomenal, [station president Colleen] Brown said. Further research showed that more than 60 percent of the households in WFMY's six-county market did not include children." The scheduling change meant that *Garfield & Friends* and *CBS Storybreak* would not be shown on Saturdays by the affiliate and that *Beakman's World* would be shifted to air at 6:30 AM. See Pressle 1994.

75. In 1988 WCBS shifted *The CBS Evening News* "to 6:30 PM from 7 PM and inserted *Win, Lose, or Draw* into the traditional slot for the network news, banking on getting better performance and making more money from the game show. Since the switch, the newscast by Dan Rather has lost some of its audience and the game show has not lived up to expectations." See Kleinfield 1989.

76. For positive reviews of the ability of *CRO* (which received partial funding from the National Science Foundation) and *Beakman's World* to teach scientific concepts, see Business Wire, 1994 and Mendoza 1993. Assessments of the educational content of NBC's educational programs were typically more negative. As one review (Mangan 1994) noted:

NBC, whose motto seems to be "Why mess with success?" keeps the same lineup for its third season with teen-oriented programming now labeled "TNBC" (the "T" stands for teen). The result is an entire Saturday morning of live-action comedies. What is new about TNBC's lineup is this: According to NBC Entertainment executives Warren Littlefield and John Miller, the entire lineup is now considered FCC friendly. That labeling may be appropriate for *Name Your Adventure* and *NBA Inside Stuff*, but including *Saved by the Bell: The New Class* and *California Dreams* may be a stretch.

77. Federal Document Clearing House 1994.

78. For its Saturday programs, three NBC shows are said to be educational (*California Dreams*, *Name Your Adventure*, *Saved by the Bell*) while one is noneducational (*Running the Halls*).

79. This effect is derived by setting all variables to their mean values and estimating the change in probability of deviation when the educational program and *Nightline* deviation dummies are changed from 0 to 1.

80. The fifty-seven stations chosen for analysis were those whose local news broadcasts were summarized in a transcript file in Lexis. Chapter 7 provides a fuller description of the sample and coding.

81. The mean percentage of local news teasers devoted to crime was 9.6% and the standard deviation was 7.3%, so the change in probability of deviation is estimated by changing the percentage of local news teasers from 2% (approximately one standard deviation below the mean) to 17% (approximately one standard deviation above the mean).

82. For a detailed examination of policies designed to improve children's educational programming, see Minow and LaMay 1995 Jordan 1996, and Krotoszynski 1997.

83. Federal Communications Commission 1996, p. 3.

84. Sunstein 1996, p. 914.

85. Turner does have a reputation of trading off profits for a personal interest in programming in some areas. In assessing the direction of HBO under Ted Turner, *Daily Variety* noted (Dempsey 1996):

It looks as though Ted Turner will be overseeing HBO, at least for the next five years, but the question is: Which Ted Turner? Will HBO's executives find themselves dealing with Ted as Dr. Jekyll, the astute businessman who'll exercise a benign hands-off policy so the network can continue to rack up record cash flows and harvest bushels of rewards? Or will Mr. Hyde rear his unsightly head, the Ted Turner who second-guesses his executives, micromanages programming decisions and insists that the network produce series, movies and specials on American Indian history or environmental concerns.

86. The diminishing role that local ownership plays in television station ownership was noted in the debate over the Telecommunications Act of 1995, during which Representative Manton noted, "Seventy-five percent of the stations in the country are group owned. And more than 90 percent of those are owned by groups headquartered in cities other than where their stations are located." See Manton 1995.

87. In the language of principal-agent models, agents have freedom to pursue interests other than those of the principal to the degree that there is "hidden action" or "hidden information" that makes it difficult for principals to observe this divergence. Since scheduling, ratings, and returns to advertising buys in terms of audiences purchased are

readily observed, it may be difficult to rely on the pursuit of norms among managers in this area. Managers willing to provide support for children's education will also face the decision of whether the money lost through scheduling educational programming or buying advertising on these shows would yield a higher impact on children if it were spent directly on educational programs in schools.

88. Public goods are goods that are characterized by "nonrivalness" (i.e., consumption of the good by one person does not reduce the amount available for consumption by another person) and "nonexcludability" (i.e., individuals cannot be excluded from consuming the good even if they have not paid for the good). Goods that have these characteristics may be underprovided for in the private market.

CHAPTER 4
PROGRAMMING VIOLENCE

1. National Television Violence Study 1996b, p. I-85. The NTVS examined whether a program had nine or more violent interactions without controlling for the length of the show, so that one reason movies have more violent interactions in this analysis is that they are longer in duration than shows in other programming genres. The calculation of violent acts per hour from the NCTV data in chapter 1 confirms that theatrical films have a much higher mean rate of violent acts per hour than that for prime-time network broadcast series. The NTVS found (1997a) that 61% of the programs in its sample for the 1995–96 television season contained violence, indicating that the prevalence of violence did not change much between the 1994–95 and the 1995–96 television seasons.

2. The UCLA Center for Communication Policy report (1995, p. 77) concluded: "A large majority of the violence on broadcast television that raises concerns can be found in theatrical films. Unlike the other areas [of programming], there has been no improvement here. Possibly owing to the large number of violent films coming out of Hollywood, television theatricals are as big a problem as they have ever been." In its second report, which focused on the 1995–96 season, the center (1996, p. 88) found: "Most of the gruesome, gory and truly gratuitous violence is still found in theatrical films, particularly action films. But there is considerably less of it this year on broadcast television."

3. For movies rated by critics on the one- to four-star scale, movies with violent indicators generally earned lower critical ratings. Mean star ratings were 2.0 for films with violent indicators versus 2.2 for those without on premium channels ($T = 7.0$), 2.3 for films with violent indicators versus 2.4 for those without on basic cable channels ($T = 5.1$), and 2.3 for films with violent indicators versus 2.5 for those without on broadcast networks ($T = 1.2$).

4. *Seinfeld* is frequently described as a show "about nothing." For example, a 1996 review of the program states:

"A show about nothing": that was the catch-phrase for "Seinfeld" that got generated . . . in its first season. Set in Manhattan—still, after all these years, the real psychic capital of America—it traces the meanderings of four people through their lives, four people who happen to share an addiction to the same mediocre neighborhood diner, the same anxiety about their lives' futures—and mutual affection. Nothing does happen in most of the episodes, in fact, except for quibbling and quarreling among the four major characters.

See McConnell 1996, p. 19.

5. For the November 1993 sweeps period, for Saturday from 1–4 PM the rating for

children 2–11 was 19.2 versus 9.3 for 1–4 PM on Monday through Friday. See Nielsen 1994a.

6. The programming information in *What's On Tonite!* was produced by New Century Productions of Kattskill Bay, N.Y. The information was shipped free to Internet users each day who requested the data from editor@paperboy.com. This programming guide (in the same manner as printed programming guides) did not identify the source of its ratings information. No indication was given whether the content indicators for theatrical films shown on network television, for example, reflected an assessment of the edited version shown on broadcast television or the unedited version shown in theaters or on premium channels. Of the MPAA-rated films, approximately 3% were films released prior to 1968, so these ratings may reflect assessments of MPAA categories that were applied retroactively to movies released before the MPAA began to rate new releases.

7. Nearly a third of the films in the sample were not rated under the MPAA system. Of these unrated films, 34% were released in the 1990s, which suggests that they were made-for-television or cable productions. Nearly half (53%) of the nonrated films were released prior to the year that the MPAA first started to rate films (1968), so these may be considered theatrical releases from earlier eras. The viewing guide provided indicators for content such as violence or adult situations, but these were primarily provided for theatrical movies previously rated by the MPAA. Note that theatrical films may be more likely to contain the content defined by the warning indicators than films made for broadcast television or earlier Hollywood releases.

8. Some unrated films in the sample, e.g., those without MPAA ratings, did have content indicators for violence. Of 3,603 unrated films, 360 had violent content indicators, 344 indicators for adult language, 370 indicators for adult situations, and 205 for nudity. When these 3,603 films were defined as violent or nonviolent based on genre, 1,548 were in "violent" genres.

9. For the full sample of movies ($N = 11,603$), the distribution of movies by total warning indicators was zero warnings, 30.4%; one, 10.9%; two, 22.7%; three, 21.4%; and four, 14.6%. In terms of star ratings by critics, 8.8% were not rated, 13.8% had one star, 43.2% two stars, 30.1% three stars, and 4.1% four stars. In terms of MPAA ratings, 31.1% were not rated, 3.4% were G, 20.4% PG, 13.4% PG-13, 31.7% R, and .1% NC-17. The warnings total is the sum of the number of indicators for violence, adult situations, adult language, or nudity that a movie received in the program guide.

10. For the sample of rated movies ($N = 7,989$), the content breakdowns were violent, 63.0%; violent indicator, 63.0%; adult language, 78.5%; adult situations, 67.4%; and nudity, 33.8%. Total warnings were zero, 5.2%; one, 14.5%; two, 31.3%; three, 29.4%; and four, 19.6%. The star ratings distribution was not rated, 3.6%; one star, 18.0%; two stars, 46.7%; three stars, 28.9%; and four stars, 2.9%. The MPAA ratings distribution was 4.9% G, 29.6% PG, 19.4% PG-13, 46% R, and .1% NC-17.

11. Although the sample included sixteen movies on PBS, these were not included in the analysis of broadcast network films so that this category can be used to examine the behavior of the four main commercial broadcast networks. Ideally, one would want to consider the audiences for the movies on broadcast networks versus premium or basic cable channels, but ratings data for individual movies on premium or basic cable are not publicly available.

12. For discussion of the different property rights of broadcast and cable networks, see Carter, Franklin, and Wright 1994 and Franklin and Anderson 1995.

13. Table A4.2 shows that broadcast and basic cable channels are similar in the percentage of violence, nudity, and adult situations in the theatrical movies they show. In

terms of violence, 67.4% carried violence indicators on premium channels versus 57.6% of those on broadcast television. Of the MPAA-rated films on premium channels 38.4% had indicators of nudity versus 27.3% for broadcast films. Premium channels still rely more on films with four content warnings, which accounted for 25.9% of their rated films versus 13.4% on broadcast and 8.1% on basic cable. Basic cable channels, which include some outlets focused on families and children, were the most likely to broadcast G or PG films. Among MPAA-rated movies, 11.1% of basic cable offerings were rated G (versus 4.7% for broadcast, 1.6% for premium) and 38.5% were rated PG (versus 27.3% for broadcast and 24.9% for premium). Even among the set of rated movies, premium channels were still more likely to use R-rated films (50.4%), although the gap with broadcast (40.7%) or basic (38.1%) is much narrower when these channels are compared only on the use of MPAA-rated films.

14. In the *1995–96 Family Guide to Prime Time Television* released by the Parents Television Council, network shows were rated so that family friendly shows received a green light in the program guide, shows with a mixed message were labeled with a yellow light, and shows that rely on "gratuitous sex, explicit dialogue, violent content or obscene language" received a red light. In this ranking, Fox received the highest number of "red light" shows seven versus five for CBS and three for ABC (Boston Herald 1995). Journalists' accounts of the Fox programming strategy frequently referred to the network's "sleazy image" (Pergament 1995). In discussing his attempt to reposition the network during the 1995–96 season, Fox President John Matoian said that, "I've tried to reduce sophomoric [content] across the board. I think the mistake this network made was, it tended to latch onto what worked. For example: sex. And did it for its own sake. It never had a real reason to be other than what it was." See Pergament 1995.

15. See Lowry 1996, p. F1.

16. Part of the reason that Fox is an outlier in terms of broadcast content is that the network is more likely to rely on theatrical films (which carry content indicators in the viewing guide) than the other three networks, which generally use made-for-television movies for the majority of their films. For Fox 60% of the movies carried MPAA ratings in the program guide, versus 52% for ABC, 22% for CBS, and 32% for NBC. If one compares only the MPAA-rated films used by the four broadcast networks (see table A4.3), Fox is an outlier only on language and adult situations. For rated films, 85.3% of the Fox offerings had indicators of adult language and 73.5% had indicators of adult situations. ABC ranks first in the percentage of rated films with violent indicators (61.4%).

17. According to one assessment of Lifetime's programming (Battaglio 1996), "Lifetime targets women 18–49 but skews toward the higher end of the demographic. The average Lifetime viewer is 39 years old and has 2.3 children."

18. Note that Comedy Central does blank out the use of some adult language in its comedy programs. As one article noted (Pacheco and Kalish, 1996):

A stand-up performance by Dennis Miller aired on Comedy Central a few weeks ago, and if you watched it with the closed captions it was hard not to notice that even though the naughty words were beeped out on the audio track, they were spelled out in their entirety in the closed captions. The f-word, the s-word and a couple of TV no-no's describing body parts were captioned. The program, "Dennis Miller: Black and White," was produced by HBO in 1990 and licensed to Comedy Central. HBO's policy is not to censor any language, but Comedy Central doesn't air four-letter words.

19. If one restricts the analysis only to the sample of 7,984 MPAA-rated films shown in the early evening and prime time by these basic cable channels, the span of programming narrows in terms of use of violence (ranging from 34% to 83%), adult language (35% to 85%), adult situations (23% to 83%), and nudity (0 to 50%). Looking at each channel's use of MPAA-rated films in table A4.3, it is still true that WGN (81.3%) and the Science Fiction Channel (83.2%) select high proportions of films with violence indicators and that Disney (34.3%) and Comedy Central (37.0%) use films with lower percentages of violence. Note that when the Family Channel does program an MPAA-rated film, it tends to contain violence (62.8%). In terms of nudity use, Bravo (40.4%) and USA (37.2%) are still at one end of the spectrum and the Family Channel (0%) is at the other. When Lifetime does use an MPAA-rated film, the channel is likely to select one with adult situations. This female-targeted channel actually has the highest percentage of MPAA-rated films with adult situations, 82.8%. Note also that its use of MPAA-rated films with nudity (34.5%) also places it at the higher end of this type of programming. Lifetime's use of MPAA-rated films that rely on violence (37.1%) is still among the lowest of any channel on basic cable and is much lower than those for rated films on broadcast television.

20. Even among R-rated films in the sample, the number of warning indicators per film has increased over time from 2.7 for R-rated films in the 1970s to 2.9 for those in the 1980s to 3.3 for those released in 1995.

21. If one analyzes only MPAA-rated films, the relative positions among the premium channels remain fixed, with Cinemax on the high end and Encore much lower in the use of violent or sexual content. If one compares the use of content in rated films, the gap between individual broadcast and individual premium channels narrows. If one compares broadcast networks and Encore in their use of MPAA-rated films, Encore would rank the lowest in terms of use of films with violent indicators—46.5% for Encore, versus 51.4% for the lowest broadcast network (NBC) and 61.4% for the highest broadcast outlet (ABC). Encore's use of adult language would place it in the middle of the broadcast networks, while its use of adult situations is greater than broadcasters except for Fox. Its use of nudity would place it fourth in the broadcast spectrum. Thus in terms of MPAA-rated films, Encore's attempts to develop a nonviolent brand image would place it within the lower part of the broadcast network spectrum in terms of controversial programming.

22. See Schatz 1995, p. A41.

23. The use of nudity in Cinemax films has caused critics to use the phrase "Cinemax skin flicks" in their reviews of popular culture (see Petrek 1995, Whitehead 1995). Both HBO and Cinemax are owned by the same parent company, Time Warner. The differences in content selections of the two channels demonstrate how a company may pursue two different market segments by establishing different brand identities for these outlets.

24. Most of the films without critical ratings were recent. Of those without a critics' rating in the sample, 76% were made in 1995 or 1996.

25. In describing a programming switch planned for the basic cable channel USA, the director of programming indicated in January 1995 that the channel was going to diversify from the "thriller/woman-in-distress genres it has become known for." See Katz 1995.

26. Cinemax advertises its use of "low-budget" movies as part of its market niche. In 1995 the channel had a month long "Troma Festival," which began with showing Troma Films' productions *Toxic Avenger I* and *Toxic Avenger II*. According to the president of Troma Films, "We're like Disney in that we have our own studio and our own brand identity. Our fans know what to expect from the Troma name." This brand identity

means that what "one can expect is scantily clad, buxom women, plenty of gratuitous violence, cheesy special effects and hokey dialogue." See Belcher 1995, p. 1.

27. If one restricts the analysis in table A4.4 to the use of MPAA-rated films only, several contrasts emerge in comparing the broadcast networks and the premium channels. In the selection of MPAA-rated films, Fox uses the highest percentage of R-rated films (67.6%) in the entire spectrum of broadcast, basic, and premium channels. Among premium channels, Cinemax has the highest reliance on R-rated films (62.3%). Encore programs a majority of its films as PG (56.4%). HBO, Cinemax, Showtime, and the Movie Channel all choose R-rated movies the most frequently, followed by PG-13 movies, and then PG. For ABC and CBS, however, this pattern is reversed. These networks rely first on R and then on PG movies, followed by PG-13. The difference between subscriber decisions that influence premium incentives and the advertiser incentives faced by these two broadcast networks may account for the reversal of PG and PG-13 uses.

28. Note that these calculations relate MPAA ratings to the content indicators of the movies as indicated in the viewing guide for television, indicator ratings that may or may not reflect edits made for television. The analysis takes as given the content indicators stated in the viewing guide, which would be the information accessible to a parent trying to decide what a PG or PG-13 movie contained.

29. This difference of proportion, although small in magnitude, is statistically significant ($Z = -2.3$). Cantor, Harrison, and Kremar (1996) note that the PG-13 rating was not introduced until 1984, so that PG movies from the post 1984 era could be expected to contain less objectionable content than PG movies prior to this time period. They found for a sample of films shown on television from the post-1984 period (p. 32):

Although these two ratings are still not distinguishable in terms of language content (with "PG" again slightly exceeding "PG-13" in adult language), a slightly higher portion of "PG-13" than "PG" movies had violence codes, and "PG-13" had a heavier weighting of "V = Violence" relative to "MV = Mild Violence."

30. The difference between the mean number of warnings for PG movies (1.9) and PG-13 (2.3) is statistically significant at the .01 level.

31. If one defines violent films as those in violent genres, then movies in violent genres that earned four stars accounted for 1.8% of the films in the sample.

32. See Nielsen 1993b.

33. In Z tests of difference of proportions for each of the four indicators and the definition of violence based on genre, none of the differences of proportions is statistically significant at the .1 level.

34. Note that in Z tests of use of rated films with four warnings the difference between sweeps and nonsweeps months was not statistically significant for the broadcast, basic cable, or premium channels.

35. For WGN, $Z = -3.1$ for use of violent films in nonsweeps versus sweeps months (.01 level) and $Z = -3.9$ for the use of films with violent indicators (.01 level).

36. Z test values for the difference of violent movies in nonsweeps versus sweeps months were $-.85$ for ABC, 1.08 for CBS, -3.6 (.01 level) for Fox, and 2.37 for NBC (.05 level).

37. Z test values for the difference of proportions of movies with violent indicators were not statistically significant for ABC, CBS, Fox, or NBC.

38. Fox weekday programming for its affiliates runs from 8 PM through 10 PM so that its movies start at 8 PM. For the other network affiliates programming from the parent

network runs from 8 PM through 11 PM, with movies often starting at 9 PM and running until 11 PM.

39. For WGN's use of adult situations $Z = -1.4$ and for nudity $Z = -1.6$ (statistically significant at the .10 level).

40. For adult situations the Z tests were ABC, $Z = -1.8$ (.10 level); CBS, $Z = 1.8$ (.10 level); Fox, $Z = .8$; NBC, $Z = .7$. For nudity the Z tests were ABC, $Z = -2.4$ (.05 level); CBS, $Z = -.2$; Fox, $Z = -.6$; and NBC, $Z = 2.5$ (.05 level).

41. The films on Disney that carried nudity indicators were *Baby: Secret of the Lost Legend*, *Continental Divide*, *Running Brave*, *The Anderson Tapes*, and *The Three Musketeers*.

42. Shales 1993, p. B1.

43. Zurawik 1994, p. D1.

44. Hutcheson 1993, p. A1.

45. Zurawik 1994, p. D1.

46. For November 1993 the average rating for ABC's *NFL Monday Night Football* was 7.3 for women 18+ and 15.1 for men 18+. See Nielsen 1994b.

47. See chapters 3 and 4 in Owen and Wildman 1992 for a discussion of the relationship between the structure of channel ownership and program diversity. Both TNT and TBS were owned by Turner Broadcasting in 1995.

48. TNT's Monday Nitro block competes against the USA network's *WWF Monday Night Raw*, a professional wrestling program. See Brown 1995a and Business Wire 1995.

49. Channels in Britain may still run into trouble if they broadcast controversial material soon after 9 PM. For example (Hellen 1992): "Melvyn Bragg's *A Time To Dance*, about a middle-aged bank manager's affair with a teenager, was censured by the BSC [Broadcasting Standards Council] for the timing of a rape scene. It was shown on BBC1 at 9.05 PM—after the adult viewing watershed but still seen by many children."

As of 1992, Britain had a watershed hour of 9:00 PM, versus 10:30 PM for Italy and France and 11 PM for Germany.

50. See Nielsen 1994a, pp. 44–45. The average total rating for Monday through Friday for 8:00–8:30 PM for children 2–11 was 33.2 and for teens 12–17 it was 31.9.

51. The 24-hour movie data came from the same Internet viewing guide described earlier, *What's on Tonite.* Differences in data format and availability meant that the 24-hour data covered the dates April 1 to May 26, 1995 and July 17, 1995 to January 9, 1996.

52. For November 1993, the total ratings for children 2–11 from 1–4 PM were 9.3 for Monday–Friday, 19.2 for Saturday, and 17.8 for Sunday. The figures for teens 12–17 were 7.4 for Monday–Friday, 19.4 for Saturday, and 20.0 for Sunday. See Nielsen 1994a.

53. The Z statistics for difference of proportion for the noon to 2 PM blocks for Monday through Friday versus Saturday were -1.71 (statistically significant at .1) for violence and -2.34 (at .05) for nudity. For 2–4 PM these figures were -3.29 (at .05) for violence and -1.57 for nudity. For the comparison between the weekday afternoons and Sunday afternoons, only violence in the 2–3:59 PM block was statistically significant ($Z = -1.92$, at .10 level).

54. $Z = 2.13$, statistically significant at .05 level.

CHAPTER 5
ADVERTISING

1. Much of the analysis in this chapter first appeared in my essay "Does Viewer Discretion Prompt Advertiser Discretion? The Impact of Violence Warnings on the Tele-

vision Advertising Market" in *Television Violence and Public Policy*, edited by James T. Hamilton. Ann Arbor: University of Michigan Press, 1998. Permission to draw upon that material is gratefully acknowledged.

2. See Mathis 1996, p. A1.

3. Ibid.

4. Zoglin 1996, p. 58.

5. Landler 1996, p. B1.

6. See the reanalysis of Times Mirror polling data in chapter 2. The original polling information was published in Times Mirror Center for the People and the Press 1993.

7. Companies targeting young demographic groups may seek product tie-ins with violent movies. Prewitt 1991 describes how the Subway sandwich chain developed a promotional campaign with the producers of *Terminator 2*, a violent film starring Arnold Schwarzenegger. Subway had product placements in the film, promoted the movie in the sandwich stores with a special meal package linked to the movie, and used a 32-ounce Pepsi cup marked with the movie logo. As a spokesman for Subway put it, "The demographics of this movie work out well for us by appealing to our customer, a male 18 to 34 years old."

8. National Television Violence Study 1996a, p. 20.

9. For the fall 1993 sweeps period, the AFA's top twelve sponsors of violence on prime time, listed in order, were Chrysler Corp., ConAgra, Burroughs Wellcome, Grand Metropolitan, Unilever, Miles Inc., Helene Curtis Industries, Campbell Soup, Pepsico, Ciba-Geigy, J. C. Penny, and Clorox. For the May 1995 sweeps the AFA based its "Dirty Dozen" ratings on incidents of sex, violence, and profanity in the shows that companies sponsored. The group listed the "12 Top Sponsors of Prime-time Filth" as Visa USA, Anheuser-Busch, Sara Lee, Toyota Motor Sales, MasterCard International, Paramount Communications, Maybelline, Adolph Coors, MCI Communications, Bristol-Myers Squibb, Unilever, and Coca-Cola. See American Family Association 1993, 1995.

10. The AFA called for a boycott of Unilever, maker of Elizabeth Arden cosmetics and Close-Up toothpaste, for sponsoring *NYPD Blue*, a show which Reverend Wildmon described as an attempt to "open the doors of sexual nudity on prime-time television." The AFA "claims to have changed the advertising policies of some of the mightiest corporations in America, including Burger King, Clorox, and SC Johnson. Pepsi pulled a 'sacrilegious ad' featuring Madonna and cancelled sponsorship of her world tour after AFA lobbying." See Olins 1995.

11. Mermigas 1996, p. 2.

12. Nielsen 1996b.

13. Landler 1996, p. B1.

14. Ibid.

15. Federman (1996, p. 19) notes, "According to Don Ohlmeyer, West Coast President of NBC, the network loses between a quarter of a million to a million dollars in advertiser pull-out whenever an advisory is placed on a movie of the week. He also notes that some of that loss is made up by other advertisers who aren't bothered by an advisory."

16. This is a simplified description of advertising decisions. For models of advertising purchases that take into account the frequency of exposures of a given group to particular messages, see Rust 1986.

17. A rating for a demographic group is defined as the percentage of the number of people in that group watching a program. A program's share for a demographic group is the percentage of the members of that group watching television at a given time that are watching the particular program.

18. The figures for violent programs on network affiliated broadcast stations include

both programming they receive from the network and the other fare such as syndicated shows that they air.

19. This point was noted at a meeting of academics I attended with members of the TV Ratings Executive Committee in Washington, D.C., on September 17, 1996.

20. For information on parents' reaction to different rating system proposals, see Cantor, Stutman, and Duran 1996. This report, entitled *What Parents Want in a Television Rating System: Results of a National Survey*, was sponsored by the National PTA, Institute for Mental Health Initiatives, and the University of Wisconsin–Madison and released during the debate over the formation of the industry rating system.

21. Figure 5.1 is based on the figure on page 126 in *Video Economics*, Bruce M. Owen and Steven S. Wildman, Cambridge, Mass.: Harvard University Press, Copyright 1992 by the President and Fellows of Harvard College.

22. The placement of a warning on a program may or may not cause the advertising price received by the broadcaster to drop. Consider first ads that have already been sold in the "upfront" market. The warning may cause some companies that fear controversy to withdraw from their commitment close to airtime. If the network is able to find advertisers who are indifferent to the warning that are willing to buy this time, the price will not drop. If there are not advertisers willing to pay the previous price, then the broadcaster will have to lower the price to sell the commercial time. In terms of spot market sales, assume there are a set of firms just willing to pay a price X to advertise on the movie. The addition of the warning may then deter some of these companies, but there may still be a number of firms willing to pay this price. If not, the broadcaster may have to lower the price to sell the time on the program with an advisory.

23. In 1994 broadcast television donated $113.9 million in time to Advertising Council public service campaigns. See Elliott 1995, p. D9.

24. See Spitzer 1996 for a discussion of the impact of the V-chip on programming.

25. See UCLA Center for Communication Policy 1995, p. 77.

26. Federal Document Clearing House 1995. This news conference transcript is available in the Lexis News file.

27. National Television Violence Study 1996b, p. I-145. Note that the description of movie genre data is based on films aired on broadcast television (which are often edited), basic cable, and premium cable (which are often unedited). The results did not further distinguish between movies shown on broadcast versus cable.

28. See Simmons Market Research Bureau 1994. Simmons data provide product usage demographics for specific products, for example, the Buick Le Sabre automobile. For those advertised products which were not found in the Simmons study, the commercial was linked to the closest product category information. For example, since there was no product specific information on Golden Crisp Cereal in the Simmons study, demographic information was collected on the general users of cold breakfast cereal.

29. The distribution by genre of prime-time network broadcast movies for 1987–93 was drama, 46%; comedy, 13%; crime drama, 13%; adventure, 6%; comedy drama, 5%; mystery 4%; fantasy, 3%; western, 3%; thriller, 3%; other, 3%; and science fiction, 2%. Film genre was determined by the program's listing in *TV Guide*.

30. Note that for nine of the films listed as originally made for television, the Internet viewer's guide also listed MPAA ratings for these films and indicators of film content.

31. For the theatrical films shown in prime time, the distribution by rating is 1% unrated, 4% G, 30% PG, 24% PG-13, and 41% R.

32. A difference of means test between ratings for 1987–93 versus 1995 is statistically significant at the .01 level for each of the ratings categories in table 5.1.

33. Media buyers explicitly describe programs such as Sunday night movies as often more oriented toward women than men. Describing the shift of the science fiction program *X-Files* by Fox to Sunday evening, one media buyer said, "I think '*X-Files*' will get creamed. That move is a big mistake, because in the fourth quarter of the year TNT and ESPN will have sports to lure male viewers from '*X-Files*,' and the other networks' movies are pretty female-oriented." See Littlefield 1996, p. F9.

34. Of the 357 movies scheduled between May 1, 1995, and February 29, 1996, a total of 252 were coded for commercial content. All movies were recorded and coded that aired during prime time on the four major broadcast networks from May 1 through December 31, 1995 (except for those that were preempted or experienced a recording error). From January 1 through February 29, 1996, only those movies that had a violence indicator or warning were coded. These additional films were coded to increase the size of the comparison sets to test the impact of warning labels. The results in the paper are thus presented as subsample comparisons rather than for the sample as a whole because the sample is intentionally weighted to focus on violent films.

35. The UCLA Center for Communication Policy report (1995, p. 72) notes that a "large number of made-for-television movies have ominous or threatening titles that imply the show will be violent, whether or not it actually is violent."

36. These figures are comparable with previous estimates of nonprogram minutes. In November 1992 there were 13.5 minutes of nonprogram content per hour of prime time on the four major networks. See Jensen 1993, p. 33.

37. Movies and videos were distinguished from the category of product ads because the Simmons data collected for product ads was much more detailed than the data available on consumer demographics for the particular films advertised. Data on general movie and video use were used in analysis of the consumer demographics for movie and video ads.

38. According to an official at Coors Brewing, the company tries to avoid advertising on "family shows" so that they avoid advertising to children and pregnant women. Supporting violent programs may ironically be part of a policy to reduce exposure of children to alcohol advertising. See Bhat 1996, p. 25.

39. Note that the statements here refer to the proportion of a product's consumers made up by different categories of consumers. The assertion that products advertised on violent films with theatrical warnings were more likely to be used by males means that males accounted for a higher mean percentage of the consumers of products advertised on violent theatrical films with warnings (49.6%) than the mean percentage of consumers of products advertised on nonviolent theatrical films (49.2%). These statements do not refer to the absolute number of males who use products advertised on these two different groups of movies. Comparisons are rather made on the basis of what fraction of a product's consumers are in different demographic categories.

40. Since the Simmons data were used at the product specific level (e.g., what percentage of consumers use a particular brand) and category level (e.g., what percentage of consumers use this category of good), the figure on mean adult usage represents an average of both product-specific and category-specific use. Unlike the other percentages that refer to what fraction of a product's consumers are from a particular group of consumers, the "total adult use" percentage does convey information about the absolute number of adult consumers for a product since this is the percentage of adult consumers in the Simmons survey that use the product or product category.

41. The Z statistics for the difference of proportion of male products are: theatrical nonviolent (29%) versus theatrical violent with warnings (39%), Z = −2.5; theatrical

violent with warning versus theatrical violent without warnings (38%), $Z = .2$; made-for-television without warning (32%) versus made-for-television with warning (31%), $Z = .2$; made-for-television with warning versus "violent" made-for-television without warning (28%) $Z = .8$.

42. National Television Violence Study 1996a, p. 20.

43. Second quarter prime-time ratings based on coverage homes for each network for May 29 to June 25, 1995, were 2.4 for TNT, 2.2 for USA, and 1.9 for TBS. See Brown 1995b, p. 20.

44. The "crime" series included were on TNT *Chips, How the West Was Won, Kung Fu, Starsky and Hutch,* and *Wild, Wild West,* on TBS *Matlock,* on USA *Knight Rider, Macgyver, Magnum, P.I., Silk Stalkings,* and *Tekwar,* and on WKFT *High Tide, Legendary Journeys of Hercules, Renegade, The Extraordinary,* and *Vanishing Son.* The mystery series were *Forever Knight* (WKFT), *In the Heat of the Night* (TNT), *Murder, She Wrote* (USA), and *Perry Mason* (TBS). The children's series were *Tattooed Teenage Alien Fighters* (USA) and *VR Troopers* (WKFT).

45. Assessing TNT's programming in June 1995, *Mediaweek* noted: "Arguably the boldest stroke made by Siegel [the network president] et al. came last January when TNT yanked its *Bugs Bunny* cartoon block in access (6–8 PM) in favor of more-adult fare, such as the '70s period piece *Starsky and Hutch* and *In the Heat of the Night.* The latter . . . has hit somewhat of a nerve at the net, increasing the number of adults 25–54 tuning in to the daypart by 52%, and women 25–54 by 58 percent. 'It's not just a bunch of blue-hairs watching,' notes Siegel. . . . TNT's *'Saturday Nitro,'* which features an action movie—often of a campy nature—scheduled from 10 PM to midnight, is up 24 percent in men 18–49, 21 percent in women 18–49 and 23 percent in adults 18–49." See Burgi 1995, p. 25.

46. For discussion of the impact of channel ownership on program diversity, see Owen and Wildman 1992, chaps. 3 and 4.

47. Within cable series there are also evident audience differences. Ads on cable crime series had a higher mean percentage of product users in the 18–24 and 25–34 demographic categories, while ads on mystery programs had a higher mean percentage of product users in the 55–64 and 65+ age groups.

48. Additional evidence that warnings on basic cable movies do not generate the advertiser backlash observed in broadcast films includes the facts that for products advertised on violent cable movies with and without warnings the percentage of male consumers is identical (50.2%) and that there is no statistical difference in the percentage of users without children in the home (56.7% for movies without warnings vs. 56.6% for those with warnings). In contrast, for broadcast films movies with warnings had products advertised that had a higher percentage of male users and a higher percentage of users without children than violent movies without warnings.

49. In describing its results of monitoring *NYPD Blue* eighteen times during the 1994–95 television season, the UCLA Center for Communication Policy report (1995, p. 59) noted, "Envisioned as broadcast television's first R-rated drama, *NYPD Blue* consistently deals with violent themes in a responsible manner. Famous for its use of seminudity and explicit (for network television) language, the show was never found to be irresponsible in its use of violence."

50. See Laurence 1993.

51. See Elliott 1993, p. D20.

52. Coe and Jessel 1993.

53. Elliott 1993.

54. See Nielsen 1994e, p. 5.

55. The regression equation used to estimate the expected advertising price for a program in prime-time broadcast network television in November 1993 was:

Expected advertising price per 30-second ad (in 000$) = −7.4 (6.8) + 2.0e − 3 (5.2e − 3) Men 18–34 viewers + 1.5e − 2 (4.3e − 3) Women 18–34 + 1.7e − 2 (3.3e − 3) Men and Women 35–49 + 1.1e − 3 (1.2e − 3) Men and Women 50+.

Note that standard errors are in parentheses, adjusted R^2 = .71, and the number of viewers in each demographic group is given in 000s. Ad prices were modeled as a function of adult viewing demographics since earlier analysis revealed that children and teens are not the advertising targets for these programs. The model indicates that the number of women 18–34 and number of viewers 35–49 are statistically significant determinants of prime-time advertising prices.

56. Robins 1995, p. 1.

57. Ibid.

58. The November 1995 expected advertising price equation was:

Expected advertising price per 30 second ad (in 000$) = −3.5 (8.6) + 5.7e − 3 (7.2e − 3) Men 18–34 viewers + 2.0e − 2 (5.2e − 3) Women 18–34 + 2.1e − 2 (3.1e − 3) Men and Women 35–49 − 4.6e − 4 (1.8e − 3) Men and Women 50+.

Standard errors are in parentheses, adjusted R^2 = .72, and the number of viewers in each demographic group is given in 000s. Ad price and ratings data were from Nielsen 1996b.

59. Consider that 357 films over the sample period × .14 carry warnings × .02 shift in ads from paid advertising to promos × 77 ads per movie × $100,000 per ad = $7.7 million in forgone ad revenue. This calculation is an approximation, for it ignores the fact that advertiser backlash could cause some ads to be sold at a lower price rather than shifted to promos and ignores the additional revenues that network promotions for shows may generate as they translate into more viewers in the long run. The decision by networks to use some commercial slots for internal promotions indicates that these spots yield positive returns that show up in rates for the advertised programs.

1. See Nielsen 1993c. For men 18+, on average for November 1992 these viewers watched 9:26 hours during prime time and 30:41 hours for the entire week. For women 18+, on average for November 1992 these viewers watched 10:10 hours during primetime and 34:47 hours total each week. Prime time is defined as Monday–Saturday 8–11 PM and Sunday 7–11 PM

2. Media Dynamics 1994, p. 85.

3. Figure 6.1 is based on the figure in Owen and Wildman 1992, p. 44. Reprinted by permission of the publisher from *Video Economics*, Bruce M. Owen and Steven S. Wildman, Cambridge, Mass.: Harvard University Press, Copyright 1992 by the President and Fellows of Harvard College.

4. Rational anticipation of the syndication market also leads some producers to avoid topical references that may not spark audience recognition over time. For example, 'Wind Dancer Productions, the production company behind 'Home Improvement,' 'Thunder Alley' and the upcoming 'Buddies,' has a policy limiting topical references. 'A

name like 'Newt,' which is so unbelievably hot now, may have no significance in six years," says Billy Riback, a consulting producer for the three series. It's dangerous to rely on that humor." See Karlin 1995, p. 3.

5. Another consideration involving program costs and scheduling is the option that a channel has of repeating a program rather than purchasing an additional show. Wildman and Lee (1989) conclude that the "smaller the share of audience that a channel can attract with the first showing of a program, the greater the financial appeal of repetition as a programming strategy." A programmer will trade off the savings from repeating a show with the potential number of viewers who would not view the program a second time. The smaller the channel's initial share when the program airs, the smaller the pool of viewers removed from potentially seeing it during the second showing. Wildman and Lee find in an analysis of 1989 data that the average showing per program episode over the course of a month varied as predicted by the market share of a channel. The average showing per program episode over the course of a month was 1.0 for network affiliates, versus 1.7 for basic cable, 3.9 for pay cable, and 19.3 for pay per view. This affects analysis of the offerings of violent programming by channel. A prime-time broadcast network may air a violent movie only once, compared with multiple airings of a violent film on basic or pay cable over the course of the month. The multiple airings, however, are in part a function of the smaller audiences attracted on basic and premium channels. Analysis of the externalities generated by program scheduling should thus attempt to take into account the size of the viewership of shows by both children and adults.

6. See Gerbner, Morgan, and Signorielli 1994, p. 5. The authors note, "Idle threats, verbal abuse, or gestures without hurting or killing (or threatening to do so) are not coded as violence." See also Gerbner 1994b for an expanded discussion of the market for television violence.

7. National Television Violence Study 1996a, p. ix.

8. The National Coalition on Television Violence data are not ideal measures of indicators of the dangers posed by violence in television programming. The coalition did not report intercoder reliability measures that academic studies such as the NTVS report use to indicate the degree that coders agree on the application of the definition of violence. The measurement used, violent acts per hour, is not linked to specific research results that indicate how this may influence viewer behavior (in contrast to the NTVS study, which identified contextual variables that the research literature indicates affect the influence of a program's violent content). The "bias" of measures derived from an advocacy group is also open to question. Despite these possible objections, I believe the NCTV figures are the best data publicly available on historical patterns of violence in specific programs. I use the data not to indicate the relative impact on children or other viewers of violent content. I rather use the information to identify which shows are in general "violent" so that I can test hypotheses about ratings and costs. The data on violence counts were collected from multiple issues of the NCTV newsletter, such as NCTV 1990.

9. This difference is statistically significant, with $T = 2.4$ for the difference of means test.

10. $T = 20.5$ for the difference of means test between the average number of violent acts per hour in violent programming genres versus the average number of violent acts per hour in nonviolent programming genres.

11. See Guttman 1994.

12. Kiesewetter 1996.

13. The differentiation among products even extends to brand identities established by

particular actors who are associated with violence. Action adventure film star Sylvester Stallone notes that what makes a successful film "is the perfect blending of men and material. But I don't think anyone's ever going to accept me in a comedy—ever, ever, ever. I'm a commodity. If you go to the store and grab a can of Stallone, you open it up and see Steve Martin—you don't want that." See Guttman 1994.

14. In response to the release of the National Television Violence Study, the director of research for NBC (Horst Stipp) indicated that the broadcast networks were already presenting less violence than in past years (Storm and Seplow 1996). Jack Valenti, the president of the MPAA, indicated in 1995 that "there is less violence in the cinema and primetime TV than there has been in a decade." See Galloway 1995. For a discussion on the potential changes over time in incentives to use violent content, see Frank and Cook 1995.

15. Historical data on prime-time broadcast programs, genres, and mean season television household ratings used in this chapter were graciously supplied by William J. Adams. For analysis of network programming strategies and use of different genres of programming, see Adams 1993 and Wakshlag and Adams 1985. Figures were updated through the 1993 season from ratings listed in *Variety*. In 1972 in prime-time broadcast network programming there were 21.4 hours in violent series programming, 30.5 hours in nonviolent series, and 23.5 hours in movie programming. In 1993 the figures were 20.0 hours in violent series, 67.0 hours in nonviolent series, and 20.0 hours in movie programming.

16. National Television Violence Study 1996a, p. 19.

17. In comparing the analysis of their sample of programs for the 1994–95 season with those from the 1995–96 season, the NTVS researchers concluded (1997b, p. 157): "Neither the overall prevalence of violence across programs nor the contextual features involved in presenting televised violence changed appreciably. Indeed . . . not a single measure among our key contextual variables shifted as much as 5% on an absolute scale from Year 1 to Year 2."

18. These data are from the annual "Primetime at a Glance" issues of *Variety*.

19. Disputes about movie costs have arisen in Hollywood because of contract terms that call for some individuals to be paid in part based on a film's "net profits." See Parker 1995, which describes disputes over the profitability of *Coming to America, Forrest Gump*, and *Indecent Proposal*. The author of the book that served as the basis for *Indecent Proposal*, for example, agreed to sell the movie rights for approximately $120,000 and 2 percent of the net profits. Yet according "to the studio's net profit accounting, 'Indecent Proposal' is $35.7 million in the red despite $250 million in worldwide ticket sales." The book's author noted, "It's kind of shocking to me that after all this time has transpired there's not a penny left for the author."

20. This fee generally gives the network the right to air an episode twice. Producers may also earn revenue from selling a program into syndication in the United States or abroad.

21. The T statistic for the difference of means test is 1.8, which indicates that the mean production fees are statistically different at the .1 level of significance.

22. The difference of means T statistic is 2.0 (statistically significant at .05) for the production fees per hour and -3.0 (significant at .01) for the program deficits per hour.

23. The viewership specification used in table A7.1 was used to estimate the probability that a person in the Times Mirror survey indicated that he or she subscribed to cable television. The variables white, east, city, town, suburb, heavy television viewership, and violence viewership were positive and statistically significant. Those relating to

income categories and age 18–34 were negative and statistically significant. The "moderate increase" in the violence viewership index is an increase by one standard deviation in the value of the index.

24. National Television Violence Study 1996b, p. 1-83.

25. Jicha 1996, p. 4D.

26. Lorando 1995, p. E1.

27. Note that within the top five premium cable program sample, there are no statistically significant differences in household ratings if the programs are compared on the basis of indicators for violence, adult language, adult situations, and nudity. For example, the mean rating for the movies with a violence indicator is 2.5 versus 2.5 for the other programs and movies without a violence indicator.

28. UCLA Center for Communication Policy 1995, p. 111.

29. National Television Violence Study 1996a, p. 18.

30. Center for Media and Public Affairs 1994, p. 24.

31. Sagansky continued by saying, "I see the problem in independent stations, which for years have run uncut movies. I see it in basic cable. I'm talking USA—have you seen those movies on USA?" See Hodges 1993, p. 1. Network executives have continually pointed out that independent stations run extremely violent programming. In the 1974 meeting of network executives with FCC Chairman Wiley, CBS President Arthur Taylor complained about the violent content of independent stations by singling out the same program title:

The networks are only part, and in some cases only a small part, of the problem of violence and tasteless material. There are times when CBS rejects a program only to find it turning up on other stations, to our competitive disadvantage. It seems pointless for the FCC to direct its attention to the networks alone while nonnetwork independent stations play very violent, syndicated programs such as *The Untouchables* in the late afternoon and early evening.

See Cowan 1979, p. 97. Note that Sagansky was complaining about the updated version of the series that Taylor complained about nearly 20 years earlier.

32. Data on market characteristics came from Nielsen 1993a, which provides detailed definitions for each variable. The percentages for professional, blue-collar, and service workers refer to the percent of the employed adult population. The percent nonwhite refers to the percentage of the population aged 2+. The gender-age percentages are defined in the following way—of adult women (18+) in the market, what percentage is 18–49, and of adult men (18+) in the market, what percentage is 18–49. Data on which markets carried the syndicated programs came from Nielsen 1994g, 1994h.

33. See Tillotson 1994, p. 1F. Tillotson describes an array of male stars as, "There's the flesh-baring David Hasselhoff and friends of 'Baywatch,' Hulk Hogan of 'Thunder in Paradise' and Fabio, romance-novel cover boy and 'himbo' king of the recently canceled 'Acapulco HEAT.' . . . Lorenzo Lamas of 'Renegade' and Grant Show of 'Melrose Place' may not run around in swim trunks all the time, but they do shed their shirts on cue, wear perpetual pouts and strike macho poses on their motorcycles. Lamas even has his own workout infomercial."

34. Violence in U.S. programming may differ in style than that used in shows in other countries. Iwao, de Sola Pool, and Hagiwara (1981) compared a sample of programming on U.S. television and a sample from Japanese television and found that programs on Japanese television showed more suffering and that "the most important violence, that

experienced by major characters, is something that arouses distress and sympathy, not something to be cheered."

35. Gerbner, Morgan, and Signorielli 1994, p. 15.

36. Some programs may be shown abroad without translation, so this approach to sampling exported programs would miss these series. If violent shows were less likely to require translation, then using the *BIB Television Programming Source Book* listing of translated programs may underrepresent the role that violent programs play in U.S. program exports.

37. Geoffrey Cowan's *See No Evil: The Backstage Battle over Sex and Violence on Television* (1979) details the controversy over television violence in the 1970s. In a meeting of broadcast network executives and FCC Chairman Wiley in 1974, the industry executives stressed that network attempts to deal with television violence and sex were hampered by competitive pressures from programming by other stations, including independent stations and PBS affiliates. Wiley responded that, "The other way of dealing with the separate station problem . . . would be to put a new question on the license-renewal form asking each station to tell us what its policy is on accepting and scheduling programs containing violence and sex" (Cowan, p. 98). The network officials strongly opposed this idea. The chairman also suggested "issuing a general policy statement outlining what we expect of licensees in guarding against sex and violence, particularly when there are large numbers of children in the audience."

38. In November 1974 FCC Chairman Richard Wiley had convened a meeting at the FCC with the presidents of ABC, CBS, and NBC to talk about television violence. During the fall the chairman had given a speech in which he said with regard to "violence and obscenity" on television that "if self-regulation does not work, governmental action to protect the public may be required" and he called for "intelligent scheduling, appropriate warnings and perhaps even some kind of industry-administered rating program." CBS President Arthur Taylor took the lead in responding to FCC pressure by proposing a revision to the National Association of Broadcaster's Television Code that would state that the first hour of prime time would be suitable for family viewing. The NAB Television Code Review Board eventually issued a policy that stated that during 7–9 PM "entertainment programming inappropriate for viewing by a general family audience should not be broadcast" and that warnings should be placed on problematic shows. The Writers Guild brought a suit against the networks and the FCC charging that the family viewing policy violated the First Amendment and that the adoption of the policy violated the Administrative Procedures Act since the policy had been adopted without a formal process of government regulatory consideration. These complaints were based on the view that the industry policy emerged from the FCC's prompting and thus constituted state action. In 1976 Judge Warren Ferguson ruled that "the adoption of the Family Viewing Policy by each of the networks constituted a violation of the First Amendment" in part because FCC Chairman Wiley "violated the First Amendment by issuing threats of government action, should industry not adopt the Family Viewing Policy, or the equivalent thereof." The networks gradually backed away from this policy. This summary of the family viewing hour is based on Geoffrey Cowan's extensive chronicle *See No Evil* (1979).

39. The court's opinion indicated "it is hard to accept the idea that the fear of federal regulation was not a powerful factor" in the networks' formulation of the Family Viewing Policy. Since the policy was viewed as a product of state action, the court concluded that "the adoption of the Family Viewing Policy by each of the networks constituted a violation of the First Amendment." See ibid., p. 230.

40. The impact of controversy on a company's willingness to sponsor a program will depend in part on the nature of a company's consumer base, a point developed more fully in chapter 5. Note that even if some companies withdraw from sponsorship of a program, this does not necessarily imply that advertising prices on the show will drop. This will depend in part on whether the companies that step in to purchase advertising on the controversial program are affected by the potential for consumer backlash. See Spitzer 1996 for a full discussion of how the V-chip may influence programming decisions.

41. Noll, Peck, and McGowan (1973) offer a detailed model of the relationships between networks, affiliates, and program suppliers that determine decisions about program creation and syndication.

42. I focus on the renewal decisions of programs in their first year because of the availability of this sample of information, which was collected by William J. Adams and used in Adams 1993.

CHAPTER 7
LOCAL NEWS AS (VIOLENT) ENTERTAINMENT?

1. This section draws in part on the discussion in Hamilton 1996 of the incentives broadcasters face in public affairs programming.

2. Downs (1957, p. 259) concludes that in "general, it is irrational to be politically well-informed because the low returns from data simply do not justify their cost in time and other scarce resources." For a debate over the empirical validity of the "rational ignorance" hypothesis, see Green and Shapiro 1994, pp. 94–97.

3. Ansolabehere, Behr, and Iyengar (1993) provide an overview of research on political coverage. Bartels (1988) demonstrates how horse race coverage may influence momentum in presidential primaries.

4. Lucas and Possner (1975) studied the extent to which viewing of local news does increase understanding of local politics. Analyzing survey data from 1968, they concluded, "Among the lower- and middle-status respondents, more frequent viewing was found to be significantly related to correct identification of the respondent's governor, senator, and congressman and to a stronger sense of understanding of local issues."

5. See Comstock and Paik 1991, pp. 181–87, for a discussion of the research by George Gerbner and others on the impact of television on beliefs about personal safety and social outcomes.

6. Assessing the influences on local news judgment has generated a significant body of research, including Atwater 1984, Berkowitz 1990, 1991, Bernstein et al. 1990, Harmon 1989, Kaniss 1991, Powers 1993, and Roberts and Dickson 1984. The potential conflicts between market demands for entertainment and journalists' perceived responsibility to inform the electorate are often emphasized in discussions of local news, as in Entman 1989, McManus 1994, and Klite, Bardwell, and Salzman 1997.

7. For a discussion of broadcasters' public interest requirements, see Ingber 1984 and Spitzer 1989.

8. The fact that the FCC monitored public affairs broadcasting did not mean that all stations complied with the spirit of public interest broadcasting requirements. Describing Ted Turner's management of the independent broadcast station WTCG (Channel 17) in the early 1970s, Goldberg and Goldberg (1995, p. 133) note:

When the ABC affiliate in Atlanta was forced by the network to run its evening news at 6:00 PM, Ted saw his chance and ran reruns of *Star Trek* against it. The results were encouraging for Channel 17. Ted presented his own news in the early hours of the morning, and as little as possible. 'As far as our news is concerned,' he admitted, 'we run the FCC minimum of forty minutes a day.'

Boyer and Wirth (1981) offer statistical evidence on the impact of FCC public interest requirements on the amount of news offered by stations. Levin (1980) and Noll, Peck, and McGowan (1973) also examine the efficacy of the FCC's public interest standards. Prisuta (1977) explores the impact of economic factors on public interest programming.

9. Nossiter 1985, p. 402.

10. Fowler and Brenner 1982, p. 210.

11. The nineteen local markets coded were Atlanta, Baltimore, Boston, Champaign & Springfield-Decatur, Chicago, Dallas–Fort Worth, Denver, Detroit, Hartford and New Haven, Los Angeles, Miami–Fort Lauderdale, Milwaukee, New York, Orlando-Daytona, Philadelphia, Richmond-Petersburg, San Francisco–Oakland–San Jose, Tampa–St. Petersburg–Sarasota, and Washington, D.C. Each weekday dinner hour news broadcast was coded for November 1 through December 1, 1993. All stories, except those for sports and weather, were analyzed. All stations and stories were coded by the same researcher. For each station one dinner hour broadcast was coded. Of the fifty-seven stations, thirty-eight had half-hour broadcasts and nineteen had 1-hour broadcasts. Where possible newscasts with the same starting time were coded within a given market, so that the coded shows were directly competing. Ratings data for local news shows were collected from Nielsen 1994f.

12. For evidence on the relation between crime coverage and crime rates, see Sheley and Ashkins 1981, Fishman 1978, and Surrette 1984. Lichter and Lichter (1983) found that violent crimes such as murder and rape accounted for a higher percentage of crimes in entertainment programs than in their percentages in FBI statistics.

13. Note that these percentages are mean percentages, that is, the average of the percentage calculated for the coverage of each station.

14. In *Market-Driven Journalism: Let the Citizen Beware?* (1994) and in other works (1990, 1992) McManus uses the case method to explore how economics influences local news decisions. He indicates (1994, p. 87) that a market theory of news production would predict that an event will be more likely to be covered the less harmful it is to broadcast investors or sponsors, the lower the cost of uncovering or reporting it, and the greater the breadth of appeal to audiences valued by advertisers. He contrasts this with a journalistic theory of news production, which would predict that an issue would be covered depending on the consequences of the story and the magnitude of the audience impacted.

15. Although sports and weather stories were not coded because they were treated differently across markets in terms of their transcription, they were included as a potential topic of story teasers.

16. The correlations are percent crime teased and percent crime (.59), percent crime teased and daily average crime stories (.61), and percent crime and daily average crime (.67). All are statistically significant at .01 level.

17. Perloff, Wartella, and Becker (1982) find that recaps in news programs increase viewer retention of information.

18. Lane 1994, p. 100.

19. Bendall 1994, p. 2B.

20. Miles 1994, p. 22.

21. Jicha 1994, p. 1E.

22. Bendall 1994, p. 2B.

23. Wilson 1994, p. 33.

24. Ibid.

25. Jeffreys 1995, p. 18. Deutsche Presse Agentur (1994) indicates that according to WSVN's accounting the station was the most profitable in Miami, with advertising revenues of $55 million.

26. McCash 1994, p. 4.

27. In a study of the four 6 PM local news broadcasts for May 23–27, 1994, conducted by the University of Miami's School of Communications, WPLG had 31.7% of its news time devoted to crime versus 30.2% for WSVN. See Bendall 1994.

28. Jicha 1994, p. 1E.

29. Deutsche Presse Agentur 1994.

30. Ratings for WTVJ were for women three for 18–34, four for 18–49, five for 18+ and for men four for 18–34, four for 18–49, and six for 18+. For WCIX, the ratings for women were two for 18–34, three for 18–34, three for 18+ and for men three for 18–34, 18–49, and 18+.

31. For a discussion of this nonparametric sign test, see Johnson and Bhattacharyya 1992, p. 590.

32. Smolowe 1993.

33. Perse (1990, 1992) divides audience motivations for watching news in part into "utilitarian" motives (e.g., information seeking) and "diversionary" motives (e.g., entertainment). She finds that seeking entertainment was associated with feeling happy after watching local news broadcasts, while seeking information was associated with feelings of anger generated by crime and government news (1990, p. 575). Ratings data for network programs in individual markets are from Nielsen 1994c.

34. Lacy, Atwater, and Qin (1989) find that as competition among local news broadcasts increased staff size and budget per newscast increased.

35. As one official for Fox described the company's emphasis on the importance of audience interest in local news (West 1994, p. 18), "We believe in locally edited news. That's not to say the lead story has to be a local story; it may very well be a national or international story. But we believe in empowering the news director to lead with whatever he thinks is of greatest interest to his community that day."

36. Hastings, 1993.

37. The probability of a station's covering the Michael Jackson crime story during November was estimated using the model in table 7.13. Changes in probability were calculated by placing all variables' values at their means except for the variable altered, whose value was placed first at one standard deviation below its mean and then one standard deviation above its mean.

38. As indicated earlier in chapter 2, a continuous variable called the violent viewership index was created by summing yes responses to ten questions in the Times Mirror survey dealing with consumption of entertainment programming. Six of these questions dealt with viewing of movies (Terminator 2, The Silence of the Lambs, Alien 3, Bloodsport, Hard to Kill, and Cape Fear) while the others dealt with viewership questions about fictional crime shows, Cops, American Gladiators, and reality crime shows in general. The index, which thus ranged from 0 to 10, had a sample mean of 3.1 and standard deviation of 2.4. Males 18–34 had a mean of 4.7, followed by 4.0 for females 18–34 and 3.4 for males 35–49, 2.7 for females 35–49, 2.1 for males 50+, and 1.5 for females 50+. The moderate increase in the index referred to in the text is an increase by a standard deviation in the value of the index. The political interest index is based on responses to questions about whether the respondent was following very closely the set

of 7 political issues listed in table A7.2. The mean for the political index was 2.5 and the standard deviation was 2.0. A moderate increase in political interests refers to a one standard deviation increase in this index. Of the sample respondents 52% reported following 2 or fewer of the 7 issues very closely.

39. The other gender difference in issue interest was the higher likelihood that women were following the creation of the health care task force. Women consistently express greater concerns over the health care issue in polling data. This was also a time when Hillary Clinton was prominent in the efforts to reform health care policy.

40. Coverage of Bosnia and Somalia during February 1993 on the three major networks was coded based on transcripts and abstracts of these news programs on Lexis and the Vanderbilt Television Archives. Visual segments and their contents were coded as indicated based on these transcripts.

41. Debates over Bosnia coverage illustrate how the print media also face the decision about balancing entertainment and information provision. According to an article in the *Columbia Journalism Review* (January 1996), the executive editor of the *Miami Herald*, Doug Clifton, noted in an in-house e-mail about one of the paper's stories about Bosnia, "I'm not sure readers cared so much that 'terrified Muslims' were 'rounded up, deported,' as our headline and story reported. Yes, I care about man's inhumanity to man, but I care more about whether this latest event brings the world or the U.S. closer to a brink. A reader—even a high-minded, liberal-thinking one with a world view—wants to know 'What does this mean to ME?'" The paper's foreign editor, who later resigned, responded that editors "rolled our editorial eyes" at such foreign coverage and they "pronounced it too complex, too alien, too boring. Can't pronounce the names. They are still killing each other; who cares." As one former editor at the paper put it, "I was taught that sometimes we have an obligation to tell the readers things they don't want to hear . . . But now we're seeing a new phenomenon, in which newspapers are trying to ally themselves with the masses in a kind of overt and deliberate and calculated way in order to deliver the information they'll want to buy." See Villano 1996.

42. See Feshbach 1972, Atkin 1983.

43. This summary of the debate over the "mean world" syndrome draws heavily upon the assessment of Comstock and Paik 1991, pp. 181–87. Their review contains extensive citations to the works examining this cultivation hypothesis.

44. In November 1993, the sample month analyzed in the local news analysis, 16% of the respondents in the *CBS News/New York Times* poll said crime was the most important issue facing the country, which placed it in a tie with unemployment for the top issue cited. Crime remained the top issue cited in these surveys throughout 1994. Polling information based on review of Roper Center at the University of Connecticut data for 1994 available online from the Lexis News file RPOLL.

45. Iyengar 1991.

46. Analyzing the results of his laboratory experiments, Iyengar (1991, p. 26) notes that individuals were less influenced by the context of coverage of crime than they were of terrorism since individuals had more familiarity with crime and were thus less likely to be affected by a given amount of coverage in the lab.

47. This chapter has emphasized the negative externalities potentially generated by crime coverage in local news. Violence may also play a role in public affairs coverage of protests, terrorism, and war. In these situations, analysts have noted that coverage of violence may sometimes serve as a desirable constraint on government action or an impetus for changes in public opinion toward particular issues. For studies of the positive and negative effects of media coverage of political issues where violence may be in-

volved, see Garrow 1978, Gitlin 1980, Paletz and Schmid 1992, Zaller 1992, Bennett and Paletz 1994, and Mickiewicz 1997.

48. See Hundt 1996.

49. For an attempt to provide British broadcasters with a code describing desirable ways to deal with coverage of violence in news (and entertainment) programming, see Broadcasting Standards Council 1989.

50. One possible policy tool to encourage the provision of public affairs coverage that would generate high positive externalities would be an end to a free grant of spectrum use and the institution of an auction for spectrum rights. The spectrum auction would "free" broadcasters of public interest requirements, which chapter 3 and this chapter suggest they will try to evade or comply with at the lowest possible cost. The spectrum proceeds could then be used to fund public broadcasting outlets, where the type of coverage is consciously shaped to generate positive externalities by informing viewers.

CHAPTER 8

DEALING WITH TELEVISION VIOLENCE

1. See Schneider and Halonen 1996, pp.1, 23, for a detailed discussion of broadcaster reactions to political pressure. This paragraph draws heavily on their collection of broadcaster assessments of television violence.

2. Ibid.

3. Ibid.

4. Ibid.

5. As early as 1971 Bork argued for treatment of media externalities as akin to pollution, stating (1971, p. 29):

pornography is increasingly seen as a problem of pollution of the moral and aesthetic atmosphere precisely analogous to smoke pollution. A majority of the community may foresee that continued availability of pornography to those who want it will inevitably affect the quality of life for those who do not want it.

6. See Edwards and Berman 1995 for a detailed analysis of proposed remedies to deal with television violence and Spitzer 1996 for an extensive analysis of the legal and economic issues surrounding the V-chip. The large legal literature on television violence includes DeLeon and Naon 1974; Krattenmaker and Powe 1978, 1994; Albert 1978; Campbell 1990; Schlegel 1993; Kim 1994; Murray 1994; Ballard 1995; Corn-Revere 1995; and Balkin 1996. Examinations of the Children's Television Act that have implications for legal treatments of television violence include Hundt 1996 and Krotoszynski 1996. For additional discussions of broad First Amendment issues, see Van Alstyne 1984, Powe 1987, Smolla 1992, and Fish 1994.

7. Sissela Bok (1994, p. 4) identifies what she terms eight "rationales" about television violence which "offer simplistic reasons for not entering into serious debate about a subject, and thus provide rationalizations for ignoring or shielding ongoing practices from outside scrutiny and interference." Two of these difficulties relate to problems of measurement (p. 4):

How can you definitively pinpoint, and thus prove, the link between viewing TV violence and acts of real-life violence?

People can't even agree on how to define "violence." How, then, can they go on to discuss what to do about it?

8. Ayres (1988) argues for more extensive analysis of broadcast content regulation using a cost-benefit framework. Posner (1986) describes explicitly how to consider the costs and benefits of regulating free speech.

9. Entman and Wildman (1992) and Baker (1996) also argue that media policy should be driven in part by the consideration of externalities (positive and negative) generated by media consumption.

10. Spitzer (1996) demonstrates that is difficult to predict the exact impact of the V-chip and rating of television content on program viewership and production.

11. Arnold (1990) traces out how the ability of voters to detect a chain of causation between congressional activity and real-world outcomes affects incentives of legislators to act on issues.

12. Wilson (1980) refers to cases where the benefits of a political alternative are dispersed and costs are concentrated as situations of entrepreneurial politics, since a political entrepreneur may be required to represent the interests of those who might enjoy the dispersed benefits.

13. Wharton 1995, p. 21.

14. Ibid.

15. Communications Daily 1995a.

16. Communications Daily 1995b.

17. As Communications Daily (1995c, p. 1) explained events:

Then, in unexpected parliamentary maneuver, Markey offered "motion to recommit," meaning send it back to committee, with instructions to include V-chip. That meant that, if adopted, bill would include both Coburn study and V-chip and legislators would have to vote up-or-down on V-chip, without cover of study. Vote was virtually reversed from before, with recommittal motion winning 224–199. . . . There was some difference of opinion whether Republicans were surprised by move, with strategists looking at it both ways.

18. Stern 1995a.

19. The ACLU voting index included the vote on the V-chip, so this vote was omitted and ACLU scores were recalculated to reflect the percentage of a representative's votes on issues identified by the ACLU that accorded with the group's position. The Christian Coalition index is similarly the percentage of a representative's votes on issues identified by the group that supported the coalition's position.

20. Machacek 1995.

21. The breakdown of votes on the technology study and the V-chip amendment was no for technology, no for V-chip: 10 Republicans (mean ACLU rating, 5; mean Christian Coalition [CC] rating, 96) and 2 Democrats (ACLU, 91; CC, 4); yes for technology, no for V-chip: 171 Republicans (ACLU, 7; CC, 95) and 16 Democrats (ACLU, 77; CC, 23); no for technology, yes for V-chip: 34 Republicans (ACLU, 13; CC, 87) and 154 Democrats (ACLU, 77; CC, 16); and yes for technology, yes for V-chip: 14 Republicans (ACLU, 9; CC, 93) and 21 Democrats (ACLU, 57; CC, 37).

22. For the no-yes Democrats (154) versus the yes-yes Democrats (21), the difference of means is statistically significant at the .01 level for both the ACLU and Christian Coalition indices. I do not attempt to separate out here the degree that a representative votes in support of the Christian Coalition because of true belief in these principles versus a desire to represent the opinions of conservative constituents (and possibly increase the odds of reelection support among these voters).

23. Mundy 1995, p. 22. The Hollings proposal was an example for some senators of

what Arnold (1990, p. 78) terms a "politically compelling" policy, one where the legislator agrees with the policy's ends, disagree's with the means used to achieve them, but votes for the policy to avoid being seen as opposing the ends of the legislation.

24. See McKenzie 1996, Wilkinson and Barton 1996.

25. See Elsner 1995.

26. Journalists covering the issue of violence on television in 1996 frequently commented on the returns to both President Clinton and Senator Bob Dole for addressing this issue. President Clinton gained significant media coverage in 1996 for two White House meetings that led to the announcement of changes in broadcaster behavior. On February 29, 1996, the president hosted a summit at the White House with entertainment industry executives on television violence. Jack Valenti, president of the MPAA, announced that day the creation of a task force that would create a voluntary rating system for television program content. These ratings would allow parents to use the V-chip to block particular programs based on their content. On July 29, 1996, President Clinton again hosted entertainment executives at a meeting at the White House where a compromise agreement was announced in which broadcasters pledged to program 3 hours of children's educational programming per week. Many journalists portrayed these efforts as attempts by the president to reach voters concerned about cultural issues. As one assessment of the president's strategy (Farrell, 1996) noted:

The "marriage gap" is particularly troublesome to Democratic strategists, says White House aide George Stephanopoulos. "In 1994 one of the single greatest determinants for voting Republican was whether you were married," he says. With issues like teen-age curfews, school uniforms and television violence, President Clinton is trying to boost his appeal with married women, and he has pulled slightly ahead of Dole among married mothers.

Senator Bob Dole also captured attention during the 1996 primary season for using television violence as a campaign issue. At a fund-raising dinner in California, Dole attacked the entertainment industry for the amount of sex and violence in both music and movies. Describing how the speech was scripted in his book *The Choice* (1996, p. 178), Bob Woodward reports:

Mari Will . . . had spent some time drafting the anti-Hollywood speech. In her conversations with Dole, she returned repeatedly to the theme of values. "The country really aches to hear about values," she said. . . . He needed to step up in a forceful and direct way if he were going to get and retain attention, particularly with conservative voters, she said. So Will had interjected some high-voltage rhetoric into the speech. Hollywood was guilty of the "mainstreaming of deviancy," with loveless sex and mindless violence. Too many of the movies and songs were "nightmares of depravity."

The speech generated front page headlines in the *New York Times* and other papers. Woodward described (p. 188) the reaction to the speech: "It was giant news. The impact was way beyond anything in Dole's entire political history. This was entirely new territory. Columns, debates, giant affection from Republicans and the right wing, and even outspoken praise from many Democrats and liberals." The Dole campaign next faced the question of what to do to follow up on the speech. Dole's advisors counseled him to let the coverage unfold and return to the issue again in the fall contest. In arguing for which topics the campaign should focus on to reach primary voters, Will proposed a combination of economic issues (e.g., taxes, budget, regulation) and cultural issues, which included Hollywood, television, schools, crime, and welfare (see Woodward 1996, p. 334).

27. National Television Violence Study 1996b, p. 1-48.

28. Dworkin (1984) notes that the two primary asbestos-related illnesses are asbestosis, a scarring of the lungs which is akin to emphysema, and mesothelioma, a lung cancer type that is only caused by asbestos.

29. See National Research Council 1993, for a summary of research on the causes of crime and possible prevention strategies.

30. Prettyman and Hook, 1987, discuss proposals to control "media-related imitative violence."

31. See Carter, Franklin, and Wright 1994, chap. 5, for a discussion of media liability for emotional and physical harm.

32. Ibid., p. 278.

33. Ibid., p. 280.

34. See Umstead 1996, p. 52, the source of all quotations here about the Missouri law.

35. Hollings 1996. In pushing for his bill, Senator Hollings urged his colleagues to stop talking about the television violence problem and take concrete steps to deal with it, saying: "Let's get down to business. Instead of dilly-dallying and talking about doing something, let's pass the bill and get this gratuitous filth off the air."

36. The UCLA Center for Communication Policy 1995 report concluded (p. 90):

Promotions raise serious concerns, particularly because they feature violence out of context. It is almost impossible for promotions to provide sufficient context for any violence that does occur. By definition, promotions feature only a small highlight of the upcoming program. Violence, as well as sex, is almost always featured as the highlight. . . . Furthermore, violent promos frequently are run during programs geared for children or on completely non-violent shows. Even shows that are virtually free of violence are promoted utilizing the merest suggestion of violence that can be gleaned from the program.

37. When violence on television has attracted controversy and government scrutiny, broadcast networks and cable networks are often urged to forgo voluntarily the use of high violent content in shows. Periodically broadcasters have pledged to reduce the amount of violence in programming. For example, in December 1992 ABC, CBS, and NBC issued a joint statement on "Standards for Depiction of Violence in Television Programs" that declared in part (see Federman 1996, p. 122):

2. Gratuitous or excessive depictions of violence (or redundant violence shown solely for its own sake) are not acceptable.

3. Programs should not depict violence as glamorous, nor as an acceptable solution to human conflict.

4. Depictions of violence may not be used to shock or stimulate the audience.

Despite these declarations, however, the networks continued to air violent programming that raised issues of concern to outside monitors. Of the 118 theatrical films shown on broadcast network television that were monitored by the UCLA Center for Communication Policy during 1994–95, 50 raised issues of concern with respect to violence.

38. Hardin 1982 discusses the prisoners' dilemma and potential solutions to these types of problems. Note that having the government coordinate a solution may be viewed as problematic since it can be seen as turning a private voluntary agreement into an instrument of state action. The 1976 Writers Guild of America, West vs. FCC decision (423 F. Supp. 1064 [1976]) that struck down the Family Viewing Policy (see subsequent discussion) made clear that the government's role in coordinating the development of this industry agreement (which was formulated by the National Association of Broadcas-

ters) turned the policy effectively into state action. The judge noted (p. 1094): "In the absence of government threats, no drastic changes would have been made. Even [CBS President Arthur] Taylor would not have locked CBS into a public commitment to the family viewing policy unless it were clear that the rest of the industry would be bound by it." The judge's description (p. 1116) of why the networks agreed to refrain from broadcasting material inappropriate for family viewing from 7–9 PM reads like an assessment of the calculations in the prisoners' dilemma solved by the intervention of a third party:

> The FCC and CBS had successfully maneuvered the two networks into a position where blockage of the proposal had become unthinkable. To block the proposal two weeks before the FCC's report to Congress would have required a degree of political masochism rarely displayed by large corporations. Here apparent corporate political benefits clearly outweighed corporate political risks. The contention that this grudging support of the NAB Code amendment arose independently of the substantial pressure generated by the imminence of the FCC report is not credible.

39. For examinations of the operation of the EPA's Toxics Release Inventory program, see Hamilton 1993 and Brehm and Hamilton 1996.

40. U.S. Environmental Protection Agency 1994, p. 182.

41. Stern 1995b.

42. Fahey 1991, examines legal issues surrounding boycotts based on advertisers' support of particular television programs.

43. Under the Telecommunications Act of 1996, the FCC had to determine whether video programming distributors had established within 1 year of the legislation's enactment voluntary rules for rating programming containing violent, sexual, or other indecent material, whether the rules were "acceptable" to the commission, and whether video programming distributors were broadcasting the ratings in signals. If the industry rated programs, then the legislation required that the ratings be carried in signals. As of July 1997, the FCC was seeking comments on whether the TV Parental Guidelines rating system developed by the industry was "acceptable." Note that if the FCC found that the industry plan was unacceptable and appointed a committee that developed an alternative methodology, there was nothing in the legislation that would require the industry to use this alternative rating system. For a description of the legislation's requirements, see Federal Communications Commission 1997.

44. Corn-Revere 1995. Spitzer (1996) provides a convincing argument that the V-chip ratings system will likely be regarded as a product of government action because of the structure of the Telecommunications Act of 1996 and pressure from politicians that led to the adoption of the "voluntary system." He concludes, however, that the ratings system would survive a constitutional challenge based on the First Amendment if the system were properly structured.

45. Federman 1996, p. 132.

46. The content advisory system used by HBO and Showtime includes ten indicators (in addition to MPAA ratings): adult language (AL), graphic language (GL), mild violence (MV), violence (V), graphic violence (GV), nudity (N), brief nudity (BN), adult content (AC), strong sexual content (SC), and rape (RP). See Rice and Brown, 1996.

47. See Cantor, Harrison, and Krcmar, 1996, for a discussion of the difficulties of determining content from MPAA ratings.

48. See Valenti, Anstrom, and Fritts 1997, for the industry's description of the initial program rating system submitted to the FCC. This letter also describes the creation of an

industry Oversight Monitoring Board, which will supervise the implementation of the system. Although the original rating system used the designation "TV-M" for "mature" programs, the industry changed this category to "TV-MA" since video game manufacturers were already using the "M" classification as part of their rating system. See Halonen 1997.

49. These responses were from a survey (sample size, 1,207 parents) conducted by Peter D. Hart Research Associates and Public Opinion Strategies between December 9–11, 1996. See Valenti, Anstrom, and Fritts 1997.

50. See Mifflin 1997. Parents may make greater use of rating information once the V-chip technology is adopted, since this may significantly reduce the effort required to shield children from harmful content. Even if parents have program content information, without a V-chip they must continually monitor a child's viewing. Access to the industry's ratings (which appear as icons at the start of programs) may be hindered currently by the reluctance of some newspapers to add to printing costs by carrying this information in their daily television grids. *TV Guide* added two to three pages per issue by publishing the ratings information each week, at an annual estimated cost of $1.5 million in extra printing expenses. See Hatch 1997.

51. National Television Violence Study 1997a, p. 35.

52. Ibid., p. 36.

53. Program episode ratings were collected from *TV Guide.* Of the 130 prime-time regularly scheduled program series, 11 had no ratings (because they were news programs), 89 had the same category ratings across episodes, and 30 programs had during the sample period two different ratings depending on episode content.

54. See Mandese 1996.

55. The Parents Television Council is a project of the Media Research Center, which describes itself as a "conservative research and education foundation dedicated to bringing political balance to the news media, and restoring family values to entertainment fare." See Parents Television Council 1996, p. 33.

56. Note that none of the prime-time broadcast network series episodes carried an M or MA rating. The first network broadcast airing to carry a TV-M rating was NBC's showing of the movie *Schindler's List* on February 23, 1997. The program was watched by an estimated audience of 65 million, which more than doubled the number of people who saw this Holocaust drama in American theaters. See Carter 1997 and Braun 1997.

57. Among programs rated as yellow by the PTC, the mean ad price for the programs carrying the higher TV-14 rating was $125,000 versus $173,000 for those rated TV-PG.

58. The distribution of episodes (those with and without advertising data) rated by TV Parental Guidelines and the Parents Television Council was the following. Of the 217 programs rated green, 170 were TV-G and 47 were TV-PG. Of the 441 yellow episodes, 51 were TV-G, 347 were TV-PG, and 43 were TV-14. Of the 201 red episodes, 4 were TV-G, 158 were TV-PG, and 39 were TV-14. The yellow episodes rated TV-14 tended to be police programs, such as *Law and Order, Nash Bridges, New York Undercover, Profiler,* and *Walker, Texas Ranger.* Red episodes rated TV-14 included *Melrose Place, Millenium, NYPD Blue, X-Files,* and *Married . . . with Children.* The programs rated red by the Parents Television Council but TV-PG by the industry included many popular comedies, such as *Friends, Seinfeld,* and *3rd Rock from the Sun.*

59. Federman 1996.

60. The market for content information to shield children from objectionable material (primarily sexual in nature) on the Internet has generated many different screens and rating systems for parents to use (Federman 1996). This is in part because advertisers

currently play less of a role in Internet content, so that labels do not generate as high a probability of "advertiser backlash" as in the broadcast television advertising market. With the shift to digital broadcasting, there may be more opportunities for ratings information from multiple sources to be transmitted to televisions, perhaps through the signals of public broadcasting stations if not through those of commercial broadcasters. Even if commercial broadcasters were reluctant to provide content information in their signals, data could be sent to televisions so that software could incorporate information on content into viewing selection mechanisms. "Downloading" information on program content in digital television signals would allow viewers to choose different ratings systems to use in screening programs.

61. Video games and Internet sites are also sources of potentially objectionable material for children. For research on the impact of violent video games on children, see Kubey and Larson 1990, Cesarone 1994, and Irwin and Gross 1995. A report by the Center for Media Education (1996) describes the potential threats to children from online marketing on the Internet. For a description of attempts by groups such as the Recreational Software Advisory Council to develop ratings for video games and Internet sites, see Roberts 1996, Recreational Software Advisory Council 1996, and Federman 1996.

62. Sunstein 1996, p. 914.

63. Demsetz and Lehn (1985, p. 1162) note:

believing that one is systematically influencing public opinion plausibly provides utility to some owners even if profit is reduced from levels otherwise achievable. These consumption goals arise from the particular tastes of owners, so their achievement requires owners to be in a position to influence managerial decisions. Hence, ownership should be more concentrated in firms for which this type of amenity potential is greater.

64. In his autobiography, Paley (1979, p. 254) quotes from a 1960 memo that he wrote to the CBS network president that stated:

CBS for years was able to maintain the kind of balance which, on the one hand, gave most of the people what they wanted and enjoyed most of the time while, at the same time, producing enough product of outstanding merit to gain for itself a reputation of quality, responsibility, etc. I know that this year we are doing more than ever before in the public affairs and news field, for which I am sure we will gain much credit.

65. See Auletta 1993, p. 46, the source of Murdoch quotations in this paragraph.

66. Goldberg and Goldberg 1995, p. 133.

67. Freeman 1995, p. E-1.

68. Laurence 1995, p. D-1.

69. Describing his reaction to *The Desperate Trail*, a violent original western aired on TNT, Turner said (Freeman 1995, p. E-1): "I was watchin' it with Jane [Fonda] and I turned it off. I thought it sucked. Listen, I told you we ain't perfect. I'm not proud of everything we air. But we ain't done nothin' like *Pulp Fiction* or *Natural Born Killers*, I can tell you that."

70. Ferguson 1995.

71. Federal Document Clearing House 1996.

72. Ibid.

73. Newton Minow emphasizes that executives at companies that sponsor television

programming should feel a responsibility to avoid advertising on violent shows. See Minow 1997.

74. Auletta 1993, p. 52.

75. Ibid., p. 53.

76. The AMA announced in September 1996 an effort to distribute its *Physician Guide to Media Violence* to 60,000 doctors. The guide provides a series of viewing guidelines that doctors can help transmit to parents. Don Ohlmeyer of NBC attacked the effort, saying (Schneider 1996, p. 1): "If you pick a bogus issue, you can seem like you're doing something. . . . Probably one or two people on some board of the AMA said, 'Let's get into this, look at all the ink this is getting. This will make it sound like we're doing something.'" For a discussion of media literacy efforts, see Thoman 1995.

77. See Sunstein 1996, for the argument that norms in part account for the racial differences in teen smoking rates.

78. Spitzer (1989) examines the rationales offered for the licensing of broadcasters.

79. Under a legislative proposal offered in 1997 by Senator Hollings, broadcasters could not show violent programming during times when children were most likely to be in the audience, unless the programming carried a rating providing parents with specific information on the violent content of the show. See Stern 1997.

80. Cowan 1979, p. 98.

81. Coase (1959) proposed auctioning spectrum frequencies as a superior way to allocate broadcasting rights.

82. In seeking comment on the ratings system developed by the industry, the FCC (1997, p. 3) indicated that the "Commission will initiate a separate proceeding shortly addressing the issues related to the 'V-chip.'" The commission could influence the development of rating systems that may serve as alternatives to the industry system by influencing the technology chosen for the V-chip.

83. Nielsen 1993c indicates that for November 1992 children 2–11 in television households averaged 23:01 hours of television viewing per week.

84. Altering the incentives that broadcasters face by changing the profits associated with violent programming is consistent with broadcast policies advocated by Coase, who noted (1966, p. 444):

I am quite certain that the broad pattern of programming will be determined by profitability. My view is that we should not bewail the fact that businessmen maximize profits. We should accept it and use it. The task which faces us (and the task of good government policy) is to devise institutional arrangements which lead the businessman, as it were by an invisible hand, to do what is desirable (by making it profitable for him to do so).

• *B I B L I O G R A P H Y* •

Adams, William J. 1993. "TV Program Scheduling Strategies and Their Relationship to New Program Renewal Rates and Rating Changes." *Journal of Broadcasting and Electronic Media*, 37:465–74.

Albert, James A. 1978. "Constitutional Regulation of Televised Violence." *Virginia Law Review*, 64:1299–1345.

Albiniak, Paige. 1997. "Ratings Get Revamped: Networks, except for NBC, Agree to Add Content Labels." *Broadcasting and Cable*, July 14, pp. 4–10.

American Family Association. 1993. *The 12 Top Sponsors of Violence on Prime-Time TV*. Tupelo, Miss.: American Family Association.

———. 1995. *AFA Dirty Dozen: the 12 Top Sponsors of Prime-Time Filth*. Tupelo, Miss.: American Family Association.

Andison, F. Scott. 1977. "TV Violence and Viewer Aggression: A Cumulation of Study Results." *Public Opinion Quarterly*, 41:314–31.

Ansolabehere, Stephen, Roy Behr, and Shanto Iyengar. 1993. *The Media Game: American Politics in the Television Age*. New York: Macmillan.

Arnold, R. Douglas. 1990. *The Logic of Congressional Action*. New Haven, Conn.: Yale University Press.

Associated Press. 1994. "TV Violence to Be Monitored and Reported." *Associated Press News Wire*, June 30.

Atkin, Charles. 1983. "Effects of Realistic TV Violence vs. Fictional Violence on Aggression." *Journalism Quarterly*, 60(4):615–21.

Atwater, Tony. 1984. "Product Differentiation in Local TV News." *Journalism Quarterly*, 61(3):757–762.

Auletta, Ken. 1993. "What Won't They Do." *New Yorker*, May 17, pp. 45–53.

Ayres, Ian. 1988. "Halfway Home: On Powe's American Broadcasting and the First Amendment." *Law and Social Inquiry*, 13:413–27.

Baker, C. Edwin. 1994. *Advertising and a Democratic Press*. Princeton, N.J.:Princeton University Press.

———. 1996. "Giving the Audience What It Wants." Working paper, University of Pennsylvania Law School, Philadelphia.

Balkin, J. M. 1996. "Media Filters, the V-chip, and the Foundations of Broadcast Regulation." *Duke Law Journal*, 45:1131–75.

Ballard, Ian Matheson, Jr. 1995. "See No Evil, Hear No Evil: Television Violence and the First Amendment." *Virginia Law Review*, 81:175–202.

Bandura, Albert, Dorothea Ross, and Sheila A. Ross. 1963. "Imitation of Film-Mediated Aggressive Models." *Journal of Abnormal and Social Psychology*, 66(1):3–11.

Bartels, Larry M. 1988. *Presidential Primaries and the Dynamics of Public Choice*. Princeton, N.J.: Princeton University Press.

Battaglio, Stephen. 1996. "Lifetime Targets Younger Crowd." *Hollywood Reporter*, April 16.

Baumol, William J., and Wallace E. Oates. 1988. *The Theory of Environmental Policy*. New York: Cambridge University Press.

Beebe, Jack H. 1977. "Institutional Structure and Program Choices in Television Markets." *Quarterly Journal of Economics*, 91:15–37.

Belcher, Walt. 1995. "Film Company Revels in Campiness; Low Budgets and Attention-Getting Titles Are Hallmarks of Troma Horror Films." *Tampa Tribune*, June 17, p. 1.

Belson, William A. 1978. *Television Violence and the Adolescent Boy*. Westmead, England: Saxon House.

Bendall, Barbara. 1994. "Study Shows Violence on Channel 7 Is Down." *Sun Sentinel* (Fort Lauderdale), June 10, p. B2.

Bennett, W. Lance, and David L. Paletz, eds. 1994. *Taken by Storm: The Media, Public Opinion, and U.S. Foreign Policy in the Gulf War*. Chicago: University of Chicago Press.

Bensman, Marvin R. 1990. *Broadcast/Cable Regulation*. Lanham, Md.: University Press of America.

Berkowitz, Dan. 1990. "Refining the Gatekeeping Metaphor for Local Television News." *Journal of Broadcasting and Electronic Media*, 34(1):55–68.

———. 1991. "Assessing Forces in the Selection of Local Television News." *Journal of Broadcasting and Electronic Media*, 35(2):245–51.

Bernstein, James M., Stephen Lacy, Catherine Cassara, and Tuen-yu Lau. 1990. "Geographic Coverage by Local Television News." *Journalism Quarterly*, 67(4):663–71.

Bhat, Madhuri. 1996. "How Should Advertising Agencies Advise Corporate Sponsors about Advertising on Violent Television in the Era of the Vchip?" M. A. thesis Sanford Institute of Public Policy, Duke University.

Bok, Sissela. 1994. "TV Violence, Children, and the Press: Eight Rationales Inhibiting Public Policy Debates." Joan Shorenstein Barone Center Discussion Paper D-16. John F. Kennedy School of Government, Harvard University, Cambridge, Mass.

Bonko, Larry. 1996. "It's Official: TV News Uses Blood to Avoid Red Ink." *Virginian-Pilot*, January 10, p. E1.

Bork, Robert H. 1971. "Neutral Principles and Some First Amendment Problems." *Indiana Law Journal*, 47:1–35.

Boston Herald. 1995. "Parents Get New TV Guide." *Boston Herald*, December 9, p. 12.

Bower, Robert T. 1985. *The Changing Television Audience in America*. New York: Columbia University Press.

Boyatzis, Chris J., Gina M. Matillo, and Kristen M. Nesbitt. 1995. "Effects of 'The Mighty Morphin Power Rangers' on Children's Aggression with Peers." *Child Study Journal*, 25(1):45–55.

Boyer, Kenneth D., and Michael O. Wirth. 1981. "The Economics of Regulation by Policy Directive: FCC Public-Interest Requirements." *Quarterly Journal of Economics and Business*, 21(1):77–96.

Braun, Neil. 1997. "Viewpoint: Why Cable Hasn't Killed Broadcasting." *Electronic Media*, March 17, p. 16.

Brehm, John, and James T. Hamilton. 1996. "Noncompliance in Environmental Reporting: Are Violators Ignorant, or Evasive, of the Law?" *American Journal of Political Science*, 40(2):444–77.

Broadcast Information Bureau. 1994. *BIB Television Programming Source Books, 1994–95*. Volume 4: *Series*. Philadelphia: North American Publishing Company.

Broadcasting Standards Council. 1989. *A Code of Practice*. London: Broadcasting Standards Council.

Brown, Rich. 1995a. "If It's Monday, It Must Be Wrestling; TNT Goes to Mat with USA over New Pro-Wrestling Series." *Broadcasting and Cable*, August 21, p. 32.

———. 1995b. "TNT Tops Prime Time for 2nd Quarter." *Broadcasting and Cable*, July 3, 20.

Burgi, Michael. 1995. "Weathering Heights." *Mediaweek*, June 19, p. 25.

Bushman, Brad, and Angela D. Stack. 1996. "Forbidden Fruit versus Tainted Fruit: Effects of Warning Labels on Attraction to TV Violence." *Journal of Experimental Psychology: Applied* 2(3):207–26.

Business Wire. 1994. "CRO Returns for a Second Season at ABC; National Science Foundation Continues Support of CTW's Ice-Age Series." *Business Wire*, June 15.

———. 1995. "Explosive and Live WCW Wrestling Comes to TNT As Centerpiece of New Weekly Monday Nitro Franchise Starting Labor Day Night." *Business Wire*, August 14.

Cable News Network. 1993. "Networks and Legislators Announce TV Violence Warnings." *News Transcript #245-1*, June 30.

Campbell, Emily. 1990. "Television Violence: Social Science vs. the Law." *Loyola Entertainment Law Review*, 10(2):413–66.

Canadian Radio-television and Telecommunication Commission. 1993. "Protecting Children While Protecting Creative Freedom: CRTC Accepts Private Broadcasters' Strengthened TV Violence Code." *CRTC News Release*, October 28.

Cantor, Joanne, and Kristen Harrison. 1996. "Ratings and Advisories for Television Programming: University of Wisconsin, Madison Study." In *National Television Violence Study: Scientific Papers, 1994–1995*, 3:1–26. Studio City, Calif.: Mediascope.

Cantor, Joanne, Kristen Harrison, and Marina Krcmar. 1996. "Ratings and Advisories: Implications for a New Rating System for Television." Paper prepared for Duke Conference on Media Violence and Public Policy, Sanford Institute of Public Policy, Duke University, Durham, N.C., June 28–29.

Cantor, Joanne, and Marina B. Krcmar. 1996. "Part II: Effects of Advisories and Ratings on Parent-Child Discussions of Television Viewing Choice." In *National Television Violence Study: Scientific Papers, 1994–1995*, 3:27–50. Studio City, Calif.: Mediascope.

Cantor, Joanne, Suzanne Stutman, and Victoria Duran. 1996. *What Parents Want in a Television Rating System: Results of a National Survey*. Madison: University of Wisconsin Communication Arts.

Carter, Bill. 1997. "TV Notes." *New York Times*, February 27, p. C17.

Carter, T. Barton, Marc A. Franklin, and Jay B. Wright. 1994. *The First Amendment and the Fourth Estate: The Law of Mass Media*. 6th Ed. Westbury, N.Y.: Foundation Press.

Center for Media and Public Affairs. 1994. *Violence in Prime Time Television, 1992–1993*. Washington, D.C.: Center for Media and Public Affairs.

Center for Media Education. 1992. *A Report on Station Compliance with the Children's Television Act*. Washington, D.C.: Center for Media Education.

———. 1996. *Web of Deception: Threats to Children from Online Marketing*. Washington, D.C.: Center for Media Education.

Centerwall, Brandon S. 1992. "Television and Violence: The Scale of the Problem and Where to Go from Here." *Journal of the American Medical Association*, 267(22):3059–63.

———. 1993. "Television and Violent Crime." *Public Interest*, III (Spring):56–71.

Cesarone, Bernard. 1994. *Video Games and Children*. Urbana, Il.: ERIC Clearinghouse on Elementary and Early Childhood Education.

Charleston Daily Mail. 1994. "Violence Deleted from TV Newscasts." *Charleston Daily Mail*, May 18, p. D5.

Chicago Tribune. 1994. "New Hearing for TV Decency Rules." *Chicago Tribune*, February 19.

Coase, Ronald H. 1959. "The Federal Communications Commission." *Journal of Law and Economics*, 2:1–40.

———. 1960. "The Problem of Social Cost." *Journal of Law and Economics*, 3:1–44.

———. 1966. "The Economics of Broadcasting and Government Policy." *American Economic Review*, 56:440–47.

Coe, Steve, and Harry A. Jessel. 1993. "'NYPD Blue': Rocky Start, on a Roll." *Broadcasting and Cable*, 123(4):18.

Committee on Communications and Media Law. 1997. "Violence in the Media: A Position Paper." *Record of the Association of the Bar of the City of New York*, 52(3): 273–342.

Communications Daily. 1995a. "'Vastly Superior' to Vchip; \$2 Million Seed Money Put Up by Networks for Viewer Control." *Communications Daily*, August 2, p. 5.

———. 1995b. "Vchip Fight Looming; House Nears Passage of Telecom Bill." *Communications Daily*, August 3, p. 1.

———. 1995c. "Networks Lose 2; House Passes Telecom Bill after Vchip Reversal." *Communications Daily*, August 7, p. 1.

Comstock, George. 1986. "Television and Film Violence." In Steven J. Apter and Arnold P. Goldstein, eds., *Youth Violence: Programs and Prospects*, pp. 178–218. New York: Pergammon.

Comstock, George, Steven Chaffee, Natan Katzman, Maxwell McCombs, and Donald Roberts. 1978. *Television and Human Behavior*. New York: Columbia University Press.

Comstock, George, and Haejung Paik. 1990. "The Effects of Television Violence on Aggressive Behavior: A Meta-Analysis." Preliminary Report to the National Research Council. S. I. Newhouse School of Public Communications, Syracuse University, Syracuse, N.Y.

———. 1991. *Television and the American Child*. San Diego: Academic Press.

Congressional Research Service. 1993. *Violence on Television: What Can Technology Do?* Washington, D.C.: Technology and Information Policy Section, CRS Science Policy Research Division.

Corn-Revere, Robert. 1995. "Television Violence and the Limits of Voluntarism." *Yale Journal of Regulation*, 12:187–205.

Cowan, Jeffrey. 1979. *See No Evil: The Backstage Battle over Sex and Violence on Television*. New York: Simon and Schuster.

Danielson, Wayne, Dominic Lasorsa, Ellen Wartella, Charles Whitney, Shannon Campbell, Saam Haddad, Marlies Klijn, Rafael Lopez, and Adriana Olivarez. 1996. "Television Violence in 'Reality' Programming: University of Texas, Austin Study." In *National Television Violence Study: Scientific Papers, 1994–1995*, 2:1–55. Studio City, Calif.: Mediascope.

DeLeon, Dennis L., and Robert L. Naon. 1974. "The Regulation of Televised Violence." *Stanford Law Review*, 26:1291–1325.

Dempsey, John. 1996. "How Will Cap'n Ted Sail HBO." *Daily Variety*, September 12, p. 28.

Demsetz, Harold, and Kenneth Lehn. 1985. "Structure of Corporate Ownership: Causes and Consequences." *Journal of Political Economy*, 93(6):1155–77.

Deutsche Presse Agentur. 1994. "Miami Hotels, TV Station Battle over Gore on News." *Rocky Mountain News*, June 19.

Dorgan, Byron. 1993. "Statements on Introduced Bills and Joint Resolutions." *Congressional Record*, May 18, 139 S 6022.

Downs, Anthony. 1957. *An Economic Theory of Democracy*. New York: Harper.

Dworkin, Terry Morehead. 1984. "Fear of Disease and Delayed Manifestation Injuries: A Solution or a Pandora's Box?" *Fordham Law Review*, 53:527–77.

Edwards, Harry T., and Mitchell N. Berman. 1995. "Regulating Violence on Television." *Northwestern University Law Review*, 89:1487–1566.

Elliot, Stuart. 1993. "A Hit Prime Time Show without Most Mainstream Advertisers? Dial 'NYPD Blue.'" *New York Times*, November 2, p. D20.

———. 1995. "Donations Up in '94 for Public Service." *New York Times*, July 24, p. D9.

Elsner, Alan. 1995. "Clinton Making Environment Key Campaign Theme." *Reuters North American Wire*. July 9.

Entman, Robert M. 1989. *Democracy without Citizens: Media and the Decay of American Politics*. New York: Oxford University Press.

———. 1990. "Modern Racism and the Images of Blacks in Local Television News." *Critical Studies in Mass Communication*, 7:332–45.

———. 1993. "Representation and Reality in the Portrayal of Blacks on Network Television News." *Journalism Quarterly*, 71(3):509–20.

Entman, Robert M., and Steven S. Wildman. 1992. "Reconciling Economic and Non-Economic Perspectives on Media Policy: Transcending the 'Marketplace of Ideas.'" *Journal of Communication*, 42(1):5–19.

Eron, Leonard D., and L. Rowell Huesmann. 1986. "The Development of Aggression in the American Child As a Consequence of Television Violence Viewing." In L. R. Huesmann and L. D. Eron, eds., *Television and the Aggressive Child: A Cross-National Comparison*, pp. 45–80. Hillsdale, N.J.: Lawrence Erlbaum Associates.

———. 1987. "Television As a Source of Maltreatment of Children." *Social Psychology Review*, 16(2):195–202.

Fahey, Patrick M. 1991. "Advocacy Group Boycotting of Network Television Advertisers and Its Effects on Programming Content." *University of Pennsylvania Law Review*, 140:647–709.

Farrell, John Aloysius. 1996. "Campaign '96: Party Draws Clout from Diversity." *Boston Globe*, August 12, p. A1.

Fay, Ann L., Stephanie D. Teasley, Britte H. Cheng, Kathleen M. Bachman, and Jennifer H. Schnakenberg. 1995. *Children's Interest in and Understanding of Science and Technology: A Study of the Effects of CRO*. Pittsburgh: Learning Research and Development Center, University of Pittsburgh.

Federal Communications Commission. 1996. *In the Matter of Policies and Rules concerning Children's Television Programming, Revision of Programming Policies for Television Broadcast Stations, Report and Order, August 8, 1996*. Washington, D.C.: Federal Communications Commission.

———. 1997. "Commission Seeks Comment on Industry Proposal for Rating Video Programming (CS Docket No. 97–55)." *FCC Public Notice*, February 7. Washington, D.C.: Federal Communications Commission.

Federal Document Clearing House, Inc. 1994. "Testimony June 10, 1994, Linda Mancuso, Vice President, Saturday Morning and Family Programs, House Energy/Telecommunications and Finance Committee, Children's Television Act." *FDCH Congressional Testimony*, June 10.

———. 1995. "Senator Simon and Others Discuss an Audit on Television Violence." *FDCH Political Transcripts*, September 20.

———. 1996. "WW-Holds News Conference with Others to Discuss Obscene Music." *FDCH Political Transcripts*, May 30.

Federman, Joel. 1993. *Film and Television Ratings: An International Assessment*. Studio City, Calif.: Mediascope.

———. 1996. *Media Ratings: Design, Use and Consequences*. Studio City, Calif.: Mediascope.

Ferguson, Ellyn. 1995. "Lieberman Challenges Time Warner's Gangsta Rap." *Gannett News Service*, June 30.

Feshbach, S. 1972. "Reality and Fantasy in Filmed Violence." In J. P. Murray, E. A. Murray, and G. Comstock, eds., *Television and Social Behavior: Television and Social Learning*, 2:318–45. Washington, D.C.: U.S. Government Printing Office.

Fish, Stanley. 1994. *There's No Such Thing As Free Speech and It's a Good Thing, Too*. New York: Oxford University Press.

Fishman, Mark. 1978. "Crime Waves As Ideology." In Ray Surette, ed., *Justice and the Media, Issues and Research*, pp. 159–80. Springfield, Il.: Charles C. Thomas Publisher.

Flynn, James, Paul Slovic, and C. K. Mertz. 1994. "Gender, Race, and Perception of Environmental Health Risks." *Risk Analysis*, 14:1101–8.

Fowler, Mark S., and Daniel L. Brenner. 1982. "A Marketplace Approach to Broadcast Regulation." *University of Texas Law Review*, 60:207–57.

Frank, Robert H., and Philip J. Cook. 1995. *The Winner-Take-All Society*. New York: Free Press.

Franklin, Marc A., and David A. Anderson. 1995. *Cases and Materials on Mass Media Law*. Westbury, N.Y.: Foundation Press.

Freedman, Jonathan L. 1984. "Effect of Television Violence on Aggressiveness." *Psychological Bulletin*, 96:227–46.

———. 1986. "Television Violence and Aggression." *Psychological Bulletin*, 100:372–78.

———. 1988. "Television Violence and Aggression: What the Evidence Shows." In S. Okamp, ed., *Applied Social Psychology Annual: Television As a Social Issue*, 8:144–62.

Freeman, John. 1995. "Turner Airs His Full-Color Views on TV, Life." *San Diego Union-Tribune*, July 11, E1.

Friedrich, L., and A. H. Stein. 1972. "Aggressive and Prosocial Television Programs and the Natural Behavior of Preschool Children." *Monographs of the Society for Research in Child Development*, 38:4, serial no. 151.

Galloway, Stephen. 1995. "Hollywood Confidential: If Americans Are Fascinated with Filmmaking, They Are Even More Fascinated with Tinseltown's Way of Doing Business." *Hollywood Reporter*, November 7.

Garrow, David J. 1978. *Protest at Selma: Martin Luther King, Jr. and the Voting Rights Act of 1965*. New Haven, Conn.: Yale University Press.

Gerbner, George. 1994a. "Highlights of the Television Violence Profile No. 16." Remarks prepared for the National Association of Television Executives Annual Conference, Miami Beach, January 27.

———. 1994b. "There Is No Free Market in Television." *Hofstra Law Review*, 22:879–84.

Gerbner, George, Larry Gross, Marilyn Jackson-Beeck, Suzanne Jeffries-Fox, and Nancy Signorielli. 1978. "Cultural Indicators: Violence Profile No. 9." *Journal of Communication*, 28(3):176–207.

Gerbner, George, Larry Gross, Nancy Signorielli, Michael Morgan, and Marilyn Jackson-Beeck. 1979. "The Demonstration of Power: Violence Profile No. 10." *Journal of Communication*, 29(3):177–96.

Gerbner, George, Michael Morgan, and Nancy Signorielli. 1994. "Television Violence Profile No. 16: The Turning Point." Unpublished manuscript.

Gerbner, George, and Nancy Signorielli. 1990. "Violence Profile 1967 through 1988–89: Enduring Patterns." Unpublished manuscript.

Gitlin, Todd. 1980. *The Whole World Is Watching: Mass Media in the Making and Unmaking of the New Left*. Berkeley: University of California Press.

Glickman, Dan. 1988. "The Television Act of 1988." *Congressional Record*, January 25, 134 H 10.

Goldberg, Robert, and Gerald Jay Goldberg. 1995. *Citizen Turner*. New York: Harcourt Brace.

Graber, Doris Appel. 1980. *Crime News and the Public*. New York: Praeger.

Green, Donald P., and Ian Shapiro. 1994. *Pathologies of Rational Choice Theory: A Critique of Applications in Political Science*. New Haven, Conn.: Yale University Press.

Greenberg, Bradley S., Robert Abelman, and A. Cohen. 1990. "Telling Children Not to Watch Television." In R. J. Kinkel, ed., *Television and Violence: An Overview*, pp. 2–22. Detroit: Mental Health Association of Michigan.

Gunther, Barrie. 1994. "The Question of Media Violence." In J. Bryant and D. Zillman, eds., *Media Effects*, pp. 163–211. Hillsdale, N.J.: Lawrence Erlbaum Associates.

Guttman, Monika. 1994. "A Kinder, Gentler Hollywood." *U.S. News and World Report*, May 9, pp. 38–46.

Halonen, Doug. 1997. "McCain Hits Hard on Violence: Fix Ratings, or Else." *Electronic Media*, March 17, p. 1.

Hamilton, James T. 1993. "Pollution As News: Media and Stock Market Reactions to the Toxics Release Inventory Data." *Journal of Environmental Economics and Management*, 28:98–113.

———. 1995. "Marketing Violence: The Impact of Labeling Violent Television Content." DeWitt Wallace Center for Communications and Journalism Working Paper Series. Terry Sanford Institute of Public Policy, Duke University, Durham, N.C.

———. 1996. "Private Interests in 'Public Interest' Programming: An Economic Assessment of Broadcaster Incentives." *Duke Law Journal*, 45:1177–92.

———. 1998. "Does Viewer Discretion Prompt Advertiser Discretion? The Impact of Violence Warnings on the Television Advertising Market." In James T. Hamilton, ed., *Television Violence and Public Policy*, chap. 8. Ann Arbor: University of Michigan Press.

Hamilton, James T., and W. Kip Viscusi. 1994. "Human Health Risk Assessments for Superfund." *Ecology Law Quarterly*, 21(3):574–611.

———. 1996. "Agency Discretion, Coalition Drift, and Social Welfare: Did the EPA Successfully Implement Superfund Legislation?" Working paper. Duke University, Durham, N.C.

Hamilton, Lee. 1996. "Television Violence." *Congressional Record*, February 1, 142 E 124.

Hapkiewicz, Walter G., and Robert D. Stone. 1974. "The Effect of Realistic versus Imaginary Aggressive Models on Children's Interpersonal Play." *Child Study Journal*, 4(2):47–58.

Hardin, Russell. 1982. *Collective Action*. Baltimore: Resources for the Future.

Harmon, Mark D. 1989. "Market Size and Local Television News Judgment." *Journal of Media Economics*, 2(1):15–29.

Hastings, Deborah. 1993. "Official Says No Grand Jury Probing Michael Jackson." AP *Worldstream*, November 24.

Hatch, David. 1997. "In Some Papers, Ratings aren't Fit to Print." *Electronic Media*, March 10, p. 4.

Hawkins, Robert P., and S. Pingree. 1982. "Television's Influence on Social Reality." In David Pearl, Lorraine Bouthilet, and Joyce Lazar, eds., *Television and Behavior: Ten Years of Scientific Progress and Implications for the Eighties*, vol. 2: *Technical Reviews*, pp. 224–47. Washington, D.C.: Government Printing Office.

Hellen, Nicholas. 1992. "Ban Sex before 10 PM Says Television Watchdog." *Evening Standard*, November 11, p. 3.

Hennigan, Karen M., Linda Heath, J. D. Wharton, Marilyn L. Del Rosario, Thomas D. Cook, and Bobby J. Calder. 1982. "Impact of the Introduction of Television on Crime in the United States: Empirical Findings and Theoretical Implications." *Journal of Personality and Social Psychology*, 42(3):461–77.

Hinich, Melvin J., and Michael C. Munger. 1994. *Ideology and the Theory of Political Choice*. Ann Arbor: University of Michigan Press.

Hirsch, Paul M. 1980. "The 'Scary World' of the Nonviewer and Other Anomalies: A Reanalysis of Gerber et al.'s Findings on Cultivation Analysis, Part I." *Communications Research*, 7(4):403–56.

———. 1981. "On Not Learning from One's Own Mistakes: A Reanalysis of Gerber et al.'s Findings on Cultivation Analysis, Part II." *Communication Research*, 8(1):3–37.

Hodges, Ann. 1993. "CBS Chief Wants to End Violence." *Houston Chronicle*, July 19, p. 1.

Holbert, Ginny. 1993. "'Opening Shot' Scores; Bravo Gives Intelligent Spin to Kids' Show." *Chicago Sun-Times*, August 3, p. 31.

Hollings, Fritz. 1996. "S. 470: The Children's Protection from Violent Programming Act of 1995." *Congressional Press Releases*, February 6.

Hotelling, Harold. 1929. "Stability in Competition." *Economic Journal*, 34:41–57.

Hughes, Michael. 1980. "The Fruits of Cultivation Analysis: A Reexamination of Some Effects of Television Watching." *Public Opinion Quarterly*, 44:287–302.

Hundt, Reed E. 1996. "The Public's Airwaves: What Does the Public Interest Require of Television Broadcasters?" *Duke Law Journal*, 45:1089–1129.

Huston, Aletha C., and John C. Wright. 1995. *Effects of Educational TV Viewing of Lower-Income Preschoolers on Academics Skills, School Readiness and School Adjustment One to Three Years Later*. Lawrence: Center for Research on the Influence of Television on Children, University of Kansas.

Hutcheson, Ron. 1993. "Panel Rebukes TV Execs Over 'Prime-Time Crime.'" *Houston Chronicle*, May 22, p. A1.

Ingber, Stanley. 1984. "The Marketplace of Ideas: A Legitimizing Myth." *Duke Law Journal*, 33:1–91.

Irwin, A. Rowland, and Alan M. Gross. 1995. "Cognitive Tempo, Violent Video Games, and Aggresive Behavior in Young Boys." *Journal of Family Violence*, 10(3):337–50.

Iwao, Sumiko, Ithiel de Sola Pool, and Shigeru Hagiwara. 1981. "Japanese and U.S. Media: Some Cross-Cultural Insights into TV Violence." *Journal of Communication*, 31(2):29–36.

Iyengar, Shanto. 1991. *Is Anyone Responsible?: How Television Frames Political Issues*. Chicago: University of Chicago Press.

Jeffreys, Daniel. 1995. "Stateside." *Independent*, August 29, Media, p. 18.

Jenish, D'Arcy. 1992. "Prime-Time Violence; Despite High Ratings for Violent Shows, Revulsion Is Growing over Bloodshed in TV." *MacLean's*, December 7, p. 40.

Jensen, Jeff. 1993. "Prime-Time Clutter Falls Slightly; But Commercial Time Rises." *Advertising Age*, March 8, p. 33.

Jicha, Tom. 1994. "Ostrich-sized News Simply for the Birds." *Sun-Sentinel* (Fort Lauderdale), April 19, p. E1.

———. 1996. "HBO's 'Strangers' Is Solid Drama." *Sun-Sentinel* (Fort Lauderdale), July 5, p. D4.

Johnson, Richard Arnold, and Gouri K. Bhattacharyya. 1992. *Statistics: Principles and Methods*. New York: John Wiley and Sons.

Jordan, Amy B. 1996. *The State of Children's Television: An Examination of Quantity, Quality and Industry Beliefs*. Philadelphia: Annenberg Public Policy Center, University of Pennsylvania.

Joy, J., M. Kimball, and M. Zabrack. 1986. "Television and Children's Aggressive Behavior." In T. M. Williams ed., *The Impact of Television: A Natural Experiment in Three Communities*, pp. 303–60. New York: Academic Press.

Kaniss, Phyllis C. 1991. *Making Local News*. Chicago: University of Chicago Press.

Karlin, Susan. 1995. "Topical References Can Make—or Break—a Series, Producers Say." *Electronic Media*, May 8, p. 3.

Katz, Richard. 1995. "Rod Perth: USA's New Programming Exec Wants the Network to be Known for Original Series, Not Women in Distress Films." *Multichannel News*, January 16, p. A47.

Kiesewetter, John. 1996. "TV Ratings System Will Give More Information, but Won't Change Programming." *Cincinnati Enquirer*, August 26.

Kim, Stephen J. 1994. "Viewer Discretion Is Advised: A Structural Approach to the Issue of Television Violence." *University of Pennsylvania Law Review*, 142:1431–41.

Kleinfield, N. R. 1989. "Channel 2 Plans New Show at 7 PM" *New York Times*, February 7, p. C18.

Klite, Paul, Robert A. Bardwell, and Jason Salzman. 1997. "Local TV News: Getting Away with Murder." *Harvard International Journal of Press/Politics*, 2(2):102–12.

Krattenmaker, Thomas G., and L. A. Powe, Jr. 1978. "Televised Violence: First Amendment Principles and Social Science Theory." *Virginia Law Review*, 64:1123–1297.

———. 1994. *Regulating Broadcast Programming*. Cambridge, Mass.: MIT Press.

Krotoszynski, Ronald J., Jr. 1996. "Into the Woods: Broadcasters, Bureaucrats, and Children's Television Programming." *Duke Law Journal*, 45:1193–1248.

———. 1997. "The Inevitable Wasteland: Why the Public Trustee Model of Broadcast Television Regulation Must Fail." *Michigan Law Review*, 95: 2101–38.

Kubey, Robert, and Reed Larson. 1990. "The Use and Experience of the New Video Media among Children and Young Adolescents." *Communication Research*, 17(1): 107–30.

Kunkel, Dale. 1993. *Broadcasters' License Renewal Claims Regarding Children's Educational Programming*. Submitted in FCC Docket 93–48. Santa Barbara:Department of Communication, University of California.

Kunkel, Dale, Barbara J. Wilson, Dan Linz, James Potter, Ed Donnerstein, Stacy Smith, Eva Blumenthal, and Timothy Gray. 1996. "Violence in Television Programming Overall: University of California, Santa Barbara Study." In *National Television Violence Study: Scientific Papers, 1994–1995*, 1:1–172. Studio City, Calif.: Mediascope.

Kurtz, Howard. 1994. "Sex! Mayhem! 'Now'!, In the Newsmagazine Derby, NBC's Star-Driven Vehicle Puts a Sheen on Sensationalism." *Washington Post*, March 14, p. D1.

Kushman, Rick. 1995. "Frontline Looks at the Link between TV and Violence." *Sacramento Bee*, January 9, p. C1.

Lacy, Stephen, Tony Atwater, and Xinmin Qin. 1989. "Competition and the Allocation of Resources for Local Television News." *Journal of Media Economics*, 2(1):3–14.

Landler, Mark. 1996. "TV Turns to an Era of Self-Control." *New York Times*, March 17, p. B1.

Lane, Randall. 1994. "The Dean of Tabloid TV." *Forbes*, February 28, p. 100.

Lasorsa, Dominic, Wayne Danielson, Ellen Wartella, D. Charles Whitney, Marlies Klijn, Rafael Lopez, and Adriana Olivarez. 1996. "TV Violence in Reality Programs: Differences across Genres." Paper prepared for Duke Conference on Media Violence and Public Policy, Sanford Institute of Public Policy, Duke University, Durham, N.C., June 28–29.

Laurence, Robert P. 1993. "After Storm, 'Blue' Is Back in Many Cities." *San Diego Union-Tribune*, November 8, p. E1.

———. 1995. "No Money Where Their Mouths Are." *San Diego Union-Tribune*, March 20, p. D-1.

Layne, Barry. 1993. "'Nick News' Up for Syndication." *Hollywood Reporter*, April 7.

Leading National Advertisers. 1994a. *Company Brand $, 1993*. New York: Leading National Advertisers.

———. 1994b. *Ad $ Summary, 1993*. New York: Leading National Advertisers.

Levin, Harvey J. 1980. *Fact and Fancy in Television Regulation: An Economic Study of Policy Alternatives*. New York: Russell Sage Foundation.

Leyens, Jacque-Phillipe, and Steve Picus. 1973. "Identification with the Winner of a Fight and Name Mediation: Their Differential Effects upon Subsequent Aggressive Behavior." *British Journal of Social and Clinical Psychology*, 12:374–77.

Lichter, Linda S., and S. Robert Lichter. 1983. *Prime Time Crime*. Washington, D.C.: Media Institute.

Lichter, S. Robert, and Daniel Admundson. 1992. *A Day of Television Violence*. Washington, D.C.: Center for Media and Public Affairs.

Liss, M. B., L. C. Reinhardt, and S. Fredriksen. 1983. "TV Heroes: The Impact of Rhetoric and Deeds." *Journal of Applied Developmental Psychology*, 4:175–87.

Littlefield, Kinney. 1994. "Tot Stuff is Hot Stuff in TV Programming." *Dayton Daily News*, July 6, p. B9.

———. 1996. "Ad Buyers Not Excited by Fall Schedules." *Orange County Register*, May 26, p. F9.

Loesch, Margaret. 1994. Oral Presentation of Margaret Loesch. FCC En Banc Hearing, Washington, D.C., June.

Lorando, Mark. 1995. "The Blue Tube." *Times-Picayune*, June 22, p. E1.

Lowry, Brian. 1995. "Webs Betting the House on Ad-Friendly Demos." *Variety*, April 24, p. 19.

———. 1996. "NBC's Big Piece of Smaller Pie; Peacock Wins Sweeps and Season, but Networks' Combined Prime-Time Share Drops to Lowest in History." *Los Angeles Times*, May 24, p. 1.

Lucas, William A., and Karen B. Possner. 1975. *Television News and Local Awareness: A Retrospective Look*. Santa Monica, Calif.: Rand Corporation.

Machacek, John. 1995. "Paxon Leads Effort against TV 'Violence Chip' Plan." *Gannett News Service*, August 2.

Mandese, Joe. 1996. "NBC's 'Seinfeld,' 'ER' Hit Record $1 Million Minute." *Advertising Age*, September 16, pp. 1, 52.

Mangan, Jennifer. 1994. "The New 'FCC Friendly' Shows; Networks Try to Please Kids and Government." *Chicago Tribune*, April 27, p. 3.

Manton, Thomas J. 1995. "Debate over the Markey-Klink-Montgomery Amendment to the Telecommunications Act of 1995." *Congressional Record*, 14, 141 H 8481.

Mathis, Nancy. 1996. "TV Remote Goes Back to Parents; Clinton Applauds Rating Guide Plan." *Houston Chronicle*, March 1, p. A1.

Mayberry, Peter. 1995. "Regulatory Reform Bill Stalls in Senate." *Nonwovens Industry*, 26(9):32.

McCash, Vicki. 1994. "WSVN: You Can't Argue with Success; S. Florida Broadcast Station Has Become the Envy of Others, Most of Whom Say They'd Copy Its Economic Style but Not Its Sensationalism." *Sun-Sentinel* (Fort Lauderdale), July 4, Business, p. 4.

McConnell, Frank. 1996. "Seinfeld. Television Program Reviews." *Commonweal*, February 9, p. 19.

McDonald, Daniel G. 1986. "Generational Aspects of Television Coviewing." *Journal of Broadcasting and Electronic Media*, 30:75–85.

McGuire, William J. 1986. "The Myth of Massive Media Impact: Savagings and Salvagings." In G. Comstock, ed., *Public Communication and Behavior*, 1:173–257. San Diego: Academic Press.

McKenzie, William. 1996. "Deficit Stays on Back Burner of Campaign." *St. Louis Post-Dispatch*, March 18, p. B15.

McManus, John H. 1990. "How Local News Learns What Is News." *Journalism Quarterly*, 67(4):672–83.

———. 1992. "Serving the Public and Serving the Market: A Conflict of Interest?" *Journal of Mass Media Ethics*, 7(4):196–208.

———. 1994. *Market-Driven Journalism: Let the Citizen Beware?* Thousand Oaks, Calif.: Sage Publications.

Media Dynamics. 1994. *TV Dimensions '94*. New York: Media Dynamics.

Medved, Michael. 1995. "Toy Ads Show Power of TV's Message." *Times Union*, December 17, p. E2.

Mendoza, N. F. 1993. "Cover Story: All the Elements; Sci-Guys Come Up with Sly Ways to Teach a Traditionally Dry Subject." *Los Angeles Times*, October 10, p. 4.

Mermigas, Diane. 1996. "Cable Hot in '96 Upfront Sales, BCPM Panel Says." *Electronic Media*, May 27, p. 2.

Mickiewicz, Ellen. 1997. *Changing Channels: Television and the Struggle for Power in Russia*. New York: Oxford University Press.

Mifflin, Lawrie. 1997. "Parents Give TV Ratings Mixed Reviews." *New York Times*, February 22, p. A8.

Milavsky, J. Ronald, Shelley Kessler, Horst H. Stipp, and W. S. Rubens. 1982. *Television and Aggression: A Panel Study*. New York: Academic Press.

Miles, Laureen. 1994. "All the News That's Fit for Youth; Sunbeam TV Corp.'s Youth Formula News." *Mediaweek*, May 23, p. 22.

Minow, Newton N. 1997. "The Effect of Television Violence on Children." Crown Lecture, Sanford Institute of Public Policy, Duke University, April 25.

Minow, Newton N., and Craig L. LaMay. 1995. *Abandoned in the Wasteland: Children, Television, and the First Amendment*. New York: Harper Collins.

Montgomery, Kathryn C. 1989. *Target: Prime Time, Advocacy Groups and the Struggle over Entertainment*. New York: Oxford University Press.

Mundy, Alicia. 1995. "A Block Off the Old Chip; in a Rush to Appease Pressure Groups, the Senate Is Lurching Ever Closer to TV Censorship." *Mediaweek*, August 21, p. 22.

Murray, John P. 1983. "Results of an Informal Poll of Knowledgeable Persons concerning the Impact of TV Violence." Paper presented to the APA Monitor, American Psychological Association, Washington, D.C.

———. 1994. "The Impact of Televised Violence." *Hofstra Law Review*, 22:809–25.

National Coalition on Television Violence. 1991. "Awakenings Film, Robin Williams, Jane Fonda Win Gandhi Awards. Steven Seagal, Kathy Bates Most Violent Actors." *NCTV Press Release*, March 15.

National Oceanic and Atmospheric Administration. 1993. "Panel on Contingent Valuation. Report." *Federal Register*, 58(10):4601–14. Washington, D.C.: U.S. Government Printing Office.

National Research Council. 1993. *Understanding and Preventing Violence*. Volume 1. Washington, D.C.: National Academy Press.

National Television Violence Study. 1996a. *National Television Violence Study: Executive Summary, 1994–1995*. Studio City, Calif.: Mediascope.

———. 1996b. *National Television Violence Study: Scientific Papers, 1994–1995*. Studio City, Calif.: Mediascope.

———. 1997a. *National Television Violence Study*. Volume 2: *Executive Summary*. Santa Barbara: Center for Communication and Social Policy, University of California.

———. 1997b. *National Television Violence Study*. Volume 2. Thousand Oaks, Calif.: Sage Publications.

Newsbytes News Network. 1994. "WAM! New Educational Cable Channel Coming 07/08/94." *Newsbytes*, July 8.

Nielsen Media Research. 1993a. *Nielsen Station Index: DMA Test Market Profiles, 1993*. New York: Nielsen Media Research.

———. 1993b. *Nielsen Station Index: Your Guide to Reports and Services*. New York: Nielsen Media Research.

———. 1993c. *Nielsen Station Index: National Audience Demographics, November 1992*. New York: Nielsen Media Research.

———. 1993d. *Nielsen Station Index: Reference Supplement, 1993–94, Methodology Techniques and Data Interpretation*. New York: Nielsen Media Research.

———. 1994a. *Nielsen Station Index: National Audience Demographics, November 1993*. Volume 1. New York: Nielsen Media Research.

———. 1994b. *Nielsen Station Index: National Audience Demographics, November 1993*. Volume 2. New York: Nielsen Media Research.

———. 1994c. *Nielsen Station Index: Network Programs by DMA, November 1993*. New York: Nielsen Media Research.

———. 1994d. *Nielsen Syndication Service: NSS National Audience Demographics, November 1993*. New York: Nielsen Media Research.

———. 1994e. *Nielsen Household and Persons Cost per Thousand, November 1993*. New York: Nielsen Media Research.

———. 1994f. *Nielsen Station Index: Viewers in Profile, November 1993. Various Cities*. New York: Nielsen Media Research.

———. 1994g. *Nielsen Station Index: Report on Syndicated Programs*. Volume 1: *A–K, November 1993*. New York: Nielsen Media Research.

———. 1994h. *Nielsen Station Index: Report on Syndicated Programs*. Volume 2 *L–Z, November 1993*. New York: Nielsen Media Research.

———. 1996a. *Nielsen Television Index: Special Release, Household and Persons Network Primetime Feature Film Directory, 1988–1995*. New York: Nielsen Media Research.

———. 1996b. *Nielsen Television Index: Household and Persons Cost per Thousand, November 1995.* New York: Nielsen Media Research.

Noam, Eli M. 1987. "A Public and Private-Choice Model of Broadcasting." *Public Choice,* 55:163–87.

———. 1991. *Television in Europe.* New York: Oxford University Press.

Noll, Roger G., Merton J. Peck, and John J. McGowan. 1973. *Economic Aspects of Television Regulation.* Washington, D.C.: Brookings Institution.

Nossiter, Bernard. 1985. "The FCC's Big Giveaway Show." *Nation,* October 26, p. 402.

Nyhan, David. 1994. "Three Strikes and You're Nowhere." *Boston Globe,* June 5, p. 71.

Oldenburg, Don. 1992. "Kids—TV Violence and Behavior." *Capital Times,* May 7, p. E1.

Olins, Rufus. 1995. "Moral Crusade Hits Unilever." *Sunday Times,* June 18, Business.

Olson, Mancur. 1971. *The Logic of Collective Action: Public Goods and the Theory of Groups.* Cambridge, Mass.: Harvard University Press.

Opinion Research Corporation. 1993. *Study XXII.* Washington, D.C.: Motion Picture Association of America.

Owen, Bruce M. 1975. *Economics and Freedom of Expression, Media Structure and the First Amendment.* Cambridge, Mass.: Ballinger Publishing.

Owen, Bruce M., Jack H. Beebe, and W. G. Manning, Jr. 1974. *Television Economics.* Lexington Mass.: Lexington Books.

Owen, Bruce M., and Steven S. Wildman. 1992. *Video Economics.* Cambridge, Mass.: Harvard University Press.

Pacheco, Patrick, and Jon Kalish. 1996. "Culture Vulture." *Newsday,* September 1, p. C02.

Paik, Haejung, and George Comstock. 1994. "The Effects of Television Violence on Antisocial Behavior: A Meta-Analysis." *Communication Research,* 21(4):516–46.

Paletz, David L., and Alex Peter Schmid. 1992. *Terrorism and the Media.* Newbury Park, Calif.: Sage.

Paley, William S. 1979. *As It Happened: A Memoir.* New York: Doubleday.

Parents Television Council. 1996. *1996–97 Family Guide to Prime Time Television.* Alexandria, Va.: Media Research Center.

Parker, Donna. 1995. "Par Denies 'Indecent' Charge; After Settling with Buchwald, Studio Takes on Another Accounting Flap." *Hollywood Reporter,* September 13.

Pearl, David, Lorraine Bouthilet, and Joyce Lazar, eds. 1982. *Television and Behavior: Ten Years of Scientific Progress and Implications for the Eighties.* Vol. 1: *Summary Report;* Vol. 2: *Technical Reviews.* Washington, D.C.: Government Printing Office.

Pergament, Alan. 1995. "Sly Fox to Clean Up Its Image." *Buffalo News,* July 17, p. C1.

Perloff, Richard M., Ellen A. Wartella, and Lee B. Becker. 1982. "Increasing Learning from TV News." *Journalism Quarterly,* 59(1):83–86.

Perse, Elizabeth M. 1990. "Involvement with Local Television News, Cognitive and Emotional Dimensions." *Human Communication Research,* 16:556–81.

———. 1992. "Predicting Attention to Local Television News: Need for Cognition and Motives for Viewing." *Communication Reports,* 5(1):40–49.

Petrek, Melissa Marie. 1995. Review of *Fresh Girls* by Evelyn Lau. *Austin American-Statesman,* March 5, p. 7.

Posner, Richard A. 1986. "Free Speech in an Economic Perspective." *Suffolk University Law Review,* 20(1):1–54.

PR Newswire Association. 1997. "Joint Statement of Motion Picture Association of America, National Association of Broadcasters, and National Cable Television Association." *PR Newswire,* July 10.

Powe, Lucas A., Jr. 1987. *American Broadcasting and the First Amendment.* Los Angeles: University of California Press.

Powers, Angela. 1993. "Competition, Conduct, and Ratings in Local Television News: Applying the Industrial Organization Model." *Journal of Media Economics,* 6(2):37–44.

Pottinger, Matt. 1997. "Ratings Don't Satisfy Senators." *Hollywood Reporter,* July 11.

Press Association Limited. 1994. "On Television, Friday July 8." *Press Association Newsfile,* July 6.

Pressle, Leigh. 1994. "WMFY Will Air News Programs on Weekend-Local News." *News and Record* (Greensboro, N.C.), August 27, p. B1.

Prettyman, E. Barrett, Jr., and Lisa A. Hook. 1987. "The Control of Media-Related Imitative Violence." *Federal Communication Law Journal,* 38:317–82.

Prewitt, Milford. 1991. "If It's Summer, It Must Be Time for Movie Tie-ins." *Nation's Restaurant News,* June 17, p. 12.

Prisuta, Robert H. 1977. "The Impact of Media Concentration and Economic Factors on Broadcast Public Interest Programming." *Journal of Broadcasting,* 21:321–32.

Recreational Software Advisory Council. 1996. *Content Ratings for the Internet and Recreational Software: Submission to National Telecommunications and Information Administration Report on Self Regulation.* Lexington, Mass.: Recreational Software Advisory Council.

Reiss, Albert J., and Jeffrey A. Roth. 1993. *Understanding and Preventing Violence.* Washington, D.C.: National Academy Press.

Rice, Lynette, and Rich Brown. 1996. "Networks Rolling Out TV Ratings; Broadcast and Cable Networks Are Busy Assigning Ratings for Programs." *Broadcasting and Cable,* December 30, p. 7.

Rideout, Victoria. 1996. *Making Television Ratings Work for Children and Families: The Perspective of Children's Experts.* Santa Monica, Calif.: Children Now.

Riker, William H. 1986. *The Art of Political Manipulation.* New Haven, Conn.: Yale University Press.

Roberts, Churchill L., and Sandra H. Dickson. 1984. "Assessing Quality in Local TV News." *Journalism Quarterly,* 61(2):392–98.

Roberts, Donald F. 1996. "Media Content Rating Systems: Informational Advisories or Judgmental Restrictions?" Wally Langenschmidt Memorial Lecture, South African Broadcasting Corporation, Johannesburg, South Africa, August 28.

Robins, J. Max. 1995. "TV's New Hue: True 'Blue.'" *Variety,* March 13, p. 1.

Rocky Mountain Media Watch. 1995. *Pavlov's TV Dogs: A Snapshot of Local TV News in America 9/20/95, Executive Summary.* Denver: Rocky Mountain Media Watch.

Roper Organization, Inc. 1993. *America's Watching: Public Attitudes toward Television.* New York: Roper Organization.

Roper Organization, Inc., and TVMS. 1993. *Connected to Cable: An Investigation of Television Consumption in Cable Subscriber Households.* New York: Roper Organization.

Rust, Ronald T. 1986. *Advertising Media Models: A Practical Guide.* Lexington, Mass.: Lexington Books.

Schatz, Robin. 1995. "Pay-TV Channels Reap Premium Profits." *Newsday,* May 9, p. A41.

Schlegal, Julia. 1993. "The Television Violence Act of 1990: A New Program for Government Censorship?" *Federal Communications Law Journal,* 46:187–217.

Schneider, Michael. 1996. "Industry Flinches over More Violence Flak." *Electronic Media*, September 16, p. 1.

Schneider, Michael, and Doug Halonen. 1996. "Candidates Put Heat on Media, It's TV-Bashing Season." *Electronic Media*, July 8, p. 1, 23.

Seigel, Jessica. 1993. "Under Pressure, Networks Trim Violence a Bit." *Chicago Tribune*, July 28, p. 1.

Sen, Amartya K. 1970. "The Impossibility of a Paretian Liberal." *Journal of Political Economy*, 78:152–57.

Shachar, Ron, and Bharat N. Anand. 1996. "All This and More, in the Next Episode of . . ." Yale School of Management Working Paper Series H-1. New Haven, Conn.: Yale School of Management.

Shachar, Ron, and John W. Emerson. 1996. "How Old Should Seinfeld Be?" Yale School of Management Working Papers Series H-4. New Haven, Conn.: Yale School of Management.

Shales, Tom. 1993. "Mayhem: Television's Violence Streak." *Washington Post*, May 21, p. B1.

———. 1994. "Sweeps Victory For the Violence-Weary." *Washington Post*, May 2, p. B1.

Sheley, Joseph F., and Cindy A. Ashkins. 1981. "Crime, Crime News, and Crime Views." In Ray Surette, ed., *Justice and the Media, Issues and Research*, pp. 124–40. Springfield, Il.: Charles C. Thomas Publisher.

Signorelli, Nancy, Larry Gross, and Michael Morgan. 1982. "Violence in Television Programs: Ten Years Later." In David Pearl, Lorraine Bouthilet, and Joyce Lazar, eds., *Television and Behavior: Ten Years of Scientific Progress and Implications for the Eighties*, vol. 2: *Technical Reviews*, pp. 158–73. Washington, D.C.: Government Printing Office.

Simmons Market Research Bureau. 1994 *Simmons Study of Media and Markets 1993*. New York: Simmons Market Research Bureau.

Simon, Paul. 1989. "Exemption of Certain Activities from Antitrust Laws." *Congressional Record*, May 31, 135 S 5793.

———. 1994. "The May Sweeps 1993 and 1994: Grounds for Guarded Optimism." *Congressional Record*, May 4, 140 S 5199.

Slater, Dan, and Teresa L. Thompson. 1984. "Attitudes of Parents concerning Televised Warning Statements." *Journalism Quarterly*, 61(4):853–9.

Smolla, Rodney A. 1992. *Free Speech in an Open Society*. New York: Alfred A. Knopf.

Smolowe, Jill. 1993. "The Tawdry Case of the Bobbitts of Manassas Heads for Round 2." *Time*, November 22, p. 45.

Snow, Robert P. 1974. "How Children Interpret TV Violence in Play Context." *Journalism Quarterly*, 51(1):13–21.

Spence, A. Michael, and Bruce M. Owen. 1977. "Television Programming, Monopolistic Competition and Welfare." *Quarterly Journal of Economics*, 91:103–26.

Spitzer, Matthew L. 1986. *Seven Dirty Words and Six Other Stories: Controlling the Content of Print and Broadcast*. New Haven, Conn.: Yale University Press.

———. 1989. "The Constitutionality of Licensing Broadcasters." *New York University Law Review*, 64:990–1071.

———. 1991. "Justifying Minority Preferences in Broadcasting." *Southern California Law Review*, 64:293–361.

———. 1996. "The Constitutional Law and Economics of the V-chip." Paper prepared for Duke Conference on Media Violence and Public Policy, Sanford Institute of Public Policy, Duke University, Durham, N.C.: June 28–29.

Steiner, Peter O. 1952. "Program Patterns and Preferences, and the Workability of Competition in Radio Broadcasting." *Quarterly Journal of Economics*, 66:194–223.

Stern, Christopher. 1995a. "Markey Wins on V-chip; House Vote to Support V-chip Amendment Sponsored by Rep. Ed Markey." *Broadcasting and Cable*, 125(32):10.

——. 1995b. "Senators Push for V Ban, Hit List; Television Violence." *Broadcasting and Cable*, 125(33):4.

——. 1997. "Violence Ban Eyed: Senate Move Is Attack on TV Industry's Ratings." *Daily Variety*, April 18, p. 8.

Steur, Faye B., James M. Applefield, and Rodney Smith. 1971. "Televised Aggression and Interpersonal Aggression of Preschool Children." *Journal of Experimental Child Psychology*, 11:442–47.

Storm, Jonathan, and Stephen Seplow. 1996. "Cable TV Hogs Violence, Study Says." *Times-Picayune*, February 18, p. A17.

Sunstein, Cass R. 1993. *Democracy and the Problem of Free Speech*. New York: Free Press.

——. 1996. "Social Norms and Social Roles." *Columbia Law Review*, 96:903–68.

Surette, Ray. 1984. *Justice and the Media, Issues and Research*. Springfield, Il.: Charles C. Thomas Publisher.

——. 1992. *Media, Crime, and Criminal Justice: Images and Realities*. Belmont, Calif.: Wadsworth.

Thoman, Elizabeth. 1995. *Beyond Blame, Challenging Violence in the Media*. Los Angeles: Center for Media Literacy.

Thomas, Kevin. 1992. "Prime-Time Flicks." *Los Angeles Times*, November 8, p. 7.

Thomas, Vicki, and David B. Wolfe. 1995 "Why Won't Television Grow Up?" *American Demographics*, 17(5):24–29.

Tiedge, James T., and Kenneth J. Ksobiech. 1987. "Counterprogramming Primetime Network Television." *Journal of Broadcasting and Electronic Media*, 31(1):41–55.

Tillotson, Kristin. 1994. "Hunkwatch." *Star Tribune*, June 26, p. F1.

Times Mirror Center for the People and the Press. 1993. *TV Violence: More Objectionable in Entertainment Than in Newscasts*. Washington, D.C.: Times Mirror Center for the People and the Press.

Turner, Charles W., and Leonard Berkowitz. 1972. "Identification with Film Aggressor (Covert Role Taking) and Reactions to Film Violence." *Journal of Personality and Social Psychology*, 21(2):256–64.

TV Parental Guidelines Oversight Monitoring Board. 1997. *The TV Parental Guidelines*. Washington, D.C.: TV Parental Guidelines Oversight Monitoring Board.

UCLA Center for Communication Policy. 1995. *The UCLA Television Violence Monitoring Report*. Los Angeles: UCLA Center for Communication Policy.

——. 1996. *The UCLA Television Violence Report 1996*. Los Angeles: UCLA Center for Communication Policy.

Umstead, R. Thomas. 1996. "Heavy Mo. Tax Threatens 'Ultimate' Events." *Multichannel News*, October 14, p. 52.

United Press. 1986. "Washington News." *United Press International*, September 10.

U.S. Environmental Protection Agency. 1993. *1991 Toxics Release Inventory: Public Data Release*. Washington, D.C.: U.S. EPA Office of Pollution Prevention and Toxics.

——. 1994. *1992 Toxics Release Inventory: Public Data Release*. Washington, D.C.: U.S. EPA Office of Pollution Prevention and Toxics.

U.S. House Committee on Energy and Commerce. 1994. "Survey Finds Parents Not Routinely Receiving 'Violence Advisories' in Advance of Programs." Study Released

• B I B L I O G R A P H Y •

January 14, 1994. Washington, D.C.: U.S. House Committee on Energy and Commerce, Subcommittee on Telecommunication, and Finance.

U.S. House Committee on the Judiciary. 1989. *Hearing on H.R. 1391, Television Violence Act of 1989.* Washington, D.C.: U.S. House Committee on the Judiciary, Subcommittee on Economic and Commercial Law.

U.S. Newswire. 1995. "Lieberman, Bennett Urge Corporate Leaders to Clean Up Daytime TV Talk." *U.S. Newswire,* November 10.

Valenti, Jack. 1997. "The Television Ratings System Is Simple and User-Friendly." *Los Angeles Times,* January 3, p. 9.

Valenti, Jack, Decker Anstrom, and Eddie Fritts. 1997. Letter to William F. Caton Secretary, Federal Communications Commission, January 17, 1997. In *FCC Public Notice 97-34, CS Docket No. 97-55, Commission Seeks Comment on Industry Proposal for Rating Video Programming,* Appendix. Washington, D.C.: Federal Communications Commission.

Van Alstyne, William W. 1984. *Interpretations of the First Amendment.* Durham, N.C.: Duke University Press.

Villano, David. 1996. "Has Knight-Ridder's Flagship Gone Adrift; Trouble at the Miami Herald." *Columbia Journalism Review,* 34:29–33.

Viscusi, W. Kip. 1992. *Fatal Tradeoffs.* New York: Oxford University Press.

Wakshlag, Jacob J., and William J. Adams. 1985. "Trends in Program Variety and the Prime Time Access Rule." *Journal of Broadcasting and Electronic Media,* 29(1):23–34.

Walley, Wayne. 1996. "Kids and Teens TV; To 'V' or Not to 'V'; Vchip, Ratings System Getting Mixed Reviews in Kids TV Industry." *Electronic Media,* March 11, p. 41.

Waterman, David. 1990. "Diversity and Quality of Information Products in a Monopolistically Competitive Industry." *Information Economics and Policy,* 4:291–303.

———. 1992. "'Narrowcasting' and 'Broadcasting' on Nonbroadcast Media: A Program Choice Model." *Communications Research,* 19(1):3–28.

Watkins, John J. 1990. *The Mass Media and the Law.* Englewood Cliffs, N.J.: Prentice-Hall.

Webster, James G., and Lawrence W. Lichty. 1991. *Ratings Analysis: Theory and Practice.* Hillsdale, N.J.: Lawrence Erlbaum Associates.

West, Don. 1994. "Preston Padden: Strategizing to Move Fox from Underdog to Head of Pack." *Broadcasting and Cable,* 124(42):18.

Wharton, Dennis. 1995. "V-Chip, On a Roll, Puts Industry in Pickle." *Variety,* July 17, p. 21.

White, Sylvia E. 1994. "Labeling Violence: How Useful Are Labels and How Far Can We Go?" Paper presented at the International Conference on Violence and the Media, St. John's University, New York, October 3–4.

Whitehead, Colson. 1995. "Journey through the Past Nine Months: In Which Our Trusty Critic Engages in Some Unsparing Self-Examination." *Wired,* July 4, p. 44.

Wildman, Steven S., and N. Y. Lee. 1989. "Program Choice in Broadband Environment." Paper presented at Integrated Broadband Networks Conference, Columbia University.

Wildman, Steven S., and Bruce M. Owen. 1985. "Program Competition, Diversity, and Multichannel Bundling in the New Video Industry." In E. M. Noam, ed., *Video Media Competition: Regulation, Economics, and Technology,* pp. 244–73. New York: Columbia University Press.

Wildman, Steven S., and Karla Salmon Robinson. 1995. "Network Programming and Off-Network Syndication Profits: Strategic Links and Implications for Television Policy." *Journal of Media Economics,* 8(2):27–48.

Wilkinson, Howard, and Paul Barton. 1996. "Campaign 1996: VP Choice Key for Dole, Age Makes Decision Crucial to Campaign." *Cincinnati Enquirer*, May 26, p. A1.

Williams, Redford B., Susan G. Curtain, O. Eugene Walton, John C. Barefoot, Barbara Frederickson, Michael J. Helms, Cynthia Mikuhn, and Edward C. Suarez. 1996a. "Violence in the Media: Effects of Affective Response, Gender and Hostility of the Viewer upon Neuroendocrine Reactivity." Working paper, Duke University Medical Center, Durham, N.C.

Williams, Redford B., Susan G. Curtain, O. Eugene Walton, S. Robert Lichter, John C. Barefoot, Michael P. Bates, Barbara Frederickson, Michael J. Helms, and Edward C. Suarez. 1996b. "Violence in the Media: Effects of Type of Violence Portrayed and Hostility and Gender of the Viewer upon Cardiovascular Activity." Working paper, Duke University Medical Center, Durham, N.C.

Wilson, Barbara J., Stacy L. Smith, James Potter, Dan Linz, Ed Donnerstein, Dale Kunkel, Eva Blumenthal, and Tim Gray. 1996. "Content Analysis of Entertainment Television: The 1994–95 Results." Paper prepared for Duke Conference on Media Violence and Public Policy, Sanford Institute of Public Policy, Duke University, Durham, N.C. June 28–29.

Wilson, James Q. 1980. *The Politics of Regulation.* New York: Basic Books.

Wilson, Mike. 1994. "Rock'em, Shock'em; WVSN-TV." *Quill,* 82(2):33.

WLFL TV 22. 1992. Children's Educational/Informational Programming Report (3rd Quarter, 1992). Raleigh, N.C.: WLFL-TV 22.

———. 1993. Children's Educational/Informational Programming Report (3rd Quarter, 1993). Raleigh, N.C.: WLFL-TV 22.

Wolfe, David. 1990. *Serving the Ageless Market.* New York: McGraw-Hill.

———. 1994. "Targeting the Mature Mind." *American Demographics,* 16(3):32–36.

Woodward, Bob. 1996. *The Choice.* New York: Simon and Schuster.

Zaller, John R. 1992. *The Nature and Origins of Mass Opinion.* New York: Cambridge University Press.

Zoglin, Richard. 1996. "Chips Ahoy: As a New Study Warns That Violence Saturates the Airwaves, a Technological Quick Fix Promises to Help. But Will the V Chip Really Protect Our Children?" *Time,* February 18, p. 58.

Zurawik, David. 1994. "Networks Shift Stand on Violence." *Fresno Bee,* January 25, p. D1.